SOCIAL WORK PRACTICE WITH THE LGBTQ COMMUNITY

Social Work Practice with the LGBTQ Community

THE INTERSECTION OF HISTORY, HEALTH, MENTAL HEALTH, AND POLICY FACTORS

Edited by Michael P. Dentato

OXFORD

UNIVERSITY PRESS

Oxford University Press is a department of the University of Oxford. It furthers
the University's objective of excellence in research, scholarship, and education
by publishing worldwide. Oxford is a registered trade mark of Oxford University
Press in the UK and certain other countries.

Published in the United States of America by Oxford University Press
198 Madison Avenue, New York, NY 10016, United States of America.

© Oxford University Press 2018

CIP data is on file at the Library of Congress
ISBN 978–0–19–061279–5

9 8 7 6 5 4 3
Printed by Marquis, Canada

This text is dedicated to the many lesbian, gay, bisexual, transgender, and queer friends, partners, clients, students, and scholars across the globe that I have known over the years. I am humbled by all that you have taught me about myself, being a social worker and an educator. I am inspired daily by your strength and resilience and therefore dedicate this text to you.

This text is also dedicated to my mother, Patricia A. (Garrow) Dentato, and in memory of my father, Vito J. Dentato, Jr. (1944–2010) who both provided the roots for my eventual growth as a social worker, educator, and advocate for social justice. Without their lifetime commitment to love, guidance, and unwavering support, I would not be the person I am today.

"We, the people, declare today that the most evident of truths—that all of us are created equal—is the star that guides us still; just as it guided our forebears through Seneca Falls, and Selma, and Stonewall; just as it guided all those men and women, sung and unsung, who left footprints along this great Mall, to hear a preacher say that we cannot walk alone; to hear a King proclaim that our individual freedom is inextricably bound to the freedom of every soul on Earth."

Inaugural Address by President Barack Obama, January 21, 2013

CONTENTS

PART II CONSIDERATIONS ACROSS THE LIFESPAN

PART III AFFIRMING LGBTQ PRACTICE APPROACHES

PART IV   HEALTH AND MENTAL HEALTH FACTORS

PART V   APPENDICES

ABOUT THE EDITOR

Michael Philip Dentato, PhD, MSW
Assistant Professor, School of Social Work, Loyola University Chicago
Dr. Dentato received his bachelor of arts and master of social work degrees from Fordham University in New York City. He earned his PhD in social work from Loyola University Chicago examining the impact of minority stress on substance use and sexual risk among men who have sex with men. Dr. Dentato is an assistant professor in the School of Social Work at Loyola and over the past 12 years has taught at institutions including Barry University, Ellen Whiteside McDonnell School of Social Work in Miami Shores, Florida, where he was also the BSW program director; the University of Illinois, Jane Addams College of Social Work; and the University of Chicago's School of Social Service Administration. Dr. Dentato's research and scholarship centers around three domains including (a) the assessment of health and health disparities among sexual-minority populations, (b) the preparedness of social work students to provide affirming services for the LGBTQ community, and (c) the impact of macro practice, interprofessional education, effective nonprofit leadership, and service provision for vulnerable communities. Dr. Dentato is co-principal investigator for the SBIRT training program at Loyola University Chicago, funded by The Substance Abuse and Mental Health Services Administration. He has more than 20 years of direct service and consultant experience including clinical, administrative, and policy work throughout his tenure in New York City, Miami, and Chicago.

Dr. Dentato is currently a research affiliate for the Center for Health, Identity, Behavior and Prevention Studies at New York University's Steinhardt School of Culture, Education and Human Development; Ambassador at the Institute for Transformative Interprofessional Education at Loyola University Chicago; associate editor for *Behavioral Medicine*; and an associate faculty member with the women's studies and gender studies program at Loyola University Chicago. He is the former co-chair of the Council on Social Work Education's Council on Sexual Orientation and Gender Identity and Expression, as well as former president of the board of directors for Test Positive Aware Network. Dr. Dentato resides in Chicago with his husband, Domingo Gonzales III.

ABOUT THE CONTRIBUTORS

Edward J. Alessi, PhD, LCSW

Assistant Professor, School of Social Work, Rutgers University

Dr. Alessi's scholarship (a) investigates the effect of minority stress on the mental health of sexual- and gender-minority populations, (b) examines mental health practitioners' use of affirmative practice, and (c) seeks to advance clinical practice with marginalized and oppressed populations. His research has been published in journals such as *The Journal of Sex Research, Psychotherapy, Psychotherapy Research,* and *Psychological Trauma: Theory, Research, Practice, and Policy.* Dr. Alessi also served as guest editor for the *Clinical Social Work Journal's* first special issue on clinical practice with LGBTQ populations. A clinical social worker since 2001, he has worked primarily in outpatient mental health and has been an independent practitioner since 2004. Dr. Alessi received his PhD in clinical social work from New York University and his master of science in social work from Columbia University.

Tyler M. Argüello, PhD, DCSW, LCSW, ACSW

Assistant Professor, College of Health and Human Services, Division of Social Work, California State University at Sacramento

Dr. Argüello's research and clinical work is a transdisciplinary project that concerns communicative practices, queer theory, and the production of identities, sex/ualities, and health disparities, namely HIV. Currently, Dr. Argüello studies intergenerational stress and divides within queer populations and is the principal investigator on multiple critical theory–driven and multimedia studies on HIV Stress Exchange, AIDS Survivor Syndrome, and long-term survivorship of queer men, inclusive of all HIV statuses. Dr. Argüello has been a practicing social worker for more than 20 years, primarily around community mental health and HIV. He teaches courses in difference and social justice, advanced clinical practice, psychodiagnostics, and qualitative research. He is a licensed independent clinical social worker, with a diplomate in clinical social work, and holds a BA (Spanish), BASW, MSW, and PhD (social welfare), all from the University of Washington, Seattle.

Ashley Austin, PhD, LCSW

Associate Professor and Director of the Center for Human Rights and Social Justice in the School of Social Work, Barry University

Dr. Austin's research and practice interests revolve around reducing disparities in health and well-being among sexual- and gender-diverse individuals. Dr. Austin's clinical practice and community education is rooted in a transgender affirmative framework. Dr. Austin is involved in multiple collaborations aimed at improving the delivery of transgender affirmative social work education and practice. In particular, Dr. Austin's clinical work is focused on the development and dissemination of a transgender affirmative cognitive behavioral therapy approach that targets the specific mental and behavioral health needs of gender-diverse clients. This model integrates an affirmative framework with empirically supported strategies to address minority stress and develop positive coping. Dr. Austin is also actively involved in creating a transgender-inclusive campus and community by bringing events such as the Transgender Day of Remembrance and Transgender Week of Awareness to her university's campus and advocating for gender-inclusive policies and practices.

Jean E. Balestrery, PhD, MA, MSW

Assistant Clinical Professor, Department of Sociology and Social Work, Northern Arizona University

Dr. Balestrery earned her PhD in social work and anthropology from the University of Michigan, her master of arts in anthropology from the University of Michigan, her master of social work from the University of Washington, and her bachelor of arts from Brown University. Dr. Balestrery is an interdisciplinary scholar whose research aims to improve health and social service outcomes particularly for marginalized communities. Her research, which is informed by many years of practice experience, addresses health, aging, clinical practice, service delivery systems, and intercultural communication in a diverse global society. She was selected in 2015 as a scholar-participant for the Translational Health Disparities course at the National Institute of Minority Health Disparities in Bethesda, Maryland, and as an ambassador with the Gerontological Society of America for a US–China delegation at the first annual Healthy Ageing and Society research symposium in Suzhou, China. Dr. Balestrery has addressed Native health disparities as a Spirit of Eagles Hampton Faculty Fellow and LGBTQ community issues as a councilor on the Council on Sexual Orientation and Gender Identity and Expression with the Council on Social Work Education. Strengthening linkages between research, teaching, and practice, Dr. Balestrery conducts consultations and trainings for community-based stakeholders.

Lacey D. Clark, MSW

Lecturer, Department of Social Work, Metropolitan State University of Denver

Ms. Clark received her bachelor of arts in psychology and master of social work degrees at Binghamton University in New York. Ms. Clark's social work practice experiences relate primarily to mental health issues with adults and youth, involving multiple practice modalities, including work with individuals, families, groups, and communities. Ms. Clark has engaged in collaborative research, including evaluation research and qualitative research projects on topics such as sexuality, culturally competent practice, and diversity in doctoral education. Ms. Clark has taught BSSW and MSW courses, including research methods and practice evaluation, diversity, and electives that focus on gender and sexuality. Ms. Clark's academic interests also include the role of research in social work practice, addressing issues of diversity and marginalization in the social work curriculum and classroom, and online pedagogy.

Shelley L. Craig, PhD, LCSW

Associate Professor and Associate Dean, Factor-Inwentash Faculty of School of Social Work, University of Toronto

Canada Research Chair in Sexual and Gender Minority Youth

Dr. Craig's research focuses on the social determinants of health and mental health and the impact of the service delivery system on vulnerable populations. Her primary specializations are (a) the needs of sexual- and gender-minority youth and subsequent program development and service delivery, (b) the roles and interventions used by health social workers to impact the social determinants of health, and (c) developing competent social work practitioners through effective social work education. Dr. Craig is a registered and licensed clinical social worker with a particular expertise in delivering effective services for vulnerable populations. Selected experiences over her 25 years of practice include founder and executive director of the Alliance for LGBTQ Youth, executive director of ALSO for Out Youth, medical social worker in the emergency care center of a community hospital, and director of a domestic violence shelter.

Dr. Craig has been the recipient of numerous awards, including the Inspirational Social Work Leader 2015, Ontario Association of Social Workers; Fellow, the Society for Social Work Research; the Excellence in Research Scholarship Award from the Council of Sexual Orientation and Gender Identity/Expression; National Association of Social Workers Student Social Worker of the Year; and the Gay and Lesbian Adolescent Social Services National Person of Impact. She is particularly proud that several of her students and mentees have also become Student Social Worker(s) of the Year.

Marcie Fisher-Borne, PhD, MSW, MPH

Program Director and Co-Principal Investigator of the Vaccinate Adolescents against Cancers Project, American Cancer Society

Assistant Professor, College of Natural Resources, North Carolina State University

Dr. Fisher-Borne has taught social work education for over 10 years. With a longstanding interest in health equity and intervention research, she is currently leading a cancer prevention intervention nationally at the American Cancer Society. She chose social work as a discipline because of its long history of applied, interdisciplinary, practice-based research. Her overarching research goals have been to contribute to the body of knowledge that helps practitioners to understand how interventions focused on structural change impact health outcomes for marginalized populations. Specifically, her work has focused on developing and evaluating health interventions that build community and organizational partnerships to tackle health inequalities in the United States and Global South (i.e., Central America and Asia). Through a competitive process in 2013, Dr. Fisher-Borne was awarded a contract from the American Cancer Society to assess the impact of community health advisers on reducing cancer disparities. The Cancer Disparities Reduction Collaborative is modeled on an evidence-based intervention from the Deep South Network for Cancer Control. She was contracted to evaluate the three-year pilot phase of intervention in the Deep South, in Appalachia and with the Eastern Band of the Cherokee Nation.

Megan Gandy-Guedes, PhD

Assistant Professor, Anne and Henry Zarrow School of Social Work, University of Oklahoma

Dr. Gandy-Guedes graduated with her MSW from the University of North Carolina-Charlotte and practiced as a licensed clinical social worker with children, adolescents, and adults with serious mental illness in both community and inpatient settings for more than six years before returning to school for her PhD at the School of Social Work at Virginia Commonwealth University in Richmond. In addition to her role as assistant professor at the Anne and Henry Zarrow School of Social Work at the University of Oklahoma (OU), she holds core affiliate faculty status with the OU Department of Women's and Gender Studies and is a faculty associate with the OU Knee Center for Strong Families. Her substantive area of research interest is LGBTQ populations, focusing primarily on mental health and service use, faith communities and social support, and social justice issues. Her scholarship includes the Queer Youth Cultural Competency scale, an instrument to measure LGBTQ-related cultural competency in direct-care behavioral health workers. She also explores how faith communities act as protective factors in the lives of LGBTQ people. Her teaching interests include direct clinical practice with individuals, groups, and families. Dr. Gandy-Guedes is involved at the grassroots level in community advocacy for LGBTQ people through a citizen-led initiative called Norman United.

Trevor G. Gates, PhD, LCSW

Assistant Professor, Social Work, Greater Rochester Collaborative MSW Program, College at Brockport, State University of New York

Dr. Gates holds a PhD in social work with an interdisciplinary certificate in gender and women's studies from the University of Illinois at Chicago. He is a clinical social worker and substance abuse counselor with more than 12 years of experience in community-based and hospital settings, specializing in practice with LGBTQ communities. His current research focuses on social justice issues with LGBTQ communities, organizational behavior, and strengths-based practices. He is currently conducting empirical research on the impact of workplace stigma-related experiences on LGBTQ people and the correlation of organizational tolerance for heterosexism and individual/organizational wellness. He is also interested in international issues, especially human rights issues for LGBTQ workers.

Eric Hartman, DSW, LCSW

Private Practitioner

Dr. Hartman maintains a full-time independent psychotherapy practice in New York City. After receiving his Master of Social Work from New York University (NYU), he joined a community-based organization that serves homeless and street-involved LGBTQ youth, where he worked in various clinical and administrative roles over the span of six years. During that time, he also completed an intensive clinical training program at the Psychoanalytic Psychotherapy Study Center in NYC. Subsequently, he earned a Doctor of Social Work (DSW) from Rutgers University, where his research interests included the investigation of embodied identity practices and dissociative experiences in gay men who grew up as effeminate boys. He is a recurrent invited lecturer on the topic of dissociation at NYU and Hunter College, and he teaches a course on phenomenology in the DSW Program at Rutgers University.

Kirsten Havig, MSW, PhD

Assistant Professor, Division of Social Work, University of Wyoming

Dr. Havig is an assistant professor of social work at the University of Wyoming, where she teaches courses on diversity and social justice, social welfare policy, administration, and clinical practice. Prior to accepting her position in Wyoming, Dr. Havig spent five years at the University of Oklahoma and served two years as a clinical instructor under the Federal Title IV-E Child Welfare training grant at the University of Missouri where she provided classroom instruction and other training around child sexual abuse and exploitation, child welfare policy, and children with sexual behavior problems. Her current research focuses on the commercial sexual exploitation of children; trauma, resilience, and posttraumatic growth; child welfare systems; and social justice pedagogy in social work education. She is a former faculty associate with the Oklahoma University Knee Center for Strong Families with funded research focused on the intersection of sexual exploitation and the child welfare system. Prior to working in higher education she was a licensed clinical social worker who practiced primarily with justice-involved youth and survivors of sexual trauma doing therapy, forensic interviewing, and advocacy work.

Lynn C. Holley, PhD, ACSW

Associate Professor, School of Social Work, Arizona State University

Dr. Holley is an associate professor in the School of Social Work at Arizona State University. She has conducted multicultural feminist research about diversity and oppression of several identity groups. Her current focus is on oppression of people with mental health conditions, including those who are of color and/or LGBTQ. She enjoys teaching and mentoring BSW, MSW, and PhD students. She earned her MSSW from the University of Tennessee at Knoxville and her PhD from the University of Washington at Seattle.

Ian W. Holloway, PhD, MSW, MPH

Assistant Professor, Luskin School of Public Affairs, University of California, Los Angeles

Professor Holloway's research focuses on understanding the multilevel contexts in which health risk and protective behaviors occur in order to inform theoretically driven, culturally tailored structural and social network-delivered interventions to improve the health and well-being of sexual- and gender-minority (LGBT) communities. He is the principal investigator of a study funded by the UCLA Center for AIDS Research to understand health risk behaviors among gay, bisexual, and other men who have sex with men in the Dominican Republic. Dr. Holloway is also currently collaborating on two studies funded by the National Institutes of Health. The first, titled "Social Networks and Technology Use of Transgender Women with/at High Risk for HIV," focuses on understanding how the structure and composition of transgender women's egocentric social networks influences their engagement in HIV risk and protective behaviors. The second, "Social Media for HIV Testing and Studying Social Networks," examines the efficacy of a Facebook-delivered peer education program on HIV testing behaviors of racially and ethnically diverse gay, bisexual, and other men who have sex with men.

Sid P. Jordan, JD

Doctoral Student, Luskin School of Public Affairs School in Social Welfare, University of California at Los Angeles

Sid Jordan's research and field experience has focused on the health, wellness, and self-determination of LGBTQ youth and survivors of violence. Mr. Jordan previously led one of the first federally funded demonstration projects aimed at increasing access to victim services for LGBTQ communities and has provided extensive training and consulting for health and human service organizations in the United States and Canada. Mr. Jordan's research interests include the intersections of social work and the law, community-based responses to violence and trauma, and the criminalization of LGBTQ youth and transgender people.

Brian L. Kelly, PhD, MSW, CADC

Assistant Professor, School of Social Work, Loyola University Chicago

Dr. Kelly received his BSW, MSW, and PhD in social work from University of Illinois at Chicago, Jane Addams College of Social Work. His research explores current and historical uses of recreational, art, and music-based activities in social work and related fields as sites and opportunities for strengths-based social work practice. He holds an associate degree in audio engineering from Full Sail University and incorporates audio documentary and other audio-based ethnographic methodologies in his work as means to increase strengths-based, participatory research practices. Dr. Kelly has several years of clinical experience working with individuals with substance use issues as a certified alcohol and drug abuse counselor. In addition, he has several years of practice experience working with the homeless, including adults living with HIV/AIDS and other chronic medical conditions as well as young people. Dr. Kelly is an advocate for the advancement of social work practice with groups and teaches group work and substance use courses at the graduate level.

Shaina Knepler-Foss, MSW, CADC

Alumnus, School of Social Work, Loyola University Chicago

Ms. Knepler-Foss, MSW, CADC, is a May 2016 graduate from the School of Social Work at Loyola University Chicago. She specialized in mental health and the Certified Alcohol and other Drug Counselor program. Ms. Knepler-Foss is interested in working with diverse communities to establish effective alternative treatments for individuals who are impacted by chemical and process addictions. While presently employed at a psychiatric rehabilitation center, Ms. Knepler-Foss spends her free time crocheting and exploring Chicago with her partner Eric and dog Luther.

Gayle Mallinger, PhD, MSW

Assistant Professor, Department of Social Work, Western Kentucky University

Professor Mallinger earned her MSW and PhD in social work at the University of Pittsburgh. Her research focuses on examining the influence of intersecting contexts on individual, family, and community resilience. Specifically, she investigates the determinants of social injustice and the evaluation of interventions aimed at promoting equity. Her current work is centered on the efficacy of varied pedagogical strategies in preparing social work students to successfully practice with LGBT client systems.

Lauren B. McInroy, MSW

Doctoral Student, Factor-Inwentash School of Social Work, University of Toronto

Ms. McInroy is a PhD candidate, research coordinator, and course instructor in the Factor-Inwentash Faculty of Social Work at the University of Toronto. She also holds master's in social work, bachelor of education, and bachelor of arts degrees from the University of Toronto and is a registered social worker in the province of Ontario. Lauren's research primarily focuses on the well-being of LGBTQ+ populations and the developmental and social implications of offline and online information and communication technologies on children, adolescents, and young adults. An accomplished emerging scholar with numerous publications, her dissertation research is investigating the impact of creative, community-driven online fan culture on the identity development and resilience of LGBTQ+ young people.

David A. McLeod, PhD, MSW

Graduate Coordinator and Assistant Professor, Anne and Henry Zarrow School of Social Work, University of Oklahoma

Dr. McLeod has spent the better part of the past two decades working to actively reduce violence, particularly that directed at people and communities with diminished capacities for self-protection. In addition to being an assistant professor in the University of Oklahoma (OU) Anne and Henry Zarrow School of Social Work, he holds affiliate faculty status with the OU Department of Women's and Gender Studies and the OU Center for Social Justice as well as being a faculty associate with the OU Knee Center for Strong Families. A former police detective who transitioned to become a forensic social worker, David has taught undergraduate and graduate courses in programs of social work, criminal justice, and preparing future faculty. His research is focused on the intersection of criminal behavior development, gender, and trauma. Some of Dr. McLeod's current professional activities include investigations of differential criminal behavior development, the impact of trauma on human development, neuroscience, female sexual offending, female incarceration, child sexual abuse, child protection and child protective service provision, intraprofessional and multidisciplinary collaboration, and human sex trafficking.

Natasha S. Mendoza, PhD

Assistant Professor, School of Social Work, Arizona State University

Dr. Natasha Mendoza is an assistant professor in the School of Social Work at Arizona State University (ASU). She received her MSW from the University of Wyoming and her PhD from The Ohio State University. Prior to joining ASU, Dr. Mendoza was an National Institute of Health–supported postdoctoral fellow at the Research Institute on Addictions in Buffalo, New York. Currently, Dr. Mendoza serves on the board of directors for the National Council on Alcoholism and Drug Dependence (Phoenix). Dr. Mendoza's scholarship is based on the premise that motivation to change substance use behaviors is intrinsic and a function of interpersonal relationships, occurring within the context of culture and across multiple systems (e.g., criminal justice, child protective services). Moreover, intersecting identities (i.e., gender, ethnic, and sexual orientation), physical health, and wellness are indelibly linked to behavioral health. Her work examines the ways in which identity and wellness may be an asset in recovery from substance use disorders or connected to risk factors associated with problematic use and treatment barriers. Aside from research, Dr. Mendoza is actively engaged in preparing students to work with members of the LGBTQ community and build on the empirical foundation of social work with an emphasis on evidence-based treatment of substance use disorders.

Anthony P. Natale, MSW, PhD

Associate Professor and Assistant Director, Anne and Henry Zarrow School of Social Work, University of Oklahoma

Dr. Natale is a PhD graduate from the University of Denver, Graduate School of Social Work and obtained a master of social work degree from Portland State University. His social work practice background includes community-based clinical social work, crisis mental health services, and employee assistance program delivery. Dr. Natale's primary scholarly interests include health disparities, HIV/AIDS, trauma and human development, social determinants of health, and social and public health policy.

John Orwat, PhD, LCSW

Associate Professor, School of Social Work, Loyola University Chicago

Dr. Orwat is an associate professor in the School of Social Work at Loyola University Chicago. He teaches health policy and systems in the MSW program and advanced statistics in the doctoral program. Dr. Orwat is principal investigator for the Interprofessional Practice with at-Risk Youth project, funded by the Health Resources and Services Administration, and co-principal investigator for the Screening, Brief Intervention and Referral to Treatment project, funded by Substance Abuse and Mental Health Services Administration, both at Loyola University Chicago. He has also led several health services research projects, most recently an analysis of physician quality in urban versus rural areas. Dr. Orwat holds a PhD from the Heller School of Social Policy and Management at Brandeis University and a master of arts in clinical social work from the University of Chicago, School of Social Service Administration.

G. Allen Ratliff, MSW, LCSW

Doctoral Student, University of California-Berkeley School of Social Welfare

Mr. Ratliff previously worked as the director of clinical services at the Youth Service Project, a social service agency on the west side of Chicago, and is a licensed clinical social worker in the state of Illinois. Mr. Ratliff received his BA in sociology and English from the University of Nebraska-Lincoln and his MSW from the University of Illinois at Chicago. Mr. Ratliff has several years of clinical experience working with queer, gender-nonconforming, and/or homeless young people and with youth and families affected by community violence. His research is centered on the experiences of queer and gender-nonconforming children and adolescents, with particular emphasis on the impacts of microaggressions on developmental milestones and long-term outcomes in health, education, and relationships. In his clinical practice and supervision Mr. Ratliff advocates the use of trauma-informed, harm reduction, positive youth development practices with young people affected by community violence, trauma, and discrimination.

Elizabeth B. Russell, PhD, LCSW, MSW

Clinical Associate Professor, Social Work, Greater Rochester Collaborative MSW Program, College at Brockport, State University of New York

Dr. Russell is currently a clinical associate professor at the College at Brockport, State University and was previously a tenured associate professor at Nazareth College. She has worked in a variety of practice settings including as a case manager for the chronically mentally ill, a clinical social worker in a university hospital outpatient setting, a child therapist, a sex therapist, a clinical supervisor, and a researcher at two other universities. Her main areas of interest are sexual health in practice settings, community advocacy for social justice, women and depression, and mental health. Her current research focuses on the sexual health training of social workers, online curriculum development and delivery, and women in academia. Dr. Russell received her PhD from the University of Rochester and her master of social work degree from the University of Michigan-Ann Arbor where she majored in interpersonal practice and sexual health. Her doctoral dissertation assessed mental health practitioners' knowledge, attitudes, and training in sexual health.

Kristin S. Scherrer, PhD, LCSW, MA

Associate Professor and BSSW Program Director, Department of Social Work, Metropolitan State University of Denver

Dr. Scherrer received her PhD in social work and sociology, as well as her MSW and MA in sociology from the University of Michigan and her BA in sociology and psychology from the University of Colorado at Boulder. Dr. Scherrer's research examines how age, generation, and cohort shape how individuals recognize themselves as having sexual-minority identities and how these identities affect their family relationships. Most recently, she investigated how family systems, and grandparent–grandchild relationships in particular, are affected by the discovery of a grandchild's LGBQ sexual orientation. Other research interests include bisexual and asexual identities, culturally competent practice, and gerontology. Dr. Scherrer's practice experiences have involved working with LGBQT individuals and their families, women and children who were victims of violence, and older adults and their families. Across these roles, Dr. Scherrer's clinical work has focused on how individuals and families cope with conflict and crisis. Dr. Scherrer has taught social work courses at MSU Denver, Rutgers University, and the University of Michigan, in content areas such as social work practice, diversity, advanced clinical practice with older adults, LGBT issues, international social work, group dynamics, aging and gerontological services, qualitative research, and women's issues.

Mark Smith, PhD, LCSW

Associate Professor, School of Social Work, Barry University

Dr. Smith has been a social work faculty member at Barry University for 14 years and holds the rank of associate professor. His undergraduate degree is in early childhood education (University of South Carolina) and his MSW is from San Francisco State University. He maintains a small practice specializing in clinical supervision and narrative-based work with adults, adolescents, children, and families. Dr. Smith's areas of interest and expertise include resiliency-focused clinical practice, social group work, family practice, community responses to disaster and trauma, LGBTQ youth and adults, international social work and social development, antiracist/oppressive social work pedagogy, narrative and constructivist clinical practice, spirituality, and participant-based qualitative research. He is currently a member of the board of directors for the International Association for Social Work with Groups.

Marcia Spira, PhD
Professor and Interim Associate Dean, School of Social Work, Loyola University Chicago
Dr. Spira coordinates the gero subspecialization program in the master of social work program. She teaches classes in human behavior and direct practice to students in the master's and doctoral programs. She earned her PhD in 1982 from the University of Chicago where she studied the impact of a chronic illness on family relationships. Dr. Spira has published many articles and presented at local and national conferences on individuals and families confronted with challenges and transitions throughout the life cycle. Her most recent work focuses on the shifts that occur in families challenged with the diagnosis of dementia. She also maintains a private practice.

De'Shay Thomas, MSW
Doctoral Student, School of Social Work, Arizona State University
De'Shay is a third-year doctoral student in the School of Social Work at Arizona State University. She received a BA in social work from San Diego State University and her master's degree in social work from California State University, Los Angeles. Ms. Thomas worked as a doctoral research intern and graduate research associate with the Southwest Interdisciplinary Research Center, where her work was centered in ethnic/racial minorities' health disparities in urban and rural communities. Her current research interests include behavioral health disparities, particularly in ethnic-, gender-, and sexual-minority communities. She aims to understand how social-cultural ideologies influence help-seeking processes while utilizing intersectionality and a Black feminist/womanist perspective.

Pamela A. Viggiani, PhD, LMSW
Associate Professor, Social Work, Greater Rochester Collaborative MSW Program, College at Brockport, State University of New York
Dr. Viggiani is currently an associate professor at the College at Brockport, State University of New York. She has worked in a variety of practice settings including working with at-risk elementary and middle school children and as the legislation director at the New York State chapter of the National Association of Social Workers. Her main areas of interest are oppression and privilege, cultural humility, advocacy and social justice, and children and families with disabilities. Her current research focuses on best practices for teaching cultural humility to social workers and health-care professionals and on practitioner–client relationships with refugee families that have children with disabilities. Dr. Viggiani received her PhD and her MSW from the State University of New York at Albany.

M. Alex Wagaman, PhD
Assistant Professor, School of Social Work, Virginia Commonwealth University
Dr. Wagaman received her PhD and MSW from Arizona State University. She has more than 10 years of practice experience in neighborhood and community organizing and community-based

anti-oppression education work. Dr. Wagaman has been actively involved in LGBTQ organizations and advocacy for two decades. Her research interests include participatory research and social service approaches for adolescents and young adults who are members of populations that face oppression and marginalization, including LGBTQ youth; community-based research needs of LGBTQ youth organizations; critical methodologies; and qualitative research methods. Dr. Wagaman's teaching interests include macro practice and social welfare policy.

Courtney Wilson, MSW
Alumnus, School of Social Work, Loyola University Chicago
Ms. Wilson, MSW, is a May 2016 graduate from the School of Social Work at Loyola University Chicago, where she specialized in the mental health program and co-chaired the Social Work Student Organization's LGBTQ committee. Ms. Wilson is interested in working with LGBTQ individuals, especially those experiencing complex trauma and substance abuse. Ms. Wilson spends her free time sewing and exploring Chicago on her bicycle.

Sarah R. Young, PhD, MSW
Assistant Professor, Department of Social Work, Binghamton University
Dr. Young received her PhD in social work from the University of Alabama and her MSW with a focus in community organizing from the University of Michigan. Born and raised in a rural town in upstate New York, Sarah fell in love with the Deep South and lived in Mississippi from 2008 to 2012 working as an LGBTQ youth organizer. She is co-founder and former program manager of the Mississippi Safe Schools Coalition, a youth-led LGBTQ youth advocacy group working to make school climate safer for LGBTQ youth. Dr. Young has served as adjunct faculty in the social work departments of both Mississippi State University and the University of Alabama at Birmingham. She is a former Point Foundation Scholar and was selected by the White House as an Emerging LGBTQ Leader; her dissertation focused on expanding safe schools protections for LGBTQ youth in the Deep South. Her research focuses on LGBTQ policy, community organizing in conservative and underresourced areas, and supporting the families of LGBTQ youth. She is currently an assistant professor at Binghamton University.

INTRODUCTION

Welcome to the first edition of *Social Work Practice with the LGBTQ Community: The Intersection of History, Health, Mental Health and Policy Factors* published by Oxford University Press. It has been such an honor in my role as both editor and author to complete this project, a true labor of love for all those involved. The authors combined knowledge in the field of social work and academia spans decades of direct experience in practice, policy, and research across the United States and Canada related to work with lesbian, gay, bisexual, transgender, and queer (LGBTQ) populations. There are so many unique aspects to this text far beyond understanding the long history of challenges faced by members of the LGBTQ community—along with acknowledging recent success and progress pertaining to the ongoing movement for equality. The authors have woven in international concerns and content associated with the LGBTQ movement and ongoing needs related to health, mental health, policy, and advocacy, among other areas of concern. Our hope was to have the content be applicable and useful for social work students and practitioners across the allied health and mental health professions as well as across disciplines. While each chapter has been led by members of social work faculty, there are many co-authors including doctoral and graduate students. The institutions and schools represent those from large urban cities and small rural towns across the United States and Canada. We attempt to examine the lens of practice in several ways while including relevant conceptual literature along with current empirical research in the field of LGBTQ health and mental health.

The text is broken up into five unique sections that include Section I: Overview: Building Knowledge for Practice; Section II: Considerations Across the Lifespan; Section III: Affirming LGBTQ Practice Approaches; Section IV: Health and Mental Health Factors; and Section V: Appendices. Highlights of the chapters include the following: (a) narrative that blends conceptual, theoretical, and empirical content; (b) examination of current trends in the field related to practice considerations; and (c) snapshots of concerns related to international progress and ongoing challenges related to equality and policy. The supplemental appendices included at the end of the text that include (a) signs, symbols, and subcultures; (b) notable and historical LGBTQ individuals; (c) important historical events and policy related issues; and (d) national resources, websites, and weblinks.

Additionally, as a classroom support for instructors, each chapter has a corresponding Powerpoint presentation that includes a resource list pertaining to that chapter's focus with websites, film, and video links as well as national and international organizations associated with the LGBTQ community. In addition to the resources, each Powerpoint presentation includes up to two case scenarios that directly relate to the chapter content for instructors to build on and use in class or for homework assignments.

As you read this text, it will be important to realize that practice and policy factors facing the LGBTQ community across the United States and international communities are changing daily. At the time of this writing, following soon after the results of the recent US presidential election, many of us await any potential challenges made that counter recent progress. Therefore, we suggest that you continue to seek current resources to supplement the time in which this text was written in order to best meet the needs of this widely diverse community; along with your continued education and developing competency, and to meet the needs of students in the classroom and field alike. Staying current assists with understanding most recent celebrations and accomplishments (e.g., US marriage equality and adoption laws) as well as the need to continue advocating for the ongoing promotion of social justice associated with other inequalities (e.g., employment; housing; immigration discrimination; hate crime laws; transgender rights; international policies; and ongoing forms of oppression). Thus whether you are a member of the LGBTQ community or an ally, there is great room for collaboration in supporting the ever-changing needs of this minority population within classroom settings, organizations, private practice, and far beyond.

A text such as this cannot be completed without ample acknowledgements and gratitude for all those involved throughout the various stages of publication. First it is important to acknowledge the hard work and collegiality of each of the authors within this text. It was an honor and privilege to work with so many esteemed colleagues. Second, I would also like to acknowledge my Practice with the LGBTQ Community class at Loyola University Chicago from the fall 2016 semester. They completed a critical review of all chapters and Powerpoint presentations as one of their class assignments, giving invaluable feedback to truly strengthen the overall content and flow from a social work student's perspective. Next, it was approximately two years ago at the annual program meeting of the Council on Social Work Education in Washington, D.C., that I met Dana Bliss with Oxford University Press. When I inquired about whether Oxford had a text on practice with the LGBTQ community, he replied: "No, but you should write one!" Well Dana—at long last—here it is! I owe him much gratitude for his unwavering support and guidance all along the way, along with the entire team at OUP. Thanks to my graduate assistant and amazing MSW/MA student Nikki Busch for all her work in the final stages of editing and submission, and also to my research assistant and doctoral student Melissa Iverson for her moral support along the way. A special thank you to many other folks that provided so much guidance, feedback, and support in countless ways, especially Edward Alessi, Tyler Argüello, Ashley Austin, Shelley Craig, Domingo Gonzales III, Susan Grossman, Brian Kelly, Marta Lundy, Denise Mather, Lori Messinger, Jason McVicker, Anthony Natale, John Orwat, Susan Wardzala, Darrell Wheeler, Courtney Wilson, my colleagues at the School of Social Work at Loyola University Chicago, and most importantly the many social work students who have inspired me over the years.

Michael P. Dentato, PhD, MSW, Editor
April 15, 2017
Chicago, IL

SOCIAL WORK PRACTICE WITH THE LGBTQ COMMUNITY

PART I

OVERVIEW

Building Knowledge for Practice

CHAPTER 1

A HISTORY OF COMMUNITY

Marching Toward LGBTQ Equality

Jean E. Balestrery

INTRODUCTION

It was a watershed moment for the lesbian, gay, bisexual, transgender, and queer (LGBTQ) community in 2015 when the US Supreme Court ruled in favor of legalizing same-sex marriage in the case of *Obergefell v. Hodges*. "In a long-sought victory for the gay rights movement, the Supreme Court ruled by a 5-4 vote . . . that the Constitution guarantees a right to same-sex marriage. 'No longer may this liberty be denied,' Justice Anthony M. Kennedy wrote for the majority in the historic decision. 'No union is more profound than marriage, for it embodies the highest ideals of love, fidelity, devotion, sacrifice and family. In forming a marital union, two people become something greater than once they were'" (Liptak, 2015). Culminating after many decades-long struggles, the LGBTQ community in the United States celebrated this success as a huge victory for human rights. However, the status of LGBTQ human rights, both legally and socially, varies widely across the globe.

This chapter charts the history of the LGBTQ movement and community. First, a contemporary global context relevant to LGBTQ people is presented. Next, this chapter identifies threads of an emerging LGBTQ social movement, which occur in relation to other social developments and movements during the nineteenth and twentieth centuries. Then review of the work of social scientists studying sex, or sexology, depicts a sociopolitical climate of ideological contestations occurring in association with the sex, sexuality, and gender systems. These contestations reflect co-constituting discourses in the United States and abroad that led to institutional developments for LGBTQ advocacy. Following such developments, this chapter describes important events including the 1969 Stonewall uprising and assassination of Harvey Milk that forwarded the modern LGBTQ movement. This chapter concludes with a look at ongoing celebrations and challenges relevant to LGBTQ people and communities.

A person's country of citizenship and place of residence can determine whether same-sex marriage is a legal option or whether same-sex behavior is a criminal offense. According to the United Nations, "in some 77 countries, discriminatory laws criminalize private, consensual same-sex relationships—exposing individuals to the risk of arrest, prosecution, imprisonment—even, in at least five countries, the death penalty" (United Nations Office of the High Commissioner for Human Rights [OHCHR], n.d.). The global context is marked by a wide array of legalization, discrimination, and criminalization with regard to the issue of sexual orientation and gender identity. A 2013 Pew Research Center survey of publics in 39 countries found huge variance by region on the broader issue of acceptance or rejection of the LGBTQ community. The United States is among many other countries across the globe, such as those in Europe and the Americas, that legally support same-sex marriage and more generally the LGBTQ community. However, such progress in the United States occurred in 2013 with the case of *U.S. v. Windsor* overturning the Defense of Marriage Act (DOMA), a 1996 federal law defining marriage as a union between one man and one woman and also allowing other states to not recognize same-sex marriage granted under the laws of other states. According to President Obama, DOMA "violated the Fifth Amendment's guarantee of equal protection" (Johnsen, 2013, p. 599). In the same regard, many countries still do not support same-sex marriage or more generally the LGBTQ community; among these are Muslim nations, Africa, Russia, and parts of Asia (Pew Research Center, 2015).

Russia, for example, is currently entertaining a new anti-LGBTQ bill that is being proposed in parliament, which follows a "gay propaganda" bill passed in 2013 (Editorial Board, 2016). This new bill "proposes fines of between four and five thousand rubles (USD $53–$66) for 'the public expression of non-traditional sexual relations, manifested in a public demonstration of personal perverted sexual preferences in public places' "; further, this bill states that if such public expression occur " 'on territories and in institutions, providing educational, cultural or youth services,' the offender could face an additional penalty of up to 15 days of administrative arrest" (Cooper, 2016). Through fines and jail time, this new bill criminalizes the public expression of LGBTQ behavior. Ivan Nikitchuk, one of the lawmakers introducing the bill, described it as "an effort to preserve longstanding social norms" (Editorial Board, 2016).

Despite President Putin's insistence that Russia is a safe country for LGBTQ people, this proposed new bill further threatens the safety of LGBTQ people. "Human Rights Watch documented a rise in harassment of gay people and violent attacks after passage of the 2013 law, which outlawed promotion of what the government classified as 'nontraditional sexual relationships' " (Editorial Board, 2016). Reporting for Human Rights Watch, researcher Tanya Cooper noted: "If the members of parliament have any regard at all for the country's constitution and international human rights obligations, they know that they should immediately reject this bill." President Putin signed the 2013 propaganda bill into law yet also has publicly denied that Russia has institutionalized homophobia. Prior to the 2014 Winter Olympics in Sochi, Putin "sought to dispel concerns that gay athletes and spectators could be vulnerable" and later stated: "[w]e have no persecution at all"—which was clearly not true (Editorial Press, 2016).

Yet, even in countries where same-sex marriage is legal, discrimination toward LGBTQ people continues—in some cases sexual and gender minorities can be assaulted, victimized, and murdered. Argentina is one such example; it legalized same-sex marriage in 2010, thus becoming the first Latin American country to do so. Argentina is a country in the Americas with some of the most liberal civil rights policies. For example, in 2012 the country passed gender identity legislation that supports gender-identity transitions without a psychiatric diagnosis or surgery (Gilbert, 2015). Despite the passage of this gender identity law, social hostility and unsolved murders of transgender people continue. In fact, it is troubling to note that the average life expectancy of transgender people in Argentina is only 35 years. Notably, activist messages such as "Enough transgendercide" and "Liberate us from violence" were visible at a 2015 LGBTQ march in Buenos Aires (Gilbert, 2015).

In Southeast Asia, Vietnam's communist government abolished a ban on same-sex marriage on New Year's Day in 2015 (Lewis, 2016). Yet discrimination toward LGBTQ people continues. Soon after this ban was lifted, reports were published about "ongoing insults, intimidation and beatings that young LGBT people are subjected to in the country's schools" (Lewis, 2016). For example, last year, a UNESCO report "on bullying on the basis of sexual orientation and gender identity across the Asia-Pacific referred to recent studies finding that almost half of LGBT students in Vietnam said they faced serious stigma in schools" (Lewis, 2016).

The United Nations has written an official position statement on the topic of LGBTQ rights. In 2011, the Human Rights Council adopted the first United Nations resolution on sexual orientation and gender identity known as Resolution 17/19. Following the adoption of this resolution, the OHCHR developed the first official United Nations report on the issue. By doing so, the United Nations was "expressing 'grave concern' at violence and discrimination against individuals based on their sexual orientation and gender identity" (United Nations OHCHR, n.d.). In September of 2015, 12 United Nations entities jointly developed an unprecedented statement to serve as a public call to end such violence and discrimination. In particular, this statement was a call to action aimed toward governmental bodies. At an international level, the OHCHR

> is committed to working with states, national human rights institutions and civil society to achieve progress towards the worldwide repeal of laws criminalizing LGBT persons and further measures to protect people from violence and discrimination on grounds of their sexual orientation or gender identity. (United Nations OHCHR, n.d.)

IMBRICATING SOCIAL MOVEMENTS

In the profession of social work, it is notable that lesbians were among the first generation of women leaders and activists for human rights, including Jane Addams, Ellen Star, and Mary Richmond. Now referred to as "lesbian foremothers," such recognition counters the erasure of sexuality in the historical record of the profession (Fredrikson-Goldsen, Lindhorst, Kemp, & Walters, 2009) as well as noting the critical role of social workers within various social movements. It should be noted that while engaged in various forms of same-sex intimacy and relationships, these women activists would likely not have used the contemporary term "lesbian" to self-identify during that historical period (circa 1880s–1920s). Regardless, the impact these and many other lesbian, bisexual, and transgender women had on social movements addressing poverty, equal rights (e.g., women, race, LGBTQ), and social justice across time must not be underestimated nor overlooked. As noted by Mary Richmond: "Movements more or less independent in origin may act and react upon one another in such a way as to make it difficult to unravel their beginnings" (1917, p. 33).

In the same regard, the LGBTQ movement is intertwined with other social movements occurring during the late nineteenth and early twentieth centuries throughout the United States and Europe. Among these are social Darwinism, eugenics, and moral reform campaigns. Inscribed within such movements were many labels, sexual acts, bodily characteristics, and roles deemed as sexual perversions. Such behaviors and alleged perversions were "linked to increasing anxiety about the nature of civilization and evolutionary 'progress'" (Gibson, 1997, pp. 111–112). Theories of degeneracy and pathology permeated these social movements and "[h]omosexuality was almost invariably labeled as a form of degeneration" (Gibson, 1997, p. 115). Odem (1995) helps us to further understand the intersection of societal events, perceptions, and the LGBTQ movement when noting

> Expressions of sexuality that did not conform to a marital, reproductive framework were increasingly subjected to government surveillance and control, as evidenced by a range of legal measures . . . [including] legislation prohibiting the dissemination of obscene literature, the criminalization of abortion, stringent measures targeting prostitution, and heightened legal repression of homosexuality. Such developments reflected Americans' deep anxiety about the increased potential for sexual expression outside of marriage—a situation that threatened middle-class Victorian ideals of sexual restraint and marital, reproductive sex. (p. 2)

Many of the laws associated with sex and sexuality in the United States date back to the nineteenth-century morality crusades with the passage of the first anti-obscenity law known as the Comstock Act of 1873. This act was followed by the Criminal Law Amendment Act of 1885, the Mann Act of 1910, the utilization of systematized categories during the 1950s such as "sex offender" and "child abuse," and laws circumscribing sexual behavior that contained jurisdictional power that functioned to criminalize homosexuality and the "homosexual" (Rubin, 1993, pp. 4–5).

The criminalization of homosexuality in the United States continued throughout the twentieth century, and the theory of pathology associated with "homosexuality" was codified in the emblematic "sexual psychopath" stereotyping that occurred during the 1930s. In 1952, the American Psychiatric Association (APA) published the first *Diagnostic and Statistical Manual of Mental Disorders* to classify sexual perversity and, later, "homosexuality" as clinically diagnosable disorders or "abnormal" conditions. It was not until 1973 and through the petitioning and activism of key LGBTQ leaders such as Barbara Gittings and Frank Kameny that the APA removed "homosexuality" from the manual.

Antisodomy laws provided another form of criminalizing the LGBTQ community. In fact, as of 1960 every state had an antisodomy law on record (Associated Press, 2003). It was not until the landmark case of *Lawrence v. Texas* in 2003 when the US Supreme Court ruled against a ban on same-sex sexual activity. The Supreme Court's decision striking down the sodomy law in Texas ruled: "that the law was an unconstitutional violation of privacy" (Associated Press, 2003). In doing so, the Supreme Court made same-sex sexual activity legal in every state and territory while also reversing a previous decision in 1986 to uphold an antisodomy law similar to Texas's antisodomy law.

In Europe, the Austrian-Prussian War led to the eventual establishment of the North German Confederation with a later integration of northern and southern German territories into the German Empire in 1871 (Steakley, 1997). Germany's penal code, known as Paragraph 175, noted that acts of sodomy among males were criminal offenses while imposing a "maximum of five years imprisonment for 'lewd and unnatural conduct' between males" (Hirshfeld, 2000, p. 14). In the wake of a rising women's movement and youth movement in Germany, alongside the German homosexual emancipation movement, there was a draft amendment for Paragraph 175 proposing the extension of criminalization of homosexual acts between women.

During the late nineteenth century, the famous trials of Oscar Wilde (1854–1900) influenced further developments relevant to the LGBTQ movement. Wilde, a notable British author of the time, was prosecuted and imprisoned for "gross indecency" in 1895. Wilde's behavior was strictly criminalized, as "no experts suggested at his trial that he should receive any kind of treatment for his condition" (Waters, 2006, p. 58). These unfortunate trials influenced the ideas among social scientists engaged in the scientific study of sex, or sexology, in other countries and particularly in Germany. For example, the trial of Oscar Wilde in Britain "elicited widespread discussion in Germany that at times took on nationalistic undertones" (Steakley, 1997, p. 139). Consequently, sexology emerged as an authoritarian field with various "experts" debating the issues relevant to the sex, sexuality, and gender systems. Among these "experts" was sexologist Magnus Hirschfeld who became committed to "homosexual" emancipation and was a pioneering political activist for the LGBTQ movement.

THE SCIENTIFIC STUDY OF SEX

The sexual politics of the nineteenth and twentieth centuries focused on ideological contestations whereby "expert" sexologists influenced the proliferation of labels and codified categories associated with sex, sexuality, and gender systems. Among these labels and categories were the terms: "homosexual" (see Kertbeny in Peters, 2014 and Stryker, 2008); "sexual invert" (Krafft-Ebing, 1886, 1965); "third sex" and "Urning" (see Ulrichs in Kennedy, 1997); "sexual intermediaries" and "transvestite" (see Hirschfeld in Stryker, 2008), and "step-child of nature" (Krafft-Ebing, 1886, 1965). The labels "homosexual" and "transvestite" appear to have persisted most throughout the centuries as predominant references within popular discourse.

As a label, "homosexuality" endured many definitional and theoretical renditions during the nineteenth and twentieth centuries. The historical and sociopolitical discourse on sexuality during this time period is replete with scientific contestation about homosexuality with questions pertaining to whether it is an act or a role; a condition or an identity; acquired or congenital; socially constructed or biologically based; normal or abnormal; a disease, an illness, or a crime; and whether it is a fixed condition or something that can be cured (Kennedy, 1997; Krafft-Ebing, 1886, 1965; Oosterhuis, 1997; Steakley, 1997). One can trace the inscription of homosexuality and its roots to the work of Karl Westphal, who wrote *The Contrary Sexual Feeling: Symptom of a Neuropathic (Psychopathic) Condition* (1869) thereby situating homosexuality within a paradigm of pathology. As noted by Kennedy, the association of homosexuality as a "contrary feeling" had a lasting impact: "for more than a century, most psychiatrists represented homosexuality as an illness by definition" (Kennedy, 1997, p. 39).

Karl Heinrich Ulrichs was the first among sexological researchers who argued for the biological naturalness of homosexuality in an emancipatory effort to equalize social and legal treatment for LBGTQ people. In 1864, Ulrichs published a paper coining the term "third sex" (Kennedy, 1997, p. 30). Ulrichs expanded the discourse of sexuality from a focus on acts to a focus on the nature of the individual, also pioneering the term "Urning" and scientifically theorizing homosexuality to be an inborn condition. "He was the first self-declared homosexual to speak out publicly for the civil and legal rights of homosexuals" (Kennedy, 1997, p. 38). Ulrichs spoke at the Congress of German Jurists in 1867 advocating repeal of antisodomy laws in Germany and Austria and published the first homosexual journal in 1870.

> It was in correspondence with Ulrichs that the German-born Hungarian citizen Karl Maria Kertbeny first coined the term "homosexual" in 1869, which he also intended to connote same-sex love, minus the element of gender inversion to be found in the term "urning." (Stryker, 2008, p. 37)

Kertbeny was a Hungarian journalist who "wrote passionately in opposition to Germany's anti-sodomy laws in the 19th Century" (Peters, 2014, p. 10).

Sexologists Krafft-Ebing, Havelock Ellis, and Magnus Hirschfeld emerged on the sociopolitical horizon. One of the most prominent psychiatrists of his time in central Europe, Krafft-Ebing is remembered today as the author of *Psychopathia Sexualis* and as "one of the founding fathers of scientific sexology" (Oosterhuis, 1997, p. 70). *Psychopathia Sexualis* is a compilation of over 200 case studies with autobiographical accounts of homosexuals and their experiences. Krafft-Ebing associated homosexuality ("inclination only toward the same sex") with the paradigm of pathology (Krafft-Ebing, 1886, 1965; Oosterhuis, 1997, p. 221). He treated "sexual abnormality as disease" in order to dissociate it from religious sin, criminal behavior, or lustful decadence (Oosterhuis, 1997, p. 73). Throughout the work of Krafft-Ebing and other sexologists, there was a continual blurring of categorical boundaries, contradictory suppositions, and paradoxical underpinnings.

> Despite the effort to distinguish perversion from normalcy, there was a clear tendency in *Psychopathia Sexualis* to undercut distinctions between divergent desires and to make various forms of normal and abnormal sexuality equivalent and interchangeable, thus abolishing a clear boundary between health and perversion. (Oosterhuis, 1997, p. 73)

Similar to Krafft-Ebing, Havelock Ellis is another sexologist who argued that there is a congenital aspect to homosexuality. Ellis (2006) advocated for decriminalizing "homosexuality," arguing that if homosexuality is acquired then it logically follows that heterosexuality is also acquired; hence, this acquired theory for any particular form of sexuality is specious.

Magnus Hirschfeld (1868–1935) and Sigmund Freud (1856–1939) were both sex researchers that proposed arguments against the theory of degeneracy. Hirschfeld developed a theory of sexual intermediacy and sexual variation, identifying approximately 43 million sexual types

(Steakley, 1997). The sex researcher Alfred Kinsey later expounded upon this theory of sexual variability and attached a quantitative value to this variation model by developing a scale from zero to 6 with extreme homosexuality and extreme heterosexuality on each end of this scale (Steakley, 1997). Hirschfeld was a pioneer in the institutional development of advocacy organizations for homosexuality. In 1897, he cofounded the Scientific Humanitarian Committee, "the world's first organization dedicated to the aim of ending the centuries-long legal intolerance and social opprobrium that homosexuals had suffered in western culture" (Hirschfeld, 2000, p. 14). Later in 1919, Hirschfeld established the Institute of Sexual Science in Berlin. Hirschfeld's position on the issue of homosexuality and transgenderism is one of staunch advocacy for equal treatment and rights for the LGBTQ community. "As early as 1910 he had written *The Transvestites,* the first book length treatment of transgender phenomena" (Stryker, 2008, p. 39). Freud, also arguing against the theory of degeneracy, developed a theory of psychosexual development premised upon stages of maturation. Freud identified homosexuality as a stunted type of sexual abnormality characterized by the Oedipus Complex. Freud's theory posits the metaphor of the "seed" and "soil." This metaphor proposes that the "seed" of homosexuality is present in everyone yet only certain "seeds" manifest into homosexual behavior as a result of external conditions that mix with the "soil."

Throughout the sexological literature, the instability with notions of what represented "normal" and "abnormal" in association with sex, sexuality, and gender systems remains evident. While many of these theories and notions developed in order to promote social justice for LGBTQ people, the sexological literature remained entangled in a pathological—and therefore disempowering—discourse. Consequently, it is critical for students and practitioners to consistently use empowerment-based practice skills, techniques, and language (e.g., "gay" rather than "homosexual") along with affirming practice models and approaches, as examined elsewhere throughout this text.

THE LAVENDER SCARE

The twentieth century witnessed increasingly organized political activism that marked threads of an emerging LGBTQ movement. In the United States, this activism encompassed significant events during the 1950s and 1960s, culminating in the uprising at the Stonewall Inn in New York City in 1969, while also symbolizing the beginning of the LGBTQ movement as an organized social movement (Duberman, 1993). Among such events leading up to the Stonewall uprising included the "Lavender Scare" and the emergence of the homophile movement.

The decade following World War II (1947–1957) was a period characterized as the "Red Scare" in the United States. There was widespread fear of espionage, fueled by Senator Joseph R. McCarthy's hysteria associated with the potential threat of Communists infiltrating the government, and overall grave concern for national security (Johnson, 2004). Concurrent with the Red Scare and "McCarthyism" was the anti-LGBTQ movement known as the Lavender Scare. This fear of gay men and women permeated much of society and culture during the same period of time, raising fears that "homosexuals posed a threat to national security and needed to be systematically removed from the federal government" (Johnson, 2004, p. 9).

Many historians have ignored the overlap between the fear of Communists and the fear of homosexuals. During the McCarthy years, the concept of "security risk" became a euphemism for "homosexual." However, most of those fired due to "security risks" were not necessarily those named by Senator McCarthy as Communists. The typical case involved a gay man confronted with circumstantial evidence that "he associated with 'known homosexuals' or been arrested in a known gay cruising area" (Johnson, 2004, p. 3). Consequently, there emerged a large-scale antihomosexual movement, which involved various constituencies including politicians, lawmakers, legal authorities such as the police and courts, psychiatric community, and the larger public. Sadly, reports and statistics "suggest that the total number of federal employees fired due to 'homosexuality' was well into the thousands" (Johnson, 2004, p. 166). One of those fired from his government position as an astronomer was Frank Kameny, who later worked for the remainder of his life as a tireless advocate and activist fighting against LGBTQ discrimination.

The rhetoric of those within the anti-LGBTQ movement conflated various labels such as "communist," "criminal sexual psychopath," "sexual deviant," and "homosexual," all of which triggered public anxieties and further marginalized LGBTQ people (Miller, 2002). There were a series of civil liberty violations, or witch-hunts, throughout the country whereby "homosexuals" were charged with sex crimes, were sent to mental hospitals in lieu of prison, fled out of cities and states, or were jailed. For example, such witch-hunts among "homosexual" men occurred in cities large and small such as Sioux City, Iowa, and Boise, Idaho (Miller, 2002). Many gay men and lesbians created "a sense of solidarity" whereby they would "rely upon one another in social settings requiring a display of heterosexuality" (Johnson, 2004, p. 153).

In the 1950s, the bar setting emerged as an institution and a symbolic context for the integration of public and private lives for many gay men and lesbians. Among other public settings such as the workplace, parks, bookstores, and bathhouses, bars became the center of gay and lesbian social life and the predominant location for seeking fellowship, community, prospective partners, and lovers. "The solidarity experienced by lesbians who knew each other through bars foreshadowed the later solidarity created by lesbian feminism" (Cruikshank, 1992, p. 148). Later on, lesbians who desired an alternative to the bar scene developed small social circles and clubs, such as the Daughters of Bilitis, which began as part of the larger homophile movement.

While such public settings (e.g., lesbian and gay bars and clubs) typically welcomed those within the cross-dressing, drag queen, transvestite, and transgender community, many often experienced various forms of rejection as well as heightened levels of violence and criminalization due to anti-cross-dressing laws. While public regulation of dress dates back to the colonial period in the United States, anti-cross-dressing laws emerged during the 1850s (Stryker, 2008, p. 31). Such laws emerged within the context of the first wave of feminist activism. For example, in the 1840s, feminist activist Amelia Bloomer argued that "long skirts and cumbersome undergarments were essentially a form of bondage that dragged women down, [advocating] that women wear pants like clothing instead" (Stryker, 2008, p. 35). First-wave feminism, a wave of reform spanning the nineteenth century, ultimately threatened the notion of gender conformity. Additionally, municipal ordinances making it illegal for men and women to cross-dress were enacted across various cities. For example, the following ordinance was enacted in San Francisco:

If any person shall appear in a public place in a state of nudity, or in a dress not belonging to his or her sex, or in an indecent or lewd dress, or shall make any indecent exposure of his or her person, or be guilty of any lewd or indecent act or behavior, or shall exhibit or perform any indecent, immoral or lewd play, or other representation, he should be guilty of a misdemeanor, and on conviction shall pay a fine not exceeding five hundred dollars. (Stryker, 2008, p. 32)

The rise of modern industrial cities created new and somewhat affirming environments for those identifying as transvestites, drag queens, and those within gender nonconforming communities. "The circumstances that supported the development of homosexual social worlds also applied to people who sought different ways to express their sense of gender" (Stryker, 2008, p. 34). Thus there were increased opportunities for women to work, travel, and dress as men and for men who identified as women to live anonymously and autonomously as women in urban areas away from more rural or hostile and unwelcoming communities. During the late nineteenth and early twentieth centuries, "homosexual desire and gender variance were closely associated" (Stryker, 2008, p. 34) and quite unlike the more contemporary and often unique definitions associated with gay, lesbian, and transgender identities.

THE HOMOPHILE MOVEMENT

While there were some gay and lesbian groups organizing before the 1950s, including the Society for Human Rights in Chicago (1924), such groups were not necessarily interconnected nor politically mobilized. In 1950, California State Department firings of gay men helped convince Harry Hay to found the Mattachine Society (Johnson, 2004). This society was named for the medieval Italian court jester who expressed unpopular truths from behind a mask. Mattachine originated with a vision to create social and political change for gay people along with a plan for challenging antihomosexual attacks during the McCarthy era (Adam, 1995).

Founded in 1951 in Los Angeles, the Mattachine Society reportedly had a membership of approximately 2,000 people by 1953 (Messinger, 2006, pp. 25–26). The Mattachine Society was "the first effective gay political organization in the United States, one that in its early years devoted itself to challenging and repealing repressive legislation and altering public opinion" (Rimmerman, 2008, p. 16). Notably, the Mattachine Society primarily attracted gay men because it focused on their concerns. However, ONE, Inc., another independent gay organization, would soon develop out of the Mattachine Society and be more welcoming to women. With chapters in various US cities, ONE, Inc. offered "counseling, workshops and classes focused on gay issues and published ONE, the first nationally distributed gay magazine" (Quimby & Williams, 2000, p. 168). In addition, this organization "rejected the medical term homosexual, and favored using homophile to express the notion that it was their same-sex (homo) love (philia) that united them, rather than just sexual behavior" (Quimby & Williams, 2000, pp. 172–175).

Soon after the development of the Mattachine Society, there emerged the beginnings of lesbian autonomy as members of Mattachine "negated the experience of lesbians and conspired to keep them out" (D'Emilio, 1983, p. 93). Consequently, a small group of women in San Francisco organized to affirm the lesbian experience. In 1955, Del Martin, Phyllis Lyon, and three other lesbian couples in San Francisco were instrumental leaders who began Daughters of Bilitis (DOB) (Messinger, 2006, p. 26), known as the "the first lesbian political organization" (D'Emilio, 1983, p. 101).

While the Mattachine Society primarily attracted gay men, DOB attracted a certain profile of lesbians characterized as white, middle to upper class, and professional. DOB published the first issue of its magazine for lesbians called *The Ladder* in 1956 (Messinger, 2006, p. 26). *The Ladder* was edited by Barbara Gittings, who would also be influential in working with Frank Kameny on civil protest pickets and marches, in cities such as Philadelphia and Washington, DC, against the government's refusal to hire gay men and lesbians. The DOB "laid the groundwork for lesbian feminism of the next decade by its social events, referrals, and confrontations with public officials, and by its work with accepting professionals" (Cruikshank, 1992, p. 148). The Mattachine Society and DOB were mostly focused on helping gay men and lesbians "fit" into society rather than promoting political and legal change. The collective development and sustainability of Mattachine Society, ONE, Inc., and DOB symbolized the emergence of the homophile movement, which focused on educating the public through "dispelling of myths, misinformation, and prejudice as the primary means of improving the status of lesbians and homosexuals" (D'Emilio, 1983, p. 103). The homophile movement coalesced within a larger confluence of social forces and societal events including the Kinsey studies, a growing African American civil rights movement, and the persecution of gay men and lesbians during the McCarthy era.

The personal courage among these pioneering leaders of the LGBTQ movement is not to be underestimated given the hostility of the social climate during the 1950s. It should be noted that while the Mattachine Society was initially based upon communist principles of organizing and social change, its use of militant ideology was later met with resistance. In 1953, Harry Hay was expelled from the Mattachine Society due to his advocacy of radical principles (Rimmerman, 2008). This conflict during the early years of the Mattachine Society's development illustrates the tension between the strategies of assimilation versus liberation in political mobilization efforts. In fact, the Mattachine Society's early liberationist strategy of political activism was later replaced by the assimilation and accommodation strategy. The liberation strategy is an outsider approach that aims to "'let us show you a new way of conceiving the world' strategy associated with lesbian and gay liberation" while assimilationists adopt a "'work within the system' insider approach to political and social change" (Rimmerman, 2008, p. 5). Members of the Mattachine Society and DOB grew to adopt a conformist, assimilationist approach through political activism:

> They assiduously cultivated an image of middle-class respectability and denied that they were organizations of homosexuals, instead claiming that they were concerned with the problem of the "variant." They expected social change to come through the good offices of professionals. They saw their task primarily as one of educating the professional who influenced public opinion and only secondarily as one of organizing lesbians and gay men. (D'Emilio, 1989, p. 460)

Within the broader lesbian and gay movement, the assimilationist strategy of political activism continued to prevail from 1953 until the 1969 Stonewall rebellion.

The homophile movement did much to foster a climate of safe spaces and places for gay men and lesbians to discuss and address their experiences as a marginalized and oppressed group. "The most important point about the U.S. homophile movement in the 1950s was that it managed to be born and survive at all" (Poindexter, 1997, p. 612). During that time period, the risks of coming out as LGBTQ included potential for harm to physical safety, loss of employment, loss of social supports, and rejection from family and friends, home, and community. The early pioneers of the homophile movement provided a context for social injustices to be questioned and the climate for a growing social protest movement.

THE STONEWALL INN UPRISING

During the 1940s and 1950s, there was an underground literary movement of poets and writers "who dissented from the dominant ethos of Cold War America, and who expressed through verse their opposition to the conformity and consumerism of the postwar era" (D'Emilio, 1989, p. 461). This underground movement increased in visibility, and the rebellious beat subculture began attracting national media attention. This counterculture was replete with protests against the values of Cold War society aligning with the heteronormative lifestyle (e.g., a focus on career, home and family, raising children) and the exclusion of gay men and lesbians. Therefore, the two subcultures of beat society and gay society reflected mutual imbrications. This was evident through the work of writers and poets such as Robert Duncan, Jack Spicer, Robin Blaser, and Allen Ginsberg (D'Emilio, 1989, p. 461). Ginsberg's *Howl*, a local bestseller, "openly acknowledged male homosexuality" (D'Emilio, 1989, p. 461).

During 1959 and 1960, there were two highly visible gay scandals in San Francisco that also influenced rebellious attitudes among the LGBTQ community. First, during the mayoral campaign, one candidate made public accusations of the incumbent mayor and chief of police as allowing San Francisco to become "the national headquarters of the organized homosexuals in the United States" (D'Emilio, 1989, p. 462). Second, when gay bar owners reported a history of extortion by the police to the district attorney, there followed a targeting of gay men by police.

> Felony convictions of gay men, which stood at zero in the first half of 1960, rose to twenty-nine in the next six months and jumped to seventy-six in the first six months of 1961. Misdemeanor charges against gay women and men stemming from sweeps of the bars ran at an estimated forty to sixty per week during 1961.... Every one of the bars that testified against the police department during the "gayola" inquiry was shut down. The police, backed by the city's press, also intensified surveillance of gay male cruising areas. (D'Emilio, 1989, p. 462).

Harassment by police of gay bars and patrons was not new at this time, as it had occurred during the 1950s. However, what was unique to the New York City and San Francisco police harassment and surveillance of gay men and lesbians was the social climate under which it was occurring. Because the scandals intensified public discussion of "homosexuality" and the ensuing police brutality intensified gay consciousness amidst a beat subculture rebellion, social forces coalesced to encourage the development of a politically rebellious response to increasing anti-gay sentiment.

On June 28, 1969, the Stonewall Inn in New York City's Greenwich Village neighborhood was raided by police—a symbolic event representing the beginning of the modern LGBTQ movement. While the 1950s have been characterized by historian John D'Emilio as "something of a national coming-out experience for gays and lesbians," the Stonewall rebellion of 1969 marks the birth of the lesbian and gay rights movement (Miller, 2002, p. 107). Many other bars in New York had been raided by the police, yet the Stonewall riots became symbolic:

> What made Stonewall a symbol of a new era of gay politics was the reaction of the drag queens, dykes, street people, and bar boys who confronted the police first with jeers and high camp and then with a hail of coins, paving stones, and parking meters. By the end of the weekend, the Stonewall bar had been burned out, but a new form of collective resistance was afoot: gay liberation. (Adam, 1995, p. 81)

A few days after the events at Stonewall, a counterculture and radical activist group called the Gay Liberation Front (GLF) organized. In addition, several women and transgender activists such as Sylvia Rivera and Marsha Johnson had actively participated in the events at Stonewall and later cofounded a group named Street Transvestite Action Revolutionaries (STAR), dedicated to helping young homeless transgender women of color and drag queens. While fewer than 50 lesbian and gay organizations existed before Stonewall, more than 800 lesbian and gay groups were in existence by 1973 (D'Emilio, 1989).

Stonewall initiated a new phase of gay and lesbian politics following nearly 20 years of the homophile movement. "The new leaders in the emerging gay rights movement considered the traditional accommodating approach of the early homophile movement slow and dated because of the less conservative approach of other movements" (Poindexter, 1997, p. 613). The leaders of the post-Stonewall movement supported heightened visibility and "coming out" among all LGBTQ individuals as a source of political mobilization as well as to be more assertive in advocacy and activism similar to other movements of the time pertaining to race (civil rights) and gender (feminism).

THE 1970s

After the Stonewall rebellion, significant events reflected increasing political activism among the LGBTQ movement that included the lesbian feminism movement (1970s), the Save Our Children campaign (1977) followed by the Briggs Amendment in California, and the assassination of Harvey Milk in San Francisco (1978).

LESBIAN FEMINISM

By the 1970s, identity politics associated with "lesbian" and "lesbianism" erupted with a new, growing intensity of collective emotion and political mobilization. "It would have been impossible to mobilize large numbers of lesbians before 1970: the taboos were too strong and the fears too great" (Cruikshank, 1992, p. 150). Gay liberation and women's liberation created the conditions for lesbian liberation politics.

> For many radical lesbians, the women's liberation movement of the 1960s was too bourgeois, too homophobic, and still too focused on how women needed to operate in a man's world. It made women who loved women invisible. In 1970 a group known as the Radicalesbians brought gay liberation and feminism together by arguing that a separatist world was the highest form of feminism and would lead to the complete elimination of patriarchy. For Radicalesbians, lesbianism was not merely a desire or a sexual object choice, but a deliberate rejection of heterosexuality in a patriarchal world. (Shneer & Aviv, 2015, p. 232).

On May 1, 1970, a group of lesbian feminist leaders known as the "Lavender Menace" preempted the regularly scheduled 2nd Congress to Unite Women in order to address lesbianism (Echols, 1991). Outcomes included adoption of resolutions by the Lavender Menace and *The Woman Identified Woman*—the Radicalesbian position paper aiming to allay feminists' fears of lesbianism (Echols, 1991). The beginning of lesbian feminism is associated with the founding of "The Furies" in 1971 in Washington, DC, followed by other lesbian feminist groups that began forming in urban areas throughout the United States (Taylor & Whittier, 1998). While both radical and liberal heterosexual feminists viewed women's liberation and sexual liberation as distinct from one another, lesbian feminists did not. Lesbian feminists promoted the slogan "the personal is political" and recast lesbianism as a political agenda rather than a collective identity agenda (Taylor & Whittier, 1998, p. 352). The early 1970s witnessed the emergence of a "separatist" agenda and lesbian-specific community centers, groups, and issues. In the late 1970s and early 1980s, particular events culminated to give impetus for lesbians to join gay men in a unified struggle for civil rights, ultimately resulting in organizing the March on Washington for Lesbian and Gay Rights in October of 1979.

SAVE OUR CHILDREN CAMPAIGN

After an ordinance passed in Dade County, Florida, in 1977, which prohibited discrimination based on sexual orientation, evangelist singer Anita Bryant led an antigay campaign with the Save Our Children organization (Adam, 1995). This campaign resulted in the repeal of Florida's antidiscrimination ordinance on June 7, 1977. In response to this repeal, lesbians and gay men organized a boycott of orange juice (as Bryant was the spokesperson for the Florida Citrus Commission at that time) and raised funds to fight Bryant's anti-gay crusade.

BRIGGS AMENDMENT

The day after Florida's antidiscrimination ordinance was repealed, California State Senator John Briggs made a public announcement that he would introduce formal legislation to ban lesbians and gay men from teaching in California's public schools. In response to this announcement, activists organized a coalition to fight the Briggs Amendment-Proposition 6, which they successfully defeated in 1978. This coalition was one of the lesbian and gay community's "most successful organizing campaigns" where they "worked together in a display of solidarity that overcame gender divides to help defeat the amendment" (Rimmerman, 2008, pp. 27–28). While previous generations of LGBTQ leaders adopted a more assimilationist strategy in coordinated political activism during the coalitions of the 1950s and early 1960s, later generations adopted a larger and more confrontational liberationist strategy, such as those opposing the Save Our Children campaign and the Briggs Amendment. Shortly after the successfully organized effort to defeat the Briggs Amendment, the lesbian and gay community experienced the unfortunate assassination of the first openly gay elected official.

THE ASSASSINATION OF HARVEY MILK

After running for the San Francisco Board of Supervisors in 1973 and 1975, as well as the California State Assembly in 1976, Harvey Milk's eventual victory in 1977 for the San Francisco Board of Supervisors was "sweet indeed" (Thompson, 1994, p. 166). Harvey Milk was San Francisco's first openly gay supervisor and "came to symbolize the gay community's determination to be part of the political process" (Thompson, 1994, p. 166). Milk was an advocate for many marginalized communities, including the LGBTQ community, racial and ethnic minorities, and the elderly. He worked to develop a politically united coalition across lines of difference: "Milk had become one of the most popular politicians in San Francisco and had achieved wide voter recognition throughout the state" (D'Emilio, 1989, p. 469). Yet, shortly after his victory, Harvey Milk and San Francisco Mayor George Moscone, an ally and supporter of the gay community, were shot to death on November 27, 1978, in City Hall by former city supervisor Dan White as an act of political vengeance:

> White, a veteran, former cop and firefighter, was the most conservative member of the Board of Supervisors and notoriously antigay. His 1977 campaign included rhetorical attacks on "social deviates." The only supervisor to vote against the gay rights ordinance, he also supported the Briggs initiative. White and Milk stood at opposite ends of the political spectrum represented on the Board of Supervisors. (D'Emilio, 1989, p. 470)

White eventually turned himself in to the police, confessing to the murders. On the evening of the shootings, approximately 25,000 people gathered to walk in silence from the Castro district to City Hall in San Francisco as an honorary tribute to both Milk and Moscone. Milk was regarded "as a symbol of the aspirations of gay people to participate openly in mainstream politics and in society" (Thompson, 1994, p. 167).

Despite the gains achieved by the LGBTQ community across the United States in the 1970s, homophobia continued and erupted in antigay backlash. For example, following the Gay Freedom Day March in 1977, "five gay businesses on Castro Street were bombed" and arsonists set fire to many gay-owned businesses (D'Emilio, 1989, p. 470). In December 1978, the newly appointed Mayor Dianne Feinstein introduced an antiporn bill that became law, allowing for gay bookstores and theatres to be investigated. Ensuing police harassment and brutality occurred predominantly in locations outside the heavily concentrated gay area of the Castro neighborhood and toward less visible LGBTQ community members. Rather than target the central stronghold, police focused on the more vulnerable in the LGBTQ community: "lesbian rather than gay male bars, gay youth rather than adults, sadomasochists rather than ordinary gays, porn stores and theaters rather than 'good gay' meeting places" (D'Emilio, 1989, p. 470).

When former city supervisor Dan White was found guilty by a San Francisco jury of a lesser crime—manslaughter rather than murder—thereby yielding a lenient sentence for the shootings of Milk and Moscone, the gay community erupted with rage. Thousands of demonstrators marched to San Francisco City Hall and rioted during the White Night Riots of May 21, 1979. Gay men, lesbians, and their allies attacked property and later that night, "[t]he angry mob set police cars ablaze and barricaded members of the Board of Supervisors within the building" (Thompson, 1944, p. 182).

THE FIRST MARCH ON WASHINGTON

The first national March on Washington for Lesbian and Gay Rights was held on October 14, 1979, in Washington, DC. As noted in the opening paragraph from the official souvenir program for the march, history was being made:

> Lesbians and gay men are making history here today. But this great assemblage is more than a March and Rally. We celebrate the 10th anniversary of the Stonewall Rebellion. We reaffirm our commitment to the struggle for full human rights. We redouble our efforts to educate ourselves and others. We reach out to gay brothers and sisters. We commemorate loved ones, friends and acquaintences, the known and the unknown, who have been victims of murder and suicide. We rejoice in the pleasure of our bodies. We honor the gay men and women of the pre-Stonewall era, who survived and especially those who spoke out against prejudice and ignorance. We feel our anger and our sorrow, as well as jubilance and bliss – and the calm within. We march. We smile. We kiss and we hug. We will probably be back again. (D.C. Media Committee)

Some sources estimated 50,000 and 75,000 people attended, while other sources cite figures of 25,000 to 125,000 people in attendance. Regardless of exact numbers, the sheer size, organization, and visibility of lesbians and gays for this initial march symbolized unity, pride, political power, and, by many standards, "success" for the broader lesbian and gay liberation movement. The 1979 march was characterized by a predominantly coordinated and collaborative political activism among lesbians and gay men. However, one primary source, the "Messages on the Occasion of the Washington March, October 14, 1979," provides a contrary perspective as it noted that there was a call among some for gay male separatism. While there was much coordination, connection, and unification between lesbians and gay men during this first march, there remained divisive elements and factions, however marginal.

Around the same time as the first march in 1979, lesbians and gays of color attended the first Third World Gay and Lesbian Conference, held near Howard University (Retter, 2000). The keynote address was given by Audre Lorde, a self-identified Black lesbian feminist and renowned poet who said:

> We are also here to examine our roles as powerful forces within our communities. For not one of us will be free until we are all free, and until all members of our communities are free. So we are here to help shape a world where all people can flourish, beyond sexism, beyond racism, beyond ageism, beyond classism, and beyond homophobia. In order to do this, we must see ourselves within the context of a civilization that has notorious disrespect and loathing for any human value, for any human creativity or genuine human difference. And it is upon our ability to look honestly upon our differences, to see them as creative rather than divisive, that our future success may lie. (Byrd, Cole, & Guy-Sheftall, 2009, pp. 208–209)

In this speech, Lorde addresses the inseparability of all oppressions and poses a call to action for everyone to carry this solidarity into his or her everyday life in order to continue the struggle for civil rights. Notably, Lorde was a featured speaker at the 20th anniversary commemoration of Martin Luther King's speech at the 1963 Civil Rights March on Washington.

THE 1980s

Following such changes and challenges for the LGBTQ community throughout the decade of the 1970s, came rather significant events that would change the movement through the modern day. From the first report of those impacted by HIV and AIDS in 1981, the impact of fear, stigma and shame would impose hatred and oppression upon members of the LGBTQ community, especially among gay and bisexual men during the early years, clearly impacting all those living with HIV/AIDS over time. The inaction by local, state and national officials would call for a rise in activism throughout the decade, while thousands were dying due to bureaucracy and barriers in seeking effective medical treatments.

THE IMPACT OF HIV/AIDS

On June 5, 1981, *Morbidity and Mortality Weekly Report* published a report of the first five cases of gay men contracting pneumocystis carinii pneumonia in Los Angeles (Centers for Disease Control and Prevention [CDC], 2001). Initially referred to as "Gay Related Immune Disease" (GRID) by the CDC due to the high incidence of transmissions among gay men, public officials labeled this disease as largely a "gay" disease. Bisexual men and women were also stigmatized as a result of being perceived to spread the disease to the larger population (Messinger, 2006). There was growing public concern about HIV/AIDS that spread as hysteria among the national consciousness. However, such concerns did not appear to impact appropriate reactions from government and leader as "President Reagan did not even mention the word AIDS in public until well into his second term in office, several years into the epidemic" (Messinger, 2006, p. 32). There was a large amount of homophobia and inaction in appropriately responding to this emerging public health epidemic while thousands were innocently dying.

By 1987, the death toll from AIDS was approximately 34,500—a number derived from reported cases only and of which approximately 75% were gay men, while approximately 2,000 cases were of women, and not necessarily lesbians (Official Souvenir Program, 1987, p. 42). In addition to this death toll, there were 45,000 known HIV/AIDS cases across the United States and over 4,400 in San Francisco alone (D'Emilio, 1989, p. 472). By comparison to today, gay and bisexual men continue to be more affected by HIV than any other group in the United States, with a disproportionate number identifying within communities of color, according to the CDC (n.d.):

> In 2013, in the United States, gay and bisexual men accounted for 81% (30,689) of the 37,887 estimated HIV diagnoses among all males aged 13 years and older and 65% of the 47,352 estimated diagnoses among all persons receiving an HIV diagnosis that year. In 2013, gay and bisexual men accounted for 55% of the estimated number of persons diagnosed with AIDS among all adults and adolescents in the United States. Of the estimated 14,611 gay and bisexual men diagnosed with AIDS, 40% were blacks/African Americans; 32% were whites; and 23% were Hispanics/Latinos.

While HIV/AIDS was initially a national tragedy among the gay community, among other communities such as hemophiliacs, Haitians, and ultimately heterosexuals as well, the crisis served as an impetus for increased and intensified political activism. The strength of the LGBTQ community was evident and grew stronger during the AIDS epidemic and the continued political inaction at the local and federal level with regard to limited funding for prevention, education, research, and treatment. This activism led to a rise in HIV/AIDS and LGBTQ activist groups and the 1987 March on Washington for Lesbian and Gay Rights.

HIV/AIDS ACTIVISM

In direct response to the AIDS crisis, the AIDS Coalition To Unleash Power (ACT UP) was formed in March 1987 in New York City. According to its founding statement, ACT UP was described as a "diverse, non-partisan group united in anger and committed to direct action to end the AIDS crisis" (Rimmerman, 2008, p. 49). While many believed that ACT UP was only comprised of gay white men, it should be noted that there were also many women and people of color involved (Gamson, 1989). In the same regard, it should be noted that the lesbian and LGBT ally communities played a vital role in the early years of the HIV/AIDS epidemic whether through advocating for treatment options, participating in civil disobedience with ACT UP, or caregiving for those dying. While there remain significant challenges with regard to the prevention and treatment of HIV/AIDS among men who have sex with men (MSM), including gay and bisexual men of color, youth, and older adults, significant treatment progress has been made. Since the mid-1990s and the advent of antiretroviral therapies, many people living with HIV remain healthy due to the effectiveness of these life-saving treatments. For more information about the impact of HIV/AIDS and other sexually transmitted infections upon gay men and the LGBTQ community, see chapters 14 and 24.

1990s–TODAY: CELEBRATIONS, COMMEMORATIONS, AND CHALLENGES

Following the first march in 1979, the next three national marches for civil rights of the broader, more inclusive LGBTQ community occurred in 1987, 1993, and 2000 in Washington, DC. The March on Washington for Lesbian and Gay Rights in 1987 was premised upon an agenda of civil disobedience and demands in direct response to the 1986 Supreme Court ruling in *Bowers vs. Hardwick* upholding sodomy laws and the ongoing governmental inaction related to the HIV/AIDS crisis. One article titled, "Hundreds of Thousands Take the Gay Cause to the Nation's Capital," noted:

> With tears and laughter, anger and joy, several hundred thousand lesbians, gay men, and their supporters marched on Washington D.C. on Oct. 11 in a massive, emotion-filled demonstration to demand a federal war on AIDS and an end to homophobic discrimination. (The Advocate, 1987, p. 11)

LGBTQ PRIDE EVENTS

While the homophile movement of the 1950s attracted gatherings that were limited in size to double digits, a post-Stonewall march in 1970 to commemorate the uprising attracted 5,000 people (D'Emilio, 1989). "By the mid-1970s, the yearly marches in several cities were larger than any political demonstrations since the decline of the civil rights and antiwar movements" (D'Emilio, 1989, p. 466). Even through the present day, such yearly commemorations (pride events, marches, rallies) are typically held during the month of June to celebrate LGBTQ pride and commemorate the uprising at Stonewall.

The LGBTQ Heritage Initiative with the National Park Service is a celebration of the stories of many LGBTQ Americans. Comprised of several unique projects, this initiative explores "how the legacy of lesbian, gay, bisexual, transgender, and queer individuals can be recognized, preserved, and interpreted for future generations" (National Park Service, 2016). Among the projects in this initiative are identifying historical places of importance to the LGBTQ community, sharing of LGBTQ preservation efforts, designing a community tour, and contributing to LGBTQ oral history by gathering stories and memories among LGBTQ elders.

Additional celebrations among the LGBTQ community include honoring LGBTQ pioneering activists, such as Colonel Margarethe Cammermeyer, MA, PhD, who is a civil rights pioneer in the US military. It was during a security interview in 1989 that Colonel Cammermeyer came out as a lesbian, sparking "a series of events that ultimately ended the ban on gays in the military" (Sudermann, 2015, p. 13). Colonel Cammermeyer received the 2015 Distinguished Alumni Veteran Award from her alma mater at the University of Washington for her advocacy in the military. This notable recognition of Colonel Cammermeyer came after the long-fought battle to overturn the 1996 federal policy known as "Don't Ask, Don't Tell" prohibiting military personnel from discriminating against or harassing closeted LGB service members or applicants, as well as barring open and out LGB individuals from military service. The "Don't Ask, Don't Tell" policy was later repealed in 2010 by President Obama.

In sum, the broader LGBTQ liberation movement has not been a single, monolithic campaign over the years. Rather, the struggle and fight for LGBTQ equality has adopted various strategies of political activism to create social change. As noted earlier, such strategies have included an assimilationist approach; seeking inclusion and accommodation, as compared to a liberationist strategy; and seeking to raise awareness of new ideas and paradigms to expand beyond the status quo. In many ways, the modern-day movement and approaches related to LGBTQ advocacy, equality, and social justice will at times blend the two strategies of assimilation and liberation.

ONGOING CHALLENGES

Almost 50 years after Stonewall, the movement for LGBTQ equality continues through the present day—even after winning the long-fought battle for marriage equality with the cases of *U.S. v. Windsor* (2013), *Hollingsworth v. Perry* (2013), and *Obergefell v. Hodges* (2015). In the United States, there remain limited state and federal laws protecting LGBTQ individuals from workplace and employment discrimination, adoption laws supporting LGBTQ parents, the ability to change gender on identification documents (e.g., driver's license, birth certificates), hate-crime laws, school antibullying policies, and so on. For more information about individual state laws and policies (or lack thereof), see Human Rights Campaign (2016).

Additional challenges relevant to the LGBTQ community include advocating for anticonversion therapy laws, health equality, and tribal rights and fighting against discriminatory religious freedom laws, among others. The anti-LGBTQ movement continues to support conversion, or reparative therapy, as a method to "cure" one of their sexual orientation or gender identity. Yet such unethical practices are fully rejected by most health and mental health professions such as the APA, National Association of Social Workers, and Council on Social Work Education. Similar to other professional membership organizations, the latter issued a policy statement opposing the practice, use, or teaching of conversion and reparative therapy approaches (Council on Social Work Education 2015). Health equality is another area that continues to be a challenge for the LGBTQ community. It is estimated that 5% to 10% of the global population is LGBTQ, yet many of the health and mental health needs among LGBTQ individuals continue to be unmet. Stigma of sexuality and gender identity contributes to the reported health disparities among the LGBTQ community. There is a current call from the World Health Organization to "lead the movement to end health disparities and discrimination of LGBTQ people" (*The Lancet*, 2016, p. 95). Achieving health equality requires the elimination of oppression and discrimination directed toward the LGBTQ community. For additional information about the ongoing global challenges pertaining to human rights for LGBTQ individuals living within many oppressive nations and countries, see the International Lesbian, Gay, Bisexual, Trans and Intersex Association's website at www.ilga.org.

Further challenges facing the LGBTQ community include the issue of tribal rights unique to LGBTQ American Indian and Alaska Native peoples who are members of sovereign tribal nations. With regard to the 2015 US Supreme Court decision legalizing same-sex marriages, it is important to note that "American Indian reservations are not bound by the decision and many continue to forbid gay marriages and deny insurance and other benefits" (Fonseca, 2015). While there are reasons tribes may continue to forbid same-sex marriages, it denies many LGBTQ American Indian and Alaska Native individuals access to tribal rights and benefits. Last, at the time of this writing several states have moved to institute religious freedom bills and laws. Such laws typically claim to protect pastors from performing same-sex marriages or to protect photographers or caterers from providing wedding services for LGBTQ couples; some go so far as to allow organizations to refuse to hire LGBTQ individuals if doing so "violates" their faith (Griffin, 2015). In the same regard, some religious and faith-based schools and universities in the United States have sought exemptions from Title IX of the Education Amendments of 1972 that provide protections for students based on sexual orientation or gender identity with regard to policies related to admissions, retention, and housing, among others—ultimately allowing for the blatant discrimination of LGBTQ students (Warbelow & Gregg, 2015).

CONCLUSION

The LGBTQ movement coalesced from imbricating historical social movements. It reflects a sociopolitical global force of advocacy for all LGBTQ people. With support from the United Nations, to policy progress overturning DOMA, the LGBTQ global community continues to experience many celebrations, as well as ongoing challenges. The LGBTQ movement is comprised of many stories replete with hope, health, and healing. From the uprising at Stonewall to the marches on Washington, DC, for equality, the LGBTQ movement has increased its visibility, voice, and victories. Advocating for the human rights of all LGBTQ people is an ethical responsibility for the profession of social work and related fields of practice. Yet social workers have not always been present at critical junctures during the LGBTQ movement and its history. According to Poindexter (1997), during "the rise of the gay rights movement in the U.S., the social work profession was not a catalyst or a supporter of that effort" (p. 608). Thus social work needs to increase its awareness of the relevance of the LGBTQ movement because it is a successful example of a community organizing against oppression. The grassroots organizational tactics evident in the LGBTQ movement present an opportunity of learning for social work students, practitioners, and educators. As discrimination and oppression continue to exist for the LGBTQ community, there is ongoing need for intervention by the field of social work. Ultimately, it is through progress and each celebration relevant to the LGBTQ movement for equality that the number and degree of challenges will continue to decline.

REFERENCES

Adam, B. D. (1995). *The rise of a gay and lesbian movement*. New York: Twayne.

Associated Press. (2003, June 26). Supreme court strikes down Texas law banning sodomy. *The New York Times*. Retrieved from http://www.nytimes.com/2003/06/26/politics/26WIRE-SODO.html

Byrd, R. P., Cole, J. B., & Guy-Sheftall, B. (Eds.). (2009). *I am your sister: Collected and unpublished writings of Audre Lorde*. Oxford: Oxford University Press.

Centers for Disease Control and Prevention. (2001). HIV and AIDS—United States, 1981–2000. *Morbidity and Mortality Weekly Report, 50*(21), 430.

Centers for Disease Control and Prevention. (n.d.). HIV among gay and bisexual men. Retrieved from http://www.cdc.gov/hiv/group/msm/

Cooper, T. (2016, January 14). Dispatches: Jail time for being gay in Russia. *Human Rights Watch*. Retrieved from https://www.hrw.org/news/2016/01/14/dispatches-jail-time-being-gay-russia

Council on Social Work Education. (2015). Policy statement of conversion/reparative therapy. Retrieved from http://www.cswe.org/File.aspx?id=85010

Cruikshank, M. (1992). *The gay and lesbian liberation movement*. New York: Routledge.

D.C. Media Committee. National March! On Washington for Lesbian and Gay Rights: Official Souvenir Program, pamphlet, 1979; Washington D.C. (digital.library.unt.edu/ark:/67531/metadc276226/ : accessed April 8, 2017), University of North Texas Libraries, Digital Library, digital.library.unt.edu; crediting UNT Libraries Special Collections.

D'Emilio, J. (1983). Dual identity and lesbian autonomy. In *Sexual politics, sexual communities* (pp. 92–107). Chicago: University of Chicago Press.

D'Emilio, J. (1989). Gay politics and community in San Francisco since World War II. In M. B. Duberman, M. Vicinus, & G. Chauncey Jr. (Eds.), *Hidden from history: Reclaiming the gay and lesbian past* (pp. 466–473). New York: New American Library.

Duberman, M. (1993). *Stonewall*. New York: Dutton.

Echols, A. (1991). Lesbianism. In *Daring to be bad: Radical feminism in America 1967–1975* (pp. 210–241). Minneapolis: University of Minnesota.

Editorial Board. (2016, January 19). Fueling homophobia in Russia. *The New York Times*. Retrieved from http://mobile.nytimes.com/2016/01/19/opinion/fueling-homophobia-in-russia.html?emc=edit_th_20160119&nl=todaysheadlines&nlid=72354774&referer=

Ellis, H. (2006). *Studies in the psychology of sex*, Vol. II (3rd ed.). Charleston, SC: BiblioBazaar.

Fonseca, F. (2015, November 27). Gay marriage is legal but not on tribal lands. *Juneau Empire*. Retrieved from http://juneauempire.com/state/2015-11-27/gay-marriage-legal-not-tribal-lands

Fredrikson-Goldsen, K. I., Lindhorst, T., Kemp, S. P. & Walters, K. L. (2009). "My ever dear": Social work's "lesbian" foremothers—A call for scholarship. *Affilia: Journal of Women and Social Work, 24*(3), 325–336.

Gamson, J. (1989). Silence, death, and the invisible enemy: AIDS activism and social movement "newness". *Social Problems, 36*(4), 351–367.

Gibson, M. (1997). Clitoral corruption: Body metaphors and American doctors' constructions of female homosexuality, 1870–1900. In V. A. Rosario (Ed.), *Science and homosexualities* (pp. 108–132). New York: Routledge.

Gilbert, J. (2015, November 28). Transgender Argentines confront continued murder and discrimination. *New York Times*. Retrieved from http://mobile.nytimes.com/2015/11/29/world/americas/transgender-argentines-confront-continued-murder-and discrimination.html?emc=edit_th_20151129&nl=todaysheadlines&nlid=72354774&referer=

Griffin, L. C. (2015). So-called Religious Freedom Restoration Acts (RFRAs) protect gender and sexual orientation discrimination, not religious freedom. *USApp–American Politics and Policy Blog*. Retrieved from http://blogs.lse.ac.uk/usappblog/2015/04/13/so-called-religious-freedom-restoration-acts-rfras-protect-gender-and-sexual-orientation-discrimination-not-religious-freedom/

Hirschfeld, M. (2000). Introduction. In *The homosexuality of men and women* (pp. 11–17). Amherst, NY: Prometheus Books.

Human Rights Campaign. (2016). Maps of state laws and policies. Retrieved from http://www.hrc.org/state_maps

Johnsen, D. (2013). The Obama's administration's decision to defend constitutional equality rather than the Defense of Marriage Act. *Fordham Law Review, 81*, 599–618.

Johnson, D. K. (2004). *The lavender scare: The Cold War persecution of gays and lesbians in the federal government.* Chicago: University of Chicago Press.

Kennedy, H. (1997). Karl Heinrich Ulrichs, first theories of homosexuality. In Vernon A. Rosario (Ed.), *Science and homosexualities* (pp. 26–45). New York: Routledge.

Krafft-Ebing, R. (1886). *The psychopathia sexualis.* London: Panther.

Krafft-Ebing, R. (1965). *Psychopathia sexualis.* New York: Arcade.

Lewis, S. (2016, January 18). Same-sex marriage ban lifted in Vietnam but a year later discrimination remains. *Time.* Retrieved from http://time.com/4184240/same-sex-gay-lgbt-marriage-ban-liftedvietnam/?xid=time_socialflow_twitter

Liptak, A. (2015, June 26). Supreme Court ruling makes same-sex marriage a right nationwide. *The New York Times.* Retrieved from http://mobile.nytimes.com/2015/06/27/us/supreme-court-same-sex-marriage.html?referrer=

Messinger, L. (2006). A historical perspective. In D. F. Morrow & L. Messinger (Eds.), *Sexual orientation and gender expression in social work practice: Working with gay, lesbian, bisexual, and transgender people* (pp. 18–42). New York: Columbia University Press.

Miller, N. (2002). *Sex crime panic: A journey into the paranoid heart of the 1950s.* Los Angeles, CA: Alyson.

National Park Service. (2016, January 18). LGBTQ Heritage Initiative. US Department of the Interior. Retrieved from http://www.nps.gov/history/heritageinitiatives/LGBThistory/index.html

Odem, M. E. (1995). *Delinquent daughters: Protecting and policing adolescent female sexuality in the United States, 1885–1920.* Chapel Hill: University of North Carolina Press.

National Lesbian and Gay Civil Disobedience Action, & National March on Washington for Lesbian and Gay Rights. (1987). *Out & outraged: Non-violent civil disobedience at the U.S. Supreme Court: C.D. handbook, National March on Washington for Lesbian and Gay Rights, October 8–13, 1987.* Washington, D.C: National Lesbian and Gay Civil Disobedience Action (pp. 1–65).

Oosterhuis, H. (1997). Richard von Krafft-Ebing's "step-children of nature": Psychiatry and the making of homosexual identity. In V. A. Rosario (Ed.), *Science and homosexualities* (pp. 46–66). New York: Routledge.

Peters, J. W. (2014, March 23). The decline and fall of the "H" word. *The New York Times,* p. 10.

Pew Research Center. (2013, June 4). The global divide on homosexuality. Retrieved from http://www.pew-global.org/2013/06/04/the-global-divide-on-homosexuality/

Pew Research Center. (2015, June 26). Gay marriage around the world. Retrieved from http://www.pewforum.org/2015/06/26/gay-marriage-around-the-world-2013/

Poindexter, C.C. (1997). Sociopolitical antecedents to Stonewall: Analysis of the origins of the gay rights movement in the United States. *Social Work, 42*(6), 607–615.

Quimby, K., & Williams, W. L. (2000). Unmasking the homophile in 1950s Los Angeles, an archival record. In J. A. Boone, M. Dupuis, M. Meeker, K. Quimby, C. Sarver, D. Silverman, & R. Weatherston (Eds.), *Queer frontiers* (pp. 166–195). Madison: University of Wisconsin Press.

Radicalesbians. (1971). The woman identified woman. In D. Shneer, & C. Aviv (2015). *American queer, now and then.* Routledge (pp. 232–235).

Richmond, M. E. (1917). *Social diagnosis.* New York: Russell Sage Foundation.

Rimmerman, C.A. (2008). *The lesbian and gay movements.* Boulder, CO: Westview Press.

Retter, Y. (2000). Lesbian activism in Los Angeles 1970–1979. In J. A. Boone, M. Dupuis, M. Meeker, K. Quimby, C. Sarver, D. Silverman, & R. Weatherston (Eds.), *Queer frontiers* (pp. 196–221). Madison: University of Wisconsin Press.

Rubin, G.S. (1993). Thinking sex: Notes for a radical theory of the politics of sexuality, 1984. In L. Kauffman (Ed.), *American feminist thought at century's end: A reader* (pp. 3–64). Cambridge, MA: Blackwell.

Steakley, J. D. (1997). *Per scientiam and justitiam*: Magnus Hirschfeld and the sexual politics of innate homosexuality. In V. A. Rosario (Ed.), *Science and homosexualities* (pp. 108–132). New York: Routledge.

Stryker, S. (2008). A hundred years of transgender history. In *Transgender history* (pp. 31–58). Berkeley, CA: Seal Press.

Suderman, H. (2015, December). Distinguished Alumni Veteran Award, Grethe Cammermeyer. *Columns: The University of Washington Alumni Magazine*, p. 13.

Taylor, V., & Whittier, N. E. (1998). Collective identity in social movement communities: Lesbian feminist mobilization. In P. Nardi & B. Schneider (Eds.), *Social perspectives in gay and lesbian studies* (pp. 349–365). New York: Routledge.

The Lancet. (2016). Meeting the unique health needs of LGBTQ people: Editorial. *The Lancet, 387,* 95.

Thompson, M. (Ed.). (1994). *Long road to freedom: The advocate history of the gay and lesbian movement.* New York: St. Martin's Press.

United Nations Human Rights Office of the High Commissioner. (n.d.) Speak up: Stop discrimination. Retrieved from http://www.ohchr.org/EN/Issues/Discrimination/Pages/LGBT.aspx

Warbelow, S., & Gregg, R. (2015). Hidden discrimination: Title IX religious exemptions putting LGBT students at risk. A Report from the Human Rights Campaign. Retrieved from http://hrc-assets.s3-website-us-east-1.amazonaws.com//files/assets/resources/Title_IX_Exemptions_Report.pdf

Waters, C. (2006). Sexology. In H. G. Cocks & M. Houlbrook (Eds.), *Palgrave advances in the modern history of sexuality* (pp. 41–63). New York: Palgrave Macmillan.

CHAPTER 2

UNDERSTANDING DIFFERENCES AND DEFINITIONS

From Oppression to Sexual Health and Practice

Elizabeth B. Russell and Pamela A. Viggiani

INTRODUCTION

As our world continues to evolve, so does our social construction of language building, classification, and categorization of people, places, and things. As topics pertaining to sex, including sexuality, sexual orientation, and sexual identity, among others, become more common place in the media, classrooms, businesses, and society in general, the helping professions are often asked to assist in clarifying a variety of terms. A key factor to being an effective social worker is knowing proper terminology and the differences that exist among clients. In order to do this, time must be spent learning the differences between varieties of terms that prevail today. This chapter provides content related to the impact of prejudice, discrimination and oppression, sexual health–related terminology and definitions, theoretical foundations to understanding models of sexual health, as well as models for discussing sexual health and examples of how these appear in clinical practice with lesbian, gay, bisexual, transgender, and queer (LGBTQ) clients.

PREJUDICE, DISCRIMINATION, AND OPPRESSION

While sex, sexuality, and sexual health are natural and integral parts of life, they can sometimes come into conflict in interpersonal practice. Such issues are often related to many of the social and public health concerns that exist in health and mental health settings today. In that regard, it may be helpful to begin with a short discussion related to the impact of oppression, discrimination, and prejudice faced by members of the LGBTQ community throughout society and within practice settings.

PREJUDICE, PHOBIAS, AND STIGMA

There is little doubt that prejudicial attitudes and behaviors continue to be a part of the LGBTQ experience. The term "sexual prejudice" can be used as an umbrella term covering all negative attitudes toward the LGBTQ community (Herek, 2000). Prejudices exist with regard to every aspect of the LGBTQ identity. Common prejudices include assuming members of the LGBTQ community suffer from mental illness, are sexually deviant and/or promiscuous, are criminals, and/or are drug and alcohol abusers. Sexual prejudice stigmatizes members of the LGBTQ community. Stigma refers to

> an . . . attribute or mark (that) is not inherently meaningful; meanings are attached to it through social interaction. The meaning attached to the mark by the larger group or society involves a negative valuation. The attribute is understood by all to signify that its bearer . . . the stigmatized are not simply different from others . . . (but) their deviation (is) discrediting. (Teliti, 2015, p. 61)

Sexual prejudice and stigma result in homophobia and transphobia or a fear, disgust, or loathing of individuals who identify as lesbian, gay, bisexual, transgender, and queer. Homo- and transphobia can also be internalized and thus become a form of self-hate for members of the LGBTQ community. Further, prejudice, phobia, and stigma play into institutional and structural policies that are discriminatory, depriving LGBTQ people basic protections surrounding health, safety, housing, jobs, and public accommodations.

POWER AND POWERLESSNESS

The LGBTQ population struggles with powerlessness. The lack of power affects the ability of members of the LGBTQ population to socially function, as a sense of power is crucial to being able to feel self-directed and in control of one's life (Appleby & Cohen, 2008). Further, as a result of heterosexism and homo- and transphobia, the LGBTQ population is often blocked from gaining economic and institutional power, which in turn affects their ability to obtain and achieve financial stability and full inclusion into society (Mallon, 2008). While members of the LGBTQ community often feel individually invisible and powerless, some power has been gained through collective action within the LGBTQ rights movement that has been active throughout the latter half of the twentieth century through today. Collective action has resulted in a gradual gaining of rights in many realms, including the removal of homosexuality as a mental illness in 1973 from the American Psychological Association's *Diagnostic and Statistical Manual of Mental Disorders* and through the recent Supreme Court ruling on same-sex marriage. Despite continued and expanded grassroots and political action, the LGBTQ community still struggles with oppression, discrimination, and marginalization.

SYSTEMS OF OPPRESSION, DISCRIMINATION, AND MARGINALIZATION

LGBTQ populations suffer from multiple systems of oppression, discrimination, and marginalization. Society reinforces heterosexism and cisgenderism as normative and natural, and thus any other ways of expressing sexuality and gender have been deemed unnatural and abnormal (Marsiglia & Kulis, 2015). Heterosexism has created a culture that privileges cisgender, heterosexual individuals while oppressing all other expressions of sexuality and gender. Historically and currently, the LGBTQ population experiences both homophobia and transphobia resulting in an environment that invites discrimination as well as acts of verbal and physical aggression (Tully, 2011). Additionally, the LBGTQ community likely experiences internalized oppression as some have "unconsciously accepted heteronormative norms and derogatory cultural messages about themselves" (Margeiglia & Kulis, 2015, p. 60).

Heterosexism and cisgenderism have resulted in institutional marginalization and discrimination. Policies and laws have actively marginalized and discriminated against or excluded the LGBTQ community in the areas of housing, employment, public accommodation, and marriage. Although nationally the federal Equal Employment Opportunity Commission has extended prohibitions against employment discrimination to include sexual orientation and gender identity, these nondiscrimination policies do not include individuals employed in the private sector ("Nondiscrimination Laws," 2016). Currently, 28 states do not have nondiscrimination laws that cover sexual orientation and gender identity and an additional two states have nondiscrimination laws covering only sexual orientation and not gender identity ("Nondiscrimination Laws," 2016). In short, across 30 states, an individual can legally be fired for being lesbian, gay, bisexual, and/or transgender.

Similarly, 28 states fail to include sexual orientation and gender identity in nondiscrimination laws pertaining to housing and an additional two states have nondiscrimination laws that cover sexual orientation and not gender identity ("Nondiscrimination Laws," 2016). Therefore, individuals who are lesbian, gay, bisexual, and/or transgender may be denied housing or evicted from housing based on their sexual orientation and/or gender identity.

Oppression and marginalization are further expressed in the lack of public accommodation and nondiscrimination laws present on the federal level and within many states. Public accommodation laws are present to protect LGBTQ people from being refused service or entry and/or from facing discrimination in publicly accessible places ("Nondiscrimination Laws," 2016). These types of laws typically include public places like the workplace, school, stores, restaurants, hotels, banks, and so on ("Nondiscrimination Laws," 2016). The LGBTQ population currently has no public accommodation protection in 29 states, thus leaving them vulnerable to discrimination in many aspects of their daily lives.

Additionally, in North Carolina, Tennessee, and Arkansas, state law prohibits the enforcement of local laws protecting LGBTQ rights in employment, housing, and public accommodation, thus reinforcing the institutional and possibly interpersonal discrimination that individuals residing within these states experience ("Nondiscrimination Laws," 2016). Most recently, public accommodation has been denied to transgender students attending public schools. However, through Title IX protections, the Obama administration incorporated sexuality and transgender identity as groups protected from sex discrimination, ordering all states to "require all public school districts . . . grant transgender students access to the bathrooms that correspond with their gender identities"—while 11 states still refuse to include gender identity and are suing the administration over the directive (Margolin, 2016, para. 1). Ongoing challenges remain with regard to some faith-based institutions (e.g., colleges and universities) seeking Title IX waivers and exemptions, claiming such protections are inconsistent with their religious tenets and ultimately openly discriminating against LGBTQ students with regard to admission, housing, and financial aid, among other areas (Human Rights Campaign, 2015).

State laws against same-sex marriage were commonplace until recently. Prior to the 2015 US Supreme Court ruling that made same-sex marriage legal, 14 states still had bans on same-sex marriage (Chappell, 2015). Although the Supreme Court ruling seemed to usher in an era of more rights for the LGBTQ population, as illustrated in this section, LGBTQ individuals still face legal and institutional oppression, leaving them vulnerable to experiences of interpersonal discrimination, oppression, and continued marginalization.

THE IMPORTANCE OF ANTI-OPPRESSIVE AND AFFIRMING PRACTICE

It is of extreme importance to recognize the historic and present-day oppression and marginalization that LGBTQ individuals consistently face in many aspects of their daily lives. The experiences of the LGBTQ population do not change when they interface with the medical and mental health professions that are often dominated by individuals who have adapted oppressive and nonaffirming cultural messages and ideologies. Professionals often think in binary terms with regard to both sexuality and gender. Often social workers and other professionals have subtle homophobic practices that are unexamined and thus come into play when working with someone who identifies as LGBTQ. The "assessment and treatment of sexual minority clients can be adversely affected by therapists' overt or subtle negative attitudes" (Love, Smith, Lyall, Mullins & Cohn, 2015, p. 84). In general it has been found that heterosexist attitudes among practitioners both reduces empathy for and does harm to LGBTQ clients (Love et al., 2015).

Anti-oppressive and affirming practice must begin with self-reflection. Social workers must work in an ongoing manner by exploring their personal feelings regarding the LGBTQ community, acknowledging that they are a part of a homo- and transphobic society that has resulted in absorption of some of those phobias. Without a thorough exploration of one's own identity and biases, a social worker is unable to bring them to consciousness and continually work on being actively anti-trans- and homophobic. Affirmative, anti-oppressive care for LGBTQ clients might include the incorporation of queer theory, which recognizes that binary categories (male/female; heterosexual/gay) serve to erase or make invisible the inherent complexity of an individual's gender and sexual identity (McPhail, 2004). The incorporation of queer theory into social work practice with the LGBTQ community challenges typical systems of powers that enforce heteronormativity. This allows the practitioner to acknowledge that gender constructs often do not adequately fit our client's definitions, and therefore we have the unique opportunity to systemically queer various systems in an LGBTQ affirming manner, rather than diminish their diverse lived experiences (Alexander, 2016). Given the daily lived experiences of oppression, marginalization, discrimination, and prejudice that LGBTQ individuals live with, it is of utmost importance that social workers take a lead in providing anti-oppressive and affirming services to LGBTQ clients. Social workers' commitment to such practices are important both from a clinical standpoint in assuring that individuals receive the best and most effective treatment as well as from a social justice standpoint, assuring that all individuals are able to fully and equally participate in society and experience physical and psychological safety and security within that society (Bell, 2010). For individuals whom identify as LGBTQ, it is paramount for practitioners to be affirming, competent, and confident in their abilities to know and address the many differences across sexual expressions, behaviors, orientations, genders, and other related identities and terminologies.

SEXUAL TERMINOLOGY

Before moving forward with clinical applications and how to discuss sexual issues with clients, it important to understand all different tenets of sex-related terminology. In this section, definitions for sex-related terms are discussed along with theoretical foundations when possible. An overarching term that often appears in research, graduate education, accreditation standards, and clinical practice areas is "sexual health." Sexual health is a fundamental part of the human life cycle. According to the World Health Organization (WHO),

> Sexual health is a state of physical, emotional, mental and social well-being in relation to sexuality; it is not merely the absence of disease, dysfunction or infirmity. Sexual health requires a positive and respectful approach to sexuality and sexual relationships, as well as the possibility of having pleasurable and safe sexual experiences, free of coercion, discrimination and violence. For sexual health to be attained and maintained, the sexual rights of all persons must be respected, protected and fulfilled. (2006, p. 1)

While this definition appears comprehensive, it is also considered a working definition because as our cultures continuously evolve, as does our understanding and definitions of terminology and language. In order to understand the complexity and intersectionality of one's sexual health, awareness of the assumptions and views a person has about health are important to explore. The word "health" is a socially constructed term that changes over time and from individual to individual. Thus determining whether someone is "healthy" depends on the context and set of norms emanating from an individual's culture, medical systems, and personal beliefs, among other factors. As stated in the definition of sexual health, health is not just the absence of disease but rather the interface of an individual's physical, mental, and social well-being (WHO, 2006). In this instance, the term "sexual" describes any sexual act, behavior, attitude, belief, or influence regarding an individual's sexual life and being. In order for sexual health to be achieved and maintained, individual sexual rights, choices, attitudes, and values must be upheld. Understanding other aspects of a person's sexual life and being are important in determining an individual's overall sexual health.

SEX-RELATED TERMINOLOGY

As mentioned, the underpinnings of sexual health often reflect the cultural, historical, personal, and community attributes of a specific time in history. In order to better understand sexual health, one must be clear on the definitions of other sexual terms. Therefore, this section examines a wide variety of sex-related terminology, including gender, sexual orientation, and many others that may be helpful with regard to practice with members of the LGBTQ community.

(BIOLOGICAL) SEX

One of the first questions people are asked upon telling someone they are pregnant is: "Is it a boy or a girl?" often followed by: "Are you going to find out?" These questions indicate society's need to categorize humans and make sense of their world. When discussing one's sex, it can be defined as the biological and physiological characteristics that determine whether humans are male or female. When considering the issue of sex, it is important for clinicians to recognize that sex is a social construct assigned by heteronormative standards. "Heteronormativity" is a descriptive term that links social behavior and role expectations along with self-identity of one's genitalia. Thus, within society, there are strictly defined norms of what constitutes maleness or femaleness. These two categories are not inclusive of all people and provide only two choices for categorization: male or female. It is important to note that there are individuals who possess both male and female biological characteristics, also known as intersex. The sex of an individual should be discussed and not assumed by the clinician. There are several indicators of a person's biological sex, including sex chromosomes, gonads, internal reproductive organs, external genitalia, and biological sex (American Psychological Association [APA], 2011).

GENDER

A person's gender refers to the social construction and meaning a given culture associates with a person's attitudes, behaviors, feelings, and their assigned biological sex. Thus gender-normative or conforming behaviors are those that align with the person's assigned biological sex at birth. Gender nonconformity occurs when the behaviors, attitudes, and feelings of a person do not align with that person's biological sex (APA, 2011).

GENDER IDENTITY

How one views oneself, whether as female, male, transgender, cisgender, or a blend of these or neither, refers to one's gender identity. Gender identity includes what people call themselves and may or may not be the same as their biological sex at birth.

GENDER EXPRESSION

Gender expression is the

> way in which a person acts to communicate gender within a given culture; for example, in terms of clothing, communication patterns and interests. A person's gender expression may or may not be consistent with socially prescribed gender roles, and may or may not reflect his or her gender identity. (APA Just the Facts Coalition, 2008, p. 28)

SEXUALITY

The term "sexuality" is often an umbrella term used to describe a variety of sexual acts, behaviors, and perceived norms. According to the working definition created by the WHO (2006), sexuality is

> a central aspect of being human throughout life encompasses sex, gender identities and roles, sexual orientation, eroticism, pleasure, intimacy and reproduction. Sexuality is experienced and expressed in thoughts, fantasies, desires, beliefs, attitudes, values, behaviors, practices, roles and relationships. While sexuality can include all of these dimensions, not all of them are always experienced or expressed. Sexuality is influenced by the interaction of biological, psychological, social, economic, political, cultural, legal, historical, religious and spiritual factors.

Sexuality is an important aspect of being human and goes beyond an individual's ability to reproduce to include how humans relate to one another and view themselves. Often, an individual's sexual orientation, sexual identity, and sexual expression are all considered parts of an individual's sexuality.

SEXUAL ORIENTATION

Sexual orientation is an individual's physical and sexual attraction toward others. This may be to an individual of the same gender (gay/lesbian/homosexual), the opposite gender (straight/heterosexual), both (bisexual), asexual, or all/any (pansexual/fluid sexuality). Sexual orientation may or may not be reflected in someone's outward behaviors or appearance. Sexual behaviors do not fully define one's sexual orientation. Therefore, social workers and other practitioners should not make assumptions of a client's sexual orientation based on sexual attitudes or behaviors.

SEXUAL IDENTITY

Sexual identity is how individuals describe their own sexuality and how it is expressed. Often, sexual identity interfaces with one's sexual orientation but not always. For example, a person can have a lesbian/gay orientation and express a heterosexual identity.

SEXUAL EXPRESSION

Sexual expression is how people relate to their world in terms of sex and their sexuality. This type of expression can include how people dress, how they express sexual urges, how they relate to other people sexually, how they emotionally or physically connect with other people, their interests, and how they view the world in terms of sex, spiritual beliefs, sexual expression, and the engagement in sexual activities (with or without partner/s).

OTHER TERMS

While there are hundreds of other terms that are important, defining all of them in this chapter is not possible; however, a few key terms are included.

Ally. An ally is usually a non-LGBTQ person who supports the rights of LGBTQ people (e.g., family members, friends, coworkers, etc.). This term can also include LGBTQ individuals who are supportive of others within the LGBTQ population (e.g., a gay man who is an ally to a transgender person).

Bisexual. An individual who is attracted to both males and females.

Cisgender. A person who is not transgender. In this case, persons whose gender is the same as their biological sex are considered to be cisgender.

Gender and Privilege. Cisgender individuals experience a level of congruence in the world around them. They are often referred to as "typically gendered" individuals and benefit from gender privilege. Gender privilege is something that is not often discussed or even acknowledged by cisgender individuals, in part because this type of power is not openly discussed or acknowledged by the majority of the population (e.g., cisgender individuals; APA, 2015). Cisgender individuals often do not experience prejudice or discrimination for their gender, can shop for clothes or use gender-assigned bathrooms without question, and can participate in other activities that overtly indicate their gender without fear of retaliation. Gender privilege is a type of social privilege in which people assume that their own perspective and experiences are universal in nature (APA, 2015).

Coming Out. This is the process LGBTQ people go through when acknowledging or letting others know about their sexual orientation and/or gender identity. This process happens in different ways for different people and can occur and progress across one's entire life. It should also not be assumed that coming out experiences are the same with regard to sexual orientation when compared to gender identity. For more information about this topic, see chapter 5 in this text.

Intersex. This is a person whose sexual anatomy and/or chromosomes do not match the traditional markers of female (XX) or male (XY) (Intersex Society of North America, 2013). It is an all-encompassing term used for individuals whose reproductive and/or sexual anatomy that does not fit traditional definitions of being a male or female. Intersex is a social construct created by the medical community to reflect biological variation.

Pansexual. A person who is pansexual does not fit the binary gender model and can be attracted to individuals of all gender identities and expressions.

Sexual Dysfunctions. Sexual dysfunctions are disorders of the sexual response cycle. These can occur during any or all of the three sexual response phases: desire, arousal/excitement, or orgasm. Sexual dysfunctions include delayed ejaculation, erectile disorder, female orgasmic disorder, female sexual interest/arousal disorder, genito-pelvic pain/penetration disorder, male hypoactive sexual desire disorder, premature (early) ejaculation, substance/medication-induced sexual dysfunction, other specified sexual dysfunction, and unspecified sexual dysfunction (APA, 2013). Most important, identifying as LGBTQ does not mean a person has a sexual dysfunction.

Sexual Rights. Sexual rights are the set of human rights that are upheld and recognized by governmental laws that include the right of all persons to live a life free of coercion, discrimination, and violence (WHO, 2006). Sexual rights include protections that afford all people the ability to seek information related to sexuality, access sexual health-care services, and choose their own sexual behaviors, partners, and relationships.

THEORETICAL PERSPECTIVES

To put these terms with regard to sexuality in perspective, it is helpful to refer to several theoretical perspectives as well as the models and diagrams below for the advances in the intersectionality of gender within today's culture.

BINARY GENDER MODEL

This model is the classification of sex and gender into two categories that are both opposite and disconnected from one another. In this model, a person is either masculine or feminine, male or female (see Figure 2.1). Classification is simple and all people fit into one of two categories (male or female). In the binary gender model, sex, gender, and sexuality are assumed to be in alignment with expected societal norms. For example, a biological female would present herself as feminine and be attracted to men (heterosexual; Burdge, 2007). Individuals who do not ascribe to this alignment of classifications are not included in this model (e.g., LGBTQ among others). This narrow view of gender has been considered the norm in many societies until just a few decades ago when it was challenged (Burdge, 2007). This model is one of the bases for the heterosexism that continues to affect our educational and professional systems today. Clients seeking professional social work services often experience heterosexism and binarism on a daily basis. LGBTQ individuals who do not fit the traditional binary system of classification are discriminated against through the use of incorrect pronouns, being forced to use restrooms by sex categories rather than by gender identity or expression, and in many other ways.

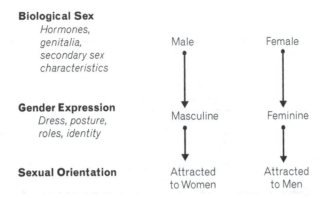

Traditional Binary Gender Model

Biological Sex
Hormones, genitalia, secondary sex characteristics

Male   Female

Gender Expression
Dress, posture, roles, identity

Masculine   Feminine

Sexual Orientation

Attracted to Women   Attracted to Men

FIGURE 2.1: Traditional binary gender model

GENDER-EXPANSIVE MODEL

While often used interchangeably, "gender" and "sex" are two very different constructs. "Gender" refers to the social construction of roles, behaviors, and attributes given to men and women in a particular society, often in Western culture to be considered binary in nature (male or female). While this is a commonly held belief, it provides a narrow, cisgender, heterosexist view of gender and sex. Often behaviors are assigned labels such as "gender-normative" (behaviors the culture associates with a specific biological sex) or "gender nonconformity" (behaviors of an individual associated with the opposite biological sex; APA, 2011).

The term "gender-expansive" has been utilized by many individuals and organizations to expand beyond the binary definition of gender (APA, 2015). Gender-expansive includes gender expression, gender identities, and perceived gender norms of a particular group or culture. The outward external appearance of one's gender identity through observable behaviors or appearance is gender expression. A person's gender expression may or may not conform to the socially con-structed or gender-assigned behaviors typically associated with being male or female. Figure 2.2 places biological sex, gender identity, gender expression, and sexual orientation on continuums that more accurately describe the sex, sexuality, and gender variations as they exist in our world and within the definition of gender-expansive. Further, viewing gender identity, gender expres-sion, and sexual orientation as being on a continuum shows the fluidity experienced in these areas by many individuals across their lifespan

BIO-PSYCHO-SOCIAL-CULTURAL PERSPECTIVE

One of the most important things a social worker can do when working with clients who present with sexual health–related issues is to not assume anything. Taking a position of curiosity is the best way to ensure effective communication that is nonjudgmental and nonassuming (Buehler, 2013). This will allow for clients to set the tone of the interactions and feel empowered to dis-cuss the topics that are most important to them with regard to their sexual health. It is impor-tant to note that not all social workers receive thorough training regarding sexual health and that

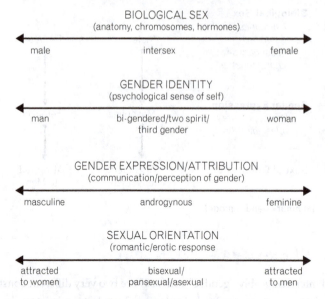

FIGURE 2.2: Diagram of sex, sexuality, and gender

additional resources, information, or continuing education may be needed to effectively work with differing sexual health–related concerns. One useful perspective for social workers to utilize when addressing sexual health concerns is a bio-psycho-social-cultural framework (Hutchinson, 2014). These dimensions can assist social workers in framing and asking questions to gather pertinent information from clients. For example, information gathered from the *biological dimension* would include questions about the genetic aspects of behavior, anatomy, and physiological responses; growth and development; and neurobiological responses of the body (Hutchinson, 2014). When assessing the *psychological dimension* of sexual health, the social worker can discuss clients' relationships with self and others, sexual expressiveness, how they view self and others, emotional reactions to stimuli, self-concept and self-esteem, as well as attitudes and behaviors about sexual issues. Because individuals are a sum of the *cultural, historical, and social influences* that shape their sexual personhood, it is important to gather information about each of these influences on a person's development and overall sexual health including gender expression, gender identity, and sexual orientation. Note that, for most clients, it is important that this framework be expanded to include socioeconomic status, educational background, intellect, spiritual and religious beliefs, media exposure, and gender socialization, among other relevant dimensions. In practice, it is the integration and interface of the bio-psycho-social-cultural factors that shape people's beliefs about themselves, their sexual health and sex life, and their relationships with others. Individuals must acknowledge all aspects of their life that might have shaped their sexual health and identity, including family of origin issues (e.g., beliefs about sexuality, relationships, roles of men and women, trauma, community influences, and role models, to mention only a few; Buehler, 2013). Understanding the influence and importance of each dimension of the bio-psycho-social-cultural framework is often captured in a full comprehensive assessment practice that can occur across many sessions with a client.

POLICY GUIDANCE FOR THE PROFESSION OF SOCIAL WORK: REJECTION OF SEXUAL CHANGE EFFORTS

Social work has a unique mission to work toward eliminating discrimination, practicing competently, and advocating for populations that have experienced oppression, including members of the LGBTQ community (Martin, Messinger, Kull, et al., 2009). Both the Council on Social Work Education (CSWE) and the National Association for Social Workers (NASW) provide guidance to the profession with regard to work with the LGBTQ community. Social workers should be prepared to practice competently across populations and contexts. The NASW Code of Ethics provides a clear mandate to all professionals to practice competently, advocate, and work toward social justice for all oppressed communities, including members of the LGBTQ community (NASW, 2008). In addition to the NASW Code of Ethics, CSWE provides clear guidance that social work students are to be educated in practicing with oppressed populations while advocating for social justice (CSWE, 2015).

Both CSWE and NASW have published documents that oppose and condemn conversion/reparative or Sexual Orientation Change Efforts (SOCE) (CSWE, 2016; NASW, 2015). SOCE refers to any intervention that:

> include(s) any practice seeking to change a person's sexual orientation, including, but not limited to, efforts to change behaviors, gender identity, or gender expressions, or to reduce or eliminate sexual or romantic attractions or feelings toward a person of the same gender. (NASW, 2015, p. 3)

NASW and CSWE provide information to social workers about SOCE and the deleterious effects SOCE has on individuals who may have experienced such treatments (CSWE, 2016; NASW, 2015). CSWE offers guidance and resources for students and professionals to practice affirmative care with LGBTQ clients (CSWE, 2015). Affirmative care provides LGBTQ individuals with a knowledge that who they are is representative of normal variations in sexual and gender identity, thus validating LGBTQ identities (Craig, Austin, & Alessi, 2013). Further, affirmative care recognizes that many within the LGBTQ community have experienced discrimination as a result of living in a homophobic and transphobic society (Craig et al., 2013).

NASW and CSWE policies on conversion therapy are reflective of the professional consensus as the majority of helping professions oppose conversion therapy (e.g., American Psychological Association, American Counseling Association, and the Association for Marriage and Family Therapy). Given that conversion therapy has often been vigorously defended by conservative Christian religious organizations, it is important to note that recently the American Association of Christian Counselors eliminated its promotion in their revised 2014 Code of Ethics. The condemnation of conversion therapy and the resulting damage it does to the LGBTQ individuals is echoed by recent federal governmental documents including a 2015 Substance Abuse and Mental Health Services Administration (2015) report titled *Ending Conversion Therapy: Supporting and Affirming LGBTQ Youth*. The report confirms that sexual and gender identity occur across a continuum and that conversion therapy is harmful to the healthy and positive development of sexual and gender identity. Finally, the Obama administration released a statement that it supported the ban of the use of conversion therapy for minors (Shear, 2015).

The social work profession provides leadership in the promotion of social justice and the elimination of oppression through advocacy for the LGBTQ community. The policies of our professional organizations clearly mandate that, as social workers, we work to support the dignity and rights of LGBTQ individuals through professional practices that are empowering and affirmative. The policies of NASW and CSWE reflect the broader professional consensus, as well as a growing recognition on the part of federal and state governments of the damage nonaffirmative practices (e.g., conversion therapy) have on members of the LGBTQ community

HEALTHY SEXUAL DEVELOPMENT: MOVING FROM STIGMA TO NORMALITY

While all people go through various stages of sexual development, discussing and defining what constitutes "healthy" sexual development can be challenging at best. What one person considers to be healthy sexual development may not align with what another person believes. When adults understand the difference between healthy and unhealthy behaviors and how their behaviors impact their lives, acknowledge their attitudes and the intersection of their beliefs with their behaviors, and realize how these impact their relationship to the world and with others, they can create more fulfilling and healthy views toward sexual health and its expression (Bueheler, 2013).

In order to be effective in working with issues of sexuality, sexual identity, and sexual health, practitioners must be aware of their own biases, the stigmas that still exist around these topics, the lack of practitioner training in addressing these complex issues, and why taboos still exist. Research indicates that sexuality is still one of the most ignored and/or taboo topics in clinical practice today (Russell, 2012). It is not uncommon for LGBTQ individuals to experience stigma and discrimination by health-care providers, including mental health providers, through the use of heteronormative language, heterosexual assumptions about partner choices by practitioners, and homophobic policies. These negative experiences and attitudes can increase a person's chance of experiencing violence and harassment, increase potential for suicide ideation, and ultimately create barriers to health and mental health care (Centers for Disease Control and Prevention, 2015). In addition to health care–related stigma, many LGBTQ youth often experience strong rejection from their families and peer groups. Ryan, Huebner, Diaz, and Sanchez (2009) indicate that LGBTQ youth who experience such rejection are eight times more likely to commit suicide, six times more like to report high levels of depression, and three times more likely to use illegal drugs or engage in risky sexual practices. Knowing how to discuss these topics and actually engaging clients in a dialogue about their experiences can lead to a more trusting, open, and effective relationship between practitioner and client system.

One of the most common questions clients ask a social worker regarding sexual behavior pertains to what is considered "normal." Therefore, it is important for social workers to be knowledgeable about typical and atypical sexual health and development for accurate assessment and effective treatment. In the same regard, social workers need to have a basic knowledge of psychosocial development and what is considered "normal" within sexual health and development. A thorough understanding and awareness of one's own biases, values, beliefs, and attitudes toward different sexual health topics, identities, and behaviors is also necessary. If social workers do not understand the biopsychosocial and cultural influences that impact their own sexual behavior, health, and biases, they are more likely to pathologize a client. Thus social workers may pathologize behaviors without merit. At all stages of clinical work, it is important for social workers to assess development and discuss a client's beliefs about sexual behaviors, gender norms, cultural expectations, family norms (past and present), how the client learned about sexually related matters, religious beliefs and influences, language and terminology used, among many other topics. All of these issues are situated in both the time and context of a society. They may change over time or they may stay the same. By using a bio-psycho-social-cultural approach to gathering information, data can be normalized and questions answered without shame or judgment.

PSYCHOSEXUAL DEVELOPMENT THEORY

While the writings of Freud have been discredited and other theories have arisen in the areas of sexual health, it is important for social workers to understand psychosexual development theory as a major contributor to sex research, interventions, and beliefs in the medical and health fields of past decades. Freud postulated that individual differences in personalities stem from differences in childhood sexual development and experiences (McLeod, 2008). He created five psychosexual stages of development that include oral, anal, phallic, latency, and genital. Freud posited that development was linear in nature, during which a specific area of a child's body (such as the mouth in the oral phase) was the focus of pleasure and thus also the dominant source of sexual arousal (Hutchinson, 2014). He suggested that if people had difficulty meeting their needs in this stage, difficulties in personality and sexual relations would subsequently occur later in their adult life. Table 2.1 provides an overview of this model and examples of how these stages might appear symptomatically later in life.

ADOLESCENCE AND SEXUAL DEVELOPMENT

While Freud's psychosexual development theory is the most widely known sexual development model of childhood, more current research has moved beyond his explanations of the latency phase for further understanding of sexual health development. Research suggests that, throughout childhood, individuals explore and are aware of sexual-related changes, behaviors, and attitudes (Johnson, 2009). Sexual development begins in utero and continues through adulthood. Social workers must know what is considered "normal" development during childhood and when behaviors are present that are of concern. Sexual development throughout childhood includes a child's physical and emotional development, as well as gender identity, behaviors, role expectations, and actions. Research indicates that same-sex attraction can exist during any phase of development but that it often begins with the onset of puberty, on average at the age of eight years old (Diamond & Savin-Williams, 2000). It is important to note that there is often variation in sexual development

TABLE 2.1 Psychosexual Development Theory

Stage	Age	Pleasure Site and Erogenous Zone	Characteristics	Manifestation of Symptoms
Oral	0 to 18 months	Mouth	Maternal dependence for food and emotional needs. The Id is the central personality. Immediate gratification is necessary.	Smoking, gum chewing, chewing hair, nail biting
Anal	18 months to 3 years	Anus	Control begins to shift to the child. Focus on toilet training. Expectations of hygiene and libido are societal standards. Child seeks pleasure and some control over behaviors/reactions from others.	Defiant behaviors, obsessive-compulsive behaviors, passive-aggressiveness, overly clean or completely disorganized (extremes)
Phallic	4 to 5 years	Genital	Body and genital exploration for sexual stimulation and pleasure; attraction to others sexually; envy of parent of opposite sex. Existence of an Oedipus or Electra Complex and the accompanying castration anxiety or penis envy; children adopt the values and characteristics of the same-sex parent, thus forming the superego.	Guilt about sexual pleasure, inferiority (women), anxiety, narcissism (men)
Latency	5 years to puberty	None	Developmental phase focusing on social relationships including family and peer relationships. Becoming more aware of environment and influences behavior.	Social disorders such as anxiety/depression
Genital	Puberty to adulthood	Genital	Sexual interest and exploration stage. This stage sparks a new interest in sexual relationships and masturbation.	Difficulties in this phase are contributed to earlier stages.

Note: Adapted from Hutchinson (2014).

based on cultural beliefs, norms, family structure, sibling placement, exposure to sexual content in the media, and other possible areas (Buehler, 2013). Ultimately, social workers and all practitioners should not assume the sexual identity or sexual orientation of any child.

Adolescence is a time of curiosity, exploration, and experimentation for many individuals. Many adolescents have difficulty transitioning from childhood to adulthood and look for ways to identify and define themselves. Healthy sexuality is an important developmental task starting at puberty and ending in the early to middle 20s. Erik Erickson (1950) postulated that adolescents must define roles and achieve ego identity, which includes sexual identity. During this part of life, peer groups become paramount, and sexual drive becomes a defining factor of life. Adolescents become decision-makers in their own lives. This is often when individuals will explore their identities and gender conformity (or nonconformity), challenge attitudes and beliefs, begin to create their own norms, explore their sexual self, and, for many, come out.

NEUROSCIENCE AND ENDOCRINOLOGY

There is evidence that genetics, neurology, and endocrinology are involved in the development of sexual orientation. For instance, there are structural differences in heterosexual adult male and female brains—such that brain structures differ in size and function depending on whether one is heterosexual male or female. As these structural differences exist, researchers have studied whether they can explain sexual orientation (Littrell, 2008). There is some evidence that the brains of gay men have some similarity to the brains of female heterosexuals and that the brains of lesbians have some similarities to the brains of male heterosexuals (Littrell, 2008). Further, twin studies have supported the inheritance of sexual orientation. In general, the studies estimate that there is between a 28% and 65% heritability of sexual orientation (Kendler, Thrornton, Gilman, & Kessler, 2000; Littrell, 2008). However, the complexity of genetics, endocrinology, and neuroscience makes the number of variables involved in the development of male and female traits and the development of sexual orientation quite large. This complexity currently does not allow the scientific community to claim that there is a definitive structural or genetic difference that determines sexual orientation. In short,

> though most neuroscientists demure from claiming that physiological processes determine sexual orientation, there are strong reasons to suspect that sexual orientation has a physiological basis. These suspicions rest on the considerable knowledge of how the fetus develops in utero; [and] observations of how sexual orientation is affected when developmental processes are perturbed. (Littrell, 2008, pp. 106–107)

There is also evidence that gender identity is influenced by genetics, hormones, and brain structure. Some individuals are born with both testes and ovaries, some have genitalia that do not coincide with what the brain is processing, and others are born with genetic mutations such as a 5-alpha reductase gene mutation, which causes a person to be born with female genitalia but to become masculine at puberty, developing a penis (Littrell, 2008). Hormonal exposure during gestation is also likely to play a role in gender identity, "as findings accumulate, a more fully articulated story is likely to emerge in the future, clarifying the role of each hormone, in each critical time period, for each of the many genderized traits and behaviors" (Littrell, 2008, p. 120). In short, while the science is not yet fully developed, it is likely that as research continues a more complete picture of the structural, hormonal, and genetic influences on both sexuality and gender will emerge.

SEXUAL ORIENTATION AND THE CASS MODEL

During the late 1960s and through the 1970s researchers began to explore theoretical stage models describing homosexual identity development (Bilodeau & Renn, 2005; Kenneady & Oswalt, 2014). The most well-known of these models was developed by Vivienne Cass in 1979. Cass discusses a model of homosexual identity formation that includes six stages (Cass, 1979, 1984; Kenneady & Oswalt, 2014). Cass created a stage model of development echoing prior researchers' conceptualization of identity development. Like all stage theories, the development process is not necessarily linear and can be quite fluid. An individual may move from one stage to the next stage and then go back to the previous stage. The Cass model of gay and lesbian identity formation incorporates the internal conflict that gay and lesbian individuals may face living in a heteronormative and homophobic society (Bilodeau & Renn, 2005). During the 1970s and early 1980s when the prevalent attitudes toward gay/lesbian individuals were largely negative, the model was presented to affirm that individuals can accept homosexuality as a positive status (Bilodeau & Renn, 2005; Cass 1979, 1984; Kenneady & Oswalt, 2014). For more information related to LGBTQ identity development, models and frameworks, see chapter 4 in this text.

Although the Cass model is probably the most well-known and oft-cited model of lesbian and gay sexual identity, it has recently been argued that it may not be valid for contemporary youth (Savin-Williams, 2015). Researchers acknowledge that while some contemporary gay and lesbian youth struggle with mental health issues as they navigate sexual identity development and reach milestones, much current research argues that the majority follow "normative" development (Savin-Williams, 2015). As Western society becomes more accepting of those who are gay and lesbian, "younger generations are increasingly accepting of sexual diversity, making same-sex sexuality categories and coming-out models less applicable" (Morgan, 2012, p. 55). In short, social acceptance of LGBTQ youth reflected in both the sociocultural indicators and recently gained legal rights suggests that there may no longer be distinct differences in sexual development between LGBTQ and heterosexual youth—rendering models such as Cass less relevant (Morgan, 2012).

Further criticism of sexual identity development models underscores a limited focus on sexual orientation rather than looking more broadly at the multifaceted nature of sexual development

(Morgan, 2012). In particular, many models of sexual development neglect to look at the vast array of individual variability (e.g., race, ethnicity, nationality, and socioeconomic status) that may influence sexual development. It is important that any "future understandings of sexual identity consider the intersection of these sociocultural and individual forces" (Morgan, 2012, p. 55). There seems to be consensus among current scholars who study sexual identity that it remains multifaceted and dynamic—therefore models should be examined through historical and a cultural contexts (Morgan, 2012).

ADULT SEXUAL DEVELOPMENT

Sexual development continues throughout adulthood and can be impacted by a variety of factors such as pregnancy, abortion, miscarriage, illness, loss of partner, environmental stressors, as well as aging. Psychological and physical changes throughout adulthood impact a person's sexual health. One of the most important developmental tasks for adults in terms of sex is learning how to communicate effectively with others including partners, doctors, health-care providers, family members, and so on (Hutchinson, 2014). In order to make choices about sexual health care but also assess risk of engaging in sexual activity and pleasure-seeking, one must be able to discuss sexuality and sexual topics openly and honestly. This is not easy for many LGBTQ individuals, and it often takes time to learn how to do it effectively. Such challenges are often raised during individual sessions or groups in which a social worker can best assist clients.

There is no one path or developmental task to master during adulthood (Buehler, 2013). For some, partnering with others will occur, and for others it will not. Perhaps an individual will change partners frequently or keep only one throughout adulthood. Sexual activity regardless of partner status will most likely change during adulthood in terms of satisfaction, ability to perform, comfort, and frequency of activity. It is common for individuals to experience discrepancies in sexual satisfaction due to an array of factors. Research indicates that there are three common factors that distinguish individuals who are satisfied sexually compared to those who are not. These include (a) accepting one's own sexuality, (b) listening to one's partner and being aware of the partner's likes and dislikes, and (c) talking openly and honestly (DeLamater & Friedrich, 2002). Discussing and normalizing discrepancies in sexual functioning and satisfaction are areas in which social workers can intervene. Completion of these developmental tasks is paramount to achieving sexual health and having healthy sexual relationships as adults.

FRAMEWORKS FOR HEALTHY SEXUAL DEVELOPMENT

It is not uncommon for social workers to have limited training in the areas of sexual health, sex, sexuality, sexual identity, and any form of sexual functioning, among other areas. There are several frameworks that can assist social workers in learning how to effectively discuss these topics with their LGBTQ clients. Researchers have identified 15 domains that constitute healthy sexual development (McKee et al., 2010):

- freedom from unwanted activity
- an understanding of consent
- education about biological aspects
- understanding of safety
- relationship skills
- agency (actions to produce a desired result)
- lifelong learning about sexual health and changes throughout development
- resilience
- open communication
- nonaggressive, positive sexual development
- self-acceptance
- awareness and acceptance that sex is pleasurable
- understanding of parental and societal values
- awareness of public/private boundaries
- competence in mediating sexual experiences such as communicating with a partner so that sexual relationships are satisfying.

This framework can assist social workers in understanding the many dimensions of sexual health and behaviors. However, it should be noted that sexuality is multilayered and multifaceted, and aspects of it are not well understood. This framework is not meant to provide a strict list of sexual health–related topics that may occur in treatment but rather a holistic approach to assessment and treatment. It is a useful tool that can and should be adapted for use with current screening and assessment tools.

THE PLISSIT MODEL

Addressing sex, sexual identity, and/or any sex-related topic can cause discomfort for the social worker as well as the client. This is the reason many social workers never even bring up the topic of sex or sexuality with their clients. Some social workers are worried that they will somehow offend their clients, not use the correct terms, not know something they should know, or make their clients feel uncomfortable. Often social workers are sensitive to instilling their own beliefs on clients and so they inadvertently avoid difficult topics. Fortunately the medical field has a useful model that can assist social workers with a framework for addressing sexual health topics with their clients. The most commonly used framework in the medical field today is the PLISSIT model (Annon, 1976). It can be applied in two ways. First, it provides clinicians with guidelines on what to address with clients; second, it gives clinicians guidelines on what is expected of them and reminds them that they do not have to have all the treatment answers. Table 2.2 provides a basic outline of the PLISSIT model.

TABLE 2.2 The PLISSIT Model

	Components	Clinician to Client	Clinician to Self
P	Permission	Ask client if it is okay to discuss sexual health. Clients are also given "permission" to engage in sexual activities (or not to) of their choice as long as they are not hurting themselves or others.	Give oneself permission as a clinician to ask about sexual health.
LI	Limited Information	Provide client with limited information.	Do not have to know everything about sexual health; ask questions and elicit information from client; provide information as needed.
SS	Specific Suggestions	Give client-specific suggestions on sexual health.	This can be in the form of homework or specific sexual health tasks, but it also can be in the form of a referral.
IT	Intensive Treatment	Provide intensive treatment that is comprehensive in nature.	This does not have to go beyond the clinician's scope of practice; it can include working with a trained sex therapist, physician, spiritual leaders, and/or other health or mental health providers.

Note: Adapted from Annon (1976).

CONCLUSION

This chapter has sought to provide an introduction to issues of oppression, stigma, and prejudice faced by members of the LGBTQ community, along with definitions, various theoretical frameworks, and basic sexual health–related information for use in social work practice. Having a thorough understanding of the key factors that impact the sexual health of members of the LGBTQ community is key to effective and affirming practice. Furthermore, social workers must know proper terminology and the differences that exist among their LGBTQ clients. In order to do this, they must spend an appropriate amount of time learning the various definitions and meanings among LGBTQ individuals that exist today. Additionally, social workers need to reflect on their own personal beliefs to assure that they remain open and objective as they counsel the many clients who seek information and help in the area of sexual health. Understanding key factors coupled with self-knowledge allows for the implementation of the basic overall framework introduced in this chapter to address sexual health–related topics. Finally, NASW and CSWE mandate that social workers develop an understanding of sexual diversity and sexual health in their practice with minority populations. This professional mandate allows social workers to use their knowledge to educate others in helping professionals and advocate on the behalf of individuals who are representative of the sexual diversity that exists in society.

REFERENCES

Alexander, K. (2016). *Queering transaffirmative care: Queer theory's placement in an affirmative clinical context* (Unpublished master's thesis). Greater Rochester Collaborative Masters Social Work Program, Rochester, NY.

American Psychological Association. (2011). *The guidelines for psychological practice with lesbian, gay, and bisexual clients.* Retrieved from http://www.apa.org/pi/lgbt/resources/guidelines.aspx

American Psychiatric Association. (2013). *Diagnostic and statistical manual of mental disorders* (5th ed.). Washington, DC: American Psychiatric Association.

American Psychological Association. (2015). Guidelines for psychological practice with transgender and gender nonconforming people. *American Psychologist, 70*(9), 832–864.

American Psychological Association Just the Facts Coalition. (2008). *Just the facts about sexual orientation and youth: A primer for principals, educators, and school personnel.* Retrieved from http://www.apa.org/pi/lgbc/publications/justthefacts.html

Annon, J. (1976). The PLISSIT model: A proposed conceptual scheme for the behavioral treatment of sexual problems. *Journal of Sex Education Therapy, 2*(2), 1–15.

Appleby, G., & Cohen, E. (2008). Social work practice with LGBTQ people in organizations. In G. P. Mallon (Ed.), *Social work practice with lesbian, gay, bisexual, and transgender people* (2nd ed., pp. 363–378). New York: Routledge.

Bell, L. A. (2010). *Theoretical foundations.* In M. Adams, W. J. Blumenfeld, C. R. Castende, H. W. Hackman, M. L. Peters, & X. Zuniga (Eds.), *Readings for diversity and social justice* (2nd ed., pp. 21–25). New York: Routledge.

Bilodeau, B. L., & Renn, K. A. (2005). Analysis of LGBT identity development models and implications for practice. In R. L. Sanlo (Ed.), *Gender identity and sexual orientation: Research, policy, and personal perspectives* (pp. 25–40). (New Directions for Student Services No. 111). San Francisco, CA: Jossey-Bass. Retrieved from https://msu.edu/~renn/BilodeauRennNDSS.pdf

Buehler, S. (2013). *what every mental health professional needs to know about sex.* New York: Springer.

Burdge, B. J. (2007). Bending gender, ending gender: Theoretical foundations for social work practice with the transgender community. *Social Work, 52*(3), 243–250.

Cass, V. (1984). Homosexual identity formation: Testing a theoretical model. *Journal of Sex Research, 20*(2), 143–167.

Cass, V. C. (1979). Homosexual identity formation: A theoretical model. *Journal of Homosexuality, 4*(3), 219–235.

Center for Disease Control and Prevention. (2015). Stigma and discrimination. Retrieved from http://www.cdc.gov/msmhealth/stigma-and-discrimination.htm

Council on Social Work Education. (2015). *Educational policy and accreditation standards for baccalaureate and master's social work programs.* Alexandria, VA: Author.

Council on Social Work Education. (2016). *Position statement on conversion/reparative therapy.* Retrieved from https://www.cswe.org/getattachment/Centers-Initiatives/Centers/Center-for-Diversity/About/Stakeholders/Commission-for-Diversity-and-Social-and-Economic-J/Council-on-Sexual-Orientation-and-Gender-Identity/CSOGIE-Resources/CSWEPositionStatementonConversion-ReparativeTherapy(003).pdf.aspx

Chappell, B. (2015, June 26). Supreme Court declares same-sex marriage legal in all 50 states. National Public Radio. Retrieved from www.npr.org

Craig, S. L., Austin, A. & Alessi, E. (2013). Gay affirmative cognitive behavioral therapy for sexual minority youth: A clinical adaptation. *Journal of Clinical Social Work, 41,* 258–266.

DeLamater, J., & Friedrich, W. (2002). Human sexual development. *Journal of Sex Research, 39*(1), 10–14.

Diamond, L. M., & Savin-Williams, R. C. (2000). Explaining diversity in the development of same-sex sexuality among young women. *Journal of Social Issues, 56,* 297–313.

Herek, G. M. (2000). The psychology of sexual prejudice. *Current Directions in Psychological Science, 9,* 19–22.

Human Rights Campaign. (2015). Hidden discrimination: Title IX religious exemptions putting LGBT students at risk. Retrieved from http://hrc-assets.s3-website-us-east-1.amazonaws.com//files/assets/resources/Title_IX_Exemptions_Report.pdf

Hutchinson, E. D. (2014). *Dimensions of human behavior* (4th ed.). Thousand Oaks, CA: SAGE.

Intersex Society of North America. (2013). *What is intersex?* Retrieved from http://www.isna.org/faq/what_is_intersex

Johnson, T. C. (2009). *Helping children with sexual behavior problems: A guidebook for professionals and caregivers* (4th ed.). Fitchburg, MA: NEARI Press Distribution.

Kendler, K. S., Thornton, L. M., Gilman, S. E., & Kessler, R. C. (2000). Sexual orientation in a U.S. national sample of twin and nontwin sibling pairs. *American Journal of Psychiatry, 157*(11), 1843–1846. Retrieved from http://dx.doi.org/10.1176/appi.ajp.157.11.1843

Kenneady, D. A., & Oswalt, S. B. (2014). Is Cass's model of homosexual identity formation relevant to today's society? *American Journal of Sexuality Education, 9,* 229–246.

Littrell, J. (2008). Incorporating information from neuroscience and endocrinology regarding sexual orientation into social work education. *Journal of Human Behavior in the Social Environment, 18*(2), 101–128.

Love, M. M., Smith, A. E., Lyall, S. E., Mullins, J. L., & Cohn, T. J. (2015). Exploring the relationship between gay affirmative practice and empathy among mental health professionals. *Journal of Multicultural Counseling & Development, 43*(2), pp. 83–96. doi:10.1002/j.2161-1912.2015.00066.x

Mallon, G. P. (2008). Knowledge for practice with gay, lesbian, bisexual & transgender people (LGBTQ). In G. P. Mallon (Ed.), *Social work practice with lesbian, gay, bisexual, and transgender people* (2nd ed., pp. 1–24). New York: Routledge.

Margolin, E. (May 25, 2016). 11 states sue Obama administration over transgender bathroom directive. NBC News. Retrieved from: http://www.nbcnews.com/news/us-news/11-states-sue-obama-administration-over-transgender-bathroom-directive-n580331

Marsiglia, F. F., & Kulis, S. (2015). *Diversity, oppression & change.* (2nd ed.). Chicago: Lyceum Books.

Martin, J. I., Messinger, L., Kull, R., Holmes, J., Bermudez, F., & Sommer, S. (2009). *Council on Social Work Education-Lambda Legal Study of LGBT Issues in Social Work.* Alexandria, VA: Council on Social Work Education. Retrieved from http://www.cswe.org/File.aspx?id=25675

McKee, A., Albury, K., Dunne, M., Grieshaber, S., Hartley, J., Lumby, C., & Mathews, B. (2010). Healthy sexual development: A multidisciplinary framework for research. *International Journal of Sexual Health, 22,* 14–19.

McLeod, S. A. (2008). *Psychosexual stages.* Retrieved from www.simplypsychology.org/psychosexual.html

McPhail, B. A. (2004). Questioning gender and sexuality binaries: What queer theorists, transgendered individuals, and sex researchers can teach social work. *Journal of Gay & Lesbian Social Services, 17*(1), 3–21.

Morgan, E. M. (2012). Contemporary issues in sexual orientation and identity development in emerging adulthood. *Emerging Adulthood, 1*(1) 52–66.

National Association of Social Workers. (2015, May). *Sexual orientation change efforts (SOCE) and conversion therapy with lesbians, gay men, bisexuals, and transgender persons.* Retrieved from http://www.socialworkers.org/diversity/new/documents/hria_pro_18315_soce_june_2015.pdf

Nondiscrimination laws. (2016). Movement Advancement Project. Retrieved from http://www.lgbtmap.org/equality-maps/non_discrimination_laws

Russell, E. B. (2012). Sexual health attitudes, knowledge and clinical behaviors: Implications for counseling. *The Family Journal, 20*(1), 90–99.

Ryan, C., Huebner, D., Diaz, R. M., & Sanchez, J. (2009). Family rejection as a predictor of negative health outcomes in white and Hispanic/Latino lesbian, gay, and bisexual young adults. *Pediatrics, 123,* 346–352.

Savin-Williams, R. C., & Cohen, K. M. (2015). Developmental trajectories and milestones of lesbian, gay, and bisexual young people. *International Review of Psychiatry, 27*(5), 357–366. doi:10.3109/09540261.2015.1093465

Shear, M. D. (2015, April 8). Obama calls for end to "conversion" therapies for gay and transgender youth. *The New York Times*. Retrieved from http://www.nytimes.com/2015/04/09/us/politics/obama-to-call-for-end-to-conversion-therapies-for-gay-and-transgender-youth.html?_r=0

Substance Abuse and Mental Health Services Administration. (2015). *Ending conversion therapy: Supporting and affirming LGBTQ youth* (HHS Publication No. 15-4928). Rockville, MD: Author. Retrieved from http://store.samhsa.gov/shin/content/SMA15-4928/SMA15-4928.pdf

Teliti, A. (2015). Sexual prejudice and sitgma of LGBTQ people. *European Scientific Journal, 11*(14), 60–69.

The White House. (2015, April 8). *Official White House response to enact Leelah's Law to ban all LGBTQ+ conversion therapy*. Washington, DC: Author. Retrieved from https://petitions.whitehouse.gov/response/response-your-petition-conversion-therapy

Tully, C. (2011). Cultural competence with lesbian, gay, bisexual and transgender persons. In D. Lum (Ed.), *Culturally competent practice: A framework for understanding diverse groups and justice issues* (4th ed., pp. 415–436). Belmont, CA: Brooks/Cole.

World Health Organization. (2006). *Sexual health—A new focus for WHO*. Geneva: Department of Reproductive Health and Research.

CHAPTER 3

ADVANCING SOCIAL AND ECONOMIC JUSTICE

*Kirsten Havig, Anthony P. Natale, David A. McLeod,
and Megan Gandy-Guedes*

INTRODUCTION

Social work is unique in that it is the only profession that can claim social justice as its organizing value and guidepost for practice (Marsh, 2005). The idea of social justice emerged as a critical concern in American life during the Progressive Era (c. 1890–1920), roughly the same time that social work itself was in its infancy as an organized profession (Miller, 1999). The importance of a social and economic justice framework for social work with lesbian, gay, bisexual, transgender, and queer (LGBTQ) populations cannot be overstated but requires operationalization to manifest in practice. It is clear that social justice is vital to social work practice, policy, and research, but it is not always clear which factors create our vision of justice or what tools we use for its promotion. This chapter provides theoretical models for understanding social and economic justice as well as concrete illustrations of the nature of injustice for LGBTQ people. The chapter concludes with recommendations for the promotion of social and economic justice in the United States and globally for LGBTQ people.

Social and economic justice for LGBTQ individuals has long been an area of disparity. For instance, in the US military, individuals could be dishonorably discharged simply for identifying as LGBTQ regardless of their military record, prior to the repeal of the Don't Ask, Don't Tell policy in 2011. Years later, some service members still report an uneasiness with trusting the systems in place to protect them, such as mental health services (Mount, Steelman, & Hertlein, 2015). Notably, as of June 2016, the military policy prohibiting transgender individuals from enlistment and service within the military had been overturned by the Department of Defense.

Discrimination in the workplace is still perfectly legal for LGBTQ individuals who live in a state without policy to protect them from discrimination based on sexual orientation or gender identity. Even in the twenty-first century, LGBTQ individuals face an unfair price for everyday living due to the costs of inequality (Movement Advancement Project, 2014). It may be important to consider the decades of financial inequality borne by same-sex couples who were unable to access the economic benefits available with legal marriage prior to the Supreme Court ruling in 2015. Such inequalities added up to paying for separate bank accounts, paying separate bills, and being treated by financial institutions as "roommates" rather than "spouses," leaving many LGBTQ individuals and families at an economic disadvantage. Transgender individuals face higher rates of unemployment (Movement Advancement Project, 2013), discrimination (Grant et al., 2010), and lack of access to health care (National Center for Transgender Equality & National Gay and Lesbian Task Force, 2009). There remain inequalities based within state governments as illustrated by the following data. As of February 2016, 49% of LGBTQ citizens live in states with few, if any, policies that pave the way for equality—including policies such as same-sex couple adoptions, religious exemption laws, and employment and housing discrimination, among others (Movement Advancement Project, 2013). Despite decades of progress, there are still many social and economic injustices faced by LGBTQ individuals within modern society.

To act on behalf of clients experiencing any type of injustice requires a critical understanding of the nature and dynamics of such injustice (e.g., discrimination, inequality, oppression, stigma). Oppression may occur at the individual level (e.g., socialization, beliefs, and behaviors); at the institutional level, (e.g., manifesting as unequal access to societal goods such as housing, employment, education, health care, media representation, and policy); and at the cultural level, (e.g., in terms of shared values, norms, roles, and expectations). Young (2001) operationalizes injustice in her work on the "five faces of oppression." These are illustrative to our discussion of LGBTQ experiences of injustice and include (a) exploitation: use of the resources of a group for the benefit of another; (b) marginalization: the "othering" of a group that results in devaluing and loss of opportunity; (c) powerlessness: often experienced as a lack of voice or influence resulting in an absence of the ability to self-determine or influence one's environment; (d) violence: as systematic harm targeting group members as an expression of hate and control; and (e) cultural imperialism: the norming of a dominant group, rendering others invisible and deviant against what is socially constructed to be right or valuable (Young 2001). Specific to the LGBTQ community, concepts of homophobia, biphobia, transphobia, and heteronormativity are relevant throughout this discussion as well. Other products of injustice often include stereotyping and stigma. Stigma has a significant impact on LGBTQ-based injustice and results in both internalized shame and external devaluation, which in turn impacts help-seeking, service participation, relationship-building, and self-concept. Ethical standards and professional guidelines for practice should assist with reducing stigma and injustice, as well as increase understanding for the pivotal role of advocacy for minority groups such as the LGBTQ community.

The National Association of Social Work (NASW) puts forth a *Code of Ethics* that sets standards for professional practice and guidelines for ethical decision-making (1999). The purpose of the *Code of Ethics* is to articulate the profession's basic values and ethical foundation. It does not prescribe beliefs or actions at the level of a particular issue but provides widely applicable principles meant to facilitate such decision-making according to generalized professional standards. Importantly, ethics also provide the profession and the general public with tools of accountability against which practical decisions may be measured. The preamble establishes social worker responsibility for the promotion of social justice and outlines that the overarching mission of the profession is "to enhance human well-being and help meet the basic human needs of all people, with particular attention to the needs and empowerment of people who are vulnerable, oppressed, and living in poverty" (NASW, 1999, para.1). The preamble clearly indicates that social justice may occur within "direct practice, community organizing, supervision, consultation, administration, advocacy, social and political action, policy development and implementation, education, and research and evaluation" (NASW, 1999, para.1)—in other words, across levels and fields of practice within the social work arena.

Despite its essential inclusion in the *Code of Ethics*, many diverse interpretations of social justice exist in the literature (Banerjee, 2005; Mitchell & Lynch, 2003). In attempting to define social justice, and its meaning for the LGBTQ population, it is helpful to first understand injustice, those who are impacted by it, and the nature of such impacts. In delineating the core principle of social justice, the *Code of Ethics* indicates that it is a social workers' duty to challenge injustices. It states that "social workers' social change efforts are focused primarily on issues of poverty, unemployment, discrimination, and other forms of social injustice" (NASW, 1999, Ethical principles section, para. 2). This passage suggests a methodology of social justice that encompasses advocacy for and partnership with clients; empowerment of people to meet their own needs and assisting others in achieving economic security; learning about and appreciating diversity; and facilitating access, inclusion, and recognition for those impacted by forces that disempower and marginalize. Highly applicable as a roadmap for work with the LGBTQ community, the *Code of Ethics* is unambiguous in placing advocacy for the marginalized at the center of social work practice.

The Social Work Dictionary, published by NASW, indicates that social justice is related to bringing about a society in which all members share the same rights, opportunities, protections, privileges, and obligations (Barker, 1995). In contrast to the *Code of Ethics*, which is intentionally broad, NASW also periodically publishes *Social Work Speaks*, with the expressed purpose of outlining the organization's stance on specific issues. The purpose of these policy statements is multifold: to define at the national level the profession's stance on critical social issues, to clarify the role that individual social workers can take in addressing them, and to establish a basis for activism and legislative advocacy rooted in social work values (NASW, 2015). The underpinning provided by *Social Work Speaks* for policy practice with the LGBT community are explored further in chapter 19 of this text.

THEORIES OF SOCIAL JUSTICE

Social justice, claimed by social work as both duty and principle, has long been the topic of political, economic, social, and legal philosophy and of constant debate within the profession. As a broad concept, social justice in society is represented by fair treatment, equity of status, access to necessities and of opportunity, and freedom from discrimination in order to maximize self-actualization for all individuals (Barsky, 2010). Reisch (2002) writes of social justice as a vehicle for redressing inequality for members of historically oppressed groups through the creation of equal opportunity and the righting of past wrongs. Young (2001) indicates that social justice is the elimination of institutionalized domination and oppression, referencing it as a means of liberation from systems that limit access and potential. While one view of social justice defines it as basic equality, in which all are treated the same, it is also thought of as important to treat everyone according to difference and to individual needs and circumstances (Barsky, 2010). Injustice, the target of such change efforts, is conceptualized as either act or omission that wrongfully prevents an individual or group's access to rights and to meeting human need (Reamer, 2006). Examples of injustices experienced by members of the LGBTQ population over the years has included legal barriers to marriage and the benefits of marriage in society; legal discrimination in the areas of housing, employment, and education access; and targeting by violence and hate speech that negatively impacts the social, emotional, physical, and vocational functioning of people.

Under the umbrella of social justice, several useful theories exist to assist social workers in operationalizing the value for the benefit of clients. As seen in Table 3.1, each of these theoretical positions addresses working toward social justice through a particular paradigm, or worldview, with designated foci and guiding principles. As this chapter continues we detail at length each of the theories depicted in Table 3.1, and later in the chapter we provide examples for applying these theories to work with and on behalf of LGBTQ people.

DISTRIBUTIVE JUSTICE

Theories of distributive justice are concerned with how a society disburses resources among its citizens, who deserves what, and by what process (Brighouse, 2004)—put simply, what society owes to its citizens. Distributive justice concerns several primary constructs including *need* (what constitutes basic and self-actualization needs and what best meets those needs), *deserving* (who deserves what share based on merit, effort, status, etc.), *fairness* (how to best address injustice), and *equality* (ensuring that no one deserving gets more or less than what is judged to be fair; Miller, 1999; Reamer, 2006). A critical challenge is to find common ground in terms of how distribution of benefit might occur and who is deserving of justice and why. Additionally, what goods are subject to distribution—jobs, material resources, opportunity, social capital—are also difficult to define (Miller, 1999). In terms of practice with LGBTQ individuals, social workers should lobby lawmakers for the passage of the Employment Non-Discrimination Act (ENDA), which would give LGBTQ individuals guaranteed access to resources derived from the workplace. Within the distributive paradigm three perspectives are often discussed: libertarian, utilitarian, and egalitarian (Barsky, 2010; Brighouse, 2004; Miller, 1999). All three are concerned with how to approach the fair distribution of resources within a society, and all incorporate a different view on how to best promote the "common good."

A *libertarian perspective* on justice emphasizes individual rights as primary and supports ownership and free market ideals over any attempt to legitimate what is seen as taking what is rightful from one and giving it to another via state interference (Brighouse, 2004; Miller, 1999). For libertarians, the role of the state should be one of benign neglect, allowing social and economic forces to play out, even if the result is increased inequality. Economic and political freedom are seen as inexorably linked, so that economic infringement such as taxation limits personal agency and liberty (Brighouse, 2004). For example, this perspective would promote the idea that social

TABLE 3.1 Theoretical Frameworks, Core Foci, and Guiding Principles

Theoretical Framework	Core Focus and Principles
Distributive Justice Paradigm	• Focused on how society distributes resources • Looks at who deserves what resources • Concerned with what society owes its citizens
Libertarian Perspective	• Focused on the importance of individual rights • The role of government should be minimized • Free markets should determine distribution of resources and access
Utilitarian Perspective	• Focused on the common good • Distribution of resources should benefit the majority of people
Egalitarian Perspective	• Focused on the importance of equal opportunity for all individuals • Stresses the importance of facilitating fairness and addressing inequality • Resources should be used to improve conditions for those with the least power before being distributed to those with greater power
Capability Approach	• Focused on the ability of people to access and make use of resources • Also concerned with what means people must use to attain resources and opportunities • Stresses the importance of person-in-environment
Intersectionality Theory	• Focused on the complex identities of individuals • Speaks to the intersection of multiple facets of individual existence and identity • Concerned with different levels of privilege in their relationship to multiple facets of an individual's identity
Procedural Justice	• Focused on policy and procedural application • The fair and equal opportunity for people to attain opportunities and resources • More concerned with process than outcome
Feminist Perspective	• Focused on how interpersonal behaviors and interactions are at the center of oppression and opportunities for empowerment • Phenomenological—a person's access to justice is related to their own personal experience and their interpretation of it • Gender, gender identity and expression, and sexual orientation are core factors associated with personal identity and have historically been used to marginalize people and foster inequality
Commutative Justice	• Focused on the relations between individuals and equity in their interactions • Particular attention is paid to reciprocity in fulfillment of obligations to one another and expectations of the relationships and dealings between individuals
Human Rights Perspective	• Focused on using Universal Declaration of Human Rights as a framework for the evaluation of access to social justice • Recognizes poverty, discrimination, and lack of education as barriers to access of social justice

constructs like marriage should not be restricted from any member of society and should be free from the regulation and intervention of the government. The libertarian view sets freedom and forced resource distribution at odds and stands in theoretical opposition to redistributive efforts such as welfare that involve the intervention of the state to assure citizens resources through redistribution of wealth (Brighouse, 2004). These ideas are antithetical to the current processes of the social work profession meant to protect and defend those most vulnerable and to help ensure that needs are met through existing distributive mechanisms, however imperfect.

The *utilitarian perspective* stresses the importance of arriving at a manner of distribution of resources that is most conducive to a common good (Barsky, 2010; Brighouse, 2004; Miller, 1999). From this perspective, social work practice with LGBTQ individuals might look like working with the Center for Disease Control and Prevention to remove the restriction for gay men to donate blood, which would thereby increase the supply of blood for the greater community. Again, a primary point of contention is that there are a variety of possible beliefs concerning what is "good." This perspective can be used to justify an unequal distribution in order to benefit the most people, such as taxation that burdens the poor less than the rich. The problem of who decides on the meaning of good remains extraordinarily problematic in our pluralistic society.

The *egalitarian perspective* on distributive justice as a path to social justice emphasizes the importance of equal opportunity and treatment of individuals as a means of redressing inequality and facilitating fairness (Barsky, 2010; Brighouse, 2004; Miller, 1999). Social work is most in line with an egalitarian view of distributive justice and its attention to inclusiveness and the impact of social status. The keystone of the egalitarian perspective is Rawls's 1971 work, *A Theory of Justice*, which highlights each individual's right to liberty and liberty within society, the idea that social justice should be applied so as to benefit those with the least power and advantage first, and the idea that equal opportunity creates the context for redressing injustice and that obligation comes with rights (Rawls, 1971).

Several criticisms of the Rawlsian model of distributive justice include questioning his assumption of equal freedom and opportunity within an inherently unequal system such as the sociopolitical and economic structure of the United States (Banerjee, 2005). Rawls does not attend to the impact of a host of social locations that disadvantage groups and individuals at a structural level, including identification with some aspect of the LGBTQ continuum. This is of particular importance to social work with a group that still experiences discrimination at the individual, institutional, and policy levels. Fair distribution of resources does not address issues of cultural-structural oppression that create and underlie inequality (Reisch, 2002). Additionally, a theory that assumes that the government accepts an obligation to create a fair and just society, and that citizens and institutions will work collectively toward this end, is not supported in reality (Banerjee, 2005). Without addressing the powerful forces of social construction and structural oppression, the continued application of Rawls to a social work profession committed to social justice falls short in providing tools to alleviate inequality (Banerjee, 2005). This is where the capabilities perspective adds some illumination. The capability approach to social justice takes into account not simply receipt of societal goods but people's ability to access and make use of them (Morris, 2002; Sen, 1999). Rawls's (1971) theory of justice as rooted in the equal distribution of social goods does not address the capability to make use of them or to "convert them into valuable functionings" (p. 368). Sen (1999) also emphasizes that it is not the products of distribution (material or social) but rather the *means* to obtaining or achieving them, for example, advocating for full accessibility to all mechanisms of higher education without discrimination based on sexual orientation or gender identity and expression. This does not mean that all LGBTQ individuals have the right to attain higher education but rather that they are guaranteed the *means* for achievement of that aim. The capability perspective minimizes the dilemma of comparing one person or group's needs and worth with any other and instead focuses on the idea of access and capacity (Brighouse, 2004; Miller, 1999). The capabilities perspective attends to person-in-environment contexts and issues of oppression, which prevent actualization and self-determination and move beyond the attainment of basic needs (Banerjee, 2005). The concept of intersectionality is particularly illustrative in this context as a tool for highlighting the differences between groups in the ability to make use of rights and protections.

INTERSECTIONALITY THEORY

Intersectionality theory provides a conceptual framework to emphasize the complex identity of every individual. This theory was initially proposed as an analytical framework emergent from the experiences of Black feminists, allowing for a more complex understanding of the many facets of intersecting identities (Crenshaw, 1991; Collins, 2000). Multiple social locations experienced by individuals including race and ethnicity, socioeconomic status, geographical location, religious affiliation, ability, and age intersect with gender identity and sexual orientation to create complex experiences of both privilege and disadvantage (Crenshaw, 1991). While some facets of identity bestow unearned privilege, others bring group-based disadvantage. A key contribution of intersectionality theory to an understanding of social and economic justice is a rejection of universal experience based on membership in any one social category; in other words, the utility of viewing an individual's experience within a socially stratified system is diminished when the complexity of identity is considered. Socioeconomic status, for instance, may be a mediating factor in terms of the capability to withstand the injustices of social inequality and must be considered to fully understand the impact for LGBTQ individuals (Billies, Johnson, Murungi, & Pugh, 2009). Highlighting the importance of the multidimensional elements of identity to understand in-group diversity around socioeconomic status reveals the fact that LGBTQ individuals may be more economically disadvantaged by policies that prevent equal access to resources or social benefits, with disproportionate impact for some. Females are more economically disadvantaged as a group and more likely to live in poverty; lesbian women and transgender individuals experience compounded disadvantages and are therefore even more likely to be in poverty (Redman, 2010). McDermott (2011) argues that class and economic justice issues have been eclipsed by an emphasis on sexual orientation and gender identity but that such concerns are critical to achieving rights and justice for LGBTQ people. Such a perspective in no way erases the reality of oppression based on gender identity or sexual orientation but makes our understanding of these categories more nuanced and acknowledges that many individuals experience multiple forms of oppression. This is important when examining the concepts of social and economic justice, such that to truly assess the injustice experienced by an individual or group, it is essential to understand the many facets of dis/advantage. In this way, it is important for social workers to improve risk assessment practices to better recognize the multiple markers of marginalization and privilege within the LGBTQ community.

PROCEDURAL JUSTICE

The concept of procedural justice brings attention to the locus of in/justice, situating it between individuals and institutions rather than as defined in relation to the state (Barry, 2005; Brighouse, 2004). Procedural justice allows for a focus on the policies and processes that guide actions, in addition to the outcomes that might be set in place to achieve (Miller, 1999). Procedures and policies do not always result in their desired outcome but have meaning in the context of human interactions. For example, not all LGBTQ couples wish to adopt children, but, prior to 2015, many were barred from doing so under certain state laws. Thus procedural justice would lead a social worker to develop legislation for uniform, national adoption and foster parenting laws with consistent processes for how placement of children is determined, regardless of parental sex, gender, sexual orientation, or gender identity. Miller outlines several qualities of just procedures that are parallel to social work values including equality of access. competence. the hearing of all sides and voices. dignity of each person. accountability and transparency. and self-determining voluntary consent. He indicates that procedural justice must be acted upon "at the moment of engagement" (p. 121), in order to promote and sustain the substantive goals of fairness and equity.

In social work, as in society, injustice and its remedies exist in terms of both individuals and groups as targets and recipients. Group-based perspectives offer useful tools for analyzing justice claims in a society in which membership in socially constructed groups (i.e., gender identity, sexual orientation) results in the experience of either relative privilege or oppression (Young, 2001). The consequences of injustice, such as poverty, have cumulative effects on those who by virtue of actual or perceived group membership are socially disadvantaged by society's structures (Barsky, 2010). The principle of participatory parity calls for all citizens to be able to act as peers in a society, with equal voice and responsibility (Brighouse, 2004). If parity is evaluated only on the basis of individual access to participation (with individual shortcomings or assets as the assumed cause) rather than in the context of the historical and intentional structures of unequal access and citizenship, the essence of both problem and solution continue to be elusive.

FEMINIST PERSPECTIVES AND COMMUTATIVE JUSTICE

The feminist perspective that *the personal is the political* points toward an approach to social justice that attends to interpersonal transactions and their connection to broader forces. Liberal feminist thought on social justice has helped to broaden the discussion from a traditional focus on distribution and the role of the state and its basic structure in formulating mechanisms for fairness (Brighouse, 2004). From this stance, interpersonal behaviors and interactions are as much the locus of in/justice as the systems and outcomes of institutions and social structures that cannot be divorced from the macro level. Practice behavior in this light may be best articulated by the words of Gandhi: You must "be the change you want to see in the world." From this perspective, it is when people strive for a world in which gender identity or sexual orientation do not create unfair hierarchies, power imbalances, and inequities that organizations that eschew injustices and demonstrate fairness and equal respect in our interpersonal transactions can be established and maintained. For social work practice with LGBTQ persons, this might look like advancing protections from, and accountability for, violence based on stereotypically gendered norms and collective action against equality. Attention to personal, or *commutative justice* (US Legal Inc., 2010) is of great value for social work as well, in that it highlights the importance of micro-level transactions to the pursuit of justice. From a perspective of commutative justice, nothing is more important than fairness and a balance of power, in the process of everyday interaction between individuals. An example of this type of justice in action is the protection of youth against bullying based on actual or perceived sexual orientation and/or gender identity and expression in schools and in the community.

HUMAN RIGHTS PERSPECTIVE

A human rights perspective offers useful insight on social justice for LGBTQ people (Fish & Bewley, 2010). The United Nations (UN) adopted the Universal Declaration of Human Rights (UDHR) in 1948, during the aftermath of the horrors of World War II. Within the document are three specific areas in which rights and freedoms are outlined: (a) political and civil rights; (b) social, economic, and cultural rights; and (c) collective rights such as the right to freedom of religion or the pursuit of personal development (United Nations, 1948). Of primary concern to social work is the second, said to be a "positive freedom" or one requiring state intervention to achieve. Three main barriers to an individual's ability to access human rights as outlined in the UDHR include poverty, discrimination based on prejudice and unequal social hierarchies, and lack of education (Mapp, 2008). Indivisible and essential in nature, these barriers are of critical importance to social work and fundamentally tied to structurally based inequity.

The UDHR is gaining recognition among American social work scholars, educators, and activists and has great promise as a tool for enhancing both conceptual understanding and real-world action for the promotion of social justice (Reichert, 2003; Wronka, 2008). A framework of social justice based not on needs but on rights represents a new lens through which to assess and advocate for just outcomes. The UDHR calls for the inclusion of all people "without distinction of any kind" (United Nations, 1948, Article 2). To date, the UN has adopted several resolutions and made declarations pertaining to the LGBTQ community (e.g., in 2011, 2014, and 2016), while recent calls for attention to the human rights of LGBTQ persons worldwide continue to emerge. The Office for the High Commissioner of the United Nations Human Rights Commission has published reports highlighting gender identity and sexual orientation as critical areas of human rights violations internationally. In 2011, a collaborative project of the UN Office for the High Commissioner for Human Rights, the UN Development Programme, the Joint UN Programme on HIV/AIDS, and the World Health Organization recognized the tension between cultural attitudes and universal human rights. The UN High Commissioner, Navi Pillay, was quoted on February 2011: "Laws criminalizing homosexuality pose a serious threat to the fundamental rights of lesbian, gay, bisexual and transgender individuals" (United Nations, 2011).

Despite the reality that the United States has not ratified the 1945 Declaration of Human Rights, the burgeoning focus of the international human rights community on LGBTQ-related injustice is encouraging. In a 2011 report commissioned by the UN Human Rights Council, the High Commissioner outlined key findings related to human rights violations committed against members of the LGBTQ population around the world. The report condemns the criminalization of consenting same-sex intimate relationships and same-sex marriage; violence perpetrated against LGBTQ individuals; discriminatory practices in employment, education, housing, health care, protection from crime, freedom of assembly, and around family structure; arbitrary arrest and imprisonment; torture and degradation; lack of legal recognition for transgender identity changes; and a lack of right of asylum for the persecuted as critical areas of LGBTQ human rights violations globally (United Nations High Commissioner for Human Rights, Office of the High Commissioner and the Secretary General Report, 2011). The report also highlights emerging responses and remedies from state and nonstate entities around the world including required training for law enforcement and others engaged in public safety efforts supported by policy change and resource investment; public information and awareness campaigns; anti-bullying and safe school initiatives; and other policy changes including pathways for transgender individuals to obtain identification reflecting their gender (United Nations, 2011). Additional recommendations include swift state responses to violence committed against members of the LGBTQ community, the repealing of laws that criminalize sexual contact between consenting same-sex adults, and the enactment of comprehensive antidiscrimination legislation that is inclusive of LGBTQ individuals. Notably, in June of 2016, the UN Human Rights Council adopted a resolution (32/2) on *Protection against Violence and Discrimination Based on Sexual Orientation, and Gender Identity*, along with mandating the appointment of an independent expert in a historic victory for the LGBTQ community as reported by the Human Rights Watch (see http://www.un.org/en/ga/search/view_doc.asp?symbol=A/HRC/RES/32/2).

NASW has taken a stand on the UDHR and its utility for social work. While the organization recognizes "the profession does not fully use human rights as a criterion with which to evaluate social work policies, practice, research, and program priorities" (NASW, 2015, p. 184), it is also made clear that the UDHR is largely a reflection of beliefs held within the profession for some 50 years before its adoption by the UN. As a result, it is the official policy of NASW to promote ratification of not only the UDHR but also other treaties such as the Covenant on Economic, Social, and Cultural Rights, taken up by the UN in 1966. NASW recognizes the importance of codifying the rights of vulnerable and oppressed populations and for establishing state accountability for enforcing these rights (NASW, 2015).

ENACTING SOCIAL AND ECONOMIC JUSTICE THEORY IN PRACTICE: SOCIAL JUSTICE AND THE ACT OF ADVANCING EQUITY

Despite the priorities set forth by policies and mission statements, theory and practice in some ways remain disconnected. Mitchell and Lynch (2003) argue that the social work profession's current paradigms of oppression and social justice are ill-equipped to support either direct practice that incorporates social justice action or the pursuit of larger, policy-based structural shifts toward equality of opportunity or resources. Almost five decades ago, several criteria for the achievement of social justice in social work practice were put forth. These included fostering a sense of belonging for clients, protection of client dignity through understanding and respect, mutuality of rights and responsibilities between clients and workers, and commitment to the belief that access to services that meet human needs is a right not an entitlement (Reynolds, 1951).

Such ideals still have relevance to the quest for social work practice that actively promotes social justice goals and are applicable across practice settings. However, ideals abound in social work and must be operationalized into specific, measureable, and observable tasks, particularly if evidence-based practice tenets are to be addressed. Practice behaviors often associated with social justice include advocacy; empowerment of clients through consciousness-raising, skill-building, and resource development; community education and organizing; legislative and media activism; social movement participation; policy analysis and development; violence intervention; diversity promotion; and program development and evaluation (Birkenmaier 2003; Birkenmaier & Berg-Weger, 2007). The promotion of social justice requires special attention to meeting the needs of vulnerable populations *and* engagement in social action to create structural change that would alter the conditions leading to discrimination and inequality—tasks that social workers have engaged in for decades (Birkenmaier, 2003; Reamer, 2006). Figure 3.1 provides a few concrete examples of the application of social justice work in LGBTQ communities and how it could connect to the theories that organize the way(s) social and economic justice are conceptualized.

The micro-macro divide in social work has concerning implications for the incorporation of social justice. Social justice concerns and social change strategies are generally perceived in terms of policy change and community work, or the macro piece of social work practice (i.e., policy analysis, development, and advocacy; community organizing and development; and the promotion of organizational change). Within a dichotomized model of social work, clinical work is thought to require neutrality and scientific objectivity (Breton, 2006; Caputo, 2002; Gibelman, 1999; Haynes, 1998; McLaughlin, 2002; Olson, 2007; Reeser & Epstein, 1990) and may as a result be considered outside the realm of social justice–promoting advocacy. Direct practice work is prescribed as a value-free approach that would be deprofessionalized by the application of a particular value orientation (Abramovitz, 1998; Hugman, 2003). Such perspectives create much confusion around the role and methods of clinical practice in the promotion of social justice goals. In some cases, the actions and behaviors associated with social justice are no longer identified as "social work" as the much discussed professional divide continues to deepen (Olson, 2007). Social justice–focused work has been labeled as "radical" social work (Andrews & Reisch, 2001; Reisch, 2002), perhaps further marginalizing such pursuits, in particular when contextualized against a backdrop of both political and social controversy surrounding the civil and human rights of LGBTQ people.

Professionalized clinical social work practice has been characterized as the perpetuation of the status quo of inequality in society, rather than as a vehicle capable of challenging societal structures (Abramovitz, 1998; Andrews & Reisch, 2001; Mitchell & Lynch, 2003; Specht & Courtney, 1994). The debate over the potential benefits and threats posed to the pursuit of social justice by professionalization is ongoing. As professionalization is not necessarily antithetical to social justice, integrative models are emerging to better represent how the promotion of social justice may be operationalized across the continuum of micro to macro practice. Social justice–promoting practice has been theorized for all levels of social work intervention, including direct clinical

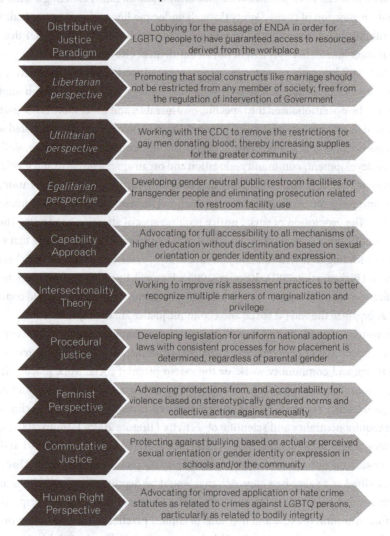

Examples of SEJ in Action

Distributive Justice Paradigm	Lobbying for the passage of ENDA in order for LGBTQ people to have guaranteed access to resources derived from the workplace
Libertarian perspective	Promoting that social constructs like marriage should not be restricted from any member of society; free from the regulation of intervention of Government
Utilitarian perspective	Working with the CDC to remove the restrictions for gay men donating blood; thereby increasing supplies for the greater community
Egalitarian perspective	Developing gender neutral public restroom facilities for transgender people and eliminating prosecution related to restroom facility use
Capability Approach	Advocating for full accessibility to all mechanisms of higher education without discrimination based on sexual orientation or gender identity and expression
Intersectionality Theory	Working to improve risk assessment practices to better recognize multiple markers of marginalization and privilege
Procedural justice	Developing legislation for uniform national adoption laws with consistent processes for how placement is determined, regardless of parental gender
Feminist Perspective	Advancing protections from, and accountability for, violence based on stereotypically gendered norms and collective action against inequality
Commutative Justice	Protecting against bullying based on actual or perceived sexual orientation or gender identity or expression in schools and/or the community
Human Right Perspective	Advocating for improved application of hate crime statutes as related to crimes against LGBTQ persons, particularly as related to bodily integrity

FIGURE 3.1: Examples of SEJ in action

practice (Mitchell & Lynch, 2003; Parker, 2003). Wronka (2008) suggests that purposeful attention to nonhierarchical, nonelitist language; a focus on strengths; and value-informed decision-making are strategies that enable professionals to act on justice in practice. Van Wormer (2004) writes about the solidarity of the helping relationship, with social worker as ally or partner rather than as expert set apart from the client. The concept of allyship is integral to building a model of socially just practice with LGBTQ people.

Aldarondo (2007) has expounded on the idea of professionalism for practice rooted in social justice and for clinical work specifically. She describes her own social justice commitment as rooted in personal experience and exposure to others' experiences of injustice; she speaks of "hearing the cry" not only for help but for justice. The promotion of social justice is viewed as one path toward healing and enhanced human well-being. Aldarondo critiques direct practice as often decontextualized and in absence of a critical awareness of the structures and systems that may be at the root of individually experienced problems. Such contextualization is a prerequisite for ethical practice with any systematically oppressed population as it reveals the personal as political; in other words, many problems for which individuals may seek the intervention of a social worker manifest at the individual level but are rooted in the social stratification that privileges some groups over others.

Liberation of the oppressed is seen as the responsibility of the privileged as well as an opportunity to help alleviate hurt and prevent future harm (Aldarondo, 2007). Other frameworks for practice exist that may enable direct practitioners to promote social justice. These include empowerment theory, queer theory, feminist practice, anti-oppressive practice, the modern settlement house model, the strengths perspective, ethnic-sensitive practice, narrative approaches, oppressor-focused intervention, critical self-reflection, and active mindfulness of power dynamics within the helping relationship (Aldarondo, 2007; Dominelli, 2002; Manning, 1997; Parker, 2003; Reichert, 2003; Swenson, 1998).

Conceptualizing the structural components of oppression allows for an analysis of client issues within a broad environmental context that includes marginalizing and privileging forces and their consequences (Wood & Tully, 2006). These structures frame our institutions and behaviors and are thought to (a) be socially constructed; (b) exist within created and maintained unequal hierarchies of oppression and privilege; (c) be dependent on socialization processes which also makes them largely invisible; (d) be understood and deconstructed through active interrogation; and (e) require the process of deconstruction and analysis of inequality and its impact on individuals, families, groups and societies in order to promote social justice (Adams et al., 2000; Wood & Tully, 2006; Young, 2001). Structural theory assumes the social construction of reality and implies that if we can create something, it stands to reason that we can also deconstruct and rebuild. Structural theory helps us to broaden our examination of person-in-environment to include systemic issues that may underlie many social problems. Even within the arena of macro work, often perceived as the locus of social justice promotion in social work, a paradigm shift is called for. Andrews and Reisch (2001) argue that policy analysis and advocacy are indispensable tools, but adapting flawed structures to meet justice needs is not enough—social workers must challenge the structures and values on which they are built.

Social workers' commitment to and action for social justice affects client populations, the agencies that provide the vehicles for service, the lives of individual professionals, the profession itself, communities, and our society at large. As all members of a society are harmed when injustice limits potential and creates division, so can all members of society benefit by the realization of social justice (van Wormer, 2004). Social justice, if seen as a driving force, creates a very different professional landscape than one informed only by the desire to help or to care—many other professions can claim these goals, so it is the intent and the values that drive the work that can distinguish social work. It is the passion for social justice that can keep alive the spirit of social change; it is neutrality and silence that will allow injustice to prevail.

There exist many challenges for social work in advocating for change and opposing a status quo that reinforces and creates inequality and oppression. Values, such as social justice, are inherently political (Reamer, 2006). Social work is a value-laden profession and one in which ethics are hailed as critical guiding forces for fair and efficacious service. Individuals who "rock the boat" by questioning policy or speaking out against prevailing political forces are at real risk of job loss, diminished status, and threats to funding and public sanction (Birkenmaier, 2003; Reisch & Andrews, 2001). Because of this a collective aversion to questioning the status quo can evolve, where social workers are rewarded, through job security, promotion, and social acceptance, for practice that is clinical, individualistic, and nonconfrontative in nature (Abramovitz, 1998; Breton, 2006; Breton, Cox, & Taylor, 2003). For social justice to become operational, members of a basic structure (society, the profession of social work) must see that there is some mutual benefit to shared participation for its realization (Miller, 1999).

CULTURAL AWARENESS AS A RELATED CONCEPT

Cultural awareness is distinct from but linked with social justice in social work and so must be attended to here, although their relationship is not always clearly articulated. Is cultural competence best thought of as one tool for promoting social justice, or is social justice a path for assuring cultural respect and recognition in social work practice? Garcia and Van Soest (2006) state that "promoting social justice for diverse individuals and populations is the foundation for culturally competent social work practice" (p. 1). NASW (2015) defines cultural and linguistic competence as requiring a "heightened consciousness and analytical grasp of racism, sexism, ethnocentrism, class conflict, and cross-cultural and intracultural diversity" (p. 62). In this light, critical consciousness around culture and its impact on groups and individuals may be interpreted as facilitating broad goals such as the pursuit of social justice. Lennon-Dearing, and Delavega (2015) call for enhanced efforts in social work through a cultural competence framework concerning LGBTQ populations. Discrimination, bullying, and harassment have negative impact for health and well-being and are often rooted in misconception, bias, and a lack of focused and consistent education around service to all populations. The need for a cultural competence approach, social contact, application of the NASW *Code of Ethics*, self-examination, a social justice frame, and use of supervision to confront and manage bias are recommended and are consistent with existing models of cultural competency (Lennon-Dearing & Delavega, 2015).

Hendricks (2003) points out the importance of learning how culture, oppression, and privilege have evolved historically and within a specific social context. Such knowledge allows us to understand not simply assumed traits of a certain social group but how membership in that group impacts and creates experiences of oppression and privilege. Active application of this knowledge to direct practice helps to demonstrate respect for diverse ways of being and to avoid unintentional participation in discrimination. Social workers must be prepared to "start where the client is" in terms of linguistic, cultural, ethnic, and other facets of identity in order to accurately understand and respond to concerns of oppression and inequity. "Culture" encompasses more than race or ethnicity and should be thought of as consisting of multiple identities such as gender, sexual orientation, religious belief, and ability (Garcia & Van Soest, 2006; Lum, 2007; NASW, 2015). These multiple identities represent in each individual positions of possible social advantage and disadvantage (Adams et al., 2007).

Empowerment theory offers an ideal framework for an examination of the meaning of social justice—the what—and the doing of social justice work—the *how*. Empowerment theory provides a lens through which we can evaluate whether and how social workers are actually equipped and enabled (i.e., empowered) to meet professional imperatives around social justice. Although emerging today across social work scholarship, empowerment theory has long been at the heart of social work (Payne, 2005). Indeed, Lee (2001) holds Jane Addams' work as the precursor of today's empowerment models, noting that settlement houses brought together a collective of disempowered minorities, both gender and ethnic, who together raised consciousness about their plight and found common solutions for and by themselves. Empowerment theory is especially salient for application with the most vulnerable groups in our society, those most in need of a social work profession committed to social justice that is committee to and capable of promoting empowerment. The main concepts of empowerment in social work practice concern partnership with and active participation of the client in consciousness-raising, overcoming barriers and oppressive forces, and the endowment of self-efficacy, a sense of belonging, and access to personal power (Payne, 2005). Empowerment is a process, not necessarily an outcome, with the goal for clients of gaining influence in their own lives and the ability to improve their circumstances (Barker, 1995).

Important to empowerment is self-understanding and the importance of consciousness-raising to the process (Gutierrez, Parsons, & Cox, 1998). Consciousness-raising involves education toward the ability to analyze the intersection between individual disempowerment with systems and structures of oppression (Gutierrez et al., 1998). Boehm (2004) differentiates two types of empowerment. First, *personal empowerment* is related to individual capacities such as the ability to look critically at the world, one's self-esteem, self-determination, a sense of responsibility, the ability to engage with others, assertiveness, and hope for the future. Second, *collective empowerment* relates to the ability to act collectively toward a shared benefit and to support one another in that struggle (Boehm, 2004). These concepts point to the applicability of the theory not only to social work practice for client empowerment but to its applicability as a lens through which to view social workers' own ability to wield influence and to act as collective change agents in the socio-political context.

SOCIAL WORKERS AS ALLIES

A key to social justice action on behalf of any marginalized and oppressed group is the willingness of members of the dominant group to stand in solidarity with others. A foundation for standing in solidarity is the ability to challenge one's own privilege and bias through reflection and self-awareness. There are myriad opportunities for social workers to stand as allies to the LGBTQ community from facilitating appropriate and sensitive service to policy advocacy (Chojnacki & Gelberg, 1995; Ji, Du Bois, & Finnessy, 2009). Washington and Evans (1991) define an ally as "a person who is a member of the dominant or majority group who works to end oppression in his or her personal and professional life through support of, and as an advocate with and for, the oppressed population" (p. 195). Ally work is a clear path to meeting the imperatives of social work ethics, but it requires proactive and targeted efforts. Ally education is important as many who wish to be allies feel they do not have the right, the credibility, the knowledge, or the skills to be effective allies (Ji et al., 2009). The same study also revealed perceptions of risk associated with standing up as an ally to the LGBTQ community, especially concerning fears of being labeled and the conflicts people experience with religion that often emerge during the ally education process. Findings, based on the sample of 11, reflected the idea that allies need skills as well as knowledge to act on this role effectively. The ally role includes actions such as learning the history of LGBTQ struggles and successes, understanding the dynamics of the coming out process, being a caring listener, showing up to support causes that may not directly impact our own lives, and standing up against discrimination and stereotyping in our own circles of influence (Ji et al., 2009). Schools of social work, entities that provide continuing education for social workers, agencies, and professional organizations can provide the instrumental knowledge and the leadership needed to prepare and support allies.

CONCLUSION

There are many strong connections between the social work profession, practice, and the pursuit of social and economic justice. Conceptualization of social justice first emerged along with the birth of social work itself, and since that time the importance of social and economic justice work has been central to the tenets of the profession. In this chapter we have explored how social work with LGBTQ populations cannot be separated from the pursuit of social justice, particularly due to the legacy of marginalization faced by the LGBTQ community. Despite progress in many areas, there remains a continued need to work toward LGBTQ empowerment in modern times. This chapter also detailed multiple theoretical perspectives on social and economic justice and explained how theoretical or paradigmatic positions can influence the methods social workers use to advocate for the improvement of conditions for LGBTQ individuals and communities. It is important to remember that just as there is an incredible amount of diversity within the LGBTQ community itself, there are a diversity of ways to conceptualize and enact the pursuit of social and economic justice and possibly endless ways to creatively apply the theories of social justice activism to the unique and contextualized problems individuals, families, and communities face within society. Even though much work has been done, and many battles have been won, the fight for social and economic justice for the LGBTQ community is far from over, and social workers will find themselves on the front lines of this struggle for many years to come.

REFERENCES

Abramovitz, M. (1998). Social work and social reform: An arena of struggle. *Social Work, 43*(6), 512–526.

Adams, M., Bell, L. A., & Griffin, P. (Eds.). (2007). *Teaching for diversity and social justice* (2nd ed.). New York: Routledge.

Adams, M., Blumenfeld, W. J., Casteneda, R., Hackman, H. W., Peters, M. L., & Zuniga, X. (2000). *Readings for diversity and social justice.* New York: Routledge.

Aldarondo, E. (Ed.). (2007). *Advancing social justice through clinical practice*. Mahwah, NJ: Lawrence Erlbaum.

Banerjee, M. M. (2005). Applying Rawlsian social justice to welfare reform: An unexpected finding for social work. *Journal of Sociology & Social Welfare, 32*(3), 35–57.

Barker, R. L. (1995). *The social work dictionary* (3rd ed.). Washington, DC: National Association of Social Workers.

Barry, B. (2005). *Why social justice matters*. Cambridge, UK: Polity Press.

Barsky, A. E. (2010). *Ethics and values in social work: An integrated approach for a comprehensive curriculum*. New York: Oxford University Press.

Billies, M., Johnson, J., Murungi, K., & Pugh, R. (2009). Naming our reality: Low-income LGBT people documenting violence, discrimination and assertions of justice. *Feminism and Psychology, 19*(3), 375–380. doi:10.1177/0959353509105628

Birkenmaier, J. (2003). On becoming a social justice practitioner. *Social Thought: Journal of Religion in the Social Services, 22*(2–3), 41–54. doi:10.1300/J131v22n02_04

Birkenmaier, J., & Berg-Weger, M. (2007). *The practicum companion for social work: Integrating class and field work* (2nd ed.). Boston: Pearson Education.

Boehm, A. (2004). Empowerment: The point of view of consumers. *Families in Society, 85*(2), 270–280.

Breton, M. (2006). Path dependence and the place of social action in social work practice. *Social Work with Groups, 29*(4), 25–44. doi: 10.1300/J009v29n04_03

Breton, M., Cox, E. O., & Taylor, S. (2003). Social justice, social policy, and social work: Searching the connection. *The Social Policy Journal, 2*(1), 3–20. doi:10.1300/J185v02n01_02

Brighouse, H. (2004). *Justice*. Cambridge, UK: Polity Press.

Caputo, R. K. (2002). Social justice: Whither social work and social welfare? *Families in Society: The Journal of Contemporary Human Services, 83*(4), 341–342.

Chojnacki, J. T., & Gelberg, S. (1995). The facilitation of a gay/lesbian/bisexual support-therapy group by heterosexual counselors. *Journal of Counseling &Development, 73*(3), 352–354.

Crenshaw, K. (1991). Mapping the margins: Intersectionality, identity politics, and violence against women of color. *Stanford Law Review, 43*, 1241–1299.

Collins, P. H. (2000). Gender, black feminism, and black political economy. *The Annals of the American Academy of Political and Social Science, 568*(1), 41–53.

Dominelli, L. (2002). *Anti-oppressive social work theory and practice*. New York: Palgrave.

Fish, J., & Bewley, S. (2010). Using human rights-based approaches to conceptualise lesbian and bisexual women's health inequalities. *Health and Social Care in the Community 18*(4), 355–362, doi:10.1111/j.1365-2524.2009.00902.x

Garcia, B., & Van Soest, D. (2006). *Social work practice for social justice: Cultural competence in action, a guide for students*. Alexandria, VA: CSWE Press.

Gibelman, M. (1999). The search for identity: Defining social work—past, present, future. *Social Work, 44*(4), 298–310.

Grant, J. M., Mottet, L., Tanis, J., Harrison, J., Herman, J. L., & Keisling, M. (2010). Injustice at every turn: A report of the National Transgender Discrimination Survey. Retrieved from http://www.thetaskforce.org/static_html/downloads/reports/reports/ntds_full.pdf

Gutierrez, L. M., Parsons, R. J., & Cox, E. O. (Eds.). (1998). *Empowerment in social work practice: A sourcebook*. Pacific Grove, CA: Brooks-Cole.

Haynes, K. S. (1998). The one hundred-year debate: Social reform versus individual treatment. *Social Work, 43*(6), 501–509.

Hendricks, C. O. (2003). Learning and teaching cultural competence in the practice of social work. *Journal of Teaching in Social Work, 23*(1–2), 73–86. doi:10.1300/J067v23n01_06

Hugman, R. (2003). Professional ethics in social work: Living with the legacy. *Australian Social Work, 56*(1), 5–15. doi:10.1093/bjsw/33.8.1025

Ji, P., Du Bois, S. N., & Finnessy, P. (2009). An academic course that teaches heterosexual students to be allies to LGBT communities: A qualitative analysis. *Journal of Gay & Lesbian Social Services, 21*, 402–429, doi:10.1080/10538720802690001

Lee, J. (2001). *The empowerment approach to social work: Building the beloved community.* New York: Columbia University Press.

Lennon-Dearing, R., & Delavega, E. (2015). Policies discriminatory of the LGBT community: Do social workers endorse respect for the NASW Code of Ethics?, *Journal of Gay & Lesbian Social Services, 27*(4), 412–435. doi:10.1080/10538720.2015.1087266

Lum, D. (2007). *Culturally competent practice: A framework for understanding diverse groups and justice issues* (3rd ed.). Belmont, CA: Brooks/Cole.

Manning, S. S. (1997). The social worker as moral citizen: Ethics in action. *Social Work, 42*(3), 223–230.

Mapp, S. C. (2008). *Human rights and social justice in a global perspective: An introduction to international social work.* New York: Oxford University Press.

Marsh, J. C. (2005). Social justice: social work's organizing value. *Social Work, 50*(4), 293–294.

McDermott, E. (2011). The world some have won: Sexuality, class and inequality. *Sexualities, 14*(1) 63–78.

McLaughlin, A. M. (2002). Social work's legacy: Irreconcilable differences? *Clinical Social Work Journal, 30*(2), 187–198.

Miller, D. (1999). *Principles of social justice.* Cambridge, MA: Harvard University Press.

Mitchell, J., & Lynch, R. S. (2003). Beyond the rhetoric of social and economic justice: Redeeming the social work advocacy role. *Race, Gender, and Class, 10*(2), 8–26.

Morris, P. M. (2002). The capabilities perspective: A framework for social justice. *Families in Society: The Journal of Contemporary Human Services, 83*(4), 365–373.

Mount, S. D., Steelman, S. M., & Hertlein, K. M. (2015). "I'm not sure I trust the system yet": Lesbian service member experiences with mental health care. *Military Psychology, 27*(2), 115–127.

Movement Advancement Project. (2013). A broken bargain for transgender workers. Retrieved from http://www.lgbtmap.org/transgender-workers

Movement Advancement Project. (2014). Paying an unfair price: The financial penalty for being LGBT in America. Retrieved from www.lgbtmap.org/unfair-price

National Association of Social Workers. (1999). *Code of ethics of the National Association of Social Workers.* Washington, DC: Author.

National Association of Social Workers. (2015). *Social work speaks* (10th ed.). Washington DC: NASW Press.

National Center for Transgender Equality, & National Gay and Lesbian Task Force. (2009). National Transgender Discrimination Survey: Preliminary findings. Retrieved from http://www.thetaskforce.org/static_html/downloads/reports/fact_sheets/transsurvey_prelim_findings.pdf

Olson, J. J. (2007). Social work's professional and social justice projects: Discourses in conflict. *Journal of Progressive Human Services, 18*(1), 45–69. doi:10.1300/J059v18n01_04

Parker, L. (2003). A social justice model for clinical social work practice. *Affilia, 18*(3), 272–288. doi:10.1177/0886109903254586

Payne, M. (2005). *Modern social work theory* (3rd ed.). Chicago: Lyceum Books.

Rawls, J. (1971). *A theory of justice.* Cambridge, MA: Belknap Press of Harvard University Press.

Reamer, F. G. (Ed.). (2006). *Social work values and ethics* (3rd ed.). New York: Columbia University Press.

Redman, L. F. (2010). Outing the invisible poor: Why economic justice and access to health care is an LGBT Issue. *Georgetown Journal on Poverty Law & Policy, 17*(3), 451–459.

Reeser, L. C., & Epstein, I. (1990). *Professionalization and activism in social work: The sixties, the eighties, and the future.* New York: Columbia University Press.

Reichert, E. (2003). *Social work and human rights: A foundation for policy and practice.* New York: Columbia University Press.

Reisch, M. (2002). Defining justice in a socially unjust world. *Families in Society: The Journal of Contemporary Human Services, 83,* 343–354.

Reisch, M., & Andrews, J. (2001). *The road not taken: A history of radical social work in the United States.* New York: Brunner-Routledge.

Reynolds, B. C. (1951). *Social work and social living.* New York: Citadel Press.

Sen, A. (1999). *Development as freedom.* New York: Knopf.

Specht, H., & Courtney, M. E. (1994). *Unfaithful angels: How social work abandoned its mission.* New York: Free Press.

Swenson, C. R. (1998). Clinical social work's contribution to a social justice perspective. *Social Work, 43*(6), 527–537.

US Legal Inc. (2010). Commutative justice. Retrieved from http://definitions.uslegal.com/c/commutative-justice/

United Nations. (1948). *Universal Declaration of Human Rights.* Retrieved from http://www.un.org/en/documents/udhr/.

United Nations. (2011). *The United Nations speaks out: Tackling discrimination on grounds of sexual orientation and gender identity.* [Brochure]. Retrieved from www.ohchr.org/EN/Issues/Discrimination/Pages/LGBTBrochure.aspx

United Nations Office for the High Commissioner for Human Rights. (2011). *Discriminatory laws and practices and acts of violence against individuals based on their sexual orientation.* Geneva: United Nations. Retrieved from www2.ohchr.org/english/bodies/hrcouncil/docs/19session/A.HRC.19.41_English.pdf

van Wormer, K. (2004). *Confronting oppression, restoring justice: From policy analysis to social action.* Alexandria, VA: CSWE Press.

Washington, J., & Evans, N. (1991). Becoming an ally. In N. Evans & V. Wall (Eds.), *Beyond tolerance: Gays, lesbians and bisexuals on campus* (pp. 195–204). Alexandria, VA: American College Personnel Association.

Wood, G. G., & Tully, C. T. (2006). *The structural approach to direct practice in social work: A social constructionist perspective* (3rd ed.). New York: Columbia University Press.

Wronka, J. (2008). *Human rights and social justice: Social action and service for the helping and health professions.* Thousand Oaks, CA: SAGE.

Young, I. M. (2001). Equality of whom? Social groups and judgments of injustice. *The Journal of Political Philosophy, 9*(1), 1–18. doi: 10.1111/1467-9760.00115

PART II

CONSIDERATIONS ACROSS THE LIFESPAN

CHAPTER 4

IDENTITY DEVELOPMENT

Tyler M. Argüello

INTRODUCTION

Foundational to this text is the assumption that objects and subjects exist and signify, either persistently or tenuously, a cultural reality of genders and sexualities. More critically, there is an inherent claim that these central elements of human experience are often encapsulated within the strategic structure of identity or identities. A variety of pathways exist to theorize and explain how identities acquire shape and occur across differing social locations. Even as this chapter is being written, contexts such as the expansion of federal marriage policy, an increase in and access to parenting, removal of restrictions in the military, and changing state and local policies for employment and housing protections are being shifted across the United States for lesbian, gay, bisexual, transgender, and queer (LGBTQ) persons. These phenomena will invariably impact the identity formations and development for LGBTQ generations now and to come.

This chapter discusses the development of LGBTQ identities, albeit artificially linear within a Western context as well as nakedly partial vis-à-vis a continually emerging knowledge base and active negotiation by individuals and communities for cultural continuance. The first section offers a discussion of important epistemological considerations when conceptualizing identity, thinking through conversations, positioning relationships, and strategizing social action. Next, various models are reviewed for their operating assumptions and logical pathways as well as measured for limitations and areas for growth. Finally, emerging areas are discussed for clinical attention and social research.

THE NATURE OF IDENTITY

ESSENTIALISM, CONSTRUCTIONISM, AND IDENTITARIAN TENDENCIES

In the quest to make meaning and order of things, philosophical positionalities need be examined. When hot topics like sexuality and gender emerge through various philosophical lenses, one effect can be the propensity to redirect the conversation into the realm of morals and values, or incite arguments on scientific merits and empirical outcomes. The task here is neither; instead, two large camps of philosophical orientations are presented in an effort to offer guideposts for the reader, intellectual abrasion for further theoretical wrangling, and traction to investigate the points of convergence and divergence, appreciating all the while the stakes of harnessing such paradigms when investigating and imagining the development of sexuality and gender (see DeLamater & Hyde, 1998; Fuss, 1989; Hart, 1984; Stein, 1999).

An essentialist perspective is one that believes in the immutable essence of sexuality and gender. There is a core reality, one that is a priori to human experience as it is with structured investigation, close scientific appreciation, and progressive uncovering that we can get at the heart of the matter, that is, one's true sexuality and gender may be known. From this angle, the elements of intrapsychic and interpersonal experiences are things that are knowable, which can be categorized, counted, and characterized by differences (Tolman & Diamond, 2001; Troiden, 1988). Essentializing perspectives often find traction in the biological and biopsychological sciences, for example, in their focus on materiality, quantities, and taxonomies. As well, essentializing arguments around sexuality and gender often commence or revert back to rhetorical maneuvers around the genetic and other natural bases for desire, motivations, and behaviors, among other experiences. Similarly, humanistic stances in clinical work and social research hold essentialist premises; no matter where one is in time or space, the fixity of the core essence of identity is intact. Stage-based models, therefore, find much animation in essentialism. These models work to form linear perspectives on developmental trajectories, ones that rely on the consolidation of identity through differentiation and integration. This is to say that essentializing self-identification of being lesbian, gay, bisexual, transgender, or queer is a process of figuring out what one is not (which is also what one is, e.g., "I am gay and therefore not bi"). More important, essentialist models adhere to a determined assumption that to fully realize what one is, requires the integration of the terms and conditions of what it means to be lesbian, gay, bisexual, transgender, or queer.

Such essentializing views on sexuality and gender are often ahistorical, devoid of politics, mired in individuality, sheltered from the circulation of power, and uncomplicated by social context. Such contingencies and differences are often points of entry and critique from a constructionist perspective. Constructionism, while often seen as a converse or opposing force, finds animation in some ways from essentializing perspectives on, or at least essentialist assumptions of, human experiences. So instead of talking about gender, we talk about *genders* or, better, *gender identities and expressions* therein. Constructionism, as a philosophical field is activated by traditions of poststructuralism and postmodernism. Instead of focusing efforts on the *what* of sexuality and gender, a constructionist perspective is concerned with the production of identities. It is believed that human experience is a reciprocal process with the social world largely constituted through language systems and cultural resources. (Some critical examples that work to construct this philosophical field could include Appadurai [1996], Butler [1990, 1993], and Foucault [1978, 1980]). As with any identity, sexuality and gender are then understood as products of systems of discourse, knowledge, and power. They are effects of the negotiation with history, space and place, available cultural categories, politics, and lived experience, among other influences. In stricter terms, a constructionist perspective on sexuality and gender would question the presumption and knowledge that develops categories of desire, fantasy, and gayness and would further direct attention to what the stakes are in context for utilizing such categories. Moreover, constructionism is concerned with the confluence and the intersection of multiple social locations. The meanings of identities are informed by and constructed by the context in which they are performed; for example, social locations afford certain possibilities and exert contingencies, given that the social world is generated through systems of power, privilege, and difference. This is to say that a constructionist perspective would seek to understand how and on what terms it means to be lesbian and a woman and a person of color, across various contexts. (For an elaborated discussion on intersectionality, see Hill-Collins [2000] or Mehrotra [2010]). Given the fluid and continually evolving nature of human experiences, constructionism sees a strategic quality to identity. Instead of holding an inner, indelible truth to hunt and find, identities in the social world function for different purposes, in different places, and to varying degrees. In a critical sense and especially for LGBTQ people who face continual marginalization, identity can be understood as a mediator between one's lived experience and the exact denial of such an existence in the public sphere (Warner, 2002).

Whether an essentializing or constructionist perspective is taken on LGBTQ identity development, what is being described is a process of *identification*, a formulation of meaning, and an integration of thoughts, feelings, behaviors, and social experiences. Identities cannot be consolidated or given life without the very act of engaging in the social world and negotiating intrapsychic and interpersonal developments. As Rowe (2014) contends, LGBTQ identities are a critical example of identification in practice, that is, making sense of some attribute portrayed as immutable yet reflexively realized over the lifespan and various spaces. Too often, this process of formation begins with the prenatal expectation that everyone is and becomes heterosexual. This is only made clear by overt and implicit messages as well as by social and material policing across the life course. LGBTQ individuals are not the only community marginalized and working to bring their identities into being. Likewise, in the struggle to exist, identity becomes a critical intention as much as it is a natural inclination. Progressively, the degree to which one can experience and live out one's identity is correlated with well-being and health promotion (see Hudson, 2015).

IDENTITY DEVELOPMENT AND DEVELOPING IDENTITIES: FORMS, FUNCTIONS, AND FRAMEWORKS

Research on LGBTQ identity has supported and reinforced a trend to regard the development of identity as a linear process from attraction, to activity, to self-identification at the group level, despite high variability at the individual level. Presented herein is a review of theories, models, and emerging considerations. Whereas some validation exists for the staged development models (Levine, 1997), others have no empirical validation (Coleman, 1982; McCarn & Fassinger, 1996; Minton & McDonald, 1984; Troiden, 1989). Often attempts to validate stages and milestones have been met with the elucidation that participants' experiences are more complex and dynamic than what models will allow, meaning there exists a great variety and order in awareness, timing, and location. (See chapter 5 for an elaborated and contingent discussion of coming out.). Still, staged models offer some points of traction and often share many similarities in the proposed progression of development. They frequently hold four meta-concepts within (Alderson, 2003; Horowitz & Newcomb, 2002):

1. Awareness, sensitization, awakening;
2. Testing, exploring, internalizing, accepting;
3. Adoption of and disclosing an identity; and
4. Identity integration, synthesis.

As helpful as these perspectives may be, they hold methodological limitations. Studies associated with LGBTQ development are problematic to the extent that they derive from self-report and retrospective accounts. Robust as they may be in the depth of narrative detail, invariably there are biases in that the reflection may minimize past experiences, obscure privilege and power, disregard or contort fluctuations and changes, and be biased by current conditions (Henry, Moffitt, Caspi, Langley, & Silva, 1994; Rosario, Schrimshaw, Hunter, & Braun, 2006; Ross, 1989). Often, they do not capture all who arrive at a LGBTQ identity through means other than (sexual) behavior, nor do they show the instability of behaviors and identifications over time. Importantly, they are typically modeled on white gay men and lesbians, then generalized to all letters in the evolving alphabet of sexualities and genders. What they tend to lack is inclusion and a more sensitive appreciation for difference by decontextualizing identities. Finally, models for LGBTQ identity development minoritize sexual identities and have the presumed end point of homosexuality, which becomes proxy for being fully integrated as an authentic, whole person.

The following sections examine several models of identity development that include D'Augelli's human development model, Cass's homosexual identity formation model, the ecological model of gay male development, the lesbian and socially oriented models, and trans* emergence for individuals and families. This is followed by a review of perspectives to further theories, inform research, and frame clinical work. These include perspectives related to a life course approach, people of color, bisexual identities, and neuroscience. Finally, emerging areas of consideration are reviewed and include rural places inhabited by LGBTQ people as well as young people and technology.

D'AUGELLI'S HUMAN DEVELOPMENT MODEL

Since the last part of the twentieth century paralleling the advent of the LGBTQ civil rights movement, one of the two most prominent models for viewing the development of LGBTQ persons has been that of D'Augelli (1994). This model of human development takes a lifespan approach as individuals come to terms with their nonheterosexual identity and the relationship they have in their development with a heterosexist society. This model focuses on six processes that may co-occur or gain more/less importance in various contexts and relationships across time and the life course for lesbian, gay, and bisexual persons that include

1. *Exiting heterosexual identity*—This process involves the personal and social recognition of one's nonheterosexual orientation. It begins with coming out to oneself and then to others and certainly is a lifelong experience of disclosures, which may decrease in frequency and intensity.
2. *Developing a personal LGB (sic) identity status*—Individuals begin to increase socioaffective stability and commence (though not complete) concretizing their identity. This is achieved and confirmed through accumulating social contact with other LGB and – affirmative people.
3. *Developing a LGB identity*—Individuals establish connections with supportive people in their social world.
4. *Becoming a LGB offspring*—Individuals renegotiate their relationships with families of origin. While some members may adapt and be supportive, each family member has their own approach to the LGB person.
5. *Developing a LGB intimacy status*—Lacking many cultural scripts, LGB persons engage in significant relationships with other like-oriented persons, often relying on context- or relationship-specific norms. This process may engage strengths of resilience, adaptation, and flexibility as much as it may induce doubt and confusion.
6. *Entering a LGB community*—This last process involves engaging in political and social action, which may happen for many but is not summarily a prerequisite for individuals within this model. To more fully engage in this process, individuals have consciousness raising about their own oppression, historically and contemporaneously. Often this can motivate resistance and action towards social justice.

D'Augelli's model points to a number of important material elements and conceptual limitations. Primary to working with these processes is the space and place in which LGB individuals have access to and inhabit. Ironically, the awareness and movement around trans* identities has foregrounded the critical importance of place (e.g., bathroom justice) in ways that this model pointed to or implied. Similarly, safety, security, time, and the availability of resources and people are important to the relationships individuals have with themselves and with those who they have invited into their developmental process. Undoubtedly, a limitation to this model is its specific focus on sexual orientation, as will be discussed in the models reviewed, identities are intersecting and dynamic. D'Augelli's model would be better supported by incorporating processes that signal the realities and potential effects of various social locations. Further, its emphasis on the individual also underscores the assumption and predominance of human agency within these phases and at large in the individual's journey and impact therein to effect well-being (Ford, Beighley, & Sanlo, 2015). That said, D'Augelli's model could be enhanced by expanding the depth and breadth of understanding around the category of sexuality itself. Rather than singularly focusing on sexual orientation, it would be a critical addition to bring attention to the process for coming to understand one's (sexual) identity, preferred sexual behaviors, and romantic orientation, among other elements that can be disarticulated within sexuality.

THE CASS HOMOSEXUAL IDENTITY FORMATION MODEL

In contrast to a process-oriented model, the second prominent but stage-based model to describe lesbian and gay (LG) development is one offered by Cass (1979, 1984), foregrounding a phenomenological understanding of the experience of LG individuals. In fact, this model is the most cited of existing models of LG development and a foundation for much work in later years (e.g., Cass, 1984; Coleman, 1982; Martin, 1991; Minton & McDonald, 1984; Troiden, 1989). While the model is stepwise in the coming out and coming to terms with a LG identity in a milieu of heterosexism, it views such identity acquisition from a strengths perspective. Each stage involves cognitive, affective, and behavioral processes, which may be accepted and integrated toward a positively integrated identity, characterized by acceptance, positive self-regard, desire to disclose, and relationships with other LGBTQ people (Kenneady & Oswalt, 2014). All the while, the model acknowledges that not every person will choose to move into the subsequent stage; such a decision, called identity foreclosure, derives from agency rather than in-/voluntary rejection and can happen within any stage. The stages of Cass's model (1979, 1996) include

1. *Pre-stage*—Individuals have awareness and recognition of heteronormativity and the minoritization of LGBTQ persons.
2. *Identity confusion*—Confusion and anxiety emerge around a person's sexual orientation, and they can engage in searching for information and understanding, or dismissing and retreating as in identity foreclosure.
3. *Identity comparison*—This stage invokes issues of self-acceptance of a LG or nonheterosexual orientation, or at least the possibility. Alienation from the mainstream and an increased experience of stigma may ensue, and individuals may seek to maintain heterosexual behaviors and/or may alter homosexual attractions and seek increased socializing.
4. *Identity tolerance*—Individuals seek to have companionship with other LGB people as their tolerance of a LG identity increases. They may maintain a public heterosexual identity, while maintaining a private homosexual one with trusted people.
5. *Identity acceptance*—Positive regard toward one's LG orientation and identity increases, along with an increased network of LGBTQ people. Individuals may engage in "passing," that is, selectively continuing to be public as heterosexual. They may disclosure their LG orientation to some heterosexual peers or families of origin.
6. *Identity pride*—Individuals in this stage increase allegiance with an LG identity as well as socializing with a LGBTQ community over heterosexual-dominated ones. Pride can be experienced and expressed as anger toward heteronormativity and homophobia. This can result in increased disclosure, social action, and demands for homosexual-affirmative attention.

7. *Identity synthesis*—As individuals move into this stage, their LG identity is further integrated into the whole of their character and into their social world on more public terms. Individuals increase interactions with non-LG persons again and relate through multiple parts of themselves, rather than exclusively or predominantly in regard to sexuality.

Similar to D'Augelli, the Cass model is not without limitations (Kenneady & Oswalt, 2014). This staged model necessarily has a staunch linear perspective on development. While components and stages resonate with some, they obfuscate the fluidity of sexuality as well as the possibility that the stages simply may not fit some peoples' lived experiences (Savin-Williams, 2011). Further, Cass focuses on lesbians and gay men at the analytical expense of other sexualities, especially with regard to bisexualities, asexuality, and beyond; it has yet to be determined how and in what ways Cass's stages map onto these various other sexualities. Co-extensive with this concern is that the Cass model draws parallels across cisgender lines in the assumption that men and women would have a similar developmental trajectory in terms of the timing of awareness, insight, behavior, and integration. Finally, other identities and their development are not intersected in the Cass model. Some emerging conceptual and empirical work is attempting to understand, for example, racial and ethnic development parallel to and co-constitutive of sexuality (Sim Chun & Singh, 2010).

ECOLOGICAL MODEL OF GAY MALE DEVELOPMENT

Alderson (2003) advanced a theory of gay male development that builds off social identity theory (see Cox & Gallois, 1996) by grounding development in an ecological paradigm, incorporating processes and developmental stages. The core of ecological theory is that human development derives from individuals themselves, their environments, and the reciprocal interactions between the two. And while typically biophysical factors are involved in such a perspective, the model here focuses more so on psychosocial (both internal and external) factors, as the intention is not on essentializing orientations but rather on identity acquisition. Moving through the phases in this model occurs when sufficient cognitive dissonance is experienced, resulting in incompatibility between cognitions, affects, and behaviors. The three concentric phases (Alderson, 2003) are as follows:

1. *Before coming out*—This phase involves a struggle between "catalysts" and "hindrances." The individual has increasing awareness of homosexual feelings (e.g., homoerotic dreams, having attractions), which can grate recognition of internalized and external homophobia. Given the accessibility and permissibility to express oneself in the local culture, this is when the individual will begin testing/exploring gay self-identification.

2. *During coming out*—Going one phase deeper within, the hallmark to this second phase is the assumption of a gay identity. Individuals reduce internalized homophobia through lived experience of what it means to be "gay" in local context, as they make meaning of their thoughts, feelings, and behaviors, resulting in an increasingly positive sexual orientation.

3. *Beyond coming out*—In this third, most center phase, individuals have committed to a gay identity for themselves and are actively working into a consolidated identity. This arises from individuals figuring out how to increase connections to oneself, to a larger gay community and a reconnection to the heterosexual world. This integration is predicated upon a positive view of oneself and being gay, having a sense of wholeness and authenticity, and enjoying a sense of community and intimacy with others. In turn, individuals also develop resiliency and capacities to deal with discrimination and prejudice.

It is important to understand that these phases sit within a sphere of global and societal influences that exert effects throughout each phase and include parental/familial, cultural/spiritual, and peers, among others.

LESBIAN AND SOCIALLY ORIENTED MODELS

Concerned with difference and overgeneralizations across LGBTQ subpopulations, models have emerged that have encouraged more attention to the identity development for women (Chapman & Brannock, 1987; Coleman, 1982; Faderman, 1984; Sophie, 1985–1986; Troiden, 1989). Early in attention to nonheterosexual identities, Lewis (1984) provided an important addition to the literature as one of the initial empirically based perspectives from and for women. Similar to other conceptualizations, Lewis describes a five-phase process for the formation of a healthy lesbian self-concept:

1. *Awareness*—A sense of being different can emerge as young as four years old for some girls; however, it may remain largely unconscious into adolescence or even young adulthood. Some may have language to verbalize such difference yet lack of a vocabulary, and ever-increasing social stigma and encouragement toward heteronormative roles are common. Isolation and withdrawal are typical in this phase.
2. *Dissonance*—During adolescence into adulthood, conflict can emerge between heteronormative socialization and attractions toward other women. Shame, anxiety, and ambivalence can increase and be met with little to no support or learning of positive coping skills. Moreover, dissonance can increase depending on where in the continuum of identity and behaviors a woman is; that is, women may have histories of heterosexual relationships.
3. *Relationships*—Movement from internal processing of identity development and making meaning of same-sex desires begins to turn outward and find traction within relationships. Relationships, then, serve multiple functions including sexual exploration, script building for roles and relations, community building, and creating nurturing and supportive networks. Coming out is common in this phase to varying degrees and may involve isolation from a larger heterosexual community. Conflicts with family may increase.
4. *Stable lesbian identity*—A stable identity coheres, which coincides with increased self-acceptance, reduced dissonance, and the acquisition of a community of friends and fictive kin. Committed relationships are common and further a developed lifestyle.

5. *Integration*—Acceptance and openness occurs increasingly for the lesbian woman, as a positive self-concept concretizes. While more coming out may occur, it is not separate from the pain that may also continue in doing so as an active negotiation with an oppressive culture exists.

Going further, McCarn and Fassinger (1996) introduced a model for lesbian identity development that brought attention to the differences that lesbians encounter, attending to more than intrapsychic conflicts and resolutions. While their model started with theorizations about lesbians, soon after its introduction into the literature, it was validated for gay men (Fassinger & Miller, 1996). Motivated by critical perspectives in ethnic and womanist models of identity development, McCarn and Fassinger proposed continuous and circuitous developmental phases that built on gaps in the literature by looking at both internal and social processes. This approach disarticulates varying attitudes toward self, other LGBTQ people, and heterosexual people as well as privileges individual identity formation as coextensive and in dialectical relation with others. Moreover, disclosure or coming out is not an index for effective integration or movement through phases. The phases are as follows, noting importantly that each phase has an individual component for development as well as a group one:

1. *Awareness*—In this first phase, the individual has un-/conscious recognition of difference and calls into question compulsory heteronormativity. Related, on a group level, the individual increases realization that a minority identity and community exist, which is not predicated upon confronting social oppression due to that minority status.
2. *Exploration*—The individual actively examines feelings toward other women but does not require sexual encounters. Simultaneously, she will explore her attitudes about the larger LGBTQ community by gathering more knowledge and begin clarifying her position toward and membership within such a community.
3. *Deepening/commitment*—The woman increases a sense of self as a sexual being and gains greater clarity around intimacies and identities. One's identity becomes more secure and externalized. Parallel to this, a deeper appreciation for the value and oppression of a larger LGBTQ community evolves, and the individual enters into that matrix of social forces with willingly and actively negotiating consequences, conflicts, and a possible increasing sense of sisterhood and solidarity.
4. *Internalization/synthesis*—In this final phase, the woman has a greater sense of internal consistency and self-acceptance across time, relationships, and social contexts. One's sexuality is integrated into a larger sense of oneself. Likewise, a sense of belonging to a minority group has become internalized (that is not also necessarily politicized) and is understood across contexts, relationships, and institutions.

While this model tends to be intrapsychic with social dynamics in the making of identity, there remains a linearity, despite its incitement of phases, that presumes a normativity of integration or optimal outcome, and social politics about one's minority sexual orientation. In a word, one's sexual orientation is *just one* part of a fully integrated, mature citizen. Cox and Gallois (1996) complicate this implication by taking a social identity perspective on homosexual identity development. They look at these same issues and yet focus on the social or group-based aspects of identity and the negotiations with social structures. This involves two evolving processes: self-categorization and social comparison. In the first, individuals gradually adopt a homosexual identity and incorporates this into their personal and/or social identity through sexual behaviors, desires, social relations, and politics, among other socially available discourses and behavior. Likewise, the second process involves the person comparatively assessing the homosexual subpopulation as well as the social categories, which leads to a calculus for one's self-esteem and valuation of homosexual categorization and one's positionality with the larger heteronormative culture. While Cox and Gallois allow for a greater appreciation of the reciprocal influences of the social world, the social identity model foregrounds the identity acquisition and does not tend to understanding initial motivations for being gay in the first place.

TRANS* EMERGENCE

Up to this point, the focus has been on the development of sexual identities, albeit intersecting with other social locations and inscribed with contingencies and difference. Predominant in this understanding of coming into sexual identity is the phenomenon of coming *out*, held by some paradigms as a normativizing[1] step and within others a functional phenomenon pregnant with both conflict and liberation. With regard to gender variance, theories and models for understanding and directing practice are materializing; chapter 16 unpacks the current state of science and applied practice with the transgender and gender nonconforming community. For the purposes here, it is important to consider that a similar consideration has been made around the becoming—or emerging—of gender variance. The Transgender Emergence Model (Lev, 2004) is a six-staged model that looks at how trans* people come to understand their identity. Lev, a social worker, is writing from a therapeutic stance, and this model examines what the individual is going through along with the responsibilities of the counselor—as noted in the following six stages:

1. *Awareness*—Initially, gender-variant people are often in great distress as they come to more conscious awareness and engagement with their gender identity. This phase can be overwhelming, involve a dysphoria around one's gender and sex (but does not always), and bring up vulnerabilities and difficulties in coping akin to dealing with traumatic stress. Often, the therapeutic task is the normalization of the experiences involved in emerging as transgender.

2. *Seeking information/reaching out*—In the second stage, people seek to gain education and support about trans* identities and experiences, which can be exhilarating as much as informative and can involve more risk-taking. The therapeutic task is to facilitate linkages and encourage outreach.

3. *Disclosure to significant others*—Next, trans* persons engage in disclosing their identity to significant others (e.g., spouses, partners, family, friends). The therapeutic task involves

---

1 The suffix *–izing* speaks to a critical understanding of the term in question. That is, normativizing speaks to the social process that reifies what is the norm, in this case the social expectation, compulsion, and even perceived obligation to come out.

supporting the trans* person to continue with trusted supports, work through conflict, and integrate in the family and/or support system. This stage, and those forward, may involve loss and grief.

4. *Exploration: Identity and self-labeling*—The fourth stage involves the exploration of and living out in real time various trans* identities and modes of gender expression, including roles, clothing, language, and mannerisms. The therapeutic task is to support the articulation and comfort with one's gendered identity and ways of expression. This stage may involve struggles with depression and harmful coping strategies.

5. *Exploration: Transition issues and possible body modification*—This stage involves exploring options for and making decisions for consolidating transition, identity, presentation, and body modification. The therapeutic task is the resolution of the decision and advocacy toward their manifestation.

6. *Integration: Acceptance and posttransition issues*—In this final stage, trans* people are able to incorporate and synthesize their transgender identity into their overall personhood and find expression in their lived daily life. The therapeutic task is to support adaptation to transition-related issues.

Parallel to the individual trans* person's experience in developing their identity, family and other trusted support networks have an emergence of their own (Lev, 2004). While awareness may be avoided, this issue is brought to the forefront during stage 3 (disclosure to significant others) of the trans* person's emergence, catalyzing development in the support system. These four stages include

1. *Discovery and disclosure*—Discovery of gender-variant feelings, identities, behaviors, and histories may come accidentally or intentionally. Nonetheless, it is often met more with shock and betrayal, as well as concern for children in the family system.

2. *Turmoil*—While some family and support systems are accepting, more commonly those in the trans* person's family system work through emotional lability, relationship distress, and struggles with coping effectively. This is when many reach out to professionals for support.

3. *Negotiation*—The next stage involves working out boundaries and engaging in a process to accept, adapt to, work through, and resolve transition. This often involves determining effective ways and timing to work with institutions (e.g., schools, medical centers) and be "out" in public settings.

4. *Finding balance*—In this final stage, the family and support system may not have fully resolved their issues nor does the trans* person fully have to transition. Rather, balance here signals that the trans* person is no longer marginalized; they are included back into the normative life of the system and increasingly accepted. Each family system decides its own boundaries and effective solutions, and not all family systems survive this process.

Implicitly embedded in considerations about the nature, emergence, and development of trans* identities is a medicalized perspective on gender and its nonconformity to both dominant normative views on gender (i.e., cisgenderism) and mental health. While the psychiatric and larger community of behavioral health professionals declassified sexual orientation as a mental disorder in 1973, gender dysphoria is still included in the latest, fifth edition of the *Diagnostic and Statistical Manual of Mental Disorders* (*DSM-5*; American Psychiatric Association, 2013). Using gender as an object to clinically categorize has shifted over the years in the *DSM*, just as the norms by which to pathologize have also been shifting. Among many changes to the *DSM*, the fifth edition foregrounds a "spectrum" paradigm for mental disorders as well as gives primacy to a brain-based etiology for all included disorders, to the extent that this is known and available in research. No matter how helpful or progressive this next iteration of the classification manual is, the power to classify and its espoused categories cannot be disentangled from the sociocultural effects it certainly has and will have. Classifying conditions as mental disorders (or behavioral health problems) suggests an error in psychological processing and that faulty mechanisms are biological in basis (Wakefield, 2013). This reifies a staunch claim that mental disorders are actually brain diseases, no matter how unproven the ideology, and therefore the best interventions are biomedical in nature. Moreover, this investment in genetics and neurobiology ironically becomes tenuous with the expansion and contraction of diagnostic categories. This continual recasting of what is disordered eclipses more proper attention to the problems of daily living, which may be intrapersonal, interpersonal, systemic, or ecologic. In the case of gender (and sexuality), this pathologizing—or deviance—perspective has endured in various formations with the transformations in dominant social and cultural norms (Perone, 2014).

In the *DSM-5*, "gender identity disorder" has been replaced with "gender dysphoria," a shift that focuses on one's distress about identity incongruence rather than targeting the incongruence itself. Similarly, gender dysphoria for children has been included as a separate category. The final remaining disorder from previous iterations is that of transvestic disorder, positioned under paraphilias. Even with these further transformations in diagnostic capacities, several limitations exist (Lev, 2004; Perone, 2014). The *DSM-5* continues to reify cisgenderism and binarism of gender identity and expression, instead of keeping in step with a more dynamic understanding of gender as a constellation of possibilities. Next, the focus on distress about one's incongruence completes a circular logic by entrapping attention still to intrapsychic processes and failings, rather than tending to the system of norms in the first place. Third, the normative understandings of masculinity and femininity and the policing of normative roles and expectations not only continues cissexism; it also invokes heterosexism in the continued conflation of sexuality with gender (Lev, 2004); for example, childhood gender nonconformity is often associated with an adult sexual orientation that is LGB (Bailey & Zucker, 1995; Bem, 1996; Lippa, 2000).

A LIFE COURSE MODEL

Holding together essentialism and constructionism and blending numerous fields of inquiry into human development and the social world (e.g., biology, psychology, anthropology), a life course model of identity foregrounds attention to the social ecology of development positioned within historical timeframes. Life course models argue that human experiences are embedded in and shaped by time and place over the entirety of one's lifetime (Elder, 1998), which then determines and allows for behavioral possibilities and categories of identification. Life course theorists posit there are five cohorts for modern LGBTQ people (Cohler, 2007; Cohler & Galatzer, 2000; McAdams, Josselson, & Lieblich, 2006):

1. *Pre–World War II*—An era of industrializing and urbanizing communities, offering networks, neighborhoods, and identities for (emerging) LGBTQ people;
2. *Post–World War II*—A time of sexual liberation and civil rights including LGBTQ awareness, advocacy, and growing activism;
3. *Post-Stonewall*—Policy and cultural practices gain traction to legitimize LGBTQ persons in US and Western societies, including declassifying homosexuality as a mental illness;
4. *AIDS*—A historically traumatic event and era that brought a loss of a generation (or more) of largely gay men and people of color; this monumental event also cohered the LGBTQ community in various ways along with brought revolutionary trends and strategies to sexual health practices as well as social and health justice activism, policy, and clinical practice;
5. *Post-AIDS*—A more recent era only coming into analysis and one that shows empirical trends; still, it offers attention to a cohort of LGBTQ persons adapting to intergenerational stress, technology, and various new legal rights and social benefits, among other social changes.

These life course theorists further argue that time and place offer opportunities and constraints as well as have effects on various age cohorts or generations. The individual is in a continual, dialectical process between human agency and developmental agency, biology and culture, and oneself and society. Specifically, with regard to sexual orientation, life course theorists discuss a "sexual lifeway," appreciating the fluidity and responsiveness of identity (Hammack, 2005). Motivating this approach are three propositions: (a) individuals possess a biological disposition to respond affectively to members of a particular sex, (b) this disposition is reflected in sexual desire, and (c) a subjective understanding of one's desire in the context of a specific cultural model of human sexuality leads to behavioral practices and identity assumption. Therefore, one's biology (e.g., genes, hormones, neurology) contributes to sexual desire, and this in turn informs one's identity, behavior, and sexual subjectivity (e.g., self-schema or internalized cultural model of sexuality). This individual process is encased in a social ecology of development (e.g., culture/society/history) that influences and informs identity. One's subjectivity dawns with the recognition of desire and onset of puberty. That time frame evokes an active negotiation and lifelong process of an engagement with the storied life of the social world, and thus making meaning of oneself, coming out and having identity, and engaging in behavior congruent with desire.

Complementing this approach is the earlier work of Kimmel (1990; Kimmel & Sang, 1995). While his initial research and clinical work around aging and adulthood of LGBTQ persons occurred well before Hammack's work, Kimmel extends the theoretical and empirical attempts to understand the various identity formations and developmental pathways of LGBTQ persons. Extending Levinson's model of adult development, Kimmel attends to psychosocial shifts as LGBTQ persons move from adolescence into adulthood, fronting the diversity within and across sexual orientations. Kimmel's work is important in many ways in that it focuses on the strengths that can develop through struggles LGBTQ people have with the sense of differentness, interacting with homophobia, and experiencing difference as they grow. Among advantages are a life continuance, self-reliance, industrious, and building a chosen family and trusted support network.

RACIAL AND ETHNIC IMPERATIVES

The human development of identity is not circumscribed to one's sexuality and gender. There are multiple identities that are in development over a lifetime, especially those related to race and ethnicity as well as the coalescing and development of multiple identities. From an intersectional standpoint, attention to multiple identities becomes imperative in appreciating the differences and conflicts that LGBTQ people of color face. As discussed in this text, not all LGBTQ identities are the same, and so for people of color, it is important to resist homogenization. People of color are a diverse social category and constituted by many social locations. An important task that any LGBTQ people of color experiences is walking within multiple worlds. This requires negotiating allegiances with various communities, navigating multiple social and cultural boundaries, and reconciling social roles and expectations. This experience incurs more stress when considering various oppressive forces that occur internally (e.g., internalized racism) and externally (e.g., ethnocentrism) and that arise from membership in two oppressed groups (e.g., Latino gay man) or multiple ones (e.g., lesbian woman of color; Chan, 1989; Diaz, 1997; Green, 1994; Icard, 1986; Loicano, 1989; Morales, 1989; Walters, Evans-Campbell, Simoni, Ronquillo, & Bhuyan, 2006).

In the area of theorizing and research on identity construction, racial and ethnic identities have received some attention (Cross, 1995; Helms, 1990, 1992, 1995; Phinney, 1990, 1992). There is also some work related to the intersection of racial and ethnic development with that of sexuality (e.g., Adams & Phillips, 2009; Rosario, Schrimshaw, & Hunter, 2004). Walters & Simoni (1993) found that models for ethnic identity development share similarities with those of gay and lesbians in terms of identity being a calculus of an individual and social experiences. Moreover, evidence exists that positive racial and ethnic identity predicts life satisfaction and further that the integration of an LGBTQ identity with one's ethnic identity is positively correlated with lower psychological distress, greater social supports, and better self-esteem and efficacy (Crawford, Allison, Zamboni, & Soto, 2002). To that end, the central premise of many dominant models (as discussed herein) on coming out as a transformative moment, catalyst for identity integration, and index of mental health may not be the most effective analytic. Instead, it is argued that coming out amidst navigating multiple identities can be critically understood as a *becoming* or *coming home* to who someone is (Walters, Evans-Campbell, Simoni, Ronquillo, & Bhuyan, 2006). This mirrors other critical perspectives on coming out as an experience of "coming in" or inviting in (Hammoud-Beckett, 2007). Moreover, the other major mainstream models on LGBTQ identity development lack an analytic for appreciating the continual, lifelong process that LGBTQ people of color face in negotiating multiple social locations as well as the cumulative and synergistic effects of stress-coping and empowerment.

Building off a model of stress and coping paradigm (Lazarus, 1980) and existing mental health research, Walters and Old Person (2008) offer the Identity Attitude Matrix Model as a practice paradigm when working with LGBT people of color (LGBTOC). Instead of a predictive pathway or teleological description of identity integration, this model proposes an "orthogonal approach" to understand the degrees to which LGBTOC align with coexisting identities. Similar to previous models within this chapter, it is ecological in nature and appreciates the parallel processes of identity construction between the self and the social. These processes manifest as two matrices: one for self-identity attitude and one for group identity attitude. Within each matrix, one axis indicates the gay attitude (positive or negative), while the other axis indicates the racial attitude (positive or negative). Given the orthogonal nature of this rubric, there are a possible 16 permutations, or "constellations." However, Walters and Old Person (2008) argue that three primary, common constellations manifest for LGBTOC: (a) combined positive identity attitudes (gay+, race+); (b) mixed positive and negative identity attitudes (gay+, race- or gay-, race+); or (c) combined negative identity attitude (gay-, race-). Depending on the person's rating, an appreciation can be made of the areas of strength and vulnerability as well as ways in which the LGBTQ person of color may be coping in response to stress and conflicts in allegiances. For example, if someone is experiencing a combined negative identity attitude, it can explored how a negative evaluation of oneself and one's group identities can be contributing to membership conflicts as well as coexisting health and mental health conditions, such as anxiety or depression (see chapter 21 for more content related to LGBTQ people of color and mental health conditions). Similar to other process-based paradigms, it is helpful to be mindful that these attitudes and combinations therein change over time and may, in fact, spiral back through earlier constellations depending on sociocultural and historical circumstances.

BISEXUALITIES

Commonly lacking in sexual identity models is the negotiation toward and development of bisexuality. The models discussed here may resonate with some individuals; however, they too often negate thorough attention to those who experience their sexuality as something other than or beyond predominantly homosexual or heterosexual. In part, this is often facilitated by the rampant levels of stigma against the bisexual community (Eliason, 1996). In popular media and academic literature, bisexual people are cast as (a) having a confused identity, meaning they "can't make a choice"; (b) being promiscuous; (c) being incapable or afraid to commit and have a long-term relationship; (d) being on their way to a true homosexual identity or are stunted in some way developmentally; (e) denying one's true sexual orientation; and (f) serving as a vector of disease transmission (especially HIV) into the heterosexual population.

Later in this text, chapter 15 reviews current scientific knowledge and applied practice strategies with the bisexual community. Still, the development of such an identity and lived phenomenon is inadequately theorized and fully understood. While attention and some research increases, only one model exists to describe the development of a bisexual identity (Weinberg, Williams, & Pryor, 1994), positing four stages: (a) initial confusion (akin to other LG models); (b) finding and applying the label; (c) settling into the identity; and (d) continued uncertainty, which references common periods of doubt about one's sexual identity. This assertion may arise from the myths and stereotypes or general lack of social support. Likewise, there is no commonly accepted definition for bisexuality. Like other sexual orientations, it can be an identity as defined through desire, behavior, and self-identification. To that end, some argue the bisexuality exists as a capacity to have relations with others of various genders, regardless of the self-identification of the person as bisexual (Firestein, 1996). The lack of definition makes the estimations of bisexuality difficult. At large, it is known that bisexuality is much more common than what most people believe. US estimates range between 0.7% and 1.1% of the population (Gates, 2011; Ward, Dahlhamer, Galinsky, & Joestl, 2014); up to 8.2% of US adults report same-sex sexual behavior in their lifetime, and up to 11% acknowledge some same-sex sexual attraction. In the mid-twentieth century, Kinsey and colleagues (Kinsey, Pomeroy, & Martin, 1948; Kinsey, Pomeroy, Martin, & Gebhard, 1953) argued a model of sexual identity, as defined through a spectrum of behaviors, along a six-point scale from exclusively heterosexual (zero) through exclusively homosexual (six). The model has been much criticized due to its original development being based on the behaviors of men; yet the model and the notion of a continuum of behavior have had much influence culturally. It points to the fact that sexuality is not a fixed point nor simply binary. Taking this further, Klein (1993) developed a sexual orientation grid. Klein too argued that one's identity falls on a continuum. However, the valuation of one's identity is a function of two major experiences. In grid format, one axis indicates sexual orientation in time (i.e., past, present, ideal); the other axis charts seven elements of identity (i.e., sexual attraction, sexual behavior, fantasies, emotional preference, social preference, hetero/homo lifestyle, and self-identification). Combined, people plot their gender preference for all the categories (i.e., 1 equals other sex only, 2 other sex mostly, 3 other sex somewhat more, and so forth to 7 which is same sex [gay or lesbian] only).

NEUROSCIENCE AND THE NATURE OF SEXUAL ORIENTATION

Lines of inquiry and empirical research exist that attempt to explain the origins of sexual identity and behaviors, pre- and postnatally. Driving these projects is an essentializing perspective on human sexuality along with apparent intra- and intergroup differences between the sexes. For cisgender men, it appears that there is a more typical bimodal distribution for sexuality; that is, men more frequently identify as either gay or straight (Bailey, Dunne, & Martin, 2000; Gates, 2011; Pattatuci & Hamer, 1995). For cisgender women, there appears to be a multimodal distribution, with more women as straight, lesbian, as well as bisexual (Veniegas & Conley, 2000; Kitzinger & Wilkinson, 1995). This apparent dichotomy for men and differences from women continue to encourage a tendency to naturalize sexuality and invest in a taxonomic schema to differentiate and explain on the basis of biology. Research into psychobiological determinations point to underlying variations in genetics (e.g., fraternal birth order), somatics (e.g., non-righthandedness), neuroanatomy (e.g., brain structure and neural pathways), neuropsychology (e.g., cognitive performance), and neurodevelopment (e.g., maternal stress during pregnancy; Rahman & Wilson, 2003). Likewise, though minimally evidenced and poorly theorized, attention has been given to psychosocial developmental experiences that lead to adult homosexual orientations, such as parental influences (Bailey, Barbow, Wolfe, & Mikach, 1995; Golombok & Tasker, 1996), context and culture-bound same-sex behavior (LeVay, 1991), or same-sex peers (Bem, 1996). Overall, the psychobiology research into human sexuality has indicated that variations exist within and across sexes and that much more understanding of the differences is merited. More critically, limitations are clear in terms of the nature of the science and the cultural implications. Implicit to a neuroscientific approach to sexuality and identity is an assumption of the bionormativity in and the homogenizing of the development of human beings. In kind, variations in sexuality are positioned as disruptions of a presumed natural and linear trajectory. While more genetic and anatomical information may be helpful over time with research, this sort of material knowledge sits within an ecological context that is already laden with extreme stigma and marginalization around matters of sexuality and gender. So increased methodological rigor and utilization of more specific and sensitive technologies would fortify scientific studies of this kind, as well provide critical attention to the psychosocial correlates that influence and effect biopsychosocial development.

RECOGNIZING MARGINS WITHIN MARGINS

The following section will examine factors related to identity development among two unique populations within the larger LGBTQ community, including those that live in rural areas, and young people.

RURAL SPACES, QUEER PLACES

A body of literature exists documenting and narrating the existence of LGBTQ persons in urban spaces, practically naturalizing a metropolitan landscape in the scenes of identity construction and lived experiences of queer communities (see Chauncey, 1994; Levine, 1998; Kennedy & Davis, 1993). Less attention has been paid to, though is emerging for, LGBTQ people in rural areas (see Howard, 1999; Johnson, 2007). In fact, in the early years of the twenty-first century, rural areas across the United States experienced a 51% increase in same-sex couples, partly attributed to increased "outness," more acceptance, and a willingness to be counted in surveys (Gates, 2006). Still, within mainstream LGBTQ culture, narratives and divides exist between urban and rural communities. Commonly, rural LGBTQ people are seen as "unmarked identities in marked spaces" and ones who are oppressed and desperate to flee to urban locations and their liberation and freedom; or, conversely, they adhere to an internalized homophobia and lead "boring" lives (Brekhus, 2003). Research in rural settings indicates that LGBTQ people do claim nonheterosexual identities, oftentimes within an isolating and intolerant atmosphere, all the while experiencing a reported quality of life replete with a slower pace, connections with the outdoors, close social and familial relationships, as well as isolation, being closeted, and lacking a public LGBTQ community (Boulden, 2001; Coby & Welch, 1997; Kirkey & Forsyth, 2001; McCarthy, 2000; Oswald & Culton, 2003).

Amidst these conditions, there too are responsive strategies to negotiate coming into and performing LGBTQ identities. In Kennedy's (2010) research, similarities and differences were noted across "native" versus "transplants" to rural areas in the ways in which participants discussed managing their identities. Strategies employed included selective or implicit disclosure, compartmentalizing, engaging in passing behaviors, rejecting as well as affirming LGBTQ identities, and actively negotiating religious beliefs. Annes and Redlin (2012) extend these narratives by describing the ways in which rural gay men rely on strategies of essentialized and naturalized standpoints for their sexual orientation and within that actively internalized staunch binarized gender roles, or engage in "effeminophobia." Finally, in another qualitative study, Kazyak (2011) documents how rural LG people underscore the importance of being a "good person" and engaging in a "live and let live" mentality as they maintain close-knit social connections. This is paralleled by the experience of negotiating an anonymity as well as visibility, fortified by embodying discourses of rural LGBTQ people leading "boring" and married lives whereas urban dwellers enjoy excitement, activism, and large community celebrations (e.g., LGBTQ pride parades).

YOUNG PEOPLE

Phased or staged models may be helpful in making sense of the coming out and identity development process for young people. However, they are not only a cohort in and of themselves, but young LGBTQ people are a new cohort in many respects. Nowadays, young people are growing up in a time when sexual diversity is "normative, acceptable, and even desirable" (Savin-Williams, 2011, p. 673). Conventional identitarian–based categorizations and aspirations, captured in the ever-evolving sexuality alphabet of LGBTQ, may not be the most effective ways for self-identification and exploration for today's young people (Morgan, 2013). Young people today have choices beyond a bi- or trimodal understanding of sexual orientation; in some estimates, there are more than a dozen different subgroups (Thompson & Morgan, 2008; Vrangalova & Savin-Williams, 2012; Weinrich & Klein, 2002; Worthington & Reynolds, 2009). (For further content surrounding queer identities, see chapter 17.) Simultaneously, this increasing ability to self-define and have a more personalized experience in development (as opposed to older/elder LGBTQ who voice more private, singular, and sociopolitically connected narratives) is increasingly associated with emerging transgenerational divides. This is to say, in what some call a "post-gay era," there is a possible difficulty in cohering a LGBTQ identity that is social in-part and by nature, and therefore this disconnection from generations prior and a collective psychology contributes to a silencing or, worse, loss of gay narratives altogether (Rowe, 2014; Weststrate & McLean, 2010).

Instead of staged models, a perspective of differential developmental trajectory (DDT) may be more effective for young generations, now and to come (Savin-Williams, 2005, 2011; Savin-Williams & Diamond, 2000). DDT signals the variability inherent within and across all people, the milestones that occur across the life course, and the probabilistic pathways that occur through space and time. It is predicated upon a refutation of longstanding assumptions in modeled identity paradigms that (a) life progresses stepwise in stages, (b) diversity and complexity should be minimized, and (c) young people can be understood through empirical research based in those who self-identity as gay. Alternatively, DDT proposes four tenets to conceptualize the emerging sexuality and self-identification of young people:

1. Same-sex attracted teens are similar to all others in their developmental trajectories. Young people share ecologic and biopsychosocial similarities in their development across the life course. Focusing on homoeroticism unnecessarily marginalizes, minoritizes, and objectifies them.
2. Same-sex attracted teens are dissimilar from their heterosexual peers in their developmental trajectories as well. Seemingly contradictory to the first point, young people who hold same-sex attraction experience different influences by the fact of growing up within a heterocentric, heteronormative, and homophobic culture, which in turn effects psychology.
3. There is high variability within same-sex-attracted young people, just as with other-sex-attracted (e.g., straight) peers.
4. The developmental trajectory of anyone is similar to that of no one who has ever lived. There is a great possibility of trajectories, pathways, and points of arrival in solidifying one's sexual orientation.

Coextensive with this rubric is the reality that young people and their development is wedded with technology and the Internet (Harper, Bruce, Serrano, & Jamil, 2009). Research is emerging on the effects of an interconnected culture through ever-expanding access and use; however, this body of literature is slow to attend to young LGBTQ people specifically (Browne, Lim, & Brown, 2009). Whereas early research suggested correlations between Internet use, social isolation, and decreased well-being, other work has indicated increased social competence (Kraut et al., 1998; Turow, 1999; Valkenburg & Peter, 2008). The rise of various platforms, formats, and devices challenge these findings. In fact, empirical findings are now indicating that young people's use of technology and increasing interconnections online have a number of strategic and helpful advantages in terms of social and sexual development (Downing, 2013; Gross, 2004; Schmitt, Dayanim, & Matthias, 2008). Among others, these include increasing self-expression and mastery of identity, increasing off-line interconnections with peers, and experimenting with identities (Huffaker & Calver, 2005; McKenna & Bargh, 1998; Mesch & Talmud, 2006).

In particular, LGBTQ young people's use of the Internet has increasingly shown to be interconnected with well-being. Harper, Bruce, Serrano, and Jamil (2009) found that gay and bisexual male youths' Internet use helped to explore their identity and become knowledgeable about the larger LGBTQ community, to connect with other LGBTQ people, and to gain self-acceptance and share their identity—rather than online activity being solely a vector for sexual risk. This had the effect of increasing self-awareness, self-acceptance, comfort, and facilitating the coming out process. While the general sentiment that the Internet is linked with anonymity and a certain amount of risks, a more empowering perspective directs attention to the fact that this aspect of modern life offers a critical safe space for LGBTQ young people. As much as young people can be inundated and affected by technology and what comes across their screens, their comfort with and acceptance of self and their identity ultimately facilitates agency and choice (Harper et al., 2009).

CONCLUSION

Presented here have been prominent models used in theory, research, and practice to make sense of the identity development of LGBTQ people. Additional perspectives (i.e., life course) and considerations (i.e., young people) were offered to further these existing models and direct attention toward current and important conversations. As stated earlier, identity is slippery; in the case of those who are nonheterosexual, the intersecting and dynamic sign of identities has critical importance and often functions for strategic purposes. Still, there is a problem inherent within a discussion such as this one on (dominant) understandings of (LGBTQ) identity: to diagram, define, categorize, and therefore consume has the regressive potential to incite ideas about what is "normal" and, often very quickly, becomes incorporated into normalizing practices. For example, there can be a propensity to impose linear narratives onto dynamically lived experiences.

Very critically, social workers would do well to always tend to normative forces—especially related to conversations regarding identification and the well-being of communities. To facilitate this process, critical approaches like queer theory (QT) can be another helpful "tool" in the practitioner's toolbox (Argüello, 2016; Eng, Halberstam, Muñoz, 2005; Sullivan, 2003). While QT often targets sexuality, it more so critiques elements of social life that promote or prohibit the construction of identities, chiefly normativizing practices (e.g., compulsory, monogamous heterosexuality). In a sense, QT turns attention back onto the privileged norm(s) and therefore facilitates an understanding of identity as relational and the process of identification as a negotiation of the mediated relationships we have with available social categories. In turn, QT exposes the limitations of identities and unpacks naturalizing terms and tendencies.

In closing, instead of trying to reify norms and what is normative, this discussion has emphasized trends and outliers in the struggles and strengths of evolving LGBTQ identities. In turn, this can be a window into the liberation of LGBTQ identities in our modern times. LGBTQ people highlight, among many things, the fact that to be seen and have voice in the public sphere requires continual mediation. These models and perspectives reviewed here all point to the dialectical process of making exterior what is importantly an interior experience but then filtered by and set into our social landscapes. That demands a dynamic use of one's self, conceptually and materially, and the available resources in one's world to *live into* an experience that, with later reflection and strategy, often is consolidated into (an) identity. By "doing" one's own identity, whether staged, modeled, phased, or done performatively and otherwise, it is making the process and struggle sayable, knowable, and meaningful in public, as well as validating what is private. Even more, the net result of any LGBTQ identity in public, oppressed in varying ways and to varying degrees, speaks to the potential and hope for all sexualities and genders, let alone a strategic move toward social justice (see Berlant & Warner, 1998; Warner, 2002).

REFERENCES

Adams, H. L., & Phillips, L. (2009). Ethnic related variations from the Cass model of homosexual identity formation: The experiences of two spirit, lesbian and gay Native Americans. *Journal of Homosexuality, 56,* 959–976.

Alderson, K. G. (2003). The ecological model of gay male identity. *The Canadian Journal of Human Sexuality, 12*(2), 75–85.

American Psychiatric Association. (2013). *Diagnostic and statistical manual of mental disorders* (5th ed.). Washington, DC: American Psychiatric Publishing.

Annes, A., & Redlin, M. (2012). The careful balance of gender and sexuality: Rural gay men, the heterosexual matrix, and "effeminophobia." *Journal of Homosexuality, 59*(2), 256–288.

Appadurai, A. (1996). *Modernity at large: Cultural dimensions of globalization.* Minneapolis: University of Minnesota Press.

Argüello, T. M. (2016). Fetishizing the health sciences: Queer theory as an intervention. *Journal of Gay and Lesbian Social Services, 28*(3), 231–244.

Bailey, J. M., Barbow, P., Wolfe, M., & Mikach, S. (1995). Sexual orientation of adult sons of gay fathers. *Developmental Psychology, 31,* 124–129.

Bailey, J. M., Dunne, M. P., & Martin, N. G. (2000). Genetic and environmental influences on sexual orientation and its correlates in an Australian twin sample. *Journal of Personality and Social Psychology, 78,* 524–536.

Bailey, J. M., & Zucker, K. J. (1995). Childhood sex-typed behaviour and sexual orientation: A conceptual analysis and quantitative review. *Developmental Psychology, 31,* 43–55.

Bem, D. J. (1996). Exotic becomes erotic: A developmental theory of sexual orientation. *Psychological Review, 103,* 320–335.

Berlant, L., & Warner, M. (1998). Sex in public. *Critical Inquiry, 24*(2), 547–566.

Boulden, W. T. (2001). Gay men living in a rural environment. *Journal of Gay & Lesbian Social Services, 12*(3–4), 63–75.

Brekhus, W. (2003). *Peacocks, chameleons, centaurs: Gay suburbia and the grammar of social identity.* Chicago: University of Chicago Press.

Browne, K., Lim, J., Brown, G. (Eds.). (2009). *Geographies of sexualities: Theory, practices and politics.* Surrey, UK: Ashgate.

Bulter, J. (1993). *Bodies that matter: On the discursive limits of "sex."* New York: Routledge.

Butler, J. (1999). *Gender trouble: Feminism and the subversion of identity.* New York: Routledge. (Original work published 1990)

Cass, V. C. (1979). Homosexual identity formation: A theoretical model. *Journal of Homosexuality, 4,* 219–235.

Cass, V. C. (1984). Homosexual identity formation: Testing a theoretical model. *Journal of Sex Research, 20*(2), 143–167.

Cass, V. C. (1996). Sexual orientation identity formation: A Western phenomenon. In R. Cabaj & T. Stein (Eds.), *Textbook of homosexuality and mental health* (pp. 227–251). Washington, DC: American Psychiatric Press.

Chapman, B. E., & Brannock, J. C. (1987). Proposed model of lesbian identity development: An empirical examination. *Journal of Homosexuality, 14,* 69–80.

Chan, C. (1989). Issues of identity development among Asian-American lesbians and gay men. *Journal of Counseling and Development, 68*(1), 16–20.

Chauncey, G. (1994). *Gay New York: Gender, urban culture, and the making of the gay male world, 1890–1940.* New York: Basic Books.

Coby, P., & Welch, P. (1997). Rural gay men in northern New England: Life experiences and coping styles. *Journal of Homosexuality 33*(1), 51–67.

Cohler, B. J. (2007). *Writing desire: Sixty years of gay autobiography.* Madison: University of Wisconsin Press.

Cohler, B. J., & Galatzer-Levy, R. M. (2000). *The course of gay and lesbian lives: Social and psychoanalytic perspectives.* Chicago: University of Chicago Press.

Coleman, E. (1982). Developmental stages of the coming out process. *Journal of Homosexuality, 7,* 31–43.

Cox, S., & Gallois, C. (1996). Gay and lesbian identity development: A social identity perspective. *Journal of Homosexuality, 30*(4), 1–30.

Crawford, I., Allison, K. W., Zamboni, B. D., & Soto. T. (2002). The influence of dual-identity development on the psychosocial functioning of African-American gay and bisexual men. *The Journal of Sex Research, 39,* 179–189.

Cross, W. E. (1995). The psychology of nigrescence: Revising the Cross model. In J. G. Ponterotto, J. M. Casas, L. A. Suzuki, & C. M. Alexander (Eds.), *Handbook of multicultural counseling* (pp. 93–122). Thousand Oaks, CA: SAGE.

D'Augelli, A. R. (1994). Identity development and sexual orientation: Toward a model of lesbian, gay, and bisexual development. In E. J. Trickett, R. J. Watts, & D. Birman (eds.), *Human diversity: Perspectives on people in context* (pp. 312–333). San Francisco, CA: Jossey-Bass.

DeLamater, J. D., & Hyde, J. S. (1998). Essentialism vs. social constructionism in the study of human sexuality. *Journal of Sex Research, 35,* 10–18.

Diaz, R. (1997). Latino gay men and psycho-cultural barriers to AIDS prevention. In M. Levine, J. Gagnon, & P. Nardi (Eds.), *In changing times: Gay men and lesbians encounter HIV/AIDS* (pp. 221–244). Chicago: University of Chicago Press.

Downing, G. (2013). Virtual youth: Non-heterosexual young people's use of the internet to negotiate their identities and socio-sexual relations. *Children's Geographies, 11*(1), 44–58.

Elder, G. H. Jr. (1998). The life course as developmental theory. *Child Development, 69,* 1–12.

Eliason, M. J. (1996). Working with lesbian, gay, and bisexual people: Reducing negative stereotypes via inservice education. *Journal of Nursing Staff Development, 12*(3), 127–132.

Eng, D. L., Halberstam, J., & Muñoz, J. E. (2005). Introduction: What's queer about queer studies now? *Social Text, 84-85*(23, 3–4), 1–17.

Faderman, L. (1984). The "new gay" lesbians. *Journal of Homosexuality, 10,* 85–95.

Fassinger, R. E., & Miller, B. A. (1996). Validation of an inclusive model of sexual minority formation on a sample of gay men. *Journal of Homosexuality, 32,* 53–78.

Firestein, B. A. (Ed.) (1996). *Bisexuality: The psychology and politics of an invisible minority.* Thousand Oaks, CA: SAGE.

Ford, M. E., Beighley, C. S., & Sanlo, R. (2015). Student development: Theory to practice in LGBT campus work. In J. C. Hawley (Ed.), *Expanding the circle: Creating an inclusive environment in higher education for LGBTQ students and studies* (pp. 187–207). Albany, NY: SUNY Press.

Foucault, M. (1990). *The history of sexuality, Vol. 1: An introduction* (Trans. R. Hurley). New York: Vintage Books. (Original work published 1978)

Foucault, M. (1980). *Power/knowledge: Selected interviews and other writings, 1972–1977.* Edited by C. Gordon. Translated by C. Gordon, L. Marshall, J. Mepham, & K. Soper. New York: Pantheon.

Fuss, D. (1989). *Essentially speaking: Feminism, nature & difference.* New York: Routledge.

Gates, G. J. (2006). *Same-sex couples and the gay, lesbian, bisexual population: New estimates from the American community survey.* Los Angeles: Williams Institute.

Gates, G. J. (2011). *How many people are lesbian, gay, bisexual, and transgender?* Los Angeles, CA: Williams Institute.

Golombok, S., & Tasker, F. (1996). Do parents influence the sexual orientation of their children? Findings from a longitudinal study of lesbian families. *Developmental Psychology, 32,* 3–11.

Green, B. (1994). Lesbian women of color: Triple jeopardy. In L. Comas-Diaz & B. Greens (Eds.), *Women of color: Integrating ethnic and gender identities in psychotherapy* (pp. 339–427). New York: Guilford Press.

Gross, E. F. (2004). Adolescent Internet use: What we expect, what teens report. *Journal of Applied Developmental Psychology, 25*(6), 633–649.

Hammack, P. L. (2005). The life course development of human sexual orientation: An integrative paradigm. *Human Development, 48,* 267–290.

Hammoud-Becket, S. (2007). *Azima ila hayati*—an invitation in to my life: Narrative conversations about sexual identity. *The International Journal of Narrative Therapy and Community Work, 1*, 29–39.

Harper, G. W., Bruce, D., Serrano, P., & Jamil, O. B. (2009). The role of the Internet in the sexual identity development of gay and bisexual male adolescents. In P. L. Hammack & B. J. Cohler (Eds.), *The story of sexual identity: Narrative perspectives on the gay and lesbian life course* (pp. 297–326). Oxford: Oxford University Press.

Hart, J. (1984). Therapeutic implications of viewing sexual identity in terms of essentialist and constructionist theories. *Journal of Homosexuality, 9*, 39–51.

Helms, J. E. (1990). Toward a model of White racial identity development. In J. E. Helms (Ed.), *Black and White racial identity: Theory, research, and practice* (pp. 49–66). New York: Greenwood Press.

Helms, J. E. (1992). *A race is a nice thing to have: A guide to being a White person, or understanding the White persons in your life*. Topeka, KS: Content Communications.

Helms, J. E. (1995). An update of Helm's White and people of color racial identity model. In J. G. Ponterotto, J. M. Casas, L. A. Suzuki, & C. M. Alexander (Eds.), *Handbook of multicultural counseling*, (pp. 181–198). Thousand Oaks, CA: SAGE.

Henry, B., Moffitt, T. E., Caspi, A., Langley, J., & Silva, P. A. (1994), On the "remembrance of things past": A longitudinal evaluation of the retrospective method. *Psychological Assessment, 6*, 92–101.

Hill-Collins, P. (2000). Black feminist thought: Knowledge, consciousness, and the politics of empowerment (10th anniversary rev. ed.). New York: Routledge.

Horowitz, J. L., & Newcomb, M. D. (2002). A multidimensional approach to homosexual identity. *Journal of Homosexuality, 42*(2), 1–19.

Howard, J. (1999). *Men like that: A southern queer history*. Chicago: University of Chicago Press.

Hudson, K. D. (2015) Toward a conceptual framework for understanding community belonging and well-being: Insights from a queer-mixed perspective. *Journal of Community Practice, 23*(1), 27–50.

Huffaker, D. A., & Calvert, S. L. (2005). Gender, identity, and language use in teenage blogs. *Journal of Computer-Mediated Communication, 10*(2). doi/10.1111/j.1083-6101.2005.tb00238.x/full

Icard, L. (1986). Black gay men and conflicting social identities: Sexual orientation versus racial identity. *Journal of Social Work and Human Sexuality, 4*(1–2), 83–93.

Johnson, C. (2007). Camp life: The queer history of "manhood" in the civilian conservation corps, 1933–1937. *American Studies, 48*(2), 19–35.

Kazyak, E. (2011). Disrupting cultural selves: Constructing gay and lesbian identities in rural locales. *Qualitative Sociology, 34*, 561–581.

Kenneady, D. A., & Oswalt, S. B. (2014). Is Cass's model of homosexual identity formation relevant to today's society? *American Journal of Sexuality Education, 9*(2), 229–246.

Kennedy, E. L., & Davis, M. (1993). *Boots of leather, slippers of gold: The history of a lesbian community*. New York: Penguin Books.

Kennedy, M. (2010). Rural men, sexual identity and community. *Journal of Homosexuality, 57*(8), 1051–1091.

Kimmel, D. C. (1990). *Adulthood and aging* (3rd ed.). New York: John Wiley.

Kimmel, D. C., & Sang, B. E. (1995). Lesbians and gay men in midlife. In A. R. D'Augelli & C. J. Patterson (Eds.), *Lesbian, gay, and bisexual identities over the lifespan* (pp. 190–214). New York: Oxford University Press.

Kinsey, A. C., Pomeroy, W. B., & Martin, C. E. (1948). *Sexual behavior in the human male*. Philadelphia: W. B. Saunders.

Kinsey, A. C., Pomeroy, W. B., Martin, C. E., & Gebhard, P. H. (1953). *Sexual behavior in the human female*. Philadelphia: W. B. Saunders.

Kirkey, K., & Forsyth, A. (2001). Men in the valley: Gay male life on the suburban-rural fringe. *Journal of Rural Studies, 17*(4), 421–441.

Kitzinger, C., & Wilkinson, S. (1995). Transitions from heterosexuality to lesbianism: The discursive production of lesbian identities. *Developmental Psychology, 31*, 95–104.

Klein, F. (1993). *The bisexual option: A concept of one hundred percent intimacy* (2nd ed.). New York: Harrington Park Press.

Kraut, R., Patterson, M., Lundmark, V., Kiesler, S., Mukophadhyay, T., & Scherlis, W. (1998). Internet paradox: A social technology that reduces social involvement and psychological well-being? *American Psychologist, 53*, 1017–1031.

Lazarus, R. (1980). The stress and coping paradigm. In L. Bond & J. Rosen (Eds.), *Competence and coping during adulthood* (pp. 28–74). Hanover, NH: University Press of New England.

LeVay, S. (1991). A difference in hypothalamic structure between heterosexual and homosexual men. *Science, 253*, 1034–1037.

Lev, A. I. (2004). *Transgender emergence: Therapeutic guidelines for working with gender-variant people and their families.* New York: Haworth Press.

Levine, H. (1997). A further exploration of the lesbian identity development process and its measurement. *Journal of Homosexuality, 34*, 67–76.

Levine, M. (1998). *Gay ghetto.* In P. M. Nardi & B. E. Schneider (Eds.), *Social perspectives in lesbian and gay studies* (pp. 194–206). New York: Routledge.

Lewis, L. A. (1984). The coming-out process for lesbians: Integrating a stable identity. *Social Work, 29*(5), 464–469.

Lippa, R. A. (2000). Gender related traits in gay men, lesbian women, and heterosexual men and women: The virtual identity of homosexual-heterosexual diagnosticity and gender diagnosticity. *Journal of Personality, 68*, 899–926.

Loicano, D. K. (1989). Gay identity issues among Black Americans: Racism, homophobia, and the need for validation. *Journal of Counseling and Development, 68*, 21–25.

Martin, H. P. (1991). The coming-out process for homosexuals. *Hospital & Community Psychiatry, 42*, 158–162.

McAdams, D. P., Josselson, R., & Lieblich, A. (Eds.). (2006). *Identity and story: Creating self in narrative.* Washington, DC: American Psychological Association.

McCarn, S. R., & Fassinger, R. E. (1996). Re-visioning sexual minority identity formation: A new model of lesbian identity and its implications for counseling and research. *The Counseling Psychologist, 24*(3), 508–534.

McCarthy, L. (2000). Poppies in a wheat field. *Journal of Homosexuality, 39*(1), 75–94.

McKenna, K. Y. A., & Bargh, J. A. (1998). Coming out in the age of the Internet: Identity "demarginalization" through virtual group participation. *Journal of Personality and Social Psychology, 75*(3), 681–694.

Mehrotra, G. (2010). Toward a continuum of intersectionality theorizing for feminist social work scholarship. *Affilia, 25*(4), 417–430.

Mesch, G., & Talmud, I. (2006). The quality of online and offline relationships: The role of multiplexity and duration of social relationships. *The Information Society, 22*, 137–148.

Minton, H., & McDonald, G. (1984). Homosexual identity formation as a developmental process. *Journal of Homosexuality, 9*, 91–104.

Morales, E. S. (1989). Ethnic minority families and minority gays and lesbians. *Marriage and Family Review, 14*, 217–239.

Morgan, E. M. (2013). Contemporary issues in sexual orientation and identity development in emerging adulthood. *Emerging Adulthood, 1*, 52–66.

Oswald, R. F., & Culton, L. S. (2003). Under the rainbow: Rural gay life and its relevance for family providers. *Family Relations, 52*(1), 72–81.

Pattatucci, A. M. L., & Hamer, D. H. (1995). Development and familiality of sexual orientation in females. *Behaviour Genetics, 25*, 407–420.

Perone, A. K. (2014). The social construction of mental illness for lesbian, gay, bisexual, and transgender persons in the United States. *Qualitative Social Work, 13*(6), 766–771.

Phinney, J. S. (1990). Ethnic identity in adolescents and adults: Review of research. *Psychological Bulletin, 108,* 499–514.

Phinney, J. S. (1992). The multigroup ethnic identity measure: A new scale for use with diverse groups. *Journal of Adolescent Research, 7,* 156–176.

Rahman, Q., & Wilson, G. D. (2003). Born gay? The psychobiology of human sexual orientation. *Personality and Individual Differences, 34,* 1337–1382.

Rosario, M., Schrimshaw, E. W., & Hunter, J. (2004). Ethnic/racial differences in the coming-out process of lesbian, gay, and bisexual youths: A comparison of sexual identity development over time. *Cultural Diversity and Ethnic Minority Psychology, 10,* 215–228.

Rosario, M., Schrimshaw, E. W., Hunter, J., & Braun, L. (2006). Sexual identity development among gay, lesbian, and bisexual youths: Consistency and change over time. *Journal of Sex Research, 43*(1), 46–58.

Ross, M. (1989). Relation of implicit theories to the construction of personal histories. *Psychological Review, 96,* 341–357.

Rowe, M. (2014). Becoming and belonging in gay men's life stories: A case study of a voluntaristic model of identity. *Sociological Perspectives, 57*(4), 434–449.

Savin-Williams, R. C. (2005). *The new gay teenager.* Cambridge, MA: Harvard University Press.

Savin-Williams, R. C. (2011). Identity development among sexual-minority youth. In S. J. Schwartz, V. L. Vigoles, & K. Luyckx (Eds.), *Handbook of identity theory and research,* (pp. 671–689). New York: Springer.

Savin-Williams, R. C., & Diamond, L. M. (2000). Sexual identity trajectories among sexual-minority youths: Gender comparisons. *Archives of Sexual Behavior, 29,* 607–627.

Schmitt, K. L., Dayanim, S., & Matthias, S. (2008). Personal homepage construction as an expression of social development. *Developmental Psychology, 44*(2), 496–506.

Sim Chun, K. Y., & Singh, A. A. (2010). The bisexual youth of color intersecting identities development model: A contextual approach to understanding multiple marginalization experiences. *Journal of Bisexuality, 10*(4), 429–451.

Sophie, J. (1985–1986). A critical examination of stage theories of lesbian identity development. *Journal of Homosexuality, 12,* 39–51.

Stein, E. (1999). *The mismeasure of desire: The science, theory, and ethics of sexual orientation.* New York: Oxford University Press.

Sullivan, N. (2003). *A critical introduction to queer theory.* New York: New York University Press.

Thompson, E., & Morgan, E. M. (2008). "Mostly straight" young women: Variations in sexual behavior and identity development. *Developmental Psychology, 44,* 15–21.

Tolman, D. L., & Diamond, L. M. (2001). Desegregating sexuality research: Cultural and biological perspectives on gender and desire. *Annual Review of Sex Research, 12,* 33–74.

Troiden, R. (1988). *Gay and lesbian identity: A sociological analysis.* Dix Hills, NY: General Hall.

Troiden, R. R. (1989). The formation of homosexual identities. *Journal of Homosexuality, 17,* 43–74.

Turow, J. (1999) *The Internet and the family: The view from the parents—the view from the press* (Report Series No. 27). Philadelphia: Annenberg Public Policy Center of the University of Pennsylvania.

Valkenburg, P. M., & Peter, J. (2008). Adolescents' identity experiments on the Internet: Consequences for social competence and self-concept unity. *Communication Research, 35*(2), 208–231.

Veniegas, R. C., & Conley, T. D. (2000). Biological research on women's sexual orientations: Evaluating the scientific evidence. *Journal of Social Issues, 56,* 267–282.

Vrangalova, Z., & Savin-Williams, R. C. (2012). Mostly heterosexual and mostly gay/lesbian: Evidence for new sexual orientation identities. *Archives of Sexual Behavior, 41,* 85–101.

Wakefield, J. C. (2013). DSM-5 and clinical social work: Mental disorder and psychological justice as goals of clinical intervention. *Clinical Social Work Journal, 41,* 131–138.

Walters, K. L., Evans-Campbell, T., Simoni, J., Ronquillo, T., & Bhuyan, R. (2006). "My spirit in my heart": Identity experiences and challenges among American Indian two-spirit women. *Journal of Lesbian Studies, 10*(1/2), 125–149.

Walters, K. L., & Old Person, R. (2008). Lesbians, gays, bisexuals, and transgender people of color: Reconciling divided selves and communities. In G. P. Mallon (Ed.), *Social work practice with lesbian, gay, bisexual, and transgender people* (2nd ed., pp. 41–68). New York: Routledge.

Walters, K. L., & Simoni, J. M. (1993). Lesbian and gay male group identity attitudes and self-esteem: Implications for counseling. *Journal of Counseling Psychology, 40*, 94–99.

Ward, B. W., Dahlhamer, J. M., Galinsky, A. M., & Joestl, S. S. (2014). Sexual orientation and health among U.S. adults: National Health Interview Survey, 2013. *National Health Statistics Reports, 77*, 1–10.

Warner, M. (2002). *Publics and counterpublics.* New York: Zone Books.

Weinberg, M. S., Williams, C. J., & Pryor, D. W. (1994). *Dual attraction: Understanding bisexuality.* New York: Oxford University Press.

Weinrich, J. D., & Klein, F. (2002). Bi-gay, bi-straight, and the bi-bi: Three bisexual subgroups identified using cluster analysis of the Klein Sexual Orientation Grid. *Journal of Bisexuality, 2*, 111–139.

Weststrate, N. M., & McLean, K. C. (2010). The rise and fall of gay: A cultural-historical approach to gay identity development. *Memory, 18*(2), 225–240.

Worthington, R. L., & Reynolds, A. L. (2009). Within-group differences in sexual orientation and identity. *Journal of Counseling Psychology, 56*, 44–55.

CHAPTER 5

THE COMING OUT PROCESS

Mark Smith, Tyler M. Argüello, and Michael P. Dentato

INTRODUCTION

This chapter covers the pivotal process of *coming out* in the lives of lesbian, gay, bisexual, transgender, and queer (LGBTQ) individuals, including the construction, declarations, and consolidation of identities that incorporate a sexual and/or gender minority orientation. Beginning with a general review of how identities are formed through social interactions, the chapter covers coming out during adolescent and young adult years, mid-life, and older adulthood. Similarities and differences between experiences of gay males, lesbians, bisexuals, and transgender individuals are explored as well as the experiences of LGBTQ individuals from the lens of intersectionality and various environmental contexts: rural versus urban settings; racial, ethnic, and cultural identities; socioeconomic status; and the opportunities and constraints posed by close family relationships. Well-established models that provide structural, stage-based descriptions of the coming out process are reviewed as well as some of the exciting ways contemporary LGBT identities are being mediated via online and social media access.

In contemporary American society, individuals who experience same-sex attraction or gender nonconforming self-identities are expected to "come out of the closet" and declare this status publically. Presumably, this declarative act of coming out enables individuals to live more truthfully and openly, leads to greater happiness, and ameliorates many potential physical and mental/emotional health concerns (Cox, Dewaele, van Houtte, & Vincke, 2011; D'Augelli & Grossman, 2001; Herek, 1988; Meyer, 2003; Proctor & Groze, 1994; Remafedi, 1987). This imperative to come out constitutes a primary event differentiating LGBTQ individuals from heterosexual or cisgender individuals, as it is unnecessary to "come out" as straight or gender-conforming if one has membership with, or conforms to, dominant social norms. The intricate strategies and emotional efforts employed by previous generations to hide same-sex or gender nonconforming inclinations constituted a central countercultural characteristic: membership in underground and secret societies (Katz, 1976; Marcus, 1992; Martin, 1982). Today the strategies and social negotiations involved in the coming out process, for many individuals, has replaced the secret countercultural aspect of identities of previous years and are the new central point of identity construction for sexual and gender minority lives (Gray, 2009; McKenna & Bargh, 1998; Pascoe, 2011).

Central to identity consolidation is the series of decisions and actions involved with coming out and the processes by which LGBTQ individuals come to acknowledge and accept their sexual orientations and gender identities and ultimately decide to disclose this realization of difference(s) to others (Goffman, 1963). Like others who embody socially stigmatized or minority status, LGBTQ individuals are often caught in a complicating dilemma; they must weigh the inherent advantages of disclosing core information about themselves against the significant risks of public exposure and possible discrimination, rejection, or physical assault (D'Augelli, Hershberger, & Pilkington, 1998; Herek, 1988).

UNDERSTANDING IDENTITY FORMATION AS SOCIAL NARRATIVE

For contemporary social scientists, *identity formation* is no longer a discrete developmental achievement but a descriptive label for an ongoing process of continually locating oneself and being located within specific social contexts (Somers, 1994; Taylor, 1992). The process of constructing and establishing identities is understood to be an interactive, relational, and ongoing dynamic that involves engaging in a variety of narrative and performative actions (Butler, 2015; Goffman, 1959). Identities, or self-depictions, are not fixed, essential, or inevitable but are fluid constructions that help one navigate social spaces and organize personal experiences (Somers, 1994). Individuals declare and perform these self-presentations in order to position themselves in relation to social contexts (Goffman, 1959; Butler, 2015). For LGBTQ individuals, this involves various forms of coming out, or narratively declaring one's distinction from what is understood to be the dominant norm (Klein, Sepekoff, & Wolf, 1985). Navigating the confluence of racial, gender, cultural, sociopolitical, religious, and other contextual influences that impact the construction of personal identities presents a challenging task for anyone. However, the process can become even more complex and demanding for those LGBTQ individuals who also are racial/ethnic minorities, multiethnic, and/or from unique cultural or religious backgrounds— especially those that are powerfully heterocentric, homophobic, condemning, or non-accepting. While coming out as LGBTQ represents a challenge to or rejection of dominant social norms for anyone, the existential undertaking involved in doing so while contradicting strongly imposed norms of family, community, culture, ethnicity, and religion become undertakings of exceptional courage and determination. However, the intricate pathways individuals utilize to navigate coming out amidst powerful contextual norms appear to have a marginal impact on the actual stages of coming out involved.

Grov, Bimbi, Nanin, and Parsons (2006) focused on an urban, multiethnic population ($N = 2,733$) of lesbian, gay, and bisexual young adults, confirming that younger cohorts of both men and women (18- to 24-year-olds) initiated sexual experiences with same-gendered partners at an earlier age than previous cohorts and came out to themselves and to others at earlier ages. Women appeared to begin the process at slightly later ages than men, reporting that they began having same-sex involvement and came out to self and others about two years later than men. However, these authors found that there were no significant racial or ethnic differences in age of coming out to self or others; yet people of color were less likely to be out to their parents. Some research findings note that race and ethnicity had little effect on the coming out process in terms of timing or decisions made about disclosure (D'Augelli, Hershberger, & Pilkington, 1998; Newman & Muzzonigro, 1993; Savin-Williams, 1989) however, Cramer and Roach (1988) found that deeply held cultural beliefs and the influence of traditional values held by individuals and their families did make a difference. For people of color, racial identity may be what matters most, and sexual minorities of color may seek solidarity not with other LGBTQ colleagues but with their identified racial communities with whom they experience more critical membership (Icard, 1986).

Therefore, for some individuals coming out as LGBTQ may be less important than maintaining membership in cultural, ethnic, community identities. Similarly, when reviewing the coming out experiences of gay males and lesbians, some differences are noted, but generally they align with the predominant models (Anderson & Mavis, 1996; Chapman & Brannock, 1987; de Monteflores & Shultz, 1978; Golden, 1987). For transgender individuals, differences from major coming out models were primarily in terms of the timing of their coming out processes (Devor, 2013; Lev, 2004). While unique challenges faced by LGBTQ individuals of minority ethnic, racial, cultural, and religious orientations are discussed in other chapters in this text, this chapter concentrates on what appears to be the more common and typical processes of coming out across life stages and circumstances.

A selection of theoretical frames structure this chapter's discussion of the development and social declaration of coming out and sexual identity/gender identity development: (a) the psychological, social, cognitive, and sexual developmental theories associated with typical (heterosexual and cisgender) processes of human growth and maturation and (b) the various stage-based models that purport to offer a normative pattern of coming out for sexual minority and gender variant individuals. To begin, the next section examines adolescent developmental processes and coming out for LGBTQ people.

ADOLESCENT DEVELOPMENT AND COMING OUT

Traditional developmental theories of human growth and maturation describe adolescence as a transitional stage during which the young person confronts unique opportunities and challenges leading to maturation. Erikson (1963) considered the ultimate goal of the adolescent stage to be establishment of a secure identity, or a positive but realistic appraisal of the self, which then allows for the ability to genuinely merge with another in an intimate relationship. Erikson identified three essential challenges of this period: (a) the establishment of positive reciprocal relationships with a group of peers, (b) the achievement of emotional independence from parents or primary caretakers, and (c) the progressive move toward a recognizable self-identity. Bowlby (1969) proposed that the quality of parental attachment is a crucial variable in the development of a secure and stable sense of self. Internalized representations of these secure parental connections allow the individual to form stable "self-models," or mental representations of the self (Bowlby, 1973).

However, poor parental attachments can lead to negative internal self-models, which predispose the individual to interpret disappointments and losses as personal failures, thereby increasing vulnerability to depression and other mental health problems.

Holtzen, Kenny, and Mahalik (1995) suggested that disclosing one's sexual or gender orientation to parents can be viewed as an act the child hopes can be contained and supported within a secure-based parental attachment. Disruptions of trust, due to incapacity of the parental bond to accommodate a child's personal disclosure, can precipitate negative views of the self and of the future and contribute to the risk of depression, suicide, and other negative self-enactments. The degree to which a young person is able to accept or embrace parts of the self that are distinctly different from others is predicated on the belief that he or she will ultimately be accepted and loved despite those differences (Malyon, 1981). If the young person has the perception that an important but divergent feature of his or her inner world will be vigorously rejected, "exploration of possible identities is thwarted by [anticipated] devaluation" (Jackson & Sullivan, 1994, p. 97). When there is an intense sense of aversion toward one's perception of self, the adolescent's struggle with identity can become a retreat into "valiant but doomed attempts toward greater conventionality and social conformity" (Coleman, 1985, p. 33). For LGBTQ youth, the dread of rejection of crucial and undeniable core aspects of their identity—sexual and gender identities—often results in a variety of desperate coping or hiding strategies (Martin, 1982). Various coping strategies and ego defenses employed by LGBTQ youth who are struggling with emerging counter-normative identities are explored in the next section.

DEFENSES EMPLOYED BY LGBTQ ADOLESCENTS

Malyon (1981) formulated a series of three "ego defensive" strategies or stages adolescents are likely to employ when dealing with the unwelcome realization that they may be LGBTQ. The three strategies include (a) repression or denial, (b) suppression, and (c) acceptance and disclosure. While these strategies or stages were intended to describe adolescent coming out processes, which is when most LGBTQ individuals make public declarations of sexual orientation and gender identity (Cox, Dewaele, van Houtte, & Vincke, 2011), the patterns described are also representative in the coming out struggles encountered at any age.

REPRESSION/DENIAL

The first adaptive strategy is *repression* or *denial*, in which one simply refuses to accept one's emerging same-sex attractions or gender-variant inclinations. Over time, this requires greater and greater expenditure of intrapsychic energy and often results in long-term emotional costs. At this early stage, individuals may engage in emotional constriction or relational avoidance, disregard personal needs, have overly compliant and overachieving behaviors, or exhibit an avoidant and destructive pattern of excessive caretaking of others at the expense of self-needs. The tendency toward overachieving, excessive caretaking, and people-pleasing is seen as an attempt to compensate for a sense of inadequacy and conceal or "undo" the shameful secret of one's urges

(Isay, 1989). LGBTQ individuals who contend with powerful aversive reactions to the emerging awareness of their sexual and gender identities are at risk of developing emotional and psychic bankruptcy.

SUPPRESSION

A second adaptive mechanism Malyon (1981) identified is the use of *suppression*, which also results in truncation of the identity formation process. Efforts by LGBTQ individuals to suppress unwelcome desires are inevitably doomed to failure as libido increases and sexual pressures mount. In the struggle to suppress sexual desires and attractions, individuals may devise intricate strategies to avoid social situations where unwanted feelings are likely to arise. Social evasion, avoidance of settings where same-sex peer groupings are likely to occur, and absorption in activities in order to keep one's mind off "bad" thoughts are typical activities engaged in to help suppress sexual urges (Rosario et al., 1996; Savin-Williams, 1998). Some efforts to suppress forbidden desires involve near-fanatical involvement in religious practices and activities, overzealousness in athletic or academic competitions, and time-intensive absorption in social clubs and extracurricular activities as ways to avoid same-sex or gender-variant urges. Other youth may attempt to "undo" their emerging same-sex urges by indulging in heterosexual relationships. Some young lesbians seek confirmation that they are not gay by becoming pregnant as a form of public proof. Other adolescents choose to enter into a sexual moratorium, strategically waiting until they are away at college or safely out on their own before allowing themselves the normalizing experiences of exploring sexuality and gender nonconforming expression (Chapman, & Brannock, 1987; Sullivan & Schneider, 1987). Ultimately, the failure to suppress unwelcome thoughts and urges often results in an intensifying sense of self-loathing that may lead to self-destructive behaviors. Concurrent with this failure to suppress is the mounting human need for authenticity and personal integrity that pushes for self-acceptance and self-disclosure (Smith & Gray, 2009). For many people the reason they report finally deciding to come out is because they "just couldn't keep living a lie" (Savin-Williams, 1989).

ACCEPTANCE AND DISCLOSURE

Malyon's third adaptive mechanism is *acceptance and disclosure*. Most LGBTQ individuals clearly remember the time they first told someone about their sexual orientation or gender identity. For many, this significant event results in self-acceptance of their identity as an LGBTQ person exemplified with feelings such as: "[I] finally became myself" (Savin-Williams, 1989). However, along with the numerous benefits of acceptance and disclosure there are significant risks to negotiate. Besides the very real challenges associated with family rejection, loss of friends, physical violence, and expulsion from home (D'Augelli, & Grossman, 2001; Herek, 1988; Hetrick & Martin, 1987), LGBTQ individuals who disclose must then face additional implications of their decision for the rest of their lives. It is important to note that the coming out process does not simply end after the first "coming out" but rather continues across the lifespan within different social circles and settings (e.g., school, work, social events, entering a nursing home or assisted living facility). The next section describes the most well-established models of coming out. These include the models described by Troiden (1979, 1989) and Cass (1984); models for lesbian coming out by Golden (1996) and McCarn and Fassinger (1996); and models of transgender coming out by Lev (2004) and Devor (2013).

PROMINENT COMING OUT MODELS

This chapter exploring issues surrounding the coming out process extends the conversation begun in chapter 4, which examines identity development for LGBTQ individuals. The following narrative enhances that discussion, as the models presented herein review stages, phases, and processes for coming out specifically rather than squarely focusing on how an LGBTQ identity at large is produced. It is helpful to keep in mind that coming out, while complicated and contextual, is contentiously considered one major milestone and source of great struggle in the larger process of identity development for LGBTQ individuals across their lifetime of experiences. At times, some of the narrative may appear duplicative; however, the aim here is to better understand the many ways individuals may or may not come out, especially in response to various situational, familial, and environmental forces.

TROIDEN'S HOMOSEXUAL IDENTITY
DEVELOPMENT MODEL

Troiden (1979, 1989) used the metaphor of "sexual scripts" to explain how sexual identity development occurs and how it impacts the coming out process. These "sexual scripts" inform the individual about what is desired or perhaps not so desired in terms of sexual partners (*the who*), what is and is not proper sexual behavior (*the what*), what are permissible and nonpermissible settings (*the where*), what are acceptable and unacceptable motives for having sex (*the why*), and sanctioned and discredible sexual techniques (*the how*). Troiden (1989) felt the stigma associated with homosexuality makes adolescent identity formation and coming out difficult because (a) it creates a context of guilt and secrecy that discourages gay adolescents from discussing their emerging orientation with either peers or family, (b) it isolates gay youth from other nonsexual normalizing adolescent activities, and (c) it isolates gay youth from other gay individuals who may serve as positive role models, as peer support, and as a means to disconfirm negative stereotypes. While previous generations of LGBTQ youth were exposed to the specifics of social and cultural sexual scripts primarily through indirect observation of LGBTQ adults in their lives, peer communication, and relationships, recent generations of youth obtain messages about such norms primarily via television, movies, the Internet, and other media sources. An important point to make about sexual and gender minority identities is that both are considered to be malleable and fluid concepts that can undergo various changes across the lifespan.

Troiden proposed a four-stage model for homosexual identity acquisition: (a) sensitization, (b) identity confusion, (c) identity assumption, and (d) commitment. The first stage, *sensitization*, describes the awareness individuals have when they begin to realize that they are different from peers and from normative media depictions. This usually occurs prior to puberty and is not usually labeled as sexual differentness or as homosexuality at this point. Following this stage, and typically brought on by the onset of puberty, an individual is likely to experience *identity confusion*. During this period initial experiences of same-sex attraction, arousal, or activity occur along with an absence of heterosexual arousal. Beginning awareness of this distinction usually leads to concerns about whether or not these sensations are indications of homosexuality, which can bring about the onset of considerable inner turmoil, anxiety, and confusion. At this stage the young person usually develops a great need for privacy and perhaps engages in some form of social isolation, and the beginning of self-labeling is initiated, in a sense of coming out to self. Stage 3 involves *identity assumption,* the period during which homosexual identity is established, coming out and disclosure to significant others is accomplished, sexual experimentation is undertaken, and identification with the homosexual subculture is established. Troiden's last stage is *commitment,* during which one's sexual minority status is adopted and integrated into one's life, there is often a commitment to a same-sex relationship, and one's sexual orientation is considered valid and satisfying.

THE CASS MODEL

Vivienne Cass (1984) offered a slightly different view of coming out processes from Troiden (1989). This model was more fully explored in chapter 4 yet here is revisited briefly to examine the function of coming out. Cass emphasized that gay or lesbian sexual identity and coming out is a linear, step-wise process and at the same time the result of an accumulation of small tacit choices (see Nuehring & Fein, 1978) made across an extended time period. In the same fashion, Savin-Williams (1998) describes how many of the young gay male respondents of his research did not experience a dramatic awareness of their sexual orientation and that there was no sudden shift to a new identity; rather, they felt the process to be a gradual, continuous endeavor.

Cass (1979) initially identified a six-stage model for coming out for lesbians and gay men that included (a) identity confusion, (b) identity comparison, (c) identity tolerance, (d) identity acceptance, (e) identity pride, and (f) identity synthesis. *Identity confusion* describes the period in which an individual's increasing awareness of sexual minority attractions comes into conflict with the perception of heterosexual behaviors and results in a general sense of confusion. In *identity comparison*, individuals begin to increase their acceptance that they differ significantly from the norm and that they represent a minority. Subsequently, the individual may come to accept a sense of alienation and isolation from others. In many ways, this comparison with others may help individuals realize they are uniquely different, animating a coming out to self. *Identity tolerance* involves the stage when individuals begin to accept their discrepant identity and increase a sense of commitment to their sexual minority status. At this point, individuals are likely to seek out community resources and information online as well as cultivate contacts within the larger LGBTQ community. In addition, this is when individuals first manage to come out to trusted supports. In *identity acceptance* individuals have mostly accepted their sexual minority identity and have managed coming out among many, if not most, of their significant relationships. Their interactions with the LGBTQ community are frequent and integrated. *Identity pride* describes the stage in which individuals mostly identify as members of the LGBTQ community with a focus on how they are perceived within this community, rather than the mainstream (heteronormative) one. This may prompt political frustration and anger with heterosexist, homophobic, and transphobic discrimination. Finally, *identity integration* involves a stage when individuals are more comfortable interacting with heterosexuals without having to hide or be ambiguous about their orientations or relationships and deftly managing both public and private identities (Cass, 1979).

LESBIAN COMING OUT

Feminist scholars have convincingly established that presumptions of a singular pathway for coming out and identity development among males and females is flawed and, in fact, reflective of the politics of maintaining male privilege. Likewise, assuming that lesbian women establish sexual identities and come out the same as gay men is dubious. Chapman and Brannock (1987) proposed a five-stage model of lesbian coming out and identity development, which subsequent theorists have consistently built upon, including (a) *same-sex orientation,* during which there is an awareness of being different from peers due to as yet unnamed attractions and a "special connection" felt with other women; (b) *incongruence,* during which there is the first undeniable recognition that feelings toward other women are sexual, while coupled with a sense of confusion regarding the lack of desire when faced with expectations to date boys/men; (c) *self-questioning/exploration,* during which one begins to think, "I might be a lesbian" while acting on strong physical/sexual attractions with other women; (d) *self-identification,* during which there is acknowledgement that "I am a lesbian," and the individual feels okay about it; and (e) *choice of lifestyle,* during which there is a conscious decision to seek women as long-term love/sexual mates, accompanied with a sense of belonging to the lesbian community.

McCarn and Fassinger (1996) proposed a four-stage model arising from an extended study of lesbian women that incorporated both individual awareness and group awareness. The first stage, *awareness,* underscores the coming out process to one's self, and it involves the individual awareness of feeling or being different ("I feel pulled toward women in ways that I don't understand") as well as a group orientation ("I had no idea there were so many lesbian/gay people out there"). The second stage, *exploration,* involves awareness and exploration of strong erotic feelings for other women or, usually, a particular woman: ("The way I feel makes me think I'd like to be sexual with a woman") as well as a group awareness of ("Getting to know lesbian/gay people is scary but exciting"). The third stage, *deepening/commitment,* involves a personal commitment to increase self-knowledge and -fulfillment as well as to begin coming out to others and make concrete choices about sexuality. This involves self-awareness ("I clearly feel more intimate sexually and emotionally with women than with men") and a group awareness ("I get angry about how I and others have been mistreated because of being a lesbian"). Finally, the last stage involves *internalization/synthesis* of love for women into one's overall identity. This is represented by such statements as "I am deeply fulfilled by my relationships with women" and a group sense of cohesion and membership in a lesbian community ("I feel connected and active in the lesbian community"). See chapter 4 for further critique of lesbian coming out and identity development models.

As with coming out processes associated with sexual orientation, the first stage for transgender individuals is to come out to self. This means acknowledging one's own gender identity, recognizing that one is unlike the majority of others, and deciding how and to whom to express this difference. Similar to coming out as lesbian, gay, or bisexual, deciding to disclose to others involves a series of decisions. First one needs to educate oneself about being transgender, what it means, what it involves, and especially what potential dangers may be involved in disclosing. Also, coming out as transgender may be similar to coming out as LGB in that it is crucial to anticipate what it will mean to specific and important relationships. However, as a cautionary note, practitioners should not assume that coming out experiences are always similar when working with sexual minorities when compared to gender minorities.

The onset of puberty is also a critical time for gender nonconforming youth whose experiences of self may be distinctly dissimilar from the gender they were assigned at birth. Awareness of discrepancy between one's felt gender and one's birth identified gender occurs quite young, perhaps as early as two or three years old (Brill & Pepper, 2008; Lev, 2004). While early years can be difficult for children who do not conform to socially sanctioned gender representations, the emergence of puberty and the beginning of the adolescent stage are when the most acute sense of gender dysphoria is often experienced. The degree of dismay, disgust, or rejection about the transformations happening physically, along with heightened gender-specific behavior expectations that accompany adolescent years, generally prompt young transgender individuals to seek help, if sources of support are available. The intensity of this felt dysphoria is often potent enough that young transgender individuals are compelled to declare difference from cisgender peers and family, thus *coming out* as transgender or gender-variant (Mallon, 1999).

Arlene Istar Lev (2004) proposes a six-stage model for the process of transgender identification. Again, some of this content may be duplicative of chapter 4, however note how the model specifically tends to transgender individuals, their families, and clinicians. Lev's model simultaneously describes identity development milestones, including the process of coming out as transgender, as well as the responsibilities of a clinician to best assist their clients in coming out *and into* their identity. Attention here is on the individual's experiences; see chapter 16 for a fuller discussion about practitioner responsibilities and the coming out process for caregivers and families.

Lev's model begins with the first stage of *awareness*, which describes coming out to oneself, when gender nonconforming individuals are often in significant distress about the discrepancy between who they feel themselves to be and who society says they are. In the second stage of *seeking information/reaching out*, gender-variant individuals seek education and support about the meaning of transgender identities and experiences, what the implications might be for them, and how others have managed various transition processes. The third stage involves *disclosure to significant others* (e.g., partners, family, friends, coworkers). The fourth stage involves *exploration of personal identity and self-labeling*; here, transgender individuals explore and construct for themselves various trans* identities. The fifth stage involves the *exploration of transition issues and possible body modification*. In concurrence with identity wishes and desires articulated in the previous stage, individuals begin to explore options of body modification and transition for more consonant identity expression and presentation. The sixth and final stage is *integration, acceptance,* *and posttransition,* in which gender-variant individuals have successfully integrated a transgender identity, that is, their felt and lived experiences involve a full and sustained coming out across all contexts of their lives.

Devor (2013) articulates an alternative 14-stage model for coming out as a gender-variant person that mostly follows Lev's (2004) six stages. However, Devor disarticulates the six stages described by Lev into additional subprocesses. For example, Lev's first stage, *awareness,* becomes four separate stages defined by Devor that include (a) abiding anxiety, (b) identity confusion about originally assigned gender and sex, (c) identity comparisons about originally assigned gender and sex, and (d) discovery of transsexualism. Devor's model does not identify supportive and professional tasks that may be indicated at each stage, and while more exhaustive in its delineation of transgender identity acquisition processes, many consider Lev's model sufficiently comprehensive. Therefore continued discussion related to the Devor model is left to the reader for further exploration elsewhere.

RURAL SETTINGS, INTERSECTING COMPETING IDENTITIES, AND COMING OUT ONLINE

Pubertal changes provide dramatic demarcation separating the sexual latency of childhood from the period during which one becomes the fully sexualized individual of late adolescence and early adulthood. Likewise, this is a crucial period for gender nonconforming individuals who must contend with the hormonal changes of puberty. While adolescence provides a convenient focus for coming out processes, it is important to recognize that individuals come out across the lifespan. Further, no two experiences of navigating the identity process of coming out occur in the same manner for LGBTQ individuals. Many other factors govern the timing, as well as sense of social permission for coming out, including those that may relate to where one lives (e.g., urban vs. rural location); the impact of competing identities (e.g., pubertal changes, race/ethnicity, socioeconomic status, HIV status); and the role of social media and use of online resources (e.g., websites, apps).

RURAL AND URBAN SETTINGS

For those living within rural settings, alternative identity acts, practices, and performances may take precedence over the need to publically come out as LGBTQ (D'Augelli, & Preston, 2002; Sears, 1991; Yarbrough, 2003). For individuals living in small rural communities that value close connections and conservative values, the discovery and acknowledgment of same-sex desires or gender nonconforming realities may prompt individuals to delay or completely avoid coming out. This may be partly due to lack of access to the availability of supports found in more vibrant LGBTQ communities and amenities found in urban settings. In the same regard, other occupational, religious, or family/cultural ties may be considered more important to publicly affirm than personal declarations of sexual orientation or gender identity. Rurally located individuals with same-sex desires and behaviors or gender-variant orientations may simply decline to self-identify because they feel media-driven portrayals of urban LGBTQ cultures simply do not represent them and their lived realities (D'Augelli & Preston, 2002; Gray, 2009). Some rural-based individuals report that tacit acceptance of nonheterosexual and gender-variant identities are relatively common in small communities as long as discretion and overall congruence with community life is presented. Belonging to the local community may take precedence over any perceived need to have same-sex or gender nonconforming identities assume centrality.

COMPETING IDENTITIES

It would be expected that managing multiple identities based on sexuality, race/ethnicity, religion, and other intersecting factors would significantly increase the difficulty of typical tasks associated with identity development and coming out. Wallace et al. (2002) found that among LGBTQ people of color, the primacy of sexual identities remained secondary to other identities and roles: racial/ethnic identities may be prioritized over sexual identity in response to the many psychosocial and environmental barriers associated with race, ethnicity, and socioeconomic status. The importance of retaining membership "with one's own people" and the special sense of support and belonging this membership affords are especially noted in groups that collectively experience the greatest sense of social marginalization and discrimination (Grov, et al., 2006). Other researchers contend that for many LGBTQ persons of color, the conflict between strong social prohibitions about atypical gender and sexual orientations increases the necessity of alienating and distancing oneself from racial, ethnic, cultural, and religious identities (see LaSala, Jenkins, Wheeler, & Fredricksen-Goldsen, 2008; Meyer, 2010; Nabors et al., 2001; Velez, Moradi, & DeBlaere, 2015).

Negotiating coming out as LGBTQ while also identifying as religiously observant has its own unique struggles. The virulent antigay and transphobic rhetoric of most religious doctrine is among the most damaging and condemning of all social messages an LGBTQ person encounters (Mahaffy, 1996) across the lifespan. To be disapproved of by friends and/or family is one thing, but to be told or believe that "God hates fags" or that one is an "abomination" presents a deep dilemma for many LGBTQ individuals. Over the years, members of the LGBTQ community who choose to come out publically may have been expelled from their church, synagogue, or mosque. The moral and spiritual crisis of faith that comes from feeling excluded from one's core belief system requires a special kind of courage and determination. Oswald (2002) described the importance of *intentionality* and *redefinition* as essential processes in coming out among religiously affiliated individuals. It should be noted that while significant barriers and challenges remain within some religious and faith-based groups, the number of LGBTQ-affirming religious institutions has expanded exponentially over the past few decades. Furthermore, the important and often pivotal role that faith and religion have played within the lives of LGBTQ individuals, couples, and families cannot be underestimated or overlooked. Assisting LGBTQ clients with integrating their various identities (e.g., religious and sexual orientation) may be one of the most challenging tasks faced by practitioners (see Dessel & Bolen, 2014).

THE ROLE OF SOCIAL MEDIA AND ONLINE RESOURCES

A recent and major factor in the coming out process for contemporary LGBTQ individuals is the availability of Internet resources and online chat rooms (Egan, 2000). Coming out in the digital era provides immensely expanded formats for exploring and constructing nonheteronormative and gender-variant identities (Bond, Hefner, & Drogos, 2009; Craig & McInroy, 2014; Gray, 2009; Hillier & Harrison, 2007; Pascoe, 2011). Merely typing key words into search engines (e.g., gay, trans, queer, or coming out) results in immediate access to a teeming world of information including pointers to help with issues related to coming out, dating, sex, being out at school or work, dealing with religious issues, safety precautions and health risks, nearby support groups, and online connections with others. However, despite greater social openness and acceptance of the sexual lives of adolescents, frank discussions between adults and youth about sex, especially nonheterosexual sexuality, remains a rarity. Therefore, most young people rely on online information, including pornography, to learn about sexuality (Tanton et al., 2015).

An additional factor when considering Internet-mediated identity processes is the ready access not only to pornography but to the hazardous landscape of online dating, sex sites, and phone apps. Concerns about the deleterious effect such exposure might have for young people just beginning to develop their sexual identities has been examined by neuroimaging technology (Love, Laier, Brand, Hatch, & Hajela, 2015). Exposure to such quantities and varieties of erotic sexual material has the potential to grossly distort beliefs about healthy human sexuality and negatively impact beliefs about intimate interpersonal relationships (Griffiths, 2001). While dangers of privacy and sharing personal information online persist, the advantages of being able to connect with others and share identity narratives minimizes the isolation and loneliness LGBTQ individuals living in rural and/or socially restrictive settings may experience (Blais, Craig, Pepler, & Connolly, 2008).

Disclosing sexual orientations and gender-variant identities online provides an opportunity to integrate coming out narratives without the very real risks that doing so in real life might have. For most young LGBTQ individuals today, the first disclosures of suspected sexual orientation or gender variance take place in conversations with "trusted friends" online (Craig & McInroy, 2014; Egan, 2000; Hillier & Harrison, 2007). Further, most first-time gay male or lesbian love affairs are transacted entirely through online connections (Bond, Hefner, & Drogos, 2009). As with sexual minority youth, transgender and gender nonconforming youth typically first locate information about themselves and about transgenderism through Internet searches and websites rather than from family members and peers. It is important to recognize that concerns about the existence of a dichotomy between public and private spaces, as well as virtual versus real life, are often confusing concepts for contemporary adolescents. As individuals who have always had access to online and Internet interactions, today's adolescents and young adults are able to easily shift from online to offline spaces and recognize that online interactions are an important and integrated part of their social lives (Alexander & Losh, 2010; Gray, 2009). LGBTQ youth recognize that one advantage of coming out online is that they can do so without fear of reprisal and rejection from families and friends. However, what remains evident is that social media and Internet-based content can provide both avenues of support or potential stress and strain for

LGBTQ youth. Therefore, social workers, practitioners, educators, and family members/care-givers alike should work alongside LGBTQ youth to insure they are receiving helpful and sup-portive messages and content, as well as assist with sorting through nonaffirming, derogatory, or hurtful images and materials.

COMING OUT AT LATER STAGES ACROSS THE LIFESPAN

Coming out across the lifepan can have unique implications, challenges, as well as opportunities for members of the LGBTQ community, especially when considering those within the stages of mid-late adulthood or older adulthood.

MID-LATE ADULTHOOD

Coming out as LGBTQ after adolescence or young adulthood typically follows the same pat-terns and processes as when it occurs during earlier developmental periods (Hunter, 2005; Lee, 1991). However, some of the distinguishing features of coming out in mid-life (e.g., early, mid-, or later adulthood) may involve an extra focus on coming to grips with losses that may have resulted from a lifetime of concessions and compromises made in the effort to "pass" as heterosexual or as gender-conforming. The perilous negotiations of coming out amidst the contexts of long-standing primary relationships, which may include marital partners and children, typically adds additional stressors to the process. Many individuals who decide to come out in mid- or later life must con-tend with a sense of having lived a lie—having lied about themselves to others they care about, as well as to themselves. Friend (1991) proposed that the construction of an affirmative gay/lesbian identity was dependent on the ability to challenge or question the validity of negative internalized heterosexist ideologies. A major part of coming out for those in mid- or older life periods involves reconciliation of previous generations' ideas about what being LGBTQ entails with the relative degree of acceptance present within contemporary society.

Some LGBTQ adults who come out later in mid-life often undergo a pseudo-adolescent period of excessive sexual experimentation and public declarations that might have been preventable had their adolescence been less emotionally constricted by fear, stigma, and internalized homophobia (D'Augelli & Grossman, 2001). Many people from an earlier historical period who look back on their coming out process describe this period of trying to suppress their homosexual or gender nonconforming feelings as one of extreme loneliness and dread (Cox, Dewaele, van Houtte, & Vincke, 2011; Malyon, 1981; Savin-Williams, 1998). They describe a deep sense of dejection that accompanied such efforts as staying home from parties or after-school activities in order to avoid being "found out," obsessively engaging in religious prayer or spiritual practices hoping to cleanse themselves of sinful thoughts, forcing themselves to date or have sex with opposite-sex partners in order to maintain a cover, and feeling the loneliness of having to pretend to be something they increasingly knew they were not. Coming to grips with the grief involved in lost adolescence and young adulthood is often part of the process of the prolonged process of coming out in mid-life, as is the perceived sense of betrayal of loved ones. On the other side of disclosure is the acquisition of a newfound sense of integrity and authenticity.

OLDER ADULTHOOD

The decision to come out as LGBTQ in later life (older or very old adulthood) occurs as the result of multiple social, environmental, and personal factors. As with previous developmental periods, the push for establishing greater personal integrity often motivates the senior LGBTQ individual to seek authentic disclosure and acceptance. This may be experienced with heightened urgency as end-of-life tasks and decisions approach. It may be that certain seniors feel they now have little to lose as a consequence of coming out, as they are widowed, retired, or with grown children so that disclosure is less likely to threaten careers, reputations, or relationships. Coming out in later years is often distinguished from the way the coming out process is navigated in earlier periods across the lifespan in that there is typically less deliberation, strategizing, and/or agonizing about disclosure (Grov et al., 2006). Rather, LGBTQ seniors are likely to make a sudden announcement to family members or close friends.

Even though we live in a time of progressive social change with increased visibility and inclusion of LGBTQ people, it is important to remember that today's LGBTQ older adults came of age in an era that was far less affirming of their identities (Dentato, Orwat, Spira & Walker, 2014). For LGBT elders who come out late in life, or who have come out in earlier periods of life, distinct memories of adversity and social discrimination remain vivid. Seniors, in particular, are likely to remember a sociopolitical time when being LGBTQ was an underground affair and subject to random law enforcement and harmful psychiatric interventions (D'Emilio, 2012; Katz, 1976). For those who managed to come out in a positive and affirmative manner, many developed their own systems of support, affirming communities, and "families of choice." However, the effects of a lifetime of marginalization, social stigma, and prejudice should not be underestimated. Members of this generation came into maturity believing that hiding—presenting as heterosexual and/or gender conforming—was essential to physical, social, and financial survival and safety. Therefore, any assumptions to perceived advantages of being "out" may not be as apparent with older generations of LGBTQ adults.

Another important factor to consider related to the lived identities of older LGBTQ adults and seniors is the legacy of the HIV/AIDS pandemic. For many older LGBTQ individuals who lived through the early years while suffering multiple losses of loved ones, partners, and close friends, along with "discredited" grief processes (Goffman, 1963), intense stigmatization and discrimination surrounding the diagnosis, large-scale caregiver fatigue, and inexplicable survivor's guilt may have left many of them with challenged interpersonal capacities and a lack of resilience and/or coping skills. This must be contrasted to other LGBTQ older adults who emerged from this crisis with an enhanced sense of coping skills, resilience, pride, and self-determination to live their lives with strength and courage (Wierzalis, Barret, Pope, & Rankin, 2006). For many older LGBTQ individuals considering coming out, the shadow of HIV/AIDS may continue to impact or affect their decision to do so.

A different perspective related to coming out is important to explore when related to discussions surrounding LGBTQ seniors seeking assistance with health or mental health care systems. Due to generational experiences of discrimination, stigma, and disrespect, LGBTQ seniors are likely to be suspicious of health-care workers, mental health practitioners, personal care assistants, nursing home staff, and others. Many older adults having lived a secretive and private life, such that their LGBTQ identities were previously hidden, may be faced with the daunting decision to come out to home caregivers, nursing staff members, and administrators or to go back in the closet and recloset themselves due to perceived or actualized stigma and oppression. For more information about the impact of coming out and navigating systems for LGBTQ older adults, chapter 10 in this text.

IMPLICATIONS FOR PRACTICE

Respectful, responsive, and informed practice with LGBTQ individuals who are in the process of coming out requires attention to several key factors. First, and perhaps foremost, is the recognition that coming out, or declaring an LGBTQ identity to self and to others, should be an incredibly powerful act of self-assertion and individual empowerment. In essence, coming out is verbally asserting one's claim of ownership of the self and right to publically declare: "This is who I am!" Therefore, deciding how, to whom, and when to come out constitutes important components of a highly individualized and personal process. Because each individual is uniquely impacted by a vast array of factors such as cultural values, racial and ethnic identifications, religious or spiritual affiliations, family dynamics, experiences of external discrimination and internalized oppression, and access to accepting and receptive communities, the pathways one forges toward public disclosure and integration of an LGBTQ identity are complex, personal, and idiosyncratic. Unfortunately, the ability to choose how, when, and to whom to come out can be denied when an individual is "outed." Adolescents and adults who are "caught" or discovered engaging in LGBTQ relationships face sudden exposure and subsequently lose the ability to manage or control their own disclosure processes. This can severely dampen the positive emotional and developmental effect of coming out by establishing a sense of shame, fear, and disapproval regarding these core identities (D'Augelli, Hershberger, & Pilkington, 1998). Likewise, practitioners who attempt to coerce, direct, or overly influence LGBTQ individuals regarding what they "should" do are wrong-headed and potentially damaging (Morrow, 2004). Individual clients need help exploring decisions about disclosure, especially anticipating potential implications and responses from family and friends. Practitioners need to be ready to balance providing emotional support for the courage it takes to consider coming out with suggesting caution and thoughtful actions about potential repercussions or the need to remain closeted due to safety concerns.

Deciding to come out constitutes an important developmental milestone often seen as a distinctive marker in the life of an LGBTQ individual. A second important realization necessary for practitioners to convey is that while this milestone is truly significant, coming out is actually the first in an ongoing series of disclosures that will continue throughout the lifespan (Morrow, 2004). As distinct from those who identify as heterosexual or cisgender, LGBTQ individuals must continue to "come out" in new social settings and wherever heteronormative and cisgender assumptions dominate. The important implications for practitioners and therapists is related to effectively communicate with their clients that the coming out process involves a series of skills that becomes more refined over time and with practice.

A third practice implication that it is crucial for practitioners working with LGBTQ clients managing the coming out process is to be able to skillfully assess their client's psychosocial functioning. It is important to help clients realistically assess risks and consequences of coming out given the contexts of their social environments and significant relationships (or lack thereof). Being able to engage in authentic and genuine self-representation is clearly associated with improved health and mental health outcomes (Remafedi, 1987); however, it is important to accurately assess for any potential harm that may result from coming out. In fact, some practitioners may have to support clients through periods of remaining closeted to insure their safety (e.g., a youth risking being kicked out due to hostile parents). However, along with identifying any potential risks associated with coming out, it is often quite helpful to identify and mobilize networks of supportive family, friends, and allies.

While assessing psychosocial and environmental contexts is necessary, a fourth key practice implication is the importance of assessing a client's overall LGBTQ identity development. While narratively disclosing one's sense of self is a crucial component of identity construction and consolidation, doing so before one is ready can result in unfortunate negative outcomes. Occasionally, adolescents and others across the age spectrum can impulsively fix upon a transient sexual orientation or gender identity that may be part of overall identity explorations (Rosario et al., 1996; Ryan & Futterman, 1998). Encouraging clients to more fully examine their inclinations regarding sexual orientations and gender identities is in no way meant to suggest the practitioner should actively discourage coming out. However, engaging clients in thoughtful reflection and encouraging informed decisions about coming out can often prevent unnecessary stress, avoid disruption and damage to important relationships, and avert potential harm. Often, it becomes necessary for the practitioner to provide direct guidance and education regarding accurate knowledge about LGBTQ issues (Morrow, 2006). Dispelling misconceptions and dangerous stereotypes that clients may have about LGBTQ identities and lives is important, especially as they prepare to come out to self and to others. Preparing to come out implies the need to be well equipped with accurate information so that one can calmly answer concerns and questions posed by family and friends while also countering potential prejudices and negative concepts. For example, in previous eras, disclosures by gay males were usually met with questions about whether they were living with HIV/AIDS (Paxton, 2002). Ultimately, being prepared for such questions (whether realistic or not) helps the individual to better manage the process of coming out. Providing family members and friends with information about reputable websites and/or local support groups such as PFLAG can be quite helpful, timely, and relevant.

A fifth recommendation involves Ben-Ari's (1995) suggestion that individuals frame their coming out narrative in positive terms, rather than with angry, hostile, or frightening language. Friends and family members are more likely to show support and acceptance when they can feel their son, daughter, or friend is happy and at peace, rather than upset or dismayed about their sexual orientation or transgender identity. Signorile (2003) suggests that LGBTQ individuals explain that the reason they are disclosing something as private as sexual orientation or gender identity to family or close friends is because of the love and importance one feels for those being disclosed to. However, it is also important that the practitioner help prepare the LGBTQ individual for reactions from family and friends that may not be immediately supportive. Professionals might suggest that those disclosing consider how long it has taken them to come to accept their own sexual orientation or gender identity, which may help with being patient with friends and loved ones who may be just now confronted with this news. Along the same line of thought, practitioners may want to consider some form of assessment related to understanding existing or underlying mental health diagnoses or challenges with their LGBTQ clients. This may provide some level of insight related to understanding any additional barriers to the coming out process, communication challenges, or how their clients will navigate receiving negative responses.

In light of the previous discussion on assessment, a sixth practice implication involves the need for practitioners to pay particular attention to the safety of LGBTQ individuals following the first disclosure. Proctor and Groze (1994) caution that even when a young person or adult experiences a supportive and positive coming out reception, the risk of suicide and self-harm is extremely high in the hours and days following the actual coming out. The sense of not being able to turn back, or having sealed one's fate with the public disclosure, can result in sudden remorse, fear, depression, and suicidal ideation. This becomes even more perilous when individuals are met with rejection, expulsion from the home, losing their status at work, or when they have been publicly "outed" by someone else.

Finally, an important point in discussing coming out is the recognition that both gender identities and sexual identities are understood to be malleable and fluid concepts and likely to undergo changes across the lifespan. Similar to other aspects of identity, sexual orientation, and to a lesser degree gender identity, are both constantly in responsive interaction with one's interpretations of the shifting values and beliefs in the larger social environment regarding what it means to be male or female and what it means to be LGBTQ.

CONCLUSION

This chapter's discussion focused on the central features of a pivotal aspect of identity development known as coming out as an LGBTQ individual. Attempting to succinctly capture this complex process unfortunately leads to gross oversimplifications and reductionist depictions. Various models describing the general patterns and processes associated with coming out were presented with an emphasis that each person who undertakes public disclosure of LGBTQ identities does so not in accordance with any of these set models or stages but rather in a unique and idiosyncratic manner. Before discussing these models of coming out, the chapter began with an overview of how the construction of identities occurs within the context of social interactions and how verbal self-statements constitute an essential means by which identities are consolidated.

While the coming out process may follow generally established patterns and processes, important differences are noted when undertaken during adolescence, mid-life, or in later years. Likewise, coming out as a gay male, lesbian, bisexual, or transgender individual constitutes distinctive factors and considerations that are important for clinicians to take into account as they work with individuals who are somewhere in the process of coming out. Risks and concerns important to consider that can result from disclosure were identified and recommendations for helping clients plan for and safely manage these kinds of disclosures were provided. Practitioners are urged to pay special attention to the ways various environmental contexts impact the development of sexual and gender identifications, specifically rural versus urban settings; the intersections with racial, ethnic, and cultural identities; religious affiliations; as well as the opportunities and constraints posed by one's relationship with family members, friends, and community connections. Some of the exciting ways contemporary LGBTQ identities are being mediated by online and social media access was discussed as a promising area for future research and inquiry. A final section on implications for practice outlined general guidelines and recommendations for working with LGBTQ individuals preparing to come out or who may be in the midst of the process.

REFERENCES

Alexander, J., & Losh, E. (2010). A YouTube of one's own? "Coming out" videos as rhetorical action. In C. Pullen & M. Cooper (Eds.), *LGBT identity and online new media* (pp. 37–50). New York: Routledge.

Anderson, M. K., & Mavis, B. E. (1996). Sources of coming out: Self-efficacy for lesbians. *Journal of Homosexuality, 32*(2), 37–52.

Ben-Ari, A. (1995). Coming out: A dialectic of intimacy and privacy. *Families in Society: The Journal of Contemporary Human Services, 76*(5), 306–314.

Blais, J. J., Craig, W. M., Pepler, D., & Connolly, J. (2008). Adolescents online: The importance of Internet activity choices to salient relationships. *Journal of Youth Adolescence, 37*, 522–536.

Bond, B. J., Hefner, V., & Drogos, K. L. (2009). Information-seeking practices during the sexual development of lesbian, gay, and bisexual individuals: The influence and effects of coming out in a mediated environment. *Sexuality & Culture, 13*, 32–50.

Bowlby, J. (1969). *Attachment and loss: Vol. I, Attachment.* New York: Basic Books.

Bowlby, J. (1973). *Separation: Anxiety and anger: Vol. II.* New York: Basic Books.

Brill, S. & Pepper, R. (2008). *The transgender child: A handbook families and professionals.* San Francisco, CA: Cleis Press.

Butler, J. (2015). *Senses of the subject.* New York: Fordham University Press.

Cass, V. C. (1979). Homosexual identity formation: A theoretical model. *Journal of Homosexuality, 4*(3), 219–235.

Cass, V. C. (1984). Homosexual identity formation: Testing a theoretical model. *The Journal of Sex Research 20*(2), 143–167.

Chapman, B. E., & Brannock, J. C. (1987). Proposed model of lesbian identity development: An empirical examination. *Journal of Homosexuality, 14*(3–4), 69–80.

Coleman, E. (1985). Developmental stages of the coming out process. In J. Gonsiorek (Ed.), *A guide to psychotherapy with gay and lesbian clients* (pp. 31–43). New York: Harrington Park Press.

Cox, N., Dewaele, A, van Houtte, M., & Vincke, J. (2011). Stress-related growth, coming out, and internalized homonegativity in lesbian, gay, and bisexual youth. An examination of stress-related growth within the minority stress model. *Journal of Homosexuality, 58*(1), 117–137.

Craig, S. L., & McInroy, L. (2014). You can form a part of yourself online: The influence of new media on identity development and coming out for LGBT youth. *Journal of Gay & Lesbian Mental Health, 18*, 95–109.

Cramer, D. W., & Roach, A. J. (1988). Coming out to Mom and Dad: A study of gay males and their relationships with their parents. *Journal of Homosexuality,15*(3–4), 79–91.

D'Augelli, A. R., & Grossman, A. H. (2001). Disclosure of sexual orientation, victimization, and mental health among lesbian, gay, and bisexual older adults. *Journal of Interpersonal Violence, 16,* 1008–1027.

D'Augelli, A. R., Hershberger, S. L., & Pilkington, N. W. (1998). Lesbian, gay, and bisexual youths and their families: Disclosure of sexual orientation and its consequences. *American Journal of Orthopsychiatry, 68,* 361–371.

D'Augelli, A. R., & Preston, D. B. (2002). Rural men who have sex with men: An exploratory study of sexual orientation characteristics and adjustment patterns. *Journal of Rural Community Psychology,* E-5 (2).

D'Emilio, J. (2012). *Sexual politics, sexual communities.* Chicago: University of Chicago Press.

de Monteflores, C., & Shultz, S. J. (1978). Coming out: Similarities and differences for lesbians and gay men. *Journal of Social Issues, 34,* 59–72.

Dentato, M. P., Orwat, J., Spira, M., & Walker, B. (2014). Examining cohort differences and resilience among the aging LGBT community: Implications for education and practice among an expansively diverse population. *Journal of Human Behavior in the Social Environment, 24*(3), 316–328.

Dessel, A. B., & Bolen, R. M. (2014). *Conservative Christian beliefs and sexual orientation in social work: Privilege, oppression, and the pursuit of human rights.* Alexandria, VA: CSWE Press.

Devor, A. H. (2013). Witnessing and mirroring: A fourteen-stage model of transsexual identity formation. *Journal of Gay and Lesbian Psychotherapy, 8*(1–2), 41–67.

Egan, J. (2000, Dec. 10). Lonely gay teen seeking same: How Jeffrey found friendship, sex, heartache—and himself—online. *The New York Times Magazine,* pp. 110–118.

Erikson, E. (1963). *Childhood and society.* New York: Norton.

Friend, R. A. (1991). Older lesbian and gay people: A theory of successful aging. In J. A. Lee (Ed.), *Gay midlife and maturity* (pp. 99–118). Binghamton, NY: Harrington Park Press.

Griffiths, M. (2001) Sex on the Internet: Observations and implications for internet sex addiction, *The Journal of Sex Research, 38*(4), 333–342.

Goffman, E. (1959). *The presentation of self in everyday life.* New York: Anchor Books/Doubleday.

Goffman, E. (1963). *Stigma: Notes on the management of spoiled identity.* Englewood Cliffs, NJ: Prentice Hall.

Golden, C. (1987). Diversity and variability in women's sexual identities. In Boston Lesbian Psychologies Collective (Eds.), *Lesbian psychologies: Explorations and challenges* (pp. 18–34). Urbana: University of Illinois Press.

Gray, M. L. (2009). Negotiating identities/queering desires: Coming out online and the remediation of the coming-out story. *Journal of Computer-Mediated Communication, 14,* 1162–1189.

Grov, C. Bimbi, D. S., Nanin, J. E., & Parsons, J. T. (2006). Race, ethnicity, gender, and generational factors associated with the coming-out process among gay, lesbian, and bisexual individuals. *Journal of Sex Research, 43*(2), 115–121. doi:10.1080/00224490609552306

Herek, G. M. (1988). Stigma, prejudice, and violence against lesbians and gay men. In J. C. Gonsiorek & J. D. Weinrick (Eds.), *Homosexuality: Research implications for public policy* (pp. 60–80). Newbury Park, CA: SAGE.

Hetrick, E. S., & Martin, A. D. (1987). Developmental issues and their resolution for gay and lesbian adolescents. *Journal of Homosexuality 14*(1–2), 25–43.

Hillier, L., & Harrison, L. (2007). Building realities less limited than their own: Young people practicing same-sex attraction on the Internet. *Sexualities, 10*(1), 82–100.

Holtzen, D. W., Kenny, M. E., & Mahalik, J. R. (1995). Contributions of parental attachment to gay or lesbian disclosure to parents and dysfunctional cognitive processes. *Journal of Counseling Psychology, 42*(3), 350–355.

Hunter, S. (2005). *Midlife and older LGBT adults: Knowledge and affirmative practice for the social services.* New York: Haworth Press.

Icard, L. (1986). Black gay men and conflicting social identities: Sexual orientation versus racial identity. *Journal of Social Work and Human Sexuality, 4*, 83–93.

Isay, R. (1989). *Being homosexual: Gay men and their development.* New York: Avon Books.

Jackson, D., & Sullivan. R. (1994). Developmental implications of homophobia for lesbian and gay adolescents: Issues in policy and practice. *Journal of Gay and Lesbian Social Services, 1*(3–4), 93–109. doi:10.1300/J041v01n03_04

Katz, J. (1976). *Gay American history: Lesbians and gay men in the U.S.A.* New York: Crowell.

Klein, F., Sepekoff, B., & Wolf, T. J. (1985) Sexual orientation: A multi-variable dynamic process. *Journal of Homosexuality, 11*(1–2), 35–49.

LaSala, M. C., Jenkins, D. A., Wheeler, D. P., & Fredriksen-Goldsen, K. I. (2008). LGBT faculty, research, and researchers: Risks and rewards. *Journal of Gay and Lesbian Social Services, 20*(3), 253–267. doi:10.1080/10538720802235351

Lev, A. I. (2004). *Transgender emergence: Therapeutic guidelines for working with gender-variant people and their families.* Binghamton, NY: Haworth Press.

Love, T., Laier, C., Brand, M., Hatch, L., & Hajela, R. (2015). Neuroscience of Internet pornography addiction: A review and update. *Behavioral Science, 5*(3), 388–433. doi:10.3390/bs5030388

Mahaffy, K. A. (1996). Cognitive dissonance and its resolution: A study of lesbian Christians. *Journal for the Scientific Study of Religion. 35*(4), 392–402.

Mallon, G. P. (1999). *Social services with transgender youth.* Binghamton, NY: Haworth Press.

Malyon, A. K. (1981), The homosexual adolescent: Developmental issues and social bias. *Child Welfare, 60*(5), 321–330.

Martin, A. D. (1982). Learning to hide: The socialization of the gay adolescent. *Adolescent Psychiatry, 10*, 52–65.

Marcus, E. (1992). *Making history: The struggle for gay and lesbian equal rights, 1945–1990.* New York: HarperCollins.

McCarn, S., & Fassinger, R. (1996). Revisioning sexual minority identity formation: A new model of lesbian identity and its implications for counseling and research. *The Counseling Psychologist, 24*(3), 508–534.

McKenna, K. Y., & Bargh, J. A. (1998). Coming out in the age of the Internet: Identity "demarginalization" through virtual group participation. *Journal of Personality and Social Psychology, 75*(3), 681–694.

Meyer, I. H. (2003). Prejudice, social stress, and mental health in lesbian, gay, and bisexual populations: Conceptual issues and research evidence. *Psychological Bulletin, 129*(5), 674–697.

Meyer, I. H. (2010). Identity, stress, and resilience in lesbians, gay men, and bisexuals of color. *The Counseling Psychologist, 38*(3), 442–454. doi:10.1177/0011000009351601

Morrow, D. F. (2004). Social work practice with gay, lesbian, bisexual, and transgender adolescents. *Families in Society, 85*(1), 91–99.

Morrow, D. F. (2006). Coming out as gay, lesbian, bisexual, and transgender. In D. F. Morrow, & L. Messinger, (Eds.), *Sexual orientation & gender expression in social work practice: Working with gay, lesbian, bisexual & transgender people.* (pp. 129–149). New York: Columbia University Press.

Nabors, N. A., Hall, R. L., Miville, M. L., Nettles, R., Pauling, M. L., & Ragsdale, B. L. (2001). Multiple minority group oppression: Divided we stand? *Journal of the Gay and Lesbian Medical Association, 5*(3), 101–110.

Newman, B. S., & Muzzonigro, P. G. (1993). The effects of traditional values on the coming out process of gay male adolescents. *Adolescence, 28*(109), 213–126.

Nuehring, E. M., & Fein, S. B. (1978). Tacit choices: A process of becoming. *Pacific Sociological Review, 21*(2), 159–171.

Oswald, R. F. (2002). Resilience within the family networks of lesbians and gay men: Intentionality and redefinition. *Journal of Marriage and Family, 64*(2), 374–383.

Pascoe, C. J. (2011). Resource and risk: Youth sexuality and new media use. *Sexuality Research and Social Policy, 8*, 5–17.

Paxton, S. (2002). The paradox of public HIV disclosure. *AIDS care: Psychological and Socio-Medical Aspects of AIDS/HIV, 14*(4), 559–567. doi:10.1080/09540120208629674

Proctor, C. D., & Groze, V. K. (1994). Risk factors for suicide among gay, lesbian, and bisexual youths. *Social Work, 39*(5), 504–513.

Remafedi, G. (1987). Adolescent homosexuality: Psychosocial and medical implications. *Pediatrics, 79*(3), 331–337.

Rosario, M., Meyer-Bahlburg, H. F. L., Hunter, J., Exner, T. M., Gwadz, M., & Keller, A. M. (1996). The psychosexual development of urban lesbian, gay, and bisexual youths. *Journal of Sex Research, 33*(2), 113–126.

Ryan, C., & Futterman, D. (1998). *Lesbian and gay youth: Care and counseling.* New York: Columbia University Press.

Savin-Williams, R. (1989). Parental influence on the self-esteem of gay and lesbian youth: A reflected appraisals model. *Journal of Homosexuality, 18*(1/2), 93–109.

Savin-Williams, R. L. (1998). *". . . And then I became gay:" Young men's stories.* New York: Routledge.

Sears, J. T. (1991). *Growing up gay in the south: Race, gender and journeys of the spirit.* Binghamton, NY: Harrington Park Press.

Signorile, M. (2003). *Queer in America: Sex, the media, and the closets of power.* Madison: University of Wisconsin Press.

Smith, M. S., & Gray, S. W. (2009). The courage to challenge: A new measure of hardiness in LGBT adults. *Journal of Gay & Lesbian Social Services, 21*(1), 73–89. doi:10.1080/10538720802494776

Somers, M. (1994). The narrative constitution of identity: A relational and network approach. *Theory and Society, 23*(5), 605–649. doi:10.1007/BF00992905

Sullivan, T., & Schneider, M. (1987). Development and identity issues in adolescent homosexuality. *Child and Adolescent Social Work, 4*(1), 13–24.

Tanton, C., Jones, K. G., Macdowall, W., Clifton, S., Mitchell, K. R., Datta, J., . . . Wellings, K. (2015). Patterns and trends in sources of information about sex among young people in Britain: Evidence from three National Surveys of Sexual Attitudes and Lifestyles. *British Medical Journal, 34.* doi:10.1136/bmjopen-2015- 007834.

Taylor, C. (1992). *Sources of the self: The making of the modern identity.* New York: Cambridge University Press.

Troiden, R. R. (1979). Becoming homosexual: A model of gay identity acquisition. *Psychiatry, 42,* 362–353.

Troiden, R. R. (1989). The formation of homosexual identities. *Journal of Homosexuality, 17*(3–4), 43–73.

Velez, B. L., Moradi, B., & DeBlaere, C. (2015). Multiple oppressions and the mental health of sexual minority Latina/o individuals. *The Counseling Psychologist, 43*(1), 7–38. doi:10.1177/0011000014542836

Wallace, B., Carter. R., Nanin, J., Keller, R., & Alleyne, V. (2002). Identity development for "diverse and different others": Integrating stages of change, motivational interviewing, and identity theories for race, people of color, sexual orientation, and disability. In B. Wallace & R. Carter (Eds.), *Understanding and dealing with violence: A multicultural approach* (pp. 41–91). (Roundtable Series on Psychology and Education 379). Thousand Oaks, CA: SAGE.

Wierzalis, E. A., Barret, B., Pope, M., & Rankin, M. (2006). Gay men and aging: Sex and intimacy. In D. Kimmel, T. Rose, & S. David (Eds.) *Lesbian, gay, bisexual, and transgender aging: Research and clinical perspectives,* (pp. 91–109). New York: Columbia University Press.

Yarbrough, D. J. (2003). Gay adolescents in rural areas: Experiences and coping strategies, *Journal of Human Behavior in the Social Environment, 8*(2–3), 129–144.

CHAPTER 6

TRAUMA IMPACTS ON LGBTQ PEOPLE

Implications for Lifespan Development

Megan Gandy-Guedes, Kirsten Havig, Anthony P. Natale, and David A. McLeod

INTRODUCTION

Incredible advances have been made in recent decades that have helped us to understand more about the impact of trauma on the lives of individuals, families, and communities. In this chapter we examine how experiences of trauma intersect with the lives of those within the lesbian, gay, bisexual, transgender and queer (LGBTQ) community. We begin this exploration by defining and conceptualizing trauma and exploring its impact on individuals across the lifespan. From there we go on to quantify the experience of trauma in the lives of people in the LGBTQ community and to explore the many ways that trauma can influence identity development. It should be explicitly understood that this chapter does not take a position suggesting trauma to be a direct influencing factor with regard to the development of sexuality or gender identity. Rather, the intention is to communicate how trauma is related to social constructs, such as restricted access to services or resources or disparate exposure to physical and/or sexual violence. Additionally, it is the aim of this chapter to demonstrate how trauma is directly related to personalized experiences of marginalization for those within the LGBTQ community. The chapter closes with a discussion of trauma-informed care for LGBTQ people through exploring the assessment of affirming theoretical frameworks and therapeutic tools that may be used with individuals, groups, families, and communities.

DEFINING TRAUMA AND ITS IMPACT

Trauma is a highly complex, individualized, and personalized phenomenon that has been defined as an event or series of events or situations that are shocking, terrifying, and/or overwhelming and that produce intense and overpowering feelings of fear or helplessness (Gillece, 2009). With this highly subjective conceptualization of trauma, it is important to take into account the phenomenological nature of the experience; each individual person, family, group, or community can experience trauma in their own personalized and individualized way, and therefore it becomes a more complicated endeavor to attempt to define which experiences qualify as traumatic in any generalizable type of way. What one person may interpret as a traumatic experience another individual with similar life experiences may not interpret as traumatic. It is also important to note that events do not have to be quantifiably *real* in order to be traumatic. Perceptions of traumatic events are highly important when understanding this phenomenon, in that an event need only be perceived to be threating or harmful in order for the results to trigger the same biological traumatic symptoms in the human body (Perry & Pollard, 1998; Perry & Szalavitz, 2007).

Human responses to trauma can be highly varied and may be physiological, psychological, emotional, and spiritual in nature. Along the continuum of physiological responses, human beings can respond to trauma through hyperarousal, which can include dilated pupils, as well as increases in muscle contraction, heart rate, and blood pressure, among other symptoms (Perry & Szalavitz, 2007). It is important to note that physiological and psychological responses to trauma do not operate in isolation. Ties manifesting as behavioral responses can be related to trauma and the physiological characteristics that manifest as a result of it. Classic conceptualizations of *fight, flight, or freeze* responses to adverse situations are directly related to the biological release of cortisol, and the hormones dopamine, epinephrine, and norepinephrine (Perry & Szalavitz, 2007). When people come under stress as related to the conceptualization of being involved in a situation they perceive as traumatic, it is an actual autonomic response to release these hormones at higher levels. This can result in marked shifts in behavior and in psychological functioning. In addition to conditions such as hypervigilance, increased anxiety, and high levels of depression, a common psychological response to trauma is known as dissociation that manifests as a perceived emotional and mental detachment from a significant traumatic event (Carrion & Steiner, 2000; DePrince & Freyd, 2007).

These reactions to stress or trauma are absolutely vital to the survival of human beings and the ability to manage dangerous or threatening situations. However, when states of hyperarousal are maintained for significant durations of time, problematic physiological manifestations of trauma can develop. It is these prolonged and complex experiences of trauma that can produce not only problematic behavioral outcomes in the lives of individuals but also physical manifestations of trauma that can include long-term impacts on neurodevelopment (Perry & Pollard, 1998). Complex trauma can most broadly be defined as a series of acute traumatic experiences, originating from multiple sources, and often manifesting over the trajectory of one's life. Complex trauma has the potential to create exponentially negative impacts as the totality of these traumatic experiences can be far more harmful to the development of a person than the sum of the individual parts (Courtois, 2004; Lawson, Davis, & Brandon, 2013; Wamser-Nanney & Vandenberg, 2013). Complex trauma for children may also involve experiences such as abuse, perpetrated by those trusted to protect and to provide care, compounding the impact of that traumatic experience (Cook, Blaustein, Spinazzola, & van der Kolk, 2003). Research has indicated repeated exposure to traumatic events can lead to persistent and lifelong maladaptive coping mechanisms with specific impairment related to the control of one's cognitive processing, reasoning skills, and problem-solving (Alisic, Jongmans, van Wesel, & Kleber, 2011; Pflugradt & Allen, 2010).

Some of the most important research with regard to trauma, and its impact on the trajectories of people's lives, may be found in the Adverse Childhood Experiences study. This study sample included over 17,000 participants and tracked their lives for multiple decades, allowing for Felitti and colleagues (1998) to document the epidemiological and neurobiological effects of trauma in modern society. The study examined numerous types of traumatic events that occurred in the lives of the participants during childhood that were measured and compared to health, mental health, and behavioral outcomes of the participants' adult lives. The study found overwhelming results to support the notion that traumatic events in early life can disrupt neurodevelopment and have prolonged influence throughout the trajectories of one's life, particularly in terms of their impact as social determinants of health (Foege, 1998). When childhood traumatic exposure occurs, research has also found significant disruptions in social, emotional, and relational capacities along with disruption in cognitive functioning (Dube et al., 2003). The implications of these experiences of trauma and complex trauma are far-reaching. Research has continuously found the effects of prolonged trauma throughout the early lifespan to be correlated with the adoption of lifelong risk-taking and health risk behaviors, comorbid disease and disability, social and relational problems, and even compromised health and early death (Anda et al., 2006; Felitti et al., 1998). Andersen and Blosnich (2013) reported that compared with heterosexual individuals, gay, lesbian, and bisexual individuals have twice the rates of adverse childhood experiences and concluded that sexual minority individuals have increased exposure to multiple developmental risk factors beyond physical, sexual, and emotional abuse. Sexual minority individuals have higher rates of childhood sexual assaults, childhood physical assaults, and emotional maltreatment when compared with their heterosexual peers (Meyer, 2010).

It is important to understand the impact of trauma within the historical context of an individual's life. This is primarily due to the way the trauma leaves its mark. While highly subjective, the effects of trauma on the human brain are both sequential and hierarchical in nature (Perry & Pollard, 1998; Perry & Szalavitz, 2007). This means that traumatic experiences from earlier in life impact reactionary and behavioral patterns and ultimately have an influence on the manner by which an individual manages newer or more recent traumatic experiences. This is particularly important because of the way the brain manages trauma. Trauma has a direct impact on the ability of the brain to coordinate automatic responses to situational events in people's lives (Kaufman, Plotzkey, Nemeroff, & Charney, 2000). Physiological problems manifest in the cerebellum's coordination of depressive or effective responses, the limbic systems control of motor regulation, and the ability of the cerebral cortex to process and organize conscious thought (Kaufman et al., 2000). Quite literally, the psychological perceptions of traumatic experiences impact the physiological responses of the human brain and alter the behavioral mechanisms people employ to manage new traumas, as well as nontraumatic events, as they move forward in life.

This is not to say that human beings are left unable to manage traumatic experiences. In fact, psychological and physiological responses to trauma are the incredible importance in the day-to-day lives of people. The human brain, through its response to traumatic events, demonstrates remarkable adaptation and accommodation to challenges throughout a host of differential environments (Allen, 1995). Physiologically, however, it is the same chemicals that allow for amazing resilience in coping and defense mechanisms that can also have detrimental effects on a person's ability to accurately assess levels of threat or the appropriateness of engagement in high-risk behavior or to engage in healthy and appropriate relational activities. The differentiating factor in how responses to trauma manifest, either negatively or positively, is largely dependent on the meaningfulness associated with how one processes their own experience of trauma and their reactions to it (Appleby, Colon, & Hamilton, 2011). Therefore, how one responds to and makes meaning of a personalized traumatic experience is highly important.

Undoubtedly, the impact of trauma is far-reaching. As a phenomenon, traumatic experiences can occur in isolation. Oftentimes, however, the trauma LGBTQ individuals have experienced is prolonged and significant, originating in their youth and following them into adulthood. While this could be associated to some degree with traumatic experiences in families of origin, the trauma experienced in the LGBTQ community extends to school and workplace settings, faith communities, and other community-based relational settings and can manifest largely through oppression, marginalization, lack of protection, and deprivation from social capital and community-based resources and protections (Root, 1992). Perhaps most important to conceptualize when addressing experiences of trauma within the LGBTQ community is the fact that the experiences of trauma and resilience associated with those experiences are highly personalized and individualized. Far more research is needed to learn more on how the oppressive structures of a heteronormative society can manifest as traumatic in the LGBTQ community. When exploring the complexity of these issues, perhaps some broader amount of perspective may be gained by learning more about unique experiences of particular subgroups of people who identify as LGBTQ.

INCIDENCE AND PREVALENCE

Any discussion of LGBTQ discrimination incidence or prevalence must include the disclaimer that it is safe to assume that discriminatory experiences are woefully unreported or underreported (Meyer, 2003). Stigma and shame are powerful motivators for not coming forward, along with having to manage the uncertainty of knowing whether responses by police, investigators, advocates, or other systems of care will be supportive and affirming. For some, this can increase their trauma and risk by revealing their sexual orientation or gender identity.

ASSAULT ON LGBT PEOPLE

The National Coalition of Anti-Violence Programs (2010) reveals that extreme violence directed at LGBTQ people has remained consistent, with a noteworthy upward trend in severity of violence among certain groups. For example, transgender women, people of color, and gay men face the highest risks for being murdered. Another noteworthy trend is that survivors are not reporting violence to the police citing fear of hostility. The report revealed that transgender survivors were 3.7 times more likely to experience police brutality compared to nontransgender survivors. They are also seven times more likely to experience physical violence when interacting with the police compared to non-transgender people (National Coalition of Anti-Violence Programs, 2010).

The most vulnerable groups for sexual violence are transgender people, gay men, people of color, and undocumented individuals (Rothman, Exner, & Baughman, 2011). The most vulnerable LGBTQ people impacted by sexual violence are those with identities intersecting multiple forms of oppression (e.g., gender identity, race, sexual orientation; Purdie-Vaughns & Eibach, 2008). Incidences of violence often occur in spaces such as the workplace and/or emergency shelters, which are often regarded as safe spaces (National Coalition of Anti-Violence Programs, 2010). Physical violence against LGBTQ individuals is higher in the workplace, including incidents of physical violence against transgender men and sexual violence against lesbian women (Rothman et al., 2011).

INTIMATE PARTNER VIOLENCE

Intimate partner violence is defined as a pattern of behavior where one intimate partner dominates, coerces, or isolates another intimate partner in order to maintain power and control over the partner in the relationship (Rothman et al., 2011). There are various strategies employed by perpetrators to exert control, including abuse that is psychological or emotional, economic, physical, verbal, sexual, or reproductive, as well as through isolation and intimidation.

Estimates range between 2,500 to 5,000 instances of intimate partner violence occur annually in the United States among LGBTQ people (Heintz & Melendez, 2006). Statistics related to intimate partner violence among LGBTQ individuals are generally considered underreported given the degree of stigma that LGBTQ communities face in reporting and/or receiving support. In fact, the number of incidents related to intimate partner violence increased to the highest level ever recorded in 2012 (Walker, 2015). LGBTQ people of color, youth, gay men, and transgender people are most likely to suffer injuries that require medical attention as a result of intimate partner violence (Rothman, et al., 2011). Trends among members of the transgender community show the highest growth of partner violence, particularly with regard to sexual violence (Stotzer, 2009). Transgender survivors are the most likely to receive threats of intimidation and harassment as well (Walker, 2015).

When seeking support for intimate partner violence, LGBTQ individuals face multiple barriers in leaving their violent relationships. They often face pervasive institutional discrimination and homophobia and/or transphobia while receiving less than adequate support from health-care agencies or domestic violence shelters (Walker, 2015). This is particularly true for transgender survivors and even more so for transgender survivors of color (Walker, 2015). It is clear that intimate partner violence complicates the experience of trauma for LGBTQ individuals.

THE ETIOLOGY OF LGBTQ TRAUMA: FEAR AND HATE

It is critical to explore the unique context of LGBTQ experiences of trauma. Homophobia and transphobia fuel hostile environments for LGBTQ individuals in the classroom, workplace, public spaces, social services, healthcare settings, and within their homes (Tomsen & Mason, 2001). Anderson and Blosnich (2013) point out that gender nonconforming behavior is in direct opposition to societal norms. Evidence indicates that adults and peer groups resort to physical violence to correct or censor gender nonconforming behavior of others (Zou, Andersen, & Blosnich, 2013). Mediators such as gender nonconformity may explain the higher prevalence of childhood trauma among LGBTQ people (Balsam, 2002; D'Augelli, Grossman, & Starks, 2008). It is important to note that LGBTQ individuals that are also people of color or who have varying abilities may face additional forms of oppression. Just as the many facets of identity intersect, so too do the forces of discrimination and stigma resulting from membership of minority groups (Purdie-Vaughns & Eibach, 2008) or multiple minority groups.

Trauma experienced by LGBTQ individuals comes in a variety of forms across the lifespan. As children, LGBTQ individuals experience high rates of adverse traumatic experiences with their families, peers and caretakers (Balsam, Lehavot, Beadnell, & Circo, 2010). LGBTQ youth and young adults are disproportionality represented among the homeless population, which produces significant trauma; stemming from the rejection from family of origin and the experience of homelessness (Ray and Berger, 2007). As adults, LGBTQ individuals experience trauma though high rates of hate crimes including verbal, physical and sexual assaults, in addition to intimate partner violence among LGBTQ couples (Corliss, Cochran and Mays, 2002). As older adults, LGBTQ individuals face new challenges in discrimination in housing, social care, and healthcare thereby continuing vulnerability to trauma across the lifespan (Addis, Davies, Greene, et al., 2009).

MULTILEVEL TRAUMA

Root (1992) explains trauma on three different levels, and this conceptualization can be useful when applied to LGBTQ populations: *direct trauma* (that which is experienced directly by the individual); *indirect trauma,* such as hearing about or witnessing another person's traumatic experience; and *insidious trauma,* which encompasses an oppressive cultural narrative (such as that experienced by LGBTQ people in a homophobic and transphobic society) (as cited in Balsam, 2003).

In direct trauma, the LGBTQ individual may experience trauma based on their sexual orientation or gender identity. This trauma has different effects than with a heterosexual or cisgender person who experiences trauma, because it will very likely influence the LGBTQ person's sense of self in relation to their sexual orientation and/or gender identity. Indirect trauma is likened to secondary trauma, when one experiences a trauma response to hearing about someone else's trauma experience. This can happen in a one-on-one basis when LGBTQ individuals reach out to each other for support, or it can happen when LGBTQ individuals view news and media coverage of hate crimes and systemic traumas enacted upon the LGBTQ community. Insidious trauma is related to the heterosexist and cisgenderist influences of society. The systematic marginalization and oppression of LGBTQ individuals creates an "othering" experience, which over time can become a source of trauma. Re-traumatization can be ongoing due to the transphobic and homophobic influences in society, which helps explain why the trauma is "insidious." Until these societal influences are lessened, LGBTQ individuals face ongoing re-traumatization. The previous examples provide ways that trauma can be categorized into the three levels; which help explain the same situation from different angles. For instance, transgender individuals experiencing violence due to their gender identity or expression cuts across all three types of trauma as illustrated in Figure 6.1 below.

Although the direct trauma is closer to the individual, the insidious and indirect traumas act as umbrellas to cast a shadow over the individual experience. The complexity captured in these three levels of trauma provides a useful way to distinguish LGBTQ trauma from heterosexual/cisgender

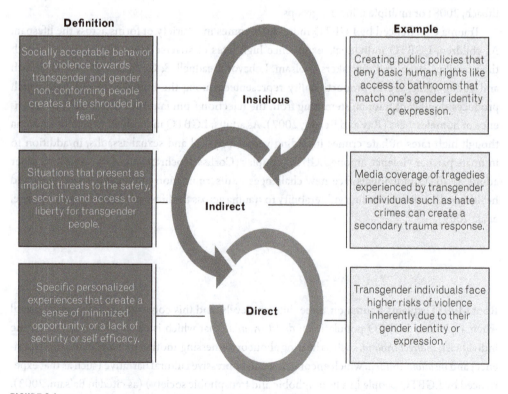

FIGURE 6.1: Violence against transgender people (three levels)

trauma experiences. That is not to say that there are not similarities. Indeed, the beginning of the chapter described biological processes that are considered universal to all humans. The psychological effects are also similar—secrecy, shame, impact on functioning, and other psychological responses to trauma can be seen in both the LGBTQ community and in the heterosexual/cisgender community. Another similarity can be seen among racial minorities and women. There may be a compounding effect due to a person's multiple minority identities. For instance, a woman who is bisexual and African-American has three minority identities based on gender, sexual orientation, and race. Research has found that racism and sexism contribute to racial minorities' experiences of distress over and above that of heterosexism/cisgenderism alone (Szymanski & Meyer, 2008).

The experience of systematic exclusion and powerlessness among racial minorities and women provides a meaningful parallel with the experiences of LGBTQ individuals. Although racism and sexism are not exactly the same as heterosexism or cisgenderism, there are many similarities because of the unique stressors experienced by people within minority populations. For LGBTQ people who cross multiple minority identities, the trauma can be experienced differently. Sometimes a person's racial identity is more salient to their experience of trauma than is their sexual orientation. Thus, there is a need for the practitioner to carefully evaluate trauma experiences of LGBTQ people of color when compared to people who have differing marginalized identities such as HIV status, ability/disability, socioeconomic status and so on.

TYPES OF TRAUMA

LGBTQ individuals experience abuse, assault, victimization, and bullying simply due to their identity. Even *perceived* LGBTQ identity is at play when an aggressor targets an individual that they believe to be LGBTQ, whether or not that individual does indeed identify as such. There are too many tragic examples of youth suicide due to victimization based on actual or perceived LGBTQ identity, some at the age of nine or even younger. Thus the importance of addressing trauma and violence towards LGBTQ individuals is salient across LGBTQ and non-LGBTQ communities. Microaggressions, defined as verbal or physical slights, insults, or acts of violence (Meyer, 2003), can help to explain an interpersonal level of "insidious trauma" and has a cumulative effect on one's identity development (Richmond, Burnes, & Carroll, 2011).

People with childhood exposure to trauma may struggle in their sexual and/or gender identity development because of the difficulty of separating out the trauma experience from one's LGBTQ identity. This is particularly relevant for those who have experienced childhood sexual abuse. There is no causal link between childhood sexual abuse and a non-heterosexual and/or transgender identity (Walker, Hernandez & Davey, 2012). However, there is an explanation that suggests a young person's gender non-conforming behavior can result in becoming a target for abuse, which links back to homophobia and transphobia (Austin & Craig, 2015; D'Augelli, Grossman, & Starks, 2006; Roberts, Rosario, Corliss, Koenen, & Austin 2012). Yet it is mistakenly viewed by some as a causal linkage between sexual abuse and LGBTQ identification. Indeed, dangerous assertions have been made by discredited sources that link pedophilia to a gay or lesbian sexual orientation. These assertions, denounced by major professional organizations (e.g., American Psychological Association, 2005; American Psychiatric Association, 2013; National Association of Social Workers, 2005), have contributed to the marginalization of survivors and to the continued oppressive stereotypes of

LGBTQ individuals. The trauma is mistakenly associated with one's sexual or gender identity rather than societal ills based on homophobia, transphobia, or personal violence (Richmond, Burnes, & Caroll, 2011) and may lead LGBTQ people to avoid, repress, or delay their sexual orientation or gender identity development. Some LGBTQ individuals, particularly lesbians and bisexual women, have reported experiencing sexual abuse by someone who is trying to "fix" their sexual orientation, which is referred to as "corrective rape" or sometimes "curative rape" (Potgieter, 2006). Literature documents this as a problem for lesbian and bisexual women in South Africa in particular and asserts that it is caused by an effort to coerce them to conform to traditional gender roles in South African society (Moffett, 2006; Morrissey, 2013; Msibi, 2009). This type of victimization is particularly troubling because not only is it sexual assault, but it is also motivated by homophobia. A hate crime such as this is influenced by a sense of power over another person's body and illustrates the intersectional dimensions present within this form of trauma.

Reparative therapy (also known as conversion therapy or sexual orientation change efforts) is a denounced and harmful practice in which a therapist guides an individual to change their orientation/identity from LGBTQ to heterosexual and/or cisgender. This treatment has induced trauma, and it is illegal in certain states for mental health practitioners to use such methods (Movement Advancement Project, 2015). This is especially prevalent in religious-based trauma wherein individuals seek *ex-gay* therapy to attempt to change their sexual orientation or gender identity according to their religious beliefs. Some extreme and unethical techniques have historically been involved in reparative therapy, including shock therapy, isolation from others for prolonged periods, and withholding of affection or even nourishment (White, 1994). However, at times there may be religious exemptions written into these laws, so that religious-based counselors or leaders can still practice reparative therapy—leaving many LGBTQ people (especially youth) vulnerable and without protection by the law.

TRAUMA AND IDENTITY DEVELOPMENT

Trauma has the power to radically impact an individual and the way they operate in the world. This is especially concerning for LGBTQ individuals regarding their lifespan and identity development as well as their resources for coping.

ONSET OF TRAUMA AND LIFESPAN/ DEVELOPMENTAL ISSUES

LGBTQ individuals can experience different levels and types of trauma depending on their age of identity disclosure. For instance, children or adolescents who are dependent on their family for support and nurturance could likely experience trauma differently than an LGBTQ adult because they are in a relatively powerless position. This situation may lead youth to either be rejected from their home or leave on their own accord to avoid abuse, which is supported by the disparate rate of homelessness among LGBTQ youth (United States Interagency Council on Homelessness,

2013). Trauma experienced in childhood impacts other areas of development as well. For instance, if an LGBTQ youth experiences bullying or victimization at school, such a hostile environment might likely influence the decision to drop out. If an LGBTQ youth drops out of school, they may face additional challenges related to unemployment, criminal charges for truancy, and difficulty accessing resources.

The age of coming out may be related to the number of victimization experiences. For example, the younger an LGBTQ individual comes out, the more instances of victimization that person may experience over time (D'Augelli, 2003). This is likely because there is more time for victimization experiences to occur over one's lifetime. Experiences of trauma or harassment during the childhood or adolescent years could lead individuals to suppress their identity due to self-hatred or attempts at conforming to a cisgender identity (Levitt & Ippolito, 2014b). This would result in adults who have dealt with the struggle over their identity for years while compounding the effects of different types of trauma, especially indirect and insidious trauma. Individuals who avoid disclosure of their LGBTQ identity until adulthood also may experience negative outcomes.

The insidious trauma is one effect, but the shame and isolation from carrying around a secret can lead to increased levels of depression and anxiety. It also impacts individuals' access to support systems—if individuals isolate from others due to having a secret identity, they are inherently going to have fewer support systems available to them. Also, because identity development models emphasize connection with the LGBTQ community as part of successful identity development, LGBTQ adults who do not disclose their identity status may lack that important connection to community along with progress in their identity development.

IMPACT OF TRAUMA ON IDENTITY DEVELOPMENT

One's sense of self (e.g., self-concept, self-worth, self-esteem) is an important aspect of identity development. Trauma can negatively impact an LGBTQ person's sense of self by stigmatizing it. If the trauma is sexual in nature, sometimes the sense of self can be impacted by the person thinking or believing that the trauma "caused" his or her sexual orientation or gender identity. If the trauma is physical in nature, the sense of self can become shrouded in fear due to the association between the violent experience and the self-identity and can prevent people from fully developing their identity or staying "in the closet." When trauma is insidious and diffused across society and culture, one's sense of self is impacted by the overarching message that one's internal identity is second-class and sometimes even unwanted or perceived as a societal ill. This can have a devastating effect upon one's sense of self, so much so that some LGBTQ individuals have taken their own lives to escape from the traumatic experience.

Even when trauma is not directly associated with one's sexual orientation or gender identity, such as trauma associated with service in the military, trauma from a natural disaster, or nonrelated sexual or physical assault, the ability of LGBTQ individuals to rebound from such trauma is influenced by their access to coping mechanisms and support systems. The unfortunate reality for many LGBTQ people is that they have been stunted in their growth of coping skills and social support because of being ostracized from family and community due to homophobia and/or transphobia. When LGBTQ individuals face trauma, no matter the association, they face a steeper climb toward healing and recovery than their non-LGBTQ counterparts (Boskey, 2014; D'Augelli, 2003).

Coming out is an important identity milestone. Trauma can impact this milestone by hindering, prolonging, or preventing it all together. However, sexual orientation or gender identity–based trauma has been found in some instances to facilitate coming out and lead to greater self-acceptance. Coming out may facilitate or hinder healing from traumatic events for LGBTQ individuals. Sometimes coming out is empowering, thus creating a sense of internal and external pride (Balsam, 2002, 2003). The more common impact of trauma on identity development is that individuals might doubt their LGBTQ identity due to the false belief that their trauma "caused" their sexual orientation or gender identity. As stated elsewhere in this chapter, there is no empirical evidence that leads to the conclusion that childhood trauma "causes" an LGBTQ identity. Some individuals postpone coming out because of the fear that their LGBTQ identity will be conflated with their abuse history (Salmon, 2014). This can have an impact on the identity development process, since coming out is an important milestone. On the other hand, LGBTQ-identified individuals who are already out may avoid disclosure of their abuse history for the same fear of conflation.

If individuals are already out and past the "coming out" stage of identity development, they can experience retraumatization because their fully developed identity is suddenly questioned due to the disclosure of a childhood abuse history. This fear of disclosure has detrimental effects because it postpones the healing process from trauma—the longer people wait to address their abuse history in a therapeutic environment, the longer the detrimental effects can make an impact on their overall well-being and functioning. When LGBTQ-identified adults seek treatment for childhood sexual trauma, the healing process may be hindered if the focus is on causation. LGBTQ individuals who wait to disclose their history of abuse often experience a heightened sense of shame, marginalization, and isolation because of the compounding effects of heterosexist and cisgender norms within society. They already face a certain degree of shame and secrecy due to their LGBTQ identity, thus when another layer of shame and secrecy is added to that LGBTQ-identity layer, individuals may face even more of those negative emotional states.

The degree of "outness" can influence an individual's experience of victimization such as hate crimes and intimate partner violence. If individuals are not out, they may be able to avoid hate crimes, but they face a risk if an abusive partner uses the threat of outing them as a form of coercion in the relationship (Balsam, 2002). To avoid victimization, LGBTQ people have had to learn how to "pass" as non-LGBTQ and how to assess situations and settings for safety and determine the degree to which they can be their authentic self (Levitt & Ippolito, 2014a). Unfortunately, gender nonconformity is associated with more experiences of trauma (Lehavot, Molina, & Simoni, 2012). Experiences of trauma related to one's gender identity or expression can lead individuals to reject their transgender identity or expression (Testa et al., 2012), so individuals may conceal their transgender identity or expression due to the anticipation of future victimization.

In general, when someone experiences trauma, the results are often a sense of powerlessness, uncertainty, and other detrimental self-cognitions. When these trauma responses are combined with the challenges of developing an LGBTQ identity, it is easy to understand how complex the recovery process can be for LGBTQ people who have experienced trauma. One study ($N = 81$) found that perception of one's identity can influence the experience of and coping responses to victimization (Willoughby, Doty & Malik, 2010). With a focus on young lesbians, gay men, bisexual men and women, and queer-identified individuals, the study found that those individuals who had a negative view of their sexual orientation had greater psychological distress than those who did not have a negative view of their identity. This highlights the importance of helping individuals to instill a positive identity as early as possible, because it can act as a buffering effect toward the negative aspects of trauma.

COPING WITH TRAUMA

Experiencing abuse can lead to higher suicidal ideation and attempts (Mustanski & Liu, 2013). Indeed, the LGBTQ population has higher incidences of suicide attempts and reports of suicidal ideation (Centers for Disease Control and Prevention, 2014). Transgender youth are especially vulnerable (Boskey, 2014). Some might seek ways to escape from the physical and psychological pain, which can be positive (e.g., involvement in school, work, extracurricular activities) or negative (e.g., drug and alcohol use, risky health behaviors; Levitt & Ippolito, 2014b). However, it is important to note that LGBTQ individuals are not inherently suicidal; most LGBTQ individuals experience no suicidality in their lifetime.

Sometimes LGBTQ survivors of trauma can benefit from embracing their sexual orientation and/or gender identity, rather than avoiding it (Salmon, 2014). Rivera (2002) noted that LGB youth who experienced peer victimization and had posttraumatic stress disorder (PTSD) symptoms were more accepting of their sexual orientation—which may be explained by the victimization forcing them toward greater self-awareness and self-acceptance. Robohm, Litzenberger, and Pearlman (2003) found that lesbians and bisexual women ($N = 227$) who had childhood sexual abuse experiences were more likely to report satisfaction with their sexual orientation than those who did not experience abuse. Thus there may be a level of resiliency in the midst of experiencing negative traumatic effects. For transgender people of color, one study ($N = 11$) found that trauma survivors were able to cope with the aftereffects of trauma due to the resiliency developed by pride in both their racial identity and their gender identity (Singh & McKleory, 2010).

Social support is an important factor for LGBTQ individuals who are coping with trauma. For lesbian youth who were victimized, those who had greater familial support had more positive outcomes than those with little or no support in a study of 206 participants by D'Augelli (2003). The same is likely true for others in the LGBTQ community. Social support grants access to things like emotional coping, resources such as counseling due to health-care coverage and ability to pay, and the overall sense of having someone "on your side." Thus when social supports are limited for LGBTQ people, their ability to cope with trauma is also negatively influenced.

TRAUMA-INFORMED CARE
FOR LGBTQ PEOPLE

Trauma experienced at the individual level is connected to the aggregate harm caused by discrimination against a social group. Anderson, Danis, and Havig (2011) indicate that trauma represents psychological oppression when rooted in violence such as child abuse and hate crimes. Recognition of the ways in which trauma is a reflection of wider oppressive forces is valuable to a trauma-informed approach to work with LGBT individuals or at the organizational level. The ability to make connections beyond the micro level where trauma often manifests is important to understanding key contextual and historical factors that impact the traumatic exposure of today and that, if unheeded, may be recapitulated in the very services designed to heal that trauma.

Historical trauma refers to the longitudinal and targeted oppression and marginalization of a group based on group membership (Braveheart & DeBruyn, 1995) and may help contextualize trauma across space and time. The concept has been developed as a lens through which to contextualize and understand the impact of oppression over time for Native Americans in the United States and has also been applied to highlight the impact on African Americans, members of the Jewish community, and other groups for whom systematic and structural discrimination has persisted over time. The impact of historical trauma for individuals and groups is alienation, damaged trust for privileged groups/oppressors, compounded impact of micro-level drama that occurs against a backdrop of aggregate oppression, and negative results of depression and a loss of self-efficacy (Braveheart & DeBruyn, 1995). As a group, LGBTQ persons have experienced such oppression, cemented by discriminatory laws and practices aimed at limiting freedom and denial of rights. Trauma experienced at the individual level may be connected to structural oppression and resulting trauma, making this historical lens an important consideration for fully understanding violence experienced by LGBTQ people.

The Substance Abuse and Mental Health Services Administration (SAMHSA, 2015), the federal agency charged with improving the quality and availability of prevention, treatment, and rehabilitative services for mental health and substance abuse treatment, is a leader in the promotion of trauma-informed practices. It provides guidelines for engaging in trauma-informed practice at the clinical, organizational, and policy levels and offers information specific to unique and vulnerable populations, including those who identify as lesbian, gay, bisexual, queer, questioning, transgender, or Two-Spirit.

Broadly, SAMHSA recommends that trauma-informed practices must (a) recognize the impact of violence and victimization on an individual's development and coping strategies; (b) center recovery from trauma as a primary goal of intervention and in doing so; (c) utilize an empowerment model or approach in work with people who have been disempowered by traumatic exposure that (d) prioritizes client choice, voice, and control; and (e) insure such practice efforts are firmly rooted in relational collaboration. The importance of creating safety, respect, and trust within the therapeutic relationship, first and foremost with attention to minimizing the possibility of retraumatization, cannot be overstated when providing care. For a population impacted by a shared history marked by discrimination (sometimes from those responsible for providing care and service), doubly impacted by personal trauma exposure, the social worker's first task is establishing trust, without which healing cannot occur. Further, the value of an emphasis on strengths and resilience (versus an approach in which trauma response and adaptation may be pathologized) is also key to both trauma recovery as well as trust building with historically oppressed persons. Significant to the process of trauma intervention is cultural sensitivity that reflects an understanding of and value for each person's unique location, experience, and context. Of particular importance here, when outlining trauma-informed principles, SAMHSA recommends that organizations actively incorporate knowledge of cultural, historical, and gender issues into practice, noting the importance of an organization that eschews stereotypes; attends to the power of language to bias and inclusion; values cultural strengths and resilience, and acknowledges the impact of historical trauma for oppressed and marginalized groups (SAMHSA, 2015). It is at this intersection that trauma-informed care meets culturally competent practice, and such a focus is of particular importance when working with LGBTQ clients.

While the hallmarks of traumatic response include disturbances that may be lifelong, are subjective and unique to an individual, and often overwhelm one's sense of safety, trust, and meaning in the world, a strengths-based frame sheds different light on the aftermath of trauma. The concept of resilience is important to any discussion of traumatic exposure and helps to illustrate those internal and external protective factors that serve to strengthen individuals and communities. Along with posttraumatic stress, posttraumatic growth (PTG) occurs because of—not in spite of—the experience of a traumatic event (Anderson et al., 2011; Saakvitne, Tennen, & Affleck, 1998; Tedeschi & Calhoun, 1995, 1996). It is essential for social workers engaged in trauma-informed practice to be well-versed in the negative outcomes as well as the potential for personal growth and meaning-making stemming from trauma. Skill-building in the areas of assessing for resilience factors and evidence of PTG, eliciting strengths-based reflection with clients, and using these factors of survivorship to promote client health and well-being are central for trauma-informed practice.

Resilience is a foundational concept to a strengths-based perspective on work with populations impacted by trauma and adversity. Resilience is often defined as the ability to rebound after a challenge or difficulty and as the ability to withstand stress through internal and external resources and attributes (Fraser, Richman, & Galinsky, 1999). Internal individual traits such as personality and supportive cultural assets have a complex interactive relationship with key contextual factors such as one's own history, economic resources, and the capacity of the environment to support positive coping to create potentially protective psychological armor. Resilience among LGBTQ people is a key facet to social work intervention and should be proactively identified and built upon as a foundation for hope and growth (Beasley, Jenkins, & Valenti, 2015; Kwon, 2013). Studies have focused on examining key resilience factors and reveal the importance of social support and community to enhancing both resilience and PTG; this is of particular interest when examining the impact of LGBTQ-related organizations and social movements and their benefit not only for the political promotion of equality and justice but also for strength and healing in the midst of individual and community-level adversity and trauma. There are standardized tools available to assist social workers in measuring client resilience (Windle, Bennett, & Noyes, 2011).

PTG is a relatively new concept in the scholarly literature, with much research to date focused on growth of survivors of interpersonal trauma such as sexual assault or exposure to domestic violence (Anderson et al., 2011). PTG is marked by experiences such as improvement in personal coping strategies based on lessons emergent from traumatic exposure; finding personal inner strengths; finding a deeper sense of purpose or meaning to life; arriving at a sense of clearer goals and priorities for one's life; gratitude and appreciation for life, relationships, and other valued elements; and enhanced motivation to give back and to help others (Helgeson, Reynolds, & Tomich, 2006; Linley & Joseph, 2004; Saakvitne et al., 1998). Empirical research supports the existence and benefits of PTG among individuals exposed to trauma, including interpersonal violence (Kunst, Winkel, & Bogaerts, 2010); however, scholarship is still emerging that establishes the nature of the relationship between PTG and PTSD (Schuettler & Boals, 2011). Recovery from trauma is a highly subjective and nonlinear process, and social workers wishing to intervene with survivors at the individual, family, and community level should include assessment for and action around the promotion of PTG as it has been demonstrated as key not only to healing after trauma but as a protective factor for retraumatization. Unfortunately, as discussed, the LGBTQ population as a whole has been found to experience traumatic events at a higher rate compared with the general population, so trauma work infused with an understanding of PTG is both a necessity and a pathway to supportive practice with the community. The value of a strengths-based approach with historically oppressed populations is clear, as discussed earlier in this chapter.

Social work practice with LGBTQ people focused on trauma is enhanced by a PTG perspective. Clinicians can build upon a survivor's resilience and capacity for growth by viewing adversity as an opportunity for growth, while at the same time acknowledging the impact of trauma as it manifests for each individual. The Posttraumatic Growth Inventory (Tedeschi, & Calhoun, 1996) is a useful tool for social workers to explore with clients the growth and meaning behind a past traumatic experience. While not yet applied or studied at the aggregate (group, community) level, it is clear how concepts relevant to PTG may have benefit to a better understanding of and appreciation for the strengths and survival of LGBTQ populations.

CONCLUSION

This chapter began by defining trauma and exploring the impact on various forms of development including psychological, biological, and neurological. It addressed the disparities faced by LGBTQ individuals as a result of increased rates of trauma as compared to their heterosexual and/ or cisgender counterparts. The impact of trauma on identity development was explored, as was the influence of age of onset. The chapter concluded with an overview of trauma-informed practice and suggestions on how PTG and resilience should inform strengths-based social work practice with LGBTQ survivors of trauma.

REFERENCES

Addis, S., Davies, M., Greene, G., MacBride-Stewart, S., & Shepherd, M. (2009). The health, social care and housing needs of lesbian, gay, bisexual and transgender older people: A review of the literature. *Health & Social Care in the Community, 17*(6), 647–658.

Alisic, E., Jongmans, M. J., van Wesel, F., & Kleber, R. J. (2011). Building child trauma theory from longitudinal studies: A meta-analysis. *Clinical Psychology Review, 31*(5), 736–747.

Allen, J. G. (1995). *Coping with trauma: A guide to self-understanding.* Washington, DC: American Psychiatric Press.

Anda, R. F., Felitti, V. J., Bremner, J. D., Walker, J. D., Whitfield, C. J., Perry, B. D., & Giles, W. H. (2006). The enduring effects of abuse and related adverse experiences in childhood. *European Archives of Psychiatry and Clinical Neuroscience, 256*(3), 174–186.

Andersen, J. P., & Blosnich, J. (2013). Disparities in adverse childhood experiences among sexual minority and heterosexual adults: Results from a multi-state probability-based sample. *PLOS One, 8*(1), e54691.

Anderson, K. M., Danis, F. S., & Havig, K. (2011). Adult daughters of battered women: Recovery and post-traumatic growth following childhood adversity. *Families in Society, 92*(2), 154–160. doi:10.1606/1044-3894.4092.

Appleby, G. A., Colon, E., & Hamilton, J. (2011). *Diversity, oppression, and social functioning: Person-in-environment assessment and intervention.* Boston: Allyn & Bacon.

Austin, A., & Craig, S. L. (2015). Transgender affirmative cognitive behavioral therapy: Clinical considerations and applications. *Professional Psychology: Research and Practice, 46*(1), 21–29.

Balsam, K. F. (2002). Traumatic victimization in the lives of lesbian and bisexual women. *Journal of Lesbian Studies, 7*(1), 1–14.

Balsam, K. F. (2003). Trauma, stress, and resilience among sexual minority women: Rising like the phoenix. *Journal of Lesbian Studies, 7*(4), 1–8.

Balsam, K. F., Lehavot, K., Beadnell, B., & Circo, E. (2010). Childhood abuse and mental health indicators among ethnically diverse lesbian, gay, and bisexual adults. *Journal of Consulting and Clinical Psychology, 78*(4), 459–568.

Beasley, C. R., Jenkins, R. A., & Valenti, M. (2015). Special section on LGBT resilience across cultures: Introduction. *American Journal of Community Psychology, 55*(1–2), 164–166. doi:10.1007/s10464-015-9701-7

Boskey, E. R. (2014). Understanding transgender identity development in childhood and adolescence. *American Journal of Sexuality Education, 9*(4), 445–463.

Braveheart-Jordan, M., & DeBruyn, L. (1995). So she may walk in balance: Integrating the impact of historical trauma in the treatment of Native American Indian women. In Jeanne Adleman & Gloria M. Enguidanos (Eds.), *Racism in the lives of women: Testimony, theory, and guides to antiracist practice* (pp. 345–368). New York: Haworth Press.

Carrion, V. G., & Steiner, H. (2000). Trauma and dissociation in delinquent adolescents. *Journal of the American Academy of Child & Adolescent Psychiatry, 39*(3), 353–359.

Centers for Disease Control and Prevention. (2014). *LGBT youth.* Retrieved from http://www.cdc.gov/lgbthealth/youth.htm

Cook, A., Blaustein, M., Spinazzola, J., & van der Kolk, B. (Eds.). (2003). *Complex trauma in children and adolescents.* National Child Traumatic Stress Network. Retrieved from http://www.NCTSNet.org

Corliss, H. L., Cochran, S. D., & Mays, V. M. (2002). Reports of parental maltreatment during childhood in a United States population-based survey of homosexual, bisexual, and heterosexual adults. *Child Abuse & Neglect, 26*(11), 1165–1178

Courtois, C. (2004). Complex trauma, complex reactions: Assessment and treatment. *Psychotherapy, Theory, Research, Practice, Training, 41*(4), 412–425.

D'Augelli, A. (2003). Lesbian and bisexual female youths aged 14 to 21: Developmental challenges and victimization experiences. *Journal of Lesbian Studies, 7*(4), 9–29.

D'Augelli, A. R., Grossman, A. H., & Starks, M. T. (2006). Childhood gender atypicality, victimization, and PTSD among lesbian, gay, and bisexual youth. *Journal of Interpersonal Violence, 21*(11), 1462–1482.

D'Augelli, A. R., Grossman, A. H., & Starks, M. T. (2008). Gender atypicality and sexual orientation development among lesbian, gay, and bisexual youth: Prevalence, sex differences, and parental responses, *Journal of Gay & Lesbian Mental Health, 12*(1/2), 121–143.

DePrince, A. P., & Freyd, J. J. (2007). Trauma-induced dissociation. In Matthew J. Friedman, Terence M. Keane, & Patricia A. Resick (Eds.), *Handbook of PTSD: Science and practice* (pp. 135–150). New York: Guilford Press.

Dube, S. R., Felitti, V. J., Dong, M., Chapman, D. P., Giles, W. H., & Anda, R. F. (2003). Childhood abuse, neglect, and household dysfunction and the risk of illicit drug use: The adverse childhood experiences study. *Pediatrics, 111*(3), 564–572.

Felitti, M. D., Vincent, J., Anda, M. D., Robert, F., Nordenberg, M. D., Williamson, M. S., & James, S. (1998). Relationship of childhood abuse and household dysfunction to many of the leading causes of death in adults: The Adverse Childhood Experiences (ACE) Study. *American Journal of Preventive Medicine, 14*(4), 245–258.

Foege, W. H. (1998). Adverse childhood experiences: A public health perspective. *American Journal of Preventive Medicine,14*(4), 354–355.

Fraser, M. W., Richman, J. M., & Galinsky, M. J., (1999). Risk, protection, and resilience: Toward a conceptual framework for social work practice. *Social Work Research, 23*(3), 1070–5309.

Gillece, J. B. (2009). Understanding the effects of trauma on lives of offenders. *Corrections Today, 71*(10), 48–51.

Heintz, A. J., & Melendez, R. M. (2006). Intimate partner violence and HIV/STD risk among lesbian, gay, bisexual, and transgender individuals. *Journal of Interpersonal Violence, 21*(2), 193–208.

Helgeson, V. S., Reynolds, K. A., & Tomich, P. L. (2006). A meta-analytic review of benefit finding and growth. *Journal of Consulting and Clinical Psychology, 74*,797–816.

Kaufman, J., Plotsky, P. M., Nemeroff, C. B., & Charney, D. S. (2000). Effects of early adverse experiences on brain structure and function: Clinical implications. *Biological Psychiatry, 48*(8), 778–790.

Kunst, M. J. J., Winkel, F. W., & Bogaerts, S. (2010). Posttraumatic growth moderates the association between violent revictimization and persisting PTSD symptoms in victims of interpersonal violence: A six-month follow-up study. *Journal of Social & Clinical Psychology, 29*(5), 527–545.

Kwon, P. (2013). Resilience in lesbian, gay, and bisexual individuals. *Personality & Social Psychology Review, 17*(4), 371–383. doi:10.1177/1088868313490248

Lawson, D., Davis, D., Brandon, S. (2013). Treating complex trauma: Critical interventions with adults who experiences ongoing trauma in childhood. *Psychotherapy, 50*(3), 331–335.

Lehavot, K., Molina, Y., & Simoni, J. M. (2012). Childhood trauma, adult sexual assault, and adult gender expression among lesbian and bisexual women. *Sex Roles, 67*(5-6), 272–284.

Levitt, H. M., & Ippolito, M. R. (2014a). Being transgender: Navigating minority stressors and developing authentic self-presentation. *Psychology of Women Quarterly, 38*(1), 46–64.

Levitt, H. M., & Ippolito, M. R. (2014b). Being transgender: The experience of transgender identity development. *Journal of Homosexuality, 61*(12), 1727–1758.

Linley, P. A., & Joseph, S. (2004). Positive change following trauma and adversity: A review. *Journal of Traumatic Stress, 17*(1), 11–21.

Meyer, D. (2010). Evaluating the severity of hate-motivated violence: Intersectional differences among LGBT hate crime victims. *Sociology, 44*(5), 980–995.

Meyer, I. H. (2003). Prejudice, social stress, and mental health in lesbian, gay, and bisexual populations: Conceptual issues and research evidence. *Psychological Bulletin, 129*(5), 674–697.

Moffett, H. (2006). "These women, they force us to rape them": Rape as narrative of social control in post-apartheid South Africa. *Journal of Southern African Studies, 32*(1), 129–144.

Morrissey, M. E. (2013). Rape as a weapon of hate: Discursive constructions and material consequences of black lesbianism in South Africa. *Women's Studies in Communication, 36*(1), 72–91.

Movement Advancement Project. (2015). *Conversion therapy laws.* Retrieved from http://www.lgbtmap.org/equality-maps/conversion_therapy

Msibi, T. (2009). Not crossing the line: Masculinities and homophobic violence in South Africa. *Agenda, 23*(80), 50–54.

Mustanski, B., & Liu, R. T. (2013). A longitudinal study of predictors of suicide attempts among lesbian, gay, bisexual, and transgender youth. *Archives of Sexual Behavior, 42*(3), 437–48.

National Coalition of Anti-Violence Programs. (2010). *Hate violence against the lesbian, gay, bisexual, transgender and queer communities in the United States in 2009.* Retrieved from http://www.avp.org/documents/NCAVP2009HateViolence ReportforWeb.pdf

Perry, B. D., & Pollard, R. (1998). Homeostasis, stress, trauma, and adaptation: A neurodevelopmental view of childhood trauma. *Child and Adolescent Psychiatric Clinics of North America. 7*(1), 33–51.

Perry, B. D., & Szalavitz, M. (2007). *The boy who was raised as a dog: And other stories from a child psychiatrist's notebook-what traumatized children can teach us about loss, love and healing.* New York: Basic Books.

Pflugradt, D. M., & Allen, B. P. (2010). An exploratory analysis of executive functioning for female sexual offenders: A comparison of characteristics across offense typologies. *Journal of Child Sexual Abuse, 19*(4), 434–449.

Potgieter, C. (2006). Guest editorial: The imagined future for gays and lesbians in South Africa: Is this it? *Agenda, 67*(2/3), 4–8.

Purdie-Vaughns, V., & Eibach, R. P. (2008). Intersectional invisibility: The distinctive advantages and disadvantages of multiple subordinate-group identities. *Sex Roles, 59*(5–6), 377–391.

Ray, N., & Berger, C. (2007). *Lesbian, gay, bisexual and transgender youth: An epidemic of homelessness.* Washington, DC: National Gay and Lesbian Task Force Policy Institute.

Richmond, K. A., Burnes, T., & Carroll, K. (2011). Lost in trans-lation: Interpreting systems of trauma for transgender clients. *Traumatology, 18,* 45–57.

Rivera, M. (2002). Informed and supportive treatment for lesbian, gay, bisexual and transgendered trauma survivors. *Journal of Trauma & Dissociation, 3*(4), 33–58.

Robohm, J. S., Litzenberger, B. W., & Pearlman, L. A. (2003). Sexual abuse in lesbian and bisexual young women: Associations with emotional/behavioral difficulties, feelings about sexuality, and the "coming out" process. *Journal of Lesbian Studies, 7*(4), 31–47.

Root, M. P. (1992). Reconstructing the impact of trauma on personality. In Laura S. Brown, Mary Ballou, & Lenore E. A. Walker (Eds.), *Personality and psychopathology: Feminist reappraisals* (pp. 229–265). New York: Guilford Press.

Roberts, A. L., Rosario, M., Corliss, H. L., Koenen, K. C., & Austin, S. B. (2012). Childhood gender nonconformity: A risk indicator for childhood abuse and posttraumatic stress in youth. *Pediatrics, 129*(3), 410–417.

Rothman, E. F., Exner, D., & Baughman, A. L. (2011). The prevalence of sexual assault against people who identify as gay, lesbian, or bisexual in the United States: A systematic review. *Trauma, Violence & Abuse, 12*(2), 55–66.

Saakvitne, K. W., Tennen, H., & Affleck, G. (1998). Exploring thriving in the context of clinical trauma theory: Constructivist self development theory. *Journal of Social Issues, 54*(2), 279–299.

Salmon, K. A. (2014). *Just as long as you're not gay: An exploratory study with queer adults on childhood sexual victimization* (Master's thesis). Smith College, Northampton, MA.

Schuettler, D., & Boals, A. (2011). The path to posttraumatic growth versus posttraumatic stress disorder: Contributions of event centrality and coping. *Journal of Loss & Trauma, 16*(2), 180–194. doi:10.1080/15325024.2010.519273

Singh, A. A., & McKleroy, V. S. (2010). "Just getting out of bed is a revolutionary act": The resilience of transgender people of color who have survived traumatic life events. *Traumatology, 17*(2), 34–44.

Stotzer, R. L. (2009). Violence against transgender people: A review of United States data. *Aggression and Violent Behavior, 14*(3), 170–179.

Substance Abuse and Mental Health Services Administration. (2015). *SAMHSA's efforts to address trauma and violence.*, Retrieved from http://www.samhsa.gov/trauma-violence/samhsas-efforts

Szymanski, D. M., & Meyer, D. (2008). Racism and heterosexism as correlates of psychological distress in African American sexual minority women. *Journal of LGBT Issues in Counseling, 2*(2), 94–108.

Tedeschi, R. G., & Calhoun, L. G. (1995). *Trauma and transformation: Growing in the aftermath of suffering.* Thousand Oaks, CA: SAGE.

Tedeschi, R., G., & Calhoun, L. G. (1996). The Posttraumatic Growth Inventory: Measuring the positive legacy of trauma. *Journal of Traumatic Stress, 9*(3), 455–471.

Testa, R. J., Sciacca, L. M., Wang, F., Hendricks, M. L., Goldblum, P., Bradford, J., & Bongar, B. (2012). Effects of violence on transgender people. *Professional Psychology: Research and Practice, 43*(5), 452–459.

Tomsen, S., & Mason, G. (2001). Engendering homophobia: Violence, sexuality and gender conformity. *Journal of Sociology, 37*(3), 257–273.

United States Interagency Council on Homelessness. (2013). *LGBTQ youth homelessness.* Retrieved from http://usich.gov/issue/lgbt_youth/lgbtq_youth_homelessness_in_focus/

Walker, J. K. (2015). Investigating trans people's vulnerabilities to intimate partner violence/abuse. *Partner Abuse, 6*(1), 107–125.

Walker, M. D., Hernandez, A. M., & Davey, M. (2012). Childhood sexual abuse and adult sexual identity formation: Intersection of gender, race, and sexual orientation. *The American Journal of Family Therapy, 40*(5), 385–398.

Wamser-Nanney, R., & Vandenberg, B. (2013). Empirical support for the definition of a complex trauma event in children and adolescents. *Journal of Traumatic Stress, 26*(6), 671–768.

White, M. (1994). *Stranger at the gate.* New York: Plume.

Willoughby, B. L. B., Doty, N. D., & Malik, N. M. (2010). Victimization, family rejection, and outcomes of gay, lesbian, and bisexual young people: The role of negative GLB identity. *Journal of GLBT Family Studies, 6*, 403–424.

Windle, G., Bennett, K. M., & Noyes, J. (2011). A methodological review of resilience measurement scales. *Health and Quality of Life Outcomes, 9*(8), 1–18.

Zou, C., Andersen, J. P., & Blosnich, J. R. (2013). The association between bullying and physical health among gay, lesbian, and bisexual individuals. *Journal of the American Psychiatric Nurses Association, 19*(6), 356–365.

CHAPTER 7

STRENGTHS-AFFIRMING PRACTICE WITH LGBTQ YOUTH

Brian L. Kelly and G. Allen Ratliff

INTRODUCTION

This chapter is intended to provide practitioners with fundamental skills and concepts for understanding social work practice with lesbian, gay, bisexual, transgender, and queer (LGBTQ) youth. As a population subgroup, LGBTQ youth are at risk for numerous factors leading to negative health and social outcomes. LGBTQ youth are at higher risk for experiencing homelessness, HIV and other sexually transmittable infections, substance abuse, violence, family rejection, poor mental and physical health outcomes, incarceration, discrimination, and death (Andersen, Zou, & Blosnich, 2015; Balsam, Rothblum, & Beauchaine, 2005; Bouris, Everett, Heath, Elsaesser, & Neilands, 2016; D'Augelli, Pilkington, & Hershberger, 2002; Frederick, 2014; Pilkington & D'Augelli, 1995; Savin-Williams, 1994; Sterzing, Auslander, & Goldbach, 2014). These increased risk factors are consistent across the globe and are dramatically increased for female youth (Heise, Ellsberg, & Gottmoeller, 2002) and young people of color (Balsam et al., 2015; Button, O'Connell, & Gealt, 2012). Ultimately such risks are very real and can translate into trauma, anxiety, depression, and other poor mental and physical outcomes for LGBTQ youth (Burton, Marshal, Chisolm, Sucato, & Friedman, 2013; D'Augelli et al., 2002; Marshal et al., 2013).

While the purpose of this chapter is to focus on and present strengths-based and affirming approaches to social work practice with LGTBQ youth, we would be remiss to ignore the dire social environments facing many LGBTQ youth across the United States and the consequences of the stigma and violence perpetrated against these young people. Homelessness and bullying are two of the central social problems addressed by social work as a profession that have distinct impacts on LGBTQ youth.

LGBTQ young people are vastly overrepresented within youth homeless populations. Studies have shown that 15% to 48% of homeless youth identify as LGBTQ, with higher percentages of LGBTQ homeless youth living in urban areas (Rosario, Schrimshaw, & Hunter, 2011, 2012;

Van Leeuwen et al., 2006; Whitbeck, Chen, Hoyt, Tyler, & Johnson, 2004). Further, LGBTQ homeless young people experience significantly higher risks for negative outcomes associated with homelessness, including depression, posttraumatic stress disorder, sex trafficking, physical and sexual assault, HIV and other sexually transmitted infections, and substance abuse (Cochran, Stewart, Ginzler, & Cauce, 2002; Frederick, 2014; Keuroghlian, Shtasel, & Bassuk, 2014; Rosario et al., 2011, 2012; Van Leeuwen et al., 2006; Whitbeck et al., 2004). LGBTQ homeless youth consistently report family stress or violence associated with their gender identity or sexual orientation as the reason they are homeless (Rosario et al., 2012).

Bullying is an international concern for LGBTQ youth. Empirical data have shown that LGBTQ youth experience high rates of bullying (Nadal & Griffin, 2011; O'Malley Olsen, Kann, Vivolo-Kantor, Kinchen, & McManus, 2014; Sterzing et al., 2014), including a recent study of sexual minority youth ($N = 125$) in which 58.4% had been bullied within the past month (Sterzing et al., 2014). LGBTQ youth have been shown to be at almost four times the risk of bullying (odds ratio 3.92) compared to heterosexual youth ($n = 75,344$; Mueller, James, Abrutyn, & Levin, 2015). The consequences of bullying for LGBTQ young people are stark, with LGBTQ youth experiencing higher rates of suicidal ideation and depression (Bouris et al., 2016; Burton et al., 2013; Mueller et al., 2015).

As evidenced by the cited work here, these risk factors are often the subject of research, policy, and discourse on the experiences of LGBTQ youth and are at the center of a growing movement for increased awareness and funding of federal and foundation research on sexual and gender minority populations. While the heightened health and mental health risks for LGBTQ youth are important for social workers to understand, it is also important to note that they do not define LGBTQ youth. In this chapter, we promote a social work practice perspective that is strengths-affirming by advocating for practice approaches and models that emphasize the resilience, self-determination, and creativity of LGBTQ young people.

IDENTITY DEVELOPMENT, SELF-DETERMINATION, AND INTERSECTIONALITY

The development of a person's identity, in all of its shapes and complexities, starts during the stages of childhood and progresses through adolescence and into adulthood. These stages are critical with regard to physical, psychological, emotional, and social development for all individuals. This developmental range is where we focus our attention to work with LGBTQ youth in social work practice.

FLUIDITY OF IDENTITY

There is a substantial body of research describing the process by which gender identity and sexual identity develop within the mind and body (Leibowitz & Spack, 2011; Steensma, Kreukels, de Vries, & Cohen-Kettenis, 2013). Gender identity develops through childhood and adolescence (Steensma et al., 2013), but people start to solidify their gender identity at a young age, including many transgender people, even those who do not recognize their gender identity until much later in their lives. Gender identity development is a normative part of human development and experience. For most, it does not contradict the many cultural messages they receive about their gender, from family, friends, teachers, and the media. For some though, including many LGBTQ youth, recognizing and connecting to their gender identity can be a stressful, confusing time.

As children and adolescents develop, their complex identities may change quickly, especially the identities that develop primarily through social and environmental interaction. Throughout their development, children and adolescents are learning whom they find attractive, how they interact with their own bodies and identities in the course of these attractions, and how their identities fit into cultural and social narratives. LGBTQ young people experience these changes like all young people, and they are particularly vulnerable to the ways in which their identities and attractions are understood and interpreted in their social environment (Malekoff, 2014). It is important to note that adolescence is a life stage in which young people experience and respond to rapid developmental, environmental, and hormonal changes. It should come as no surprise, then, to see young people change their dress, mannerisms, interests, and other characteristics during our work with them. This same expectation of change should be applied to our understanding of the gender and sexual identities of young people. See chapter 4 in this text for additional content regarding LGBTQ identity development.

SELF-DETERMINATION AND QUEERING IDENTITY

LGBTQ identities are self-determined. While there are biological, environmental, social, and other factors involved in same-gender attraction and gender identity construction, the identity of lesbian, gay, bisexual, transgender, queer, or other labels may only be selected by the individual. It is inappropriate for anyone else to suggest how another should identify or label themselves. While social work practitioners are trained to understand and document identifying features of our clients, including factors such as gender, age, race/ethnicity, and sometimes gender identity and/or sexual orientation, it is important to ask clients how they wish to be identified in our interactions with them.

A young person who otherwise has identified as heterosexual and cisgender may decide to become sexually or romantically involved with a same-gender peer. Does this suddenly shift their identity to an LGBTQ youth? What if the same-gender relationship lasts a few weeks and this same young person is only in heterosexual relationships moving forward? It is entirely appropriate for a young person to identify as heterosexual and have same-gender sexual partners but not identify as lesbian, gay, or bisexual. It is similarly appropriate for a young person to identify as cisgender male and wear a dress or make-up. From a theoretical framework, we might recognize these two examples of young people within the wider dimension of LGBTQ identities, but it is not our place, or anyone else's for that matter, to choose young people's identity for them. Later in this chapter we discuss the importance of understanding gender fluidity in practice with LGBTQ youth. If one's practice or organization expects documentation of sexual or gender identity of a young person, the best course of action is to ask the young person how they would like to be identified. Being transparent with youth will go a long way toward building strong relationships that may have therapeutic benefits.

INTERSECTIONALITY

Developing a sense of one's gender and sexual identity is a complicated process that does not happen in a vacuum. Not only do young people receive constant messages from their social environment about how to feel or love, but they interact with their social world in a more complex context than just their gender or sexuality. Gender and sexuality are deeply interconnected with cultural messages attached to a person's race, ethnicity, language, immigration status, and ability/disability. The process of understanding how to integrate these identities may be a confusing, anxiety-provoking process (Parks, Hughes, & Matthews, 2004; Rosario, Schrimshaw, & Hunter, 2004). A young person's set of identities is unique, and how those identities are developed, perceived, and expressed is unique as well. It is impossible to describe the multiple variations of identities among LGBTQ youth, but we have chosen a few important examples to build an understanding of the intersectionality of identities experienced by LGBTQ young people. The examples include those associated with immigrant/migrant status, race, ethnicity, and ability/disability.

UNDOCUQUEER

The identities of immigrant youth, and undocumented young people in particular, is a vertex of unique and powerful experiences for LGBTQ youth. Some LGBTQ young people who are undocumented use the label "undocuqueer" to emphasize the overlooked vulnerabilities and needs for undocumented people and their families. Undocuqueer identity and activism is a movement to recognize the ways in which LGBTQ identities are consistently ignored in the wider narrative of immigration, or how immigration status is ignored in the discourse on LGBTQ rights (for additional information see Undocuqueer, 2013).

LATINX

Many languages emphasize gender within vocabulary, in names, pronouns, labels, nouns, and other modes of speech. The use of gender-neutral pronouns and labels is important to many genderqueer and gender nonconforming young people. Latinx is a label for people from Latin American countries. Unlike Latino, Latina, or Latin@, the word "Latinx" moves beyond a gender binary when referring to Latinx people. While this label is new, it is gaining increasing use among LGBTQ Latinx youth (for more information see Reichard, 2015).

LGBTQ YOUTH LIVING WITH DISABILITIES

People living with disabilities are rarely discussed and/or framed as sexual beings, let alone individuals who may experience same-sex desire and/or gender identity fluidity. LGBTQ young people living with disabilities are even less likely to be discussed and/or framed in consideration of their sexuality or gender identity. This pervasive silence perpetuates the marginalization of LGBTQ youth living with disabilities, from both the perspective of LGBTQ people and within the dialogue on creating spaces that are accessible and welcoming for people with disabilities. LGBTQ youth living with disabilities often encounter prejudicial attitudes and acts of discrimination based on the intersection(s) of their disability, gender identity, and sexuality in schools, places of employment, social service agencies, and the larger LGBTQ community (Duke, 2011). LGBTQ youth living with disabilities are a highly diverse population and their evocative message to the masses is gaining ground: "We're here! We're [young, disabled, and] queer! Get used to it!" (Duke, 2011, p. 46).

BLACK LIVES MATTER

The Black Lives Matter movement was started after the shooting of Michael Brown and subsequent national protests focused on the reactions of police brutality in his hometown of Ferguson, Missouri. In the United States, Black Lives Matter has grown into a national movement of young people working toward broad goals of social and economic justice for people of color. Unlike previous civil rights movements and affiliated organizations, Black Lives Matter is inclusive of LGBTQ people and promotes gender and sexuality within its areas of activism and advocacy (for more information see Black Lives Matter, n.d.; Dalton, 2015). LGBTQ youth of color are active members of Black Lives Matter at local and national levels. Many of the Black Lives Matter leaders are young queer women, a stark contrast to the Black Freedom Struggle of the twentieth century, which silenced gay black leaders, such as Bayard Rustin (D'Emilio, 2003).

LANGUAGE AS PRACTICE

The words we use to refer to people are fundamental components in developing effective, safe, and supportive environments. Social workers are often the stewards of respectful, inclusive language in creating affirming environments for their clients, which is a role of vital importance for LGBTQ young people. There are many ways to refer to people, in talking to them and/or about them, some of which may damage relationships and lose young people's trust and respect. In this section we review the language associated with LGBTQ young people and our responsibility in respecting that language. How we talk to and about young people suggests how we understand them, rife with the possibility for helping or harming.

CONFIDENTIALITY AND EXPECTATIONS OF COMING OUT

As social workers, we "meet clients where they are" and engage with them in their context and with respect for their self-determination. LGBTQ young people may not be interested in coming out to family, friends, or others in their environment. This decision may be based on a number of factors, and it highlights the importance of remembering that coming out is not the goal for every LGBTQ youth. For some people, especially LGBTQ youth, coming out may be dangerous, problematic, or painful. If LGBTQ young people do not want to come out, our goal is to work with them and maintain their confidentiality and safety at all times. If LGBTQ young people are unwilling to

come out due to fear of violence, our role is to support them in creating opportunities to reinforce their safety and the confidentiality of their identity. In the same regard, if an LGBTQ youth
appears unaware of the potential for a negative reaction by a family member, caregiver, friend, or
environment (e.g., school), it is our role to assist that youth with understanding safety factors and
support in *not coming out*. This may appear to be disempowering or counterintuitive as practitioners but in fact may provide safer and more appropriate guidance. There are other reasons why
LGBTQ youth might decline to come out, including social environment, religious context, financial support, or simple lack of interest. Regardless of the reason, it is important to create supportive
relationships and environments that respect clients' decisions regarding others' knowledge of their
sexual and gender identities. For more information about coming out experiences unique to the
LGBTQ community and to review models of coming out, see chapter 5 in this text.

LEARNING AND VALIDATING INCLUSIVE LANGUAGE

Before speaking to the specifics of language use with LGBTQ youth, it is important to consider the
process by which inclusive language is learned and validated. When a young person comes to an
agency, school, or private practice, a first step in building a supportive relationship with that young
person is to treat them with respect. The simplest way to ensure that language is respectful is to ask;
however, there is not always an appropriate place or time to ask. Asking for more information must
not put the young person under a microscope, especially if other people (i.e., peers and adults) are
around. In times like these, best practice suggests using context clues to make our best guess as to
the right course of action, always confirming with the young person later if this was in fact the best
tactic.

Learning and validating inclusive language occurs on micro, mezzo, and macro levels. Micro-level
interactions offer optimal ways to learn the language of an individual (Quinlivan & Town, 1999).
One-on-one meetings, intake appointments, therapy sessions, and other person-level interactions
provide an opportunity to ask questions and get to know a person. This is the perfect time to ask a
young person's name, pronouns, and other information that will help build a safe and positive relationship. Mezzo-level interactions, such as facilitating therapy or psychosocial groups in schools or
hospitals with families or others may be more difficult to determine and establish language norms
for young people, particularly in situations when different people know certain pieces of information
about a young person (e.g., a mother knows her son uses female pronouns but the father does not).

Building an agency culture that learns and validates inclusive language may reduce the anxiety
or awkwardness that might emerge when determining how to refer to people and their relationships. It is common in groups, trainings, and meetings to start with introductions, which provide
an excellent opportunity to get to know people and hear how they refer to themselves. More agencies and organizations are including gender pronouns in their introductions for groups or meetings. As a social worker, we might be in the best position to normalize language. For example, we
may introduce ourselves as follows:

"Hi! My name is Allen and I use he/him/his or they/them/their pronouns."
"Hello, my name is Brian and I use he/him/his pronouns."

Including pronouns in introductions normalizes validating inclusive language for everyone and provides an opportunity to learn pronouns of others.

The macro level provides additional opportunities for learning and validating inclusive language, for example by using current events and modeling to demonstrate respectful language. For the first time in US history there are many well-known LGBTQ figures across fields, increasingly even within professional sports, and LGBTQ-related topics (e.g. marriage, adoption, art, etc.) are more prominent in media and contemporary discourse. This creates the opportunity for social workers to refer to these current events using respectful language, names, pronouns, and discussion when working with clients, especially in group settings with young people.

While the current narratives on LGBTQ issues tend to be positive and affirming, there are many situations in which hostility against LGBTQ people may emerge in conversation. The heterosexist, transphobic nature of historical discourse on LGBTQ people and interests continues to be promoted by significant portions of the US government and citizens (e.g., state appeals and lawsuits to recent federal legislation legalizing gay marriage as well as ongoing antitrans legislation at the regional and state level). These negative discourses are at the center of the potential for recurring microaggressions, which are subtle or covert acts of emotional or physical violence against LGBTQ people and other minority groups (Nadal & Griffin, 2011; Nadal et al., 2011). Microaggressions may be difficult to notice by the untrained eye, but it is important to acknowledge them and their destructive power in predominantly hetero- and cisnormative environments. One of the most iconic microaggressions experienced by queer youth is the daily experience of hearing "that's so gay" from their peers. Microaggressions may also be intended as "positive" comments, such as a gay male youth being asked about fashion or to be a shopping buddy, which may serve to essentialize and/or tokenize the youth.

PRONOUNS

At this time, it may be helpful and important to extend the discussion about the importance of understanding pronouns and pronoun usage for practice with LGBTQ youth. Pronouns exist to streamline language, using simple, one-syllable words to refer to a person instead of their multisyllabic names. This function exists in many languages and tends to be centered on a person's gender. This historically based linguistic function emphasizes a binary construction of gender (see Butler [1990] for a critique of this model). This is problematic for a number of reasons, but most relevant to our discussion is how pronouns impact young people. For most of us the pronouns "he," "she," "her," "his," and so on are instinctual; they roll off the tongue without a second thought. We are socialized to understand certain clothing, style, accessories, or mannerisms as attributes of a certain gender, so when we see or meet someone we use pronouns that match our assumptions of gender. For most people this works out just fine, but problems arise when our assumptions of people's gender-based pronouns do not match their actual self-identified gender and corresponding pronouns.

Social workers may be anxiously wondering, "How do I know which pronouns to use?" The most inclusive and validating response is simply to ask the person. Of course the context of the question is critical, people should be asked for their pronouns in a safe, supportive environment.

Most often, this would be in a private and comfortable one-on-one conversation. There may be times when this question comes up in a group setting. Including and validating the practice of stating pronouns in the culture of an organization may diminish the anxiety of asking and telling a person's pronouns. An additional inclusive and validating practice is the inclusion of pronouns in email signatures, which may serve to normalize the process for an organization and young clients.

While most people, including LGBTQ youth, tend to use conventional gender binary pronouns (i.e., he/him/his, she/her/hers), the use of gender-neutral pronouns is a growing and affirming practice. Most notable of these is the use of the singular "they/them/their(s)" while other people use created pronouns like "zie/zir/zir(s)." The pronouns that have been intentionally crafted for their gender neutrality, such as the "zie" and "hir" root pronouns, are usually the most difficult to adopt into common language (Poon, 2015). Becoming comfortable with using pronouns requires thoughtful practice and patience. While the most commonly used pronouns are easiest for us to use, familiarizing ourselves with gender-neutral pronouns will demonstrate commitment to inclusion of clients who use crafted gender-neutral pronouns (Alexander et al., 2014; Leap, 2007).

The most prominent English-language gender-neutral pronoun is the singular "they." A common critique to using "they" is the application of a plural pronoun applied to an individual may create confusion, but rest assured the use of "they" as a singular pronoun has long been supported by linguists. In fact, the American Dialect Society voted the singular "they" as the society's 2015 Word of the Year (American Dialect Society, 2016) and in 2015 the Washington Post Style Guide updated its rules to not only allow "they" but to prioritize its use (Walsh, 2015). When working with LGBTQ young people, "they" is a frequently used pronoun. Building it into the lexicon of one's social work practice will enable one to demonstrate competence in understanding gender and pronouns.

If a young LGBTQ person uses unfamiliar pronouns like "zie" and "hir," there are several online resources available that describe the appropriate application of tenses for these pronouns (Poon, 2015). While first inclination might be to ask the client to teach which pronouns to use, this approach places the impetus for education on the client, not on the social worker. Self-education is a professional responsibility for social workers. While social workers may need to ask LGBTQ youth to clarify and correct language, educating ourselves ahead of time will demonstrate a commitment to creating safe, inclusive, accepting relationships with all clients, especially those who experience marginalization due to their sexual and gender identities.

NAMES

In many cultures, names are associated with gender. In American culture some names are understood as gender neutral, but the majority of names have distinct gender implications. Sarah, Mary, Brenda, Rachel, and Susan are understood to be female names, while Michael, Brian, David, Terrance, and Samuel are understood to be male names. Gender-neutral names are less clear in their gender interpretation. For queer and gender nonconforming young people, the assumption of gender in names may be problematic. Names, especially legal names, are assigned at birth and are often associated with the sex that has been assigned to the newborn. Over time a young person may express gender differently than their sex assigned at birth, which may create problems for that young person when others assume their gender from their name.

In order to avoid this tension, some LGBTQ youth, especially genderqueer and gender non-conforming young people, use names other than their legal names. Some youth use a name that avoids or corrects gender implications, while others use names that better connect to their identity, personality, and experiences. These names might be conventional names, sometimes tied to their legally assigned names. For example, a young person assigned as female and named Louisa at birth might change his name to Louis and use he/him/his pronouns to better match his gender. The same person might use the shortened Lou and use they/them/their pronouns, or any variation of these names or pronouns. Other people might use names completely void of connection to their legal names, gender conventions, and other traditional naming conventions.

There are many times in which social workers are required to complete documentation using a client's legal name. These requirements are often inescapable, mandated by funders, institutions, and laws. It is important to gather mandated information from LGBTQ young people without marginalizing their names and identities. In conversation, use a young person's chosen name and pronouns. In contexts where a young person's legal name must be used, use clarity to differentiate when the use of a legal name is needed and when asking for that person's name. For example, in working with an LGBTQ youth on completing an application for housing that requires their legal name you might say: "For this form I need to use your legal name, but I want to know what name I should call you when I'm talking to you." Additionally, agencies may consider including separate lines for "Legal Name" and "Preferred Name." Doing so contributes to an affirming organizational culture of inclusivity and validation, by signaling to agency staff young people's preferred and legal names for documentation.

Social workers are positioned to interact with a variety of systems and can serve as a model for other service providers on how to refer to queer and gender nonconforming young people. There are important times when a social worker may consider using a young person's legal name outside of specifically legal contexts. Many parents, teachers, peers, or others might be unaware of a young person's identity or have negative or aggressive feelings against LGBTQ people, same-gender relationships, or gender nonconformity. In these situations, use language that is safest for the young person. When working with LGBTQ youth, take time to privately review when and with whom to use preferred and legal names or pronouns. Also, ask young people to keep you updated if situations change, giving you the opportunity to support their process and reinforcing to your clients the importance you place on respecting their identity, confidentiality, and safety.

ROMANTIC AND SEXUAL RELATIONSHIPS

Social work practice with LGBTQ youth must include an understanding of romantic and sexual relationships and how to talk about them. Same-sex or same-gender romantic relationships are no different than opposite-gender relationships, aside from the cultural and institutionalized environments that impact them. Stigma, political discourse, religion/spirituality, coming out experiences, and family support are areas in which same-gender relationships are often treated differently than opposite-gender relationships (Hatzenbuehler, 2009; Istar Lev, 2010; Rosario et al., 2004). Communication, attraction, shared interests, shared values, and other parts of romantic relationships are all components of both same- and opposite-gender relationships. Using gender-neutral language in reference to a young person's special someone may be tricky as relational terms are often gendered. For example, "boyfriend" or "girlfriend" and "husband" or "wife" are words that connote the type of relationship and the gender of the partner involved, whereas language like "significant other," "partner," "spouse," or similar terms are inclusive of all genders.

It is important to ask young people about their relationships from a gender-neutral perspective, especially when first getting to know them. For example, instead of asking a young woman whether she has a boyfriend, asking her if she is "dating anyone" creates space to include other responses (e.g., a girlfriend). In practice situations where information about the gender or sex of a person's sexual partners is needed (e.g., sexual health and/or sexual behavior intake and/or assessment questions) ask directly: "Have your sexual partners been male, female, both, or other?" Or more simply, "Tell me about your sexual partners."

The types of relationships that young people are creating, particularly LGBTQ young people, also challenge conventional assumptions of relationships. Queer young people are often involved in nonmonogamous, polyamorous, open, or communal relationships (D'Augelli, Rendina, Sinclair, & Grossman, 2007). The assumption that a young person has only one sexual/romantic partner, or that having a monogamous, long-term relationship is the ideal, may not apply to all youth. Further, the notion that monogamy is the only healthy relationship option may be communicated through heteronormative social work practice that prioritizes relationships and long-term commitment. Idealizing relationship milestones like engagement, marriage, and having children perpetuates the belief that these are the singular goals of romantic interactions. Social work practice approaches that consider nonmonogamous, polyamorous, open, or communal relationships allow for more inclusive and validating practice with LGBTQ youth. For more information on LGBTQ dating, relationships and coupling, see chapter 8.

FLUIDITY OF IDENTITY AND IMPACT ON LANGUAGE

As previously noted, the fluidity of gender and sexual identity is broadening. It is important for social workers to understand how to work with young people whose gender and sexual identity is fluid (Council on Social Work Education, 2015). The following practice example provides a model of respectful and transparent communication with a gender fluid, nonconforming young person. It also models acceptance and celebration of this fluidity. This example is compiled from the authors' actual practice experience in the field working with LGBTQ youth.

PRACTICE EXAMPLE

A young person named Rick identified as queer, used male pronouns, and dressed in traditionally masculine clothing. One day Rick showed up to a group session wearing a skirt and tube top, lipstick, heels, and a beautiful blonde wig. During introductions, which are done every week in group, Rick introduced herself as "Rihanna" and used she/her pronouns. The next day Rick came to group wearing his baggy jeans, t-shirt, and introduced himself as Rick. The following week Rick came to an individual therapy session wearing her Rihanna clothing. When asked what name she was using today, Rihanna said "If I'm wearing girl clothes then call me Rihanna; if I wear boy clothes call me Rick." In the session that followed she stated that she knew she could come as Rihanna or as Rick and it would be okay because she knew that people at the agency could "keep up." In this practice example with Rihanna the social worker provided her the space to explore her gender fluidity and be whoever she wanted to be, whenever she felt so.

Utilizing such an open and affirming approach in our practice with LGBTQ youth may not always be easy, come naturally, or make us comfortable as practitioners. However, true empowerment of our clients should imply that we remain open to all those that are fluidly expressing their gender and identities in alternating ways, sometimes within the midst of one week such as Rick/Rihanna, to create a strong therapeutic alliance as well as support them in any way possible. At the same time, managing worker bias, assumptions, and stereotypes may mean seeking support through supervision or continuing education or engaging in our own therapy to address personal and professional challenges.

GRAPPLING WITH LANGUAGE AND MAKING MISTAKES

Language mistakes are a normal part of practice when working with young people whose gender and sexual identity may be fluid. If a mistake is made and a young person is addressed using an incorrect name or pronoun, the best response is to apologize to the person as soon as possible and assure them that you will make your best effort to do better next time. Just as using chosen names and pronouns can create unsafe situations for youth in contexts when their name and gender is unwelcome or disrespected, avoid bringing attention to any misnaming or misgendering that occurs toward clients when it would be unsafe for them if you did. Using the previous example, accidentally calling Lou "she" when they use they/them/their pronouns would have different connotations depending on the context. If you called Lou "she" in front of other staff members without Lou present, you may correct yourself and move on. However, calling Lou "she" when in conversation with their unaccepting mother may not be a mistake; it might be what Lou needs to keep them safe when they are at home.

RECOMMENDED MODELS FOR PRACTICE

In the following section we review three recommended practice models that promote the development and implementation of inclusive and validating programs, services, and support systems for LGBTQ young people. The models are positive youth development (PYD), trauma-informed care, and harm reduction. While these models are by no means exhaustive or exclusive, they offer foundational practices for building successful relationships with LGBTQ youth.

POSITIVE YOUTH DEVELOPMENT

PYD is an asset-based, holistic approach to working with young people. It equally incorporates young people's biological (e.g., health management), intellectual (e.g., educational and vocational skills), emotional, and psychological health (e.g., confidence and motivation), as well as their social development (e.g., sense of connectedness and integration; US Department of Health and Human Services, 2007). PYD contrasts prevention-oriented approaches to working with young people, whereby social workers emphasize the prevention of youth problems. Rather, PYD promotes positive development and factors that facilitate the healthy development and well-being of young people (Small & Memmo, 2004). Several prominent youth-serving organizations have adopted PYD models into their structure, including Big Brothers Big Sisters, National 4-H, and Mobility International (Forrest-Bank, Nicotera, Anthony, & Jenson, 2015; Mueller et al., 2011; Sanders, Munford, Thimasarn-Anwar, Liebenberg, & Ungar, 2015; Zarrett & Lerner, 2008). PYD promotes the idea that in order for young people to achieve positive outcomes they must be respected as individuals; their skills, identities, experiences, and motivations must be included and celebrated in society. PYD (Damon, 2004; Dotterweich, 2006) is built on the following beliefs:

1. Young people are a positive, respected, valuable asset to society; youth are integral to the success of their families, school, neighborhoods, communities, and society.
2. Young people are active, engaged participants in their own lives. As experts of their own experiences, youth-focused programs must be built with youth as leaders, decision-makers, planners, spokespeople, and implementers.
3. Healthy development in young people requires the opportunity to experiment and make mistakes within environments that are safe and inclusive.
4. Young people need opportunities to participate in activities that build skills, self-efficacy, a sense of belonging, and respect for others.
5. Youth crave an active examination of issues of social justice, identity, power and privilege, and collaboration.

The Five Cs represent a distillation of the central outcomes for PYD models, with the understanding that positive youth development programs aim for these outcomes from program development to implementation and then evaluation. The Five Cs of PYD (Dotterweich, 2006; Lee & Shek, 2010) are

1. Competence: The motivation and ability to engage in healthy personal practices.
2. Confidence: A sense of mastery, future opportunity, and self-efficacy.
3. Character: A sense of responsibility, individuality, and insight.
4. Connection: Belonging to a community that is safe and structured.
5. Contribution: Involvement as active participant and decision-maker.

PYD emphasizes concepts that are central to creating inclusive spaces for LGBTQ young people. These concepts include framing LGBTQ youth as experts of their own experiences, respecting their identities, and creating safe and inclusive environments for them. An effective, authentic PYD model will be inherently inclusive of the needs of LGBTQ youth by providing safe, structured environments for participants that affirm their individual identities and experiences, while advocating for social justice within young people's communities. An authentic PYD model will recognize, include, and celebrate LGBTQ identities and same-gender relationships. Youth programs that utilize PYD models and seek to ensure the inclusion of LGBTQ youth must find ways to demonstrate an environment of safety and security for young LGBTQ participants. Safe zone training stickers (e.g., rainbow flags, pink triangles, safe zone messaging and logos, etc.) strategically placed on agency and office walls and doors, gender-neutral inclusive and validating language, and gender and sexuality affirming organizational cultures support PYD models that holistically engage LGBTQ youth. For more information on PYD, see Dotterweich (2006).

TRAUMA-INFORMED CARE

A trauma-informed care model recognizes that people are distinctly impacted by complex trauma and these experiences should be addressed in social service programming. LGBTQ youth are unfortunately at higher risk for a constellation of victimization experiences that lead to complex trauma, such as microaggressions, bullying, hate crimes, physical and emotional violence, domestic violence, and child abuse or neglect due to their sexual and gender identities (Axelsson, Modén, Rosvall, & Lindström, 2013; Dank, Lachman, Zweig, & Yahner, 2013; Grossman et al., 2009; Langenderfer-Magruder, Walls, Whitfield, Brown, & Barrett, 2015; Nadal et al., 2011; O'Malley Olsen et al., 2014; Roberts, Rosario, Slopen, Calzo, & Austin, 2013; Russell, Franz, & Driscoll, 2001; Sterzing et al., 2014; Sterzing, Hong, Gartner, & Auslander, 2016). Additionally, LGBTQ youth experience higher rates of polyvictimization (e.g., victimization from multiple sources and typologies), which increases their experiences of complex trauma.

When non-LGBTQ youth experience one form of victimization (e.g., bullying), there may be a safe place to escape the violence (e.g., the bullied youth can go home and escape the bullying). LGBTQ youth are less likely to have access to safe spaces due to increased rates of family nonacceptance, violence, and/or homelessness (Ray, 2006; Rosario et al., 2012). Complex trauma is attributed to a wide range of negative results, including affective disorders, internalizing behaviors (e.g., isolation), externalizing behaviors, (e.g., violence, delinquent behaviors), substance use, sexual risk-taking, revictimization, metabolic or immune disorders, and others (Gabowitz, Zucker, & Cook, 2008; Price, Higa-McMillan, Kim, & Frueh, 2013; Steinberg et al., 2014; Wonderlich et al., 2011a). Young people affected by complex trauma present to social service providers with behaviors that may include fighting, disobedience, hypervigilance, emotional dysregulation, and suspicion, among others.

Trauma-informed care emphasizes three core approaches to addressing complex trauma (Bath, 2008; Ko et al., 2008) that include safety, connections, and emotional regulation. *Safety* addresses the impact of complex trauma on people's fundamental sense of when, where, and with whom they can be genuinely safe. *Connections* address the inhibited ability to establish and maintain functional relationships after experiencing complex trauma. *Emotional regulation* approaches address the diminished function of impulse control, emotionally stability, and self-efficacy. A trauma-informed care model of practice with LGBTQ youth will work to address experiences of interpersonal, community, and systemic violence and disenfranchisement. The three core practices of trauma-informed care will provide the opportunity for LBGTQ young people to address the impacts of complex trauma through safety, connection, and emotional stability (Dittmann & Jensen, 2014; Fava & Bay-Cheng, 2013; Weiner, Schneider, & Lyons, 2009; Wonderlich et al., 2011b).

For LGBTQ young people, safety is paramount. Providers should include sexual orientation and gender identity/expression in their policies and protocols that address safety, inclusion, and antidiscrimination. Any incidence of antigay or antitrans behavior or homophobic/transphobic language must be immediately addressed. Such behaviors might come from other program participants, staff, visitors, administrators, or guests. LGBTQ youth must know and feel that they are physically, psychologically, and emotionally safe from violence.

In building positive, healthy connections with LGBTQ young people, particular attention must be attended to demonstrating respect for pronouns, names, relationships, and the unique cultural context of LGBTQ youth. Recognizing how an LGBTQ identity is integral to young people will foster a culture that signifies that they are safe to build authentic relationships. This can be demonstrated in simple daily interactions, such as asking about a significant other/partner, collaborating with a supportive teacher, or checking in about a difficult interaction with a peer, parent, or caregiver.

Emotional regulation can be a difficult skill to learn and implement, particularly for young people whose neurology is still developing impulse control and emotional regulation. For LGBTQ young people, the hyperarousal that leads to emotional dysregulation is often triggered by attacks (real or perceived) focused on the young person's sexual or gender identity. When an outburst, aggression, or other instance of emotional dysregulation occurs, an intentional response to the incident should be clear to address specific behaviors that a young person can work toward, while validating the triggering event and the emotions associated with it (Fava & Bay-Cheng, 2013; Habib, Labruna, & Newman, 2013).

HARM REDUCTION

LGBTQ youth use substances (e.g., alcohol and other drugs) at higher rates than their heterosexual, cisgender peers (Chow et al., 2013; Kelly, Davis, & Schlesinger, 2015). Substance use is also highly correlated to bullying, which as mentioned previously LGBTQ youth experience at higher rates than their heterosexual counterparts (Sterzing et al., 2014). In addition, transmission rates for HIV are highest in young men who have sex with men (MSM) and young people who are trans-identified, particularly transgender women. Young black MSM and transgender women of color experience the highest rates of HIV seroconversion in the United States (Baral et al., 2013; Millett, Peterson, Wolitski, & Stall, 2006). While these risk areas may not be the priority for some youth-serving programs, implementing harm reduction practices into program models provides opportunities for inclusive, accepting relationships with LGBTQ young people who might be at a higher risk for substance use or sexual risk-taking.

Born out of the substance abuse treatment community, harm reduction was developed as a model for approaching and treating drug and alcohol abuse. In direct contrast to more widely known treatment models that emphasize total abstinence from drug/alcohol use, harm reduction practices do not focus treatment on whether or not a client is using substance. Rather, they focus on the implementation of incremental practices introduced to reduce the harm that substance use creates within a client's life (Little, Hodari, Lavender, & Berg, 2008; Marlatt, 1996). In this way, harm reduction follows the foundational social work adage of "meeting clients where they are"—a priority for any work with LGBTQ young people within social service systems.

Within sexual health education models, especially those relating to HIV prevention, the practice of risk reduction is highly effective in reducing HIV and other sexually transmissible infections in youth (Pedlow & Carey, 2003). Unlike abstinence-only or abstinence-focused sexual health education, comprehensive sexual health education recognizes that most people will engage in sexual activity. Risk reduction promotes the identification and reduction of risks for sexual transmission of infections. Counselors and educators using a risk reduction model support their clients in identifying high-risk behaviors and strategizing on how to reduce those risks. Harm reduction and risk reduction practices are centered on a client's fundamental right to self-determination, recognizing the diversity of human behavior and the relativistic understanding of human uniqueness (Little et al., 2008).

Harm reduction practices offer several important ways of engaging and working with LGBTQ young people. As previously noted, LGBTQ youth often experience stigma and discrimination centered on their identities. Harm reduction models center on the acceptance of clients, "meeting the client where they are," and prioritizing client self-determination (Little et al., 2008). Harm reduction approaches offer social workers important opportunities to work with LGBTQ youth from a foundation of acceptance, which allows young people to play an important and collaborative role in our work with them.

PRACTICE ESSENTIALS

While a particular practice setting may not be conducive to any of these models, perhaps due to size, management, funding, and so on, the models embody several basic ideas that may be distilled into practice essentials in working with LGBTQ youth. In the following section we present these practice essentials and hope you will incorporate them into your own work with LGBTQ youth.

AFFIRMING AND CELEBRATING SELF-DETERMINATION

Young people intrinsically demand acceptance. Social workers must approach all work, regardless of the client population, from the understanding that clients are the experts on their own lives. Social workers are stewards of support, education, and social justice. LGBTQ young people face significant adversity, and it is imperative they not experience it within our practice settings

(Bonvicini & Perlin, 2003; Crisp & McCave, 2007). Thus the tenet of self-determination fully applies as a valuable practice essential. LGBTQ youth have been socialized to understand the social tensions that have been placed upon their identities and will be sensitive to any approach that does not include them as full, valuable participants of the program. As social workers, we should approach our practice with attention to affirmation of the unique and diverse identities of LGBTQ youth.

WORKING TO REDUCE HARM

LGBTQ young people experience disproportionate levels of risk vulnerability. Every day LGBTQ youth experience complex traumas that impact their mental and physical health. Social workers must recognize that LGBTQ youth are at higher risk for harm, both external and internal, and work to create practices that are safe, inclusive, and understanding of this harm. That said, working to reduce harmful and risky behaviors, such as alcohol and substance abuse and/or unprotected sex, must be done in a thoughtful and client-centered way that does not infringe upon the young person's identity or relationships (Adelson, 2012; Duncan, Hatzenbuehler, & Johnson, 2014; Fava & Bay-Cheng, 2013; Leibowitz & Spack, 2011; Pedlow & Carey, 2003).

CREATING SUPPORT

Humans are relational beings; our brains are designed to interact with others. We build relationships for many reasons, and our relationships protect us from harm and provide us with networks of resources and supports. Young people need supportive peers, adults, and health and mental health care systems. Having stable, supportive connections reduce the risks for violence, substance use, poor health, and other outcomes. For LGBTQ youth, who are already more vulnerable to risk and often experience decreased familial support, these connections are vital to achieving positive outcomes throughout life. Mentors, social workers, teachers, coaches, staff members, clinicians, peers, and other supportive relationships create opportunities for LGBTQ youth to have safe spaces to grow and thrive.

WELCOMING THE WHOLE PERSON

LGBTQ youth are greater than their sexuality, their gender identity, and any prejudice and discrimination they may experience as a result of heterosexist, homophobic, and transphobic attitudes, practices, and policies within their social environments. Working within a group setting provides practitioners with opportunities to "welcome the whole" LGBTQ youth and help them identify and develop narratives of resilience and strength (Malekoff, 2014). In addition, groups offer practitioners opportunities to harness important therapeutic factors, such as the instillation of hope and universality (Yalom & Leszcz, 2005), which may serve as important protective and/or promotive functions by letting LGBTQ youth know, if they are struggling with their identity, life does get better and they are certainly not alone in their struggles.

CONCLUSION

Social work practice with LGBTQ youth is exciting and dynamic. Attention to the universal, normative child, adolescent, and young adult developmental milestones as well as the specific needs of LGBTQ young people's sexual and gender identities calls for greater attention to inclusive and validating language, as well as affirming practices, policies, and organizational cultures. In addition, social workers are called to engage with understanding and attentiveness to the fluidity of sexual and gender identity development processes for LGBTQ youth, never categorizing or labeling young people without their input. Positive youth development, trauma-informed care, and harm reduction practice models provide practitioners with important approaches and techniques to ensure social work practice is grounded in affirming the experiences LGBTQ youth and recognizing their inherent strengths. Consideration of inclusive and validating language, along with use of these practice models, and related essential practice skills leads to increased opportunities for strength-affirming practice with LGBTQ youth.

REFERENCES

Adelson, S. L. (2012). Practice parameter on gay, lesbian, or bisexual sexual orientation, gender nonconformity, and gender discordance in children and adolescents. *Journal of the American Academy of Child & Adolescent Psychiatry, 51*(9), 957–974. doi:10.1016/j.jaac.2012.07.004

Alexander, S. C., Fortenberry, J. D., Pollak, K. I., Bravender, T., Østbye, T., & Shields, C. G. (2014). Physicians' use of inclusive sexual orientation language during teenage annual visits. *LGBT Health, 1*(4), 283–291. doi:10.1089/lgbt.2014.0035

American Dialect Society. (2016, January 8). *2015 word of the year is singular "they."* American Dialect Society. Retrieved from http://www.americandialect.org/2015-word-of-the-year-is-singular-they

Andersen, J. P., Zou, C., & Blosnich, J. (2015). Multiple early victimization experiences as a pathway to explain physical health disparities among sexual minority and heterosexual individuals. *Social Science & Medicine, 133*, 111–119. doi:10.1016/j.socscimed.2015.03.043

Axelsson, J., Modén, B., Rosvall, M., & Lindström, M. (2013). Sexual orientation and self-rated health: The role of social capital, offence, threat of violence, and violence. *Scandinavian Journal of Public Health, 41*(5), 508–515. doi:10.1177/1403494813476159

Balsam, K. F., Molina, Y., Blayney, J. A., Dillworth, T., Zimmerman, L., & Kaysen, D. (2015). Racial/ethnic differences in identity and mental health outcomes among young sexual minority women. *Cultural Diversity and Ethnic Minority Psychology, 21*(3), 380–390. doi:10.1037/a0038680

Balsam, K. F., Rothblum, E. D., & Beauchaine, T. P. (2005). Victimization over the life span: A comparison of lesbian, gay, bisexual, and heterosexual siblings. *Journal of Consulting and Clinical Psychology, 73*(3), 477–487. doi:10.1037/0022-006X.73.3.477

Baral, S. D., Poteat, T., Strömdahl, S., Wirtz, A. L., Guadamuz, T. E., & Beyrer, C. (2013). Worldwide burden of HIV in transgender women: A systematic review and meta-analysis. *The Lancet Infectious Diseases, 13*(3), 214–222. doi:10.1016/S1473-3099(12)70315-8

Bath, H. (2008). The three pillars of trauma-informed care. *Reclaiming Children and Youth, 17*(3), 17–21.

Black Lives Matter. (n.d.). *About Black Lives Matter network.* Retrieved from http://blacklivesmatter.com/about/

Bonvicini, K. A., & Perlin, M. J. (2003). The same but different: Clinician–patient communication with gay and lesbian patients. *Patient Education and Counseling, 51*(2), 115–122. doi:10.1016/S0738-3991(02)00189-1

Bouris, A., Everett, B. G., Heath, R. D., Elsaesser, C. E., & Neilands, T. B. (2016). Effects of victimization and violence on suicidal ideation and behaviors among sexual minority and heterosexual adolescents. *LGBT Health, 3*(2), 153–61doi:10.1089/lgbt.2015.0037

Burton, C. M., Marshal, M. P., Chisolm, D. J., Sucato, G. S., & Friedman, M. S. (2013). Sexual minority-related victimization as a mediator of mental health disparities in sexual minority youth: A longitudinal analysis. *Journal of Youth and Adolescence, 42*(3), 394–402. doi:10.1007/s10964-012-9901-5

Butler, J. (1990). *Gender trouble: Feminism and the subversion of identity.* New York: Routledge.

Button, D. M., O'Connell, D. J., & Gealt, R. (2012). Sexual minority youth victimization and social support: The intersection of sexuality, gender, race, and victimization. *Journal of Homosexuality, 59*(1), 18–43. doi:10.1080/00918369.2011.614903

Chow, C., Vallance, K., Stockwell, T., Macdonald, S., Martin, G., Ivsins, A., . . . Duff, C. (2013). Sexual identity and drug use harm among high-risk, active substance users. *Culture, Health & Sexuality, 15*(3), 311–326. doi:10.1080/13691058.2012.754054

Cochran, B. N., Stewart, A. J., Ginzler, J. A., & Cauce, A. M. (2002). Challenges faced by homeless sexual minorities: Comparison of gay, lesbian, bisexual, and transgender homeless adolescents with their heterosexual counterparts. *American Journal of Public Health, 92*(5), 773–777. doi:10.2105/AJPH.92.5.773

Council on Social Work Education. (2015). *Educational policy and accreditation standards.* Retrieved from http://www.cswe.org/File.aspx?id=81660

Crisp, C., & McCave, E. L. (2007). Gay affirmative practice: A model for social work practice with gay, lesbian, and bisexual youth. *Child and Adolescent Social Work Journal, 24*(4), 403–421. doi:10.1007/s10560-007-0091-z

Dalton, D. (2015, October 11). How 4 Black Lives Matters activists handle queerness and trans issues. *The Daily Dot.* Retrieved from http://www.dailydot.com/politics/black-lives-matter-queer-trans-issues/

Damon, W. (2004). What is positive youth development? *The ANNALS of the American Academy of Political and Social Science, 591*(1), 13–24. doi:10.1177/0002716203260092

Dank, M., Lachman, P., Zweig, J. M., & Yahner, J. (2013). Dating violence experiences of lesbian, gay, bisexual, and transgender youth. *Journal of Youth and Adolescence, 43*(5), 846–857. doi:10.1007/s10964-013-9975-8

D'Augelli, A. R., Pilkington, N. W., & Hershberger, S. L. (2002). Incidence and mental health impact of sexual orientation victimization of lesbian, gay, and bisexual youths in high school. *School Psychology Quarterly, 17*(2), 148–167. doi:10.1521/scpq.17.2.148.20854

D'Augelli, A. R., Rendina, J., Sinclair, K. O., & Grossman, A. H. (2007). Lesbian and gay youth's aspirations for marriage and raising children. *Journal of LGBT Issues in Counseling, 1*(4), 77–98. doi:10.1300/J462v01n04_06

D'Emilio, J. (2003). *Lost prophet: The life and times of Bayard Rustin.* New York: Simon & Schuster.

Dittmann, I., & Jensen, T. K. (2014). Giving a voice to traumatized youth—Experiences with trauma-focused cognitive behavioral therapy. *Child Abuse & Neglect, 38*(7), 1221–1230. doi:10.1016/j.chiabu.2013.11.008

Dotterweich, J. (2006). *Positive youth development resource manual.* Retrieved from https://ecommons.cornell.edu/bitstream/handle/1813/21946/PYD_ResourceManual.pdf?sequence=2

Duke, T. S. (2011). Lesbian, gay, bisexual, and transgender youth with disabilities: A meta-synthesis. *Journal of LGBT Youth, 8*(1), 1–52. doi:10.1080/19361653.2011.519181

Duncan, D. T., Hatzenbuehler, M. L., & Johnson, R. M. (2014). Neighborhood-level LGBT hate crimes and current illicit drug use among sexual minority youth. *Drug and Alcohol Dependence, 135*, 65–70. doi:10.1016/j.drugalcdep.2013.11.001

Fava, N. M., & Bay-Cheng, L. Y. (2013). Trauma-informed sexuality education: recognizing the rights and resilience of youth. *Sex Education, 13*(4), 383–394. doi:10.1080/14681811.2012.745808

Forrest-Bank, S. S., Nicotera, N., Anthony, E. K., & Jenson, J. M. (2015). Finding their way: Perceptions of risk, resilience, and positive youth development among adolescents and young adults from public housing neighborhoods. *Children and Youth Services Review, 55*, 147–158. doi:10.1016/j.childyouth.2015.05.015

Frederick, T. (2014). Diversity at the margins: The interconnections between homelessness, sex work, mental health, and substance use in the lives of sexual minority homeless young people. In D. Peterson & V. R. Panfil (Eds.), *Handbook of LGBT communities, crime, and justice* (pp. 473–501). New York: Springer.

Gabowitz, D., Zucker, M., & Cook, A. (2008). Neuropsychological assessment in clinical evaluation of children and adolescents with complex trauma. *Journal of Child & Adolescent Trauma, 1*(2), 163–178. doi:10.1080/19361520802003822

Grossman, A. H., Haney, A. P., Edwards, P., Alessi, E. J., Ardon, M., & Howell, T. J. (2009). Lesbian, gay, bisexual and transgender youth talk about experiencing and coping with school violence: A qualitative study. *Journal of LGBT Youth, 6*(1), 24–46. doi:10.1080/19361650802379748

Habib, M., Labruna, V., & Newman, J. (2013). Complex histories and complex presentations: Implementation of a manually guided group treatment for traumatized adolescents. *Journal of Family Violence, 28*(7), 717–728. doi:10.1007/s10896-013-9532-y

Hatzenbuehler, M. L. (2009). How does sexual minority stigma "get under the skin"? A psychological mediation framework. *Psychological Bulletin, 135*(5), 707–730. doi:10.1037/a0016441

Heise, L., Ellsberg, M., & Gottmoeller, M. (2002). A global overview of gender-based violence. *International Journal of Gynecology & Obstetrics, 78*(Suppl. 1), S5–S14. doi:10.1016/S0020-7292(02)00038-3

Istar Lev, A. (2010). How queer!—The development of gender identity and sexual orientation in LGBTQ-headed families. *Family Process, 49*(3), 268–290. doi:10.1111/j.1545-5300.2010.01323.x

Kelly, J., Davis, C., & Schlesinger, C. (2015). Substance use by same sex attracted young people: Prevalence, perceptions and homophobia. *Drug and Alcohol Review, 34*(4), 358–365. doi:10.1111/dar.12158

Keuroghlian, A. S., Shtasel, D., & Bassuk, E. L. (2014). Out on the street: A public health and policy agenda for lesbian, gay, bisexual, and transgender youth who are homeless. *American Journal of Orthopsychiatry, 84*(1), 66–72. doi:10.1037/h0098852

Ko, S. J., Ford, J. D., Kassam-Adams, N., Berkowitz, S. J., Wilson, C., Wong, M., . . . Layne, C. M. (2008). Creating trauma-informed systems: Child welfare, education, first responders, health care, juvenile justice. *Professional Psychology: Research and Practice, 39*(4), 396–404. doi:10.1037/0735-7028.39.4.396

Langenderfer-Magruder, L., Walls, N. E., Whitfield, D. L., Brown, S. M., & Barrett, C. M. (2015). Partner violence victimization among lesbian, gay, bisexual, transgender, and queer youth: Associations among risk factors. *Child and Adolescent Social Work Journal, 33*, 55–68. doi:10.1007/s10560-015-0402-8

Leap, W. (2007). Language, socialization, and silence in gay adolescence. In K. E. Lovass & M. M. Jenkins (Eds.), *Sexualities & communications in everyday life: A reader* (pp. 95–105). Thousand Oaks, CA: SAGE.

Lee, T. Y., & Shek, D. T. L. (2010). Positive youth development programs targeting students with greater psychosocial needs: A replication. *The Scientific World Journal, 10*, 261–272. doi:10.1100/tsw.2010.3

Leibowitz, S. F., & Spack, N. P. (2011). The development of a gender identity psychosocial clinic: Treatment issues, logistical considerations, interdisciplinary cooperation, and future initiatives. *Child and Adolescent Psychiatric Clinics of North America, 20*(4), 701–724. doi:10.1016/j.chc.2011.07.004

Little, J., Hodari, K., Lavender, J., & Berg, A. (2008). Come as you are: Harm reduction drop-in groups for multi-diagnosed drug users. *Journal of Groups in Addiction & Recovery, 3*(3–4), 161–192. doi:10.1080/15560350802424845

Malekoff, A. (2014). *Group work with adolescents: Principles and practice.* New York: Guilford Press.

Marlatt, G. A. (1996). Harm reduction: Come as you are. *Addictive Behaviors, 21*(6), 779–788.

Marshal, M. P., Dermody, S. S., Shultz, M. L., Sucato, G. S., Stepp, S. D., Chung, T., . . . Hipwell, A. E. (2013). Mental health and substance use disparities among urban adolescent lesbian and bisexual girls. *Journal of the American Psychiatric Nurses Association, 19*(5), 271–279. doi:10.1177/1078390313503552

Millett, G. A., Peterson, J. L., Wolitski, R. J., & Stall, R. (2006). Greater risk for HIV infection of black men who have sex with men: A critical literature review. *American Journal of Public Health, 96*(6), 1007–1019. doi:10.2105/AJPH.2005.066720

Mueller, A. S., James, W., Abrutyn, S., & Levin, M. L. (2015). Suicide ideation and bullying among US adolescents: Examining the intersections of sexual orientation, gender, and race/ethnicity. *American Journal of Public Health, 105*(5), 980–985. doi:10.2105/AJPH.2014.302391

Mueller, M. K., Phelps, E., Bowers, E. P., Agans, J. P., Urban, J. B., & Lerner, R. M. (2011). Youth development program participation and intentional self-regulation skills: Contextual and individual bases of pathways to positive youth development. *Journal of Adolescence, 34*(6), 1115–1125. doi:10.1016/j.adolescence.2011.07.010.

Nadal, K. L., & Griffin, K. E. (2011). Microaggressions: A root of bullying, violence, and victimization toward lesbian, gay, bisexual, and transgender youths. In M. A. Paludi (Ed.), *The psychology of teen violence and victimization* (pp. 3–22). Santa Barbara, CA: Praeger.

Nadal, K. L., Issa, M.-A., Leon, J., Meterko, V., Wideman, M., & Wong, Y. (2011). Sexual orientation microaggressions: "Death by a thousand cuts" for lesbian, gay, and bisexual youth. *Journal of LGBT Youth, 8*(3), 234–259. doi:10.1080/19361653.2011.584204

O'Malley Olsen, E., Kann, L., Vivolo-Kantor, A., Kinchen, S., & McManus, T. (2014). School violence and bullying among sexual minority high school students, 2009–2011. *Journal of Adolescent Health, 55*(3), 432–438. doi:10.1016/j.jadohealth.2014.03.002

Parks, C. A., Hughes, T. L., & Matthews, A. K. (2004). Race/ethnicity and sexual orientation: Intersecting identities. *Cultural Diversity and Ethnic Minority Psychology, 10*(3), 241–254. doi:10.1037/1099-9809.10.3.241

Pedlow, C. T., & Carey, M. P. (2003). HIV sexual risk-reduction interventions for youth: A review and methodological critique of randomized controlled trials. *Behavior Modification, 27*(2), 135–190. doi:10.1177/0145445503251562

Pilkington, N. W., & D'Augelli, A. R. (1995). Victimization of lesbian, gay, and bisexual youth in community settings. *Journal of Community Psychology, 23*(1), 34–56. doi:10.1002/1520-6629(199501)23:1<34::AID-JCOP2290230105>3.0.CO;2-N

Poon, L. (2015, September 28). *"Ze" or "they"? A guide to using gender-neutral pronouns.* Retrieved from http://www.citylab.com/navigator/2015/09/ze-or-they-a-guide-to-using-gender-neutral-pronouns/407167/

Price, M., Higa-McMillan, C., Kim, S., & Frueh, B. C. (2013). Trauma experience in children and adolescents: An assessment of the effects of trauma type and role of interpersonal proximity. *Journal of Anxiety Disorders, 27*(7), 652–660. doi:10.1016/j.janxdis.2013.07.009

Quinlivan, K., & Town, S. (1999). Queer pedagogy, educational practice and lesbian and gay youth. *International Journal of Qualitative Studies in Education, 12*(5), 509–524. doi:10.1080/095183999235926

Ray, N. (2006). *Lesbian, gay, bisexual and transgender youth: An epidemic of homelessness.* New York: National Gay and Lesbian Task Force Policy Institute and the National Coalition for the Homeless. Retrieved from http://www.thetaskforce.org/static_html/downloads/reports/reports/HomelessYouth.pdf

Reichard, R. (2015, August 29). Why we say Latinx: Trans & gender non-conforming people explain. *Latina.* Retrieved from http://www.latina.com/lifestyle/our-issues/why-we-say-latinx-transgender-non-conforming-people-explain#1

Roberts, A. L., Rosario, M., Slopen, N., Calzo, J. P., & Austin, S. B. (2013). Childhood gender nonconformity, bullying victimization, and depressive symptoms across adolescence and early adulthood: An 11-year longitudinal study. *Journal of the American Academy of Child & Adolescent Psychiatry, 52*(2), 143–152. doi:/10.1016/j.jaac.2012.11.006

Rosario, M., Schrimshaw, E. W., & Hunter, J. (2004). Ethnic/racial differences in the coming-out process of lesbian, gay, and bisexual youths: A comparison of sexual identity development over time. *Cultural Diversity and Ethnic Minority Psychology, 10*(3), 215–228. doi:10.1037/1099-9809.10.3.215

Rosario, M., Schrimshaw, E. W., & Hunter, J. (2011). Homelessness among lesbian, gay, and bisexual youth: Implications for subsequent internalizing and externalizing symptoms. *Journal of Youth and Adolescence, 41*(5), 544–560. doi:10.1007/s10964-011-9681-3

Rosario, M., Schrimshaw, E. W., & Hunter, J. (2012). Risk factors for homelessness among lesbian, gay, and bisexual youths: A developmental milestone approach. *Children and Youth Services Review, 34*(1), 186–193. doi:10.1016/j.childyouth.2011.09.016

Russell, S. T., Franz, B. T., & Driscoll, A. K. (2001). Same-sex romantic attraction and experiences of violence in adolescence. *American Journal of Public Health, 91*(6), 903–906.

Sanders, J., Munford, R., Thimasarn-Anwar, T., Liebenberg, L., & Ungar, M. (2015). The role of positive youth development practices in building resilience and enhancing wellbeing for at-risk youth. *Child Abuse & Neglect, 42*, 40–53. doi:10.1016/j.chiabu.2015.02.006

Savin-Williams, R. C. (1994). Verbal and physical abuse as stressors in the lives of lesbian, gay male, and bisexual youths: Associations with school problems, running away, substance abuse, prostitution, and suicide. *Journal of Consulting and Clinical Psychology, 62*(2), 261–269. doi:10.1037/0022-006X.62.2.261

Small, S., & Memmo, M. (2004). Contemporary models of youth development and problem prevention: Toward an integration of terms, concepts, and models. *Family Relations, 53*(1), 3–11. doi:10.1111/j.1741-3729.2004.00002.x

Steensma, T. D., Kreukels, B. P. C., de Vries, A. L. C., & Cohen-Kettenis, P. T. (2013). Gender identity development in adolescence. *Hormones and Behavior, 64*(2), 288–297. doi:10.1016/j.yhbeh.2013.02.020

Steinberg, A. M., Pynoos, R. S., Briggs, E. C., Gerrity, E. T., Layne, C. M., Vivrette, R. L., . . . Fairbank, J. A. (2014). The national child traumatic stress network core data set: Emerging findings, future directions, and implications for theory, research, practice, and policy. *Psychological Trauma: Theory, Research, Practice, and Policy, 6*(Suppl. 1), S50–S57. doi:10.1037/a0037798

Sterzing, P. R., Auslander, W. F., & Goldbach, J. T. (2014). An exploratory study of bullying involvement for sexual minority youth: Bully-only, victim-only, and bully-victim roles. *Journal of the Society for Social Work and Research, 5*(3), 321–337. doi:10.1086/677903

Sterzing, P. R., Hong, J. S., Gartner, R. E., & Auslander, W. F. (2016). Child maltreatment and bullying victimization among a community-based sample of sexual minority youth: The meditating role of psychological distress. *Journal of Child & Adolescent Trauma, 9*(4), 283–293. doi:10.1007/s40653-016-0101-4

Undocuqueer. (Producer). (2013). *Undocuqueer manifesto.* [YouTube Video]. Retrieved from https://www.youtube.com/watch?v=ANlKTdTWp4s

US Department of Health and Human Services. (2007). *Promising strategies to end youth homelessness.* Retrieved from https://www.acf.hhs.gov/sites/default/files/fysb/youth_homelessness.pdf

Van Leeuwen, J. M., Boyle, S., Salomonsen-Sautel, S., Baker, D. N., Garcia, J. T., Hoffman, A., & Hopfer, C. J. (2006). Lesbian, gay, and bisexual homeless youth: An eight-city public health perspective. *Child Welfare, 85*(2), 151.

Walsh, B. (2015, December 4). The Post drops the "mike" — and the hyphen in "e-mail." *The Washington Post.* Retrieved from https://www.washingtonpost.com/opinions/the-post-drops-the-mike--and-the-hyphen-in-e-mail/2015/12/04/ccd6e33a-98fa-11e5-8917-653b65c809eb_story.html

Weiner, D. A., Schneider, A., & Lyons, J. S. (2009). Evidence-based treatments for trauma among culturally diverse foster care youth: Treatment retention and outcomes. *Children and Youth Services Review, 31*(11), 1199–1205. doi:10.1016/j.childyouth.2009.08.013

Whitbeck, L. B., Chen, X., Hoyt, D. R., Tyler, K. A., & Johnson, K. D. (2004). Mental disorder, subsistence strategies, and victimization among gay, lesbian, and bisexual homeless and runaway adolescents. *Journal of Sex Research, 41*(4), 329–342. doi:10.1080/00224490409552240

Wonderlich, S. A., Simonich, H. K., Myers, T. C., LaMontagne, W., Hoesel, J., Erickson, A. L., . . . Crosby, R. D. (2011a). Evidence-based mental health interventions for traumatized youth: A statewide dissemination project. *Behaviour Research and Therapy, 49*(10), 579–587. doi:10.1016/j.brat.2011.07.003

Wonderlich, S. A., Simonich, H. K., Myers, T. C., LaMontagne, W., Hoesel, J., Erickson, A. L., . . . Crosby, R. D. (2011b). Evidence-based mental health interventions for traumatized youth: A statewide dissemination project. *Behaviour Research and Therapy, 49*(10), 579–587. doi:10.1016/j.brat.2011.07.003

Yalom, I. D., & Leszcz, M. C. (2005). *The theory and practice of group psychotherapy* (5th ed.). New York: Basic Books.

Zarrett, N., & Lerner, R. M. (2008). *Ways to promote the positive development of children and youth: Research-to-results* (Publication #2008-11). Retrieved from: http://www.childtrends.org/wp-content/uploads/2013/01/Youth-Positive-Devlopment.pdf

CHAPTER 8

DATING, RELATIONSHIPS, AND FAMILY ISSUES

Michael P. Dentato, Tyler M. Argüello, and Mark Smith

INTRODUCTION

Over the past 20 years, the landscape has been rapidly changing with regard to understanding lesbian, gay, bisexual, transgender, and queer (LGBTQ) dating styles and patterns, relationships and the composition of various forms of coupling and family systems, and related evolving definitions, whether described in the literature or, quite importantly, defined by individuals and communities themselves. A good amount of this evolution has been quite public and recent due to changes in various US local and federal policies associated with adoption, marriage equality, and the continued evolution of positive societal sentiment for the LGBTQ community. In fact, a poll conducted by Gallup ($N = 1,024$) reported that support for same-sex marriage increased from 27% in 1996, to over 60% in 2014, with over 63% in favor of same-sex adoption (Gates, 2015b; McCarthy, 2015). However, there remain a number of significant challenges related to the overall movement for full LGBTQ equality across the United States (e.g., workplace discrimination, transgender rights, hate crimes legislation, immigration laws), as explored in other chapters of this text. Similar and more extensive human rights and LGBTQ social justice challenges remain across the globe (e.g., Sudan, Mauritania, Russia, India, Iran, Iraq, and Saudi Arabia, among others), with regard to decriminalizing homosexuality and hostility toward the transgender community; while a good number of European and South American countries have made significant progress with regard to expansion of marriage equality and hate crimes legislation (see http://ilga.org/what-we-do/lesbian-gay-rights-maps/; BBC News, 2014; Wilkinson & Langlois, 2014). Other challenges pertain to the lack of scholarly research that evaluates the robustness and diversity of relationships, coupling, family patterns, and styles within the LGBTQ community (Umberson, Thomeer, Kroeger, Lodge, & Xu, 2015). Therefore, fully understanding the depth and breadth of LGBTQ relationships and the compositions of various family structures has implications for effective and

affirming practice with this diverse community. Along the same line of thought, it is vitally important that social workers and practitioners approach these topics with fluidity and an open mind
related to understanding and utilizing frameworks of practice that do not always align with heteronormative styles and patterns of dating, coupling, and family dynamics. This chapter begins with
a glimpse of current statistics related to LGBTQ couples and families across the United States
and then moves into a conversation about heteronormativity and homonormativity, followed by
examining the formation of relationships and relationship types, socialization styles, and settings,
along with highlighting key lifespan considerations (e.g., marriage, separation, divorce, adoption,
children/adolescents, older adults). The chapter then looks at unique practice issues when working with bisexual and transgender couples and families and concludes with best practices for therapy with LGBTQ couples and families.

A SNAPSHOT OF CURRENT NUMBERS

According to the William's Institute evaluation of 2010, US Census data, Gallup surveys, and other
reports, there are an estimated 8.2 million LGBT adults in the United States, with an estimated
3 million LGBT adults that have somewhere between one and two children (Gates, 2013). The
same report by Gates notes that there are an estimated 650,000 same-sex couples living in the
United States. Despite an increase in positive societal support for same-sex parenting, interesting
trends over the past 16 years have demonstrated that fewer same-sex couples are reporting raising
children (Gates, 2015b). This may be related to LGBTQ individuals coming out earlier than previous age cohorts due to the alleviation of societal stigma and less likelihood to engage in opposite-
sex relations that produce children—as evidenced by some LGBTQ individuals from older
generations (Gates, 2015b). In that regard, an estimated 37% of LGBT adults have had a child at
some point during their lifetime, and as many as 6 million children and adults in the United States
have an LGBT parent (Gates, 2013). When it comes to adoption and foster care, same-sex couples
are more likely than opposite-sex couples to adopt and foster children, with figures estimated at
16,000 LGBT couples/families adopting 22,000 children and 2,600 LGBT couples/families fostering 3,400 children (Gates, 2013). Last, a many children being raised by same-sex individuals or
couples may actually be their grandchildren, siblings, or other children whether related or unre-
lated to one of the partners/spouses (Gates, 2013).

DEFINING FAMILY

In their review of literature associated with LGBT families, Moore and Stambolis-Ruhstorfer
(2013) note that the very definition of the term "family" can be an obstacle to understanding the
vast number of LGBTQ couplings and families across the United States. While many LGBTQ
couples and families are changing the traditional terms of what defines and comprises a "family," a good amount of research in this area limits the exploration of such fluid or broad-based
discussions and rather endorses more rigid and typical nuclear same-sex and "homo-nuclear"

(Power et al., 2012) formations, thus favoring two-parent heteronormative family characteristics (Peterson, 2013). In the same regard, most existing research on LGBTQ families and households typically centers around couples rather than single-parent families, typically with a primary focus on members of the lesbian and/or gay community when compared to the dearth of research and information on bisexual, transgender, or queer communities (Moore & Stambolis-Ruhstorfer, 2013). Definitions of LGBTQ couplings or families are often fraught with multiple challenges due to heteronormative ideologies, histories, relationship structures, and assumptions. Similarly, the short- and long-term impact of oppression, stigma, and internalized homophobia/transphobia among members of the LGBTQ community that do establish relationships may create additional unique strain or stressors (Hatzenbuehler, McLaughlin, Keyes, & Hasin, 2010; Graham & Barnow, 2013) that is not experienced by heterosexual couplings (Connolly, 2014). In fact, when examining interpersonal connections and the association of minority stress upon LGBTQ relationship quality, one study (N = 90) found higher levels of discrimination and internalized homophobia were associated with less positive perceptions of relationship quality among lesbian participants (Otis, Riggle, & Rostosky, 2006).

Hopkins, Sorensen, and Taylor (2013) note that, historically, there have been many unique ways in which lesbians and gay men defined and constructed families (Carrington, 1999; D'Emilio, 1983; Weston, 1991) separately from their biological families and relationships. Such unique and alternative formations may have included kinship networks established with family members of "choice," which are comprised of friends, allies (Weston, 1991), partners, and lovers, among others (Hopkins et al., 2013). Other factors pertaining to understanding the uniqueness of coupling and families relates to assessing racial/ethnic backgrounds, socio-economic status, and urban/rural locations. Gates (2012) analyzed data from the America Community Survey (2004–2009) and the US Census (2000) and noted that (a) it was more likely that children were being raised within racial/ethnic minority same-sex homes; (b) it was more common that children were being raised by LGBTQ parents/couples (43%) who did not complete a high school education; and (c) 20% of these families were living in poverty. Notably, single LGBT adults raising children were found to be *three times more likely* to have household incomes at the poverty threshold when compared to their non-LGBT counterparts, and married and partnered couples were *twice as likely* to be at the same poverty threshold (Gates, 2013). However, these numbers continue to change, especially in one analysis of demographics pertaining to same-sex households from the American Community Survey of 2013 by Gates (2015a). There were stark differences when comparing married (n = 3,102) to unmarried (n = 5,238) same-sex couples related to income and poverty, raising children, geographic location, racial/ethnic status, and gender, among other factors (Gates, 2015a). Legalizing same-sex marriage has had a positive impact on increasing household incomes among same-sex couples, while decreasing the likelihood for poverty when compared to nonmarried same-sex couples (Gates, 2015a). Specifically, Gates (2015b) found that married same-sex couples had a median household income approximately 27% higher than unmarried same-sex couples, while poverty rates were less likely for those married (4%) compared to those unmarried (18%). The same analysis underscored that 27% of married same-sex couples had children under 18 years of age (71% with female couples), compared to 15% of unmarried same-sex couples (77% with female couples; Gates, 2015a).

OPPRESSION, STIGMA, AND PREJUDICE

For LGBTQ individuals who want to come together socially, sexually, and otherwise, they must endeavor to do so within a climate that is often inhospitable, resulting in negative effects on their lives and livelihood (Rosario, Schrimshaw, & Hunter 2009, 2012). The reasons for such a climate varies as much as the people themselves; though, while most commonly positioned as a phobia (e.g., homophobia, biphobia, transphobia), it is less accurately explained by fear (Herek, 2009). That said, such phobias do exist and often have more overt expressions, such as verbal and physical violence. These violent and traumatic experiences, while discussed in more detail in chapter 6, continue against LGBTQ people even with legal and cultural advances. For recent trends and tracking, see the work of the National Coalition of Anti-Violence Programs (Waters, Jindasurat, & Wofle, 2016).

Parallel to overt violence, this inhospitable heterosexist climate can be interrogated through understanding the terms of sexual prejudice, which is an ideological system that motivates denigration and discrimination against any identities, relationships, behaviors, and beyond that are not cisgendered and heterosexual (Reed & Valenti, 2012). Effectively, this system nullifies, marginalizes, and stigmatizes LGBTQ individuals and their relationships. Theoretical and empirical work has been conducted to identify the motivations and processes of sexual prejudice, such as the Sexual Prejudice Scale (Chonody, 2013). When biases are targeted against members of the LGBTQ community, as in the case of biases motivated by religious fundamentalism and sexism, having social relationships (e.g., both LGBTQ and allies) has been found to be helpful in buffering against such prejudice, though less effective in moderating gender-biased forms (Cunningham & Melton, 2013).

Increasing attention must be given to the ways in which various prejudices and privileges synergize with LGBTQ sexualities and genders as well as, ultimately, within their partnerships and relationships. Central to this analysis is tending to the ways in which racism and ethnocentrism factor into LGBTQ relations, both inside and outside of the bedroom. Such dynamics have been found to contribute to hypersexualizing people of color, stereotyping bodies (e.g., penis size), objectifying through microaggressive terms (e.g., Rice Queen, Tranny), presumptive positioning in sexual situations (e.g., top or bottom, fem or dom), idolizing hyper-cismasculinity and policing gender, as well as idealizing a white, "nonracialized" norm, among other effects (Giwa & Greensmith, 2012; Han 2007, 2015). Given these racialized forces, Reed and Valenti (2012) centered attention on how Black lesbians ($N = 14$) responded to sexual prejudices in order to manage their identities. Their study found that women engaged in "passing" behaviors (e.g., having relationships with men), increasingly chose (LGBTQ) families and social support, and actively fought back against antagonizing people and messages (Reed & Valenti, 2012).

Race is not the only synergizing force with sexual prejudice that affects LGBTQ relationships. Theoretical and empirical research has interrogated the "ontology of gender" (Gustavson, 2009) held by lesbians and gay men, suggesting numerous enduring stigmatized beliefs about bisexuality, including that bisexual people are simply in a transitional phase of their sexuality, are typically nonmonogamous, and are unsuitable partners for whom gender truly does frame their sexual practices (Feinstein, Dyar, Bhatia, Latack, & Davila, 2016). From another angle, Erickson (2016) investigated the ways in which normativizing beliefs around sexuality mis-/align with disabilities and foster "cultures of undesirability" (p. 13), that is, positioning disabled people and their bodies outside the terms of desirability.

The terms for who and what is desirable is at the heart of LGBTQ relationships, inflected with the everyday expressions of an inhospitable and oppressive climate. Just as it is presumed that normativizing forces exert stress on and within LGBTQ relationships, their relationships also embody resilience. Operario, Burton, Underhill, and Sevelius (2008) confront the assumptions and ideologies of researchers and service providers when considering the identities and behaviors of men who have sex with transgender women; these men include those who self-identify as straight, bisexual, gay, and not identified. Findings from their work underscores an important call for more fluidity around sexual orientations, as well as interrogating the rampant desires of professionals to concretize sexualities and make behaviors, identities, and desires equivalent variables. In fact, LGBTQ identities and enacted relationships can be liberating in many ways for themselves, as well as our larger culture. Galupo, Lomash, and Mitchell (2016) interrogated the veracity of two common measures for sexual orientation (the Kinsey Scale and the Klein Sexual Orientation Grid), exposing the limits of such instruments and conceptualizations. The researchers found that participants preferred more disaggregation of sexual and romantic aspects of attraction, and they challenged the implicit binary assumption of gender and opted for a broader dimensional explication of genders (e.g., attraction to masculine, feminine, androgynous, and gender nonconforming individuals).

EMBRACING HETERONORMATIVE PATTERNS AND CREATING QUEER FORMATIONS

A foundational concept in today's cannon of gender, LGBTQ, and queer studies is that of heteronormativity. Its origins are often attributed to melding second-wave feminist critiques of modern economies and production (see Rubin, 1997) with queer theory–animated critiques of the "heterosexual matrix" (Butler, 1990) and other heteropatriarchal structures that organize and essentialize bodies, sexualities, genders, and daily lives (Warner, 1991, 1993). A critical analysis of heternormativity works to unpack taken-for-granted social practices and policies that position certain behaviors as natural and normal, which then are given protection and currency in society—namely, the production of heterosexuality—at the expense of other ways of being and organizing (e.g., any other sexualities, genders). This privileging of one identity in turn legitimates a compulsory, utopian vision of sexuality and gender (Herz & Johansson, 2015; Iantaffi & Bockting, 2011); this largely has meant someone who is monogamous, cisgendered, heterosexual, procreative, and coupled, or, better yet, married.

Accordingly, over the past few decades, scholars have been concerned with an increasing liberalism of sorts in LGBTQ communities, and they have applied queer theory and specifically heteronormativity in the context of a mobilizing LGBTQ constituency across the US legal and political landscape, one that has mounted traction especially around marriage equality and military policies. The concept of *homonormativity* has emerged from queer theory, one that embeds a largely white, able-bodied, neoliberal, LGBTQ-identified subject in contemporary discourses, a subject who replicates heteronormativity through their own modern relationships as well as demands and practices in US culture (Duggan, 2002, 2003). From this perspective, homonormativity critiques the reproduction of heterosexuality in (new) contexts, as well as looks to uncover how discourses around sexuality and gender (e.g., obligatory heterosexuality) explore and propagate ideas and practices that support the modern nation-state (e.g., policies to protect certain domestic spaces and lives but not others), in all of its hierarchies and modernizing tendencies, domestically and abroad (Eng, Halberstam, & Muñoz, 2005; Puar, 2005; Reddy, 2005). In turn, queer scholars have harnessed homonormativity to offer an extended critique of LGBTQ people and related institutions who have furthered "gay marriage," politically and practically, arguing that such a singular agenda anesthetizes LGBTQ people (and beyond) into passively accepting alternative forms of inequality in return for domestic privacy and freedom to consume (Martin & Manalansan, 2005). More recently, some literature has enhanced this critique by seeking to "lighten the load" on the shoulders of LGBTQ people, who have become easily targeted, vilified, and marginalized in these cultural wars over rights and access to civil institutions (Weber, 2015).

This approach to understanding the role of intersecting identities, empowerment, and forces of stigma, discrimination, and oppression is imperative in concert with critiques of gay marriage, especially given the stakes involved. In earlier chapters, attention has been given to the various disparities and oppressions that LGBTQ people have endured and continue to face, individually and collectively (Institute of Medicine, 2011). These disparities and the marginalization of LGBTQ desires and arrangements do not cease to exist when we set them into the frame of relationships and how we have them (i.e., social, sexual, romantic, otherwise). As is discussed in more detail later, parallel to the critiques of gay marriage within the LGBTQ community, attention has been given to the ways in which oppressive forces, such as racism and homophobia (Bryant, 2008; Han, 2007), can in fact express and reproduce hetero/homonormativity. This becomes especially important to consider after the June 2015 US Supreme Court decision in *Obergefell v. Hodges*, declaring unconstitutional state-level bans on "same-sex marriages" and effectively grounding the *expansion* of "marriage," legally and ideologically. With its stepwise progress, there has been research emerging regarding the health benefits and overall effects on well-being of legal marriage for LGBTQ individuals and couples.

At-large, being in a dyadic relationship has been shown to be positively associated with psychological benefits for LGBTQ couples, such as increased life satisfaction and lower levels of depression (Horwitz, White, & Howell-White, 1996; Kim & McKenry, 2002; Marks & Lambert, 1998; Strohschein, McDonough, Monette, & Shao, 2005; Williams, 2003). There have also been tangible benefits found for married LGBTQ couples that contribute to overall well-being (e.g., insurance, tax incentives; Herek, 2006). Previous public health research demonstrated that US states with bans on the expansion of marriage equality had an association with LGBTQ people experiencing increased mood and anxiety conditions as well as decreased individual overall well-being (Buffie, 2011; Hatzenbuehler et al., 2010; MacIntosh, Reissing, & Andruff, 2010; Riggle, Rostosky, & Horne, 2010). Quite critically, Tatum (2017) provides findings that show increased legal marriage benefits for LGBTQ people are associated with redressing minority stress—*regardless* of relationship status; this is to suggest that even just living, coupled or not, within a climate of increased rights and recognition can have positive effects on well-being. Echoing this are the earlier findings of Whitton, Kuryluk, and Khaddouma (2015) that indicated having legal and social ceremonies to formalize LGBTQ relationships has effects on satisfaction and stability, and important to these models are relationship commitment and support within their communities.

The Beyond Same-Sex Marriage (2008) collective, as one example, argued for a new strategic vision for (LGBTQ) families and relationships. In response to a presumed singular endeavor for gay marriage, this collective has argued for committed action guided by more inclusive principles, including recognition and respect for all chosen relationships; legal enfranchisement for a wider range of household configurations; separating benefits and relationship recognition from a conjugal requirement; freedom from narrow definitions of sexual lives and gender identities and expressions; and recognition of the interdependence with other marginalized communities, who may collectively or individually not be LGBTQ (e.g., older people, immigrant communities, single parents, prisoners, people with disabilities, and poor people). In another way, LGBTQ relationships in all their forms may be helpful models of both progress and tradition, as well as subversion for how to arrange and organize relationships, domestically and publicly. As is being unfolded throughout this chapter and text, LGBTQ relations hold the potential to be indices for how to experience and enact affiliations, intimacies, orientations, romances, and beyond—whether married or not.

PORTRAYALS AND IMAGES OF LGBTQ RELATIONSHIPS

LGBTQ individuals grow up in heteronormative and cisgendered social environments in which patterns and ideals of opposite-sex romantic and sexual relationships dominate their environment (e.g., within school curriculum, television, movies) and overall lifespan development. It is also the expectation that while being born into and growing up within heterosexual families with heteronormative ideals that all youth will therefore (by default) also be heterosexual (Valentine & Skelton, 2003). Although the portrayal of celebrated same-sex romantic unions can be found throughout history and within the classical literature, prior to the later years of the twentieth century, dominant sexuality and gender narratives acted to suppress or deny the historical evidence of nonheterosexual relationships. In fact, throughout history (e.g., prior to the 1990s), many lesbian and gay male couples worked diligently to conceal their partner's sex and gender whether by altering their names (e.g., Barbara being called "Bob" during public conversations) or through the use of a "cover" (e.g., a gay male bringing a female to family or work functions— also known as a "beard"). Historically, same-sex and gender-variant relationships of famous individuals have usually been minimized or else presented as evidence of either a pathological mental disorder or some tragic personal flaw (e.g., Joan of Arc, Walt Whitman, Oscar Wilde, Pytor Ilyich Tchaikovsky). Until recently, younger LGBTQ generations had few if any nonheterosexual or transgender models from which to emulate healthy relationships (Mustanski, Greene, Ryan, & Whitton, 2015). Many families of origin, images portrayed within the media, schools, churches, and legal institutions all staunchly promote a narrowly defined and almost exclusively heterosexual and cisgendered standard and language for relationships (Potârcă, Mills, & Neberich, 2015). Unlike some other minority communities (e.g., racial/ethnic, religious, differently abled) who may access numerous social support systems and environmental settings that can help moderate or prepare them as members of these groups, most LGBTQ youth enter childhood and adolescence without models or such preparation for their developing sexual minority or gender-variant identities. Fortunately, over the past few decades as the social, legal, and cultural climates continue to evolve, society has begun in some ways to treat LGBTQ individuals, same-sex couples, and queer relationships in the same fashion as their heterosexual and opposite-sex couple counterparts—meaning that some differences between the two types of couples have narrowed (Gates, 2015b). In the same manner, there has been an increase in positive images of lesbian and gay individuals, couples, and families represented within the media (Gross, 2012) and via various famous and "out" couples and families, while there continues to be a lack of visible representation of bisexual, transgender, and queer communities, families, and couples (Cashore & Tuason, 2009).

DATING, SOCIALIZATION, AND MEETING OTHERS

LGBTQ individuals often meet other members of their own community in similar patterns, styles, and settings as those from many other communities. Such connections may be made via friends, family, and extended family members, whether in school or college, within religious institutions, through parent groups/networks, or at bars, clubs, and sports teams, and via social media (Miller, 2015), among other venues (Valentine & Skelton, 2003). What may be most notable is how such heteronormative styles and traditional settings have evolved with the continued broadening acceptance of the LGBTQ community across the United States. Historically, due to extreme societal oppression of LGBTQ relationships, at times including various forms of verbal harassment and physical victimization (Andersen, Zou, & Blosnich, 2015) or family/peer rejection (Savin-Williams, 1996), individuals were forced to hide their relationships or seek companionship solely within private settings such as a home or social settings such as a bar or club (Chaney & Brubaker, 2014). Such stigma and oppression increased the need for secrecy of LGBTQ relationships and the creation of slang, terminologies, and code words for socialization. Examples relate to having "gaydar" (e.g., knowing or sensing another person may be LGBTQ) or partaking in "cruising" whereby seeking partners for sexual or intimate relations in public settings such as parks, the streets, or public bathrooms (especially among gay and bisexual men and men who have sex with men [MSM]). Meeting, socializing, and dancing at predominately gay and lesbian bars and clubs were the main venues through which socialization occurred (and often still occurs) for many LGBTQ individuals and couples. However, these settings were often run by the mafia and raided by the police (e.g., Stonewall Inn). Such barriers and challenges with seeking connectivity through public and private venues has clearly evolved over the past 10 years with the advent and use of social media apps and websites (e.g., Scruff, Grindr, HER, Tinder, Match.com; (Miller, 2015; Simon Rosser, West, & Weinmeyer, 2008).

As quickly as new technology has come on the market, it has given rise to continually evolving purposes for sex and sexuality, regardless of the intended use of the technology itself. LGBTQ young people, for example, have used the Internet as a primary place to locate not only each other but also information about sexual health (Magee, Bigelow, DeHaan, & Mustanski, 2012). This is significant given that the inhospitable heteronormative climate in which they grow up virtually erases any developmental and health knowledge specific to their needs. Some empirical attention has been given to how lesbians self-identify and negotiate their identities and relationships on niche dating sites. Hightower (2015) determined, among many things, that the politics around lesbian identities are in flux (as compared to previous generations) and that the site's users did a lot of creative work to represent their identities, such that the connections online worked as a foundation for building real-world relationships.

Gay and bisexual men, especially, have been consistent earlier adopters and users of new technology to network, socially and sexually; this fact coupled with the HIV epidemic has caused researchers to be interested in their online practices as well as attempt to harness new technologies for sexual health, harm reduction, and prevention of HIV/AIDS. (For a comprehensive review, see Grov, Breslow, Newcomb, Roseberger, & Bauermeister, 2014.) Research is emerging that chronicles the virtual behaviors of LGBTQ people, in particular social (e.g., Facebook) as well as sexual networking (e.g., Grindr) applications. Miller (2015) argues that social technology is the "modern-day gay bar"—at least possibly for MSM who have shown to increasingly use technology to satisfy a spectrum of social gratifications (e.g., friends, dating, chatting, networking) and allowed for a latitude of behaviors independent of having to claim specific (sexual) identities (e.g., men exploring same-sex sexuality without decidedly claiming a "gay" identity). In fact, this seems to be particularly meaningful and powerful for gay and bisexual men and MSM: social and sexual networking work hand in hand. In other words, sexual networking sites could be viewed as a nexus of the physical and digital world that gives form and real-time functions to LGBTQ relationships (Roth, 2016), all the while being part of the modern project of globalization, fueled by advertising and marketing. Some men have voiced the fact that they use social and sexual networking applications simultaneously to strategically manage multiple identities (e.g., professional versus personal lives) and to garner a sense of credibility when virtually cruising on other networking sites (Gudelunas, 2012).

Grosskophf and colleagues (2014) found that a sample of MSM ($N = 126$) in New York City who used both the Internet and mobile apps tended to be younger, had higher incomes, and had a positive sexual identity; what did not hold significant in their analyses were sensation-seeking and internalized homophobia, which are often positioned as challenges for prevention related to transmission of HIV/AIDS and sexually transmitted infections. Other research has shown that MSM who use apps tend to have more lifetime sexual partners and lower levels of self-control yet did not have more incidences of unprotected anal intercourse, though they did have increased rates of other sexually transmitted infections, specifically gonorrhea and chlamydia (Beymer et al., 2014; Beymer, Rossi, & Shu, 2016; Lehmiller & Loerger, 2014). While there is a bevy of ever-evolving and available mobile applications, Beymer and colleagues (2016) found that most MSM used only one app, with just over 25% using two apps, and around one-sixth using three or more apps.

In this age of rapidly developing technology and the endurance of the HIV epidemic, app users and apps themselves can too often be veiled as landscapes of drugs and disease transmission. Moreover, with the sociopolitical focus of LGBTQ sexualities and relationships monopolized by couplehood, state recognition, and compulsory monogamy, more critical appreciation might be given to the potential for digital worlds and relationship-building (Race, 2015a, 2015b). Mobile devices and apps allow for coconstructed fantasies and an endless potential for encounters, which may or may not ever be realized in earnest or to full satisfaction. Still, they offer an *infrastructure of intimacy*—a mediated human geography replete with erotic, social, and communal potentials (Race, 2015a). Last, they also provide a space for *stranger sociability*, or an ability to be in public seeking pleasure, possibility, and connections, all while unburdened by normative structures (Warner, 2002).

RURAL AND URBAN COMMUNITY SETTINGS

LGBTQ couples and families reside across the United States and globe within a wide array of urban, suburban, and rural settings. Historically, LGBTQ individuals relocated to urban cities and neighborhoods in search of community and safety. In some major cities, the ghettoizing of neighborhoods (e.g., the West Village in New York City, Boystown in Chicago, or the Castro district in San Francisco) by the LGBTQ community has ultimately led to the gentrification of such areas (Valentine & Skelton, 2003). Oppositely, there are many LGBTQ individuals, couples, and families that prefer to reside within non-predominate LGBTQ neighborhoods or cities (Simon Rosser, West, & Weinmeyer, 2008) whether due to personal preference or higher expenses associated with renting or purchasing homes. While members of the LGBTQ community may find it liberating to visit urban locations for socialization and connectivity, it is likely that such a setting may not resonate with them as they prefer to reside in a less urban city or neighborhood (Annes & Redlin, 2012; Kazyak, 2011). It is also important to assess the wide range of LGBTQ-affirming policies and protections (or lack thereof) available within various cities, counties, and states and the environmental or systemic impact of broadening or limiting the potential for socialization, dating, mating, and coupling across the United States. Many LGBTQ couples and families live within states that still do not afford full protections for their relationships and children (e.g., workplace discrimination, public accommodations, housing, hate crimes, bullying, gender marker changes on identification documents, and inconsistent laws protecting sexual orientation and/or gender identity as a minority class; see Lambda Legal: http://www.lambdalegal.org/in-your-state and Human Right Campaign: http://www.hrc.org/state_maps). Ultimately, understanding how the places in which LGBTQ individuals, couples, and families reside can impact their overall quality of life remains necessary. One study of older LGBTQ adults ($N = 1,201$) living in rural areas found a decreased likelihood for coming out, being guarded about their identity with family and friends, and lower levels of income (Lee & Quam, 2013). Social workers and all practitioners should be acutely aware of the environments in which LGBTQ couples, children, and families live and the impact of residing in such locations (e.g., self-esteem, isolation, coming out, substance use, sexually transmitted infections) on their overall development or health and mental health needs (Oswald & Culton, 2003; Wienke & Hill, 2013; Willging, Salvador, & Kano, 2006).

TRADITIONAL AND UNIQUE RELATIONSHIP FORMATIONS

For all the contentious debates regarding LGBTQ people and their relationships, less is known about how such couplings develop, whether or not they ever formalize into partnerships or marriage. As has been discussed, dyadic romantic relationships have been found to be protective factors and to improve overall health for LGBTQ people (Bauermeister et al., 2010; Peplau & Fingerhut, 2007), yet their foundational assumptions and approaches are based on heteronormative understandings of relationships (Macapagal, Greene, Rivera, & Mustanski, 2015). Akin to the models discussed earlier regarding individual identity development in chapter 4, two main camps of thought have been used in understanding LGBTQ relationship development. Staged models attempt to explain a linear sequence, from attraction through the ending of a relationship (e.g., Levinger, 1980), whereas more process-oriented models focus on interpersonal dynamics that animate a relationship, such as closeness, trust, and commitment (e.g., Rusbult, 1980; Wieselquist, Rusbult, Foster, & Agnew, 1999). Complicating these models, Macapagal and colleagues (2015) conducted a mixed-methods investigation of young LGBT couples ($N = 36$) to better understand the confluence of the development of sexual and gender identities and their emergence into adulthood. Whereas there were numerous findings similar to heterosexist staged and process models, such as a similar progression to more overt gestures of commitment (e.g., engagement), LGBT relationships held important differences, including the level of outness to family and friends, which was associated with levels of support; more explicit discussions about nonmonogamy/monogamy; cohabitation by choice or encouraged due to lack of family support; explicit family planning through adoption and assisted technologies; and contending with external stressors, such as relationship disapproval and parallel management of sexual, gender, and racial identities (Macapagal et al., 2015).

EXPECTATIONS OF MARRIAGE AND MONOGAMY

From a homonormative critique, the apparent singular agenda, as of late, in US LGBTQ politics has focused on marriage—but this has also eclipsed a wider dialogue about other relationship formations, sociabilities, intimacies, attachments, and scenes of association. Implicit in the debate about marriage is a privileging presumption that LGBTQ people will have a developmental trajectory toward a formalized relationship (i.e., becoming married); embedded within that is another assumption that they would desire and invariably commit to monogamy within that couplehood. In truth, monogamy is but one strategy for organizing one's (sexual) behaviors and congealing one's (dyadic) relationship. Despite (or maybe exactly for) the fact that monogamy is normative, there is a scant literature base about its benefits and drawbacks (Moors, Matsick, Ziegler, Rubin, & Conley, 2013). Accordingly, much stigma exists against nonmonogamy, especially when intersected with LGBTQ identities, as can increasingly be seen in mass media portrayals of oversexualized or overeroticized individuals, in pathologizing assessments by clinicians, in moral indictments by conservative politicians, or in allegations in its role in fomenting the continued HIV epidemic (Conley, Moors, Matsick, & Ziegler, 2013). Still, some empirical attention is mounting with regard to variations to monogamy.

Conley and colleagues (2013) have more recently engaged in discussions surrounding *consensual nonmonogamy* (CNM), that is, sexual and/or romantic relationships alongside the primary relationship (e.g., married, dating) with one committed partner. While local terms are forever proliferating for such arrangements, a continuum does exist, at least for this emerging area of research (Moors et al., 2013), including terms like "closed" (full monogamy), "poly" or polyamorous (usually connoting physical *and* romantic relations with others), "monogamish" (a couple playing *together* with others), "open" (connoting extra-dyadic physical play *or* romantic relations, together or separately), "swingers" (usually in a heterosexual context, similar to monogamish or open), or "swollies" (or poly swingers). The terms and understanding of CNM (and the like) can be confused with relationship processes of fidelity, commitment, and loyalty. CNM can often be set in contraindication to relational roles like parenthood or family, as well as to other formations such as threesomes ("thruples") or couples dating couples. It is important to note that CNM (and the like) are not the same as actual nonmonogamy (e.g., cheating), which would include all relationship arrangements that are not reported, kept from a primary partner, or otherwise held secret.

Even more so, when people hear of these variations to dyadic monogamy, it can be easily lost that such arrangements are not new to LGBTQ people or their heterosexual counterparts. Gay men (or more generally MSM) have often been the targets of scrutiny around monogamy due to the HIV epidemic. To that end, Prestage and colleagues (2008) have given extended attention over time to such arrangements, especially in the context of negotiating safety and risk, and they found fair consistency. Still, outside of purposes for public health, researchers have attempted to estimate how typical monogamy is for LGBTQ people, with many (non-population-based) estimates ranging from as low as 18% (in the 1980s) to more recently just under 75% (Bricker & Horne, 2007), which happens to be the convergence point of most estimates. So while monogamy seems more typical, CNM appears commonplace too, and more similarities than differences appear to exist across relational arrangements. In fact, Bricker and Horne (2007) showed that monogamous and nonmonogamous gay couples had many similarities: the spread between partners' ages, the number of previous (sexual) partners, the frequency of sex with primary partner, relationship satisfaction, and histories with attempting CNM. Hosking (2014) dovetails these findings, showing that both types of arrangements evidenced similar commitment, passion, and intimacy. Moreover, partners in open relationships did not show significant jealousy; rather, importance was placed upon a mutually agreed-on set of rules for CNM arrangements (Hosking, 2014).

Often stigmatized and misunderstood as on the continuum of romance, "fuckbuddies," "hookups" or "friends with benefits" are other common sexual and social formations for some LGBTQ people. These relationships are often beyond casual sexual encounters as they more often extend a sense of friendship among LGBTQ folks (Bricker & Horne, 2007; Hughes, Morrison, & Asada, 2005; O'Connor, 1992; Nardi, 1992; Wilksinson et al., 2012). As discussed previously, gay men (or, in a larger frame, MSM) have had a long history with public environments to meet, engage in sex, and develop community (e.g., urban neighborhoods, parks, truck stops). That said, it should be noted that lesbians (or, in a larger frame, women who have sex with women) have also had a history with public sex environments; however, it is less discussed and differently policed (e.g., see the history of Toronto's Pussy Palace; Gallant & Loralee, 2001; Lamble, 2009; Valverde, 2007).

Coextensive with such public sex environments are private sex parties (Meunier, 2014), which have taken on more popularity and meaning given the HIV epidemic, new online and mobile technologies, and policies that have closed many public venues like bathhouses. Regularly, these places are cast as scenes for public sex that are impersonal, exclusionary, and risk-laden; contesting this, Meunier (2013) ethnographically documented the various forms and functions of these environments. Private sex parties are more ground-up responses to the decline of other public sex venues and often reflect the values of those who organize them. Instead of excluding, most parties are public, cater to preferences (e.g., fetishes), adhere to rules of conduct, and are scenes for communing, as much as indulging, sexual interests. This is consistent with similar findings in another urban sample of gay men who frequented both public and private sex environments. Higa (2008) found that men ($N = 17$) did not simply populate spaces around the city to fulfill sexual needs: they sought and found fellowship and a sense of community, all the while some experiencing a deep sense of compassion in what would otherwise be dubbed anonymous acts.

SUBCULTURE BEHAVIORS, COMMUNITIES, AND RELATIONSHIPS

Members of the LGBTQ community may or may not find certain subculture behaviors and relationships to be appealing or relevant for their encounters with other partners, whether married or unmarried. Some subculture and/or fetish behaviors may include those associated with bondage, discipline, and sadomasochism (BDSM); paraphilia; other fetishisms; participation within the leather, bear, and/or house/ball communities; or an attraction to younger or older partners, among other relationships and subculture groups. What is important to note is that such attraction to subculture behaviors and relationships is not unique to the LGBTQ community or other minority groups. In fact, some research demonstrates that the majority of people engaging in BDSM behavior are typically identified as white and well-educated (Sheff & Hammers, 2011). Furthermore, the perpetuation of stigmatizing and labeling (e.g., pathological, compulsive, addicted, compulsive) individuals and couples who engage in such behaviors promotes oppression, stigma, and shame (Herbert & Weaver, 2015), all the while contradicting the use of an empowerment perspective. In fact, framing such subculture behaviors and relations as normative is atypical of most social worker and practitioner assessment and treatment practices, which should consistently embrace diversity and empower clients, promote self-determination, and utilize a strengths perspective (Williams, 2016). Additionally, such diverse communities and behaviors are typically stigmatized, marginalized, and oppressed by those within the health and mental health professions (Moser & Kleinplatz, 2005). Expanding knowledge of diverse subculture behaviors and communities among LGBTQ populations may also assist with education, prevention, and treatment of alcohol and substance use addictions (Halkitis, Levy, Moreira, & Ferrusi, 2014) as well as sexually transmitted infections (e.g., HIV/AIDS), especially among gay and bisexual men, MSM (Prestage, Brown, & De Wit, 2015), and members of queer and transgender communities (Lyons et al., 2015). In fact, one study of transgender women and African American MSM members ($N = 274$) of the house/ball community actually found greater likelihood for increased social support for safer sexual behavior and positive social networks, along with greater likelihood for HIV testing (Arnold, Sterrett-Hong,

Jonas, & Pollack, 2016). Similar findings in a study by Kubicek, McNeeley, Holloway, Weiss, and Kipke (2013) provides further evidence of resiliency and increased social support systems among African American MSM members ($N = 263$) of house/ball communities.

PORNOGRAPHY

Another aspect of LGBTQ coupling and relationships relates to the various roles and usages of pornography. It is not a new debate to referee the merits and the public health effects of this contentious continuum of media, from "erotica" to "hardcore" pornography (Calderone, 1972; Howard, 2016). Often the debates shuttle between "good versus bad" or "pro- versus antiporn," and get mired in political, legal, and moralistic debates, leaving little defined and much open to research (Corneau & Van der Meulen, 2014). In fact, despite how ubiquitous porn is argued to be in the lives of LGBTQ individuals and couples (and generally among all adults), few empirical studies have been conducted on LGBTQ pornography specifically. What is known gets taken up and dichotomized across the anti/pro debate. For example, scholars argue gay porn perpetuates homophobic and masculinist stereotypes and biases (Kendall, 1999), contributes to unrealistic body images and dissatisfaction (Duggan & McCreary, 2004), furthers sexual racism (Kendall & Funk, 2003), and contributes to high-risk sexual practices (e.g., unprotected anal intercourse; Stein, Silvera, Hagerty, & Marmor, 2012). Alternatively, gay porn can be seen as a tool of liberation and resistance to heteronormativity (Champagne, 1995), a more equitable and reciprocal exchange (Dyer, 1994), a channel through which to provide information and education (Watney, 1997), and a way to depict and validate multiple sexualities (Chatterjee, 2001). Additionally, porn has been a typically targeted channel through which to educate gay men (and LGBTQ people) about safer sex and sexually transmitted infections (Leonard, 2012; Scott-Sheldon & Johnson, 2006).

This brings in an even more important debate about the value of porn, especially for LGBTQ people. Albury (2014) argues for a critical literacy of porn and for it to be part of sex education. This is to say, rather than focusing contentious debates on what porn *really* teaches (and what "it" *is*), conversations about porn may have more traction when intersected with discussions about a spectrum of sexual practices, how people and sexuality find and gain self-representation, and what sorts of knowledge are included or not, which goes beyond sexuality. For example, Erickson (2016) studies and produces *queercrip* porn that seeks to make transparent conversations about how *cultures of undesirability* are produced through the intersections of sexual prejudices and other social injustices, such as ableism and racism. In response, she both creates and researches porn that visualizes and represents the lived desires of bodies, voices, and identities that are not only marginalized by our modern culture but also specifically by porn itself. Given its intention for resistance and subversion, Erickson sees her work as collaboratively making space for the *lust of recognition*— that is to recognize "hotness" in both our positive sides and each other's "cripness" (p. 19).

SEXUALITY, GENDER, AND COMPULSIVITY

Turning attention to psychobiology, Peterson and colleagues (2010) looked at both heterosexual and lesbian women's sexual response, considering stimulus, affective reaction, and sexual history.

Whereas men are largely gender-defined in their sexual response (e.g., gay men respond to other male stimuli), women's responses were more complex and nuanced. Their work points to a growing body of research (see Rullo, Strassberg, & Israel, 2010) that suggests women's feelings, identities, and behaviors may change over time and may be determined in part by context, partner availability, and political ideology. Moreover, women's sexual response may be influenced but not strictly defined by self-identified sexual orientation.

Parallel to this, Kelly, Bimbi, Nanin, Izienicki, and Parsons (2009) interrogated the sexual compulsivity of a community sample ($N = 1,543$) of gay, lesbian, and bisexual men and women. Given the scant attention in the literature to women, and especially nonheterosexual women, this study provides acknowledgement of a continuum of sexual behaviors for lesbians and bisexual women (as well as male counterparts), which include having sex with alcohol or drugs, engaging in a host of "specialized sexual behaviors" (e.g., water sports, fisting, ass play, BDSM, exhibitionism), and other behaviors such as group sex. Also, this work showed that within gender groups, sexually compulsive men tended to use more substances and alcohol before sex, and sexually compulsive women tended to concentrate on more "kinky" behaviors (e.g., water sports, exhibitionism, BDSM). It should be noted that little research exists related to understanding lesbian and bisexual women's "kink" tendencies and behaviors, apart from conjoining them to a compulsivity, which runs the risk of reifying cissexist heteronormativity as well as continuing the pathologization of LGBTQ sexualities. Tomassilli, Golub, Bimbi, and Parsons (2009) similarly did find a range of "kinky" behaviors among a comparable community sample ($N = 347$) finding that more than 40% of women had participated in kinky behaviors, suggesting that such behaviors are not uncommon for lesbians and bisexual women. Moreover, kink behaviors were associated with women who came out younger or were younger at their first same-sex sexual experience, suggesting that experience and time are key elements to coming into one's own sexuality.

It is important to acknowledge that one of the ways that oppression of LGBTQ people, couples, and relationships continues is through essentializing them into their identities. This is not to blithely and microaggressively argue that sexuality and gender are "just one piece" of LGBTQ people. Instead, a more liberatory way to read LGBTQ sexual behaviors and identities is to unpack their functions. Wilkinson and colleagues (2012) direct attention to a community-based model for LGBTQ attachments. Their empirical research ($N = 3,198$) exposes the fact that attachment for gay men to one another and to a larger community was not relegated simply to sexual encounters; rather, their need for and attachment to a LGBTQ community was personal, that is, a function of sex, love, friendship, belonging, and place. In fact, sex-driven models to explain gay sexual behaviors was less helpful in analyzing their large-scale survey results. For example, gay men engaged in higher rates of socializing activities and civic engagement, rather than frequenting public sex venues; as well, almost three-quarters of the men who visited online gay sex sites were just as interested in making friends as they were in locating a casual sex partner. They also found a democratization of sociability in that the men befriended and relied on all other LGBTQ people, heterosexual friends, and families. In the face of social fragmentation in our modern culture due to mounting individualism and identitarian politics, these results provide provocative evidence for LGBTQ solidary beyond sexuality.

ESTABLISHING FAMILIES

There are a variety of ways through which LGBTQ individuals and couples may become parents and create families. Whether through adoption, foster or kinship care, insemination, surrogacy, having a child or children from a previous heterosexual relationship/family, shared parenting or custody agreements, there are myriad ways in which families can be established (Mallon, 2013). As noted earlier in this chapter, such family formations are not unlike those of the heterosexual community. However, many biases remain with the assumption that families be comprised of two opposite-gender parents (e.g., one mom and one dad) in order to create a "healthy" or "normal" environment for any child regardless of that child's sexual orientation or gender identity. While the literature and research in this area has found such assumptions to be invalid and unsubstantiated (Manning, Fettro, & Lamidi, 2014; Moore & Stambolis-Ruhstorfer, 2013; Perrin et al., 2013; Siegel et al., 2013), oppression toward LGBTQ couples and families continues today (Cahill & South 2002; Diaz-Serrano & Meix-Llop, 2016; Friedman et al., 2013; Meyer, 2003) and can be further compounded by the intersectionality of socioeconomic status, perceived gender/gender identity, race/ethnicity, religion, and other such factors. The gender, sexual orientation, and/or gender identity of a child's parent(s) is less likely to negatively impact their development when compared to the quality and caliber of the parental relationships, economic and social supportive systems, and the parent(s)' overall feelings of security and competence (Perrin et al., 2013). In the same regard, one longitudinal study of female same-sex couples ($N = 95$) and opposite-sex couples ($N = 95$) with children in the age range between 6 and 17 years old found no major differences within the households on family relationships or child outcomes, even with female same-sex couples reporting more stress (Bos, Knox, van Rijn-van Gelderen, & Gartrell, 2016). Additionally, a meta-analysis of 33 published and unpublished studies examining the impact of same-sex individuals and couples found positive outcomes (e.g., parent/child relations, positive psychological adjustment) among children ($N = 5,272$) within nontraditional family structures (Fedewa, Black, & Ahn, 2015). This research affirms the work of Biblarz and Savci (2010) underscoring the fact that children of same-sex couples fare well, if not sometimes better than, children living within opposite-sex family structures. While some children living with LGBTQ, foster, or adoptive parents may have to face unique stressors and navigate issues such as bullying and/or the coming out and disclosure process with their peers, teachers, or others, overall they can be more compassionate and accepting of diverse family structures and identities when compared to children not raised by LGBTQ parents or caregivers (Cody, Farr, McRoy, Ayers-Lopez, & Ledesma, 2017).

ADOPTION AND INSEMINATION

Among the typical ways through which LGBTQ people become parents, adoption and the use of assisted reproductive technologies (e.g., donor insemination, surrogacy) are two common methods typically sought (Moore & Stambolis-Ruhstorfer, 2013). One study of lesbian, gay, and heterosexual parents ($N = 130$) examined reasonings, differences, and similarities related to decisions to adopt with results demonstrating challenges with fertility for heterosexual couples and same-sex couples preferring adoption over other types of childbearing overall and as the first route to becoming parents (Jennings, Mellish, Tasker, Lamb, & Golombok, 2014). The same study found that heterosexual women and lesbians were motivated to adopt due to challenges with fertility and insemination, treatment failure, miscarriages, or death of an infant, such that adoption offered the greatest potential for parenting (Jennings et al., 2014). Another fascinating discovery in this research related to gay fathers and lesbian mothers showing more interest in adoption due to the lack of concern related to the biological or genetic kinship of their potential children when compared to heterosexual couples (Jennings et al., 2014). When examining why single and partnered women (including heterosexuals, bisexuals, and lesbians) preferred donor insemination rather than adoption, Goldberg and Schieb (2015) found that participants ($N = 50$) noted reasons that pertained to interests in biological parenting and having genetic links to their child(ren), challenges with adoption associated with costs/expenses and unpredictability of the process, perceptions of problems with adopted kids, and legal, organizational, and systemic barriers.

Nonetheless, it is clear that gay men and lesbians endorse wanting children (DeLair, 2000; Gates, 2013), or, better framed, they have "procreative consciousness" or a felt sense of self that enjoins both identities as parents and LGBTQ people (Berkowitz, 2007; Berkowitz & Marsiglio, 2007). Lesbians, in particular, have shown to spend more time thinking about becoming parents as well as having a stronger desire to do so versus heterosexual women (Bos, van Balen, & van de Boom, 2003; Greenfeld, 2015). Some of the largest barriers that persist for LGBTQ people to becoming parents and parenting are sexual prejudice and heterosexist stigma, state and federal laws, and their own families of origin who show decreased support and outright opposition, especially those who are notably religious (DeLair, 2000; Greenfeld, 2015; Moore & Stambolis-Ruhstorfer, 2013; Perin, Pinderhughes, Mattern, Hurley, & Newman, 2016).

A number of disclaimers need to be made regarding this body of literature, however. Most of it is in the context of the United States and other predominantly white, Western nations. The main context for such work is in cisgendered lesbian or gay-identified dyadic couples, while single-parent households or other relationship formations (e.g., thruples), including those headed by people who identify as transgender, bisexual, or queer, receive little to no attention. Similarly, additional investigation should be conducted with regard to LGBTQ parents and parenting in the context of a LGBTQ-identified person staying within a heteronormative household or couplehood with a different-sex partner.

RAISING (LGBTQ) CHILDREN IN LGBTQ HOUSEHOLDS

With the opening of sperm banks' doors to lesbians in the 1980s there has been a veritable lesbian "baby boom" with a gay male version following closely thereafter due to increasing adoption rights (Bos et al., 2016). Since then, literature has also been booming regarding the effects of LGBTQ parents on their children, as well as on the parents themselves. Overall, little differences have been shown in the development and mental/health outcomes of children raised in LGBTQ households (Ariel & McPherson, 2000; Bos et al., 2016; Bos, van Balen, & van den Boom, 2003, 2004, 2005; Crouch, McNair, & Waters, 2016; Greenfeld, 2015; Hines, 2006; Perin et al., 2016; Starks, Newcomb, & Mustanski, 2015). This also holds true for adopted children through the child welfare system (Goldberg, Kinkler, Moyer, & Weber, 2014) and those donor-conceived (Zweifel, 2015). Generally, children in LGBTQ households develop well (e.g., temperament, mood, aptitude, coping), their parents contribute beneficially to their mental health, and LGBTQ couples show more equity in their roles in the household (Bos et al., 2016; Crouch, McNair, & Waters, 2016). Moreover, this research argues that child health is not dependent on the gender of the parents or their biological connection. Similar to heterosexual households, children in LGBTQ homes are similarly impacted by income, regional environment, the relationship between the parents, and, quite importantly, the stability of the family over time.

All the while, LGBTQ parents and caregivers often parent in similar ways to their heterosexual counterparts and in some ways more effectively. LGBTQ parents contend with similar needs to have more re-/connection with their partners, as well as generally have support from trusted networks (Goldberg et al., 2014). Gay men, while less researched around parenting, have shown to perform similarly to lesbians and heterosexual women (Biblarz & Savci, 2010), and they indicate less depression and parental stress as opposed to heterosexual men (Greenfeld, 2015). Lesbians tend to be less interested in conforming to heteronormative parenting styles, all the while spending more time justifying their quality of parenting (Bos et al., 2004). Similarly, transgender parents have found benefits for themselves and their families by challenging gender norms, which can deepen intimacies (Hines, 2006). Interestingly, for children who themselves are LGBTQ growing up with and having strong attachments with LGBTQ parents can be a protective factor, including increasing positive mental health development and prolonging the commencement of dating relationships (D'Augelli, Rendina, Sinclair, & Grossman, 2007; Starks et al., 2015).

All this said, it is important to unhinge both hetero/homonormative assumptions and privilege from parenthood and the practice of parenting. This body of research is not aimed at or showing that LGBTQ parents are simply "the same" as heterosexual parents (see Lev, 2010). LGBTQ households are many things including, quite importantly, permutations of parenting performance, which is only now starting to become understood by empirical research. LGBTQ households and parents continue to develop new structures of intimacy and affiliation, contextualized responses to enduring stigma and prejudice, unique solutions for mounting trusted supports, and creative avenues for being in community. One of the most radical strengths and potentials for LGBTQ families may, in fact, be the ability to be outside of the singular drive to procreate, that is, to create a future through child rearing, or replication of one's heredity. Instead, LGBTQ people fall out of heteronormative timelines for household construction, parenthood, and expectations of development (Halberstam, 2005). As well, LGBTQ people have more investments in, as Edelman (2004) contends, *reproductive futurity*—or the potential for a social world that is more just and simply better due to their participation in parenting, community, and refuting heteronormativity.

SEPARATION, DIVORCE, AND REBUILDING
INTIMATE RELATIONSHIPS

When relationships among LGBTQ couples and families begin to dissipate due to myriad challenges (e.g., poor communication, intimacy, adultery, finances, childcare), the eventual need for break-up, separation, or divorce may be inevitable. Such life transitions for LGBTQ couples and families often create "turning points" (Muraco & Fredriksen-Goldsen, 2016) in which changes may bring stress and strain yet also new pathways for self-growth and development. In a study ($n = 33$) of lesbian and gay adults over the age of 50, major turning points identified by participants included family and relationships, work-related achievements, coming out, and loss or death of a loved one (Muraco & Fredriksen-Goldsen, 2016). While the majority of participants identified beginning and ending relationships as the most common turning point, lesbians noted that the end of their relationships was more of a turning point for them than gay men. Lesbian respondents also maintained relationships/friendships with their former partners post-separation more so than gay male respondents (Muraco & Fredriksen-Goldsen, 2016). This study provides some important considerations for practitioners and social workers related to assessing and understanding the impact of significant turning points across the lifespan for their LGBTQ clients, most especially during expected or unexpected changes (e.g., separation/ divorce, loss/death). Monitoring and measuring a client's ability to manage such potential stress and strain countered by an ability to cope and adapt as well as maintain resilience and hardiness is essential.

Historically, without the legal sanctioning of LGBTQ relationships via marriage, domestic partnerships, or civil unions, such relationships were often perceived as "less than" opposite-sex couplings and therefore in many ways were not legitimized. Such challenges of legitimacy were evidenced in research conducted before the legalization of marriage for same-sex couples. One study ($N = 32$) of gay men married in Iowa found mixed results with regard to the impact of positive family reactions (Ocobock, 2013). While marriage did result in greater relationship recognition and legitimacy (from in-laws as well), along with increased family support and inclusion, some participants re-experienced rejection from nonsupportive family members along with some noting new experiences of rejection from previously supportive family members (Ocobock, 2013). With evolving mindsets both within and outside of the LGBTQ community, along with long-fought federal recognition of such relationships, comes the need to more clearly understand how separations are managed whether formally via a divorce or informally via a short/long-term separation. There is little (if any) long-term data to assist with understanding the various factors causing separations and divorces that may be similar to opposite-sex relationships or unique to same-sex couples and partnerships. Limited literature in this area often focuses on assessing the impact of lesbian and gay parenting after a post-heterosexual separation or divorce and the related impact upon their children (Tasker, 2013). One study of separated lesbian couples ($N = 40$) found that shared custody of their children was important especially in cases where one mother legally adopted the other partner's birth child and that there was no difference in their children's well-being and development with coparenting and shared custody situations (Gartrell, Bos, Peyser, & Rodas, 2011). A larger study ($N = 3,009$) comparing stability related to marriage and longevity among same-sex and opposite-sex couples found the break-up rate to be similar for both types of couples (Rosenfeld, 2014). Similarly, the predictors for decreasing relationship dissolution related to the longevity of the marriage or partnership (as those with a lengthier time together were less likely to divorce or separate) as well as the quality of the relationship(s) and household income (Rosenfeld, 2014). Other reasons for relationship dissolution were highlighted in a study of heterosexual, lesbian, and gay male adoptive parents by Goldberg and Garcia (2015) in which they found couples ($N = 190$) who adopted older children were at higher risk for separation/divorce, as well as those feeling less prepared for adoption and those with very high or very low preadoption relationship maintenance behaviors. However, the study found no difference between adoptive same-sex and opposite-sex couples related to the odds of ending their relationships (Goldberg & Garcia, 2015). The implications of this study by Goldberg and Garcia may assist social workers, practitioners, and adoption placement staff with assessing parental readiness to adopt, discussing the impact on existing relationships (e.g., not adopting to repair a broken or strained relationship), and providing ample supportive services to reduce the potential for separation or divorce to benefit both same-sex and opposite sex couples and their children alike.

There are a number of programs and services that can assist LGBTQ couples and families faced with divorce, separation, and/or reunification that extends beyond couples, family, or marital counseling. Depending on local and state resources, there may be school-based support groups for children with separated or divorced parents, divorce educational classes, and workshops and mediation services (Gustavsson & MacEachron, 2014). Ultimately, when LGBTQ couples break up, separate, or divorce, there may be a wide variety of implications pertaining to their overall health and mental health, financial stability/instability, social and familial relationships, and welfare of their children that social workers and practitioners must be effectively prepared to attend to.

UNIQUE LIFESPAN PERSPECTIVES

It is important not only to assess how dating and relationships may be uniquely different for segments of the LGBTQ community but also across age cohorts and stages of lifespan development. A study of older LGBTQ adults ($N = 2,560$) acknowledging the impact of discriminatory experiences over one's lifetime provides important insight into perceptions of the quality of life among adults over the age of 50 when compared to younger generations that have been raised in more accepting community and family environments (Fredriksen-Goldsen, Kim, Shiu, Goldsen, & Emlet, 2015). Such lifetime experiences of prejudice, oppression, and discrimination likely have a negative impact on overall quality of life as well as myriad health and mental health factors (Fredriksen-Goldsen, Kim, Barkan, Muraco, & Hoy-Ellis, 2013; Fredriksen-Goldsen et al., 2015). Thus it may be helpful to briefly look at two unique LGBTQ age cohorts, specifically youth and older adults for insight into how relationships differ across the lifespan for members of the LGBTQ community.

LGBTQ youth begin to develop romantic and sexual attractions for others about the same time and age as their heterosexual and cisgender peers—while also believing that these are norma-tive developmental patterns (Savin-Williams & Cohen, 2015). For the most part, LGB youth often first recognize emerging sexual orientations when they begin to experience sexual attrac-tions for another (Martos, Nezhad, & Meyer, 2015); however, transgender youth may be less likely to engage in sexual exploration as they may experience significant distress or anxiety if dysphoria about their bodies is intense (Steensma, Kreukels, de Vries, & Cohen-Kettenis, 2013). What remains distinctly different is the absence of appropriate social supports, cultural endorse-ments, and familial guidance about how such relationships might evolve and develop over time. For example, sex education programs and textbooks in schools typically and exclusively con-tain heterosexual-oriented content punctuated with heteronormative language—without any mention of variability in sexual orientations or gender expressions. While progress on this front has been slow, recently the state of California's educational system approved inclusion of topics related to the LGBTQ community and history within their elementary, middle, and high school statewide curriculum (Resmovits, 2016). In the same fashion, public and private school systems should progressively act in assisting LGBTQ youth with their overall development, from navigat-ing the coming out process, to strengthening family and peer relations, as well as dealing with the often complicated processes of dating, coupling, sex, and sexuality. Insuring that schools all have effectively trained and LGBTQ-affirming counselors, educators, and administrators is essential, along with establishing and sanctioning clubs or groups such as Gay/Straight Alliances (GSAs) or Queer/Straight Alliances (QSAs).

When most heterosexual and cisgendered youth first develop romantic relationships and begin to date others, they can usually expect to benefit from positive appraisals from valued adults and peers. Such behaviors are seen as positive markers of healthy developmental progression. For LGBTQ youth, these developmental events are conjoined with the need to come out to friends and family—also involving the prospect of facing realistic fears of disapproval, rejection, physical violence, or homelessness. Because same-sex relationships can be viewed as serious violations of familial, cultural, or religious core values, the negative stereotypes and false assumptions of these relationships focus inordinate attention on sexual behaviors rather than on the development of affectionate relationships and emotional attachments.

Quite often, few families are prepared to provide guidance or support for adolescents navigat-ing the emotional minefield of same-sex romantic relationships, dating, sexuality, and inevitable heartbreak. Paradoxically, support from various systems (e.g., family, peers, school) is exactly what is required to counter negative health and mental health outcomes (e.g., helplessness, hopeless-ness, loneliness, suicide ideation) for LGBTQ youth (McConnell, Birkett, & Mustanski, 2015). This can be even more challenging for some racial/ethnic, rural, religious, and other family sys-tems with LGBTQ children. As LGBTQ youth begin to explore emotional attachments and romantic alliances, the often powerful and internalized negative messages received from family, religions, and cultures related to certain morality, propensity for poor mental health and addiction, general unhappiness, legal prohibitions, and physical danger may significantly impact their early relationships and must be countered by positive messages and imagery about their development as young adults. Self-rejection and the inability to fully accept oneself as capable of having healthy relationships as inherently good adversely affects one's ability to form and maintain stable and lasting relationships (LeBlanc, Frost, & Wight, 2015).

OLDER ADULTS

LGBTQ older adults (65 years and older) have unique needs to be met that include quality-of-life issues associated with safety, security, and long-term life planning (Fredriksen-Goldsen et al., 2015; Knauer, 2010). As discussed in chapter 10, older adults in the LGBTQ community may have relied strongly on their friends and families of choice throughout their lives without children or other family supports (Gabrielson, 2011). When needs increase for older LGBTQ adults across several areas (e.g., medical, health and mental health care, legal, religious and spiritual needs, housing, socialization) reliance on various systems of care (e.g., medical professionals, counselors, assisted living facilities, faith-based institutions) is necessary to insure such needs are not addressed in isolation (Orel, 2014). However, at times such professionals and systems are not affirming or fully understand the unique needs of older LGBTQ adults (Crisp, Wayland, & Gordon, 2008; Hughes, Harold, & Boyer, 2011), and therefore issues related to stigma, oppression, isolation, and hopelessness may arise. If family care is unavailable due to distance or previously fractured relationships, social workers and other practitioners must intervene, advocate, and insure the safety of all older LGBTQ adults at all times. It should also not be assumed that older LGBTQ adults do not seek relationships, partnerships, intimacy, or sex (Syme, 2014). In fact, older LGBTQ adults do seek intimate and relational connections whether living independently at home or within various care systems. In that regard, assisted living facilities may create and foster hostile environments whether caused by staff or other residents, therefore affirming practice skills and trainings (Crisp et al., 2008) are essential—as well as the constant monitoring for any type of bullying, homo-/transphobia or potential for verbal or physical neglect and/or abuse. Along with agencies and staff members, state and local licensing boards should be trained to insure the facilities they oversee are affirming, nurturing, safe, and caring environments for all their residents (Crisp et al., 2008; Gabrielson, 2011; Hillman & Hinrichsen, 2014). There is much promise as some larger cities (e.g., Chicago, New York, Palm Springs) are opening (or have opened) housing facilities for LGBTQ elders.

Long-term planning includes insuring that an older LGBTQ individual's health, mental health, housing, and financial needs are secure. While costly for many individuals, it is essential to insure that wills and living wills are created with legal oversight (via power of attorney) meeting state requirements in which an older LGBTQ person resides, medical directives created and healthcare proxies are identified who respect and will carry through with last wishes, and requirements for estates are met (Arthur, 2015; Knauer, 2010). There are a number of national organizations that can assist LGBTQ individuals, couples, and families with such needs including AARP, SAGE, LAMBDA Legal, and HRC among other agencies, hotlines, and networks at the national and local level.

Last, when a member of the LGBTQ community is dying, or faced with bereavement or death of a spouse, partner, child, family member, friend, or pet, social workers and practitioners must allow for management of expected or anticipated losses (Walter, McCoyd, & Walter, 2015) and an appropriate grieving period and process—which varies widely based on each individual's reactions and resilience, healing, and coping mechanisms (Hooyman & Kramer, 2013)—and arrange for outside services or care if available and necessary (e.g., hospice, pastoral or grief counseling; Arthur, 2015). Such needs described in this section on older adults may be similar to those outside of the LGBTQ community; however, years of stigma, oppression, and trauma may exacerbate an individual, couple, or family's ability to navigate the often complex and complicated systems of care (Fredriksen-Goldsen et al., 2015). Social workers must ensure that older LGBTQ adult's needs are met with regard to wills and estates, short- or long-term housing needs, or health and mental health care—all while life expectations extend for many people well into their 70s, 80s, and beyond.

IMPLICATIONS FOR PRACTICE

This section examines some of the implications for practice with LGBTQ couples and with regard to family therapy. To begin this discussion, it may be helpful to look at two specific LGBTQ community examples, such as some of the unique challenges that may be faced by bisexual and transgender couples and families.

THE BISEXUAL COMMUNITY

As mentioned earlier in this chapter, the bisexual community is often not widely discussed within the literature or research associated with dating and family formations when compared to lesbians and gay men. As noted by Biblarz and Savci (2010), there are a good number of questions that remain unanswered with regard to fully appreciating and understanding the dynamics of bisexuality related to dating, coupling, and various family formations. Such questions pertain to parental reactions to their child's bisexual identity compared to a gay or lesbian identity; parenting patterns, styles, and formations (e.g., bisexual men and women having children with same-sex or opposite-sex partners); and how children and their bisexual parent(s) navigate relationships if there are shifts in same-sex or opposite-sex partners across the lifespan (Biblarz & Savci, 2010).

Notably, the bisexual community is exposed to multiple levels of oppression and marginalization not only from the heterosexual community but often from the LGBTQ community as well (Scherrer, 2013). Even while faced with such challenges, we do know that, for many bisexual adults, there is a strong and clear definition of their identity that clearly defies existing oppressive and stereotypical biases associated with assuming bisexuality is inauthentic, transitional, or a duplicitous identity (Scherrer, 2013). As examined and underscored by Diamond (2009), bisexuality is clearly a sexual orientation not unlike that of those identifying as gay or lesbian. In a study of bisexual parents ($N = 48$) in Australia and New Zealand, researchers found that participants noted challenges not unlike non-bisexual families pertaining to discipline, finances, balancing life, work and family needs, and seeking more quality time, among other common factors (Power et al., 2012). Bisexual parenting is likely quite similar to gay and lesbian parenting when in the context of a same-sex relationship or with a single parent, yet such parenting formations and styles are likely uniquely different from those of same-sex couplings, especially when in the context of a heterosexual relationship (Power et al., 2012). In one study of LGBTQ children ($N = 19$) with lesbian and bisexual mothers, researchers found themes associated with parents having a positive influence on their child(ren)'s discovery of their own sexual or gender identities; children experiencing fears resulting from heterosexism and societal scrutiny of their lesbian or bisexual mother(s) identities along with pressures to be to be gender-conforming or heterosexual; and the role of parental social support either in supporting them with their own LGBTQ identity formation and disclosure or having little impact on the same (Kuvalanka & Goldberg, 2009). For the sake of practice with the bisexual community, social workers and all practitioners should monitor their attitudes, values, and beliefs about bisexuality as well as for underlying biphobia and fully understand how development, social relationships, and sexual health may be unique for members of the bisexual community (Scherrer, 2013) when compared to their lesbian, gay, or heterosexual counterparts. While there remains a need for more knowledge on many levels related to affirming practice among members of the bisexual community, for additional information (e.g., partnering, coupling, monogamy, polyamory, children, family topics), see chapter 15 in this text.

THE TRANSGENDER COMMUNITY

Members of the transgender and gender nonconforming community seek partners and families in the same form and fashion as other members of the LGBQ community, yet there sadly remains a dearth of information about their lived experiences (Blumer, Green, Knowles, & Williams, 2012). There are substantial challenges faced by transgender individuals, couples, and families that pertain to discrimination, transphobia, access and utilization of health care and mental health care services, general safety concerns, a lack of resources and affirming care systems, and fractured systems of family, peer, and community care (Downing, 2013; Grossman & D'Augelli, 2006). Practitioners must be aware of these challenges as well as how developmental stages (e.g., adolescence, adulthood, older age) and topics associated with dating, coupling, marriage, and separation uniquely impact members of the transgender community (e.g., school nondiscrimination policies, changing name and/or gender identification markers on a birth certificate or driver's license, residing in an assisted living facility or nursing home, and so on.). Other unique facets associated with transgender dating, coupling, and family formations that social workers and practitioners should be aware of relate to not making assumptions about their partnerships or binary constructions of gender, gender identity, and sexual orientation (Giammattei, 2015). In fact, transgender individuals may define themselves in many ways such as transman, transwoman, or transgender along with ascribing to a sexual orientation that may include heterosexual, lesbian, gay, bisexual, asexual, pansexual, and so on (Giammattei, 2015). While transgender relationships can be widely defined, partnerships may have unique challenges such as those pertaining to coming out and disclosure of one's transgender identity. For example, when one member of a couple has to disclose their evolving or changing gender identity, gender expression, or sexual orientation to a partner, there may be a need for some form of counseling to assist the couple through the process (Lev, 2013).

Strong therapeutic alliances with transgender clients are helpful so that gender identity discussions or topics related to reassignment surgery are not avoided or delayed by married or partnered couples fearing rejection or child custody issues, among other challenges (Lev, 2013; Lewins, 1995). Gender transition discussions with children are equally important—regardless of whether the couple is staying together or separating, along with ensuring that both parents and extended family members are supportive—limiting interparent conflict as much as possible during the process (Giammattei, 2015; White & Ettner, 2004). Most important, it should be noted that many transgender couples and families have the same challenges as their LGBQ and heterosexual counterparts (e.g., communication challenges, managing finances, child care, sexual relations; Giammattei, 2015; Lev, 2013). For more information about practice with members of the transgender community (e.g., impact of trauma, parenting a transgender or gender nonconforming child), see chapter 16.

COUPLES THERAPY

To understand the unique challenges that LGBTQ couples face, it is important to assess some of the key components of living as a member of a minority community. Some of those challenges directly relate to existing within a heteronormative society over the short term and one's lifetime and managing stressors associated with oppression, stigma, homo/trans/biphobia, family stressors, trauma, and other systemic challenges. While one should not assume that LGBTQ couples have faced such obstacles whether individually or collectively over time, social workers and practitioners should seek clarity related to the presenting problem(s) from each partner and apply the framework of a person-in-environment model while using the strengths perspective to create an affirming therapeutic alliance—always underscoring the couple's resilience (Lev, 2015). At the same time, caution must be applied and practitioners should base decisions on the best route for therapy along with the LGBTQ couple in a mutual partnership. Avoiding assumptions is essential as the issues a couple may be struggling with (e.g., communication, financial, childcare, work) may be simply "just that"—and may have nothing to do with either partner's sexual orientation, gender identity, or gender expression. When available, LGBTQ couples typically seek affirming LGBTQ therapists or groups for therapeutic services. The manner in which they can or cannot locate such important resources may relate to their health insurance coverage and costs associated with copayments, urban versus rural locations, personal referrals that can speak to the practitioner's reputation and history of work with the LGBTQ community, office location, and hours.

Practitioners should be familiar with the unique norms and cultures of the LGBTQ community to effectively practice and avoid stereotyping, making heterosexist assumptions, and pathologizing what each couple may consider "normal" within the parameters of their relationship (Bepko & Johnson, 2000). To expand on content discussed earlier in this chapter, the uniqueness of what defines a "couple" outside of the typical realm of heteronormative frameworks may be important to understand with each LGBTQ couple in the early stages of intake (Heck, Flentje, & Cochran, 2013) and assessment prior to treatment or during the first few sessions. Social workers and practitioners should insure that they are consistently on the same page with the couple in understanding terms, definitions, and meanings. Therefore, embracing a LGBTQ couple's unique queer narratives and relationship structure while deconstructing hetero- and homonormative frameworks and paradigms is essential to be an affirming social worker and practitioner (Hudak & Giammattei,

2014). Oppositely, to not engage in such a conversation with a LGBTQ couple might create significant barrier; for example, a lesbian couple describing challenges with fidelity in a polyamorous relationship is likely much different than a lesbian couple describing challenges with fidelity in a monogamous relationship, and so on.

It would not be atypical for therapists and practitioners seeing LGBTQ couples to use many common tools (e.g., ecomaps, genograms) as well as to manage typical conflictual issues and defense mechanisms (e.g., sexuality, power, scapegoating, triangulation) while tuning in to the couple's unique norms, values, and meanings related to monogamy, sex, relations with biological family compared to family of choice, and so on (Bepko & Johnson, 2000). Models and theoretical approaches that have been found to be most effective in working with LGBTQ couples may include behavioral approaches (e.g., cognitive behavioral therapy), psychodynamic approaches (e.g., Bowen's family systems), social constructionist (e.g., narrative, solution focused), or systemic approaches (e.g., brief/strategic, structural; see Gurman, Lebow, & Snyder, 2015). Lastly, and yet likely of utmost importance, practitioners should always utilize the lens of relational intersectionality to understand LGBTQ couple's multiple identities (e.g., gender, race, ethnicity, sexual orientation, gender identity, and beyond) as critical to understanding the unique lived experiences of couples seeking therapy (Addison & Coolhart, 2015). Such an intersectional approach to couple's therapy with LGBTQ clients implies that the unique and often complex identity of each individual will intersect within their partnership as a couple—therefore social workers, therapists, and practitioners: "must not only understand how each individual's multiple identities intersect, but also how each partner's complex identities overlap with and intersect with one another" (Addison & Coolhart, 2015, p. 442).

FAMILY THERAPY

Whether discussing individuals, couples, or families, it is indicated that practitioners enact an ethic of acceptance with their LGBTQ clients as well as create a space that is validating, affirmative, and open to the re-/narration of lived experiences (see Davies, 1996; Tilsen & Nylund, 2010). Consistent with one subtheme across this chapter, when it comes to locating practice models for LGBTQ families there is a paucity of research and empirically validated translation of existing models into these, admittedly, varied familial contexts (LaSala, 2013). This certainly is a function of another subtheme: heteronormative assumptions about family and heterosexist standpoints have occluded this work and made the conversation inhospitable to other ways of relating outside of domesticity, romance, and monogamy. LaSala (2013) documents the evolution of the family in clinical practice with LGBTQ people, arguing for three waves in modern practice. The first wave was a gestalt of "blaming the family" such that family dysfunctions were looked at as the cause for nonnormative and pathological variants in their children (e.g., gay children being diseased). The second wave was a period of "avoiding the family" in that LGBTQ people largely looked outside families of origins for community, support, and affiliation; they created what is commonly discussed as "families of choice." Finally, in the third wave, the family became a "resource" such that families have been more affirmative toward sexual and gender differences as well as been a protective factor against a heterosexist and prejudiced environment.

Despite the lack of empirically validated specific practice models and approaches, recommendations responsive to LGBTQ families do exist, as have been discussed. Quite succinctly, Boggis (2012) provides a self-reflective agenda based on having worked with LGBTQ people for more than 20 years. Boggis recommends practitioners tend to a number of areas, including the effects of an invalidating legal and social climate; dialogues about deciding to become parents and then announcing those decisions to extended family; tendencies to revert to the proverbial closet as a coping strategy, especially within heterosexist environments; planning scripts and strategies for how to incorporate more people at the table, per se, such as donor dads or surrogate participants; intentional bonding rituals for nonbiological parents; active strategies to cultivate community and coping with potential loss of LGBTQ connections due to newly assembled roles as parents; intentional practices to blend cultures (e.g., racial/ethnic, immigrant); and tending to re-/narrating dialogues around LGBTQ parents and/or children coming out within the family system, as well as other communities. It would also be endemic to these efforts that practitioners continually check their own heterosexist biases and hetero/homonormative standpoints. Bernstein (2000) even formalizes that last crucial point into a model of self-reflective and ethical practice, called the cultural literacy model, especially useful for when heterosexual practitioners are working with LGBTQ families.

Other researchers and practitioners dovetail these recommendations. Braverman (2015) directs attention to the multiple roles and ethics that mental health practitioners invariably have to navigate when working with families in reproductive health clinics, including shuttling among being one who provides assessments and psychoeducation to being a gatekeeper of services. Degges-White and Marszalek (2007) argue for practitioners to be competent in the legal and social service systems that in-/directly affect LGBTQ families and from there facilitate explicit conversations about division of labor within the home. Another essential discussion would be around sexual scripts for nonmonogamous agreements, which includes practitioners also assessing their own preconceived notions (Degges-White & Marszalek, 2007; Hosking, 2013). Parallel to these elements for dialogue, Singh and McKleroy (2010) make the argument for a continual, multifaceted cultural assessment, one that considers intersecting forces and effects of histories (current or past) of trauma and violence, experiences with families of origin, gender and racial/ethnic oppressions, access to resources (e.g., health care), spirituality and religious resources, as well as connections with a chosen community, among other elements. Given these considerations, LaSala (2013) does argue for the existing modes of clinical practice of structural and strategic family therapy to be adapted and deployed in doing family therapy work with LGBTQ people.

CONCLUSION

This chapter examined some of the many facets of coupling, partnering, and family structures relevant to practice with the LGBTQ community. By no means exhaustive, this chapter began by looking at snapshots related to recent numbers of LGBTQ couples, families, and child care relationships across the United States. This was followed by a discussion of the many challenges faced by LGBTQ couples and families due to historical, social, and structural/systemic forces over time (e.g., family, religion, policy, oppression from within the LGBTQ community). Social workers must remain open with regard to understanding the unique definitions of couplings and family formations among the LGBTQ community. "Family" can no longer be characterized as two opposite-sex, cisgender, biological parents with two heterosexual children, living behind the proverbial white picket fence, driving a mini-van. Understanding both traditional and nontraditional structures and frameworks remains essential for practitioners to effectively work with their LGBTQ clients. Such structures may align directly with existing heteronormative styles, while oppositely other couples and families may outright reject or, better yet, transform such relationships and form their own structures, terms, and meanings. What is most fascinating and challenging is that research and literature remains new and evolving with regard to our understanding of LGBTQ couples and families. Similarly, the expansion of marriage equality in the United States in 2015 will likely transform such dialogues about LGBTQ families and couples in the years ahead. Globally, there remains room for significant progress among many nations and countries that continue to be challenged with the promotion of human rights for their LGBTQ citizens, couples, children, and families.

REFERENCES

Addison, S. M., & Coolhart, D. (2015). Expanding the therapy paradigm with queer couples: A relational intersectional lens. *Family Process, 54*(3), 435–453.

Albury, K. (2014). Porn and sex education, porn as sex education. *Porn Studies, 1*(1–2), 172–181.

Andersen, J. P., Zou, C., & Blosnich, J. (2015). Multiple early victimization experiences as a pathway to explain physical health disparities among sexual minority and heterosexual individuals. *Social Science & Medicine, 133,* 111–119.

Annes, A., & Redlin, M. (2012). Coming out and coming back: Rural gay migration and the city. *Journal of Rural Studies, 28*(1), 56–68.

Ariel, J., & McPherson, D. W. (2000). Therapy with lesbian and gay parents and their children. *Journal of Marital and Family Therapy, 26*(4), 421–432.

Arnold, E. A., Sterrett-Hong, E., Jonas, A., & Pollack, L. M. (2016). Social networks and social support among ball-attending African American men who have sex with men and transgender women are associated with HIV-related outcomes. *Global Public Health,* 1–15.

Arthur, D. P. (2015). Social work practice with LGBT elders at end of life: Developing practice evaluation and clinical skills through a cultural perspective. *Journal of Social Work in End-of-Life & Palliative Care, 11*(2), 178–201.

Bauermeister, J. A., Johns, M. M., Sandfort, T. G., Eisenberg, A., Grossman, A. H., & D'Augelli, A. R. (2010). Relationship trajectories and psychological well-being among sexual minority youth. *Journal of Youth and Adolescence, 39,* 1148–1163.

BBC News. (2014, February 10). Where is it illegal to be gay? *BBC News.* Retrieved from http://www.bbc.com/news/world-25927595

Bepko, C., & Johnson, T. (2000). Gay and lesbian couples in therapy: Perspectives for the contemporary family therapist. *Journal of Marital and Family Therapy, 26*(4), 409–419.

Berkowitz, D. (2007). A sociohistorical analysis of gay men's procreative consciousness. *Journal of GLBT Family Studies, 3,* 157–190.

Berkowitz, D., & Marsiglio, W. (2007). Gay men: Negotiating procreative, father, and family identities. *Journal of Marriage and Family, 69,* 366–381.

Bernstein, A. C. (2000). Straight therapists working with lesbians and gays in family therapy. *Journal of Marital and Family Therapy, 26*(4), 443–454.

Beymer, M. R., Rossi, A. D., & Shu, S. B. (2016). Assessing self-control and geosocial networking app behavior among an online sample of men who have sex with men. *Journal of Urban Health 93*(4), 698–708. doi:10.1007/s11524-016-0056-7

Beymer, M. R., Weiss, R., Bolan, R. K., Rudy, E. T., Bourque, L. B., Rodriguez, J. P., & Morisky, D. E. (2014). Sex on demand: Geosocial networking phone apps and risk of sexually transmitted infections among a cross-sectional sample of men who have sex with men in Los Angeles County. *Sexually Transmitted Infections, 90*, 567–572.

Beyond Same-Sex Marriage. (2008). Beyond same-sex marriage: A new strategic vision for all our families and relationships. *Studies in Gender and Sexuality, 9*, 161–171.

Biblarz, T. J., & Savci, E. (2010). Lesbian, gay, bisexual, and transgender families. *Journal of Marriage and Family, 72*(3), 480–497.

Blumer, M. L., Green, M. S., Knowles, S. J., & Williams, A. (2012). Shedding light on thirteen years of darkness: Content analysis of articles pertaining to transgender issues in marriage/couple and family therapy journals. *Journal of Marital and Family Therapy, 38*(Suppl. 1), 244–256.

Boggis, T. (2012). The real modern family. . . can be real complicated. *Journal of Gay & Lesbian Mental Health, 16*(4), 353–360.

Bos, H. M. W., Knox, J. R., van Rijn-van Gelderen, L., & Gartrell, N. K. (2016). Same-sex and different-sex parent households and child health outcomes: Findings from the National Survey of Children's Health. *Journal of Developmental & Behavioral Pediatrics, 37*, 179–186.

Bos, H. M. W., van Balen, F., & van den Boom, D. C. (2003). Planned lesbian families: Their desire and motivation to have children. *Human Reproduction, 18*(10), 2216–2224.

Bos, H. M. W., van Balen, F., & van den Boom, D. (2004). Experience of parenthood, couple relationship, social support, and child-rearing goals in planned lesbian mother families. *Journal of Child Psychology and Psychiatry, 45*(4), 755–764.

Bos, H. M. W., van Balen, F., & van den Boom, D. C. (2005). Lesbian families and family functioning: An overview. *Patient Education and Counseling, 59*, 263–275.

Bricker, M. E., & Horne, S. G. (2007). Gay men in long-term relationships. *Journal of Couple and Relationship Therapy, 6*(4), 27–47.

Bryant, K. (2008). In defense of gay children? "Progay" homophobia and the production of homonormativity. *Sexualities, 11*(4), 455–475.

Buffie, W. C. (2011). Public health implications of same-sex marriage. *American Journal of Public Health, 101*(6), 986–990.

Butler, J. (1999). *Gender trouble: Feminism and the subversion of identity*. New York: Routledge. (Original work published 1990)

Cahill, S., & South, K. (2002). Policy issues affecting lesbian, gay, bisexual, and transgender people in retirement. *Generations, 26*(2), 1–6.

Cashore, C., & Tuason, M. T. G. (2009). Negotiating the binary: Identity and social justice for bisexual and transgender individuals. *Journal of Gay & Lesbian Social Services, 21*(4), 374–401.

Calderone, M. S. (1972). "Pornography" as a public health problem. *American Journal of Public Health, 62*(3), 374–376.

Carrington, C. (1999). *No place like home: Relationships and family life among lesbians and gay men*. Chicago: University of Chicago Press.

Champagne, J. (1995). *The ethics of marginality: A new approach to gay studies*. Minneapolis: University of Minnesota Press.

Chaney, M. P., & Brubaker, M. (2014). The impact of substance abuse and addiction in the lives of gay men, adolescents, and boys. In M. Kocet (Ed.), *Counseling gay men, adolescents, and boys: A strengths-based guide for helping professionals and educators* (pp. 109–128). New York: Routledge.

Chatterjee, B. B. (2001). Last of rainmacs: Thinking about pornography in cyberspace. In D. S. Walls (Ed.), *Crime and the Internet* (pp. 74–99). New York: Routledge.

Chonody, J. M. (2013). Measuring sexual prejudice against gay men and lesbian women: Development of the Sexual Prejudice Scale (SPS). *Journal of Homosexuality, 60*(6), 895–926.

Cody, P. A., Farr, R. H., McRoy, R. G., Ayers-Lopez, S. J., & Ledesma, K. J. (2017). Youth perspectives on being adopted from foster care by lesbian and gay parents: Implications for families and adoption professionals. *Adoption Quarterly, 20*, 98–118.

Conley, T. D., Moors, A. C., Matsick, J. L., & Ziegler, A. (2013). The fewer the merrier?: Assessing stigma surrounding consensually non-monogamous romantic relationships. *Analyses of Social Issues and Public Policy, 13*(1), 1–30.

Connolly, C. M. (2014). Clinical issues with same sex couples: A review of the literature. In J. Bigner & J. L. Wetchler, J. L. (Eds.), *Relationship therapy with same-sex couples* (pp. 3–12). New York: Routledge.

Corneau, S., & Van der Meulen, E. (2014). Some like it mellow: On gay men complicating pornography discourses. *Journal of Homosexuality, 61*, 491–510.

Crisp, C., Wayland, S., & Gordon, T. (2008). Older gay, lesbian, and bisexual adults: Tools for age-competent and gay affirmative practice. *Journal of Gay & Lesbian Social Services, 20*(1-2), 5–29.

Crouch, S. R., McNair, R., & Waters, E. (2016). Impact of family structure and sociodemographic characteristics on child health and wellbeing in same-sex parent families: A cross-sectional survey. *Journal of Pediatrics and Child Health, 52*, 499–505.

Cunningham, G. B., & Melton, E. N. (2013). The moderating effects of contact with lesbian and gay friends on the relationships among religious fundamentalism, sexism, and sexual prejudice. *Journal of Sex Research, 50*(3–4), 401–408.

D'Augelli, A. R., Rendina, H. J., Sinclair, K. O., & Grossman, A. H. (2007). Lesbian and gay youth's aspirations for marriage and raising children. *Journal of LGBT Issues in Counseling, 1*(4), 77–98

D'Emilio, J. (1983). *Sexual politics, sexual communities: The making of a homosexual minority in the United States, 1940–1970*. Chicago: University of Chicago Press.

Davies, D. (1996). Towards a model of gay affirmative therapy. In D. Davies & C. Neal (Eds.), *Pink therapy: A guide for counsellors and therapists working with lesbian, gay, and bisexual clients* (pp. 24–31). Buckingham, UK: Open University Press.

Degges-White, S., & Marszalek, J. (2007). An exploration of long-term, same-sex relationships. *Journal of LGBT Issues in Counseling, 1*(4), 99–119.

DeLair, C. (2000). Ethical, moral, economic, and legal barriers to assisted reproductive technologies employed by gay men and lesbian women. *DePaul Journal of Healthcare Law, 4*, 147–192.

Diamond, L. M. (2009). *Sexual fluidity: Understanding women's love and desire*. Cambridge, MA: Harvard University Press.

Diaz-Serrano, L., & Meix-Llop, E. (2016). Do schools discriminate against homosexual parents? Evidence from a randomized correspondence experiment. *Economics of Education Review, 53*, 133–142.

Downing, J. B. (2013). Transgender-parent families. In A. E. Goldberg, & K. R. Allen, (Eds.). *LGBT-parent families: Innovations in research and implications for practice* (pp. 105–115). New York: Springer.

Duggan, L. (2002) The new homonormativity: The sexual politics of neoliberalism. In R. Castronovo & D. D. Nelson (Eds.), *Materializing democracy: Toward a revitalized cultural politics* (pp. 175–194). Durham, NC: Duke University Press.

Duggan, L. (2003). *The twilight of equality? Neoliberalism, cultural politics, and the attack on democracy.* Boston: Beacon Press.

Duggan, S. J., & McCreary, D. R. (2004). Body image, eating disorders, and the drive for muscularity in gay and heterosexual men: The influence of media images. *Journal of Homosexuality, 47*(3–4), 45–58.

Dyer, R. (1994). Idol thoughts: Orgasm and self-reflexivity in gay pornography. *Critical Quarterly, 36*(1), 49–62.

Edelman, L. (2004). *No future: Queer theory and the death drive*. Durham, NC: Duke University Press.

Eng, D. L., Halberstam, J., & Muñoz, J. E. (2005). Introduction: What's queer about queer studies now? *Social Text, 84–85*(23, 3–4), 1–17.

Erickson, L. (2016). Transforming cultures of (un) desirability: Creating cultures of resistance. *Graduate Journal of Social Science, 12*(1), 11–22.

Fedewa, A. L., Black, W. W., & Ahn, S. (2015). Children and adolescents with same-gender parents: A meta-analytic approach in assessing outcomes. *Journal of GLBT Family Studies, 11*(1), 1–34.

Feinstein, B. A., Dyar, C., Bhatia, V., Latack, J. A., & Davila, J. (2016). Conservative beliefs, attitudes towards bisexuality, and willingness to engage in romantic and sexual activities with a bisexual partner. *Archives of Sexual Behavior, 45*(6), 1535–1550. doi:10.1007/s10508-015-0642-x.

Fredriksen-Goldsen, K. I., Kim, H. J., Barkan, S. E., Muraco, A., & Hoy-Ellis, C. P. (2013). Health disparities among lesbian, gay, and bisexual older adults: Results from a population-based study. *American Journal of Public Health, 103*(10), 1802–1809.

Fredriksen-Goldsen, K. I., Kim, H. J., Shiu, C., Goldsen, J., & Emlet, C. A. (2015). Successful aging among LGBT older adults: Physical and mental health-related quality of life by age group. *The Gerontologist, 55*(1), 154–168.

Friedman, S., Reynolds, A., Scovill, S., Brassier, F. R., Campbell, R., & Ballou, M. (2013). *An estimate of housing discrimination against same-sex couples*. Retrieved from https://papers.ssrn.com/sol3/papers.cfm?abstract_id=2284243

Gabrielson, M. L. (2011). "We have to create family": Aging support issues and needs among older lesbians. *Journal of Gay & Lesbian Social Services, 23*(3), 322–334.

Gallant, C., & Loralee, G. (2001). Pussies bite back: The story of the women's bathhouse raid. *Torquere: Journal of the Lesbian and Gay Studies Association, 3*, 152–167.

Galupo, M. P., Lomash, E., & Mitchell, R. C. (2017). "All of my lovers fit into this scale": Sexual minority individuals' responses to two novel measures of sexual orientation. *Journal of Homosexuality, 64*(2), 145–165.

Gartrell, N., Bos, H., Peyser, H., Deck, A., & Rodas, C. (2011). Family characteristics, custody arrangements, and adolescent psychological well-being after lesbian mothers break up. *Family Relations, 60*(5), 572–585.

Gates, G. J. (2012). Family formation and raising children among same-sex couples. *National Council of Family Relations, 51*(1).

Gates, G. J. (2013). *LGBT parenting in the United States*. Los Angeles, CA: Williams Institute. Retrieved at: http://williamsinstitute.law.ucla.edu/wp-content/uploads/LGBT-Parenting.pdf

Gates, G. J. (2015a). *Demographics of married and unmarried same-sex couples: Analyses of the 2013 American Community Survey*. Los Angeles, CA: Williams Institute. Retrieved from http://williamsinstitute.law.ucla.edu/research/census-lgbt-demographics-studies/demographics-of-married-and-unmarried-same-sex-couples-analyses-of-the-2013-american-community-survey/

Gates, G. J. (2015b). Marriage and family: LGBT individuals and same-sex couples. *The Future of Children*, 67–87.

Giammattei, S. V. (2015). Beyond the binary: Trans-negotiations in couple and family therapy. *Family Process, 54*(3), 418–434.

Giwa, S., & Greensmith, C. (2012). Race relations and racism in the LGBTQ community of Toronto: Perceptions of gay and queer social service providers of color. *Journal of Homosexuality, 59*, 149–185.

Goldberg, A. E., & Garcia, R. (2015). Predictors of relationship dissolution in lesbian, gay, and heterosexual adoptive parents. *Journal of Family Psychology, 29*(3), 394.

Goldberg, A. E., Kinkler, L. A., Moyer, A. M., & Weber, E. (2014). Intimate relationship challenges in early parenthood among lesbian, gay, and heterosexual couples adopting via the child welfare system. *Professional Psychology: Research and Practice, 45*(4), 221–230.

Goldberg, A. E., & Scheib, J. E. (2015). Why donor insemination and not adoption? Narratives of female-partnered and single mothers. *Family Relations, 64*(5), 726–742.

Greenfeld, D. A. (2015). Effects and outcomes of third-party reproduction: Parents. *Fertility and Sterility, 104*(3), 520–524.

Gross, L. (2012). *Up from invisibility: Lesbians, gay men, and the media in America.* New York: Columbia University Press.

Grosskophf, N. A., LeVasseur, M. T., & Glaser, D. B. (2014). Use of the Internet and mobile based "apps" for sex-seeking among men who have sex with men in New York City. *American Journal of Men's Health, 8*(6), 510–520.

Grossman, A. H., & D'Augelli, A. R. (2006). Transgender youth: Invisible and vulnerable. *Journal of Homosexuality, 51*(1), 111–128.

Graham, J. M., & Barnow, Z. B. (2013). Stress and social support in gay, lesbian, and heterosexual couples: Direct effects and buffering models. *Journal of Family Psychology, 27*(4), 569.

Grov, C., Breslow, A. S., Newcomb, M. E., Rosenberger, J. G., & Bauermeister, J. A. (2014). Gay and bisexual men's use of the internet: Research from the 1990s through 2013. *Journal of Sex Research, 51*(4), 390–409.

Gudelunas, D. (2012). There's an app for that: The uses and gratifications of online social networks for gay men. *Sexuality & Culture, 16*, 347–365.

Gurman, A. S., Lebow, J. L., & Snyder, D. K. (Eds.). (2015). *Clinical handbook of couple therapy.* New York: Guilford Press.

Gustavson, M. (2009). Bisexuals in relationships: Uncoupling intimacy from gender ontology. *Journal of Bisexuality, 9*(3–4), 407–429.

Gustavsson, N., & MacEachron, A. (2014). Gay divorce. *Social Work, 59*(3), 283–285.

Halberstam, J. (2005). *In a queer time and place: Transgender bodies, subcultural lives.* New York: New York University Press.

Halkitis, P. N., Levy, M. D., Moreira, A. D., & Ferrusi, C. N. (2014). Crystal methamphetamine use and HIV transmission among gay and bisexual men. *Current Addiction Reports, 1*(3), 206–213.

Han, C.-S. (2007). The don't want to cruise your type: Gay men of color and the racial politics of exclusion. *Social Identities, 13*(1), 51–67.

Han, C-S. (2015). *Geisha of a different kind.* New York: New York University Press.

Hatzenbuehler, M. L., McLaughlin, K. A., Keyes, K. M., & Hasin, D. S. (2010). The impact of institutional discrimination on psychiatric disorders in lesbian, gay, and bisexual populations: A prospective study. *American Journal of Public Health, 100*, 452–459.

Heck, N. C., Flentje, A., & Cochran, B. N. (2013). Intake interviewing with lesbian, gay, bisexual, and transgender clients: Starting from a place of affirmation. *Journal of Contemporary Psychotherapy, 43*(1), 23–32.

Herbert, A., & Weaver, A. (2015). Perks, problems, and people who play: A qualitative exploration of dominant and submissive BDSM roles. *The Canadian Journal of Human Sexuality, 24*(1), 49–62. doi:10.3138/cjhs.246749

Herek, G. M. (2006). Legal recognition of same-sex relationships in the United States: A social science perspective. *American Psychologist, 61*, 607–621.

Herek, G. M. (2009). Sexual prejudice. In T. Nelson (Ed.), *Handbook of prejudice, stereotyping, and discrimination* (pp. 441–467). New York: Psychology Press.

Herz, M., & Johansson, T. (2015). The normativity of the concept of heteronormativity. *Journal of Homosexuality, 62*(8), 1009–1020.

Higa, D. (2008). *Gay men's brief sexual connections: Settings, processes, meanings, and ethics* (Unpublished doctoral dissertation). University of Washington, Seattle.

Hightower, J. L. (2015). Producing desirable bodies: Boundary work in a lesbian niche dating site. *Sexualities, 18*(1–2), 20–36.

Hillman, J., & Hinrichsen, G. A. (2014). Promoting an affirming, competent practice with older lesbian and gay adults. *Professional Psychology: Research and Practice, 45*(4), 269–277.

Hines, S. (2006). Intimate transitions: Transgender practices of partnering and parenting. *Sociology, 40*(2), 353–371.

Hooyman, N. R., & Kramer, B. J. (2013). *Living through loss: Interventions across the life span.* New York: Columbia University Press.

Hopkins, J. J., Sorensen, A., & Taylor, V. (2013). Same-sex couples, families, and marriage: Embracing and resisting heteronormativity. *Sociology Compass, 7*(2), 97–110.

Horwitz, A. V., White, H. R., & Howell-White, S. (1996). Becoming married and mental health: A longitudinal study of a cohort of young adults. *Journal of Marriage and Family, 58*(4), 895–907.

Hosking, W. (2013). Agreements about extra-dyadic sex in gay men's relationships: Exploring differences in relationship quality by agreement type and rule-breaking behavior. *Journal of Homosexuality, 60*(5), 711–733.

Hosking, W. (2014). Australian gay men's satisfaction with sexual agreements: The roles of relationship quality, jealousy, and monogamy attitudes. *Archives of Sexual Behavior, 43*, 823–832.

Howard, J. (2016, July 15). Republicans are calling porn a "public health crisis," but is it really? CNN. Retrieved from http://www.cnn.com/2016/07/15/health/porn-public-health-crisis/

Hudak, J., & Giammattei, S. V. (2014). Doing family: Decentering heteronormativity in "marriage" and "family" therapy. In Thorana Nelson & Hinda Winawer (Eds.), *Critical topics in family therapy* (pp. 105–115). Dordrecht: Springer.

Hughes, A. K., Harold, R. D., & Boyer, J. M. (2011). Awareness of LGBT aging issues among aging services network providers. *Journal of Gerontological Social Work, 54*(7), 659–677.

Hughes, M., Morrison, K., & Asada, K. J. (2005). What's love got to do with it: Exploring the impact of maintenance rules, love attitudes and network support on friends with benefits relationships. *Western Journal of Communication, 69*(1), 49–66.

Iantaffi, A., & Bockting, W. O. (2011). Views from both sides of the bridge? Gender, sexual legitimacy and transgender people's experiences of relationships. *Culture, Health & Sexuality, 13*(3), 355–370.

Institutes of Medicine. (2011). *The health of lesbian, gay, bisexual, and transgender people: Building a foundation for better understanding.* Washington DC: Author.

Jennings, S., Mellish, L., Tasker, F., Lamb, M., & Golombok, S. (2014). Why adoption? Gay, lesbian, and heterosexual adoptive parents' reproductive experiences and reasons for adoption. *Adoption Quarterly, 17*(3), 205–226.

Kazyak, E. (2011). Disrupting cultural selves: Constructing gay and lesbian identities in rural locales. *Qualitative Sociology, 34*(4), 561–581.

Kelly, B. C., Bimbi, D. S., Nanin, J. E., Izienicki, H., & Parsons, J. T. (2009). Sexual compulsivity and sexual behaviors among gay and bisexual men and lesbian and bisexual women. *Journal of Sex Research, 46*(4), 301–308.

Kendall, C. N. (1999). Gay male pornography/ gay male community: Power without consent, mimicry without subversion. In J. A. Kuypers (Ed.), *Men and power* (pp. 195–213). New York: Promotheus Books.

Kendall, C. N., & Funk, R. E. (2003). Gay male pornography's "actors": When "fantasy" isn't. *Journal of Trauma Practice, 2*(3–4), 93–114.

Kim, H. K., & McKenry, P. C. (2002). The relationship between marriage and psychological well-being: A longitudinal analysis. *Journal of Family Issues, 23*(8), 885–911.

Knauer, N. J. (2010). Gay and lesbian elders: Estate planning and end-of-life decision making. *Florida Coastal Law Review, 11*, 2011–2016.

Kubicek, K., McNeeley, M., Holloway, I. W., Weiss, G., & Kipke, M. D. (2013). "It's like our own little world": Resilience as a factor in participating in the ballroom community subculture. *AIDS and Behavior, 17*(4), 1524–1539.

Kuvalanka, K. A., & Goldberg, A. E. (2009). "Second generation" voices: Queer youth with lesbian/bisexual mothers. *Journal of Youth and Adolescence, 38*(7), 904–919.

LaSala, M. C. (2013). Out of the darkness: Three waves of family research and the emergence of family therapy for lesbian and gay people. *Clinical Social Work Journal, 41*, 267–276.

Lamble, S. (2009). Unknowable bodies, unthinkable sexualities: Lesbian and transgender legal invisibility in the Toronto women's bathhouse raid. *Social & Legal Studies, 18*(1), 111–130.

LeBlanc, A. J., Frost, D. M., & Wight, R. G. (2015). Minority stress and stress proliferation among same-sex and other marginalized couples. *Journal of Marriage and Family, 77*(1), 40–59.

Lee, M. G., & Quam, J. K. (2013). Comparing supports for LGBT aging in rural versus urban areas. *Journal of Gerontological Social Work, 56*(2), 112–126.

Lehmiller, J. J., & Loerger, M. (2014). Social networking smartphone applications and sexual health outcomes among men who have sex with men. *PLOS One, 9*(1), 1–6.

Leonard, W. (2012). Safe sex and the aesthetics of gay men's HIV/AIDS prevention in Australia: From Rubba Me in 1984 to F** k Me in 2009. *Sexualities, 15*(7), 834–849.

Lev, A. I. (2010). How queer!—The development of gender identity and sexual orientation in LGBTQ-headed families. *Family Process, 49*(3), 268–290.

Lev, A. I. (2013). *Transgender emergence: Therapeutic guidelines for working with gender-variant people and their families.* New York Routledge.

Lev, A. I. (2015). Resilience in lesbian and gay couples. In Karen Skerrett & Karen Fergus (Eds.), *Couple resilience* (pp. 45–61). Dordrecht: Springer Netherlands.

Levinger, G. (1980). Toward the analysis of close relationships. *Journal of Experimental Social Psychology, 16*(6), 510–544.

Lewins, F. (1995). *Transsexualism in society: A sociology of male-to-female transsexuals.* South Melbourne: Macmillan Education Australia.

Lyons, T., Shannon, K., Pierre, L., Small, W., Krüsi, A., & Kerr, T. (2015). A qualitative study of transgender individuals' experiences in residential addiction treatment settings: Stigma and inclusivity. *Substance Abuse Treatment, Prevention, and Policy, 10*(1), 1–6.

MacIntosh, H., Reissing, E. D., & Andruff, H. (2010). Same-sex marriage in Canada: The impact of legal marriage on the first cohort of gay and lesbian Canadians to wed. *Canadian Journal of Human Sexuality, 19*, 79–90.

Macapagal, K., Greene, G. J., Rivera, Z., & Mustanski, B. (2015). "The best is always yet to come": Relationship stages and processes among young LGBT couples. *Journal of Family Psychology, 29*(3), 309–320.

Magee, J. C., Bigelow, L., DeHaan, S., & Mustanski, B. S. (2012). Sexual health information seeking online: A mixed-methods study among lesbian, gay, bisexual, and transgender young people. *Health Education & Behavior, 39*(3), 276–289.

Mallon, G. (2013, June 11). Lesbian, gay, bisexual, and transgender (LGBT) families and parenting. In *Encyclopedia of social work.* Retrieved from http://socialwork.oxfordre.com/view/10.1093/acrefore/9780199975839.001.0001/acrefore-9780199975839-e-158.

Manning, W. D., Fettro, M. N., & Lamidi, E. (2014). Child well-being in same-sex parent families: Review of research prepared for American Sociological Association Amicus Brief. *Population Research and Policy Review, 33*(4), 485–502.

Marks, N. F., & Lambert, J. D. (1998). Marital status continuity and change among young and midlife adults: Longitudinal effects on psychological well-being. *Journal of Family Issues, 19*(6), 652–686.

Martin F., & Manalansan, I. V. (2005). Race, violence, and neoliberal spatial politics in the global city. *Social Text, 84–85*(23, 3–4), 141–156.

Martos, A. J., Nezhad, S., & Meyer, I. H. (2015). Variations in sexual identity milestones among lesbians, gay men, and bisexuals. *Sexuality Research and Social Policy, 12*(1), 24–33.

McCarthy, J. (2015, May 20). *Record-high 60% of Americans support same-sex marriage.* Gallup. Retrieved from http://www.gallup.com/poll/183272/record-high-americans-support-sex-marriage.aspx

McConnell, E. A., Birkett, M. A., & Mustanski, B. (2015). Typologies of social support and associations with mental health outcomes among LGBT youth. *LGBT Health, 2*(1), 55–61.

Meunier, É. (2014). No attitude, no standing around: The organization of social and sexual interaction at a gay male private sex party in New York City. *Archives of Sexual Behavior, 43,* 685–695.

Meyer, I. H. (2003). Prejudice, social stress, and mental health in lesbian, gay, and bisexual populations: conceptual issues and research evidence. *Psychological Bulletin, 129*(5), 674.

Miller, B. (2015). "They're the modern-day gay bar": Exploring the uses and gratifications of social networks for men who have sex with men. *Computers in Human Behavior, 51,* 476–482.

Moore, M. R., & Stambolis-Ruhstorfer, M. (2013). LGBT sexuality and families at the start of the twenty-first century. *Annual Review of Sociology, 39,* 491–507.

Moors, A. C., Matsick, J. L., Ziegler, A., Rubin, J. D., & Conley, T. D. (2013). Stigma towards individuals engaged in consensual nonmonogamy: Robust and worthy of additional research. *Analyses of Social Issues and Public Policy, 13*(1), 52–69.

Moser, C., & Kleinplatz, P. (2005). Introduction to the state of our knowledge on SM. *Journal of Homosexuality, 50,* 1–15.

Muraco, A., & Fredriksen-Goldsen, K. I. (2016). Turning points in the lives of lesbian and gay adults age 50 and over. *Advances in Life Course Research, 30,* 124–132.

Mustanski, B., Greene, G. J., Ryan, D., & Whitton, S. W. (2015). Feasibility, acceptability, and initial efficacy of an online sexual health promotion program for LGBT youth: The queer sex ed intervention. *The Journal of Sex Research, 52*(2), 220–230.

Nardi, P. (1992). What friends are for: Friends as family in the gay and lesbian community. In K. Plummer (Ed.), *Modern homosexualities* (pp. 108–120). London: Routledge.

O'Connor, P. (1992). *Friendships between women: A critical review.* New York: Guilford Press.

Ocobock, A. (2013). The power and limits of marriage: Married gay men's family relationships. *Journal of Marriage and Family, 75*(1), 191–205.

Operario, D., Burton, J., Underhill, K., & Sevelius, J. (2008). Men who have sex with transgender women: Challenges to category-based HIV prevention. *AIDS and Behavior, 12,* 18–26.

Orel, N. A. (2014). Investigating the needs and concerns of lesbian, gay, bisexual, and transgender older adults: The use of qualitative and quantitative methodology. *Journal of Homosexuality, 61*(1), 53–78.

Oswald, R. F., & Culton, L. S. (2003). Under the rainbow: Rural gay life and its relevance for family providers. *Family Relations, 52*(1), 72–81.

Otis, M. D., Riggle, E. D. B., & Rostosky, S. S. (2006). Impact of mental health on perceptions of relationship satisfaction and quality among female same-sex couples. *Journal of Lesbian Studies, 10*(1-2), 267–283.

Peplau, L. A., & Fingerhut, A. W. (2007). The close relationships of lesbians and gay men. *Annual Review of Psychology, 58,* 405–424.

Perin, E., Pinderhughes, E. E., Mattern, K., Hurley, S. M., & Newman, R. A. (2016). Experiences of children with gay fathers. *Clinical Pediatrics.* Advance online publication. doi:10.1177/0009922816632346.

Perrin, E. C., Siegel, B. S., Pawelski, J. G., Dobbins, M. I., Lavin, A., Mattson, G., . . . Yogman, M. (2013). Promoting the well-being of children whose parents are gay or lesbian. *Pediatrics, 131*(4), e1374–e1383.

Peterson, C. (2013). The lies that bind: Heteronormative constructions of "family" in social work discourse. *Journal of Gay & Lesbian Social Services, 25*(4), 486–508.

Peterson, Z. D., Janssen, E., & Laan, E. (2010). Women's sexual response to heterosexual and lesbian erotica: The role of stimulus intensity, affective reaction, and sexual history. *Archives of Sexual Behavior, 39,* 880–897.

Potârcă, G., Mills, M., & Neberich, W. (2015). Relationship preferences among gay and lesbian online daters: Individual and contextual influences. *Journal of Marriage and Family, 77*(2), 523–541.

Power, J. J., Perlesz, A., Brown, R., Schofield, M. J., Pitts, M. K., McNair, R., & Bickerdike, A. (2012). Bisexual parents and family diversity: Findings from the Work, Love, Play Study. *Journal of Bisexuality, 12*(4), 519–538.

Prestage, G., Brown, G., De Wit, J., Bavinton, B., Fairley, C., Maycock, B., . . . Zablotska, I. (2015). Understanding gay community subcultures: Implications for HIV prevention. *AIDS and Behavior, 19*(12), 2224–2233.

Prestage, G., Jin, F., Zablotska, I., Grulich, A., Imrie, J., Kaldor, J., Honnor, G., & Kippax, S. (2008). Trends in agreements between regular partners among gay men in Sydney, Melbourne and Brisbane, Australia. *AIDS and Behavior, 12*, 513–520.

Puar, J. K. (2005). Queer times, queer assemblages. *Social Text, 84–85*(23, 3–4), 121–140.

Race, K. (2015a). "Party and play": Online hook-up devices and the emergence of PNP practices among gay men. *Sexualities, 18*(3), 253–275.

Race, K. (2015b). Speculative pragmatism and intimate arrangements: Online hook-up devices in gay life. *Culture, Health & Sexuality, 17*(4), 496–511.

Reddy, C. (2005). Asian diasporas, neoliberalism, and family: Reviewing the case for homosexual asylum in the context of family rights. *Social Text, 84–85*(23, 3–4), 101–120.

Reed, S. J., & Valenti, M. T. (2012). "It ain't all as bad as it may seem": Young black lesbians' responses to sexual prejudice. *Journal of Homosexuality, 59*, 703–720.

Resmovits, J. (2016, July 14). California's students will soon learn more LGBT history in schools. *L.A. Times.* Retrieved from http://www.latimes.com/local/lanow/la-me-lgbt-curriculum-california-20160714-snap-story.html

Riggle, E. D. B., Rostosky, S. S., & Horne, S. G. (2010). Psychological distress, well-being, and legal recognition in same-sex couple relationships. *Journal of Family Psychology, 24*, 82–86.

Rosario, M., Schrimshaw, E. W., & Hunter, J. (2009). Disclosure of sexual orientation and subsequent substance use and abuse among lesbian, gay, and bisexual youths: Critical role of disclosure reactions. *Psychology of Addictive Behaviors, 23*, 175–184.

Rosario, M., Schrimshaw, E. W., & Hunter, J. (2012). Homelessness among lesbian, gay, and bisexual youth: Implications for subsequent internalizing and externalizing symptoms. *Journal of Youth and Adolescence, 41*(5), 544–560. doi:10.1007=s10964-011-9681-3

Rosenfeld, M. J. (2014). Couple longevity in the era of same-sex marriage in the United States. *Journal of Marriage and Family, 76*(5), 905–918.

Roth, Y. (2016). Zero feet away: The digital geography of gay social media. *Journal of Homosexuality, 63*(3), 437–442.

Rubin, G. (1997). The traffic in women. Notes on the "political economy" of sex. In L. Nicholson (Ed.), *The second wave: A reader in feminist theory* (pp. 157–210). New York: Routledge.

Rullo, J. E., Strassberg, D. S., & Israel, E. (2010). Category-specificity in sexual interest in gay men and lesbians. *Archives of Sexual Behavior, 39*, 874–879.

Rusbult, C. E. (1980). Commitment and satisfaction in romantic associations: A test of the investment model. *Journal of Experimental Social Psychology, 16*, 172–186.

Savin-Williams, R. C. (1996). Dating and romantic relationships among gay, lesbian, and bisexual youths. In R. C. Savin-Williams & K. M. Cohen (Eds.), *The lives of lesbians, gays, and bisexuals: Children to adults* (pp. 166–180). Orlando, FL: Harcourt Brace College.

Savin-Williams, R. C., & Cohen, K. M. (2015). Developmental trajectories and milestones of lesbian, gay, and bisexual young people. *International Review of Psychiatry, 27*(5), 357–366.

Scherrer, K. (2013). Culturally competent practice with bisexual individuals. *Clinical Social Work Journal, 41*(3), 238–248.

Scott-Sheldon, L., & Johnson, B. (2006). Eroticising creates safer sex: A research synthesis. *Journal of Primary Prevention, 27*(6), 619–640.

Sheff, E., & Hammers, C. (2011). The privilege of perversities: Race, class and education among polyamorists and kinksters. *Psychology & Sexuality, 2*(3), 198–223.

Siegel, B. S., Perrin, E. C., Pawelski, J. G., Dobbins, M. I., Lavin, A., Mattson, G., . . . Martini, D. R. (2013). Promoting the well-being of children whose parents are gay or lesbian. *Pediatrics, 131*(4), 827–830.

Simon Rosser, B. R., West, W., & Weinmeyer, R. (2008). Are gay communities dying or just in transition? Results from an international consultation examining possible structural change in gay communities. *AIDS Care, 20*(5), 588–595.

Singh, A. A., & McKleroy, V. S. (2010). "Just getting out of bed is a revolutionary act": The resilience of transgender people of color who have survived traumatic life events. *Traumatology, 17*(2), 34–44.

Starks, T. J., Newcomb, M. E., & Mustanski, B. (2015). A longitudinal study of interpersonal relationships among lesbian, gay, and bisexual adolescents and young adults: Mediational pathways from attachment to romantic relationship quality. *Archives of Sexual Behavior, 44*, 1821–1831.

Steensma, T. D., Kreukels, B. P., de Vries, A. L., & Cohen-Kettenis, P. T. (2013). Gender identity development in adolescence. *Hormones and Behavior, 64*(2), 288–297.

Stein, D., Silvera, R., Hagerty, R., & Marmor, M. (2012). Viewing pornography depicting unprotected anal intercourse: Are there implications for HIV prevention among men who have sex with men? *Archives of Sexual Behavior, 41*(2), 411–419.

Strohschein, L., McDonough, P., Monette, G., & Shao, Q. (2005). Marital transitions and mental health: Are there gender differences in the short-term effects of marital status change? *Social Science & Medicine, 61*, 2293–2303.

Syme, M. (2014). The evolving concept of older adult sexual behavior and its benefits. *Generations, 38*(1), 35–41.

Tasker, F. (2013). Lesbian and gay parenting post-heterosexual divorce and separation. In A. E. Goldberg & K. R. Allen (Eds.), *LGBT-parent families: Innovations in research and implications for practice* (pp. 3–20). New York: Springer.

Tatum, A. K. (2017). The influence of same-sex marriage access on sexual minority identity, mental health, and subjective well-being. *Journal of Homosexuality, 64*(5), 638–653. doi:10.1080/00918369.2016.1196991.

Tilsen, J., & Nylund, D. (2010). Resisting normativity: Queer musings on politics, identity, and the performance of therapy. *The International Journal of Narrative Therapy and Community Work, 3*, 64–70.

Tomassilli, J. C., Golub, S. A., Bimbi, D. S., & Parsons, J. T. (2009). Behind closed doors: An exploration of kinky sexual behaviors in urban lesbian and bisexual women. *Journal of Sex Research, 46*(5), 438–445.

Umberson, D., Thomeer, M. B., Kroeger, R. A., Lodge, A. C., & Xu, M. (2015). Challenges and opportunities for research on same-sex relationships. *Journal of Marriage and Family, 77*(1), 96–111.

Valentine, G., & Skelton, T. (2003). Finding oneself, losing oneself: The lesbian and gay "scene" as a paradoxical space. *International Journal of Urban and Regional Research, 27*(4), 849–866.

Valverde, M. (2007). Bodies, words, identities: The moving targets of the criminal law. In M. Dubber & L. Farmer (Eds.), *Modern histories of crime and punishment* (pp. 224–251). Stanford, CA: Stanford University Press.

Walter, C. A., McCoyd, J. L., & Walter, P. C. A. (2015). *Grief and loss across the lifespan: A biopsychosocial perspective.* New York: Springer.

Warner, M. (1991). Introduction: Fear of a queer planet. *Social Text, 9*(4), 3–17.

Warner, M. (2002). *Publics and counterpublics.* New York: Zone Books.

Warner, M. (Ed.). (1993). *Fear of a queer planet: Queer politics and social theory.* Minneapolis: University of Minnesota Press.

Waters, E., Jindasurat, C., & Wolfe, C. (2016). *Lesbian, gay, bisexual, transgender, queer, and HIV-affected hate violence in 2015.* New York: National Coalition for Anti-Violence Programs.

Watney, S. (1997). *Policing desire: Pornography, AIDS and the media.* Minneapolis: University of Minnesota Press.

Weber, S. (2015). Daring to marry: Marriage equality activism after Proposition 8 as challenge to the assimilationist/radical binary in queer studies. *Journal of Homosexuality, 62*(9), 1147–1173.

Weston, K. (1991). *Families we choose: Lesbians, gays, kinship.* New York: Columbia University Press.

White, T., & Ettner, R. (2004). Disclosure, risks and protective factors for children whose parents are undergoing a gender transition. *Journal of Gay & Lesbian Psychotherapy, 8* (1–2), 129–145.

Whitton, S. W., Kuryluk, A. D., & Khaddouma, A. M. (2015). Legal and social ceremonies to formalize same-sex relationships: Associations with commitment, social support, and relationship outcomes. *Couple and Family Psychology, 4*(3), 161–176.

Wienke, C., & Hill, G. J. (2013). Does place of residence matter? Rural–urban differences and the wellbeing of gay men and lesbians. *Journal of Homosexuality, 60*(9), 1256–1279.

Wieselquist, J., Rusbult, C. E., Foster, C. A., & Agnew, C. R. (1999). Commitment, pro-relationship behavior, and trust in close relationships. *Journal of Personality and Social Psychology, 77,* 942–966.

Wilkinson, J., Bittman, M., Holt, M., Rawstorne, P., Kippax, S., & Worth, H. (2012). Solidarity beyond sexuality: The personal communities of gay men. *Sociology, 46*(6), 1161–1177.

Wilkinson, C., & Langlois, A. J. (2014). Special issue: Not such an international human rights norm? Local resistance to lesbian, gay, bisexual, and transgender rights—Preliminary comments. *Journal of Human Rights, 13*(3), 249–255.

Williams, D. J. (2016). The framing of frequent sexual behavior and/or pornography viewing as addiction: Some concerns for social work. *Journal of Social Work.* Advance online publication. doi:abs/10.1177/1468017316644701

Williams, K. (2003). Has the future of marriage arrived? A contemporary examination of gender, marriage, and psychological well-being. *Journal of Health and Social Behavior, 44*(4), 470–487.

Willging, C. E., Salvador, M., & Kano, M. (2006). Pragmatic help seeking: How sexual and gender minority groups access mental health care in a rural state. *Psychiatric Services, 57*(6), 871–874.

Zweifel, J. E. (2015). Donor conception from the viewpoint of the child: Positive, negatives, and promoting the welfare of the child. *Fertility and Sterility, 104*(3), 513–519.

CHAPTER 9

EMPLOYMENT, STRESS, AND THE STRENGTHS PERSPECTIVE

Trevor G. Gates

INTRODUCTION

The workplace is an important part of everyday life for many Americans, including those within the lesbian, gay, bisexual, transgender, and queer (LGBTQ) community. Because the workplace is an important life domain, the well-being of LGBTQ workers is of interest to practitioners in the helping professions. The workplace is an important site of social welfare policy and practice because employment is an integral part of social identity in the United States: "The very fabric of our life revolves around work . . . [t]he type of food we eat, the neighborhood we live in, the clothes we wear, and how we socialize—all somehow are related to our work" (Berry, 2005, p. ix).

Yet LGBTQ workers are not able to equally experience all of the privileges and benefits of the workplace because some work environments tolerate discrimination and other disparate treatment of LGBTQ workers. The Williams Institute, a think tank on sexual orientation law and public policy, estimates that between 16% to 68% of LGB people report experiencing employment discrimination and other forms of disparate treatment (Badgett, Lau, Sears, & Ho, 2007). In a number of employment-related studies, LGBTQ people were less likely to be selected for employment than other candidates (Crow, Fok, & Hartman, 1998; Horvath & Ryan, 2003; Hebl, Foster, Mannix, & Dovidio, 2002; Weichselbaumer, 2003). However, the experience of employment discrimination in hiring seems to be less pronounced in certain urban metropolitan areas (Bailey, Wallace, & Wright, 2013).

There are promising examples that employment circumstances are improving for LGBTQ workers (Gates & Rodgers, 2014; Hewlett, Sears, Sumberg, & Fargnoli, 2013; Parco & Levy, 2012). The purpose of this chapter is to explore the changing conditions affecting LGBTQ employment discrimination and other forms of disparate treatment in the United States. Specifically, key historical events, including Title VII of the Civil Rights Act of 1964, evidence of an end to institutionalized discrimination in federal employment, and progress toward employment protections in the United States, will be examined to highlight the changing context of practice and policy. Additionally, this chapter examines the extent that experiences of discrimination differ among LGBTQ workers, especially the degree which the worker is "out," their sex and/or gender identity, as well as the social position and geography of the worker.

STRENGTHS PERSPECTIVE

The theoretical perspective guiding this chapter is the strengths perspective. The strengths perspective in social work practice is based on the assumption that individuals, groups, and communities are more than their problems or struggles. Instead of focusing on "human deficits, what is broken, gone wrong, or failed" (Blundo, 2001, p. 297), practitioners operating from a strengths perspective seek to highlight and build on assets, resources, and supports that individuals, groups, and communities already possess (Munford & Sanders, 2005). Those assets that individuals, groups, and communities possess can be drawn on to overcome great obstacles. Those strengths may be "obscured by the stresses of the moment, submerged under the weight of crisis, oppression, or illness but, nonetheless, they abide" (Saleebey, 2009, p. 15). Though LGBTQ workers have experienced marginalization in American society, the LGBTQ community and its allies have fought back and changed the dominant paradigm of oppression (D'Emilio, 1998; Haider-Markel, & Meier, 1996). Though the LGBTQ community has often had competing priorities, from sexual liberation to family equality, it has demanded the attention of communities, medical and social service organizations, and policymakers, advocating for basic human and social justice (Genke, 2004; Herek, 1991). These important efforts illustrate the great strengths of LGBTQ individuals and communities (Gates & Kelly, 2013).

HISTORICAL TRENDS IN EMPLOYMENT AND LGBTQ RIGHTS

LGBTQ workers and their allies have fought for and achieved significant gains in workplace protections. Several key historical events provide significant context to the status of LGBTQ workplace rights in the United States. Though there has been progress during the past decade recognizing the contributions of LGBTQ workers, explicit workplace protections have been a more recent phenomenon. Central developments, including Title VII of the Civil Rights Act of 1964, challenges to pervasive discrimination in civil service and the military, and efforts to pass an Employment Non-Discrimination Act (ENDA), provide evidence that progress can be made to advance LGBTQ workers equality. Yet those advances toward equality have been gradual. On the one hand, there is growing interest in protecting LGBTQ workers just like any other protected class of people. On the other hand, current state laws in the United States provide only a patchwork of protections for

LGBTQ workers based on sexual orientation or gender identity. (See Human Rights Campaign [HRC]: http://www.hrc.org/state_maps.)

TITLE VII OF THE CIVIL RIGHTS ACT OF 1964

An important piece of legislation that has set the stage for protecting LGBTQ workers is Title VII of the Civil Rights Act of 1964. Title VII, which prohibits discrimination and other forms of disparate treatment based on race, color, religion, sex, or national origin, applies to all employers in the United States with 15 or more workers. Though Title VII was surely not the first proposed piece of legislation that would protect workers on race, color, religion, sex, or national origin, President John F. Kennedy and other important civil rights leaders of the era called for comprehensive employment-based protections as the next plausible steps in correcting the wrongs of slavery and other injustices of the past. In a speech urging Congress to address widespread civil rights issues in the United States, Kennedy (1963) noted, "[Discrimination in] employment is especially injurious both to its victims and to the national economy. It results in a great waste of human resources and creates serious community problems" (n.p.).

Title VII has been interpreted broadly to protect workers from various adverse employment decisions that might be made because of race, color, religion, sex, or national origin. This includes adverse decisions in hiring, firing, and compensation based solely on the worker's protected status. It also includes protection from adverse decisions in times of promotion, transfer, and layoffs. Disability leaves, fringe-benefit programs, and retirement decisions can also not be made because of race, color, religion, sex, or national origin. Important to the spirit of Title VII is the assumption that minorities have a constitutional right to protection in the workplace and that the government has an interest in ensuring such protections.

Though Title VII provided an important foundation for later employment-based measures, many years passed before Title VII was used as a mechanism for protecting LGBTQ workers. Several lawsuits were brought before the Supreme Court that took to task the issue of Title VII and under what circumstances it applied to LGBTQ workers. For example, in 1977 in *Holloway v. Arthur Anderson and Company*, the Court rejected a transgender plaintiff's claim of sex discrimination under Title VII, stating that Congress had only intended to protect a person's birth sex (Holt, 1997). Similarly, in *Desantis v. Pacific Telephone and Telegraph Company* in 1979, the Court rejected the petitioner's claim, stating that a sex discrimination claim cannot apply to homosexuals (Rivera, 1980). However, in *Joseph Oncale v. Sundowner Offshore Services, Inc.* (1998), the Court ruled in favor of the plaintiff. In the claim, Oncale claimed that his male co-workers pervasively harassed him and assaulted him based on his perceived sexual orientation identity. Though the Court ruled that a violation of Title VII occurred and that men can sexually harass other men, the larger question about the extent of LGBTQ harassment was never fully addressed in the decision (Faley et al., 2006; McDonald, Ravitch, & Sumners, 2006; Paetzold, 1999).

To date, Title VII has not included explicit protections for LGBTQ workers. Yet the advocacy efforts of LGBTQ workers and their allies have prompted a widening of existing law. The Equal Employment Opportunity Commission (EEOC, 2015), an agency of the US government enforcing federal employment discrimination laws, holds that discrimination based on sexual orientation and gender identity constitutes discrimination based on sex. In *Mia Macy v. Department of Justice* (2012) and *David Baldwin v. Department of Transportation* (2015), the EEOC accepted claims from the petitioners that argued that Congressional action is unnecessary to apply sex discrimination claims to sexual orientation and gender identity. Rather, language of "sex discrimination" is simply plain language that can be reasonably applied to a variety of circumstances. They argued that the plain language of Title VII does not name specific types of cultural or religious groups either, yet few would question the application of the law to a variety of people of different faith backgrounds.

CHALLENGES TO DISCRIMINATION IN THE CIVIL SERVICE AND MILITARY

The US federal government has not, however, always been willing to extend protections to LGBTQ workers. Some members of the federal government once openly treated LGBTQ workers with outright contempt. During the 1950s, Senator Joseph McCarthy prompted widespread fear about a variety of hidden subcultures in federal government, particularly people he perceived to be social "deviants" like communists and homosexuals (Frank, 2014). McCarthy believed that homosexuals and communists were immoral and great security risks, and his crusade against homosexuals and communists led to the questioning of thousands of workers perceived to be among their ranks (Johnson, 2004). During this time, hundreds of federal civil service workers perceived to be homosexuals, communists, or sympathizers were terminated from their federal positions (Escoffier, 1985). Termination from federal employment for these reasons often had lasting impact on these workers, as being labeled a communist or LGBTQ person carried with it much stigma. Many terminated workers became separated or distanced from their families and found themselves unable to work in their chosen careers; several others committed suicide (Johnson, 2004).

LGBTQ workers also found themselves unwelcome in branches of the armed forces under similar assumptions that homosexuals were immoral and not to be trusted. In the 1980s, the Department of Defense stated that "homosexuality is incompatible with military service" and that the presence of LGBTQ service members affected the armed force's ability to maintain trust, order, discipline, and morale among the troops (Sinclair, 2009, p. 703). Critics of LGBTQ people serving openly in the military said that LGBTQ people could not possibly begin to serve effectively alongside their straight counterparts. Of course, like many other professions, LGBTQ people have always been part of military ranks, even if their presence was concealed (Britton & Williams, 1995).

The narrative surrounding LGBTQ people being unsuitable for military service did not continue to resonate with all of the populace and indeed some politicians and policymakers. In the early 1990s, President Bill Clinton actively courted the LGBTQ community as voters and promised to eliminate the ban on LGBTQ people in the military (Halley, 1999). Clinton's efforts were unsuccessful and resulted in a compromise with conservatives called Don't Ask Don't Tell (DADT), a law that allowed LGBTQ people to serve in the military without the threat of harassment and discharge provided that they did so discreetly and without engaging in sex (Di Mauro,

2001; Frank, 2009). Protection, however, was only an illusion. During the Clinton administration and subsequent administrations, the military discharged more LGBTQ people after the passage of DADT than prior to the law (Gates & Rodgers, 2014; Rivera, 1998).

DADT remained the military policy in the United States for more than 17 years until 2010, when the policy was repealed by Congressional action (Don't Ask, Don't Tell Repeal Act, 2010; Parco & Levy, 2010). LGBTQ service members and their allies demanded that President Barack Obama make good on his promise to repeal DADT. President Obama's administration, though sympathetic to LGBTQ equality issues generally and particularly to adopting policy that would allow military service by people who were publically LGBTQ, continued to defend DADT until the law was repealed (White House, 2011). Today, members of the armed forces cannot be separated from service solely because of their sexual orientation identity. However, until June of 2016, gender identity could still be the basis for separation. Previously, the argument was that gender dysphoria, defined as a marked difference between a person's gender identity and the gender that would be assigned by others, is a diagnosed mental health condition in the current version of the *Diagnostic and Statistical Manual of Mental Disorders* (American Psychiatric Association, 2013; Quam, 2015). Problematic in this blanket characterization of gender variance as a mental health condition is that not all transgender people experience "dysphoria" or any impairment in psychosocial functioning because of their gender identity. Therefore, in June of 2016, the US Department of Defense (DOD) announced that transgender individuals could openly serve in the military, overturning their previously oppressive and prohibitive policy (Cronk, 2016). The DOD also issued a series of instructions (DOD Instruction 1300.38) describing how transgender members of the US military could actively serve, as well as providing a construct through which gender transitioning could occur while serving, providing procedures for gender marker changes in the Defense Enrollment Eligibility Reporting System, and specifying medical treatment provisions for active and reserve members (DOD, Special Report 2016). For more information, see the US DOD website (http://www.defense.gov/News/Special-Reports/0616_transgender-policy).

Other advocacy efforts of LGBTQ workers and allies have resulted in further protections for certain LGBTQ workers. More recently, there has been positive policy changes protecting the rights of LGBTQ workers in civil service. In 2014, President Barack Obama signed Executive Order 13672, which extended workplace protections to LGBTQ workers employed by or seeking jobs with federal contractors (Department of Labor, 2014; White House, 2014). Civilian workers were already protected based on sexual orientation per President Bill Clinton's Executive Order 13087 (1998).

Executive Order 13672 adds sexual orientation and gender identity to other already protected classes of workers under the employ of contracting companies doing business with the federal government. As workers employed as federal contractors include almost 28 million workers, or 20% of the workforce (HRC, 2014), Obama's executive order carries considerable weight for better protecting LGBTQ civil service workers.

EMPLOYMENT NON-DISCRIMINATION ACT

Executive Order 13672 was necessary because LGBTQ workers are not explicitly protected under current law in the United States. Though Title VII of the Civil Rights Act of 1964 has been interpreted to protect LGBTQ workers because of sex discrimination (EEOC, 2015), especially concerning federal workers, sexual orientation and gender identity are not protected classes. A comprehensive Employment Non-Discrimination Act or ENDA (2013), which would explicitly protect LGBTQ workers has, to date, failed to pass both the House and Senate—as have various forms of antidiscrimination laws for LGBTQ laws failed for the past 40 years (Gates & Saunders, 2015; National Gay and Lesbian Taskforce, 2014). Meanwhile, a significant number of LGBTQ workers report some form of employment discrimination or disparate treatment at work (Badgett et al., 2007).

Comprehensive nondiscrimination policies for LGBTQ workers have been more successful within individual corporations and some state and local governments. Corporations in the United States have, to some extent, taken the lead in providing comprehensive protection for LGBTQ workers. At present, most Fortune 500 companies, which reportedly employ more than 25 million people collectively, offer some form of antidiscrimination policies protecting LGBTQ workers (HRC, 2015). Many cities and approximately half of the states in the United States offer explicit protections in their policies based on sexual orientation, gender identity, or both (American Civil Liberties Union, 2015). Interestingly, the District of Columbia, home to the federal government, capital of the United States, and a large LGBTQ community (Gates & Newport, 2013), offers some of the nation's most comprehensive protections for LGBTQ citizens. The Washington DC Human Rights Act identifies 19 protected traits, including sexual orientation and gender identity/ expression, which are protected in housing, employment, education, and public accommodations (District of Columbia Office of Human Rights, 2015). However, in places where LGBTQ identities are not explicitly protected under law, some LGBTQ workers may experience discrimination and/or be subject to disparate treatment without a clear mechanism for protecting their rights (Badgett et al., 2007; Cunningham-Parmeter, 2015; Kaplan, 2014; Soucek, 2014).

PROTECTIVE FACTORS IN THE WORKPLACE

Laws that protect LGBTQ workers, however, are only a start in changing their overall experience in the workplace, hiring and promotion processes, retention, benefits, and so on. There are several significant protective factors that influence the day-to-day experiences of LGBTQ individuals across workplace settings, which includes an organizational commitment to protecting LGBTQ workers. Generally, organizations that make a formal commitment to take care of and protect the health and well-being of workers promote an organizational culture that is attentive to the needs of others as an inherent part of the culture and mission of the company (Mearns & Hope, 2005). A growing body of research has found, for LGBTQ workers specifically, the presence of formal and informal policies and practices protecting people from discrimination based on sexual orientation and gender identity, the more comfortable LGBTQ workers will feel there (Button, 2001; Griffith & Hebl, 2002; King, Mohr, Peddie, Jones, & Kendra, 2017; Ragins, 2004).

Huffman, Watrous-Rodriguez, and King (2008) found a relationship between workplace support and job and other life satisfaction in a convenience sample ($N = 99$) of lesbian, gay, and bisexual-identified workers in the Southwest. In the sample, Huffman and colleagues found that support at work was multidimensional and affected outcomes on multiple life domains. A relationship was found between supervisor support and job satisfaction. Perhaps more telling was the impact of co-worker support, which was not just correlated with job satisfaction. Rather, it was correlated with *overall life satisfaction* for the worker. Participants with strong co-worker support were more likely to perceive that the "conditions of [their] life [was] excellent" than participants who felt that they lacked the support of their colleagues (Huffman et al., 2008, p. 245).

Colleague support can come from a range of sources and need not necessarily be the support of other LGBTQ-identified workers. Rumens' (2011) study of the role and meaning of gay male friendship in the workplace found that social relationships at work significantly affected the emotional and social well-being of gay male workers. Participants in the study ($N = 33$) were just as likely to form enduring and significant friendships with both LGBTQ and straight people of both genders. Challenging cultural stereotypes that gay men are likely to form friendships primarily with other gay men and with women, several study narratives indicated that some of the most meaningful bonds were with heterosexual men. One participant, particularly, noted that his sexual orientation was only one part of who he was and that mutual care and support were more important bonds of friendship at his workplace than necessarily shared sexual orientation identity (Rumens, 2011).

Supportive organizational climates benefit not only the LGBTQ worker but also the organization as a whole. Brenner, Lyons, and Fassinger (2010) found that LGBTQ workers in supportive climates spend less time at work focusing on self-preservation and more time engaging in altruistic, collaborative behavior. They care not only about themselves but also about the organization. LGBTQ workers who feel the support of their organizations tend to demonstrate a higher commitment to the organization and may go beyond what is normally required of their job performance to meet the organizational mission (Brenner et al., 2010). In essence, protecting LGBTQ workers may have advantages for all involved, including LGBTQ people, non-LGBTQ people, and the organization itself.

Additionally, because LGBTQ workers employed at supportive organizations tend to have higher job satisfaction and better relationships with their supervisors and co-workers, they may be more likely to stay employed with the organization (Tejeda, 2006). While these feelings may be attributed to a variety of factors, including the actual work performed for the organization, there is evidence that supportive organizations are good for the careers of LGBTQ workers. Those LGBTQ workers who work in supportive environments tend to feel recognized for their talents, feel as though their careers are moving forward, and feel as if they have excellent advancement potential (Hewlett et al., 2013).

DIFFERENCES IN LGBTQ WORKER EXPERIENCES

While there is some evidence of gradual improvement in law, policy, and experience of LGBTQ workers across the United States, it is important to recognize differences in the individual experiences of workers as it can vary. For example, the worker's degree of outness, as well as the intersection of sex and gender identity, likely affects individual LGBTQ worker experiences. Additionally, geography and social position may also influence the experiences of individual LGBTQ workers.

OUTNESS AT WORK

Outness refers to the extent which an LGBTQ person has disclosed his or her LGBTQ identity to one or more people. The decision about whether to "come out" to work colleagues is often one that LGBTQ workers spend much time fretting over, as the consequences of coming out can either be positive or negative (Gusmano, 2008). Weighing the pros and cons of this decision can cause anxiety and fear for LGBTQ workers (Ragins, Singh, & Cornwell, 2007), especially when workers feel as though their jobs can be at stake simply because they have decided to be open and honest with their supervisors and colleagues.

However, once the LGBTQ worker has decided to come out to some or all of their colleagues, there can be positive psychosocial outcomes. LGBTQ workers, particularly those who work in supportive workplaces with nondiscrimination policies and informal practices that protect LGBTQ workers, are more likely to be out and are more likely to have a strong commitment to their organizations (Bouzianis, Malcolm, & Hallab, 2008; Day & Schoenrade, 2000; King, Reilly, & Hebl, 2008). These workers are less likely to internalize negative attitudes toward LGBTQ people and tend to experience greater psychological wellness within their organizations (Bowleg, Burkholder, Teti, & Craig, 2008; Gates, 2014).

SEX AND GENDER IDENTITY

The intersection of other social and cultural identities affects LGBTQ worker experiences. One of the most significant differences in experiences can be attributed to sex, gender identity, and gender expression. Transgender individuals are often included in discourse regarding sexual minority communities (i.e., "LGBTQ" workers), yet gender identity and expression are different from sexual orientation identity (Kuper, Nussbaum, & Mustanski, 2012; Sudore, 2015). Transgender workers, though often included in statistics about discrimination statistics, typically experience discrimination at rates higher than lesbian, gay, and bisexual workers (Badgett et al., 2007). Transgender workers experience disproportionate rates of unemployment, underemployment, and other career challenges that can hinder full participation in the workplace (Irwin, 1999; Kirk & Belovics, 2008).

Several empirical studies also highlight important distinctions among lesbian and gay male workers. Gay males, particularly those who do not conform to traditional stereotypes of masculinity, tend to experience more workplace discrimination than lesbians (Crow, Fok, & Hartman, 1998; Luhtanen, 2003; Ratcliff, Lassiter, Markman, & Snyder, 2006). This may be because of a pervasive culture that privileges maleness and discounts the experiences of the feminine and/or anyone who rejects traditional forms of masculinity (Embrick, Walther, & Wickens, 2007; Herek, 2000; Gillingham, 2006).

SOCIAL POSITION AND GEOGRAPHY

An LGBTQ worker's social position also affects workplace experiences. A popular misconception is that LGBTQ people are "Dual Income No Kids" (DINKs), meaning that LGBTQ people have no children and thus have income to spend frivolously (Badgett, 1998). This misconception is largely driven by consumer market research and bears little reality to the lived experiences of many LGBTQ workers (Black, Gates, Sanders, & Taylor, 2000; Mallon, 2001; McDermott, 2006; Oldfield, Candler, & Johnson, 2006). In reality, LGBTQ workers are found across the lower, middle, and upper classes, with many LGBTQ workers belonging to the lower or working classes (Anastas, 1998; Appleby, 2001; Badgett, 1998).

Geography may also influence the experiences of LGBTQ workers. Rural LGBTQ communities tend to be tightly knit, and sometimes invisible communities emerge in otherwise conservative communities (Lindhorst, 1998). Some LGBTQ workers gravitate toward a more urban environment because they perceive that the city is a more welcoming environment for LGBTQ people (Annes & Redlin, 2012). While this may indeed be true for some LGBTQ workers, there is some empirical evidence to the contrary. LGBTQ people living in rural communities may experience well-being at the same or higher levels than LGBTQ people living in urban communities (Kirkey, & Forsyth, 2001; Lewis, 2014; Wienke & Hill, 2013).

IMPLICATIONS FOR PRACTICE

Social workers can play an important role in helping address the issue of LGBTQ workplace discrimination. A first step is to help leverage organizational resources to create an inclusive atmosphere valuing the unique contributions of LGBTQ workers. This move toward inclusivity can be expanded by actively recruiting qualified LGBTQ workers to the organization. LGBTQ workers bring a unique perspective to the workplace, and efforts should be made to actively include them among the organizational ranks. Additionally, efforts should be made to improve the conditions for LGBTQ workers already working within the organization. Mandatory training and staff development that includes affirming LGBTQ content is an essential step. However, efforts should also be made to improve the day-to-day lived experiences of LGBTQ individuals. Another tangible step to make LGBTQ workers feel more included in the workplace would include the use gender-neutral language within employment documents and manuals when discussing family and/or spousal topics. There are also more implicit steps that can be taken to make LGBTQ worker feel more comfortable. For example, if the norm in the office is to informally discuss family life with co-workers and supervisors; then said co-workers and supervisors should ask similarly interested questions related to the lives of LGBTQ workers. Of course, as with any other workers, the organization should respect the boundaries of individual LGBTQ workers, including but not limited to the decision to come out at work. The provision and location of gender-neutral bathrooms is another critical move in which organizations can provide affirming workplace environments, especially for members of the transgender and gender nonconforming community.

Social workers can also play a role in employee assistance programs (EAP) and human resources initiatives for LGBTQ workers. LGBTQ workers experiencing workplace discrimination might first come into contact with EAP and human resource professionals. Social workers, EAP professionals, and human resource professionals should actively work to foster a work environment that respects the unique contributions that LGBTQ workers make to the workplace. When needed and appropriate, social workers and EAP should also provide counseling and referrals for workers experiencing distress related to the environment of the workplace.

CONCLUSION

LGBTQ workers continue to experience discrimination and other forms of disparate treatment. The extent to which an LGBTQ worker is out, as well as other factors including sex, gender identity, social position, and geography may all influence whether they encounter negative treatment. Regardless, despite numerous challenges that are often faced on a daily basis, LGBTQ workers manage to survive and thrive. They openly serve in a variety of occupations in a variety of workplaces, including the military and civil service. LGBTQ workers and their allies have successfully advocated for nondiscrimination policies within certain states and federal employment, sometimes prompting a widening of existing civil rights law to further protect the rights of LGBTQ workers. Though additional progress must be made in the United States to realize full civil rights protections in the workplace, efforts made by LGBTQ workers and their allies provide evidence that these protections will become a reality.

REFERENCES

American Civil Liberties Union. (2015). *Non-discrimination laws: State by state information.* Retrieved from http://www.aclu.org/map/non-discrimination-laws-state-state-information-map

American Psychiatric Association. (2013). *Diagnostic and statistical manual of mental disorders* (5th ed.). Washington, DC: Author.

Anastas, J. W. (1998). Working against discrimination: Gay, lesbian and bisexual people on the job. *Journal of Gay and Lesbian Social Services, 8*(3), 83–98. doi:10.1300/J041v08n03_07

Annes, A., & Redlin, M. (2012). Coming out and coming back: Rural gay migration and the city. *Journal of Rural Studies, 28*(1), 56–68. doi:10.1016/j.jrurstud.2011.08.005

Appleby, G. A. (2001). Ethnographic study of gay and bisexual working-class men in the United States. *Journal of Gay and Lesbian Social Services, 12*(3–4), 51–62. doi:10.1300/J041v12n03_04

Badgett, M. V. L. (1998). *Income inflation: The myth of affluence among gay, lesbian, and bisexual Americans.* New York: Policy Institute of the National Gay and Lesbian Task Force.

Badgett, M. V. L., Lau, H., Sears, B., & Ho, D. (2007). *Bias in the workplace: Consistent evidence of sexual orientation and gender identity discrimination.* Los Angeles, CA: Williams Institute. Retrieved from http://williamsinstitute.law.ucla.edu/wp-content/uploads/Badgett-Sears-Lau-Ho-Bias-in-the-Workplace-Jun-2007.pdf

Bailey, J., Wallace, M., & Wright, B. (2013). Are gay men and lesbians discriminated against when applying for jobs? A four-city, internet-based field experiment. *Journal of Homosexuality, 60*(6), 873–894.

Berry, P. A. (2005). Foreward. In S. H. Akbas & P. A. Kurzman (Eds.), *Work and the workplace: A resource for innovative policy and practice* (pp. ix–xiv). New York: Columbia University Press.

Black, D., Gates, G., Sanders, S., & Taylor, L. (2000). Demographics of the gay and lesbian population in the United States: Evidence from available systematic data sources. *Demography, 37*(2), 139–154. doi:10.2307/2648117

Blundo, R. (2001). Learning strengths-based practice: Challenging our personal and professional frames. *Families in Society: The Journal of Contemporary Human Services, 82*(3), 296–304. doi:10.1606/1044-3894.192

Bowleg, L., Burkholder, G., Teti, M., & Craig, M. L. (2008). The complexities of outness: Psychosocial predictors of coming out to others among black lesbian and bisexual women. *Journal of LGBT Health Research, 4*(4), 153–166. doi:10.1080/15574090903167422

Bouzianis, B., Malcolm, J. P., & Hallab, L. (2008). Factors associated with sexual identity disclosure in the workplace by gay men and lesbians: A couples study. *Gay and Lesbian Issues and Psychology Review, 4*(3), 166–175.

Brenner, B. R., Lyons, H. Z., & Fassinger, R. E. (2010). Can heterosexism harm organizations? Predicting the perceived organizational citizenship behaviors of gay and lesbian employees. *Career Development Quarterly, 58*(4), 321–335. doi:10.1002/j.2161-0045.2010.tb00181.x

Britton, D. M., & Williams, C. L. (1995). "Don't Ask, Don't Tell, Don't Pursue": Military policy and the construction of heterosexual masculinity. *Journal of Homosexuality, 30*(1), 1–21. doi:10.1300/J082v30n01_01

Button, S. B. (2001). Organizational efforts to affirm sexual diversity: A cross-level examination. *Journal of Applied Psychology, 86*(1), 17–28. doi:10.1037/0021-9010.86.1.17

Cronk, T. M. (2016). *Transgender service members can now serve openly, Carter announces.* Retrieved from http://www.defense.gov/News/Article/Article/822235/transgender-service-members-can-now-serve-openly-carter-announces

Crow, S. M., Fok, L. Y., & Hartman, S. J. (1998). Who is at greatest risk of work-related discrimination—women, blacks, or homosexuals? *Employee Responsibilities and Rights Journal, 11*(1), 15–26. doi:10.1023/A:1027319915725

Cunningham-Parmeter, K. (2015). Marriage equality, workplace inequality: The next gay rights battle. *Florida Law Review, 67,* 1099–1156.

David Baldwin v. Department of Education. (2015). Retrieved from http://www.eeoc.gov/decisions/0120133080.pdf

Day, N. E., & Schoenrade, P. (2000). The relationship among reported disclosure of sexual orientation, antidiscrimination policies, top management support and work attitudes of gay and lesbian employees. *Personnel Review, 29*(3), 346–363. doi:10.1108/00483480010324706

D'Emilio, J. (1998). *Sexual politics, sexual communities* (2nd ed.). Chicago: University of Chicago Press.

Di Mauro, D. (2001). Regulation: Sexual behavior. In Neil J. Smelser & Paul B. Baltes (Eds.), *International encyclopedia of the social and behavioral sciences* (pp. 12970–12974. Amsterdam: Elsevier.

District of Columbia Office of Human Rights. (2015). *Protected traits in DC.* Retrieved from http://ohr.dc.gov/protectedtraits

Don't Ask Don't Tell Repeal Act. (2010). Retrieved from http://www.congress.gov/111/plaws/publ321/PLAW-111publ321.pdf

Embrick, D. G., Walther, C. S., & Wickens, C. M. (2007). Working class masculinity: Keeping gay men and lesbians out of the workplace. *Sex Roles, 56*(11), 757–766. 10.1007/s11199-007-9234-0

Employment Nondiscrimination Act. (2013). Retrieved from http://www.congress.gov/bill/113th-congress/senate-bill/815/text

Equal Employment Opportunity Commission. (2015). *Facts about discrimination in federal government employment based on marital status, political affiliation, status as a parent, sexual orientation, and gender identity.* Retrieved from http://www.eeoc.gov/federal/otherprotections.cfm

Escoffier, J. (1985). Sexual revolution and the politics of gay identity. *Socialist Review, 15*(4), 126–196.

Executive Order 13087. (1998). Retrieved from http://archive.opm.gov/er/eo13087.htm

Faley, R. H., Knapp, D. E., Kustis, G. A., & Dubois, C. L. Z., Young, J., & Polin, B. (2006). Estimating the organizational costs of sexual harassment: The case of the US Army. *Journal of Business and Psychology, 30*(5), 557–577. doi:10.1023/A:1022987119277

Frank, N. (2009). *Unfriendly fire: How the gay ban undermines the military and weakens America.* New York: Macmillan.

Frank, W. (2014). *Law and the gay rights story: The long search for equal justice in a divided democracy.* New Brunswick, NJ: Rutgers University Press.

Gates, G. J., & Newport, F. (2013). *LGBT percentage highest in DC, lowest in North Dakota.* Retrieved from http://www.gallup.com/poll/160517/lgbt-percentage-highest-lowest-north-dakota.aspx

Gates, T. G. (2014). Assessing the relationship between outness at work and stigma consciousness among LGB workers in the Midwest and the resulting implications for counselors. *Counseling Psychology Quarterly, 27*(3), 264–276. doi:10.1080/09515070.2014.886998

Gates, T. G., & Kelly, B. L. (2013). LGB cultural phenomena and the social work research enterprise: Toward a strengths-based, culturally anchored methodology. *Journal of Homosexuality, 60*(1), 69–82. doi:10.1080/00918369.2013.735939

Gates, T. G., & Rodgers, C. G. (2014). Repeal of Don't Ask Don't Tell as a "policy window": A case for the passage of the Employment Non-Discrimination Act. *Journal of Discrimination and the Law, 14*(1), 5–18. doi:10.1177/1358229113500419

Gates, T. G., & Saunders, M. C. (2015). Bella Abzug, queer rights, and disrupting the status quo. *Journal of Social Change, 7*(1), 69–82. doi:10.5590/JOSC.2015.07.1.06

Genke, J. (2004). Resistance and resilience: The untold story of gay men aging with chronic illnesses. *Journal of Gay and Lesbian Social Services, 17*(2), 81–95. doi:10.1300/J041v17n02_05

Gillingham, P. (2006). Male social workers in child and family welfare: New directions for research. *Social Work, 51*(1), 83–85.

Griffith, K. H., & Hebl, M. R. (2002). The disclosure dilemma for gay men and lesbians: "Coming out" at work. *Journal of Applied Psychology, 87*(6), 1191–1199. doi:10.1037/0021-9010.87.6.1191

Gusmano, B. (2008). Coming out or not? How nonheterosexual people manage their sexual identity at work. *Journal of Workplace Rights, 13*(4), 473–496.

Haider-Markel, D. P., & Meier, K. J. (1996). The politics of gay and lesbian rights: Expanding the scope of the conflict. *Journal of Politics, 58*(2), 332–349. doi:10.2307/2960229

Halley, J. (1999). *Don't: A reader's guide to the military's anti-gay policy.* London: Duke University Press.

Hebl, M. R., Foster, J. B., Mannix, L. M., & Dovidio, J. F. (2002). Formal and interpersonal discrimination: A field study of bias toward homosexual applicants. *Personal and Social Psychology Bulletin, 28*(6), 815–825. doi:10.1177/0146167202289010

Herek, G. (1991). Stigma, prejudice, and violence among lesbians and gay men. In J. C. Gonsiorek & J. D. Weinrich (Eds.), *Homosexuality: Research implications for public policy* (pp. 60–80). Newbury Park, CA: SAGE.

Herek, G. M. (2000). The psychology of sexual prejudice. *Current Directions in Psychological Science, 9*(1), 19–22. doi:10.1111/1467-8721.00051

Hewlett, S. A., Sears, T., Sumberg, K., & Fargnoli, C. (2013). *The power of "out" 2.0: LGBT in the workplace.* New York: Center for Talent Innovation.

Holt, K. W. (1997). Re-evaluating Holloway: Title VII, equal protection, and the evolution of a transgender jurisprudence. *Temple Law Review, 70,* 283–319.

Horvath, M., & Ryan, A. M. (2003). Antecedents and potential moderators of the relationship between attitudes and hiring discrimination on the basis of sexual orientation. *Sex Roles, 48*(3–4), 115–130. doi:10.1023/A:1022499121222

Huffman, A. H., Watrous-Rodriguez, K. M., & King, E. B. (2008). Supporting a diverse workforce: What type of support is most meaningful for lesbian and gay employees? *Human Resource Management, 47*(2), 237–253. doi:10.1002/hrm.20210

Human Rights Campaign. (2014). *An important step toward workplace equality: An Executive Order on federal contractors.* Retrieved from http://www.hrc.org/resources/entry/an-important-step-toward-workplace-equality-an-executive-order-on-federal-c

Human Rights Campaign. (2015). *LGBT equality at the Fortune 500.* Retrieved from http://www.hrc.org/resources/lgbt-equality-at-the-fortune-500

Irwin, J. (1999). *The pink ceiling is too low: Workplace experiences of lesbians, gay men, and transgender people.* Sydney: Australian Centre for Lesbian and Gay Research.

Johnson, D. K. (2004). *The lavender scare: The Cold War persecution of gays and lesbians in the federal government.* Chicago: University of Chicago Press.

Kaplan, D. M. (2014). Career anchors and paths: The case of gay, lesbian, and bisexual workers. *Human Resource Management Review, 24*(2), 119–130. doi:10.1016/j.hrmr.2013.10.002

Kennedy, J. F. (1963). *Special message to the Congress on civil rights February 28, 1963.* Retrieved from http://www.presidency.ucsb.edu/ws/?pid=9581

King, E. B., Mohr, J. J., Peddie, C. I., Jones, K. P., & Kendra, M. (2017). Predictors of identity management: An exploratory experience-sampling study of lesbian, gay, and bisexual workers. *Journal of Management, 43*(2), 476–502. doi:10.1177/0149206314539350

King, E. B., Reilly, C., & Hebl, M. (2008). The best of times, the worst of times: Exploring dual perspectives of "coming out" in the workplace. *Group & Organization Management, 33*(5), 566–601. doi:10.1177/1059601108321834

Kirk, J., & Belovics, R. (2008). Understanding and counseling transgender clients. *Journal of Employment Counseling, 45*(1), 29–43.

Kirkey, K., & Forsyth, A. (2001). Men in the valley: Gay male life on the suburban-rural fringe. *Journal of Rural Studies, 17*(4), 421–441. doi:10.1016/S0743-0167(01)00007-9

Kuper, L. E., Nussbaum, R., & Mustanski, B. (2012). Exploring the diversity of gender and sexual orientation identities in an online sample of transgender individuals. *Journal of Sex Research, 49*(2–3), 244–254. doi:10.1080/00224499.2011.596954

Lewis, N. M. (2014). Rupture, resilience, and risk: Relationships between mental health and migration among gay-identified men in North America. *Health and Place, 27*, 212–219. doi:10.1016/j.healthplace.2014.03.002

Lindhorst, T. (1998). Lesbians and gay men in the country: Practice implications for rural social workers. *Journal of Gay and Lesbian Social Services, 7*(3), 1–11. doi:10.1300/J041v07n03_01

Luhtanen, R. K. (2003). Identity, stigma management, and well-being: A comparison of lesbians/bisexual women and gay/bisexual men. *Journal of Lesbian Studies, 7*(1), 85–100. doi:10.1300/J155v07n01_06

Mallon, G. P. (2001). Oh, Canada: The experience of working-class gay men in Toronto. *Journal of Gay and Lesbian Social Services, 12*(3–4), 103–117. doi:10.1300/J041v12n03_08

McDermott, E. (2006). Surviving in dangerous places: Lesbian identity performances in the workplace, social class and psychological health. *Feminism and Psychology, 16*(2), 193–211. doi:10.1177/0959-353506062977

McDonald, J. L., Ravitch, F. S., & Sumners, P. (2006). *Employment discrimination law: Problems, cases, and critical perspectives.* Upper Saddle River, NJ: Pearson.

Mearns, K., & Hope, L. (2005). *Health and well-being in the offshore environment: The management of personal health.* Aberdeen, UK: Health and Safety Executive.

Mia Macy v. Department of Justice. (2015). Retrieved from http://www.eeoc.gov/decisions/0120120821%20Macy%20v%20DOJ%20ATF.txt

Munford, R., & Sanders, J. (2005). Working with families: Strengths-based approaches (pp. 158–173). In M. Nash, R. Munford, & K. O'Donoghue (Eds.), *Social work theories in action.* Philadelphia: Jessica Kingsley.

National Gay and Lesbian Taskforce. (2014). *Historic victory: U.S. Senate passes Employment Non-Discrimination Act.* Retrieved from http://www.thetaskforce.org/historic-victory-u-s-senate-passes-employment-non-discrimination-act/

Oldfield, K., Candler, G., & Johnson, R. G. (2006). Social class, sexual orientation, and toward proactive social equity scholarship. *American Review of Public Administration, 36*(2), 156–172. doi:10.1177/0275074005281387

Paetzold, R. L. (1999). Same-sex sexual harassment, revisited: The aftermath of Oncale v. Sundowner Offshore Services, Inc. *Employee Rights and Employment Policy Journal, 3*(2), 259–260.

Parco, J. E., & Levy, D. A. (2012, September). DADT, RIP: Why the anti-gay policy vanished without ill effects. *Armed Forces Journal.* Retrieved from http://www.armedforcesjournal.com/dadt-r-i-p/

Quam, K. (2015). Unfinished business of repealing Don't Ask, Don't Tell: The military's unconstitutional ban on transgender individuals. *Utah Law Review, 3,* 721–741.

Ragins, B. R. (2004). Sexual orientation in the workplace: The unique work and career experiences of gay, lesbian and bisexual workers. *Research in Personnel and Human Resources Management, 23,* 35–120.

Ragins, B. R., Singh, R., & Cornwell, J. M. (2007). Making the invisible visible: Fear and disclosure of sexual orientation at work. *Journal of Applied Psychology, 92*(4), 1103–1118. doi:10.1037/0021-9010.92.4.1103

Ratcliff, J. J., Lassiter, G. D., Markman, K. D., & Snyder, C. J. (2006). Gender differences in attitudes toward gay men and lesbians: The role of motivation to respond without prejudice. *Personality and Social Psychology Bulletin, 32*(10), 1325–1338. doi:10.1177/0146167206290213

Rivera, R. (1980). Recent developments in sexual preference law. *Drake Law Review, 30*(2), 311–346.

Rivera, R. R. (1998). Our straight-laced judges: Twenty years later. *Hastings Law Journal, 50,* 1179–1198.

Rumens, N. (2011). *Queer company: The role and meaning of friendship in gay men's work lives.* Surrey, UK: Ashgate.

Saleebey, D. (2009). Power to the people. In D. Saleebey (Ed.), *The strengths perspective in social work practice* (pp. 1–23). Boston: Pearson.

Sinclair, G. D. (2009) Homosexuality and the military: A review of the literature. *Journal of Homosexuality, 56*(6), 701–718. doi:10.1080/00918360903054137

Soucek, B. (2014). Perceived homosexuals: Looking gay enough for Title VII. *American University Law Review, 63,* 715–788.

Sudore, R. (2015). Trans* sensitivity in re-entry programs: Recommendations for social justice advocacy. *Journal of Social Work Values and Ethics, 12*(2), 11–19.

Tejeda, M. J. (2006). Nondiscrimination policies and sexual identity disclosure: Do they make a difference in employee outcomes? *Employee Responsibilities and Rights Journal, 18*(1), 45–59. doi:10.1007/s10672-005-9004-5

Weichselbaumer, D. (2003). Sexual orientation discrimination in hiring. *Labor Economics, 10*(6), 629–642. doi:10.1016/S0927-5371(03)00074-5

White House. (2011). *Statement by the president on the repeal of Don't Ask, Don't Tell.* Retrieved from http://www.whitehouse.gov/the-press-office/2011/09/20/statement-president-repeal-dont-ask-dont-tell

White House. (2014). *Executive Order: Further amendments to Executive Order 11478, Equal Employment Opportunity in the federal government, and Executive Order 11246, Equal Employment Opportunity.* Retrieved from http://www.whitehouse.gov/the-press-office/2014/07/21/executive-order-further-amendments-executive-order-11478-equal-employment

Wienke, C., & Hill, G. J. (2013). Does place of residence matter? Rural–urban differences and the wellbeing of gay men and lesbians. *Journal of Homosexuality, 60*(9), 1256–1279. doi:10.1080/00918369.2013.806166

CHAPTER 10

AGING WITHIN THE LGBT COMMUNITY

An Exploration of Life's Challenges

Marcia Spira, John Orwat, and Shaina Knepler-Foss

INTRODUCTION

It is estimated that among the general aging population, there are approximately 1.5 million lesbian, gay, bisexual, and transgender (LGBT) Americans who are over the age of 60 (Alpert, 2015).
Due to the retiring Baby Boomer population this number is anticipated to grow exponentially over
the next few decades, to an estimated 3 million individuals by the year 2030 (Henning-Smith,
Gonzales, & Shippee, 2015), which will represent approximately 20% of the overall population
(US Census Bureau, 2010). As social norms and values continue to shift toward recognition and
acceptance of the LGBT community there remains a critical need to address the continued challenges created by discriminatory attitudes and practices. According to the Institute of Medicine
Committee on Lesbian, Gay, Bisexual, and Transgender Health Issues and Research Gaps and
Opportunities (IOM, 2011), there is almost no published research on LGBT individuals who are
over the age of 85. The IOM report goes on to state that research conducted has disproportion-
ally focused on gay men and lesbians, frequently ignoring the plight of even more marginalized
members of the LGBT community, such as transgender individuals. In the same regard, many
best practices and interventions for older adults are typically based on heteronormative models
of aging, as the field of gerontology and other related disciplines have seldom researched LGBT
aging concerns and issues.

In the absence of sufficient research associated with older LGBT adults and areas of practice
related to health and mental health, certain conclusions should be regarded as speculative. In fact,
it is important that practitioners realize that reliance on the personal narratives of older LGBT
individuals can often provide legitimacy far beyond the current discussion. This chapter provides

an overview of the unique challenges and opportunities in life faced by LGBT older adults, including health and mental health, family issues, housing and long-term care (LTC), abuse and neglect, legal concerns, and loss, grief, death, and dying. Analysis of these issues is approached from the life course perspective, an approach that frames issues of aging within historical, cultural, sociological, and political contexts.

SOCIOHISTORICAL RELEVANCE

From the highest levels of government policy to the most micro-level health-care encounter, pronounced homophobia and transphobia still exists today. Regardless of the broadening acceptance of LGBT issues over the past 40 years, many LGBT older adults continue to experience a number of significant obstacles and are still denied services on the basis of sexual orientation or gender identity (Fredricksen-Goldsen, Kim, Shiu, Goldsen, & Emlet, 2015). Examining such factors through a life course perspective (Bronfenbrenner, 1979) may best assist with understanding the profound impact of differences among generational age cohorts (Wethington, 2005) along with understanding implications for well aging among LGBT older adults. Current models of aging do not always consider the life course experience of older LGBT individuals who have often demonstrated extraordinary strength and resilience in the face of extreme biopsychosocial challenges over time.

The life course perspective describes developmental processes and outcomes that are uniquely shaped by social trajectories across the lifespan, with implications related to early choices and decision-making (Eckenrode & Gore, 1990; Moen, Dempster-McClain, & Williams, 1992). Knowledge and understanding of an individual's recall of prior life events is essential to best understand the breadth and depth of the later years of aging (Elder, 1994). Common components of the life course perspective include the interplay of life and historical times, the timing of lives, linked or interdependent lives, and human agency utilized in decision-making processes (Bronfenbrenner, 1979; Elder, 1994). It is therefore relevant to continue research and a dialogue about the application of such components related to the life course perspective when examining older LGBT adults and generational cohort differences related to health, risk behaviors, perceptions of well aging, and how these concepts change over time (Wethington, 2005).

Older LGBT individuals may have life histories of closeting their identities in order to protect their families, jobs, and safety. These individuals grew up in communities that imposed restrictions and oppression on many minority groups, including racial, sexual, and gender minorities, among others. After World War II, most states recognized homosexuality as a socially threatening disease (Messinger, 2006), and experimental harmful treatment procedures included shock therapy, lobotomy, and genital mutilation. During this time, homosexuality was often connected with treason and communism, including dismissal of many government employees and police raids on gay bars, resulting in the humiliating publication of detainees' names in military reports and local newspapers (Messinger, 2006).

Following three nights of protest and civil unrest during the summer of 1969 in New York City at the Stonewall Inn (Spencer, 1995) came significant historical, social, cultural, and legal changes for members of the LGBT community. Examining and understanding LGBT older adults within such contexts as the historical and social realms (Clunis, Fredriksen-Goldsen, Freeman, & Nystro, 2005; Fredriksen-Goldsen & Muraco, 2010) remains important. Practitioners should also take into account the culture, politics, and social mores of the era in which older LGBT adults came of age—when compared to the era in which they currently live—to best understand their uniquely lived experiences and needs. Prior to the significant social and legislative changes that followed the uprising at Stonewall, homosexuality had been pathologized in the American Psychiatric Association's third edition of the *Diagnostic and Statistical Manual of Mental Disorders* as a mental disorder. This was further compounded by antigay legislation and social propaganda resulting in LGBT individuals risking job loss, family separation, social standing, and even personal safety. Some LGBT individuals may have been threatened by institutions from which safety is expected—such as policing practices that led to brutality, arrest, and exposure (Atkins, 2003; Weststrate & McLean, 2010; Williams & Freeman, 2007). As recent as 1998, several state-level sodomy laws criminalized same-sex acts and were used to discriminate against and marginalize members of the LGBT community before such laws were struck down (Elze, 2006).

One of the most significant challenges faced by generations of gay and bisexual men was surviving the initial years of the HIV/AIDS epidemic during the 1980s and early 1990s prior to the advent of effective antiretroviral medications. The initial lack of appropriate response from the government and society to this health-care crisis affirmed the marginalization and impact of invisibility on the LGBT population. For example, the Food and Drug Administration approval of new and effective medications remained slow despite evidence that this treatment had the potential to save lives. This systemic discrimination from local, state, and federal authorities had both disempowering and empowering impacts: it emboldened advocacy groups (e.g., ACT-UP and Queer Nation) and spurred momentum to establish access to care and medications, while greater barriers may have been formed with distrust of the medical and health-care systems. The picture is complicated for those who survived the early years of the HIV/AIDS epidemic—as many continue to live healthy lives with antiretroviral medications—or for those not infected with HIV, who may suffer from survivor guilt (Halkitis, 2013). There remains a dearth of long-term research and understanding related to the implications of living more than two decades with HIV/AIDS, on or off antiretroviral therapies, along with challenges related to physical and mental health outcomes (Burgoyne, Rourke, Behrens, & Salit, 2004), including adding the typical complexities of aging.

The uprising at Stonewall, followed by several marches for LGBT equality in Washington, D.C., and protests in support of the HIV/AIDS community, along with other key events ushered in an era of increased visibility and activism for members of the LGBT community over the past 40 years. These events, along with related psychosocial factors have had a profound impact on the lived identities of older LGBT adults (Vaccaro, 2009; Weststrate & McLean, 2010). Witnessing and/or participating in such events likely affected the physical and mental health of many generations of LGBT individuals, as well as impacted the manner in which they seek *or do not seek* health and mental health care services. Ultimately, such experiences may differ significantly among members of the aging LGBT community when compared to younger LGBT individuals, or non-LGBT counterparts, thus providing a unique opportunity for continued examination from a life course perspective.

Recent advances and ongoing struggles for civil rights (e.g., marriage equality, the need for a national employment nondiscrimination act, transgender equality) have promoted greater levels of visibility and acceptance for members of the LGBT community. Regardless, the endurance of lifetime intolerance and discriminatory practices experienced by older LGBT adults likely has potential long-term consequences on self-esteem, self-image, coping, and management of life stressors. Such challenges include barriers to access and utilizations for health and mental health care, discriminatory practices with regard to securing housing and employment, caregiving and LTC assistance, legal matters, and substance use and addiction, among other areas of concern (Grossman, 2006).

AGE COHORTS

Among literature exploring birth cohort differences and maturational factors, it remains evident that the larger social context plays a significant role in sexual identity development (Floyd & Bakeman, 2006; Parks, 1999; Rosenfeld, 1999). The collective attitudes of community and society alike, which can be reflected through policies as well as behaviors, greatly influences self-perception among LGBT individuals. Such positive and negative messages can impact an LGBT individuals' internalization of the meanings and feelings about their particular personal attributes, including sexual identity. Several studies have explored the dynamics and impact of societal perspectives on the characteristics of LGBT cohorts born before and after pivotal events that have changed the social perception of homosexuality and given rise to broader acceptance of sexual identities (Allen & Roberto, 2016; Fredriksen-Goldsen et al., 2015; Rosenfeld, 1999; Vaccaro, 2009). Through understanding older LGBT adults as age groups or identity cohorts (Parks, 1999; Rosenfeld, 1999), greater insight is achieved with regard to differing perspectives on the need for advocacy, issues related to social justice (e.g., employment, housing, immigration status, relationships), and the discrepant perceptions of disclosure management related to coming out or remaining closeted. Rosenfeld's (1999) study divided participants ($N = 37$) into a pre-Stonewall cohort (defined as a more passively silent group stigmatized by homosexuality) and a post-Stonewall cohort (which viewed homosexuality as a status imbued with political and moral meanings). The researcher noted:

> Such membership in identity cohorts may introduce intra-generational, inter-cohort tensions to social worlds in which inter-generational tensions already exist, causing identity cohort members to be estranged not only from members of other generations but from certain members of their own. (Rosenfeld, 1999, p. 138)

Vaccaro's (2009) study ($N = 49$) identified some intergenerational similarities along with stark differences between several age cohorts, including Baby Boomers (born circa 1940s–1960s), Generation X (born circa 1960s–1980s), Millennials (born circa 1980s–2000s), and their own lived experiences related to coming out, family, relationships, activism, prejudice, and experiences of discrimination. It is important to note that compared to a cross-generational assessment, such differences might exist among members of the same age cohort who experience similar historical events yet have divergent reactions based on geography, race, socioeconomic status, and other factors (Fullmer, 2006).

Such an examination of age cohort similarities and differences is essential for understanding best practices and service provision as well as ongoing research in the field of LGBT aging. Myriad factors impact an LGBT individual's lived experiences from perceptions of support, to expectations for acceptance or rejection, as well as the ability to develop resilience (Butler, 2004) and an ability to cope and adapt. In addition to aging LGBT cohorts managing such aforementioned stressors is the potential for minority stress factors associated with perceived or actual experiences of prejudice, discrimination, and/or harassment (Meyer, 2003). Throughout history, tension has also existed between subgroups within the LGBT community itself. For example, lesbians were excluded from gay organizations and bars; transwomen were expelled from lesbian organizations; bisexuals were excluded from the broader gay and lesbian movements; class divisions went mostly overlooked; and men and women of all kinds were excluded from a variety of groups on the basis of being too visibly "butch" or "femme" (Messinger, 2006). In the same regard, despite the increasing presence of celebrities and politicians becoming more public about their role as LGBT allies or openly as members of the LGBT community, ageism still persists. Most LGBT stereotypical character depiction within the media is typically of young, handsome, and virile adults. Despite Vaccaro's (2009) study finding that more intergenerational similarities existed than each cohort might expect, it is clear that the older generations of LGBT adults may feel somewhat devalued by, estranged from, or invisible to both the mainstream LGBT community and society as a whole.

Depending on the level of isolation and invisibility (Reid, 1995) experienced by older LGBT adults, it may be important to consider differing age cohort perceptions (Elder, 1994) related to self-identity, access, privilege, and power (Van Wagenen, Driskell, & Bradford, 2013). In spaces where LGBT supportive attitudes are not readily expressed, many older LGBT individuals may feel the need to conceal their identity—or go back into the closet—even after years of living out, for fear of discrimination (Persson, 2009; Stein, Beckerman, & Sherman, 2010). It should be noted that contradictory messages of inclusion and exclusion within the community or at the workplace likely required differential expressions of an individual's lived identities. Older LGBT persons who could be open about sexual identity in the community may have remained closeted at work or vice versa. Additionally, bearing such stress over time may increase the potential for risk behaviors related to substance use, sexual risk, and suicide ideation or attempt, among other factors (Elze, 2006; Logie, Bridge, & Bridge, 2007).

In addition to stressors associated with identifying as LGBT lies the intersection or affiliation with other intersecting identities (e.g., race, gender identity, disability, HIV status). Such multiple identities might impact chronic stressors such as oppression and discrimination or potentially amplify risks associated with acute stressors including victimization or hate crimes (Elze, 2006). Alone, such risks are significant enough, but recent research continues to emphasize the relationship between poor health and mental health outcomes (Fredricksen-Goldsend et al., 2015). Thus practitioners working with the aging LGBT community must be competent and keenly aware of a multitude of typical and atypical aging and birth cohort–related factors. The risk is that practitioners may overlook key factors that could critically enhance and strengthen the therapeutic alliance when working with aging members of this diverse minority population.

HEALTH AND MENTAL HEALTH: UNDERSCORING STRENGTHS AND RESILIENCE

Health and mental health care disparities have been identified among members of the LGBT community. Wight, LeBlanc, and Badgett (2013) found that stigma, expectations for rejection, experiences of discrimination, internalized homophobia, and the need to conceal one's identity may create levels of stress leading to poorer mental health outcomes among LGBT individuals. Personal experiences of discrimination among older LGBT adults may lead to a general distrust of health and mental health professionals, resulting in lower likelihood of seeking services and help (Fredriksen-Goldsen et al., 2015; Hughes, Harold, & Boyer, 2011; Xavier, Bradford, & Honnold, 2007). Additional identification with minority factors such as race, gender, class, and socioeconomic status may compound external barriers to health and mental health care. Such mistrust of the government, health, and mental health care sectors by many minority groups has been compounded over the years as a result of the unethical Tuskegee syphilis studies conducted from the 1930s to the 1970s to governmental inaction at the beginning of the HIV/AIDS crisis in the 1980s (Laurencin, Christensen, & Taylor, 2008) among other traumatizing historical events.

RACE/ETHNICITY

Concerns about the intersectionality of sexual orientation and race are often excluded from conversations on health and mental health outcomes. Additionally, current research is insufficient, especially in the form of understanding long-term health outcomes for LGBT racial/ethnic minorities (Rogers, Rebbe, Gardella, Worlein, & Chamberlin, 2013). As the IOM (2011) discusses, a lack of foundational understanding regarding health disparities among older LGBT individuals of color can create patterns of systemic oppression and gaps in adequate health care (Fredriksen-Goldsen, 2011) For instance, the committee ascertains that there is an increased likelihood of higher body mass index among African American and Latina lesbian and bisexual women (IOM, 2011). The availability of LGBT health-care providers adequately trained to provide competent and nonjudgmental services for LGBT racial minority populations is essential to maintenance of high-quality care.

SEXUAL HEALTH

Many older LGBT adults have been sexually active throughout their lives and continue healthy sexual behavior, especially with reduced risk of pregnancy and availability of erectile dysfunction medications. However, many professionals assume older LGBT adults are not sexually active, and many sexual health and education campaigns overlook this group (Emlet, 2004; Simone & Appelbaum, 2008). Older LGBT adults from some age cohorts may find it difficult to volunteer information regarding sexual health or behavior (Emlet, 2004, 2006) due to the sexually repressed or conservative values of the era during which they matured. This is often compounded by attitudes and societal messages often suggesting or assuming that older adults are not or should not be sexual. However, it is important to understand that aging can bring changes that affect sexual arousal and vulnerability to sexually transmitted infections (STIs). Decreased arousal can evoke feelings of insecurity in one partner, with the other partner feeling less attractive as a result. For lesbians or transwomen, thinning of the vaginal walls and decreased or delayed lubrication of the vagina increases the risk of tearing, which, combined with decreased immune functioning, places them at risk for STIs (Levy-Dweck, 2005). Social attitudes about masculinity have fueled the popularity of erectile enhancement medications, resulting in older men having more sexual partners than ever before (Levy-Dweck, 2005). An education and communication gap between professionals and the aging LGBT community risks not only the opportunity to express affirmation and acceptance of the client's sexual identity but the chance to screen for STIs, including HIV/AIDS, and the opportunity to clearly understand their unique needs.

HIV/AIDS

The number of deaths among older adults (age 65+) from HIV/AIDS has increased more than any other age group, with African Americans overrepresented in all age groups (Centers for Disease Control and Prevention, 2012). Many older LGBT adults are not voluntarily tested for myriad reasons, including stigma surrounding age, sexuality, and HIV status, combined with an overall perceived lack of risk (Emlet, 2004; Simone & Appelbaum, 2008). Similarly, health-care professionals may not consider an older adult to be at risk for HIV and credit symptoms to the natural weakening of the immune system associated with the aging process (Levy-Dweck, 2005; Simone & Appelbaum, 2008). As a result, many older adults who are diagnosed with HIV/AIDS are found to have a lower CD4 (T-cell) count than their younger counterparts at time of primary diagnosis and are therefore at higher risk for HIV/AIDS-related complications (Heckman et al., 2001; Simone & Appelbaum, 2008). Ultimately it remains urgent to diagnosis HIV infections at an earlier stage while preventing new infections among this age group—both goals that can be accomplished through education and training for the older LGBT community as well as ongoing professional development for those working in the field of aging. Regardless of HIV status, intervention efforts with members of the aging LGBT community should focus on understanding diverse cultures, norms, lifestyles, and experiences (Strombeck & Levy, 1998) while building on knowledge gained from effective interventions for behavior change among younger cohorts and sensitivity to sociocultural contexts (Coon, Lipman, & Ory, 2003). Notably, there remains a dearth of long-term research and understanding related to the implications of living 20 or more years with HIV/AIDS, whether on antiretroviral therapies or not, along with challenges related to physical and mental health outcomes (Burgoyne et al., 2004).

STRENGTHS AND RESILIENCE

When examining the struggles faced by LGBT older adults, it is important to understand that while these experiences may have been difficult or painful for many, they do not always result in long-term suffering (IOM, 2011). Such assumptions of associated pathology are problematic and offer limited insight related to the many positive and affirming aging experiences of LGBT adults and other vulnerable communities (Fredricksen-Goldsen, 2011; Logie et al., 2007). This is clearly evidenced in earlier literature and research describing positive psychosocial functioning among older gay men and lesbians (Berger, 1984; Berger & Kelly, 1986; Gray & Dressel, 1985) noting favorable feelings about aging (Whitford, 1997), appearance (Gray & Dressel, 1985), and sexuality (Pope & Schulz, 1990). Subsequent studies found older gay male and lesbian adults ($N = 108$) to be no more depressed than heterosexual counterparts (Dorfman et al., 1995); and a majority of gay and lesbian adults ($N = 416$) notably rated their mental health as excellent or good (D'Augelli & Grossman, 2001). Though social discrimination, homophobia, and ageism can have negative effects on older LGBT adults, such challenges have underscored a multitude of coping mechanisms and resilience (Butler, 2004) among members of this often oppressed community (Smith, McCaslin, Chang, Martinez, & McGrew, 2010). In light of overwhelming social and political discrimination, members of the LGBT community from the "Greatest" and Baby Boomer generations were particularly active in fighting for equality and the rights of the modern LGBT movement (Messinger, 2006). It is important to note that many older LGBT individuals may have mastered coping and management of life situations involving stigma due to repeated encounters, ultimately preparing them to adapt better with the stigmas typically associated with aging (Fullmer, 2006).

Communication gaps between practitioners and older LGBT adults may increase the risk for not effectively expressing affirmation and acceptance of the client's sexual identity along with the chance to screen for STIs and the opportunity to clearly understand the unique needs of diverse generational cohorts (Henning-Smith et al., 2015; IOM, 2011). As previously noted, regardless of age cohort or client population, sex and sexuality are important topics to discuss with older LGBT adults, as practitioners otherwise risk ignoring vulnerabilities that can have broad reaching implications for well-being as well as physical and emotional health. Ultimately, practitioners would be wise to effectively demonstrate empathy—along with underscoring resilience from a strengths perspective—during their work with older LGBT adults, rather than solely emphasizing histories of stigma and oppression.

RELIGION AND SPIRITUALITY

The value of religious practice and spiritual belief seems to be indisputable for older LGBT adults. Religion is associated with an organized set of institutionalized communal experiences (Wood & Conley, 2014), while spirituality refers to a set of beliefs that provides meaning and cohesiveness of self and connection (Frankl, 1961; Love, Bock, Jannarone, & Richardson, 2005). Religious practice may reduce stress, improve well-being, and augment social engagement through membership within a community. Religious and spiritual practices have been recognized as a source of coping with life challenges among older adults (Ellor, 2013). In fact, Stanley et al. (2011) found strong preferences for the inclusion of religion and spirituality in the treatment of anxiety and depression among older adults. Similarly, Noronha (2015) found that older adults aged more productively through spiritual and cultural interests. Levin and Hein (2012) noted that older adults facing adversity such as housing and health concerns had better psychosocial and health outcomes as a result of religious identification and spiritual beliefs.

However, religion and spirituality may have both positive and negative effects on LGBT individuals (Fallon et al., 2013). Sherry, Adelman, Whilde, and Quick (2010) discussed the conflict created between the anti-LGBT doctrine of some religious traditions and the important value of religion and spirituality to LGBT individuals. Many LGBT older adults have experienced a long history of religious oppression, complicating access to religious and spiritual resources for coping with life's challenges. For years LGBT individuals may have been excluded from participation in religious rituals, while others may have been traumatized (i.e., sexual abuse, reparative or conversion therapy). Consistent with homophobic societal views, religious institutions viewed LGBT adults as deviant, excluding them from participation in rituals, creating a sense of alienation from religion and the potential for low self-esteem (Bowers, Minichiello, & Plummer, 2010).

Wood and Conley (2014) explored the loss of religious and spiritual identity among LGBT individuals, finding that a bifurcation of religious identity and sexual orientation proves detrimental to LGBT adults who have continued to suffer discrimination within religious institutions. A Pew study (2013) found that 29% of LGBT individuals felt unwelcome in houses of worship despite the wider acceptance of the LGBT community. The history of persecution of LGBT individuals may promote a tendency to compartmentalize or deny their religious and/or spiritual identify from public view (Rodriguez cited in Wood & Conley, 2014). This separation of the two identities typically leads to reconciliation by abandoning one or the other. The best outcome, of course, would be an integration of the two identities, in which LGBT individuals can obtain a harmonious and cohesive sense of self (Wood & Conley, 2014). In fact, addressing the integration of such separate identities may be essential with regard to practitioners working with LGBTQ clients struggling with their religious beliefs and sexual orientation or gender identity.

Practitioners should also be aware that membership within a religious community has a social engagement component as well as it can be positively associated with coping, end-of-life concerns, increased self-esteem, and self-acceptance while also enabling individuals with health concerns (i.e., HIV, cancer) to cope more effectively (Siegel & Schrimshaw, 2002). Another essential matter pertains to the encouragement of all practitioners to be aware of their personal biases about the LGBT community that may be based in religious ideology. A study by McGeorge, Carlson, and Tommey (2014) notes the importance of including religious and spiritual content in family therapy training programs. Students who received training from a spiritual framework were more accepting of work with the LGBT community from an affirmative perspective and less likely to support reparative therapies. It remains evident that acknowledgment of religious and spiritual aspects of an older LGBTQ adult's identity may underscore important resources. Reconciling personal values or conflicts associated with one's religious and spiritual identity with LGBTQ older adult clients may be essential for effective treatment and care (Fallon et al., 2013).

FAMILIES OF ORIGIN AND FAMILIES OF CHOICE

Shifting social norms have challenged the traditional definitions of family as well as the diversity of family structures but have not completely eradicated the biases and barriers that LGBT individuals face (Allen & Roberto, 2016). Relatedly, we have limited knowledge with regard to older LGBT adults and relations with families of origin compared to families of choice, which may hinder the ability to construct and ascertain patterns related to the meaning and structure of how "family" is defined (Allen & Roberto, 2016). Nevertheless, there is some evidence suggesting that older LGBT adult experiences are similar to non-LGBT older adults, as their families of choice, origin, and procreation exist within both normative and nonnormative family structures (Allen & Roberto, 2016). However, there are distinctive characteristics among older LGBT adults that differ from their non-LGBT counterparts, such as a higher probability of living alone, being less likely to be married or have children (Erosheva, Kim, Emlet, & Fredriksen-Goldsen, 2015), as well as an increased likelihood of facing conflict with their family of origin (Henning-Smith et al., 2015). Additionally, serious family or personal problems may arise from disclosure of an older adult's LGBT identity (D'Augelli & Grossman, 2001).

Despite recent federal policies supporting same-sex marriage, there are still governmental institutions that may not necessarily comprehend the unique nontraditional family structures that may be present within the LGBTQ community. Allen and Roberto (2016) discuss the social and legal constraints on the definition of families within the LGBT community before the social changes starting in the 1990s through the present. Such constraints may have included no guarantee for reliance on biological ties for support, both instrumentally and emotionally. Heteronormative definitions and societal assumptions associated with family structures and relationships are still typically applied to members of the LGBT community, whether in the mass media or with agency policies and forms and so on. Ultimately, definitions of family of origin should be expanded to include not only those that LGBT adults have with their aging parents and adult siblings but also relationships with same-sex partners, same- or different-sex partners, children, and grandchildren.

COMING OUT FACTORS

The current cohort of older LGBT individuals came out at a time when sexual minority status was treated as illegal (Allen & Roberto, 2016). Older LGBT individuals may have closeted their sexual identity and attempted to live within societal and familial norms of heterosexual marriage and family early in life, coming out at a much later time. Other facets of coming out, whether to adult children or grandchildren, can be complex; and an LGBT individual's relationship with older parents may also be complicated. For instance, the desire of LGBT individuals to care for aging parents may be shunned or declined by nonaccepting parents.

Families of origin continue to face similar challenges confronted by members of the LGBT community (Allen & Roberto, 2016) with regard to coming out. Specifically, the coming out process is a transition that has implications for family, extended family, and friends alike. The historical and life cycle timing of the coming out process is significant in understanding the impact of this transition on various family systems. In fact, parents may experience a parallel process to their LGBT family member's disclosure of sexual orientation. Parents may feel challenged with the need to reconcile expectations for their children and themselves that revolve around heteronormative family relations and structures. Parents can also be reluctant to disclose their child's identity in the coming out process with their friends and extended family as they struggle with their own process of acceptance or nonacceptance. While older LBGT adult children have likely lived with recognition of their sexual orientation for many years before disclosing to parents and family members; their parents and family members have likely had (at the time of disclosure) far less time to reorganize their experience. Therefore, while parents may come to terms with the coming out process parallel to that of their children, the timing is not often congruent with the adult child's experience. While the literature does demonstrate that the majority of gay and lesbian older adults ($N = 1,200$) do receive some level of acceptance and support from their families of origin (Metlife, 2010), practitioners should be sensitive to parents who need time to process the life transition with their older LGBT adult child.

Relationships and connections are critical for older LGBT individuals. A strong and comprehensive network for socialization and support has shown to have a positive impact on health and mental health outcomes (Erosheva et al., 2015). Furthermore, these support networks provide many of the same functions as families of origin. Many LGBT individuals prefer to receive support and care from families of choice, as they are able to eliminate the need to desexualize or hide evidence of their sexual orientation and lifestyle (Cronin, Ward, Pugh, & Price, 2011; Fredriksen-Goldsen, 2011). Notably, many members of the LGBT community rely on various kinship networks of friends, allies, and families of choice to provide elements of support—when not provided by families of origin—in response to life events such as a major illness (Muraco & Fredriksen-Goldsen, 2014).

Expectations remain hopeful that family relationships will increasingly become less stressful and more visibly supportive due to changes with the social and political climate across the United States. Family members are often key allies for older LGBT adults who can also impact policy reform on many levels. Policies at the local and federal levels can both positively (e.g., marriage equality) and negatively (e.g., workplace discrimination, religious freedom laws) impact the LGBT community. Ultimately, there are a multitude of reasons for families of origin to support and celebrate their aging LGBT family members despite any history of conflict or oppression.

LONG-TERM CARE: HEALTH AND PROVIDER CONCERNS

While there are many similarities with regard to care needs for LGBT older adults in comparison to heterosexual older adults, there are also many psychosocial issues that are unique and must be accounted for (Stein et al., 2010). Additionally, some studies suggest that LGBT individuals face greater risk of needing LTC than their heterosexual counterparts (Fredriksen-Goldsen et al., 2015; IOM 2011). Explanations for these findings are a bit speculative; however, it is hypothesized that this dichotomy could be related to a larger percentage of LGBT older adults frequently domiciling alone and being less likely to have families that can provide care (Stein et al., 2010). This is compounded by discrimination and barriers in the health-care field that LGBT older adults often face (Stein et al., 2010). Concern over care is heightened by policies that require disclosure of sexual orientation, gender or gender identity, and the additional fear of a negative response by providers. Many LTC facilities also typically assume that all of their clients are heterosexual or in heteronormative relationships with typical family structures. As a result, this lack of recognition by providers of older LGBT individual's needs can limit care (Kimmel, 2014). In the same regard, programming to meet the health-care needs of aging LGBT individuals can be unintentionally biased and discriminatory (Rogers et al., 2013) while also based in heteronormative ideology. While all aging individuals share similar challenges, the vulnerability of minority status and systemic oppression may create an unsafe environment for older LGBT individuals in programs such as reminiscence groups within LTC facilities. The stress of censorship may lead to higher levels of anxiety and concerns about needing to re-closet their true selves (Almack, Seymour, & Bellamy, 2010; IOM, 2011; Stein et al., 2010).

LTC facilities are often unwelcoming to LGBT older persons, and health-care workers often lack training to address the specific health needs of their diverse residents (Henning-Smith et al., 2015). Policies that continue to prohibit same-sex partners from living together in LTC housing must be challenged and spaces created with the same fairness afforded to heterosexual couples. Service providers should also be aware of advance planning and health directives to meet the specialized needs of their sexual minority clients. In the same fashion, intake, assessment and care plans should always include language and measures to treat all clients with respect regardless of their gender identity or sexual orientation. It is imperative that all LTC and service providers receive ongoing training for their work with older LGBT adults, as the National Senior Citizens Law Center (2011) recognized that many still need protection from discrimination and mistreatment based on gender identity and sexual orientation. Another important national organization is Services and Advocacy for GLBT Elders (SAGE), which provides services and trainings along with policy advocacy to raise awareness and visibility of older LGBT adults. Most notably, the federal government has recently supported funding for a SAGE technical assistance resource center, which promotes appropriate LTC support systems for LGBT elders (see http://www.sageusa.org/programs/nrc.cfm).

It is also important to be aware of the many unique and specific patterns of health-care needs for marginalized groups within the older LGBT adult population. Some unique concerns may relate to gender, gender identity, race/ethnicity, socioeconomic status, rural/urban location, or other sociodemographic differences. For example, lesbians are reported to have higher rates of health risk behaviors, including smoking, drinking, and obesity, that places them at greater risk for diseases (e.g., cardiovascular disease) when compared to their heterosexual counterparts (D'Augelli & Grossman, 2001; Hughes & Evans, 2003; Tang et al., 2004). Similarly, older lesbians may face increased forms of discrimination as their gender, sexual minority status, and age may serve as a triple threat correlated with decreased resources and a lack of social connections (Gabrielson, 2011).

While some LGBT individuals might prefer to accept care from families of choice in order to eliminate the necessity to hide their sexual orientation, the high costs associated with such care has often included significant financial burdens and limited choices. However, one key benefit stemming from changes in marriage equality laws will be to insure the protection of an LGBT spouse's finances when a spouse needs to enter a LTC facility or needs other home health-care services. Such financial benefits and options have not previously been available to same-sex couples prior to marriage equality.

ABUSE AND NEGLECT

Older LGBT adults commonly face high levels of discrimination, abuse, stigma, and neglect (Fredriksen-Goldsen et al., 2015; D'Augelli & Grossman, 2001). Although potentially appearing in many forms, studies illustrate that it is most frequently experienced in the form of physical attacks, abuse by caregivers, financial exploitation, and prejudice and hostility within institutional care facilities (American Psychological Association, 2009; Fredriksen-Goldsen et al., 2015; Grossman et al., 2014). While this topic is markedly underresearched, one study showed that on average LGBT older adults ($N = 2,560$) experience an average of four occurrences of discrimination, in the form of verbal and physical violence (Fredriksen-Goldsen et al., 2015). Transgender adults over the age of 50 have an even higher average of verbal and physical violence occurrences (Fredriksen-Goldsen et al., 2015); however, the extent of research on violence experienced by older transgender adults remains limited (Xavier et al., 2007). Experiencing a lifetime of abuse, stigmatization, victimization, or neglect can potentially lead to internalized homophobia and myriad health challenges (i.e., sexual risk behavior), as well as negative outcomes associated with mental health (D'Augelli & Grossman, 2001) among older LGBTQ adults. Oppositely, the provision of support and affirming services for LGBTQ older adults can result in better health and mental health outcomes along with lower rates stress, strain, and internalized homophobia (Rogers et al., 2013).

Self-abuse and self-harm are considerable risks for older LGBT individuals who have lived in a society that breeds contempt and discrimination. As a group greatly impacted by risk for suicide in general, older adults have a higher national average, with LGBT older adults accounting for an even higher percentage (Haas & Lane, 2015) of suicide attempt or completion. LGBT individuals are at an increased risk over the course of their lives to experience and endure interpersonal violence within intimate relationships and through hate crimes and violence by other LGBT people (D'Augelli & Grossman, 2001). Caregiver abuse against older LGBT individuals, at home with family or in nursing homes, raises additional cause for concern. While older adults face the normal challenges of aging, LGBT individuals are at a higher risk of abuse due to their sexual orientation or gender identity (Cook-Daniels, 1998), as well as other related minority statuses associated with race, religion, socioeconomic status, and so on.

As generations of older LGBT adults have suffered various forms of hospitalization, criminalization, and demoralization, they may be hesitant to be open and transparent about their sexual orientation or gender identity (Almack et al., 2010). Furthermore, many older LGBT adults have been subjected to varying levels of abuse and neglect by family, the government, and social service organizations—especially with regard to fair treatment and equal protections—allowing for access and eligibility to needed services (Rogers et al., 2013). Through both discriminatory practices and the nonexistence of necessary services and resources, this population continues to be neglected and marginalized and to face numerous barriers and access within a number of settings. Practitioners should assess for neglect and abuse as part of the typical intake and assessment process when working with older LGBT adults as well as be sensitized to how it has impacted them over the lifespan.

LEGAL CONCERNS

The 1996 Defense of Marriage Act (DOMA)—since ruled unconstitutional in the 2013 case of *U.S. v. Windsor*—was a federal law that prohibited the recognition of same-sex marriage on the federal level, regardless of the marriage laws in any specific state, and allowed states to refuse to recognize such marriages from other states. The impact of DOMA was that same-sex spouses were ineligible for receiving over 1,138 federal benefits, regardless of the legality of their marriage in their state of residence. Such benefits included survivor benefits for veterans, social security, property rights, and immigration, all of which can be based on an individual's legal marital status (Goldberg, 2009; Human Rights Campaign, 2016). Further, any benefits extended by the state were not recognized on the federal level so that, for example, the additional cost of a family health insurance benefit incurred a federal tax, which was not the case with marriage between opposite-sex partners. The repeal of DOMA has provided opportunities for LGBT couples to enjoy the benefits of marriage previously denied, such as having access to spousal employer pensions, health insurance, and survivor/death benefits.

While DOMA has been ruled unconstitutional, extensive discrimination and inequality continues to impact those members of the LGBT community who choose to marry. While same-sex marriage is legal on a federal level, a number of states and county clerks have attempted to create discriminatory barriers (i.e., refusal to issue marriage licenses to same-sex couples). Additionally, the legalization of marriage still requires LGBT individuals to assume and abide by a heteronormative structure to attain status for federal and state benefits. As marriage equality is celebrated by the LGBT community as a civil rights accomplishment, some may continue to reject it as a heteronormative structure. This may be especially true for older LGBT adults who have spent a lifetime building families within hostile sociopolitical systems—thus creating alternative pathways to acknowledge their partner and long-term relationship and commitment. Sensitivity to family structures outside of heteronormative marital models in policy and clinical practice is important despite recent civil rights accomplishments.

Many of the legal concerns faced by LGBT individuals emerge as they reach the end of their life. Through having families of choice versus families of origins, LGBT older adults may lack an individual with legal authority to make decisions. A 2006 study of 40- to 61-year-olds ($N = 1,000$) by MetLife and the American Society for Aging's Lesbian Gay Aging Issues Network demonstrated that over half of their participants did not have any kind of legal documents that addressed their own health-care wishes and decisions, such as living wills or advanced directives. The long history of ineligibility may make some reluctant to apply for available benefits. Such uncertainties attest to the importance of end-of-life planning so that the LGBT person's wishes can be honored (Kimmel, 2014). Such plans and end-of-life documents, including living wills, estate plans, and health-care directives, must be completed while the individual is able to make competent decisions. It is also important to establish documentation and forms that are friendly and affirming for members of the LGBT community and same-sex couples and inclusive of diverse family structures. Additional legal concerns faced by older LGBT adults may be associated with social and economic injustices, workplace discrimination, and immigration status, among other factors. Additional information on these topics may be found in chapters 3 and 9 of this text.

GRIEF, LOSS, DEATH, AND DYING

At the end of life, older LGBTQ individuals may be faced with incomplete grief buried from their experience with multiple losses over time, especially those who lived through the HIV/AIDS crisis. Many suffer survivor's guilt and continue to mourn the loss of intimate friends who died from AIDS before the availability of antiretroviral drug therapies (Almack et al., 2010; Halkitis, 2013). Many may have experienced multiple losses and experienced a form of chronic grief for not only their personal losses but for the loss of their community as a whole (IOM, 2011).

LGBT older adults may have had a closeted relationship and be unable to openly address their loss and grief (Fenge, 2014). Additionally, there may be limited social acknowledgement or disregard for their grief, which can hinder emotional closure and the ability to adjust and move on after the loss of a loved one (McNutt & Yakushko, 2013). This can be especially apparent within religious communities, where the nature of the relationship may not be accepted and can potentially cause conflict (McNutt & Yakushko, 2013). Furthermore, specific rituals associated with end of life and bereavement may be inaccessible to LGBT individuals (i.e., attending a memorial service, wake, or burial; LGBT affirming grief counseling groups). Practitioners should always be sensitive to referrals for LGBTQ affirming hospice and palliative care (Farmer & Yancu, 2015) or a bereavement group sensitive to the needs of a grieving LGBTQ older adult, to provide the appropriate level of support necessary (Almack et al., 2010).

BEST PRACTICE CONSIDERATIONS

Intervention efforts with members of the aging LGBT community should focus on an understanding of diverse cultures, norms, lifestyles, and experiences (Strombeck & Levy, 1998) while building on knowledge gained from effective interventions for behavior change among older age cohorts and sensitivity to sociocultural contexts (Coon et al., 2003). Models and theories of older adult development that inform interventions are not usually inclusive of the unique biopsychosocial issues confronted by older LGBT adults as outlined throughout this chapter. Therefore it is critical to integrate affirming training models and advocacy methods for older LGBT adults in order to promote empowerment and establish a foundation of trust (Rogers et al., 2013). Additional understanding may be enriched by further research into the culture and history of LGBT communities and working to help facilitate trust between the LGBT community and social service agencies (Rogers et al., 2013). Affirming models and best practices begin with practitioner self-reflection and expanding knowledge of diverse LGBT identities. The synthesis of self-knowledge and awareness of the life course for LGBT clients may translate into practices that recognize the reciprocal impact of the provider and client subjectivities. The end result of these practice processes is to develop more accepting and nonjudgmental views that acknowledge and address the potentially different life courses and experiences of LGBT clients. Clinical providers in health and mental health must be trained in culturally attuned responses to nonheteronormative family configurations and social networks (Jann, Edmiston, & Ehrenfeld, 2015). Acceptance of sexual minorities must extend beyond an intellectual embrace and integrate empathic attunement to the life histories and experiences of older LGBT individuals.

Health and behavioral health-care systems are moving toward integrated care and comprehensive training programs to maximize quality and effectiveness as well as patient-centered care (Jann et al., 2015). For LGBT older adults, as with all older adults, the value of integrated care is more significant than ever before, as people are living longer with more complicated illnesses. Integrated health care has shown significant improvements related to the complexity of diagnostics and treatment of health and behavioral health conditions, often complicated by other treatments as well as psychosocial issues (Jann et al., 2015; Sabin, Riskind, & Nosek, 2015).

However, such care should include professionals well versed and competent in addressing in the unique concerns of LGBT individuals (Jann et al., 2015) to include differences in family structures, long-term use of medications, sensitivity of substance abuse, mental health screenings, and so on. Examples of unique health discussions with LGBT clients that practitioners should consider include mammography and cervical cancer screens for transgender individuals, discussions related to safer sexual practices with older LGBTQ adults, and assessment for related health or mental health issues.

Policymakers and researchers are increasingly calling for universal screening for depression, substance abuse, and anxiety. Use of screens by health and behavioral health professionals should be sensitive in language and assumptions related to members of the LGBT community. Furthermore, universal screening for issues related to sexual behavior and relationship violence is critical (D'Augelli & Grossman, 2001). The use of universal systems within health-care settings sensitive to the unique concerns of LGBT older adults is crucial such that such screening, assessment, and treatment is seen as a critical component of care.

In the creation of specific services and activities that meet the developmental needs of older LGBT adults, unique aspects of their life course should always be considered—for example, consideration of the unique stories brought to reminiscent groups by LGBT older adults, the potential for reading groups oriented to LGBT issues, and an overall review of opportunities for congregation that support the unique socialization and community needs of older LGBT clients. Such opportunities should consider issues related to inclusion and not reinforce feelings of vulnerability or exclusion. It is important for older LGBT adults to tell their stories (i.e., narrative therapy or group models of practice) while practitioners provide opportunities for listening and processing. Through taking advantage of these opportunities, practitioners can not only increase their own understanding of older LGBT adults but also learn historical perspectives and events in time that may be otherwise lost forever. Last, professionals should continuously strive for ongoing opportunities related to professional education, advocacy for older LGBT adults, and the creation of sustainable change (Rogers et al., 2013) for their older LGBTQ clients.

CONCLUSION

This chapter examined some of the key practice and policy factors facing the diverse and growing LGBTQ older adult population. In order to effectively expand knowledge and understanding related to the many factors facing older LGBT adults (e.g., legal, psychosocial, well aging, health-care issues), educators and practitioners alike must ensure the expansion and effective infusion of such topics across settings that include the classroom (Craig, Dentato, Messinger, & McInroy, 2016; Gezinski, 2009; Logie et al., 2007), field placements (Messinger, 2011), and agencies and counseling offices while measuring competency whenever possible. This may be accomplished through ongoing discussions related to best practices, social justice, and the need for policy change in order to increase knowledge of LGBT aging (McFarland & Sanders, 2003), lifespan, and psychosocial issues.

ACKNOWLEDGMENTS

This chapter was adapted from a previously published article: Dentato, M. P., Orwat, J., Spira, M., & Walker, B. (2014). Examining cohort differences and resilience among the aging LGBT community: Implications for education and practice among an expansively diverse population. *Journal of Human Behavior in the Social Environment, 24*(3), 316–328.

REFERENCES

Allen, K. R., & Roberto, K. A. (2016). Family relationships of older LGBT adults. In D. A. Harley & P. B. Teaster (Eds.), *Handbook of LGBT elders* (pp. 43–64). Dordrecht: Springer.

Almack, K., Seymour, J., & Bellamy, G. (2010). Exploring the impact of sexual orientation on experiences and concerns about end of life care and on bereavement for lesbian, gay and bisexual older people. *Sociology, 44*(5), 908–924.

Alpert, J. (2015). Out, proud and old: LGBT seniors more likely to age alone. WBUR Common Health. Retrieved from http://commonhealth.wbur.org/2015/01/lgbt-seniors-age-alone

American Psychological Association. (2009). *Elder abuse and neglect: In search of solutions.* Retrieved from http://www.apa.org/pi/aging/elder/abuse.html

Atkins, G. L. (2003). *Gay Seattle: Stories of exile and belonging.* Seattle, WA: University of Washington Press.

Berger, R. M. (1984). Realities of gay and lesbian aging. *Social Work, 29*(1), 57–62.

Berger, R. M., & Kelly, J. J. (1986). Working with homosexuals of the older population. *Social Casework, 67*(4), 203–210.

Bowers, R., Minichiello, V., & Plummer, D. (2010). Religious attitudes, homophobia, and professional counseling. *Journal of LGBT Issues in Counseling, 4*(2), 70–91.

Bronfenbrenner, U. (1979). *The ecology of human development: Experiments by nature and by design.* Cambridge, MA: Harvard University Press.

Burgoyne, R. W., Rourke, S. B., Behrens, D. M., & Salit, I. E. (2004). Long-term quality-of-life outcomes among adults living with HIV in the HAART era: The interplay of changes in clinical factors and symptom profile. *AIDS and Behavior, 8*(2), 151–163.

Butler, S. S. (2004). Gay, lesbian, bisexual, and transgender (GLBT) elders: The challenges and resilience of this marginalized group. *Journal of Human Behavior in the Social Environment, 9*(4), 25–44.

Centers for Disease Control and Prevention. (2012). *Estimated HIV incidence in the United States 2007–2010.* HIV Surveillance Supplemental Report, 17(4). Retrieved from http://www.cdc.gov/hiv/topics/surveillance/resources/reports/#supplemental.

Clunis, D. M., Fredricksen-Goldsen, K. I., Freeman, P. A., & Nystrom, N. (2005). *Lives of lesbian elders: Looking back, looking forward.* Binghamton, NY: Haworth Press.

Cook-Daniels, L. (1998). Lesbian, gay male, bisexual and transgendered elders: Elder abuse and neglect issues. *Journal of Elder Abuse & Neglect, 9*(2), 35–49.

Coon, D. W., Lipman, P. D., & Ory, M. G. (2003). Designing effective HIV/AIDS social and behavioral interventions for the population of those age 50 and older. *JAIDS: Journal of Acquired Immune Deficiency Syndromes, 33,* S194–S305.

Craig, S. L., Dentato, M. P., Messinger, L., & McInroy, L. B. (2016). Educational determinants of readiness to practise with LGBTQ clients: Social work students speak out. *British Journal of Social Work, 46*(1), 115–134.

Cronin, A., Ward, R., Pugh, S., King, A., & Price, E. (2011). Categories and their consequences: Understanding and supporting the caring relationships of older lesbian, gay and bisexual people. *International Social Work, 54*(3), 421–435.

D'Augelli, A. R., & Grossman, A. H. (2001). Disclosure of sexual orientation, victimization, and mental health among lesbian, gay, and bisexual older adults. *Journal of Interpersonal Violence, 16*(10), 1008–1027.

Dorfman, R., Walters, K., Burke, P., Hardin, L, Karanik, T., Raphael, J., . . . Silverstein, E. (1995). Old, sad and alone: The myth of the aging homosexual. *Journal of Gerontological Social Work, 24*(1/2), 29–44.

Eckenrode, J., & Gore, S. (1990). Stress between work and family (Plenum Series on Stress and Coping). New York: Plenum Press.

Elder, G. H. (1994). Time, human agency and social change: Perspectives on the life course. *Social Psychology Quarterly, 57*(1), 4–15.

Ellor, J. W. (2013). Religion and spirituality among older adults in light of DSM-5. *Social Work and Christianity, 40*(4), 372–383.

Elze, D. E. (2006). Oppression, prejudice, and discrimination. In D. Morrow & L. Messinger (Eds.), *Sexual orientation & gender expression in social work practice: Working with gay, lesbian, bisexual, & transgender people* (pp. 43–77). New York: Columbia University Press.

Emlet, C. (2004). HIV/AIDS and aging. *Journal of Human Behavior in the Social Environment, 9*(4), 45–63.

Emlet, C. (2006). "You're awfully old to have this disease": Experiences of stigma and ageism in adults 50 years and older living with HIV/AIDS. *The Gerontologist, 46*(6), 781–790.

Erosheva, E., Kim, H., Emlet, C., & Fredriksen-Goldsen, K. (2015). Social networks of lesbian, gay, bisexual, and transgender older adults. *Research on Aging, 38*(1), 98–123.

Fallon, K. M., Dobmeier, R. A., Reiner, S. M., Casquarelli, E. J., Giglia, L. A., & Goodwin, E. (2013). Reconciling spiritual values conflicts for counselors and lesbian and gay clients. *Adultspan Journal, 12*(1), 38–53.

Farmer, D. F. & Yancu, C. N. (2015). Hospice and palliative care for older lesbian, gay, bisexual and transgender adults: The effect of history, discrimination, health disparities and legal issues on addressing service needs. *Palliative Medicine and Hospice Care, 1*(2), 36–43.

Fenge, L. (2014). Developing understanding of same-sex partner bereavement for older lesbian and gay people: Implications for social work practice. *Journal of Gerontological Social Work, 57*(2-4), 288–304.

Floyd, F., & Bakeman, J. (2006). Coming-out across the life course: Implications of age and historical context. *Archives of Sexual Behavior, 35*(3), 287–296.

Fredriksen-Goldsen, K. I. (2011). Resilience and disparities among lesbian, gay, bisexual, and transgender older adults. *Public Policy & Aging Report, 21*(3), 3–7.

Fredriksen-Goldsen, K. I., Kim, H. J., Shiu, C., Goldsen, J., & Emlet, C. A. (2015). Successful aging among LGBT older adults: Physical and mental health-related quality of life by age group. *The Gerontologist, 55*(1), 154–168.

Fredriksen-Goldsen, K., & Muraco, A. (2010). Aging and sexual orientation: A 25-year review of the literature. *Research on Aging, 32*(3), 372–413.

Fullmer, E. M. (2006). Lesbian, gay, bisexual, and transgender aging. In D. Morrow & L. Messinger (Eds.), *Sexual orientation & gender expression in social work practice: Working with gay, lesbian, bisexual, & transgender people* (pp. 286–303). New York: Columbia University Press.

Gabrielson, M. (2011). "We have to create family": Aging support issues and needs among older lesbians. *Journal of Gay & Lesbian Social Services, 23*(3), 322–334.

Gezinski, L. (2009). Addressing sexual minority issues in social work education: A curriculum framework. *Advances in Social Work Practice, 10*(1), 103–113.

Goldberg, N.G. (2009). *The impact of inequality for same-sex partners in employer-sponsored retirement plans.* Los Angeles, CA: Williams Institute.

Gray, H., & Dressel, P. (1985). Alternative interpretations of aging among gay males. *The Gerontologist, 25,* 83–87.

Grossman, A. (2006). Physical and mental health of older lesbian, gay, and bisexual adults. In D. Kimmel, T. Rose, & S. David (Eds.), *Lesbian, gay, bisexual, and transgender aging: Research and clinical perspectives* (pp. 53–69). New York: Columbia University Press.

Grossman, A., Frank, J., Graziano, M., Narozniak, D., Mendelson, G., El Hassan, D., & Patouhas, E. (2014). Domestic harm and neglect among lesbian, gay, and bisexual older adults. *Journal of Homosexuality, 61*(12), 1649–1666.

Haas, A. P., & Lane, A. (2015). Collecting sexual orientation and gender identity data in suicide and other violent deaths: A step towards identifying and addressing LGBT mortality disparities. *LGBT Health, 2*(1), 84–87.

Halkitis, P. N. (2013). *The AIDS generation: Stories of survival and resilience.* New York: Oxford University Press.

Heckman, T., Kochman, A., Sikkema, K., Kalichman, S., Masten, J., Bergholte, J., . . . Catz, S. (2001). A pilot coping improvement intervention for late middle-aged and older adults living with HIV/AIDS in the USA. *AIDS Care, 13*(1), 129–139.

Henning-Smith, C., Gonzales, G., & Shippee, T. (2015). Differences by sexual orientation in expectations about future long-term care needs among adults 40 to 65 years old. *American Journal of Public Health, 105*(11), 2359–2365.

Hughes, C., & Evans, A. (2003). Health needs of women who have sex with women. *British Medical Journal, 327*(7421), 939–941.

Hughes, A. K., Harold, R. D., & Boyer, J. M. (2011). Awareness of LGBT aging issues among aging services network providers. *Journal of Gerontological Social Work, 54*(7), 659–677.

Human Rights Campaign. (2016). *Overview of federal benefits granted to married couples.* Retrieved from http://www.hrc.org/resources/an-overview-of-federal-rights-and-protections-granted-to-married-couples

Institute of Medicine Committee on Lesbian, Gay, Bisexual, and Transgender Health Issues and Research Gaps and Opportunities. (2011). *The health of lesbian, gay, bisexual, and transgender people: Building a foundation for better understanding.* Washington DC: National Academies Press.

Jann, J., Edmiston, E., & Ehrenfeld, J. (2015). Important considerations for addressing LGBT health care competency. *American Journal of Public Health, 105*(11), E8.

Kimmel, D.C. (2014). Lesbian, gay, bisexual, and transgender aging concerns. *Clinical Gerontologist, 37*(1), 49–63.

Laurencin, C. T., Christensen, D. M., & Taylor, E. D. (2008). HIV/AIDS and the African-American community: A state of emergency. *Journal of the National Medical Association, 100*(1), 35–43.

Levy-Dweck, S. (2005). HIV/AIDS fifty and older. *Journal of Gerontological Social Work, 46*(2), 37–50.

Levin, J., & Hein, J. F. (2012). A faith-based prescription for the surgeon general: Challenges and recommendations. *Journal of Religion and Health, 51*(1), 57–71.

Logie, C., Bridge, T. J., & Bridge, P. D. (2007). Evaluating the phobias, attitudes, and cultural competence of master of social work students toward LGBT populations. *Journal of Homosexuality, 53*(4), 201–221.

Love, P., Bock, M., Jannarone, A., & Richardson, P. (2005). Identity interaction: Exploring the spiritual experiences of lesbian and gay college students. *Journal of College Student Development, 46*(2), 193–209.

McFarland, P., & Sanders, S. (2003). A pilot study about the needs of older gays and lesbians. *Journal of Gerontological Social Work, 40*(3), 67–80.

McGeorge, C. R., Carlson, T. S., & Toomey, R. B. (2014). The intersection of spirituality, religion, sexual orientation, and gender identity in family therapy training: An exploration of students' beliefs and practices. *Contemporary Family Therapy, 36*(4), 497–506.

McNutt, B., & Yakushko, O. (2013). Disenfranchised grief among lesbian and gay bereaved individuals, *Journal of LGBT Issues in Counseling, 7*(1), 87–116.

Meyer, I. H. (2003). Prejudice, social stress, and mental health in lesbian, gay and bisexual populations: Conceptual issues and research evidence. *Psychological Bulletin, 129,* 674–697.

Messinger, L. (2006). A historical perspective. In D. Morrow & L. Messinger (Eds.), *Sexual orientation & gender expression in social work practice: Working with gay, lesbian, bisexual, & transgender people* (pp. 18–42). New York: Columbia University Press.

Messinger, L. (2011). A qualitative analysis of faculty advocacy on LGBT issues on campus. *Journal of Homosexuality, 58*(9), 1281–1305.

MetLife. (2006). *Out and aging: The MetLife study of lesbian and gay baby boomers.* Westport, CT: MetLife Mature Market Institute.

MetLife. (2010). *Still out, still aging: The MetLife study of lesbian, gay, bisexual, and transgender baby boomers.* Westport, CT: MetLife Mature Market Institute.

Moen, P., Dempster-McClain, D., & Williams, R. M. Jr. (1992). Successful aging: A life-course perspective on women's multiple roles and health. *American Journal of Sociology, 97*(6), 1612–1638.

Muraco, A., & Fredriksen-Goldsen, K. I. (2014). The highs and lows of caregiving for chronically ill lesbian, gay, and bisexual elders. *Journal of Gerontological Social Work, 57*(2–4), 251–272.

Noronha, K. J. (2015). Impact of religion and spirituality on older adulthood. *Journal of Religion, Spirituality & Aging, 27*(1), 16–33.

Parks, C. A. (1999). Lesbian identity development: An examination of differences across generations. *American Journal of Orthopsychiatry, 69*(3), 347–361.

Persson, D. I. (2009). Unique challenges of transgender aging: Implications from the literature. *Journal of Gerontological Social Work, 52*(6), 633–646.

Pew Research Center (2013, June). *A survey of LGBT Americans.* Retrieved from http://www.pewsocialtrends.org/2013/06/13/a-survey-of-lgbt-americans/

Pope, M., & Schulz, R. (1990). Sexual attitudes and behavior in midlife and aging homosexual males. *Journal of Homosexuality, 20*(3–4), 169–177.

Reid, J. D. (1995). Development in late life: Older lesbian and gay lives. In A. R. D'Augelli & C. J. Patterson (Eds.), *Lesbian, gay, and bisexual identities over the lifespan: Psychological perspectives* (pp. 215–240). New York: Oxford University Press.

Rogers, A., Rebbe, R., Gardella, C., Worlein, M., & Chamberlin, M. (2013). Older LGBT adult training panels: An opportunity to educate about issues faced by the older LGBT community. *Journal of Gerontological Social Work, 56*(7), 580–595.

Rosenfeld, D. (1999). Identity work among lesbian and gay elderly. *Journal of Aging Studies, 13*(2), 121–144.

Sabin, J., Riskind, R., & Nosek, B. (2015). Health care providers' implicit and explicit attitudes toward lesbian women and gay men. *American Journal of Public Health, 105*(9), 1831–1841.

Sherry, A., Adelman, A., Whilde, M. R., & Quick, D. (2010). Competing selves: Negotiating the intersection of spiritual and sexual identities. *Professional Psychology: Research and Practice, 41*(2), 112–119.

Siegel, K., & Schrimshaw, E. W. (2002). The perceived benefits of religious and spiritual coping among older adults living with HIV/AIDS. *Journal for the Scientific Study of Religion, 41*(1), 91–102.

Simone, M., & Appelbaum, J. (2008). HIV in older adults. *Geriatrics, 63*(12), 6–12.

Smith, L. A., McCaslin, R., Chang, J., Martinez, P., & McGrew, P. (2010). Assessing the needs of older gay, lesbian, bisexual and transgender people: A service-learning and agency partnership approach. *Journal of Gerontological Social Work, 53*(5), 387–401.

Spencer, C. (1995). *Homosexuality in history*. New York: Harcourt Brace.

Stanley, M. A., Bush, A. L., Camp, M. E., Jameson, J. P., Phillips, L. L., Barber, C. R., ... Cully, J. A. (2011). Older adults' preferences for religion/ spirituality in treatment for anxiety and depression. *Aging & Mental Health, 15*(3), 334–343.

Stein, G., Beckerman, N., & Sherman, P. (2010). Lesbian and gay elders and long-term care: Identifying the unique psychosocial perspectives and challenges. *Journal of Gerontological Social Work, 53*(5), 421–435.

Strombeck, R., & Levy, J. A. (1998). Educational strategies and interventions targeting adults age 50 and older for HIV/AIDS prevention. *Research on Aging, 20*(6), 912–936

Tang, H., Greenwood, G.L., Cowling, D.W., Lloyd, J.C., Roeseler, A.G., & Bal, D.G. (2004). Cigarette smoking among lesbians, gays, and bisexuals: How serious a problem? (United States) *Cancer Causes & Control, 15*(8), 797–803.

US Census Bureau. (2010). *The older population, 2010*. Retrieved from www.census.gov/population/www/ socdemo/age/

Vaccaro, A. (2009). Intergenerational perceptions, similarities and difference: A comparative analysis of lesbian, gay, and bisexual millennial youth with generation X and Baby Boomers. *Journal of LGBT Youth, 6*(2–3), 113–134.

Van Wagenen, A., Driskell, J., & Bradford, J. (2013). "I'm still raring to go": Successful aging among lesbian, gay, bisexual, and transgender older adults. *Journal of Aging Studies, 27*(1), 1–14.

Wight, R. G., LeBlanc, A. J., & Badgett, M. (2013). Same-sex legal marriage and psychological well-being: Findings from the California health interview survey. *American Journal of Public Health, 103*(2), 339–346.

Weststrate, N. M., & McLean, K. C. (2010). The rise and fall of gay: A cultural-historical approach to gay identity development. *Memory, 18*(2), 225–240.

Wethington, E. (2005). An overview of the life course perspective: Implications for health and nutrition. *Journal of Nutrition Education and Behavior, 37*(3), 115–120.

Williams, M. E., & Freeman, P. A. (2007). Transgender health. *Journal of Gay & Lesbian Social Services, 18*(3–4), 93–108.

Whitford, G. (1997). Realities and hopes for older gay males. *Journal of Gay & Lesbian Social Services, 6*(1), 79–95.

Wood, A., & Conley, A. (2014). Loss of religious or spiritual identities among the LGBT population. *Counseling and Values, 59*(1), 95–111.

Xavier, J. M., Bradford J., & Honnold J. (2007). *The health, health-related needs, and life-course experiences of transgender Virginians*. Richmond, VA: Virginia Department of Health.

PART III

AFFIRMING LGBTQ PRACTICE APPROACHES

CHAPTER 11

AFFIRMING AND STRENGTHS-BASED MODELS OF PRACTICE

Trevor G. Gates and Brian L. Kelly

INTRODUCTION

Affirming and strengths-based practice with lesbian, gay, bisexual, transgender, and queer (LGBTQ) individuals and communities started to become more mainstream in the 1970s and 1980s and continues today. Whereas stigmatization of LGBTQ individuals and communities was once the accepted norm, most mainstream professional organizations in social work and allied helping professions today treat LGBTQ identity as part of the normal spectrum of human experience and support affirming and strengths-based models of practice with LGBTQ communities (American Counseling Association, 2013; American Psychological Association [APA], 2008; Council on Social Work Education [CSWE], 2015; National Association of Social Workers, 2005). In this chapter, we describe affirming and strengths-based practice with LGBTQ individuals and communities and consider the context in which these practice models emerged. Additionally, we explore the various theoretical and practice models that are the foundation of affirming and strengths-based practice with LGBTQ communities and consider the efficacy of these service approaches.

DEFINING AFFIRMING AND STRENGTHS-BASED PRACTICE

LGBTQ-affirmative and strengths-based practice refers to the range of practice models that create a safe, supportive environment for individuals to express their sexual orientation and varied gender identities and expressions. Grounded in the assumption that LGBTQ identities are normal and expected parts of the human experience, LGBTQ-affirmative practice acknowledges and affirms individuals' identities without assuming the individual is "struggling" with their identity or that the core of the individual's psychosocial issues is related to sexual orientation or gender identity and expression (Van Den Bergh & Crisp, 2002). Rather, affirmative social workers acknowledge LGBTQ identities as an important part of life that may or may not be directly impacting the client's presenting issues and work to help clients integrate their LGBTQ identities with the rest of their life (Lebolt, 1999; Malyon, 1982).

Affirmative and strengths-based practice models also acknowledge that, while LGBTQ individuals may seek services when experiencing pain, stress, and losses, they have a wealth of ideas, competencies, and resources that they can draw upon in their time of need (Munford & Sanders, 2005; Saleebey, 2009). LGBTQ individuals may have experienced injury or have been victimized because of who they are, yet LGBTQ individuals are not victims (Baines, 2007; Gates & Kelly, 2013; Saleebey, 2009). They are capable change-agents who have experiences from which they can draw from (Dominelli, 2002; Weick, Kreider, & Chamberlain, 2009) for coping, adaptation, and resilience.

Likewise, affirmative and strengths-based practice means that the practitioner openly supports all LGBTQ individuals and communities. LGBTQ affirmative practice approaches celebrate sexual orientation and gender identity/expression, promote cultural competence in working with LGBTQ communities, and provide judgment-free spaces for LGBTQ clients to explore who they are (Crisp & McCave, 2007; Hill, 2009; Yarlzouse & Beckstead, 2011). Social workers who use LGBTQ-affirmative practice approaches recognize that, while some LGBTQ people have experienced challenges as a result of their environment, overall LGBTQ individuals are resilient and able to overcome these challenges (Crisp & McCave, 2007; Kort, 2008). LGBTQ identities are not aberrations or a problem; they are, in fact, quite ordinary. Affirmative and strengths-based practice blends the micro, mezzo, and macro by supporting individual LGBTQ individuals while actively speaking out when individuals, groups, institutions, and communities treat them with less than the full dignity they deserve.

HISTORICAL INFLUENCES

Serving LGBTQ individuals with dignity has not always been the social and cultural norm. Practice approaches that affirm LGBTQ identities are, more or less, recent phenomena within the helping professions. These approaches have been shaped by sociohistorical factors, as well as scholarship and research over the last fifty years.

DECLASSIFICATION OF HOMOSEXUALITY
FROM THE DSM

Prior to the 1970s, homosexuality was classified as a mental illness in the APA's *Diagnostic and Statistical Manual for Mental Disorders* (DSM), which is widely utilized for mental health classification. In 1973, homosexuality was officially declassified as a mental illness. The third edition of the DSM reclassified sexual orientation disturbance as ego-dystonic homosexuality, a mental health disorder only when the individual experiences distress because of his or her same-sex desire (APA, 1980). Eventually, ego-dystonic homosexuality was removed (APA, 1994; Stein, 2001). However, gender identity and expression variance remain represented in the DSM. In the fifth edition, gender dysphoria results when individuals experience a conflict between their birth sex and their gender identity, resulting in clinically significant impairment in functioning (APA, 2013). Presence of a diagnosis in the DSM helps some transgender people demonstrate the "medical necessity" of chemical transition (hormone therapy or other procedures that assist with feminization or masculinization of the body), surgical transition (sexual reassignment surgery/gender confirmation surgery, including phalloplasty, vaginoplasty, and breast enhancement or reduction), and other services that help makes the body consistent with the individual's identified gender identity. Yet the gender dysphoria diagnosis continues to be challenging in that it unnecessarily pathologizes gender variance instead of seeing gender variance as a normal part of the human experience.

A small but enduring group of mental health professionals continues to see LGBTQ behavior and identity as problematic. For example, organizations such as National Association for Research and Therapy of Homosexuality (NARTH) and the now-defunct Exodus International support the practice of conversion, reparative, or ex-gay therapies, which purport to help individuals change their sexual orientation identities into heterosexual ones (Bright, 2007). NARTH (2015) believes that such as LGBTQ individuals have the right to claim their identity, that people who wish to "diminish their homosexuality and to develop their heterosexual potential" should have the right to do so without being stigmatized. They believe that LGBTQ individuals should have the right to choose from "all relevant therapeutic options" and particularly the right to suppress LGBTQ identities if they so choose (Kaufman, 2001, p. 441).

Yet most mainstream professional helping organizations state that sexual orientation change efforts are ineffective and harmful (American Counseling Association, 2013; APA, 2008; CSWE, 2015; National Association of Social Workers, 2005). Further, CSWE and its Council on Sexual Orientation and Gender Identity and Expression advocate against teaching conversion or ex-gay therapies in accredited bachelor's and master's level social work programs, in large part because of their incompatibility with CSWE Educational Policy and Accreditation Standards (CSWE, 2015). Several jurisdictions in the United States currently ban conversion therapy, particularly with minors (Steinmetz, 2015). To date, the US Supreme Court has refused to hear challenges of those bans, and social workers and other mental health professionals in California, Illinois, New Jersey, and Oregon may not provide conversion therapy to minors (Miller, 2015).

IDENTITY DEVELOPMENT MODELS USEFUL FOR AFFIRMING PRACTICE

Perhaps one of the most commonly cited contributions to LGBTQ affirming and strengths-based practice is the Cass model of homosexuality development. Cass (1984) proposed a six-stage model for sexual minority identity development, including identity confusion, identity comparison, tolerance, acceptance, pride, and synthesis. Strengths of the Cass model are that the individual and social worker can process through a variety of stages and there are measurable milestones and goals that can be achieved (Kort, 2008). The Cass model can also be useful for working with a variety of culturally diverse populations with some adaptations (Adams & Phillips, 2009; Degges-White, Rice, & Myers, 2000; Feldman & Wright, 2013).

However, challenges of the Cass model are its linearity and maybe incorrect assumptions about LGBTQ identity development. It assumes that men and women develop their sexual orientation identities similarly and that the experience is the same whether the individual is young or old (Kenneady & Oswalt, 2014; Rickards & Wuest, 2006). The Cass model assumes that the eventual goal is reintegration into a sexual or gender-normative society through synthesis when, in fact, some people may be unwilling or unable to do so. It also at times incorrectly assumes that everyone goes through a period of "confusion." Some LGBTQ individuals are only confused by the reaction of their families and society but never have confusion about their sexual orientation, gender identity, and/or expression.

When the Cass model is less than suitable for an individual's unique circumstances, social workers should make use of other LGBTQ identity development models. For example, a far less linear model is D'Augelli's (1994) homosexual lifespan development model, a model that emphasizes developing a public identity first with friends, family, and then to a larger community. Of course, coming out to a larger community may be what indeed occurs first, especially for people who are never able to pass as straight. They might have dealt with assumptions about their sexual orientation throughout their life. Lev's (2004) transgender emergence model, like other models, focuses on coming out to oneself and others while eventually exploring options for transitioning in appearance and/or body, to include, sometimes, physical or hormonal efforts to make the physical body congruent with the person's unique sense of gender identity and expression. Similar to the Cass model, reintegration and synthesis into society are the eventual goal of the transgender emergence model (Cass, 1984; Lev, 2004). For more information on these models of LGBTQ identity development, see chapter 4 in this text.

SEXUAL LIBERATION, HIV/AIDS, AND SEX POSITIVE INTERVENTIONS

Paving the way for affirmative practice has been the emergence of LGBTQ activism and sexual liberation movements during the twentieth century. These movements have been widely studied by scholars of LGBTQ history. Chauncey (1994) chronicles thriving same-sex desire communities in New York during the late nineteenth and early twentieth century. Boyd (2003) describes a bustling lesbian community in post–World War II San Francisco, where bars and softball leagues served important community-building roles. D'Emilio (1998) traces the work of the homophile movement during the 1950s and 1960s, a movement that made significant strides in creating spaces for homosexuals and lesbians to connect, at times for social reasons and at other times to challenge, fight, march, and speak out against the discrimination and prejudice enacted on them by the dominant heterosexist and homophobic culture. These historiographies highlight the important ways in which same-sex loving men and women throughout the first half of the twentieth century laid the foundation for significant cultural and political changes to follow in the second half of the century. In fact, D'Emilio (1998) proposes it was the homophile movement that provided the foundation for the gay liberation movement that followed it in the late 1960s and paved the way for significant LGBTQ activism, particular the Stonewall rebellion. The Stonewall Inn rebellions in Greenwich Village in New York City were a series of spontaneous riots launched by LGBTQ individuals who were responding to mistreatment by the police at the popular bar and nightclub.

A milestone in the LGBTQ rights movement, the Stonewall rebellion catalyzed a more radical, less apologetic voice in fledging LGBTQ communities of the time and become an iconic symbol of LGBTQ liberation. This unapologetic voice proactively challenged stigmatizing conceptions of LGBTQ love, relationships, and sex. The sexual revolution of the 1970s that followed opened doors for LGBTQ individuals that prior to that point were unimaginable. A platform grounded in the New Left (i.e., a political movement of the late 1960s and early 1970s that promoted civil and gender equality rights) and Gay Liberation Fronts (i.e., offshoots of the New Left focused on gay rights—see Wittman, 1997) exploded in urban areas along the coasts in cities like New York and San Francisco. As a result, many gay men experienced new and open forms of sexual freedom and liberation. Several authors of various political inclinations have documented this time period. Kramer (1978) somewhat scathingly documents this era of new and unbridled gay male sexuality made easier and more accessible through bathhouses, while Berkowitz (2003) and Feinberg (1989) describe an era of sexual liberation, albeit with consequences, including the proliferation of sexually transmitted diseases among populations of gay men. These authors describe the sexual liberation of the gay male community without sugarcoating the consequences of their behaviors, which was often sickness and disease. Still, many gay men protected their newfound sexual liberation, despite some of the consequences it presented. In this milieu, many men contracted and transmitted what would eventually be known as HIV and AIDS.

In 1983, Larry Kramer published the now infamous essay, *1,112 and Counting* (Kramer, 1989). It served as a call to action to address the then mysterious named disease, gay related immune deficiency (GRID), which was rapidly killing many gay men. It is important to note, though, that several scholars argue that other oppressed populations, including intravenous drug users, women, individuals of color, and the poor, were equally affected in the early days of the epidemic (Brier, 2009; Cohen, 1999; Treichler, 1999). As the HIV/AIDS epidemic spread throughout the 1980s, LGBTQ individuals and communities created strong and resilient networks of support. Grassroots efforts to care for, feed, and shelter those living with HIV/AIDS rose up across the nation to combat the homophobic fear and heterosexism that plagued the early years of the epidemic. Many of these grassroots efforts blossomed into local, statewide, and national advocacy campaigns, including the Gay Men's Health Crisis (see Byron, 1997) and Act Up (see Kramer, 1997). These campaigns sought to increase awareness and demand federal support for life-saving services and treatments, a necessary effort as the federal government all but ignored the epidemic until 1987 (Brier, 2009).

While the health and lives of LGBTQ individuals and communities were threatened and at times devastated by the HIV/AIDS epidemic, strength and resilience ultimately prevailed. LGBTQ communities, standing on the foundation of the homophile movement, Stonewall, the New Left and Gay Liberation Fronts, and the sexual liberation of the 1970s, demanded visibility and humane medical treatment and care. Since the mid-1990s, the outlook for those living with HIV and AIDS has vitally changed due to the valiant efforts of LGBTQ advocates and allied communities.

One of the more lasting legacies of the HIV/AIDS pandemic is the promotion of safe sex practices. In their landmark 1983 essay, "How to Have Sex in an Epidemic," Berkowitz and Callen (1997) cautioned against gay male sexual promiscuity and promoted safe sex practices, including the use of condoms. They contended that safe sex practices offered the best way to engage in sex in the era of life threatening sexually transmitted infections. While criticized by many as paranoid and puritanical at the time, this essay and the work of others provided a foundation for safe sex movements within LGBTQ and non-LGBTQ communities that have saved millions of lives. The safe sex movement continues to expand and grow as LGBTQ individuals and communities advocate for and promote sex positive attitudes toward HIV/AIDS prevention. Efforts include the promotion of condom use between individuals who are HIV-positive and individuals who are HIV-negative engaging in anal or vaginal intercourse. In addition, proponents of safe sex practices incorporate harm-reduction approaches in their work, which seek to promote the reduction of sexual behaviors that place LGBTQ individuals at risk for HIV and other sexually transmissible infections. Each of these approaches affirm LGBTQ sexual expression, while prioritizing LGBTQ individuals' health and safety. For more information about these health education, prevention, and treatment topics, see chapters 20 and 24 in this volume.

COMPLEMENTARY THERAPEUTIC APPROACHES

Several complementary practice approaches can be used or modified as a part of LGBTQ affirmative and strengths-based practice. By drawing on psychodynamic theory, social constructivist, postmodern, and narrative approaches, as well as cognitive-behavioral strategies, practitioners can serve LGBTQ populations in more comprehensive and supportive ways.

PSYCHODYNAMIC THEORY

Psychodynamic practice offers social workers important opportunities to engage LGBTQ individuals from an affirming, strengths-based perspective. While a complete review of psychodynamic theory is beyond the scope of this chapter, it is important to note that it is grounded in the psychoanalytic tradition initially developed by Sigmund Freud and further developed by his followers, including Carl Jung. Psychodynamic practice represents a broader approach to and application of Freud's work, which seeks to treat various forms of psychopathology (e.g., depression, neurosis) through a dialogical process between the individual and his or her social worker (see Freud & Gay [1995] for additional explanation of psychoanalytic theory). Much like the larger social context in which it was developed, many scholars and practitioners of psychodynamic theory framed homosexuality as a form of pathology and perversion throughout much of the twentieth century (Fairbairn, 1952; Winnicott, 1964). This oppressive and discriminatory legacy is best represented in the diagnosing of homosexuality as a form of pathology in early versions of the DSM and still lives on today in the attitudes of some analysts trained during the early to mid-twentieth century (Bartlett, King, & Phillips, 2001; Phillips, Bartlett, & King, 2001).

Despite this historical precedent, several current psychodynamic scholars and practitioners have moved beyond framing same-sex desire as pathological and problematic, or at least viewing it essentially as such. Ellis (2005) stresses the dialogical nature of psychodynamic practice and argues that it offers important opportunities for individuals to move beyond potentially pathologizing, causal descriptions of sexual identity to richer, contextualized descriptions of their sexual identity. In this more affirming psychodynamic approach, individuals are invited to consider how their sexual identities intertwine with and/or depart from other identities they embody. Mair and Izzard (2001) theoretically explore the practitioner's role in affirming approaches to psychodynamic practice with LGBTQ individuals, arguing for a person-centered approach that welcomes the whole person into the therapeutic process. This important theoretical work suggests there is greater potential for increased affirming and strengths-based psychodynamic practice with LGBTQ individuals.

A need for a shift in focus from psychoanalysis was first proposed by Austrian-born US psychiatrist Heinz Kohut's movement toward self-psychology. Kohut (1977) argued against a psychiatry based on "pathology" and for an empathic approach that focused less on the ego or individual conscious and unconscious sexual and aggressive impulses (Martin, 2008). Proponents of self-psychology aim to help the individual have a greater realization of self and to experience his or her identity, past, and relationships with maturity and congruence (Flanagan, 2008). Affirmative practice helps LGBTQ individuals make sense of their experiences of heterosexism, homophobia, and other forms of oppression and helps integrate that history into the individual's present identity (Kertzner, 1999). LGBTQ-affirmative social workers may help LGBTQ people coping with past experiences by helping them realize that, though the experience may have felt damaging, they are not a damaged person.

SOCIAL CONSTRUCTIVIST, POSTMODERN, AND NARRATIVE APPROACHES

Constructivist and postmodern approaches to social work practice with LGBTQ individuals offer opportunities for affirmation, as well as strength recognition and building. Grounded in the work of French philosopher Michel Foucault (see Chambon [1999] for further discussion of Foucault's work and its relevance to social work), postmodern and constructivist approaches to social work practice recognize that knowledge is socially constructed through time- and context-bound experiences and the meaning individuals, groups, communities, and systems place on those experiences (Payne, 2014). Within this paradigm, socially constructed knowledge is never static; it always has the potential for change as experiences and meaning attribution evolve over time. As socially constructed knowledge is enacted on, it creates realities that prioritize certain identities and ways of being over others, thereby empowering some groups while disempowering others, and ultimately creating socially constructed systems of power, privilege, and oppression. Postmodern and constructivist approaches to social work practice seek to recognize these dynamics and create opportunities for LGBTQ individuals to give voice to their experiences of oppression while also seeking to create opportunities for them to empower themselves.

Situated in Foucault's philosophical work and constructivist and postmodern approaches to clinical practice, narrative therapy evolved out of the fields of couple/marriage and family therapy in New Zealand and Australia during the late 1980s (Besley, 2002). Constructivist and postmodern couple/marriage and family therapists seeking to prioritize solutions and individual strengths developed therapist–client collaborative styles, in which clinicians work together with individuals to prioritize their lived experiences and the meaning they attach to their experiences (Walsh, 2012). Narrative therapy is the fullest realization of this model, whereby the practitioner assists individuals in retelling the story of their lives in less problem-driven and more functional and strengths-based ways (Freedman & Combs, 1996; White & Epston, 1990). Social workers practicing with LGBTQ individuals employing the principles of narrative therapy may assist individuals in retelling experiences of internalized homophobia, interpersonal homophobia and heterosexism, and systemic homophobia and heterosexism (Galarza, 2013; Saltzburg, 2007).

COGNITIVE-BEHAVIORAL APPROACHES

Cognitive-behavioral strategies are also helpful for social workers operating from a strengths and affirmative framework in their work with LGBTQ clients. Cognitive-behavioral therapy (CBT) works to develop new patterns of thinking in individuals and new behaviors to accompany those thought changes (Walsh, 2013). CBT is a widely used approach in social work that actively works to change maladaptive ways of thinking and behaving (Butler, Chapman, Forman, & Beck, 2006). CBT has been used with varying degrees of success in helping LGBTQ individuals combat internalized heterosexism, homophobia, and other troublesome thinking patterns in several different treatment studies (Austin & Craig, 2015; Craig, Austin, & Alessi, 2013; Hart, Tulloch, & O'Cleirigh, 2014; Ross, Doctor, Dimito, Kuehl, & Armstrong, 2008).

Social workers using CBT within a strengths and affirming practice paradigm should focus on patterns of thinking and behaving that are functional for LGBTQ individuals. For example, when working to reduce internalized homophobia or heterosexism, social workers should focus attention on hopes, visions, talents, and abilities (Saleebey, 2009) instead of self-defeating thoughts. Remembering and reconnecting with individuals who helped make life interesting and happy (De Jong & Berg, 2002) for the LGBTQ individual may be more productive than ruminating on maintaining relationships with unsupportive individuals. Additionally, helping the LGBTQ individual identify next steps can also be useful, as remaining fixed in negative thoughts and behaviors may hinder locating and connecting with others providing support within the community.

SOCIAL WORK AND GAY-AFFIRMATIVE APPROACHES

Gay-affirmative psychotherapy, which emerged in the 1970s and 1980s from a need for counseling practice that was free from heterosexist bias, works from the assumption that sexual orientation and gender identity/expression are normal expressions of human sexuality and identity (Kort, 2004).

Kort, a Michigan social worker specializing in gay-affirmative practice, argues that gay-affirmative services promote self-acceptance of sexual orientation and gender identity/expression (2008). He further states that affirmative practice goes beyond that of simply being tolerant or friendly to LGBTQ issues. Furthermore, it is not even enough for practitioners to be LGBTQ-identified and claim they are affirming toward the community. Affirmative practice means celebrating sexual orientation and gender identity/expression as a form of diversity that adds to the richness of our society (Kort, 2008).

Attempts have also been made in social work to measure LGBTQ-affirmative practice methods. One of the most widely used measures in social work for LGBTQ-affirmative practice is Crisp's (2006) Gay-Affirmative Practice (GAP) scale. Conceptually, GAP in social work views LGBTQ individuals from the person-in-environment perspective and recognizes that LGBTQ individuals have strengths that help them cope with homophobia and heterosexism. Further, GAP emphasizes that cultural competence is necessary in working with LGBTQ individuals, that LGBTQ identities are just as healthy as non-LGBTQ identities, that social workers should help LGBTQ individuals negotiate the challenges of deciding when and if "coming out" makes sense for them individually, and that social workers must engage in raising consciousness about the ongoing and challenging role of homophobia and heterosexism within society.

Crisp's (2006) GAP is a 30-item scale that measures beliefs ($\alpha = 0.93$) and behavioral ($\alpha = 0.94$) intentions of social workers for affirmative and strengths-based practice. Social workers responding to the GAP scale indicate their willingness to support the diverse makeup of LGBTQ families, verbalize respect, educate themselves about LGBTQ communities, and help LGBTQ individuals challenge discrimination and shame about their identity. Additionally, GAP measures social workers' willingness to talk openly about LGBTQ issues, verbalize that LGBTQ identities can be as healthy as heterosexual identities, and create a climate that encourages openness and authenticity around one's LGBTQ identity when suitable for the services being offered.

Available empirical evidence within the social work professional literature shows a trend toward affirming and strength-based practice with LGBTQ communities. Though some recent studies show evidence of negative attitudes toward LGBTQ communities among social workers and students (Kulkin, Williams, Boykin, & Ahn, 2009; Dentato et al., 2016); other studies have shown that social workers have a willingness to engage in affirmative practice (Black, Oles, & Moore, 1998; Dentato, Craig, Messinger, Lloyd, & McInroy, 2014; Logie, Bridge, & Bridge, 2007; Swank & Raiz, 2010). In a study that examined heterosexual psychologists, social workers, and marriage and family therapists ($N = 476$) engagement in affirmative practice, Alessi, Dillon, and Kim (2015) found that training interventions that help practitioners to understand the importance of affirming and strengths-based practice positively affects beliefs and engagement in affirmative practice approaches. Study participants noted that additional training on LGBTQ issues resulted in a stronger willingness and ability to practice affirmatively.

Evidence shows that social work educational settings are giving serious attention to affirming and strengths-based practices. Competency in two of CSWE's (2015) Educational Policy and Accreditation Standards note that social workers should work to understand the importance of diversity, which include both sexual orientation and gender identity/expression, on the formation of human identity. There are an encouraging number of social work faculty who are teaching LGBTQ-affirmative practice within the classroom (Chonody & Smith, 2013; Einbinder, Fiechter,

Sheridan, & Miller, 2012; Rowntree, 2014; Woodford, Luke, Grogan-Kaylor, Fredriksen-Goldsen, & Gutierrez, 2012). This evidence suggests that LGBTQ-affirmative practice is becoming a norm within some schools of social work.

CONCLUSION

Affirming and strengths-based practice models include a range of safe, supportive practice models that celebrate sexual orientation and gender identity and expression. LGBTQ individuals experience many of the joys and struggles of ordinary human experience yet are challenged by stigma-related experiences that occur in everyday life. Surely, LGBTQ liberation has brought many positive changes for individuals with various sexual orientations and gender identities and expressions. LGBTQ-affirming and strengths-based social workers and practitioners are able to assist individuals and communities to enjoy the rewards of fully participating within society. By recognizing that LGBTQ individuals and communities have a variety of interpersonal strengths and community support systems from which they may draw in times of need, practitioners are able to aid clients in identifying their own resilience and capacity for development.

REFERENCES

Adams, H. L., & Phillips, L. (2009). Ethnic related variations from the Cass model of homosexual identity formation: The experiences of two-spirit, lesbian and gay Native Americans. *Journal of Homosexuality, 56*(7), 959–976. doi:10.1080/00918360903187895

Alessi, E. J., Dillon, F. R., & Kim, H. M. S. (2015). Determinants of lesbian and gay affirmative practice among heterosexual therapists. *Psychotherapy, 52*(3), 298–307. doi:10.1037/a0038580

American Counseling Association. (2013). *LGBTQ issues.* Retrieved from http://www.counseling.org/knowledge-center/browse-by-topic/lgbtq-issues

American Psychiatric Association. (1980). *Diagnostic and statistical manual of mental disorders* (3rd ed.). Washington, DC: Author.

American Psychiatric Association. (1994). *Diagnostic and statistical manual of mental disorders.* (4th ed.). Washington, DC: Author.

American Psychiatric Association. (2013). *Diagnostic and Statistical Manual of Mental Disorders* (5th ed.). Washington DC: Author.

American Psychological Association. (2008). *Answers to your questions: For a better understanding of sexual orientation and homosexuality.* Retrieved from http://www.apa.org/topics/sexuality/sorientation.pdf

Austin, A., & Craig, S. L. (2015). Empirically supported interventions for sexual and gender minority youth. *Journal of Evidence-Informed Social Work, 12*(6), 567–578. doi:10.1080/15433714.2014.884958

Baines, D. (2007). *Doing anti-oppressive practice: Building transformative politicized social work.* Halifax, NS: Fernwood.

Bartlett, A., King, M., & Phillips, P. (2001). Straight talking: an investigation of the attitudes and practice of psychoanalysts and psychotherapists in relation to gays and lesbians. *British Journal of Psychiatry, 179*(6), 545–549. doi:10.1192/bjp.179.6.545

Berkowitz, R. (2003). *Stayin'alive: The invention of safe sex*. Cambridge, MA: Westview Press.

Besley, A. C. (2002). Foucault and the turn to narrative therapy. *British Journal of Guidance and Counselling*, 30(2), 125–143. doi:10.1080/03069880220128010

Black, B., Oles, T. P., & Moore, L. (1998). The relationship between attitudes: Homophobia and sexism among social work students. *Affilia: Journal of Women and Social Work*, 13(2), 166–189. doi:10.1177/088610999801300204

Berkowitz, R., & Callen, M. (1997). How to have sex in an epidemic. In M. Blasius & S. Phelan (Eds.), *We are everywhere: A historical sourcebook of gay and lesbian politics* (pp. 571–574). New York: Routledge.

Boyd, N. A. (2003). *Wide open town: A history of queer San Francisco to 1965*. Berkley and Los Angeles: University of California Press.

Brier, J. (2009). *Infectious ideas: US political responses to the AIDS crisis*. Chapel Hill: University of North Carolina Press.

Bright, C. (2007). *Social workers respond to clients seeking to change a homosexual orientation to a heterosexual one* (Doctoral dissertation). Retrieved from Proquest Dissertations and Theses database (UMI No. 3294306).

Butler, A. C., Chapman, J. E., Forman, E. M., & Beck, A. T. (2006). The empirical status of cognitive-behavioral therapy: a review of meta-analyses. *Clinical Psychology Review*, 26(1), 17–31. doi:10.1016/j.cpr.2005.07.003

Byron, P. (1997). AIDS and the gay men's health crisis of New York. In M. Blasius & S. Phelan (Eds.), *We are everywhere: A historical sourcebook of gay and lesbian politics* (pp. 587–593). New York: Routledge.

Cass, V. C. (1984). Homosexual identity formation: Testing a theoretical model. *Journal of Sex Research*, 20(2), 143–167. doi:10.1080/00224498409551214

Chambon, A. S. (1999). *Reading Foucault for social work*. New York: Columbia University Press.

Chauncey, G. (1994). *Gay New York: Gender, urban culture, and the making of the gay male world, 1890–1940*. New York: Basic Books.

Chonody, J. M., & Smith, K. S. (2013). The state of the social work profession: A systematic review of the literature on antigay bias. *Journal of Gay and Lesbian Social Services*, 25(3), 326–361. doi:10.1080/10538720.2013.806877

Cohen, C. (1999). *The Boundaries of blackness: Aids and the breakdown of black politics*. Chicago: University of Chicago Press.

Council on Social Work Education. (2015). *Educational policy and accreditation standards*. Retrieved from https://www.cswe.org/getattachment/Accreditation/Accreditation-Process/2015-EPAS/2015EPAS_Web_FINAL.pdf.aspx

Craig, S. L., Austin, A., & Alessi, E. (2013). Gay affirmative cognitive behavioral therapy for sexual minority youth: A clinical adaptation. *Clinical Social Work Journal*, 41(3), 258–266. doi:10.1007/s10615-012-0427-9

Crisp, C. (2006). The gay affirmative practice scale (GAP): A new measure for assessing cultural competence with gay and lesbian clients. *Social Work*, 51(2), 115–126. doi:10.1093/sw/51.2.115

Crisp, C., & McCave, E. L. (2007). Gay affirmative practice: A model for social work practice with gay, lesbian, and bisexual youth. *Child and Adolescent Social Work Journal*, 24(4), 403–421. doi:10.1007/s10560-007-0091-z

D'Augelli, A. R. (1994). Lesbian and gay male development: Steps toward an analysis of lesbians' and gay men's lives. In B. Greene & G. M. Herek (Eds.), *Lesbian and gay psychology* (pp. 118–132). Thousand Oaks, CA: SAGE.

D'Emilio, J. (1998). *Sexual politics, sexual communities* (2nd ed.). Chicago: University of Chicago Press.

Degges-White, S., Rice, B., & Myers, J. E. (2000). Revisiting Cass' theory of sexual identity formation: A study of lesbian development. *Journal of Mental Health Counseling*, 22(4), 318–333.

De Jong, P., & Berg, I. K. (2002). *Interviewing for solutions*. Pacific Grove, CA: Brooks/Cole.

Dentato, M. P., Craig, S. L., Lloyd, M. R., Kelly, B. L., Wright, C., & Austin, A. (2016). Homophobia within schools of social work: The critical need for affirming classroom settings and effective preparation for service with the LGBTQ community. *Social Work Education, 35*(6), 672–692. doi:10.1080/02615479.2016.1150452

Dentato, M. P., Craig, S. L., Messinger, L., Lloyd, M., & McInroy, L. B. (2014). Outness among LGBTQ social work students in North America: The contribution of environmental supports and perceptions of comfort. *Social Work Education, 33*(4), 485–501. doi:10.1080/02615479.2013.855193

Dominelli, L. (2002). *Anti-oppressive social work theory and practice.* New York: Palgrave Macmillan.

Einbinder, S. D., Fiechter, S., Sheridan, D. A., & Miller, D. L. (2012). Social work educators' attitudes toward gay men and lesbians: A national assessment. *Journal of Gay and Lesbian Social Services, 24*(2), 173–200. doi:10.1080/10538720.2012.669746

Ellis, M. L. (2005). Sexual languages/cultural bodies: Transforming psychoanalysis. *Psychodynamic Practice, 11*(4), 405–415. doi:10.1080/14753630500387372

Fairbairn, W. R. D. (1952). *Psychoanalytic studies of the personality.* New York: Routledge.

Feinberg, D. B. (1989). *Eighty sixed.* New York: Penguin Books.

Feldman, S. E., & Wright, A. J. (2013). Dual impact: Outness and LGB identity formation on mental health. *Journal of Gay and Lesbian Social Services, 25*(4), 443–464. doi:10.1080/10538720.2013.833066

Flanagan, L. M. (2008). The theory of self psychology. In J. Berzoff, L. M. Flanagan, & P. Hertz (Eds.), *Inside out and outside in: Psychodynamic clinical theory and psychopathology in contemporary multicultural contexts* (2nd ed., pp. 161–188). Lanham, MD: Rowan & Littlefield.

Freedman, J., & Combs, G. (1996). *Narrative therapy.* New York: W. W. Norton.

Freud, S., & Gay, P. (1995). *The Freud reader.* New York: W. W. Norton.

Galarza, J. (2013). Borderland queer: Narrative approaches in clinical work with Latina women who have sex with women (WSW). *Journal of LGBT Issues in Counseling, 7*(3), 274–291. doi:10.1080/15538605.2013.812931

Gates, T. G., & Kelly, B. L. (2013). LGB cultural phenomena and the social work research enterprise: Toward a strengths-based, culturally anchored methodology. *Journal of Homosexuality, 60*(1), 69–82. doi:10.1080/00918369.2013.735939

Hart, T. A., Tulloch, T. G., & O'Cleirigh, C. (2014). Integrated cognitive behavioral therapy for social anxiety and HIV prevention for gay and bisexual men. *Cognitive and Behavioral Practice, 21*(2), 149–160. doi:10.1016/j.cbpra.2013.07.001

Hill, N. L. (2009). Affirmative practice and alternative sexual orientations: Helping clients navigate the coming out process. *Clinical Social Work Journal, 37*(4), 346–356. doi:10.1007/s10615-009-0240-2

Kaufman, B. (2001). Why NARTH: The American Psychiatric Association's destructive and blind pursuit of political correctness. *Regent University Law Review, 14*, 423–442.

Kenneady, D. A., & Oswalt, S. B. (2014). Is Cass's model of homosexual identity formation relevant to today's society? *American Journal of Sexuality Education, 9*(2), 229–246. doi:10.1080/15546128.2014.900465

Kertzner, R. (1999). Self-appraisal of life experience and psychological adjustment in midlife gay men. *Journal of Psychology and Human Sexuality, 11*(2), 43–64. doi:10.1300/J056v11n02_03

Kohut, H. (1977). *The restoration of the self.* Chicago: University of Chicago Press.

Kort, J. (2004). *Queer eye for the straight therapist: Creating an affirming practice for gay clients.* Retrieved from http://www.joekort.com/var/joekort2/storage/original/application/0b42aec2a665129e60b84c167db617d1.pdf

Kort, J. (2008). *Gay affirmative therapy for the straight clinician: The essential guide.* New York: W. W. Norton.

Kulkin, H., Williams, J., Boykin, L., & Ahn, B. (2009). Social work students and homophobia: What are their attitudes? *Journal of Baccalaureate Social Work, 14*(2), 79–88.

Kramer, L. (1978). *Faggots.* New York: Grove Press.

Kramer, L. (1989). *Reports from the Holocaust: The making of an AIDS activist.* New York: St. Martin's Press.

Kramer, P. (1997). The beginning of acting up. In M. Blasius & S. Phelan (Eds.), *We are everywhere: A historical sourcebook of gay and lesbian politics* (pp. 609–615). New York: Routledge.

Lebolt, J. (1999). Gay affirmative psychotherapy: A phenomenological study. *Clinical Social Work Journal, 27*(4), 355–370. doi:10.1023/A:1022870129582

Lev, A. I. (2004). *Transgender emergence: Therapeutic guidelines for working with gender-variant people and their families.* New York: Routledge.

Logie, C., Bridge, T. J., & Bridge, P. D. (2007). Evaluating the phobias, attitudes, and cultural competence of master of social work students toward the LGBT populations. *Journal of Homosexuality, 53*(4), 201–221. doi:10.1080/00918360802103472

Mair, D., & Izzard, S. (2001). Grasping the nettle: Gay men's experiences in therapy. *Psychodynamic Counselling, 7*(4), 475–490. doi:10.1080/13533330110087723

Malyon, A. K. (1982). Psychotherapeutic implications of internalized homophobia in gay men. *Journal of Homosexuality, 7*(2–3), 59–69. doi:10.1300/J082v07n02_08

Martin, J. L. (2008). Self psychology theory. In N. Coady & P. Lehmann (Eds.), *Theoretical perspectives for direct social work practice* (pp. 199–217). New York: Springer.

Miller, J. (2015, May). Supreme Court turns away challenge to gay conversion therapy ban. *CBS News.* Retrieved from http://www.cbsnews.com/news/supreme-court-turns-away-challenge-to-gay-conversion-therapy-ban/

Munford, R., & Sanders, J. (2005). Working with families: Strengths-based approaches In M. Nash, R. Munford, & K. O'Donoghue (Eds.), *Social work theories in action* (pp. 158–173). Philadelphia, PA: Jessica Kingsley.

National Association for Research and Therapy of Homosexuality. (2015). *NARTH Institute position statements.* Retrieved from http://www.narth.com/#!narth-position-statements/c1ae

National Association of Social Workers. (2005). *National Committee on Lesbian, Gay, Bisexual, and Transgender Issues.* Retrieved from http://www.socialworkers.org/governance/cmtes/nclgbi.asp

Payne, M. (2014). *Modern social work theory.* Chicago: Lyceum Books.

Phillips, P., Bartlett, A., & King, M. (2001). Psychotherapists' approaches to gay and lesbian patients/clients: A qualitative study. *British Journal of Medical Psychology, 74*(1), 73–84. doi:10.1348/000711201160812

Rickards, T., & Wuest, J. (2006). The process of losing and regaining credibility when coming-out at midlife. *Health Care for Women International, 27*(6), 530–547. doi:10.1080/07399330600770254

Ross, L. E., Doctor, F., Dimito, A., Kuehl, D., & Armstrong, M. S. (2008). Can talking about oppression reduce depression? Modified CBT group treatment for LGBT people with depression. *Journal of Gay and Lesbian Social Services, 19*(1), 1–15. doi:10.1300/J041v19n01_01

Rowntree, M. R. (2014). Making sexuality visible in Australian social work education. *Social Work Education, 33*(3), 353–364. doi:10.1080/02615479.2013.834885

Saleebey, D. (2009). Introduction: Power to the people. In D. Saleebey (Ed.), *The strengths perspective in social work practice* (pp. 1–23). Boston: Pearson.

Saltzburg, S. (2007). Narrative therapy pathways for re-authoring with parents of adolescents coming-out as lesbian, gay, and bisexual. *Contemporary Family Therapy, 29*(1–2), 57–69. doi:10.1007/s10591-007-9035-1

Stein, T. S. (2001). Homosexuality and psychiatry. In N. J. Smelser & P. B. Baltes (Eds.), *International encyclopedia of the social & behavioral sciences* (pp. 6899–6904). New York: Elsevier.

Steinmetz, K. (2015, May). Oregon becomes third state to ban conversion therapy on minors. *Time.* Retrieved from http://www.time.com/3889687/oregon-conversion-therapy-ban/

Swank, E., & Raiz, L. (2010). Attitudes toward gays and lesbians among undergraduate social work students. *Affilia: Journal of Women and Social Work, 25*(1), 19–29. doi:10.1177/0886109909356058

Treichler, P. A. (1999). *How to have theory in an epidemic: Cultural chronicles of AIDS.* Durham, NC: Duke University Press.

Van Den Bergh, N., & Crisp, C. (2002). Defining culturally competent practice with sexual minorities: Implications for social work education and practice. *Journal of Social Work Education, 40*(2), 221–238. doi:10.1080/10437797.2004.10778491

Walsh, J. (2013). *Theories for direct social work practice* (3rd ed.). Belmont, CA: Cengage.

Walsh, N. (2012). Clinical views of family, normality, health, and dysfunction In N. Walsh (Ed.), *Normal family processes: Growing diversity and complexity* (4th ed., pp. 28–56). New York: Guilford.

Weick, A., Kreider, J., & Chamberlain, R. (2009). Key dimensions of the strengths perspective in case management, clinical practice, and community practice. In D. Saleebey (Ed.), *The strengths perspective in social work practice* (pp. 108–120). Boston: Pearson.

White, M., & Epston, D. (1990). *Narrative means to therapeutic ends.* New York: W. W. Norton.

Winnicott, D. W. (1964) *The child, the family and the outside world.* Harmondsworth, UK: Penguin.

Wittman, C. (1997). A gay manifesto. In M. Blasius & S. Phelan (Eds.), *We are everywhere: A historical sourcebook of gay and lesbian politics* (pp. 380–388). New York: Routledge.

Woodford, M. R., Luke, K. P., Grogan-Kaylor, A., Fredriksen-Goldsen, K. I., & Gutierrez, L. (2012). Social work faculty support for same-sex marriage: A cross-national study of US and Anglophone Canadian MSW teaching faculty. *Social Work Research, 36*(4), 301–312. doi:10.1093/swr/svs033

Yarlzouse, M. A., & Beckstead, A. L. (2011). Using group therapy to navigate and resolve sexual orientation and religious conflicts. *Counseling and Values, 56*(1–2), 96–120.

CHAPTER 12

INCORPORATING MINORITY STRESS THEORY INTO CLINICAL PRACTICE WITH SEXUAL-MINORITY POPULATIONS

Edward J. Alessi and Eric Hartman

INTRODUCTION

Population-based studies consistently show that sexual-minority populations have higher prevalence of mood, anxiety, and substance use disorders than heterosexuals (Cochran & Mays, 2000; Cochran, Sullivan, & Mays, 2003; Gilman et al., 2001; Sandfort, de Graaf, Bijl, & Schnabel, 2001; Sandfort, de Graaf, Ten Have, Ransome, & Schnabel, 2014). Meyer (2003) hypothesized that higher prevalence of psychiatric disorders among lesbian, gay, and bisexual (LGB) people is a consequence of minority stress. His minority stress theory is based on the notion that, similar to other minority groups, sexual minorities face chronic stress due to homophobic and heterosexist social conditions. Meyer's hypothesis was supported by a meta-analysis that revealed sexual minorities were about 2.5 times more likely than heterosexuals to have a mood, anxiety, or substance abuse disorder at some point in their lifetime and twice as likely to have a current disorder. The higher prevalence of psychiatric disorders among LGB populations is partially explained through the conceptual framework of minority stress (Herek & Garnets, 2007). That is, mental health problems are the result of negative social conditions produced by prejudice and discrimination (Meyer, 2003).

Studies supporting minority stress–based hypotheses have clear implications for programmatic and public policy interventions, particularly those relating to mental health service delivery. Scholars have expressed concern about the quality of mental health services that sexual and gender minority individuals receive (American Psychological Association, 2012; Haas et al., 2011).

One way to address this issue is to mandate community- and hospital-based mental health facilities that receive government funding and reimbursement from Medicaid and Medicare to adopt nondiscrimination policies (Gay and Lesbian Medical Association & LGBT Health Experts, 2001). In addition, health insurance companies should maintain provider directories that include up-to-date listings of affirmative mental health clinicians (Gay and Lesbian Medical Association & LGBT Health Experts, 2001).

However, the implications for clinical practice with sexual and gender minority individuals are less clear-cut. Although the extant empirical and clinical literature recommends that mental health practitioners recognize the impact of minority stress (prejudice events, stigma, internalized homophobia, and concealing one's sexual orientation), there is little understanding of how to systematically address it in the actual clinical situation, especially when the implications lend themselves to more programmatic and policy interventions. Increasing our knowledge in this area is necessary for developing effective treatment interventions for lesbian, gay, bisexual, and transgender (LGBT) individuals seeking counseling to deal with minority stress–related concerns. In fact, a systematic review of the LGBT psychotherapy literature revealed the need for specific interventions that help LGB clients cope with the unique challenges related to sexual orientation (King, Semlyn, Killaspy, Nazareth, & Osborn, 2007).

This chapter reviews concepts associated with minority stress and then provides suggestions for specifically incorporating minority stress theory into treatment with LGB individuals. Although researchers have used minority stress theory to understand negative mental health outcomes among transgender populations (Breslow et al., 2015; Bockting et al., 2013; Hendricks & Testa, 2012), the authors do not discuss clinical practice issues with transgender individuals. Transgender individuals contend with unique issues stemming from transphobia, requiring in-depth discussion rather than mere mention in a chapter with LGB people (Austin & Craig, 2015). Therefore, a proposed framework begins with a two-part clinical assessment process for sexual-minority individuals only.

The first part of this chapter, based on Meyer's (2003) minority stress model, examines the effects of prejudice events, stigma, internalized homophobia, and sexual orientation concealment. Based on the work of Hatzenbuelher (2009), the second half of the chapter examines the client's general psychological processes, including coping/emotional regulation, social/interpersonal, and cognitive processes, which may be elevated by minority stress. These include coping abilities, social support, and maladaptive self-schemas, respectively (Hatzenbuelher, 2009). The inclusion of Hatzenbuelher's work is a necessary component of the framework because it helps clinicians to understand how LGB clients manage the various components of minority stress. Following the assessment process, the framework suggests using an LGB-affirmative treatment approach. In order to demonstrate the use of the framework, we apply it to the treatment of a Black man who identifies as gay.

This framework offers an innovative approach to LGB clinical practice because it (a) provides a systematic, not general, way to address minority stress in the actual clinical situation; (b) highlights the clinical utility of examining the specific components of minority stress (e.g., stigma, internalized homophobia) as well as the client's general psychological processes, thus offering a comprehensive treatment approach; and (c) demonstrates the use of LGB-affirmative psychotherapy for clients struggling with minority stress, with specific attention to LGB clients of color.

THE MINORITY STRESS MODEL

LGB individuals routinely encounter stressful events not usually experienced by heterosexuals (Herek & Garnets, 2007). Typically involving prejudice and discrimination, these events are the hallmark of minority stress, which is defined as "a state intervening between the sequential antecedent stressors of culturally sanctioned, categorically ascribed inferior status, social prejudice and discrimination, the impact of these environmental forces on psychological well-being, and consequent readjustment or adaptation" (Brooks, 1981, p. 107). Because prejudice and discrimination occur unexpectedly, LGB people must constantly readjust to living in a homophobic social environment. Brooks (1981) argued that "'readjustment' becomes, in a sense, adaptation to a perpetual state of stress" (p. 78). When adaptation fails, a pathological stress response such as depression or anxiety may result. Numerous studies have demonstrated the relationship between various forms of sexual orientation discrimination and negative mental health outcomes among LGB populations (Lewis, Derlega, Griffin, & Krowinski, 2003; Huebner, Rebchook, & Kegeles, 2004; Mays & Cochran, 2001; Warner et al., 2004). Furthermore, sexual minorities encounter high rates of sexual and physical assault (Heidt, Marx, & Gold, 2005; Rothman, Exner, & Baughman, 2011; Tjaden, Thoennes, & Allison, 1999), which is associated with depression, anxiety, and posttraumatic stress disorder (PTSD) (Gold, Dickstein, Marx, & Lexington, 2009; Gold, Marx, & Lexington, 2007; Heidt et al., 2005).

Meyer (2003) proposed that LGB people encounter minority stress "along a continuum from distal stressors, which are typically defined as objective events and conditions, to proximal personal processes, which are by definition subjective because they rely on individual perceptions and appraisals" (p. 676). Four specific minority stress processes provide the framework for Meyer's model: (a) chronic and acute prejudice-related events, (b) the expectation of minority stress and the vigilance this expectation requires (stigma), (c) the internalization of negative societal attitudes (internalized homophobia), and (d) concealment of sexual orientation. The minority stress model also discusses coping and social support. Although it highlights the ameliorating effects of individual coping in determining the effect on mental health (Meyer, 2003), it focuses more on minority group coping. Specifically, minority group members, including LGB people, frequently cope with minority stress by maintaining strong connections to their community. This allows minority group members to evaluate themselves based on others who are similar rather than different. As a result, the minority group helps to provide a reappraisal of the stressful condition, which may in turn improve mental health (Meyer, 2003).

MINORITY STRESS AND LGB PEOPLE OF COLOR

Holding more than one minority identity can exacerbate minority stress. Herek and Garnets (2007) proposed that LGB individuals who hold two or more stigmatized identities experience prejudice in majority group contexts (e.g., being Black, a woman, and a lesbian) and in minority community settings (e.g., homophobic responses from Black heterosexuals and racial prejudice from White lesbians). Meyer, Schwartz, and Frost (2008) found that Black and Latino LGB individuals were more likely than White LGB individuals to experience stressful events, including those involving racial/ethnic prejudice, though Black and Latino LGB individuals were no more likely than White LGB individuals to experience stressful events involving sexual orientation prejudice.

Few studies have compared prevalence of mental health disorders among White LGB people and LGB people of color, and, among these studies, findings were mixed. Meyer, Dietrich, and Schwartz (2008) found that Black and Latino LGB participants ($N = 388$) did not have higher prevalence of mood, anxiety, and substance abuse disorders than White LGB participants. Black LGB participants had fewer psychiatric disorders than both White and Latino LGB participants. However, more Black, and especially Latino, LGB participants reported a history of suicide attempts than White participants. Suicide attempts occurred at an earlier age for Black and Latino participants, which may suggest that they coincided with a coming-out period. Using the same sample, Alessi, Meyer, and Martin (2013) found that Black and Latino LGB individuals did not have higher prevalence of PTSD than White LGB individuals. However, when the authors allowed stressful events that did not pose threat to life or physical integrity to qualify toward a PTSD diagnosis, Latino LGB individuals had higher prevalence of PTSD than both White and Black LGB individuals.

While findings from these two studies were inconsistent with minority stress theory, Alessi et al. (2013) suggested that they were not surprising. Studies that compared prevalence of mental disorders between White and Black individuals showed similar findings. It is possible that strong family and community networks may help to buffer the effects of traumatic events among Black individuals (Allen, 1996). They may also cope with traumatic events in ways that do not outwardly convey their levels of psychological distress. For example, one study showed that Black women used binge eating to cope with negative affect related to traumatic experiences. (Harrington, Crowther, & Shipherd, 2010). Despite the nature of these contradictory findings, clinicians should be aware that LGB people of color face the "cultural complexities" of holding two minority statuses (Smith, 1997, p. 282). In fact, one study demonstrated that discrimination based on sexual orientation and gender identity contributed to depression and anxiety among sexual and gender minority individuals of color ($N = 200$), which in turn impacted suicidal ideation among this population (Sutter & Perrin, 2016). In this study, racism was also directly associated with mental health but was not linked to suicidal ideation (Sutter & Perrin, 2016). These findings suggest that it is critical to understand the impact of multiple identities on the mental health of LGB people of color.

GENERAL PSYCHOLOGICAL PROCESSES

The minority stress model is used to partially explain the connection between group-specific processes and negative mental health outcomes among LGB people. Group-specific processes refer to both distal (objective prejudice events) and proximal (stigma, internalized homophobia, and concealment of sexual orientation) stressors (Meyer, 2003). Generally, identifying as a sexual-minority person leads to higher levels of stress, which in turn confers increased risk for psychopathology. However, comprehensive approaches to clinical practice with LGB clients (and heterosexual clients, for that matter) require an understanding of more than group-specific processes. It is also important to understand the role of general psychological processes when conducting clinical interventions with LGB individuals (Hatzenbuehler, 2009). General psychological processes refer to the client's coping/emotional regulation, social/ interpersonal, and cognitive processes, which may be elevated by minority stress (Hatzenbuehler, 2009). As discussed earlier, these include coping abilities, social support, and maladaptive self-schemas, respectively.

According to Hatzenbuehler (2009), LGB individuals encounter excess levels of stress due to their marginalized status; this stress in turns creates elevations in general psychological processes that confer risk for psychopathology. Hatzenbuehler proposed a psychological mediation model in which the relationship between minority stress (i.e., distal stressors) and psychopathology is mediated by general psychological processes. His psychological mediation model builds on Meyer's (2003) minority stress model as well as studies demonstrating elevated general psychological process among LGB populations compared to heterosexual populations. Researchers are beginning to examine the role of potential mediators in the relationship between minority stress and mental health outcomes among LGB people, though studies have yet to examine the role of general psychological processes specifically. For example, Wight, LeBlanc, de Vries, and Detels (2012) found that sense of personal mastery partially mediated the relationship between gay-related stressors (as well as aging-related stressors) and depressive symptoms among 202 older adult gay men. Another study (Lehavot & Simoni, 2011) showed that social support and spirituality mediated associations between minority stressors (i.e., sexual orientation victimization, internalized homophobia, and concealment) and mental health among lesbians ($N = 1,381$), though there were direct links between victimization and substance abuse and internalized homophobia and substance abuse. Feinstein, Goldfried, and Davila (2012) found that internalized homophobia and rejection sensitivity mediated the relationship between discrimination experiences and symptoms of depression and social anxiety among 467 LGB participants, suggesting that perceptions and appraisals play a role in determining mental health outcomes following such experiences.

A discussion of Hatzenbuehler's (2009) psychological mediation model and Meyer's (2003) minority stress model offers the foundation for a comprehensive approach to clinical practice by identifying how group-specific factors and the elevation of general psychological processes contribute to mental health problems among LGB people. An LGB person's general psychological processes are likely to reflect the way in which he or she manages prejudice, stigma, internalized homophobia, and concealment/disclosure. Along the same line, Hatzenbuehler asserts that "exclusive focus on either process alone—without consideration of their interrelationships—may hinder the development of effective theory on the determinants of mental health disparities among sexual minorities, as well as prevention and intervention efforts with this population" (p. 707).

APPLICATION OF THE MINORITY STRESS FRAMEWORK

This section presents the application of the minority stress framework for clinical practice with LGB clients. The case example highlights the complexities that may emerge when working with clients struggling with minority stress and also discusses the challenges faced by LGB clients of color, particularly those identifying as Black.

BACKGROUND

Steven, a 26-year-old Black man employed as a data analyst at a large digital marketing firm, identified social anxiety, anger management, and difficulty navigating the world of sex and dating as his primary reasons for seeking treatment.[1] Steven identifies as gay, presents with a muscular frame, and dresses in understated, traditionally masculine-style clothing. When he is at ease, he is an animated speaker, but when he feels anxious, he tends to speak in a low voice and exhibits constricted body language (e.g., arms crossed or one hand partially covering his mouth). His anger management problem is characterized by the occurrence of verbal outbursts in which he shouts at people when he perceives that they are mistreating or misunderstanding him. These incidents include states of high physiological arousal (e.g., heart pounding and hands shaking) and a decreased capacity to control his impulse to yell. After such incidents, he feels embarrassed by his behavior and remorseful about its impact on others.

Steven grew up in a mid-size, predominantly White suburban city in a lower-middle-class home with his two parents and a younger sister. He described being considerably underweight as a child and was physically and verbally bullied by his peers due to his small stature. From first grade through high school he was harassed and taunted on a daily basis. Steven attributes these childhood experiences to his persistent body image problems and a general distrust of people he does not know well. He tends to avoid social engagements that involve more than one or two friends and feels very nervous or "on edge" during the rare occasions when he goes out to the bars. He expresses difficulty forming romantic relationships and attributes this to experiences of feeling rejected by other gay men after coming out at age 20. He felt devalued by many of the White gay men that he encountered in his community, and, consequently, he decided to move to a larger city with more racial diversity at age 23. After his move, Steven joined a gym, became interested in bodybuilding, and developed a fit, muscular build through diet and exercise. While he noticed more positive attention since the change in his appearance, he continued to worry about not being big enough and experienced chronic fear of being rejected due to his size and skin color.

Steven has a core group of close friends and speaks to his family regularly, although he has never come out to his parents or sister. He denies feelings of shame about his sexual orientation yet admits that he has difficulty coming out to anyone outside of an exclusively gay environment. When he is not experiencing anxiety or anger, he has a warm smile, a sharp sense of humor, and a tendency to be generous to others.

MINORITY STRESS ASSESSMENT

EXPOSURE TO PREJUDICE EVENTS

Stressful events involving prejudice can be acute or chronic. Acute stressful events cause a significant change in a person's life, while chronic stressful events consist of everyday discrimination

1. Identifying information was changed to protect the client's privacy.

(e.g., being treated with less respect or receiving poor services) and stigma (which will be discussed in detail later; Meyer, Schwartz, & Frost, 2008). Although Steven had not encountered any recent acute prejudice events, he was bullied throughout his childhood and experienced racial discrimination in the gay community in the years after coming out. As a result, Steven spent most of his time alone and continues to use isolation as a way to cope with minority stress as an adult. To fully understand the developmental processes of LGB individuals, clinicians should be aware of the effects of discrimination (i.e., homophobia) on clients' childhood and adolescent experiences as well as the compounding effects of prejudice based on other minority identities.

STIGMA

Stigmatized individuals are faced with the dilemma of continually having to discern what others are thinking about them, and they are likely to interpret their daily interactions as being undermined by the dominant group (Goffman, 1963). Steven grapples with multiple experiences of stigma relating to his race, sexual orientation, and body image. He fears being rejected because of his body and anticipates being ignored or disrespected for being a Black, gay male. He enters most social situations with the belief that he will be rejected and as a result appears detached, quiet, or tense. It is not uncommon for stigmatized individuals to maintain a high degree of vigilance in their interactions with the dominant group. This is not necessarily pathological. In fact, this vigilance can be protective; it may help LGB people cope with negative appraisals and also motivates them to seek out positive social supports (Kaufman & Johnson, 2004). For Steven, it is problematic because he overestimates threats of being rejected based on his body size in situations that are otherwise LGB-affirming.

INTERNALIZED HOMOPHOBIA

Internalized homophobia is defined as "the gay person's direction of negative social attitudes toward the self" (Meyer & Dean, 1998, p. 161). Steven does not present with the common manifestations of internalized homophobia. For instance, he does not specifically avoid contact with other LGB people. On the contrary, he feels quite comfortable socializing in exclusively gay environments, although he retains a degree of anxiety about being rejected due to his race and physical appearance even in these environments. He also does not wish he were heterosexual; in fact, he celebrates aspects of gay culture, such as reading gay literature and viewing LGBT-related films, and he has an affirmative stance toward his own same-sex desire. Steven's positive attitude toward his gay identity should be considered one of his strengths. Despite growing up in contexts (family, school, and community) where homophobia was pervasive, internalized homophobia does not cause him much distress. He attributes this to the counseling that he received in college when he first came out. Steven learned early in his adult life that because he grew up in a culture embedded in heterosexist traditions and symbols, he had to work hard to challenge his own heteronormative thinking.

Although Steven does not struggle with internalized homophobia to the extent that he struggles with stigma, early developmental experiences and continued exposure to a heterosexist society may impact the way in which he sees himself (Meyer, 2003). Steven acknowledges that the lasting effects of internalized homophobia may account for part of his fears about being too skinny, which may be linked to his anxiety about being perceived by others as effeminate and therefore gay. His peers used antigay slurs (e.g., "faggot" and "sissy") to tease and harass him for behaving differently than the other boys. In a study (Szymanski & Gupta, 2009) that examined the effects of internalized homophobia and internalized racism among lesbian, gay, bisexual, and questioning Black adults, both variables were unique predictors of self-esteem. However, when internalized homophobia and internalized racism were examined in relation to psychological distress, only internalized homophobia predicted psychological distress. The authors suggested that this might be due to the participants' belief that the Black community is intolerant of homosexuality. This needs to be kept in mind when working with Steven because it may have contributed to his decision to conceal his sexual orientation in some contexts.

SEXUAL ORIENTATION CONCEALMENT

Steven's need to conceal his sexual orientation from his family and co-workers may be connected to being bullied throughout childhood as well as other experiences of homophobia. Although Steven has not come out to any family members, he assumes that his parents and extended family know because they no longer ask him questions about his dating life. Steven feels that he should not have to come out in a formal way—since heterosexuals do not have to—but he is aware that he leaves out details of his life when he is with his family members or co-workers. He has struggled to find a way to deal with this issue. At work, when his co-workers converse about dating and relationships, he remains silent because he worries about the risk of having an angry explosion in the event that someone "says something stupid" regarding his sexuality. While concealing one's sexual orientation may offer protection from a hostile social environment, those who conceal must also contend with the ongoing threat of discovery. Pachankis (2007) proposed that this threat leads to four specific psychological responses: (a) vigilance, suspiciousness, and preoccupation (cognitive); (b) shame, guilt, anxiety, and depression (affective); (c) social avoidance, the need for feedback, and impaired relationships (behavioral); and (d) identity ambivalence, negative view of self, and diminished self-efficacy (self-evaluation). Steven manifests these psychological responses on a daily basis. He recognizes that concealing his sexual orientation prevents him from having authentic relationships with people, which in turn increases his feelings of disconnection from others. At the same time, it is likely that past experiences of being judged or feeling different have been integrated into Steven's defensive system, making hiding feel necessary for self-protection (Drescher, 1998).

ASSESSMENT OF GENERAL PSYCHOLOGICAL PROCESSES

COPING/EMOTIONAL REGULATION

Steven frequently uses avoidance as a way to contend with multiple experiences of stigma. For example, he avoids approaching men whom he finds attractive, and he isolates at home, working on solitary projects, such as reading or playing video games. He also avoids mirrors in order to prevent feeling ashamed about being too thin. This behavior paradoxically reinforces his belief that he is much smaller than he is because he does not take in the image of his actual size. He also engages in rumination, which is a risk factor for depression and anxiety (Hatzenbeuhler, 2009). For example, he will spend hours thinking about whether someone he spoke to online is interested in dating him or only wants him for sex.

SOCIAL/INTERPERSONAL

Steven has a few close gay male friends, which helps him feel connected to the LGB community. His friends encourage him to go out with them, and they support him in his efforts to date. Yet he also feels alienated from them because of his conflicts about dating and his obsessive fears about his physical appearance. He would like to be more open with them, but he experiences difficulty in social situations in which he perceives high risks of being judged or rejected. Although isolating himself and being private during childhood and adolescence was an adaptive response for dealing with a hostile social environment, it is now associated with loneliness for Steven.

COGNITIVE

Steven has a number of negative self-schemas associated with the core belief that he is unlovable (Beck, 2011). Concerns about his body type, shame about his anger, and the need to conceal his sexual orientation in some contexts strengthen these negative self-schemas. He believes that he is always at risk of exploding because of someone's judgment of him, and he feels this way even when he is around other LGB people. He expresses doubt that he will ever feel comfortable enough to date someone long term without feeling judged by the person.

AN EXAMINATION OF LGB-AFFIRMATIVE TREATMENT

The therapeutic approach used with Steven was integrative, incorporating techniques from cognitive and psychodynamic psychotherapy. The social worker used cognitive techniques to modify the client's core beliefs about rejection, enhance coping skills, and offer encouragement and support, while he used psychodynamic techniques to maintain a nonjudgmental stance, evoke negative affective states, and process the client-therapist relationship (Jones & Pulos, 1993). Integrating these approaches provides clinicians with the tools to deal with the complex problems frequently encountered in community mental health and private practice settings.

Engaging Steven in the therapeutic process was difficult at first. He resisted the social worker's attempts to connect with him out of concerns about being judged. Having a gay-identified social worker eased some of these concerns, and Steven gradually became more at ease. Regardless of the therapist's sexual orientation or racial identity, however, the use of affirmative psychotherapy techniques can help to foster collaboration, regardless of the therapist's sexual orientation or racial identity (Davies, 1996). King et al.'s (2007) systematic review of the affirmative counseling literature revealed that therapists' sexual orientation was less important to LGB clients than the therapist's attitudes, knowledge, and practice skills. On the other hand, social workers should not assume that questions about their sexual orientation relate to resistance or transference issues on the part of the client. LGB clients may inquire about the social worker's sexual orientation as a way of discerning whether it is safe to discuss LGB-related issues. Therapists should evaluate a client's need to know about their sexual orientation and be prepared to disclose when appropriate and/or necessary (Drescher, 1998).

LGB-affirmative psychotherapy is not an independent practice approach. Its purpose is to enhance existing treatment models (e.g., cognitive-behavioral, psychodynamic, or humanistic; Davies, 1996). However, LGB-affirmative psychotherapy differs from traditional treatment modalities. The LGB-affirmative practitioner "celebrates and advocates the validity of lesbian, gay, and bisexual persons and their relationships" (Tozer & McClanahan, 1999, p. 736). According to King et al. (2007), clients' experiences of LGB-affirmative therapy usually involve "therapy in which homosexuality and bisexuality are regarded positively, prejudice is avoided, the stress of externalised and internalised anti-homosexual bias is recognized, and there is sensitivity to [LGB] development, culture and lifestyles" (p. 32). Social workers should not underestimate the importance of using affirmative approaches. Practicing without discriminating is not the same as practicing affirmatively (Crisp, 2006).

ADDRESSING STIGMA

Helping clients cope with stigma is an important affirmative psychotherapy technique. For example, the social worker normalized Steven's anger about working with colleagues who made inappropriate comments about homosexuality. The social worker informed him that the workplace should be free of discrimination and harassment and that there were options for dealing with this situation if he chose to (e.g., reporting it to his supervisor or informing his colleagues that these remarks made him uncomfortable). Using the social worker's authority to counter harsh criticism against LGB people deprograms stereotypes about homosexuality (Davies, 1996). Indeed, there is concern that treatment with LGB clients is overly focused on intrapsychic processes and thus fails to acknowledge how macro-level forces shape their feelings, attitudes, and behaviors (Glassgold, 2007; Russell & Bohan, 2006). Additionally, Steven contends with stigma related to his racial identity. Focusing on the challenges related to these intersecting identities (i.e., identifying as Black and gay) was integral to helping Steven deal with his isolation. The social worker conveyed that he understood the struggles that Steven experienced as a Black gay man. Acknowledging the challenges of living with both sexual orientation and race-related stigma helped Steven to see that he had internalized negative attitudes about his sexual desires not as a generic repudiation of his homosexuality but about the conflicts he experienced when he felt attracted to men of other races.

BUILDING A RELATIONSHIP

However, before the social worker could explore this further, he and Steven had to build a strong therapeutic relationship. This was particularly important because Steven exhibits an anxious attachment style. Because his anxiety was organized around anticipating rejection, the social worker strengthened the therapeutic relationship by periodically checking in to see whether Steven felt validated, accepted, and understood. A willingness to hear the client's concerns and complaints helps to facilitate the therapeutic holding environment (Drescher, 1998), which is essential for treatment.

Attachment-based approaches may be especially helpful for LGB clients with intimacy problems, because the therapist functions as "a conduit through which new, secure, [cognitive working models] of attachment can be created between therapist and client" (Sherry, 2007, p. 223). The facilitation of these new internal working models may decrease shame and guilt and enable the client to connect with others in new ways. It may be helpful to create these new internal working models before suggesting that clients, for example, attend LGB social events, because they may not be ready to develop close relationships with others (Sherry, 2007). Using exposure techniques before these new working models are in place may increase feelings of failure and thus precipitate more anxiety in future exposure exercises.

SEXUAL ORIENTATION DISCLOSURE

Holding two minority statuses complicated Steven's concerns about self-disclosure. Deep family connections may exacerbate sexual orientation conflict when one's cultural community (e.g., religious institutions, extended family) does not accept homosexuality (Smith, 1997). To maintain connections to the larger cultural community, some LGB individuals of color, such as Steven, remain closeted to family members (Greene, 1994). Coming out to family members may present numerous challenges, since there is a possibility of losing one's racial/ethnic support system as a result of identifying as LGB (Szymanski & Gupta, 2009). Early sexual identity development models (Cass, 1979, 1984; Troiden, 1979) conceptualized homosexual identity development as a stage process in which individuals progress from feeling different to acceptance of their homosexual identity (Loiacano, 1989). However, these models may not account for cultural variations among LGB individuals of color who may place less emphasis on coming out than White individuals (Loiacano, 1989). Furthermore, some individuals, regardless of their race/ethnicity, may not identify with the stages in these sexual identity development models at all.

Thus the social worker proceeded cautiously when discussing issues of disclosure. Steven's hesitation about coming out to his parents was understandable, given his parents' silence about his dating life. Practitioners should not minimize racial/ethnic minority clients' concerns about coming out to members of their racial/ethnic community (Liddle, 2007). Social workers should monitor their countertransference when addressing disclosure issues, since there is the risk of pushing clients to come out before they are ready (Alessi, 2008). This can result in unintended consequences, which some clients may be unequipped to deal with. Due to intense pressure to "please" the therapist, some clients may also terminate treatment (Alessi, 2008). Exploring Steven's concern about coming out to his family members allowed the social worker and Steven to understand what family means to him (Jacobo, 2001) and whether or not he felt it was important for him to come out to his parents. Focusing on this conflict helped Steven to cope with some of his concerns about coming out. Some LGB people may decide not to reveal their sexual orientation in certain contexts, even if they completely accept their LGB identity, indicating that outness may be influenced by situational and environmental circumstances rather than internal conflict (Frost & Meyer, 2009).

FOCUS ON COPING

Improving Steven's coping processes was a primary focus of treatment. While avoidance may be adaptive in the short term, it inadvertently reinforced Steven's notion that he could not cope effectively with dating or with interpersonal conflict. Because Steven used avoidance to cope with anxiety-provoking situations, the social worker used cognitive-behavioral techniques to help reduce and manage his anxiety. For example, Steven started using self-talk strategies. He would tell himself that he was not trapped or stuck in a situation and that he was free to leave at any time. This strategy, combined with his increased awareness of and ability to regulate his physical arousal state, helped him to realize that he could handle more than he had previously estimated. The social worker also helped Steven to use mindfulness exercises to increase his awareness of his bodily states, helping him to understand how his body reacts during different stages of emotional arousal (McKay, Wood, & Brantley, 2007). He learned to regulate his anger by attending to his physiological hyperarousal and practicing relaxation techniques. Mindfulness training was also used to create a more realistic sense of his present adult body in order to challenge his automatic negative thoughts relating to his size.

IMPROVING SOCIAL SKILLS

As Steven's ability to cope with stress improved, treatment shifted toward helping Steven improve his social skills. The social worker helped him identify places in the community that would allow him to meet new people. In order to do this, social workers should be aware of affirmative resources in the LGB community (Alessi, Dillon, & Kim, 2015). Steven subsequently visited a number of LGB-related venues. Unlike the events he usually attended, which were primarily geared toward men of color, these new places were more racially and ethnically mixed. Despite his concerns about rejection, he was amenable to using exposure techniques to cope with his fears when trying to approach someone he was attracted to. Steven practiced approaching guys, engaging in casual conversation, and occasionally asking some of them to go out on dates. After experiencing some rejection when men did not show interest in him, he and the social worker spent a significant amount of time processing his shame, disappointment, and frustration. Eventually Steven made several new friends and had one dating relationship that lasted more than three months.

PROCESSING THE THERAPEUTIC RELATIONSHIP

Furthermore, analyzing the client–therapist relationship provided Steven with information about how he interacts with others. For example, at times, he responded to the social worker with a sarcastic and irritable tone, offering an example of how he might interact with others outside of the therapeutic space. This led to the shared realization that Steven's irritability stemmed from his need to protect himself from those who could reject him. As discussed previously, Steven's fears of rejection stemmed from negative self-schemas associated with the core belief that he was unlovable. He struggled with feelings of loneliness and, at times, felt he had too many "issues" to overcome. The belief that he was "crazy" was projected onto the social worker, which in turn contributed to

Steven's belief that the social worker was judging him in such a way. As their work progressed, it was important to help Steven identify these projections as his own automatic thoughts, as well as to challenge the cognitive distortions that exacerbated Steven's tendency to attack himself. In order to help him expand his capacity for imagining how others perceived him, the social worker began to ask him how he thought he was being experienced by the social worker at various points during sessions (Fonagy, 2000). Doing this allowed him to doubt his conviction that the social worker thought he was "crazy."

Although Steven became much more comfortable with his identity, he continued to struggle with minority stress. The dynamic interplay between minority stress and a LGB client's general psychological processes can maintain negative outcomes (Hatzenbuehler, 2009). For example, Steven's difficulty coping with stigma exacerbates it, which then makes it harder for him to cope. Since he frequently feels judged, he will react in either an avoidant or hostile way toward the people he believes are judging him, even in the therapeutic space. This behavior often results in the other person reacting in kind by treating him coldly or with hostility, affirming his belief that he is unlovable. As Steven worked to disrupt this vicious cycle, he learned that others tended to perceive him as warm and generous. He was also surprised to discover that some of the people he had conflict with admired him for his kindness and intelligence. In this regard, he made notable improvements in how he saw himself and how he imagined others perceived him. However, Steven's avoidant behaviors would require longer-term treatment to help him further develop his coping skills for managing the effects of minority stress and attachment-related anxiety.

CONCLUSION

This chapter reviewed the tenets of minority stress theory and provided a specific case example to demonstrate how the minority stress framework can be used in practice with LGB individuals. The client struggled primarily with stigma and concerns related to sexual orientation concealment. His coping/emotional regulation, social/interpersonal, and cognitive processes were impaired by stigma-related experiences, making it difficult for him to manage minority stress. Although Steven's anxiety and depression decreased and his social functioning improved for a period of time, without the use of objective measures (e.g., symptom scales) it is difficult to know the actual effect of treatment and whether assessing Steven through the lens of the minority stress framework enhanced treatment in any way. Social workers should be aware that LGB clients enter mental health treatment to deal with a number of problems, not just sexual orientation-related issues (King et al., 2007), which can make it difficult to fully understand the impact of minority stress on the client's psychosocial functioning. The differential impact of each minority stress component (e.g., stigma, internalized homophobia) is not always evident and does not affect all clients equally. Thus there is a possibility that clinicians might under- or overestimate the impact of minority stress. As Newcomb and Mustanski (2010) stated: it is preferable to assess the impact of minority stress "with each client rather than making assumptions about the detrimental effects of these variables" (p. 1028). In a similar vein, while sexual-minority individuals share common minority stressors, the identities and experiences of lesbian and bisexual women should be differentiated from the identities and experiences of gay and bisexual men (Fassinger & Arseneau, 2007). Further research is needed to develop an assessment tool that can reliably assess minority stress among LGB clients seeking mental health treatment. This assessment tool should also be able to capture the effects of living with more than one minority identity. In the meantime, applying the minority stress framework to clinical practice provides a starting point for understanding the impact of a hostile social environment on the psychosocial functioning of LGB people.

ACKNOWLEDGMENTS

This chapter was adapted from a previously published article: Alessi, E. J. (2014). A framework for incorporating minority stress theory into treatment with sexual minority clients. *Journal of Gay & Lesbian Mental Health, 18*, 47–66.

REFERENCES

Alessi, E. J. (2008). Staying put in the closet: Examining clinical practice and countertransference issues in work with gay men married to heterosexual women. *Clinical Social Work Journal, 36*, 195–201. doi:10.1007/s10615-007-0092-6

Alessi, E. J., Dillon, F. R., & Kim, H. M. (2015). Determinants of lesbian and gay affirmative practice among heterosexual therapists. *Psychotherapy, 52*, 298–307. doi:10.1037/a0038580

Alessi, E. J., Meyer, I. H., & Martin, J. I. (2013). PTSD and sexual orientation: An examination of criterion A1 and non-criterion A1 events. *Psychological Trauma: Theory, Research, Practice, and Policy, 5*, 149–157. doi:10.1037/a0026642

Allen, I. M. (1996). PTSD among African Americans. In A. J. Marsella, M. J. Friedman, E. T. Gerrity, & R. M. Scurfield (Eds.), *Ethnocultural aspects of posttraumatic stress disorder: Issues, research, and clinical applications* (pp. 209–238). Washington, DC: American Psychological Association.

American Psychological Association. (2012). Guidelines for psychological practice with lesbian, gay, and bisexual clients. *American Psychologist, 67*, 10–42. doi:10.1037/a0024659

Austin, A., & Craig, S. L. (2015). Transgender affirmative cognitive behavioral therapy: Clinical considerations and applications. *Professional Psychology: Research and Practice, 46*, 21–29. doi:10.1037/a0038642

Beck, J. S. (2011). *Cognitive behavior therapy: Basics and beyond* (2nd ed.). New York: Guilford Press.

Bockting, W. O., Miner, M. H., Swinburne Romine R. E., Hamilton A., & Coleman E. (2013). Stigma, mental health, and resilience in an online sample of the US transgender population. *American Journal of Public Health, 103*, 943–951. doi:10.2105/AJPH.2013.301241.

Breslow, A. S., Brewster, M. E., Velez, B. L., Wong, S., Geiger, E., & Soderstrom, B. (2015). Resilience and collective action: Exploring buffers against minority stress for transgender individuals. *Psychology of Sexual Orientation and Gender Diversity, 2*, 253–265. doi:10.1037/sgd0000117

Brooks, V. R. (1981). *Minority stress and lesbian women.* Lexington, MA: Heath.

Cass, V. C. (1979). Homosexual identity formation: A theoretical model. *Journal of Homosexuality, 4*(3), 219–235.

Cass, V. C. (1984). Homosexual identity formation: Testing a theoretical model. *Journal of Sex Research, 20*, 143–167.

Cochran, S. D., & Mays, V. M. (2000). Relation between psychiatric syndromes and behaviorally defined sexual orientation in a sample of the US population. *American Journal of Epidemiology, 151,* 516–523.

Cochran, S. D., Sullivan, J. G., & Mays, V. M. (2003). Prevalence of mental disorders, psychological distress, and mental health services use among lesbian, gay, and bisexual adults in the United States. *Journal of Consulting and Clinical Psychology, 71,* 53–61. doi:10.1037/0022-006X.71.1.53

Crisp, C. (2006). The gay affirmative practice scale (GAP): A new measure for assessing cultural competence with gay and lesbian clients. *Social Work, 51,* 115–126. doi:10.1093/sw/51.2.115

Davies, D. (1996). Towards a model of gay affirmative therapy. In D. Davies & C. Neal (Eds.), *Pink therapy: A guide for counsellors and therapists working with lesbian, gay, and bisexual clients* (pp. 24–40). Buckingham, UK: Open University Press.

Drescher, J. (1998). *Psychoanalytic therapy and the gay man.* Hillsdale, NJ: Analytic Press.

Fassinger, R. E., & Arseneau, J. R. (2007). "I'd rather get wet than be under that umbrella:" Differentiating the experiences and identities of lesbian, gay, bisexual, and transgender people. In K. J. Bieschke, R. M. Perez, & K. A. DeBord (Eds.), *Handbook of counseling and psychotherapy with lesbian, gay, bisexual, and transgender clients* (2nd ed., pp. 19–49). Washington, DC: American Psychological Association.

Feinstein, B. A., Goldfried, M. R., & Davila, J. (2012). The relationship between experiences of discrimination and mental health among lesbians and gay men: An examination of internalized homonegativity and rejection sensitivity as potential mechanisms. *Journal of Consulting and Clinical Psychology, 80,* 917–927. doi:10.1037/a0029425

Fonagy, P. (2000). Attachment and borderline personality disorder. *Journal of the American Psychoanalytic Association, 48,* 1129–1146. doi:10.1177/00030651000480040701

Frost, D. M., & Meyer, I. H. (2009). Internalized homophobia and relationship quality among lesbians, gay men, and bisexuals. *Journal of Counseling Psychology, 56,* 97–109. doi:10.1037/a0012844

Gay and Lesbian Medical Association & LGBT Health Experts. (2001). *Healthy people 2010 companion document for lesbian, gay, bisexual, and transgender (LGBT) health.* San Francisco, CA: Gay and Lesbian Medical Association.

Gilman, S. E., Cochran, S. D., Mays, V. M., Hughes, M. Ostrow, D., & Kessler, R. C. (2001). Risk of psychiatric disorders among individuals reporting same-sex sexual partners in the National Comorbidity Survey. *American Journal of Public Health, 91,* 933–939. doi:10.2105/AJPH.91.6.933

Goffman, E. (1963). *Stigma: Notes on the management of spoiled identity.* Englewood Cliffs, NJ: Prentice-Hall.

Gold, S. D., Dickstein, B. D., Marx, B. P., & Lexington, J. (2009). Psychological outcomes among lesbian sexual assault survivors: An examination of the role of internalized homophobia and experiential avoidance. *Psychology of Women Quarterly, 33,* 54–66.

Gold, S. D., Marx, B. P., & Lexington, J. M. (2007). Gay male sexual assault survivors: The relations among internalized homophobia, experiential avoidance, and psychological symptom severity. *Behaviour Research and Therapy, 45,* 549–562. doi:10.1016/j.brat.2006.05.006

Greene, B. (1994). Ethnic minority lesbians and gay men: Mental health and treatment issues. *Journal of Consulting and Clinical Psychology, 62,* 243–251. doi:10.1037/0022-006X.62.2.243

Glassgold, J. M. (2007). "In dreams begin responsibilities": Psychology, agency, and activism. *Journal of Gay and Lesbian Psychotherapy, 11* (3/4), 37–57. doi:10.1300/J236v11n03_03

Haas, A. P., Eliason, M., Mays, V. M., Mathy, R. M., Cochran, S. D., D'Augelli, A. R., . . . Clayton, P. J. (2011). Suicide and suicide risk in lesbian, gay, bisexual, and transgender populations: Review and recommendations. *Journal of Homosexuality, 58*(1), 10–51. doi:10.1080/00918369.2011.534038

Harrington, E. F., Crowther, J. H., & Shipherd, J. C. (2010). Binge eating, and the "strong Black woman." *Journal of Consulting and Clinical Psychology, 78,* 469–479. doi:10.1037/a0019174

Hatzenbuehler, M. L. (2009). How does sexual minority stigma "get under the skin"? A psychological mediation framework. *Psychological Bulletin, 135,* 707–730. doi:10.1037/a0016441

Heidt, J. M., Marx, B. P., & Gold, S. D. (2005). Sexual revictimization among sexual minorities: A preliminary study. *Journal of Traumatic Stress, 18,* 533–540. doi:10.1002/jts.20061

Hendricks M. L., & Testa, R. J. (2012). A conceptual framework for clinical work with transgender and gender nonconforming clients: An adaptation of the minority stress model. *Professional Psychology: Research and Practice, 43*, 460–467. doi:10.1037/a0029597

Herek, G. M., & Garnets, L. D. (2007). Sexual orientation and mental health. *Annual Review of Clinical Psychology, 3*, 353–375. doi:10.1146/annurev.clinpsy.3.022806.091510

Huebner, D. M., Rebchook, G. M., & Kegeles, S. M. (2004). Experiences of harassment, discrimination, and physical violence among young gay and bisexual men. *American Journal of Public Health, 94*, 1200–1203. doi:10.2105/AJPH.94.7.1200

Jacobo, M. C. (2001). Revolutions in psychoanalytic theory of lesbian development. *Psychoanalytic Psychology, 18*, 667–683.

Jones, E. E., & Pulos, S. M. (1993). Comparing the process in psychodynamic and cognitive-behavioral therapies. *Journal of Consulting and Clinical Psychology, 61*, 306–316. doi:10.1037/0022-0167.55.2.221

Kaufman, J. M., & Johnson, C. (2004). Stigmatized individuals and the process of identity. *The Sociological Quarterly, 45*, 807–833. doi:10.1111/j.1533-8525.2004.tb02315.x

King, M., Semlyn, J., Killaspy, H., Nazareth, I., & Osborn, D. (2007). *A systematic review of research on counselling and psychotherapy for lesbian, gay, bisexual, and transgender people.* British Association for Counselling and Psychotherapy. Retrieved from http://www.nitherapy.net/assets/images/2012/05/BACP_LGBTreview.pdf

Lehavot, K., & Simoni, J. M. (2011). The impact of minority stress on mental health and substance use among sexual minority women. *Journal of Consulting and Clinical Psychology, 79*, 159–170. doi:10.1037/a0022839

Lewis, R. J., Derlega, V. J., Griffin, J. L., & Krowinski, A. C. (2003). Stressors for gay men and lesbians: Life stress, gay-related stress, stigma consciousness, and depressive symptoms. *Journal of Social and Clinical Psychology, 22*, 716–729.

Liddle, B. J. (2007). Mutual bonds: Lesbian women's lives and communities. In K. J. Bieschke, R. M. Perez, & K. A. DeBord (Eds.), *Handbook of counseling and psychotherapy with lesbian, gay, bisexual, and transgender clients* (2nd ed., pp. 51–69). Washington, DC: American Psychological Association.

Loiacano, D. K. (1989). Gay identity issues among Black Americans: Racism, homophobia, and the need for validation. *Journal of Counseling & Development, 68*, 21–25.

Mays, V. M., & Cochran, S. D. (2001). Mental health correlates of perceived discrimination among lesbian, gay, and bisexual adults in the United States. *American Journal of Public Health, 91*, 1869–1876. doi:10.2105/AJPH.91.11.1869

McKay, M., Wood, J., & Brantley, J. (2007). *The dialectical behavior therapy skills workbook: Practical DBT exercises for learning mindfulness, interpersonal effectiveness, emotion regulation, and distress tolerance.* Oakland, CA: New Harbinger.

Meyer, I. H. (2003). Prejudice, social stress, and mental health in lesbian, gay, and bisexual populations: Conceptual issues and research evidence. *Psychological Bulletin, 129*, 674–697. doi:10.1037/0033-2909.129.5.674

Meyer, I. H., & Dean, L. (1998). Internalized homophobia, intimacy, and sexual behavior among gay and bisexual men. In G. M. Herek (Ed.), *Stigma and sexual orientation: Understanding prejudice against lesbians, gay men, and bisexuals* (pp. 160–186). Thousand Oaks, CA: SAGE.

Meyer, I. H., Dietrich, J. H., & Schwartz, S. (2008). Lifetime prevalence of mental disorders and suicide attempts in diverse lesbian, gay, and bisexual populations. *American Journal of Public Health, 98*, 1004–1006. doi:10.2105/AJPH.2006.096826

Meyer, I. H., Schwartz, S., & Frost, D. M. (2008). Social patterning of stress and coping: Does disadvantaged status confer excess exposure and fewer coping resources? *Social Science & Medicine, 67*, 368–379. doi:10.1016/j.socscimed.2008.03.012

Newcomb, M. E., & Mustanski, B. (2010). Internalized homophobia and internalizing mental health problems: A meta-analytic review. *Clinical Psychology Review, 30*, 1019–1029. doi:10.1016/j.cpr.2010.07.003

Pachankis, J. E. (2007). The psychological implications of concealing a stigma: A cognitive-affective-behavioral model. *Psychological Bulletin, 133*, 328–345. doi:10.1037/0033-2909.133.2.328

Rothman, E. F., Exner, D., & Baughman, A. L. (2011). The prevalence of sexual assault against people who identify as gay, lesbian, or bisexual in the United States: A systematic review. *Trauma, Violence, & Abuse, 12*, 55–66. doi:10.1177/1524838010390707.

Russell, G. M., & Bohan, J. S. (2006). The case of internalized homophobia: Theory and/as practice. *Theory & Psychology, 16*, 343–366. doi:10.1177/0959354306064283

Sandfort, T. G., de Graaf R., Bijl, R. V., & Schnabel, P. (2001). Same-sex sexual behavior and psychiatric disorders: Findings from the Netherlands Mental Health Survey and Incidence Study (NEMESIS). *Archives of General Psychiatry, 58*, 85–91. doi:10.1001/archpsyc.58.1.85

Sandfort, T. G., de Graaf, R., Ten Have, M., Ransome, Y., & Schnabel, P. (2014). Same-sex sexuality and psychiatric disorders in the second Netherlands Mental Health Survey and Incidence Study (NEMESIS-2). *LGBT Health, 11*, 292–301. doi:10.1089/lgbt.2014.0031

Sherry, A. (2007). Internalized homophobia and adult attachment: Implications for clinical practice. *Psychotherapy: Theory, Research, Practice, Training, 44*, 219–225. doi:10.1037/0033-3204.44.2.219

Smith, A. (1997). Cultural diversity and the coming-out process: Implications for clinical practice. In B. Greene (Ed.), *Ethnic and cultural diversity among lesbians and gay men* (pp. 279–300). Thousand Oaks, CA: SAGE.

Sutter, M., & Perrin, P. B. (2016). Discrimination, mental health, and suicidal ideation among LGBTQ people of color. *Journal of Counseling Psychology, 63*, 98–105. doi:10.1037/cou0000126

Szymanski, D. M., & Gupta, A. (2009). Examining the relationship between multiple internalized oppressions and African American lesbian, gay, bisexual, and questioning persons' self-esteem and psychological distress. *Journal of Counseling Psychology, 56*, 110–118. doi:10.1037/a0012981

Tjaden, P., Thoennes, N., & Allison, C. J. (1999). Comparing violence over the life span in samples of same-sex and opposite-sex cohabitants. *Violence and Victims, 4*, 413–425.

Tozer, E. E., & McClanahan, M. K. (1999). Treating the purple menace: Ethical considerations of conversion therapy and affirmative alternatives. *The Counseling Psychologist, 27*, 722–742. doi:10.1177/0011000099275006

Troiden, R. R. (1979). Becoming homosexual: A model of gay identity acquisition. *Psychiatry, 42*, 362–373.

Warner, J., McKeown, E., Griffin, M., Johnson, K., Ramsay, A., Cort, C., & King, M. (2004). Rates and predictors of mental illness in gay men, lesbians, and bisexual men and women. *British Journal of Psychiatry, 185*, 479–485. doi:10.1192/bjp.185.6.479

Wight, R. G., LeBlanc A. J., de Vries B., & Detels, R. (2012). Stress and mental health among midlife and older gay-identified men. *American Journal of Public Health, 102*, 503–510. doi:10.2105/AJPH.2011.300384

CHAPTER 13

PRACTICE WITH THE LESBIAN COMMUNITY

A Roadmap to Effective Micro, Mezzo, and Macro Interventions

Gayle Mallinger

INTRODUCTION

This chapter explores social work practice with lesbian-identified women. Specifically, this chapter considers the historical and sociopolitical contexts impacting their lives across the lifespan. By definition, lesbians embody the intersection of gender and sexual orientation and are thus impacted by oppression and discrimination associated with both these identities. Practitioners must understand the unique needs of lesbians, including those further marginalized due to race/ethnicity, social-economic status, religion/spirituality, age, ability, nativity, urban/rural location, and/or veteran status. Effective social workers begin with an understanding of context critical to the population with whom they work—therefore, this chapter begins with an historical overview and the sociopolitical climate impacting lesbians in the United States. The chapter then examines the influences of community context on their lives, as well as exploring issues across the lifespan, including identity development, bullying, dating, intimate partner violence, committed relationships and building families, health and mental health, aging, illness, and issues relative to death and dying. The intersection of multiple identities is woven throughout the chapter, concluding with implications for micro-, mezzo-, and macro-level practice with lesbian clients. Note that the synonymous terms "lesbians," "lesbian-identified women," "lesbian women," and "women who identify as lesbians" are used interchangeably throughout the chapter.

THEORETICALLY INFORMED CONCEPTUAL FRAMEWORK

Feminist ethics of care, risk and resilience, and ecological theories inform the reciprocal interactions between lesbian women and the environment (Kerby & Mallinger, 2014). These theories, in combination, are useful in developing a conceptual model that considers diversity and complex systems in relation to the resilience of lesbian-identified women. These three paradigms form the basis for the model, considering the additive and interactive risks negatively influencing lesbians. In the aggregate, these theories also inform effective social work interventions.

Bronfenbrenner's (1977, 1979) theory of human ecology stresses the importance of the interactive influence of various systems on personal development. Bronfenbrenner described the ecological environment as comprised of nested systems. Microsystems refer to the interactions between the people and their immediate environment, including family, peers, and school. Mesosystems are comprised of connections between microsystems in which the person is an active participant, such as relationships with parents and teachers. Exosystems are defined as systems in which workers are not directly involved but are affected by decisions, such as administrative policies developed by the school board. Macrosystems consist of established cultural patterns that influence individuals. For example, institutional sexism and heterosexism are considered macro-level influences. A central theme of this perspective is the emphasis on the linkages among social networks. These interrelationships can serve as supports or barriers to individual development.

Risk and resilience theory can be used as a structure for explaining variations in physical and mental health outcomes for lesbian women. While the genesis of this paradigm emerged from research on children and adolescents, it is applicable to lesbians across the lifespan. Risk refers to distal (ecological environmental) and/or proximal influences (individual stressors) that place lesbians at risk for negative consequences. These risk factors often occur simultaneously and may be additive or exponential. Resilience is described as the ability to successfully manage hardships. Some women at high risk for adverse consequences surmount risk and do well despite difficult circumstances. Protective factors are defined as external factors serving to counteract, moderate, or mediate risk for negative outcomes (Fraser, Kirby, & Smokowski, 2004). Social workers operate from a strengths perspective; therefore, they should be sensitive to their lesbian client's resilience and ability to access and utilize protective factors, rather than solely focusing on risk factors.

THE APPLIED MODEL OF CARE

The applied model of care (see Figure 13.1) provides a roadmap for understanding the influences of various contexts on lesbian identity development. This conceptual model also informs social work intervention strategies for empowerment within the structural barriers that disadvantage lesbian women across the lifespan. Specifically, the model begins with an examination of the *national*

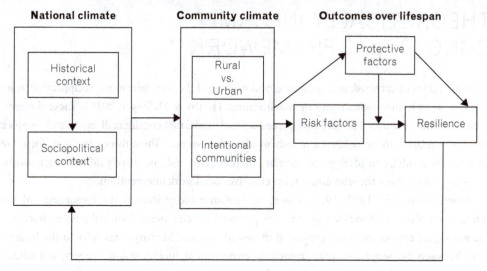

National climate   Community climate   Outcomes over lifespan

FIGURE 13.1: Applied model of care

climate influencing lesbians. The national climate is considered the combination of historical and sociocultural contexts. The national climate impacts the environment in which lesbians reside. For example, lesbian collective communities became popular during second wave feminism. The combination of national and *community climates* impact the experience of individual women. Rural and urban lesbians may have different experiences based on their locale. For example, some evidence suggests rural women are at increased risk for health and mental health issues (*outcomes*). Lesbians residing in cities have better access to medical and social work professionals. This is considered a protective factor leading to improved health/mental health outcomes.

HISTORICAL CONTEXT

Public opinion about lesbians has varied dramatically based on culture and place in time (Scasta, 1998). At certain points in history, same-sex relationships were viewed as normal expressions of human sexuality. In other eras, religious perspectives enforced the view of lesbians as sinners. Historically, the term "homosexuality" referred to gay men as well as lesbians. From the late nineteenth century through the early 1970s, homosexuality was regarded as a diagnosable mental illness. These perspectives are important, as they are the antecedents of present-day attitudes of social workers and other human service professionals.

In 1886, Richard Kraft-Ebing argued that homosexuality was not sinful; instead, same-sex relations were perversities due to genetic and environmental factors. During the same time period, Havelock Ellis, a famous sexologist, argued that homosexuality was an inborn trait (Scasta, 1998). Freud viewed homosexuality as an incurable pathology (Friedman & Downey, 1998; Scasta, 1998). Freud's followers extended the view of homosexuality as pathological and referred to same-sex attraction as thwarted heterosexuality due to a narcissistic wound occurring before the age of five. This wounding not only "guaranteed" a homosexual identity but was accompanied by borderline or narcissistic personality disorders (Friedman & Downey, 1998). This line of thinking led to the inclusion of homosexuality as a psychiatric diagnostic category in the first edition of the *Diagnostic and Statistical Manual of Mental Disorders* (1952). Not only did the American Psychiatric Association officially list homosexuality as a mental illness, the United States military and the State Department determined that homosexuals constituted a security threat (Faderman, 1982, Johnson, 2004). Individuals with "homosexual tendencies" were deemed unfit for service and were discharged from service or were mandated to mental health treatment to eradicate these propensities (Rimmerman, 2013).

Oppression gave rise to resistance in the 1960s and 1970s (Faderman, 1982; Johnson, 2004; Miller, 1995). The Stonewall rebellion sparked gay liberation. Stonewall, a gay bar located in the Greenwich Village section of New York City, was a target of frequent police raids. In June of 1969, the attack was met with mass resistance from the bar patrons. Capitalizing on the energy of the Stonewall riots, groups taking the name Gay Liberation Front were created in major cities across the United States (Miller, 1995). Among the victories for the lesbian and gay community was the removal of homosexuality as a codified, diagnosable mental illness in 1973 (Herek, 2004).

Although the events of the late 1960s brought activists together, lesbians continued to experience and marginalization in the Gay Liberation Front and within the women's movement (Samek, 2015). While first-wave feminists fought for voting rights for women, leaders in second-wave feminism concentrated on reproductive rights. Both of these waves are criticized for marginalizing women of color, working-class women, and lesbians. For example, second-wave feminist leader Betty Friedan claimed lesbian-identified women threatened the movement and politicized sexuality and referred to them as "the lavender menace" (Poirot, 2009). Lesbians also felt marginalized in the Gay Liberation Front. For example, male leaders dismissed lesbian specific issues of the time, such as such as child custody, as insignificant. Radical separatist feminists maintained lesbianism allowed women the chance to be totally free from male oppression. However, even within the radical lesbian feminist movement, women of color and working-class women were disenfranchised.

In the 1980s, the discovery of the HIV/AIDS virus and its transmission influenced the gay and lesbian community to coalesce in response to the antigay propaganda linking the sin of homosexuality with the disease. In response to the Red Cross mandate that gay men abstain from blood donations during this time, lesbians in various communities organized blood drives to replenish the supplies. Lesbians were also greatly influential in caregiving for all those impacted by HIV/AIDS and actively protested the lack of governmental response to the crisis (Hutchison, 2015). The physical devastation of AIDS, including death, heightened the awareness of lesbians and gays related to the need for legal partnership protections, such as medical decision-making and inheritance rights (Miller, 1995). Concern over the lack of legal protections continued into the 1990s. The conservative antigay agenda gained momentum during this decade, mobilizing around the reinstatement of "traditional family values" (Sullivan, 2004).

Opposition to the discourse of the "religious right" and the recognition of the need for the formation of social policies to afford equitable legal protections to gay and lesbian families emerged as the overriding, unifying agenda. Same-sex marriage, adoption by same-sex couples, and changes in discriminatory child custody laws accompanied cries for changes in policies prohibiting gay and lesbian service in the military, excluding lesbian, gay, bisexual, and transgender (LGBT) individuals from existing hate crime legislation, and the denying civil employment protections to the community (Belkin & Bateman, 2003; Lind, 2004; Sullivan, 2004). Increased visibility, technological advances, and a keen understanding of the dearth of legal protections, significantly impacted the lesbian community.

SOCIOPOLITICAL CONTEXT

The experiences of lesbian women across the lifespan are situated in pervasive sexism and heterosexism. *Sexism* is defined as the systematic subordination of women through the maintenance of patriarchal social structures, including legal, religious, and economic institutions. Glick and Fiske (2001) describe two distinct types of sexism. *Hostile sexism* is perceived as overt and takes the shape of denigrating and stereotypical remarks about women's incompetence or of resentful behavior to women who are "too powerful." *Benevolent sexism* consists of seemingly positive attitudes depicting women in need of protection. For instance, more than 50 years after the passage of the Equal Pay Act of 1963, women consistently earn less than men in the same positions and are less likely to advance professionally (Institute for Women's Policy Research, 2015). Structural barriers disadvantage women who choose to aspire to managerial positions. In addition, sexism can be overt, as described above, or more hidden. Covert sexism is synonymous with gendered microaggressions. Sue and colleagues (2007) defined microaggressions as casual comments and/or behaviors by people of privilege communicating disparaging messages to marginalized recipients. Microaggressions serve to demean and devalue individuals, whether or not they are intentional.

Heterosexism, as defined by Herek (2004), is a system of oppression that serves to stigmatize LBGTQ individuals and communities. Heterosexism includes individual antigay prejudice as well as institutional discrimination. This includes assumptions that individuals are heterosexual, such as describing couples as husband and wife instead of using gender-neutral language, such as partners. The inability of same sex couples to show public affection without fear of verbal and/or physical assault serves as another example. Institutional heterosexism can be explicit or implied. The exclusion of Jane Addams' purported long-term, intimate relationship with Mary Rozel Smith in much of social work education may be considered implicit heterosexism (Faderman, 1982). Hiring practices that exclude lesbians and gay men at sectarian agencies are explicitly heterosexist. Microaggressions against lesbians and gay men include comments that are derogatory, such as "that's so gay."

Pharr (1977), in her seminal piece, wrote specifically about the intersection of sexism and heterosexism. She referred to lesbians as woman-identified women, a term made popular following Friedan's pejorative "lavender menace" comments. To Pharr, women identified women define the abandonment of economic and sexual dependence on men. By doing so, lesbian women threaten male dominance and "compulsory heterosexuality" (p. 17). Thus, lesbian women have no support from privileged males or societal institutions. The consequences of abandoning the status quo include threats of and/or actual physical and sexual violence.

Heterosexism and sexism influence the policies affecting lesbian women. The Civil Rights Act of 1964 prohibits discrimination due to race, creed, color, or national origin and the 1990 Americans with Disabilities Act (ADA) forbids discrimination against people with disabilities. Unfortunately, there are no federal protections in place to prevent employment or housing discrimination for LGBT individuals. Notably, the past decade has given rise to several positive political changes for lesbian women and gay men.

THE REPEAL OF DON'T ASK, DON'T TELL

As previously discussed, the military banned service of gay men and lesbians, arguing homosexuality as a psychiatric illness. Following the removal of gay and lesbian identities as mental disorders, the Department of Defense continued the service ban, stating the presence of gay men and lesbians would threaten military cohesion and thereby threaten national security (Connell, 2015). Don't Ask, Don't Tell (DADT) in 1993 was a compromise policy between President Clinton, military leadership, and more conservative members of Congress. Clinton promised an end to the ban during his presidential campaign but was met with opposition; this concession and policy allowed lesbians and gay men to serve if they remained closeted. Gay rights activists fought to repeal DADT for nearly 20 years, claiming this policy violated the civil rights of lesbians and gay men serving in the military. President Obama signed the repeal of DADT into law in December 2010, and the law was officially repealed in September 2011 after appropriate military policies and procedures were put into place. In addition to allowing lesbians to remain in military service, those who were discharged under DADT are allowed to reenlist.

MARRIAGE EQUALITY

Marriage is more than the social sanctioning of a relationship. There are numerous legal and economic benefits associated with marital status. The official ban on same-sex marriage in the United States began in Maryland in 1993 with the statutory definition of marriage as the union of one man and one woman (Schmid, 2015). In 1993, however, the Supreme Court of Hawaii found it unconstitutional to deny same-sex couples the right to marry. The ruling galvanized opponents of marriage equality, ushering a wave of antigay state marriage laws throughout the nation. Consequently, President Clinton signed a federal ban on same sex marriage, the Defense of Marriage Act (DOMA), into law in 1996. As most pieces of legislation, DOMA was multifaceted. Section 3 of this law allowed states not in support of same-sex marriage to deny marital status to couples legally married in other states. Further, this section precluded same-sex couples legally married in any state to enjoy federal protections including tax benefits (Kahn, 2014).

In 2013 the US Supreme Court settled the case of the *United States v Windsor* in a landmark decision. Edith Windsor married her longtime partner in Canada and registered her marriage in New York when same-sex marriage became legal there. The following year her wife died, leaving

Windsor her entire estate. Under DOMA, the federal government did not recognize the legitimacy of Windsor's marriage. Thus she was forced to pay more than $300,000 in estate taxes. She successfully challenged the tax code inequity, and in a 5 to 4 decision, the Court overturned Section 3 of DOMA (Kahn, 2014).

Section 2 of DOMA affirmed the rights of states and territories to refuse to recognize marriages of same-sex couples wed in states allowing marriage equality. Ohio, along with Tennessee, Kentucky, and Michigan, did not recognize marriage equality. Obergefell and Arthur had legally married in 2013. Arthur suffered from a terminal illness and in fact died several months after the suit commenced. The plaintiffs asserted the Fourteenth Amendment of the Constitution required all states to recognize valid marriages performed elsewhere. The federal district court reversed previous rulings that had benefitted the plaintiffs. The Supreme Court agreed to hear the appeal and consolidated the case with other cases challenging the right to marriage equality, specifically, addressing whether the Fourteenth Amendment required states to issue marriage licenses to same-sex couples. On June 26, 2015, the Supreme Court ruled that all states must grant licenses to same-sex couples and recognize the legality of marriages performed in other states. (American Civil Liberties Union, 2016).

COMMUNITY CONTEXT

Social workers understand the importance of context critical to populations with whom they work. Like historical and sociopolitical climates, community environment also influences the lives of lesbian women in the United States. Many believe that the concept of community is physically bound. While geography can be a defining aspect of community, for example a neighborhood, it can extend to intentional communities of identity. This section specifically explores rural and urban in a geographic community context and intentional communities of identity using the Michigan Womyn's Music Festival as a brief case study.

RURAL AND URBAN LIFE

Experiences of lesbians living in rural areas are different than those residing in metropolitan/suburban areas. Although definitions of what constitutes rural may vary, descriptions often consider population density, social values, and attitudes. Thus residents of rural and urban communities have disparate experiences. The social climate for rural lesbian-identified women is often harsher than for their urban counterparts. Those in rural areas often have less access to formal resources and frequently experience social isolation. A survey of 527 lesbian-identified women living in rural areas found a lack of LGBTQ specific resources and high levels of heterosexism within rural communities (Oswald & Culton, 2003). Lesbians in rural areas are often stigmatized and experience heightened levels of discrimination due to their sexual orientation (Swank, Frost, & Fah, 2012). Social networks, including bars, clubs, and lesbian-centered agencies are extremely rare in rural areas (McCarthy, 2000). Barefoot, Smalley, and Warren (2015) surveyed 895 lesbian-identified women and found that lesbians in rural communities were significantly more likely to have higher levels of psychological distress and increased barriers to mental health services. These obstacles included actual lack of mental health facilities and fear of discriminatory treatment by providers.

The recent national climate has become more accepting of individuals with diverse sexual orientations. Increased access to technology and various forms of social media led to increased opportunities for socialization and decreased risk of negative outcomes for lesbians residing in rural settings. These changes may explain why current studies have found little differences in the health, mental health, and general welfare between lesbians in rural versus urban environments. Farmer, Blosnich, Jabson, and Matthews (2016) merged data across 10 states including information about sexual orientation from the 2010 Behavioral Risk Factor Surveillance System surveys. The researchers compared the health outcomes of 117 rural lesbians to 498 metropolitan lesbians and found no difference in health outcomes between the two. Puckett, Horne, Levitt, and Reeves (2011) interviewed 414 lesbian mothers and found urban and rural mothers had similar experiences with social support, stigma, and internalized heterosexism.

INTENTIONAL COMMUNITIES

Intentional communities are those formed in an effort to live among like-minded individuals as an alternative to mainstream society. These communities are ideologically bound but may or may not have specific geographical borders. The interests of the residents in the aggregate prevail over individual interests (Meijering, Huigen, & Van Hoven, 2007). Thus these communities provide a place where individuals feel accepted and safe.

Women's intentional communities arose during second-wave feminism. Radical lesbian separatist feminists were instrumental in creating these women-only spaces. The Michigan Womyn's Music Festival is an example of a space designed, built, and occupied by/for women. The festival, often referred to as Michfest, began in 1976 and provided space for several thousand cis-women (women whose sex assigned at birth matches their gender identity) to gather annually for workshops, concerts, and communal living on 650 acres of land in remote Michigan. The original organizers of Michfest, Lisa Vogel, her sister, Kristie Vogel, and a friend, Mary Kindig, designed the community for women to provide a space free from the oppression of the patriarchy. The festival included heterosexual and bisexual women from the beginning but was widely known as lesbian-centric.

"Festies" (those in attendance) were required to participate in work activities including trash/recycling, security, and transportation. In addition, many women arrived early to participate in the building of the physical structure, including roads, trails, kitchens, and centers, along with coordinating other logistical issues (McConnell, Odahl-Ruan, Kozlowski, Shattell, & Todd, 2016). Following the weeklong festival, women stayed to return the land to its natural state. Although Michfest lasted only one week, over its 40-year history, women participants discussed keeping the experience alive throughout the year, enabling them to survive the mainstream patriarchal culture (Morris, 2000).

Since its inception, Michigan Womyn's Festival experienced controversy. For example, lesbian separatist feminists were divided about policies regarding sadism and masochism practices on the land. There were also disagreements about the presence of male children. Arguments about attempts to address racism, ageism, and ableism were also contentious (Kendall, 2013; Trigilio, 2016). Throughout its history, Vogel, the staff, and attendees worked to ameliorate issues around intersecting identities. The festival offered camping sites for specific groups such as those over 50, clean and sober areas, and a Womyn of Color Tent. Perhaps the most controversial issue in the history of the festival centered on what many perceived to be discrimination of transgender women.

The organizers always maintained the festival was intended for women-born women (Vogel, 2014). In 1991, a transwoman had been asked to leave Michfest. Shortly thereafter, trans-activists in protest formed Camp-Trans, located across from the festival (Kendall, 2013). Over the years, many women musicians withdrew from the festival, and 40 years after it began, the Michigan Womyn's Festival held its last event in 2015.

LIFESPAN INFLUENCES

As previously discussed in this chapter, the individual development of lesbian lives is positioned in the context of sexism and heterosexism. Research regarding lesbian lives is a rather recent phenomenon. Lesbians experience many of the same lifespan risks as their heterosexual counterparts, including potential victimization due to bullying or intimate partner violence, and issues surrounding death and dying. They also share some of the potential joys including finding love, entering into long-term committed relationships, and enjoying close friendships. Other issues are specific to lesbians, including identity development and coming out processes. This section reviews the current literature as it informs best practices with lesbian clients.

CHILDHOOD AND ADOLESCENCE

Developing a healthy identity is a challenging task and is even more demanding for marginalized individuals. For female adolescents who identify as lesbian or are questioning their sexual orientation, there are additional hurdles. For many young women, adolescence is marked with close friendships, dating, and intimate relationships. However, being an out or questioning lesbian teen can alter the experience. These adolescent women may experience social isolation due to their experiences with oppression and discrimination (Bedard & Marks, 2010). Social work practitioners must be knowledgeable about the similarities and differences between heterosexual and lesbian youth to better enable them to build effective therapeutic alliances.

IDENTITY DEVELOPMENT AND COMING OUT

Identity development is one of the most critical tasks of adolescence. The formation and integration of a lesbian identity can be complicated and includes biological, psychological, and sociocultural processes. Early models of lesbian development discussed identity formation and integration as linear processes. Cass (1979) described this progression as recognizing, accepting, and ultimately affirming one's sexual orientation in six discrete stages. More recent models conceptualize sexual identity development as a continuous process, recognizing the influence of historical and cultural context (Parks & Hughes, 2007). The coming out process varies for lesbians and often happens at different developmental stages, not simply in adolescence. The decision to disclose one's sexual orientation varies by age, perceived social supports, geography, race/ethnicity, and religious/spiritual beliefs. For example, compared to White lesbians, African American and Latina females experience significant barriers disclosing their sexual orientation (Riley, 2010).

McCarn and Fassinger (1996) proposed a more inclusive model of lesbian development, distinguishing between individual identity and group identity. Phase one is described as one of awareness of one's own attraction to other women and recognition of the existence of lesbian women. This is followed by the second phase of exploration, where women examine their feelings for other women and relationships to the lesbian community. The next phase, deepening/commitment, allows the woman to internalize her identity as a lesbian and commit to the lesbian community. Finally, the internalization and synthesis phase is marked by merging her lesbian identity with her overall identity, coupled with her ability to maintain her identity as a lesbian across contexts. This conceptualization allows for women's individual and group identity occurring at different times and acknowledges cultural background.

Baiocco and colleagues (2015) surveyed 219 lesbian, gay, and bisexual youth. They reported parents' strong religious beliefs coupled with highly conservative political attitudes predicted negative outcomes for lesbian adolescents' disclosure of sexual orientation. High levels of depression and low self-esteem are associated with negative reactions to disclosure of sexual orientation (D'amico, Julien, Tremblay, & Chartrand, 2015; Ryan, Legate, & Weinstein, 2015; Solomon, McAbee, Åsberg, & McGee, 2015). Ultimately, social workers can assist parents, siblings, and others to better support lesbian youth throughout their identity development across the lifespan, as well as their coming out experiences.

BULLYING

School bullying is an extensive problem for children and youth. This victimization includes verbal harassment, intimidation, taunting, and threats of and actual physical violence. Lesbian-identified adolescents are significantly more at risk for bullying than their straight-identified peers. According to a recent national survey of 1,732 LGBT students between the ages of 13 and 20, more than half of lesbian adolescents reported feeling unsafe in school. Nearly three-quarters of those responding had experienced verbal abuse and over one-third had been victims of physical aggression due to their sexual orientation (Kosciw, Greytak, Palmer, & Boesen, 2014).

Victimization due to bullying leads to a myriad of negative outcomes, including depression, anxiety, low self-esteem, and frequent absences from school (Greene, Britton, & Fitts, 2014). For many, these adverse consequences continue long after high school graduation. The negative effects for lesbians are more pronounced than for their heterosexual peers. Often, these young women choose not to share their experience with parents or teachers due to perceived intolerance. Teachers and school administrators do not intervene, even when directly observing harassment of gay and lesbian students (Elze, 2003). The implicit message is "bullying *is* tolerated here." Social workers can directly intervene with lesbian high school students to assist them in managing the effects of bullying. In the same regard, social workers are also well positioned to advocate for institutional change within school systems and districts. School social workers can directly intervene with administration and faculty to develop and reinforce policies of zero tolerance for queer bullying (Mishna, Newman, Daley, & Solomon, 2009).

DATING AND RELATIONSHIPS

Romantic relationships during adolescence are essential to positive identity development. Dating provides young women with opportunities to explore sexual and emotional intimacy. Successful dating in adolescence is associated with improved interpersonal skills, including effective negotiation and communicating, throughout the lifespan (Furman & Shaffer, 2003). These relationships are of particular importance to young lesbian women who confront additional challenges to identity formation due to their oppressed status (Bauermeister et al., 2010). Lesbian adolescents may face increased challenges due to a limited pool of potential dating partners, especially if they reside in rural areas or communities without LGBTQ supports. In addition to the anxiety and fear of rejection accompanying asking someone out, lesbian women may worry about whether the potential romantic partner is of the same sexual orientation (Chorney & Morris, 2008). Further, if they are able to find young women to date, they are at risk for harassment and potential violence, requiring them to hide their relationships from others (Elze, 2002).

Marginalized youth may be at heightened risk of intimate partner violence. Such violence within dating relationships can include emotional, sexual, and physical abuse. Dank, Lachman, Zweig, and Yahner (2014) surveyed 5,647 adolescents across 10 schools and found lesbian teens were at significant increased risk of being victims and/or perpetrators of all forms of dating violence. Social workers should also be cognizant of a particular type of emotional threat particular to those in same-sex relationships. Lesbian teens are at risk for being "outed" by a partner or former partner. When lesbians do recognize partner violence, they may be less likely to seek services due to fear of rejection by service providers (Luo, Stone, & Tharp, 2014).

Social work practitioners can support young lesbians with successfully negotiating dating and relationships. They also may advocate for services promoting physical, sexual, and emotional health. For example, social workers may facilitate relationship enhancing skills groups for lesbian teens (Starks, Newcomb, & Mustanski, 2015). Many lesbian teens meet potential dating partners in organized environments, including recreational settings, such as softball or summer camp. In addition, social workers can discuss online safety. Service providers can also evaluate the efficacy of these programs in facilitating peer and romantic relationship development.

ADULTHOOD

Adulthood is generally believed to span from the late teenage years until the mid-60s. During this time, individuals experience biological, psychological, and social changes, including the completion of formal education, financial independence, and choice of a partner. Lesbian development occurs in the sociocultural context of oppression and thus continues to affect lesbian-identified women throughout adulthood. Discrimination in terms of culture and various social policies may negatively impact lesbian adult social and psychological growth. For example, although one in four lesbians experience workplace discrimination, there remains no federal protection for these employees (Sears & Mallory, 2013). Working-class lesbians are especially at risk for workplace harassment (Gates & Mitchell, 2013). Social workers must be knowledgeable about the cultural and policy issues to competently practice with lesbian adults.

PARTNERSHIP/MARRIAGE

As previously discussed, federal marriage equality in the United States is a very recent occurrence. However, lesbian women have entered into long-term committed partnerships for centuries. Heterosexual and lesbian dating and partnership patterns are alike in some ways and different in others. Lesbian romantic relationships are similar to those of heterosexuals with regard to intimacy, conflict resolution, expression of feelings, and satisfaction (Markey, Markey, Nave, & August, 2014). Due to differences in social norms, being single is not the same experience for straight and lesbian women (Kertzner, 2007). Relationship dynamics and family structures may also be dissimilar. Unable to rely on socially constructed gender roles, lesbian women report equal division of household chores and finances (Esmail, 2010). Unlike heterosexual couples, lesbians in partnerships agree about the value of talking and sharing intimate thoughts and report greater intimacy and compatibility (Gotta et al., 2011). Social work practitioners must understand the similarities and differences between heterosexual and lesbian unions to deliver premarital counseling, couples therapy, and other culturally competent interventions.

BUILDING FAMILIES

The definition of the American family is no longer limited to the heteronormative, two heterosexual parent varieties. Lesbian-headed families are included among the diverse constellations now considered to be nuclear family units. Although gay men and lesbians have been rearing children for centuries, these families have become increasingly more visible over the past several decades. Children raised by lesbian mothers are either born in heterosexual relationships or are planned in the context of existing same-sex relationships through adoption or donor insemination. Lesbians wanting biological children with their female partners must make deliberate decisions regarding which woman would become pregnant, using anonymous or known donors, and so on.

Several studies have explored parenting practices and parenting roles among lesbian mothers. In their study of adoptive parents, Farr and Patterson (2013) studied 104 adoptive families and found, when compared to gay male and heterosexual couples, lesbian partners were the most supportive of one another and shared household and child rearing tasks more equitably. Lesbian mothers of children born via donor insemination were also more egalitarian in sharing labor than heterosexual parents (Patterson, Sutfin, & Fulcher, 2004).

Children of lesbian mothers do not seem to differ from those parented by heterosexuals. Golombok, Spencer, and Rutter (2003) reported on the quality of parent and child relationships and the social and emotional development of seven-year-old children raised by 27 lesbian-headed families. They obtained parent and teacher ratings, as well as the children's reports on standardized instruments. They found no significant differences in the social and emotional development of children of lesbian mothers when compared to those with heterosexual parents. Wainwright, Russell, and Patterson (2004) looked at a wide array of outcomes for 44 adolescent children of same-sex couples. They found that adolescents raised in gay and lesbian households were not significantly different in personal and school adjustment than their counterparts in heterosexual households. Specifically, self-esteem, anxiety, depressive symptoms, academic achievement, autonomy, and peer relationships did not differ by family type. Adolescents raised by lesbian mothers scored significantly higher on social and academic measures, higher in self-esteem, and lower in aggressive and externalizing behaviors than their peers raised by heterosexual parents (Bos, Gelderen, & Gartrell, 2015). A meta-analysis of 33 studies found adults who were reared in lesbian-headed households were more tolerant of diversity and less likely to adhere to gender stereotypes (Biblarz & Stacey, 2010).

HEALTH AND MENTAL HEALTH

Individuals who are part of marginalized groups are at increased risk for physical health, mental health, and addiction issues. While lesbians share health risks with heterosexually identified women, there are certain factors that uniquely influence their health. For example, while heart disease is the number one killer of women, lesbians are at increased risk, due to certain lifestyle issues, including obesity, tobacco use, and lack of exercise (Hunte & Williams, 2009). Lesbians are also at heightened risk of reproductive cancers, including breast, ovarian, and endometrial cancers (Zaritsky & Dibble, 2010). This increased risk is believed to be related to null parity (never giving birth) and, for those choosing to have children, older age at first birth (Clavelle, King, Bazzi, Fein-Zachary, & Potter, 2015). These health disparities may well be multiplied for women marginalized due to race/ethnicity. In addition, lesbian-identified women may be more reluctant to seek preventative health care due to concerns around heterosexist attitudes of medical professionals. Barriers to care include availability of culturally competent services, lack of availability of care, and financial issues.

The prejudice and discrimination experienced by lesbians in their daily lives make them vulnerable to increased mental health and substance use disorders. Compared to heterosexual women, lesbian women have higher rates of depression, suicidal ideation, nonsuicidal self-injury, and actual suicide attempts (Blosnich & Andersen, 2015; Kerr, Santurri, & Peters, 2013). Lesbians with depression, anxiety, bipolar disorder, and other issues are also at risk of dual stigmas. Specifically, they are in danger of discrimination from the mental health community due to sexual orientation and from the lesbian community due to emotional and behavioral health issues. Lesbians of color experience multiple stressors due to intersections of identity, including racism within the lesbian community and heterosexism within communities of color. However, there are few differences between White and racially/ethnically diverse lesbians with regard to mental health risk (Balsam et al., 2015).

Lesbians are also at risk for increased use of alcohol, tobacco, and other drugs. Kerby, Wilson, Nicholson, and White (2005) found high rates of alcohol use among 76 lesbian respondents with nearly half reporting daily use. Lesbians begin drinking at earlier ages, and the odds of substance misuse are more than four times greater than their heterosexual counterparts (Litt, Lewis, Blayney, & Kaysen, 2013). Social work interventions with lesbian-identified women need to consider the context of bar culture within the community and assist clients in developing alternative social strategies. For example, clients could be directed to LGBTQ Internet sites and social media resources promoting sobriety strategies and support.

AGING

The needs of older lesbians are rarely addressed in the professional literature. These women are challenged by the intersection of heterosexism, sexism, and ageism. Social networks provide beneficial resources for successful aging and well-being, and, for heterosexual elders, most support comes from family related through blood or marriage. Older lesbians, however, rely on partners and friends for assistance. Lesbian seniors are more likely to live alone and often do not have children to emotionally and socially support them. In addition, they tend to have less contact with siblings and extended family. Grossman and colleagues (2014) found such barriers to social support negatively influenced successful aging, while placing older lesbians at risk for self-neglect.

Similar to their younger counterparts, elder lesbians are more likely to use tobacco, excessively drink alcohol, and suffer from obesity than heterosexual women. These risky health behaviors are related to overall poor health, including high rates of cardiovascular disease and diabetes (Fredriksen-Goldsen, Hyun-Jun, Barkan, Muraco, & Hoy-Ellis, 2013). Although elder lesbians have significant risk factors, they also are quite resilient. For example, more than 80% of lesbian older adults report engagement in regular wellness activities and almost half attend some type of religious service at least monthly (Hillman, & Hinrichsen, 2014). Social work practitioners can build upon these strengths and encourage continued connections with "chosen" family, as well as offer support services for caregivers. In addition, social workers are obligated to educate healthcare providers about issues specific to lesbian elders to improve access to care.

SOCIAL WORK PRACTICE CONSIDERATIONS

Competent social workers demonstrate the knowledge, values, skills, and cognitive/affective processes to practice with diverse populations. The gay affirmative practice model outlines guidelines for culturally competent micro, mezzo, and macro interventions with lesbian clients. For example, social workers are encouraged to not assume heterosexuality when engaging clients and recognize their own attitudes and biases toward LGBTQ individuals. In addition, adept professionals are aware that heterosexism is the problem, not the client's sexual orientation (Appleby & Anastas,

1998; Van Den Berg & Crisp, 2004). Thus gay affirmative practitioners can provide protection against potential negative consequences for LGBTQ individuals.

This chapter has reviewed historical and sociocultural information informing the lives of lesbians, as well as lifespan considerations. In addition to deepening their knowledge of contexts influencing lesbians and issues unique to LGBTQ clients, social workers must examine their own values. The following sections highlight micro, mezzo, and macro practice interventions with lesbian client systems.

MICRO-PRACTICE CONSIDERATIONS

Individual practice does not occur in a vacuum. Social workers can assist lesbian clients by acknowledging heterosexist and sexist impacts. One way to do so is to increase comfort by making sure certain language on intake forms are devoid of heterosexual language, such as asking about relationship instead of marital status. Private practitioners can add lesbian-friendly magazines or feminist newsletters to waiting-room areas. School social workers can be sensitive to the needs of adolescents struggling with issues related to coming out to family and peers. Child welfare workers can advocate for lesbian couples wanting to adopt. Most important, social workers should seek peer consultation and supervision to reduce chances of microaggressions in working with lesbian clients.

MEZZO-PRACTICE CONSIDERATIONS

Group work provides individuals with opportunities to help one another, validation and normalization of difficult issues, and the ability to learn from and obtain immediate feedback from peers. Group intervention benefit lesbian clients across the lifespan. For example, group treatment can assist gay and lesbian youth by affording the opportunity to meet others and successfully navigate identity conflicts (Yarhouse & Beckstead, 2011). Craig, Austin, and McInroy (2014) found significant increases in self-esteem and coping among the 263 multiethnic gay and lesbian adolescent participants in a school-based support group. Social workers can provide group therapy to survivors of same-sex intimate partner violence. In addition, practitioners could facilitate support groups for lesbian widows.

MACRO-PRACTICE CONSIDERATIONS

Competent social workers are cognizant of historical and current social policies and are obligated to advocate for policies advancing social and economic justice (Council on Social Work Education, 2015). Although the recent Supreme Court decision endorsed marriage equality, policies prohibiting the rights of LGBT individuals are still in place. Social workers should advocate for equity. The lack of federal employment protection places lesbians at financial risk. The Fair Housing Act does not specifically include sexual orientation as a protected status. Immigration and refugee reform is needed to assist lesbians and gay men to successfully traverse the migration and citizenship procedures.

Social work practitioners should advocate for antidiscrimination laws on the state and local levels as well. Practitioners have an ethical obligation to advocate for legislation promoting equity and against legislation in discordance with the National Association of Social Workers Code of Ethics. Effective social workers across all levels of practice should promote affirming agency policies, services, and programs. For example, school social workers can promote gay–straight alliances and lavender proms. Practitioners in health/mental health agencies serving LGBTQ individuals should actively champion increased funding for services.

CONCLUSION

Social workers providing services to lesbians should be cognizant of the risks to their successful development, while affirming and supporting these women in individual, couple, family, group, or community interventions. Additionally, social workers are obligated to vigorously advocate for policies promoting social and economic justice in schools, social service organizations, as well as local, state, and federal governmental entities. Further, ethical social work practice requires self-awareness and willingness to seek supervision to assist with biases that may negatively impact work with lesbian clients. Practitioners should also use an intersectional lens to understand the multiple disenfranchisements for lesbian women of color, working-class or impoverished lesbians, lesbians with disabilities, lesbians who do not identify as Christian, and older lesbian women. In this way, social work professionals can provide lesbian clients a safe and nurturing environment in which they may reach their full potential.

REFERENCES

American Civil Liberties Union. (2016). *LGBT rights on the docket*. Retrieved from http://www.acluohio.org/archives/cases/obergefell-v-hodges

Appleby, G. A. & Anastas, J. W. (1998). *Not just a passing phase: Social work with gay, lesbian, and bisexual people*. New York: Columbia University Press.

Baiocco, R., Fontanesi, L., Santamaria, F., Ioverno, S., Marasco, B., Baumgartner, E., . . . Laghi, F. (2015). Negative parental responses to coming out and family functioning in a sample of lesbian and gay young adults. *Journal of Child & Family Studies, 24*(5), 1490–1500. doi:10.1007/s10826-014-9954-z

Balsam, K. F., Molina, Y., Blayney, J. A., Dillworth, T., Zimmerman, L., & Kaysen, D. (2015). Racial/ethnic differences in identity and mental health outcomes among young sexual minority women. *Cultural Diversity & Ethnic Minority Psychology, 21*(3), 380–390. doi:10.1037/a0038680

Barefoot, K. N., Smalley, K. B., & Warren, J. C. (2015). Psychological distress and perceived barriers to care for rural lesbians. *Journal of Gay & Lesbian Mental Health, 19*(4), 347–369. doi:10.1080/19359705.2015.1041629

Bauermeister, J. A., Johns, M. M., Sandfort, T. M., Eisenberg, A., Grossman, A. H., & D'Augelli, A. R. (2010). Relationship trajectories and psychological well-being among sexual minority youth. *Journal of Youth & Adolescence, 39*(10), 1148–1163. doi:10.1007/s10964-010-9557-y

Bedard, K. K., & Marks, A. K. (2010). Current psychological perspectives on adolescent lesbian identity development. *Journal of Lesbian Studies, 14*(1), 16–25. doi:10.1080/10894160903058857

Belkin, A. & Bateman, G. (2003). *Don't ask, don't tell: Debating the gay ban in the military.* London: Lynne Rienner.

Biblarz, T. J., & Stacey, J. (2010). How does the gender of parents matter? *Journal of Marriage and Family, 72*(1), 3–22.

Blosnich, J., & Andersen, J. (2015). Thursday's child: The role of adverse childhood experiences in explaining mental health disparities among lesbian, gay, and bisexual US adults. *Social Psychiatry & Psychiatric Epidemiology, 50*(2), 335–338. doi:10.1007/s00127-014-0955-4

Bos, H., Gelderen, L., & Gartrell, N. (2015). Lesbian and heterosexual two-parent families: Adolescent-parent relationship quality and adolescent well-being. *Journal of Child & Family Studies, 24*(4), 1031–1046. doi:10.1007/s10826-014-9913-8

Bronfenbrenner, U. (1977). Toward an experimental ecology of human development. *American Psychologist, 32*(7), 513–531.

Bronfenbrenner, U. (1979). *The ecology of human development.* Cambridge, MA: Harvard University Press.

Cass, V.C. (1979). Homosexual identity formation: A theoretical model. *Journal of Homosexuality, 4*(3), 219–235.

Chorney, D. B., & Morris, T. L. (2008). The changing face of dating anxiety: Issues in assessment with special populations. *Clinical Psychology: Science & Practice, 15*(3), 224–238. doi:10.1111/j.1468-2850.2008.00132.x

Clavelle, K., King, D., Bazzi, A. R., Fein-Zachary, V., & Potter, J. (2015). Breast cancer risk in sexual minority women during routine screening at an urban LGBT health center. *Women's Health Issues, 25*(4), 341–348. doi:10.1016/j.whi.2015.03.014

Connell, C. (2015). Right to serve or responsibility to protect? Civil rights framing and the DADT repeal. *Boston University Law Review, 95*(3), 1015–1028.

Council on Social Work Education. (2015). *Educational policy and accreditation standards.* Washington, DC: Author.

Craig, S., Austin, A., & McInroy, L. (2014). School-based groups to support multiethnic sexual minority youth resiliency: Preliminary effectiveness. *Child & Adolescent Social Work Journal, 31*(1), 87–106. doi:10.1007/s10560-013-0311-7

D'amico, E., Julien, D., Tremblay, N., & Chartrand, E. (2015). Gay, lesbian, and bisexual youths coming out to their parents: Parental reactions and youths' outcomes. *Journal of GLBT Family Studies, 11*(5), 411–437.

Dank, M., Lachman, P., Zweig, J., & Yahner, J. (2014). Dating violence experiences of lesbian, gay, bisexual, and transgender youth. *Journal of Youth & Adolescence, 43*(5), 846–857. doi:10.1007/s10964-013-9975-8

Elze, D. E. (2002). Against all odds: The dating experiences of adolescent lesbian and bisexual women. *Journal of Lesbian Studies, 6*(1), 17–29.

Elze, D. E. (2003) Gay, lesbian, and bisexual youths' perceptions of their high school environments and comfort in school. *Children & Schools, 25*(4), 225–239.

Esmail, A. (2010). Negotiating fairness: A study on how lesbian family members evaluate, construct, and maintain fairness with the division of household labor. *Journal of Homosexuality, 57*(5), 591–609. doi:10.1080/00918361003711881

Faderman, L. (1982). *Surpassing the love of men: Romantic friendship and love between women from the renaissance to the present.* New York: William Morrow.

Farmer, G. W., Blosnich, J. R., Jabson, J. M., & Matthews, D. D. (2016). Gay acres: Sexual orientation differences in health indicators among rural and non-rural individuals. *The Journal of Rural Health, 32*(3), 321–331. doi:10.1111/jrh.12161

Farr, R. H., & Patterson, C. (2013). Co-parenting among lesbian, gay, and heterosexual couples: Associations with adopted children's outcomes. *Child Development, 84*(4), 1226–1240.

Fraser, M. W., Kirby, I. D., & Smokowski, P. R. (2004). Risk and resilience in childhood. In M. W. Fraser (Ed.), *Risk and resilience in childhood: An ecological perspective* (pp.13–66). Washington, DC: NASW Press.

Fredriksen-Goldsen, K. I., Hyun-Jun, K., Barkan, S. E., Muraco, A., & Hoy-Ellis, C. P. (2013). Health disparities among lesbian, gay, and bisexual older adults: Results from a population-based study. *American Journal of Public Health, 103*(10), 1802–1809. doi:10.2105/AJPH.2012.301110

Friedman, R. C., & Downey, J. I. (1998). Psychoanalysis and the model of homosexuality as pathology: A historical overview. *The American Journal of Psychoanalysis, 58*, 249–270.

Furman, W., & Shaffer, L. (2003). The role of romantic relationships in adolescent development. In P. Florsheim (Ed.), *Adolescent romantic relations and sexual behavior: theory, research, and practical implications* (pp. 3–22). Mahwah, NJ: Lawrence Erlbaum.

Gates, T. G., & Mitchell, C. G. (2013). Workplace stigma-related experiences among lesbian, gay, and bisexual workers: Implications for social policy and practice. *Journal of Workplace Behavioral Health, 28*(3), 159–171. doi:10.1080/15555240.2013.808066

Glick, P., & Fiske, S. T. (2001). An ambivalent alliance: Hostile and benevolent sexism as contemporary justifications for gender inequality. *American Psychologist, 56*(1), 109–118.

Golombok, S., Spencer, A., & Rutter, M. (2003). Children in lesbian and single-parent households: Psychosexual and psychiatric appraisal. *Journal of Child Psychology and Psychiatry, 24*, 551–572.

Gotta, G., Green, R., Rothblum, E., Solomon, S., Balsam, K., & Schwartz, P. (2011). Heterosexual, lesbian, and gay male relationships: A comparison of couples in 1975 and 2000. *Family Process, 50*(3), 353–376. doi:10.1111/j.1545-5300.2011.01365.x

Greene, D. C., Britton, P. J., & Fitts, B. (2014). Long-term outcomes of lesbian, gay, bisexual, and transgender recalled school victimization. *Journal of Counseling & Development, 92*(4), 406–417. doi:10.1002/j.1556-6676.2014.00167.x

Grossman, A. H., Frank, J. A., Graziano, M. J., Narozniak, D. R., Mendelson, G., El Hassan, D., & Patouhas, E. S. (2014). Domestic harm and neglect among lesbian, gay, and bisexual older adults. *Journal of Homosexuality, 61*(12), 1649–1666. doi:10.1080/00918369.2014.951216

Herek, G. M. (2004). Beyond homophobia: Thinking about sexual prejudice and stigma in the twenty-first century. *Journal of Sexuality Research and Social Policy, 1*, 6–24.

Hillman, J., & Hinrichsen, G. A. (2014). Promoting an affirming, competent practice with older lesbian and gay adults. *Professional Psychology: Research & Practice, 45*(4), 269–277. doi:10.1037/a0037172

Hunte, H. E., & Williams, D. R. (2009). The association between perceived discrimination and obesity in a population-based multiracial and multiethnic adult sample. *American Journal of Public Health, 99*(7), 1285–1292. doi.org/10.2105/AJPH.2007.128090

Hutchison, B. (2015). Lesbian blood drives as community-building activism in the 1980s. *Journal of Lesbian Studies, 19*(1), 117–128. doi:10.1080/10894160.2015.968079

Institute for Women's Policy Research. (2015). *The gender wage gap by occupation fact sheet and by race and ethnicity.* Retrieved from www.iwpr.org/pdf/C350a.pdf

Johnson, D. K. (2004). *The lavender scare: The Cold War persecution of gays and lesbians in the federal government.* Chicago: University of Chicago Press.

Kahn, R. (2014). Understanding *United States v. Windsor* and the symposium contributions using unidirectional and bidirectional models of Supreme Court decision making. *Case Western Reserve Law Review, 64*(4), 1293–1339.

Kendall, L. (2013). *The Michigan Womyn's Music Festival: An amazon matrix of meaning.* Baltimore, MD: Spiral Womyn's Press.

Kerr, D. L., Santurri, L., & Peters, P. (2013). A comparison of lesbian, bisexual, and heterosexual college undergraduate women on selected mental health issues. *Journal of American College Health, 61*(4), 185–194. doi:10.1080/07448481.2013.787619

Kerby, M. B., & Mallinger, G. (2014). Beyond sustainability: A new conceptual model. *eJournal of Public Affairs, 3*(2), 1–18.

Kerby, M., Wilson, R., Nicholson, T., & White, J. B. (2005). Substance use and social identity in the lesbian community. *Journal of Lesbian Studies, 9*(3), 45–56.

Kertzner, R. M. (2007). Developmental issues in lesbian and gay adulthood. In I. H. Meyer & M. E. Northridge (Eds.), *The health of sexual minorities: Public health perspectives on lesbian, gay, bisexual, and transgender populations* (pp. 48–64). New York: Springer.

Kosciw, J. G.; Greytak, E. A.; Palmer, N. A.; Boesen, M. J. (2014). *The 2013 national school climate survey: The experiences of lesbian, gay, bisexual and transgender youth in our nation's schools.* New York: GLSEN.

Lind, A. (2004). Legislating the family: Heterosexual bias in social welfare policy frameworks. *Journal of Sociology and Social Welfare, 31*(4), 21–35.

Litt, D. M., Lewis, M. A., Blayney J. A., & Kaysen, D. L. (2013). Protective behavioral strategies as a mediator of the generalized anxiety and alcohol use relationship among lesbian and bisexual women. *Journal of Studies on Alcohol & Drugs, 74*(1), 168–174

Luo, F., Stone, D. M., & Tharp, A. T. (2014). Physical dating violence victimization among sexual minority youth. *American Journal of Public Health, 104*(10), e66–e73. doi:10.2105/AJPH.2014.302051

Markey, P., Markey, C., Nave, C., & August, K. (2014). Interpersonal problems and relationship quality: An examination of gay and lesbian romantic couples. *Journal of Research in Personality, 51*, 1–8. doi:10.1016/j.jrp.2014.04.001

McCarn, S. R., & Fassinger, R. E. (1996). Revisioning sexual minority identity formation: A new model of lesbian identity and its implications for counseling and research. *The Counseling Psychologist, 24*(3), 508–534.

McCarthy, L. (2000). Poppies in a wheat field: Exploring the lives of rural lesbians. *Journal of Homosexuality, 39*(1), 75–94.

McConnell, E. A., Odahl-Ruan, C. A., Kozlowski, C., Shattell, M., & Todd, N. R. (2016). Transwomen and Michfest: An ethnophenomenology of attendees' experiences. *Journal of Lesbian Studies, 20*(1), 8–28. doi:10.1080/10894160.2015.1076234

Meijering, L., Huigen, P., & Van Hoven, B. (2007). Intentional communities in rural spaces. *Journal of Economic and Social Geography, 98*(1), 42–52. doi:10.1111/j.1467-9663.2007.00375.x

Miller, N. (1995). *Out of the past: Gay and lesbian history from 1869 to the present.* London: Vintage Press.

Mishna, F., Newman, P. A., Daley, A., & Solomon, S. (2009). Bullying of lesbian and gay youth: A qualitative investigation. *British Journal of Social Work, 39*(8), 1598–1614.

Morris, B. J. (2000). *Eden built by eves: The culture of women's music festivals.* New York: Alyson Books.

Oswald, R. F., & Culton, L. S. (2003). Under the rainbow: Rural gay life and its relevance for family providers. *Family Relations: An Interdisciplinary Journal of Applied Family Studies, 52*(1), 72–81.

Parks, C., & Hughes, T. L. (2007). Age differences in lesbian identity development and drinking, *Substance Use and Misuse, 42*(2-3), 361–380. doi:10.1080/10826080601142097

Patterson, C. J., Sutfin, E. L., & Fulcher, M. (2004). Division of labor among lesbian and heterosexual parenting couples: Correlates of specialized versus shared patterns. *Journal of Adult Development, 11*, 179–189.

Pharr, S. (1997). *Homophobia: A weapon of sexism.* Berkeley, CA: Chardon Press.

Poirot, K. (2009). Domesticating the liberated woman: Containment rhetorics of second wave radical/lesbian feminism. *Women's Studies in Communication, 32*(3), 263–292.

Puckett, J. A., Horne, S. G., Levitt, H. M., & Reeves, T. (2011). Out in the country: Rural sexual minority mothers. *Journal of Lesbian Studies, 15*(2), 176–186. doi:10.1080/10894160.2011.521101

Riley, B. H. (2010). GLB adolescent's "coming out." *Journal of Child and Adolescent Psychiatric Nursing, 23*(1), 3–10. doi:10.1111/j.1744-6171.2009.00210.x

Rimmerman, C. A. (2013). *Gay rights, military wrongs: Political perspectives of lesbians and gays in the military.* New York: Routledge.

Ryan, W. S., Legate, N., & Weinstein, N. (2015). Coming out as lesbian, gay, or bisexual: The lasting impact of initial disclosure experiences. *Self and Identity, 14*(5), 549–569. doi:10.1080/15298868.2015.1029516

Samek, A. A. (2015). Pivoting between identity politics and coalitional relationships: Lesbian-feminist resistance to the woman-identified woman. *Women's Studies in Communication, 38*(4), 393–420. doi:10.1080/07491409.2015.1085938

Scasta, D. (1998). Historical perspectives on homosexuality. *Journal of Gay and Lesbian Psychotherapy, 2,* 3–18.

Schmid, S. (2015). Income tax treatment of same-sex couples: *Windsor v. State Marriage Bans. Marquette Law Review, 98*(4), 1805–1840.

Sears, B., & Mallory, C. (2013). *Documented evidence of employment discrimination and its effects on LGBT people.* Retrieved from http://williamsinstitute.law.ucla.edu/research/workplace/documentedevidence-of-employment-discrimination-its-effects-on-lgbt-people/#sthash.nIfYxEtC.dpuf

Solomon, D., McAbee, J., Åsberg, K., & McGee, A. (2015). Coming out and the potential for growth in sexual minorities: The role of social reactions and internalized homonegativity. *Journal of Homosexuality, 62*(11), 1512–1538. doi:10.1080/00918369.2015.1073032

Starks, T., Newcomb, M., & Mustanski, B. (2015). A longitudinal study of interpersonal relationships among lesbian, gay, and bisexual adolescents and young adults: Mediational pathways from attachment to romantic relationship quality. *Archives of Sexual Behavior, 44*(7), 1821–1831. doi:10.1007/s10508-015-0492-6

Sue, D. W., Capodilupo, C. M., Torino, G. C., Bucceri, J. M., Holder, A. B., Nadal, K. L., & Esquilin, M. (2007). Racial microaggressions in everyday life. *American Psychologist, 62*(4), 271–286. doi:10.103770003-066X.624.271

Sullivan, M. (2004). *The family of women.* Berkley: University of California Press.

Swank, E., Frost, D. M., & Fahs, B. (2012). Rural location and exposure to minority stress among sexual minorities in the United States. *Psychology and Sexuality, 3*(3), 226–243. doi:10.1080/19419899.2012.700026

Trigilio, J. (2016). Complicated and messy politics of inclusion: Michfest and the Boston Dyke March. *Journal of Lesbian Studies, 20*(2), 234–250. doi:10.1080/10894160.2016.1083835

Van Den Berg, N., & Crisp, C. (2004). Defining culturally competent practice with sexual minorities: Implications for social work education and practice. *Journal of Social Work Education, 40*(2), 221–238.

Vogel, L. (August 1, 2014). *Michfest response to equality Michigan's call for boycott.* (Press release by Michigan Womyn's Music Festival).

Wainwright, J. L., Russell, S.T., & Patterson, C. J. (2004). Psychosocial adjustment, school outcomes, and romantic relationships of adolescents with same-sex parents. *Child Development, 75*(6), 1886–1898.

Yarhouse, M. A., & Beckstead, A. L. (2011). Using group therapy to navigate and resolve sexual orientation and religious conflicts. *Counseling & Values, 56*(1/2), 96–120.

Zaritsky, E., & Dibble, S. L. (2010). Risk factors for reproductive and breast cancers among older lesbians. *Journal of Women's Health, 19*(1), 125–131. doi:10.1089/jwh.2008.1094

CHAPTER 14

PRACTICE WITH THE GAY MALE COMMUNITY

Michael P. Dentato, Tyler M. Argüello, and Courtney Wilson

INTRODUCTION

Understanding the complex needs of the unique and widely diverse gay male community underscores the importance of practitioners to robustly examine the wide array of sociocultural, lifespan, health and mental health factors. While gay men are a subpopulation of the broader lesbian, gay, bisexual, transgender, and queer (LGBTQ) community, practitioners should realize that they have unique needs associated with their sexual orientation, gender, gender identity, and gender expression sometimes similar to their LBTQ counterparts but often separate from factors that impact LBTQ individuals. In the same fashion, while gay men may encounter similar life challenges as their nongay counterparts separate from some associations with gender and sex, there are clearly unique issues related to their sexual orientation and other intersecting factors (e.g., race and ethnicity, socioeconomic status, religion/spirituality, rural/urban setting, HIV status, etc.). This chapter starts with an examination of the relevant literature associated with cisgender gay men—defined largely as gay men who were born male, ascribe to a male gender and a gay sexual orientation, are not on the transgender spectrum, and do not identify as bisexual or heterosexual. The opening background section explores the relevant literature on this community while tying in relevant historical and sociological events from the twentieth and twenty-first centuries that have influenced their lives and culture, followed by an examination of lifespan considerations from early school age through older adulthood and death and dying; the impact of dating, marriage, and relationships; culture and subculture factors; various health and mental health needs; and best practice approaches for practitioners in the field of health and mental health and across the related disciplines of social work, mental health counseling, psychology, and other related fields. The chapter focuses on the experiences of cisgender gay men from a Western perspective and by no means is meant to imply that the experiences of gay men across the globe is identical or even similar. While some experiences may be shared (e.g., oppression, violence, coming out, etc.), the severity and significance of challenges for gay men across the world may differ from positive affirmation, complete inclusion, and civil equality within their community to the quite negative and opposite extremes of criminalization, imprisonment, or death solely due to the perception or self-identification as a gay man. Last, the term "gay men" is used throughout this chapter as the term "homosexual" has an often diagnostic, negative, or derogatory connotation, history, and meaning for many gay men. The term "homosexual" is only used when appropriate and due to referenced sources or context.

SOCIOHISTORICAL BACKGROUND

It may be helpful to begin with a discussion centering upon the impact of homophobia and heterosexism upon the lived experiences of gay men. This history chronicles unethical practices, oppression, and mistreatment, sometimes emanating directly from the medical and mental health professions. Progress over the years will also be examined due to activism and other efforts by the lesbian, gay, bisexual, transgender and queer community movement for equality.

HOMOPHOBIA AND HETEROSEXISM

Many gay men experience direct and indirect forms of homophobia while living within a heterosexist society (Pachankis & Goldfried, 2004). Such experiences begin early on and continue for much of their lives. Whether at home with their family of origin or within school settings, the workplace, or the larger community, such experiences can increase the likelihood for vulnerability, trauma, and health/mental health risks as well as heighten internalized homophobia (Miller, 2013). "Homophobia" is defined as the conscious or unconscious yet pervasive fear of homosexuals and can result in verbal and physical aggression against gay men to overt violence or psychological battering (Sears & Williams, 1997). Homophobia can be implicit or explicit, affecting gay men's attitudes about themselves and others, which may ultimately result in the fear of self-disclosure of their sexual orientation or impact their ability to seek relationships and intimacy. Institutionalized forms of homophobia may arise within the workplace or businesses that openly or subtly discriminate against gay men through written and unwritten policies (Giuffre, Dellinger, & Williams, 2008). Internalized homophobia is the process by which gay men may adopt and accept negative feelings and attitudes about themselves or homosexuality, which may manifest itself in many ways including challenges associated with mental health, relationships and intimacy, sexual risk behavior, addiction, suicide ideation, or low self-esteem, among other areas of concern (Herek, Gillis & Cogan, 2009; Meyer, 2003; Williamson, 2000). The terms "heterosexism," "heterocentrism," and "heteronormativity" refer to assumptions and processes that are integrated within mainstream society that imply that people and lifestyles are naturally heterosexual and the normal standard by which members of the LGBTQ community should be understood and evaluated (Herek, 2000; Pachankis & Goldfried, 2004; Shernoff, 2006). Various forms of homophobia, internalized homophobia, and heterosexism can have a huge impact on the health and mental health of gay men. Practitioners must understand and fully explore the history, depth, and relevance of such issues when working with gay men across practice settings.

HISTORY OF OPPRESSION

Gay men have been subject to a long history of oppression that includes institutional, societal, religious, and other forms of stigma imposed by individuals and groups. Several sociohistorical examples follow to underscore the long-term impact of oppression, stigma, and violence on gay men and gay male culture as well as to illustrate how such events have directly affected various age cohorts of gay men across time. While the context of understanding oppression on gay men is important, it should be noted that the gay male community has exhibited an exorbitant amount of collective resilience as a group as well as resilience evidenced through individual experiences. The importance of understanding individual and collective resilience as well as an ability to adapt and cope with oppression, stigma, stress, and minority status are examined later in this chapter.

THE HOLOCAUST

The Nazi occupation of Europe and subsequent extinction of 7 million members of the Jewish community during World War II was a dark time in our world's history that included the arrest, punishment, and death of members of the gay community as well (Grau & Shoppmann, 2013). Individuals identified as homosexual were persecuted as part of the Nazi moral crusade to racially and culturally purify Germany. This persecution ranged from the dismantling of the homosexual press and the closing of bars, clubs, and organizations to the internment of thousands of gay individuals within concentration camps (Grau & Shoppmann, 2013; Vetri, 1998). Gay men, in particular, were subject to harassment, arrest, incarceration, and even castration (Grau & Shoppmann, 2013). Identified by pink triangle badges placed on their prisoner uniforms, gay men were singled out as being sexual deviants (Grau & Shoppmann, 2013; Plant, 2011). The pink triangle (see Appendix A) has since been reclaimed both as a token of remembrance for those gay individuals lost during the Holocaust as well as a symbol of empowerment for the LGBTQ community (Jensen, 2002).

UNETHICAL TREATMENT APPROACHES

During the 1950s and earlier, several behavioral therapies were utilized in conjunction with harmful medical approaches to "cure" or "alter" one's sexual orientation or attraction to the same sex through use of psychopharmacology, electroshock therapy, lobotomies, or medical castration (Berrill & Herek, 1990; Murphy, 1992). The harmful impact of such archaic, violent, and trauma-inducing treatment approaches for gay men clearly resulted in multiple short- and long-term health and mental health challenges. Similarly, modern-day approaches known as conversion or reparative "therapies" have been widely rejected by most professional organizations (Jenkins & Johnston, 2004) across disciplines (e.g., American Psychiatric Association [APA], American Psychological Association, American Counseling Association, American Academy of Pediatrics, American Medical Association, National Association of Social Workers (NASW), Council on Social Work Education, and others). Conversion and reparative approaches are presently against the law in several states including California, Oregon, New Jersey, Illinois, and Washington, D.C. (Shumer, 2014). Further discussion of the negative impact of reparative/conversion "therapies" is provided in this chapter under the section on effective approaches and interventions.

THE STONEWALL REVOLUTION

Discourse centered on the role of such events as the Stonewall revolution in New York City during June of 1969 cannot be overlooked, especially with regard to the impact on gay men and the movement for LGBTQ equality. Many scholars reference the events at Stonewall as the rise of the modern LGBTQ liberation movement promoting tolerance, equality, and resistance to continued oppression to create larger national attention through protest led by LGBTQ individuals (Hall, 2010). The interesting factor about discussing Stonewall is that it lends to differences in understanding the lives of gay men and the impact of living before, during, or after the creation of this civil rights movement lasting through the modern day. While the three days of protest in New York City was predominately led by members of the transgender community along with gay men and lesbians, the long-term impact it has had on progress for LGBTQ civil rights led to the national landmark status of the Stonewall Inn bar to insure its protection and honor (Armstrong & Crage, 2006). The events at Stonewall also led to the broadened visibility of many national LGBTQ organizations including those active throughout the 1950s and 1960s such as the Mattachine Society, Daughters of Bilitis, and Gay Liberation Foundation, while certainly giving cause to modern-day organizations including the Human Rights Campaign, LAMDA Legal, GLAAD, GLSEN, and many others that can be found in Appendix C of this text.

HARVEY MILK

After the events at the Stonewall Inn during the summer of 1969, the movement for LGBTQ equality spread across the United States. Harvey Milk was an openly gay man and activist who relocated from New York City to San Francisco in 1972 and was soon elected to the San Francisco board of supervisors in 1977. Milk not only supported and promoted gay liberation but also emphasized the importance of individual rights and the need for a gay rights city ordinance and helped lead the counterattack to the Briggs Initiative, which failed by voter referendum to remove gay teachers from California's public school system (Hall, 2010). Milk and his ally Mayor George Mascone were assassinated by Dan White, a disgruntled former San Francisco city supervisor in November of 1978. White was acquitted of murder and sentenced for manslaughter due to his attorney's claims that White had eaten too much junk food and could not be held accountable for his crimes, which came to be known as the "Twinkie defense" (Shilts, 1982). The city of San Francisco held a candlelight vigil that soon erupted into civil unrest known as the White Night Riots between upset citizens and the police (Shilts, 1982). Milk's legacy continues on in many ways with the Harvey Milk Foundation run by his family and a school named in his honor for LGBTQ youth in New York City.

DIAGNOSTIC CRITERIA CHANGES

Over the years, the APA has published the *Diagnostic and Statistical Manual of Mental Disorders* (DSM) that assists practitioners across disciplines with understanding a multitude of criteria by which to measure an individual's mental health needs and create a diagnosis to assist with their care. The DSM is widely utilized by the psychiatry, psychology, and social work professions, among others—while it also has recently garnered attention for its notable limitations and flaws by the National Institutes of Mental Health (Carey, 2014). One of the biggest hurdles for the LGBTQ community stems from inclusion of homosexuality in the DSM as a mental disorder. In fact, until the third edition of the DSM was published in 1973, homosexuality was listed as a mental disorder. However with the release of the third edition, a new diagnosis titled "ego-dystonic homosexuality" was created and remained until all references to homosexuality were removed by 1987 (Morin & Rothblum, 1991). Thus the historical impact of the DSM's inclusion of diagnostic criteria labeling homosexuality as a "mental disorder" combined with other forms of societal oppression and stigma stemming from antigay legislation, employment discrimination, family stressors, and other challenges have had a profoundly negative impact on gay men (Atkins, 2003; Weststrate & McLean, 2010; Williams & Freeman, 2007). Additionally, continued challenges related to the DSM remain for members of the transgender community as "gender identity disorder" was changed to "gender dysphoria" with the publishing of the fifth edition of the DSM in 2013 (Duschinsky & Mottier, 2015).

HIV/AIDS AND ACT UP

The impact that the earliest years of the HIV/AIDS epidemic through the 1980s and early 1990s had on gay men cannot be overstated as the disease continues to devastate this minority population of men, especially those within diverse racial/ethnic backgrounds, younger gay men, and those over the age of 50 (Hall, Byers, Ling, & Espinoza, 2007). The first report of five gay men being diagnosed with pneumocystis carinii pneumonia in 1981 from the *Morbidity and Mortality Weekly Report* caused great uncertainty with regard to understanding the origins and transmission of what would ultimately become HIV/AIDS (Sepkowitz, 2001). The early 1980s were a time of great fear, stigma, moral panic, and government inaction while thousands of gay men and others (e.g., hemophiliacs, Haitians, heterosexuals) with HIV/AIDS were dying (Labra, 2015; Weeks, 1989). Potential treatments were withheld due to drug pharmaceutical bureaucracy and financial barriers to treatment and care (Isbell, 1993). This inaction led to the development of community based HIV/AIDS organizations (e.g., Gay Men's Health Crisis in 1981) as well as activist groups including ACT UP in 1987 and Queer Nation in 1990, which organized public protests to raise awareness for those living with and impacted by the epidemic (Haldi, 1999; Lune, 2007). Many gay men, members of the LBTQ community, and their allies became active leaders and members within these organizations. Protest events and marches at the Centers for Disease Control and Prevention, Wall Street, the White House, and throughout major metropolitan areas such as New York City and San Francisco can be ultimately credited with drug pharmaceuticals lowering prices for early treatments such as AZT and the movement for more rapid release of treatments such as antiretroviral therapies (ART) in the mid-1990s (Smith & Siplon, 2006). While ART treatments remain the main approach to treatment and care for those living with HIV, smaller doses taken daily are being used to prevent HIV transmission known as pre-exposure prophylaxis (PrEP; Brooks et al., 2012). Ultimately, the long-term impact of HIV/AIDS among gay men cuts across age cohorts from those that lost many of their best friends, lovers, and partners in the early years, to those that found much hope with new treatments in the mid-1990s, to the newer generations living with HIV long term and asymptomatic and lowering potential for transmission with PrEP. The majority of gay men living today have never truly known a world without HIV/AIDS, which has likely had some impact on shaping their identity, relationships, sex, sexuality, health, and mental health.

DON'T ASK, DON'T TELL, THE DEFENSE OF MARRIAGE ACT, AND MARRIAGE EQUALITY

Two significant challenges for gay men pertained to an inability openly serve as an out gay man in the military and the ability to legally marry rather than commit via domestic partnerships and civil unions. The 1994 Clinton era policy of "Don't Ask, Don't Tell" was meant to protect gay men from coming out or being outed in the military. However, the policy was flawed and often caused a negative or more hostile impact (Knauer, 2009), later to be overturned by the Obama administration in 2011. In the same regard, the Defense of Marriage Act was passed in 1996, which defined marriage as the union of one man and one woman, allowing states to refuse to recognize same-sex marriages granted under the law of other states. While several states provided some form of domestic partnership or civil union (e.g., Vermont, Illinois, and Connecticut) as early as 2000, it was not until the Commonwealth of Massachusetts became the first state to legally sanction same-sex marriage in 2004 that other states would soon follow by enacting either similar legislation for marriage or some form of domestic partnership or civil union (Pierceson, 2014). In 2011, the Obama administration refused to uphold or defend the 1996 Defense of Marriage Act (Elze, 2006; Landau, 2012), and it was ultimately struck down by the US Supreme Court in the 2013 case of *U.S. v. Windsor* (Pierceson, 2014). On June 26, 2015, the US Supreme Court ruled in favor of marriage equality across the 50 states, also ruling in favor of all states recognizing one another's marriage laws (Mills, 2015).

LIFESPAN CONSIDERATIONS

Examining the role of neuroscience upon lifespan development of gay men, as well as looking at specific stages (e.g., childhood, adulthood), may assist with understanding implications for health, wellness, mental health and practice with this diverse community. Understanding elements of intersectionality is often helpful related to sexual orientation, racial/ethnic background, culture and subculture, and sexual risk behavior, among other key areas of concern.

NEUROSCIENCE

The history of scientific inquiry regarding sexuality, including the study of neuroscience and possible biological differences among gay men, has long been fraught with the oppression and subjugation of those who identify as gay. Beginning in the late 1800s and lasting through much of the twentieth century, many individuals belonging to the medical establishment defined unacceptable sexual behaviors, such as homosexuality, as pathological brain disorders (Wolpe, 2004). Using science as justification, doctors and scientists performed castration and lobotomies and used hormonal therapies to "cure" homosexuality (Byne & Lasco, 1999; Wolpe, 2004). Science both reflects and influences culture, and it is important for practitioners to take this into consideration when attempting to find empirical support explaining homosexuality and sexual behavior (Wolpe, 2004). The medical ethicist Paul Wolpe (2002, 2004) suggests that using categories such as "heterosexual" and "homosexual" when researching differences in sexuality is not particularly helpful due to the fact this binary classification system discounts the fluidity of sexual orientation. Scientists have yet to come to a conclusion regarding biological determinants in the development of human sexuality, and the understanding of the human brain is still in its infancy (Byne & Lasco, 1999; Rahman & Wilson 2003). Research focusing on differences between heterosexual and homosexual men has pointed to fraternal birth order, differences and abnormalities in different sections of the brain, and genetic differences in the X chromosome (Rahman & Wilson, 2003). While brain science has been advancing at lightening speeds, it is imperative for scientists and mental health practitioners to reflect on the political, social, and cultural implications created with new research to inform clinical practice.

CHILDHOOD AND ADOLESCENCE

Exploring how gay men experienced childhood and the beginning stages of their sexual orientation may be significant to assist with development of treatment and understanding early experiences of stigma and oppression (Miller, 2013). Norms associated with adolescence, such as dating, mating, social groupings, and status, are framed from a heteronormative perspective and can raise feelings of isolationism and stigmatization for gay men (Miller, 2013). Many gay men have expressed that, as youth, they felt different from their peers and were treated differently by family, peers, and outsiders (D'Augelli, Grossman, & Starks, 2006). A study of 191 gay and bisexual men emphasized the role of childhood experience in the development of their adulthood relationships (Landolt, Bartholomew, Saffrey, Oram, & Perlman, 2004). This study found a significant relationship between childhood rejection and attachment anxiety in adulthood—whereas rejection from parents, siblings, and peers in childhood directly related to higher levels of attachment avoidance in both romantic and platonic relationships (Landolt et al., 2004). All of this research points to the fact that childhood and adolescence is such a pivotal developmental time in a gay man's life: impacted by positive and negative experiences affecting self-image and self-esteem with lasting consequences.

COMING OUT

Once a gay man begins the process of resolving the internal conflict of his sexual orientation being different from that of heterosexuality, the self-disclosure process can begin a process on a path toward full acceptance and integration including among family and friends (Carrioin & Lock, 1997). The disclosure process is a common and important step of the sexual identity development and integration process that occurs over time for most gay men across the lifespan (Grafsky, 2014). The initial coming out process may occur at different times and ages depending on age cohort factors and perceptions of support and safety. Additionally, the process of coming out takes place across time whether in social settings, the workplace, school, a doctor's office, a retirement home, or an assisted living facility. The impact of coming out on family and caregivers should also be considered. Assisting parents and caregivers with their gay son's coming out may be necessary as they may respond and adjust in both supportive and/or negative ways while also have a coming out process themselves (Phillips & Ancis, 2008). A more comprehensive discussion related to understanding the impact of disclosure processes and coming out stages for members of the LGBTQ community may be found in chapter 5 of this text.

BULLYING

Understanding how gay men have experienced bullying in childhood and how these experiences may have influenced their development, self-image, and self-esteem or increased their risk for challenges associated with health (e.g., obesity, smoking, drugs) and mental health (e.g., suicidality, depression) is important. Unfortunately, bullying, which is sometimes referred to as sexual orientation victimization within research literature, is a common childhood occurrence for gay men: research studies have shown that close to 80% of gay men experienced some sort of sexual orientation victimization in childhood. Bullying can arise in differing forms including physical abuse, name-calling, teasing and threats, social exclusion, and rumor spreading (Meneses & Grimm, 2012). The effects of bullying can look different for gay youth than their straight counterparts, due to a lack of support from parents or school personnel (Meneses & Grimm, 2012). The majority of gay males who experience school-based bullying often do not report it to teachers, school administration, or parents (Meneses & Grimm, 2012). Ultimately, the impact of childhood bullying cannot be ignored, as risk for mental health disorders, including suicide and suicide ideation, are high (Meneses & Grimm, 2012).

ADULTHOOD

The role of stigma and discrimination based on sexual orientation and other factors (e.g., HIV, partner, socioeconomic status) may affect gay men throughout adulthood. Living within a heteronormative culture in which expectations for adults include marriage and children, gay men have been historically barred from experiencing such milestones throughout life (Herdt, Beeler, & Rawls, 1997). In their study of lesbian and gay adult males and their development, Herdt et al. emphasized the difficult task faced in overcoming stigma based on sexuality. Further research has shown continued marginalization and oppression based on sexual orientation and the toll this has on individuals who identify as gay. In his research, Weeks (1998) coined the term "sexual citizenship," a phrase used to describe the phenomenon of citizenship being shaped by society's normative and socially accepted sexual behavior, whereby those who do not fit within this construct (e.g., gay men who are not in heteronormative marriages producing children) are consistently devalued and undermined throughout their adulthood. However, changes such as the US Supreme Court ruling on marriage equality, have the ability to completely change the scope of how gay men and their families are perceived and treated. It will be equally important to follow how this ruling at the federal level impacts the lives of adult gay men over time.

Ageism is an important factor to consider when attempting to further understand the life experiences of adult gay males, and the process of aging and the complexities that surround it are another topic of interest in the research literature. Herdt et al. (1997) found that many gay men have a significant loss of self-esteem as they age. This loss of self-esteem can be attributed to many factors. Some research has shown that the value of youth and beauty is prized higher in gay culture than in dominating cultures (Dorfman et al., 1995). In the same regard, while previous studies found large differences in societal acceptance of gay males, with those age 50 and older least likely to have accepting attitudes (Kaiser Family Foundation, 2001), evolving perceptions have been much more favorable (Lewis et al. 2015). Ultimately it may be important for practitioners to explore the impact of societal stigma and prejudice experiences among older gay men.

Gay men often create families of "choice," which are communities and individuals that often replace families of origin due to alienation and rejection. Historically, in many states gay couples were unable to legally marry or adopt children, which led them to build relationships outside of the traditional family system. One study of Chicago area of 160 lesbians and gay men found that up to two-thirds of the sample reported having a family of choice (Beeler, Rawls, Herdt, & Cohler, 1999). Another study found over half of the 145 gay men interviewed considered close friends to be "as close" or "closer" to them than family members, as well as believing personal friendships to be of great importance (de Vries & Johnson, 2002). Such families of choice, and the strong bonds that form within them, have been found to be protective against isolationism and depression (Beeler et al., 1999).

DEATH AND DYING

While the rates of HIV transmission have been steadily declining throughout the past 20 years for specific subsets of the gay community, the impact of HIV/AIDS on the lives of gay men is still a very relevant topic. In their study of 746 gay men over a seven-year period, Martin and Dean (1993) examined the impact of HIV/AIDS bereavement, finding a large loss of cohort support with diminished mental health effects of such losses over time. This fact is especially relevant in the older gay male community as they are more likely to have lost family support due to their sexual orientation combined with losing friends, lovers, and partners to HIV/AIDS, likely having long-term consequences for their supportive networks (Martin & Dean, 1993). Others have studied grief and bereavement within the gay community focusing attention on the effect disenfranchisement has on grief and loss and the lack of legitimacy this loss is given by the dominant culture (Doka, 1989). Brown, Alley, Sarosy, Quarto, and Cook (2001) underscored the fear and reality of aging and dying without strong levels of social supports, as older gay men are increasingly shut out from mainstream gay culture and left without strong support systems.

In measures to combat the isolation that many older gay men face, different community groups across the United States were formed. These included SAGE (Services & Advocacy for GLBT Elders) in New York City and GLOE (Gay and Lesbian Outreach to Elders, now New Leaf Outreach to Elders) in San Francisco, among many others. With the focus on community building within the aging gay community, these organizations have had a positive effect on the well-being of older gay men within the LGBT population (Morrow, 2001). In response to HIV/AIDS stigmatization and disenfranchisement, such projects as the AIDS Memorial Quilt were organized. This project, ongoing since 1987, stitches together quilts with the names of individuals lost due to HIV/AIDS. The project was created to be a community-building endeavor, giving those impacted by HIV/AIDS a public forum to show expressions of grief and loss (Corless, 1995).

Although the Supreme Court ruling in the matter of *Obergfell v. Hodges* may change the legal status of many gay men who have been in long-term partnerships and wish to be legally married, attention still needs to be paid to the legalities of end-of-life decisions. Previously, many gay men in long-term partnerships were faced with the lack of decision-making authority automatically granted to married heterosexual couples, further adding to experiences of oppression and disenfranchisement.

RACIAL AND ETHNIC CONSIDERATIONS

Greene (1994) explored the impact of minorities that have additional minority status (e.g., sexual, ethnic, gender, disability) and the multiple levels of oppression and discrimination that accompany such identities. Racial/ethnically diverse gay men must manage the dominant culture's racism, sexism, and heterosexism as well as that of their own ethnic group. However, such ties to their ethnic minority group may provide practical and emotional support and significance. Ongoing challenges related to often explicit homophobia within these groups may cause racial and ethnic diverse gay men to remain closeted and more vulnerable for certain risk factors (i.e., substance use, suicide ideation). Additionally, ethnic minority gay men have been disproportionately affected by HIV/AIDS. Although rates of new transmissions has been declining for White gay males, HIV has continued to greatly impact gay African American males and gay Latino males. While African Americans represent only 12% of the overall population, they accounted for 44% of new HIV/AIDS cases in 2013 (Centers for Disease Control and Prevention [CDC], 2013). Similarly, the HIV transmission rate in the gay Latino community is more than three times that of Whites (CDC, 2013). Correlates of poverty and the overall lack of HIV testing, prevention, and treatment resources has been given the most attention in the ongoing study of these unbalanced statistics related to transmission. There also has been strong momentum for advocacy, continued outreach, education, and prevention measures and programming such as *Dentengamos Juntos el HIV* (Let's stop HIV together), Act Against AIDS Leadership Initiative, and the Care and Prevention in the United States Demonstration Project. All of these health advocacy, prevention, and educational programs focus specifically on ethnic minority communities (CDC, 2013).

RELIGION AND SPIRITUALITY

There is a fine balance between understanding the historical oppression of gay men by religious groups and institutions when compared to the supportive role that religion and spirituality has upon this diverse community. Many religious institutions have a history of stigmatizing and excluding gay men from their congregations, barring gay religious leaders, and prohibiting religious ceremonies such as weddings. In a study of 66 lesbian, gay, and bisexual individuals, nearly two-thirds reported experiencing conflict through their involvement with religious institutions, resulting in ongoing negative effects including difficulty in coming out and an increase in internalized shame and depression, among other factors (Schuck & Liddle, 2000). Such marginalization and oppression can negatively impact gay identity formation along with having lasting psychological consequences (Schuck & Liddle, 2000). While many gay men view religious institutions as oppressors, it is also true that many often turn to spirituality (Tan, 2005) as an alternative to organized religion. Additionally, Tan (2005) found that individuals who express higher levels of spirituality had higher self-esteem, more self-acceptance, and better overall well-being. It is important to note that a good number of religious institutions have become "open and affirming" by openly welcoming LGBTQ congregants as well as providing the potential for leadership roles. For example, in early July of 2015, the Episcopal Church affirmed and invited same-sex couples to be married at their institutions. Exploring ways that religion and spirituality can be effectively integrated into social services and counseling experiences for gay men remains an important aspect for social workers to consider when providing care or building a therapeutic alliance.

RURAL AND URBAN LIVES

Throughout the twentieth and twenty-first centuries, gay men have been moving en masse to urban areas such as San Francisco, New York City, and Chicago. In these densely populated urban areas, gay men have created vibrant communities providing a wide range of support systems (Lindhorst, 1998). However, there are still many gay men living in rural areas out of choice or an inability to afford the expensive costs of moving to large cities (Lindhorst, 1998). Gay men living in rural areas experience a different lifestyle than those living in large cities and also have differing needs. Rural areas are traditionally more politically conservative and have inhabitants who hold moral values created in a fundamentalist religious context (Lindhorst, 1998; Mancoske & Lindhorst, 1994). Although public attitudes have improved for the LGBTQ community over the past 30 years, studies consistently show communities in rural areas continue to have homophobic attitudes (Lindhorst, 1998). This can lead to gay men in rural areas experiencing more isolation, higher levels of explicit homophobia, and smaller networks of support than their urban counterparts (Bacharach, 1987; Lindhorst, 1998). Some research has shown gay men in rural areas experience higher rates of depression and suicide compared to those living in more populated areas (Bacharach, 1987; Paulson, 1991). Typically fewer health and mental health resources exist in these areas, limiting access to necessary support (Lindhorst, 1998; Mancoske & Lindhorst, 1994). Luckily technology has enabled many rural gay men to join online communities, thus expanding support networks previously unavailable to them (Kirkey & Forsyth, 2001).

MIGRATION AND IMMIGRATION

The lives and experiences of gay men who are also migrants or undocumented immigrants is a topic that has only recently been receiving the attention it deserves. The intersection of sexual orientation and undocumented status often poses unique and difficult challenges for many

LGBTQ individuals. They often face multiple layers of oppression due to racism, homophobia, and xenophobia. Additionally, undocumented immigrants are the victims of crime, including kidnapping, rape, trauma, and verbal and physical abuse, all with an underlying fear of immigration police and being discovered as undocumented (Bianchi et al., 2007). The historical context of understanding the intersection between sexual orientation and immigration is also an important consideration when working with gay men. Specific statutes regarding naturalization and immigration laws barred members of the LGBTQ community from become legal citizens (Carro, 1989). Additionally, many undocumented immigrants come to the United States with the hope of receiving quality care for HIV/AIDS and related illnesses. However, lack of access to proper health care is a reality that many of these gay immigrants and migrants face (Manalansan, 2006). Bianchi et al. (2007) found that the reasons for immigration among gay men are extremely varied and nuanced to each individual. Some individuals come to escape conservative, homophobic countries and to achieve greater sexual freedom, while others leave their home countries due to widespread poverty, political instability, and limited educational opportunities (Bianchi et al., 2007). Understanding the social and political context of immigration choices is imperative when working with this community of individuals.

DATING AND RELATIONSHIPS

To fully understand patterns of dating for gay men, practitioners should not assume such patterns align or follow those of their nongay counterparts. In the same regard, gay men are typically raised in heteronormative environments, witnessing their opposite-sex parents' relationships (through both positive and negative aspects) while living in environments that focus on male and female dating, mating, and relating patterns affirmed through institutions such as schools, churches, and the mass media (Potârcă, Mills, & Neberich, 2015). Some progress has been made since the 1990s with more visible symbols of same-sex dating and mating through literature, movies, television, and advertising (Campbell, 2015). There remains limited research and empirical literature with regard to understanding the long-term impact of marriage and divorce or patterns that may be developing among gay couples. Negative implications associated with marriage among gay couples along with assumptions stemming from those opposed to marriage equality have yet to arise as well (Langbein & Yost, 2015).

MONOGAMY, NONMONOGAMY, AND POLYAMORY

Gay male couples may have spoken or unspoken agreements with regard to the status of their relationship, intimacy, and needs for sexual relations. Such agreements may range from monogamy to nonmonogamy or polyamory. There are also clear differences related to fidelity factors as some gay couples may openly agree to the terms of their sexual relationship while others may not or may find ways to secretly engage in sexual relations, causing infidelity. Sanchez, Bocklandt, and Vilain (2009) compared single ($n = 129$) to partnered ($n = 114$) gay men and found differences regarding concerns over traditional masculine roles and interest in casual sex. Researchers found that single men were more restrictive in affectionate behavior with other men and more interested in casual sex than partnered men. Oppositely, partnered men were more interested in success and power and were more competitive than single men.

One main difference between gay couples and opposite-sex couples is that many, but clearly not all, within the larger gay community have an easier acceptance of casual or anonymous sex, nonmonogamy, and sexual nonexclusivity, which is a clear departure from typical heteronormative views and values (Shernoff, 2006). Some of these views may have arisen due to the decades of oppression and repression of male sexuality causing gay men to socialize, date, and engage in sex in public settings while rejecting sexual patterns they may have witnessed from their parents or nongay counterparts over time as discussed in the previous paragraph (Sanchez et al., 2009). Furthermore, some of these factors and sexual inclinations may simply be due to gender (Shernoff, 2006). Mitchell, Harvey, Champeau, and Seal (2012) examined the impact of various sexual agreements made between gay male couples ($N = 144$), finding that couples demonstrated a lower risk of unprotected anal intercourse with their secondary partner when in a strictly monogamous relationship with a primary partner and a commitment to their sexual agreement. In addition, there were other factors that impacted such agreements (e.g., HIV/AIDS complacency and treatment optimism, substance use, failure to practice safe sex, etc.) as well as various relationship factors (e.g., HIV status of each partner and testing, faulted sexual agreements, perceived monogamy) that impact overall sexual risk behavior among gay male couples. Sexual agreements may include conversations surrounding trust, honesty, and negotiated safety (e.g., use of condoms); serosorting (e.g., sorting partners by HIV status); seropositioning (e.g., lessening risk by selecting HIV-negative partners for insertive and not receptive anal sex); seroconcordant status (e.g., selecting partners with the same HIV status; Mitchell et al., 2012).

CULTURE AND SUBCULTURE

Historically and currently, gay men have had a unique relationship with and within public and private spaces. As no concrete demographic exists to determine or predict one's sexuality, gay men have had to harness various forms of mediated communication in order to associate socially and sexually. Incidentally, some have claimed that gay men (and more broadly LGBTQ people) hold an innate sixth sense or "gaydar" (Shelp, 2002) to locate another gay person. Yet, more important, gay men have existed and continue to exist within social climates that range from accepting and tolerant to blatantly hostile and oppressive. Depending on the location, it may be illegal to self-identify as gay or engage in same-sex behaviors (see www.ilga.org). From that perspective, gay men are not simply a subpopulation; instead, they can better be conceptualized as a "counterpublic" (Warner, 2002) or networks of individuals and groups that continually interact with and are defined, to various extents, by normative structures and oppressive forces. Because of this, when considering the ways in which gay men participate in the public sphere, mediated communication is central. This can take the form of finding unique spaces and places (e.g., bathhouses) to socialize or find sexual partners, engaging in social and sexual behaviors (e.g., joining the leather, drag, or bondage, discipline, and sadomasochism [BDSM] communities), or actively choosing and expressing identities atypical of those expected by larger LGBTQ culture or society in general.

Few documented histories are available that illustrate the cultures that have allowed for homo-socializing over time (Boyd, 2005; Chauncey, 1995). Still, LGBTQ neighborhoods have been established around the United States and beyond, including the Castro District in San Francisco, West Hollywood in Los Angeles, Chelsea in New York City, and Boystown in Chicago. These locations allow for social and material capital to exist, social identities to find expression, and sexual encounters to occur. Especially with stricter social and legal policing, gay men have relied on a variety of strategies to connect with other gay men for socializing and sexualizing (Frankis & Flowers, 2005, 2007, 2009). Importantly, cruising among gay men has existed as a social behavior to search for sexual encounters. Public sex venues (PSV), such as bars, parks, and bathhouses, have been sanctioned and contested places where gay men can congregate, including engaging in sexual encounters. In the early days of the HIV epidemic, many cities ushered in the closing of PSVs for fear of contagion and in hope of controlling the epidemic (Woods & Binson, 2003). Parallel to PSVs, gay men have engaged in cruising in public sex environments (PSEs), which are places not originally built for sexual activity; instead, PSEs can include parks, truck stops, gyms, or public bathrooms, among other spaces. These places have historically been met with high levels of policing (see Humpheys, 1970). As of late, both PSVs and PSEs have received increased attention from public health and allied professionals in order to better understand the correlation of these locations with the continued HIV epidemic and other sexually transmitted infections (STIs; Frankis & Flowers, 2007).

In more recent times, another place that has been a prominent scene of association for gay men is online and through social media. Even before the rise of the Internet, gay men, and more generally men who have sex with men (MSM) have been early adopters of technology for social and sexual purposes. Gay men and MSM have utilized multimedia channels and, progressively, interweb spaces for seeking out sexual health information, cruising for and finding sex partners, social networking, dating, having cybersex, and consuming pornography (Grov, Breslow, Newcomb, Rosenberger, & Bauermeister, 2014). Prior to the 1990s, mediated communication among gay men centered on media such as telephone chat lines, magazines, and VHS videos. Moving into the 1990s brought about the rise of the Internet, which included online chatrooms for cruising, the development of new language for online connections (e.g., M4M), and the proliferation of sexual networking websites like Manhunt.net and Adam4Adam.com. In the early 2000s, broadband and wi-fi technologies allowed for increased interconnectivity, bringing about increases in not only sexual connections but also relationships between gay men. These connections were found to correlate Internet usage and HIV/STIs (Liau, Millet, & Marks, 2006). Public health researchers, therefore, worked to gain methodological traction for conducting research online, as well as begin rolling out more Internet-based interventions targeting gay men and high-risk behavior. Even more recently, new media has been attributed to the decline of built gay spaces and historically entrenched "gayborhoods." Parallel to this, with the advent of smartphones and tablets, even greater personalization and connectivity has developed (Grov et al., 2014). Applications for social and sexual networking have taken hold, such as Facebook, Grindr, and Scruff. Accordingly, a research focus has increased especially regarding the high-risk sexual behaviors of young MSM. Gay men now have greater choice of media spaces for connecting, especially in relation to social identities, sexual fetishes, and other behaviors. For example, apps such as Scruff allow for greater networking of bears, cubs, and otters, or those affiliated with a subculture of gay men focused on more masculine archetypes and hairier, rugged men. In the same regard, those who may be more attracted to leather, BDSM, or other fetishisms may be able to locate others with similar interests via an app when compared to the more historical venue of a bar or club.

HEALTH AND MENTAL HEALTH

A paucity of empirical population-based information exists on the health and mental health of gay men (Institute of Medicine [IOM], 2011), as data regarding sexual orientation, gender identity, and expression are not routinely and consistently collected on state and federal surveillance research projects. This concerning disparity leaves an inaccurate picture with regard to the health of gay men (and LBTQ persons at large) and is a priority for the outcomes of "Healthy People 2020" (US Department of Health and Human Services, 2013). Blosnich, Farmer, Lee, Silenzio, and Bowen (2014) were able to aggregate population-based data of adults in the United States ($N = 93,414$) from a behavioral risk factor survey across 10 states, finding that adult gay men, as compared to heterosexual peers, were nearly twice as likely to smoke, had higher odds of mental distress and life dissatisfaction, and more commonly had activity limitations due to physical, mental, and emotional problems. Alternatively, gay men utilized health-care services at a similar rate as heterosexual men and were less likely to be overweight or obese, were more likely to be vaccinated for the flu, and were more likely to undergo HIV testing than heterosexual peers. Bisexual men were 60% less likely to have ever had an HIV test (Blosnich et al. 2014).

HIV/AIDS, STIs, AND SEXUAL RISK

Whereas gay, bisexual, and other MSM are estimated to comprise 2% of the US population, they continue to be disproportionately affected by HIV (CDC, 2015). In 2010, gay and bisexual men accounted for 63% of all new HIV infections and 78% among men overall (CDC, 2015). White MSM accounted for the largest number of newly infected (38%), followed by African American MSM (36%) and Latino MSM (22%) (CDC, 2015). In 2011, 57% (or 500,022) of all people living with HIV in the United States were gay and bisexual men (CDC, 2015). In 2013, gay and bisexual men comprised 81% of new diagnoses among men (13 years and older) and 65% of all new diagnoses overall. Disproportionately, young people and African Americans (of any age) are the populations with increasing rates of new infections and diagnoses, with the latter being the most affected population in the recent years. Moreover, MSM of color account for almost three-quarters of those diagnosed with AIDS and typically have worse HIV-related health outcomes. As of 2011, of the gay and bisexual men diagnosed, 80.6% were linked to care, 57.5% were retained in care, 52.9% were prescribed antiretroviral therapies, and 44.6% had achieved viral suppression (CDC, 2015). With these medical advances, it is estimated that people living with HIV nowadays will have typical lifespans in the United States and Canada (Samji et al., 2013).

This raises a number of challenges, however, for prevention. As of 2008, it has been estimated that close to one in three gay and bisexual men do not know they are HIV positive, and, as of 2011, one in five gay and bisexual men who tested had HIV, with the prevalence increasing with age.

The main direct risk factor for transmitting HIV within this population is anal sex. Contributing to risk for acquiring HIV are a number of biopsychosocial factors, including increased numbers of sexual partners, having a committed partner, group sex environments (Grov, Rendina, Ventuneac, & Parsons, 2013), as well as homophobia, stigma, and discrimination. Adding to this calculus is perception of risk, especially for younger people, and substance use, including methamphetamines, alcohol, and injection drug use. With the increased numbers of partners, gay men are at increased risk for all other STIs, including gonorrhea, chlamydia, HPV, hepatitis, and syphilis. In 2013, MSM accounted for 75% of all new syphilis cases (CDC, 2015).

In the face of this context, attention has been paid to the ways in which gay men have negotiated risk and relationships including serosorting and other seroadaptive behaviors with prospective and regular partners (Rönn, White, Huges, & Ward, 2014). Parallel to this, gay men have factored into their sexual behavior with partners increasing attention to HIV status, viral loads, CD4 counts, and adherence to treatment. Very recently, antiretroviral drugs were approved for use by high-risk populations as another prevention method, know as pre-exposure prophylaxis (PrEP). PrEP is recommended in concert with testing, condom use, and other risk-reducing behaviors.

The politics of "barebacking," also known as condomless or unprotected anal intercourse, has garnered much attention from public health authorities among gay men experiencing "prevention fatigue" or complacency, thus being critical of the gay community's obligation to be altruistic sexual citizens (Davis, 2008). Such criticism eclipses the responsibilities of public health authorities and questions of effectiveness of health promotion efforts (Perry-Argüello, 2008).

SUBSTANCE USE, BODY IMAGE, AND MENTAL HEALTH

As a subpopulation of sexual minorities, gay men are more likely to use alcohol and other drugs, have higher rates of substance abuse, are less likely to abstain from use, and continue heavy drinking into later life (CDC, 2015; Ostrow & Stall, 2008). These behaviors not only have immediate consequences; they are correlated with an increased risk for heart disease (Ostrow & Stall, 2008; World Heart Federation, 2012). In concert with an increased risk for HPV, gay men have an increased risk for colon, testicular, and prostate cancers (Asencio, Blank, & Descartes, 2009; Heslin, Gore, King, & Fox, 2008; Substance Abuse and Mental Health Services Administration [SAMHSA], 2012). Additionally, more attention is being paid to the issues of the interplay among identity, eating, body, and sexuality for gay men. Siconolfi, Halkitis, Allomong, and Burton (2009) found in a cross-sectional sample of 219 urban gay men that body dissatisfaction was positively correlated with age and external motivations for working out (e.g., social comparisons, sexual prowess), while eating disorder scores were positively correlated with more frequent and longer exercise routines as well as anxiety, depression, ambivalence, and self-esteem related to sexual orientation. These findings dovetail existing knowledge of the link between internalized homophobia and problematic body image (Kimmel & Mahalik, 2005; Reilly & Rudd, 2006) and support a deeper analysis of the biopsychosocial consequences of the "buff agenda" that has predominated much of the mainstream Western gay culture (Halikitis et al., 2004).

In terms of mental health, an analysis of data from a national study of alcohol and related conditions ($N = 34,653$) found that sexual minorities are 1.5 to 2 times more likely to experience mood and anxiety disorders in their lifetime (Bostwick, Boyd, Hughes, & McCabe, 2010) compared to heterosexual counterparts. This is echoed and further confirmed by meta-analyses for LGB people more generally, which estimate depression, anxiety, and substance misuse are 1.5 times more common (King et al., 2008). Gay men, specifically, were more than twice as likely to have a mood or anxiety disorder in their lifetime and the past year when compared with heterosexual men. Relatedly, gay men have an increased risk for suicide ideation and attempt. Gay men (and lesbians) are estimated to be 2.47 times more likely to have attempted suicide—and gay and bisexual men specifically have a lifetime fourfold increased risk for suicide overall (King et al., 2008). A number of factors co-exist with and contribute to these rates, such as age, affiliation with gay culture(s), levels of stress, and level of outness (SAMHSA, 2012). Hatzenbuehler, McLaughlin, Keyes, and Hasin (2010) found that institutional policies, like anti-gay amendments in various US states had an impact on increased rates of mood, anxiety, and substance use disorders.

STIGMA, DISCRIMINATION, ABUSE, AND VIOLENCE

Gay men commonly experience discrimination in everyday life, which is often thought to have an impact on their mental health and overall quality of life. Bostwick, Boyd, Hughs, and West (2014) continued analysis of their work (see Bostwick et al., 2010) and found that gay men were more likely than bisexual or heterosexual men to report any discrimination in the past year, especially in health-care settings and public places (e.g., sidewalks, stores, restaurants), and being verbally assaulted—including physical threats. When racial/ethnic discrimination was added into this analysis, negative reactions to the experiences of discrimination increased as did the negative overall effect on mental health. This study illustrates the ways in which the multiple identities of individuals intersect and relate to outcomes associated with health, mental health, and other psychosocial factors.

In a study of 936 gay men, Brennan, Hellerstedt, Ross, and Welles (2007) found that one in seven participants may have been victims of childhood sexual abuse. Young sexual minorities on average experience 3.8 times more sexual abuse, 1.2 times more parental physical abuse, and 1.7 times more assaults at school (Friedman et al., 2011). Further, depression and substance abuse have been strongly correlated with experiences of interpersonal violence (e.g., physical, verbal, and sexual including unprotected anal intercourse). One study ($N = 817$) found 32% ($n = 265$) of gay men reported abuse in present or past relationships, while 54% of those same participants ($n = 144$) reported more than one type of abuse within their relationships (Houston & McKirnan, 2007).

The central role of stigma often acts as a primary motivator for health and mental health disparities among gay men, as well as other minority populations (Hatzenbuehler, Phelan, & Link, 2013). Stigma includes discrimination but speaks to a broader system of co-occurring and intersecting lived experiences of labeling, stereotyping, separations, and loss of status within settings in which power is exercised. The short- and long-term impact of stigma on housing, educational outcomes, employment, health care, and beyond are often misunderstood or understudied among sexual minorities. Psychosocial factors can mediate the relationship between stigma and health disparities and include various resources, social relationships, an ability to manage stress, and psychological and behavioral responses (e.g., coping and resilience). The first national probability-based sample of LGB adults ($N = 662$) found gay men at the greatest risk for person or property crimes based on antigay stigma, with almost 40% of the participants reporting such victimization (Herek, 2009). More generally, among LGB adults, 1 in 10 noted experiences of stigma in housing and employment, with 1 in 5 reporting crimes against person or property (Herek, 2009). Moreover, gay men are at increased risk for developing internalized homophobia, which is associated with such health issues including depression and anxiety, eating disorders, relationship problems, sexual compulsivity, substance use, and the synergizing of negative health consequences (Dew & Chaney, 2005; Frost & Meyer, 2009; Herrick et al., 2013; Lehavot & Simoni, 2011; Meyer & Dean, 1995; Wiseman & Moradi, 2010). It is important to note that higher levels of self-esteem, positive affect, and resiliency among gay men often assists with the resolution of internalized homophobia as well as other negative health and mental health consequences (Herrick, Gillis, & Cogan 2009) previously discussed.

EFFECTIVE AND BEST PRACTICE APPROACHES

Mental health practitioners across disciplines should be knowledgeable of the issues facing sexual minority populations, mindful of their own personal attitudes and histories, and judicious in selecting and implementing affirming therapeutic interventions (Kissinger, Lee, Twitty, & Kisner, 2009). While many allied professions have called for great attention to the needs and clinical issues of gay men (see APA, 2012; IOM, 2011; US Department of Health and Human Services, 2013), translations of evidenced-based interventions have yet to be widely tested and disseminated. Given the aforementioned health and mental health disparities, it understandable that many applied interventions arise from cognitive-behavior theories, as well as dominant approaches to behavior change through health promotion activities. And, as clinical research is being conducted to adapt these widely adopted interventions (see Alessi, 2014; Pachankis, 2014), the attention to process and approach are equally important. Many clinical interventions can be adapted to work with gay men (Alessi, 2014; Crisp, 2006; Meyer, 2003) and, to that end, the macro-level forces that shape feelings, attitudes, and behaviors cannot be underestimated (Glassgold, 2007; Russel & Bohan, 2006). Thus the role of the competent, affirming, and highly self-aware practitioner becomes even more critical so as to not replicate or reinforce homophobic behaviors and ideologies (Davison, 2001).

Before going any further regarding approaches and techniques, it is important to understand that the NASW (2015), the National Committee on LGBT Issues, and the Council on Social Work Education (2016) released statements that definitively denounce and reject any use of sexual orientation change efforts, such as reparative or conversion approaches. Conversion therapy has already been rejected by a number of other organizations, including the APA, American Academy of Pediatrics, American Medical Association, American Psychological Association and American Counseling Association. The states of California, Illinois, New Jersey, New York and Oregon, as well as the District of Columbia, have also banned licensed professionals from practicing conversion therapy with minors. The NASW reaffirms that such efforts are empirically unfounded and compromise the health and mental health of gay men and all LGBTQ persons. Moreover, they are in direct opposition to the NASW Code of Ethics (2008) as well as other professional ethical standards and guidelines.

THEORETICAL, AFFIRMATIVE, AND RESPONSIVE MODELS OF CARE

One longstanding approach to working with gay men, as well as persons who are lesbian or bisexual, is LGB affirmative psychotherapy (Davies, 1996). This is less a set of discrete intervention tasks as it is an interdisciplinary conceptual framework that brings together attitudes, knowledge, and skills in service of empowering gay men. The clinician approaches the client keeping in mind four central principles: (a) sexual orientation is positively regarded and supported, (b) prejudices within the clinician and in the relationship are avoided, (c) stigma is recognized and repaired, and (d) attention and sensitivity are paid to gay development, issues of lifestyle, and cultural practices (Davies, 1996; King, Semlyen, Killaspy, Nazareth, & Osborn, 2007). This perspective is then operationalized through three interlocking and complimentary processes, which include the person-in-environment perspective, cultural competency, and the strengths perspective. An ecological-based perspective allows for an understanding to emerge of the networks, resources, and relationships that the gay male client is embedded within and has been navigating. Cultural competency requires attention to knowledge, attitudes, beliefs, and skills that can be developed and deployed in order to more fully appreciate the standpoint and development of the client as well as foster increased affirmation through an engaged process of learning and growth. As Crisp (2006) astutely argues, practicing affirmatively is not synonymous with practicing without discrimination. From a gay affirmative standpoint, the clinician and client are both committed and engaged, and the clinician is not divorced from operative homonegative discourse and other oppressive forces at work in the local context. In the third aspect, a strengths perspective underscores attention to self-determination, well-being, and the health of the gay male client (versus pathologizing and other demoralizing tactics) and consciousness raising of one's own identities and social locations.

In more practical terms, a gay affirmative approach would directly espouse a number of tenets. During assessment and other phases of intervention, heterosexuality should not be assumed, no matter the legal arrangement of the client (e.g., married, domestically partnered, single). The social oppression of homophobia is just that: a societal problem, not an issue for the client to tolerate. Sexuality and sexual orientation are to be valued, accepted, and perceived as positive outcomes of an empowerment-based helping process, that is, lived experiences of becoming. Quite importantly, then, internalized homophobia must be confronted and reduced in order to increase well-being. This relates to the client as much as the clinician tending to their own homophobia and other heteronormative biases. Much of that reflection can be facilitated by increasing one's knowledge of various theories of identity development, sexuality, and stories of coming out, disclosing, and coming to terms with one's identities. And, as clients come into their own identities, it is imperative to not focus on pathologizing origins of sexuality and forcing normative ideas of coming out; rather, it is important to support the client's level of outness and experiences of disclosure (Alessi, 2008; Hunter, Shannon, Knox, & Martin 1998).

On an empirical level, minority stress theory (MST) has been developed as a model for conceptualizing the lived experiences of being a minority in society, especially gay men (Meyer, 2003). It is also an increasingly validated model to understand and explain the pathway between the continual social stress of being in a marginalized social position (i.e., living with chronic prejudices and discrimination) and the consequent health and mental health effects. The MST model is particularly apt for gay men as it draws together interdisciplinary perspectives on stress and coping, appreciating the multiple contextual factors that facilitate or work against well-being (Bostwick et al., 2014). Pachankis (2014) conducted the first participatory-based study with clinicians ($n = 21$) and consumers ($n = 20$) alike to adapt MST into an intervention program specifically for gay men. Project ESTEEM combined cognitive-behavior techniques with the conceptual framework of MST. When tested further, it will be the first adapted intervention showing the efficacy of MST in reducing mood and anxiety disorders for gay men. Similarly, Alessi (2014) has shown promising operationalization of MST in individual clinical work. Based on MST, Alessi developed a two-phase minority stress assessment process to be used with sexual-minority adults. The first part assesses prejudice events in the client's life, the nature of the client's experiences with internalized homophobia, and the extent of sexual orientation concealment. The second phase examines the client's coping strategies and emotion regulation, social and interpersonal repertoire, and nature of cognitive processing. See chapter 12 for more information about MST and its use with gay men.

Given the continued disproportionate burden that gay men bear in the HIV epidemic, the incorporation of sexuality and health behavior change strategies into existing interventions is necessary when working with this population (Spector & Pinto, 2011; also see Stampley, 2008). Unlike the work yet to be done to scale up MST and other gay-affirmative approaches, many versions of evidenced-based interventions exist that incorporate translations of behavior change theories, like the health belief model or social learning theory (Glanz, Rimer, & Viswanath, 2008), with cognitive-behavior approaches to individual and group work. These interventions all share the common goal of preventing HIV transmission, while simultaneously targeting other biopsychosocial outcomes like increased adherence, quality of life improvement, or social connections. The CDC regularly updates and disseminates these "high impact prevention" interventions via its website (https://effectiveinterventions.cdc.gov).

Third-wave cognitive-behavior therapies, or contextual psychotherapies, have been proving to be effective clinically for a number of issues, including depression, posttraumatic stress disorder, and anxieties (Boone, 2014; Dimeff & Koerner, 2007; Thompson, Luoma, & LeJeune, 2013). As an extension of more traditionally understood cognitive-behavior therapy, they incorporate and emphasize more mindfulness and acceptance in an effort to increase more effective behavioral repertoires. One in particular, acceptance and commitment therapy (ACT), continues to be supported empirically through various clinical trials (Harris, 2006; Masuda, 2014), and clinical researchers have been adapting it to more specific issues and populations (e.g., gay men). The premise of ACT is that humans experience pain and change and in turn often understandably struggle, leading to high levels of cognitive fusion and experiential avoidance. ACT aims to foster psychological flexibility to promote a more satisfying and worthwhile life. This is achieved through simultaneous processes of acceptance, mindfulness, and behavior change. Given this focus, ACT is an apt approach to target stigma, internalized homophobia, and related internalizing tendencies that commonly exist for gay men (Masuda, 2014).

Additionally, narrative therapy is an increasingly sought-after intervention utilized in working with LGBTQ populations. It has foundations in family systems work (Madigan, 2010) and builds off this approach to incorporate postmodern sensibilities around identities and critical theory commitments of tending to structural forces in the lived experiences of marginalized persons. For gay men this becomes an important method of intervention as it allows for a closer analysis of operative cultural values and worldviews and how power and privilege work in those prominent narratives both individually and collectively. To that end, narrative therapy offers a framework for understanding how the stories we hold onto impact our well-being (Behan, 1999; McLean & Marini, 2008; Tilsen & Nylund, 2010).

CLINICAL SUPERVISION

Parallel to clinical interventions and affirmative approaches, the role of clinical supervision cannot be underestimated. The entrenched prejudices and biases that exist around sexuality make an attention to self-reflexivity a continual practice that must be explored (Davison, 2001). In working with gay men, it is common that questions may arise from the client about the clinician's own sexuality. Some clients will seek out a clinician specifically because they are (or are perceived as) LGBTQ. Whereas this may be an important element for the client, it does not have to be a barrier to effective treatment. Alessi (2014) and King et al. (2007) direct attention to the value of a clinician's knowledge, attitude, and skills when working with gay men. So one does not have to be gay in order to conduct effective treatment, nor does one's sexuality guarantee success. Instead, clinicians should be willing and prepared to process such inquiries about their sexuality and should consider disclosing their own sexuality rather than immediately dismissing, avoiding, or resisting such lines of questions (Knox & Hill, 2003).

Further, it is common that cultural-based countertransference can emerge for clinicians (Spector & Pinto, 2011; Stampley, 2008) and take the form of denying client's strengths, distancing oneself and conversations from sexuality and HIV, relying on assumptions about sexuality and cultural practices too often, marshaling hetero- and homonormative assumptions about relationships and sexual practices, and avoiding topics like assessing properly for HIV-related considerations. In part or in sum, these may be effective "warning signs" that biases and prejudices are operating within the helping relationship. Prejudices held by the clinician have the ability to interfere with the efficacy of counseling, inflame countertransference and transference, lead to ineffective treatment choices, and result in treatment errors (Berkman & Zinberg, 1997; Davies, 1996; Van Den Bergh & Crisp, 2004).

ONGOING TRAINING AND EDUCATION

In keeping with an affirmative approach, social workers can engage in a number of strategies to reduce clinical errors, increase self-reflexivity, and increase well-being when working with gay men. Culturally humble practice requires continued education and training. One place to start with this is in the clinician's own local context; this is to say, social workers should be aware of the community resources, networks, organizations, and other assets that support their gay male clients and the larger LGBTQ community (Alessi, 2014; Saari, 2001). Next, social workers should locate and revisit peer-reviewed literature about the most current understandings of gay identity and psychosocial development. Parallel, grey literature (e.g., policy papers) and other cultural resources (e.g., movies, social media, non-/fiction books) are necessary tools to expand any clinician's sensitivity and acceptance of gay men—as well as work through their own process of coming to terms with sexuality, personally and professionally.

Another source of continuing education and training for social workers is the health profession itself. The clinical attention to and research projects regarding gay men and the LGBTQ community at-large have resulted in numerous allied health professions updating best practice recommendations as well as guidelines for practical training and curriculum standards (see, for example, APA, 2012; Lim, 2013; NASW, 2015; IOM, 2011). Many of these recommendations provide guidance to fostering more inclusive climates within professional programs as well as within larger university and health-care systems. Examples of such standards are (a) comprehensive nondiscrimination policies, (b) ubiquitous use of inclusive language (e.g., "partner" and/ or "spouse") and human resource policies (e.g., full health care and related domestic benefits), (c) increased data collection regarding sexuality and gender identity and expression (d) increased availability of LGBTQ content in courses, (e) opportunities for practical training with LGBTQ populations, and (f) clearly identifiable and easily accessible administrative and clinical supervision mechanisms for LGBTQ students and/or those working with LGBTQ clients to field concerns and experiences with discrimination that may arise within training programs, the university, or agency settings.

CONCLUSION

Gay men have been a visible element of the movement for LGBTQ equality for decades alongside other members of the community. Challenged by living in an often oppressive society facing a multiplicity of challenges stemming from oppression to HIV/AIDS and fighting for equal rights under law related to marriage or to serve in the armed forces, the level of resilience found among this sexual minority group is truly astounding. Practitioners working with gay men should be keenly aware of the unique challenges that they have faced specific to their race/ethnicity, age cohort, socioeconomic status, and other areas of intersectionality discussed in this chapter. Providing an affirming and supportive experience and abiding by the tenets and ethics of our professions remains essential to best meet the needs of all gay men. Working collectively in a strong therapeutic alliance is essential, as is the creation of safe spaces within therapeutic settings such that gay men will not feel vulnerable but rather empowered to work through their health and mental health needs.

REFERENCES

Alessi, E. J. (2008). Staying put in the closet: Examining clinical practice and countertransference issues in work gay men married to heterosexual women. *Clinical Social Work Journal, 36,* 195–201.

Alessi, E. J. (2014). A framework for incorporating minority stress theory into treatment with sexual minority clients. *Journal of Gay & Lesbian Mental Health, 18,* 47–66.

American Psychological Association. (2012). Guidelines for psychological practice with lesbian, gay, and bisexual clients. *American Psychologist, 67,* 10–42.

Armstrong, E. A., & Crage, S. M. (2006). Movements and memory: The making of the Stonewall myth. *American Sociological Review, 71*(5), 724–751.

Asencio, M., Blank, T., & Descartes, L. (2009). The prospect of prostate cancer: A challenge for gay men's sexualities as they age. *Sexuality Research & Social Policy, 6*(4), 38–51.

Atkins, G. L. (2003). *Gay Seattle: Stories of exile and belonging.* Seattle, WA: University of Washington Press.

Bacharach, L. L. (1987). Mental health services in rural areas. In A. Summers, J. M. Schriver, P. Sundet, & R. Meinert (Eds.), *Social work in rural areas: Proceedings of the Tenth National Institute of Social Work in Rural Areas* (pp. 106–117). Columbia: University of Missouri, School of Social Work.

Beeler, J., Rawls, T., Herdt, G. & Cohler, B. (1999). The needs of older lesbians and gay men in Chicago. *Journal of Gay and Lesbian Social Services, 9*(1), 31–49.

Behan, C. (1999). Linking lives around shared themes: Narrative group therapy with gay men. *Gecko: A Journal of Deconstruction and Narrative Ideas in Therapeutic Practice, 2,* 18–35.

Berkman, C., & Zinberg, G. (1997). Homophobia and heterosexism in social workers. *Social Work, 42,* 319–332.

Berrill, K. T., & Herek, G. M. (1990). Violence against lesbians and gay men: An introduction. *Journal of Interpersonal Violence, 5*(3), 269–273.

Bianchi, F., Reisen, C., Zea, M., Poppen, P., Shedlin, M., & Montes-Penha, M. (2007). The sexual experiences of Latino men who have sex with men who migrated to a gay epicentre in the U.S.A. *Culture, Health and Sexuality, 9,* 505–518.

Blosnich, J. R., Farmer, G. W, Lee, J. G. L., Silenzio, V. M. B., & Bowen, D. J. (2014). Health inequalities among sexual minority adults: Evidence from ten U.S. states, 2010. *American Journal of Preventive Medicine, 46*(4), 337–349.

Boone, M. S. (Ed.). (2014). *Mindfulness & acceptance in social work: Evidenced-based interventions & emerging applications.* Oakland, CA: New Harbinger.

Bostwick, W. B., Boyd, C. J., Hughes, T. L., & McCabe, S. E. (2010). Dimensions of sexual orientation and the prevalence of mood and anxiety disorders in the United States. *American Journal of Public Health, 100*(3), 468–475.

Bostwick, W. B., Boyd, C. J., Hughes, T. L., & West, B. (2014). Discrimination and mental health among lesbian, gay, and bisexual adults in the United States. *American Journal of Orthopsychiatry, 84*(1), 35–45.

Boyd, N. A. (2005). *Wide-open town: A history of queer San Francisco to 1965.* Oakland: University of California Press.

Brennan, D. J., Hellerstedt, W. L., Ross, M. W., & Welles, S. L. (2007). History of childhood sexual abuse and HIV risk behaviors in homosexual and bisexual men. *American Journal of Public Health, 97*(6), 1107–1112.

Brooks, R. A., Landovitz, R. J., Kaplan, R. L., Lieber, E., Lee, S. J., & Barkley, T. W. (2012). Sexual risk behaviors and acceptability of HIV pre-exposure prophylaxis among HIV-negative gay and bisexual men in serodiscordant relationships: A mixed methods study. *AIDS Patient Care and STDs, 26*(2), 87–94.

Brown, L., Alley, G., Sarosy, S., Quarto, G., & Cook, T. (2001). Gay men: Aging well! *Journal of Gay and Lesbian Social Services, 13*(4), 41–54.

Byne, W., & Lasco, M. (1999). The origins of sexual orientation: possible biological contributions. In J. Corvino (Ed.), *Same sex: Debating the ethics, science and culture of homosexuality* (pp. 107–120). Lanham, MD: Rowman & Littlefield.

Campbell, J. E. (2015). Gay and lesbian/queer markets/marketing. In D. T. Cook & J. M. Ryan (Eds.), *The Wiley Blackwell encyclopedia of consumption and consumer studies* (pp. 1–4). Chichester, UK: John Wiley.

Carey, B. (2014, February 3). Blazing trails in brain science. *The New York Times*, pp. D-1.

Carrion V. G., & Lock, J. (1997). The coming out process: Developmental stages for sexual minority youth. *Clinical Child Psychology and Psychiatry, 2*, 369–377.

Carro, J. (1989). From constitutional psychopathic inferiority to AIDS: What is in the future for homosexual aliens? *Yale Law & Policy Review, 7*(1), 201–228.

Centers for Disease Control and Prevention. (2013). *HIV surveillance report: Vol. 25.* Retrieved from http://www.cdc.gov/hiv/library/reports/surveillance/

Centers for Disease Control and Prevention. (2015). *Gay and bisexual men.* Retrieved from http://www.cdc.gov/hiv/group/msm/index.html

Chauncey, G. (1995). *Gay New York: Gender, urban culture, and the making of the gay male world, 1890–1940.* New York: Basic Books.

Corless, I. (1995). Saying good-bye to tomorrow. In J. Kauffman (Ed.), *Awareness of mortality: Death, value, and meaning* (pp. 171–184). Amityville, NY: Baywood.

Council on Social Work Education. (2016). *Position statement on conversion/reparative therapy.* Retrieved from http://www.cswe.org/File.aspx?id=85010

Crisp, C. (2006). The Gay Affirmative Practice Scale (GAP): A new measure for assessing cultural competence with gay and lesbian clients. *Social Work, 51*(2), 115–126.

D'Augelli, A. R., Grossman, A. H., & Starks, M. T. (2006). Childhood gender atypicality, victimization, and PTSD among lesbian, gay, and bisexual youth. *Journal of Interpersonal Violence, 21*(11), 1462–1482.

Davies, D. (1996). Towards a model of gay affirmative therapy. In D. Davies & C. Neal (Eds.), *Pink therapy: A guide for counsellors and therapists working with lesbian, gay, and bisexual clients* (pp. 24–31). Buckingham, UK: Open University Press.

Davis, M. (2008). The "loss of community" and other problems for sexual citizenship in recent HIV prevention. *Sociology of Health & Illness, 30*(2), 182–196.

Davison, G. C. (2001). Conceptual and ethical issues in therapy for the psychological problems of gay men, lesbians, and bisexuals. *JCLP/In Session: Psychotherapy in Practice, 57*(5), 695–704.

de Vries, B., & Johnson, C. (2002). Multidimensional reactions to the death of a friend in the later years. *Advances in Life-Course Research: New Frontiers in Socialization, 7*, 299–324.

Dew, B. J., & Chaney, M. P. (2005). The relationship among sexual compulsivity, internalized homophobia, and HIV at-risk sexual behavior in gay and bisexual male users of Internet chat rooms. *Sexual Addiction & Compulsivity, 12*(4), 259–273.

Dimeff, L. A., & Koerner, K. (Eds.). (2007). *Dialectical behavior therapy in clinical practice.* New York: Guildford Press.

Doka, J. (Ed.). (1989). *Disenfranchised grief: Recognizing hidden sorrow.* Lexington, MA: Lexington Books.

Dorfman, R., Walters, K., Burke, P., Hardin, L., Karanik, T., Raphael, J., & Silverstein, E. (1995). Old, sad and alone: The myth of the aging homosexual. *Journal of Gerontological Social Work, 24*(1-2), 29–44.

Duschinsky, R., & Mottier, V. (2015). The DSM-5 as political battleground: Gender identities, sexual norms and female desire. *Psychology & Sexuality, 7*(1), 1–5.

Elze, D. E. (2006). Oppression, prejudice, and discrimination. In D. Morrow & L. Messinger (Eds.), *Sexual orientation & gender expression in social work practice: Working with gay, lesbian, bisexual, & transgender people* (pp. 43–77). New York: Columbia University Press.

Frankis, J. S., & Flowers, P. (2005). Men who have sex with men (MSM) in public sex environments (PSEs): A systematic review of quantitative literature. *AIDS Care, 17*(3), 273–288.

Frankis, J. S., & Flowers, P. (2007). Examining the sexual health experiences of men who cruise public sex environments (PSEs): Sexually transmitted infections (STIs), hepatitis vaccination, and STI clinic use. *International Journal of Sexual Health, 19*(2), 45–55.

Frankis, J. S., & Flowers, P. (2009). Public sexual cultures: A systematic review of qualitative research investigating men's sexual behaviors with men in public spaces. *Journal of Homosexuality, 56*(7), 861–893.

Friedman, M. S., Marshal, M. P., Guadamuz, T. E., Wei, C., Wong, C. F., & Saewyc, E. (2011). A meta-analysis of disparities in childhood sexual abuse, parental physical abuse, and peer victimization among sexual minority and sexual nonminority individuals. *American Journal of Public Health, 101*(8), 1481–1494.

Frost, D. M., & Meyer, I. H. (2009). Internalized homophobia and relationship quality among lesbians, gay men, and bisexuals. *Journal of Counseling Psychology, 56*(1), 97–109.

Giuffre, P., Dellinger, K., & Williams, C. L. (2008). "No retribution for being gay?": Inequality in gay-friendly workplaces. *Sociological Spectrum, 28*(3), 254–277.

Glanz, K., Rimer, B. K., & Viswanath, K. (Eds.). (2008). *Health behavior and health education: Theory, research, and practice* (4th ed.). San Francisco, CA: Jossey-Bass.

Glassgold, J. M. (2007). In dreams begin responsibilities psychology, agency, and activism. *Journal of Gay and Lesbian Psychotherapy, 11*(3–4), 37–57.

Grafsky, E. L. (2014). Becoming the parent of a GLB son or daughter. *Journal of GLBT Family Studies, 10*(1-2), 36–57.

Grau, G., & Shoppmann, C. (2013). *The hidden Holocaust: Gay and lesbian persecution in Germany 1933–45.* Chicago: Routledge.

Greene, B. (1994). Ethnic-minority lesbians and gay men: Mental health and treatment issues. *Journal of Consulting and Clinical Psychiatry, 62*(2), 243–251.

Grov, C., Breslow, A. S., Newcomb, M. E., Rosenberger, J. G., & Bauermeister, J. A. (2014). Gay and bisexual men's use of the Internet: Research from the 1990s through 2013. *Journal of Sex Research, 51*(4), 390–409.

Grov, C., Rendina, H. J., Ventuneac, A., & Parsons, J. T. (2013). HIV risk in group sexual encounters: An event-level analysis from a national online survey of MSM in the U.S. *Journal of Sexual Medicine, 10*(9), 2285–2294.

Haldi, A. (1999). AIDS, anger, and activism: ACT UP as a social movement organization. In J. Freeman & V. L. Johnson (Eds.), *Waves of protest: Social movements since the sixties* (pp. 135–152). Boston: Rowman & Littlefield.

Hall, S. (2010). The American gay rights movement and patriotic protest. *Journal of the History of Sexuality, 19*(3), 536–562.

Hall, H. I., Byers, R. H., Ling, Q., & Espinoza, L. (2007). Racial/ethnic and age disparities in HIV prevalence and disease progression among men who have sex with men in the United States. *American Journal of Public Health, 97*(6), 1060–1066.

Harris, R. (2006). Embracing your demons: An overview of acceptance and commitment therapy. *Psychotherapy in Australia, 12*(4), 2–8.

Hatzenbuehler, M. L., McLaughlin, K. A., Keyes, K. M., & Hasin, D. S. (2010). The impact of institutional discrimination on psychiatric disorders in lesbian, gay, and bisexual populations: A prospective study. *American Journal of Public Health, 100*(3), 452–459.

Hatzenbuehler, M. L., Phelan, J. C., & Link, B. G. (2013). Stigma as fundamental cause of population health inequalities. *American Journal of Public Health, 103*(5), 813–821.

Herdt, G., Beeler, J., & Rawls, T.W. (1997). Life course diversity among older lesbians and gay men: A study in Chicago. *Journal of Gay Lesbian and Bisexual Identity, 2*(3–4), 231–246.

Herek, G. M. (2000). The psychology of sexual prejudice. *Current Directions in Psychological Science, 9*(1), 19–22.

Herek, G. M. (2009). Hate crimes and stigma-related experiences among sexual minority adults in the United States: Prevalence estimates from a national probability sample. *Journal of Interpersonal Violence, 24*(1), 54–74.

Herek, G. M., Gillis, J. R., & Cogan, J. C. (2009). Internalized stigma among sexual minority adults: Insights from a social psychological perspective. *Journal of Counseling Psychology, 56*(1), 32–43.

Herrick, A., Lim, S. H., Plankey, M., Chimel, J., Guadamuz, T., & Kao, U. (2013) Adversity and syndemic production among men participating in the MACS: A life-course approach. *American Journal of Public Health, 103*(2), 79–85.

Heslin, K. C., Gore, J. L., King, W. D., & Fox, S. (2008). Sexual orientation and testing for prostate and colorectal cancers among men in California. *Med Care, 46*(12), 1240–1248.

Houston, E., & McKirnan, D. J. (2007). Intimate partner abuse among gay and bisexual men: Risk correlates and health outcomes. *Journal of Urban Health, 84*(5), 681–690.

Humphreys, L. (1970). *Tearoom trade: Impersonal sex in public places.* Chicago: Aldine.

Hunter, S., Shannon, C., Knox, J., & Martin, J. I. (1998). *Lesbian, gay, and bisexual youths and adults: Knowledge for human services practice.* Thousand Oaks, CA: SAGE.

Institute of Medicine. (2011). *The health of lesbian, gay, bisexual, and transgender people: Building a foundation for better understanding.* Washington, DC: Author.

Isbell, M. T. (1993). AIDS and access to care: Lessons for health care reformers. *Cornell Journal of Law & Public Policy, 3*(1)2, 7–53.

Jenkins, D., & Johnston, L. (2004). Unethical treatment of gay and lesbian people with conversion therapy. *Families in Society: The Journal of Contemporary Social Services, 85*(4), 557–561.

Jensen, E. N. (2002). The pink triangle and political consciousness: Gays, lesbians, and the memory of Nazi persecution. *Journal of the History of Sexuality, 11*(1), 319–349.

Kaiser Family Foundation. (2001). *Inside-OUT: A report on the experiences of lesbians, gays, and bisexuals in America and the public's views on issues and policies related to sexual orientation.* Retrieved from http://www.lgbtdata.com/uploads/1/0/8/8/10884149/ds020_ksso_report.pdf

Kimmel, S. B., & Mahalik, J. R. (2005) Body image concerns of gay men: The roles of minority stress and conformity to masculine norms. *Journal of Consulting and Clinical Psychology, 73*(6), 1185–1190.

King, M., Semlyen, J., Killaspy, H., Nazareth, I., & Osborn, D. (2007). A systematic review of research on counseling and psychotherapy for lesbian, gay, bisexual, and transgender people. British Association for Counseling and Psychotherapy. Retrieved from http://www.bacp.co.uk/research/LGBT_web.pdf

Kirkey, K. & Forsyth, A., (2001). Men in the valley: Gay male life on the suburban-rural fringe. *Journal of Rural Studies, 17*(4), 421–441.

Kissinger, D. B., Lee, S. M., Twitty, L., & Kisner, H. (2009). Impact of family environment on future mental health professionals' attitudes toward lesbians and gay men. *Journal of Homosexuality, 56*(7), 894–920.

Knauer, N. J. (2009). LGBT elder law: Toward equity in aging. *Harvard Journal of Law and Gender, 32,* 1–58.

Knox, S., & Hill, C. E. (2003). Therapist self-disclosure: Research-based suggestions for practitioners. *Journal of Clinical Psychology, 59*(5), 529–539.

Labra, O. (2015). Social representations of HIV/AIDS in mass media: Some important lessons for caregivers. *International Social Work, 58*(2), 238–248.

Landau, J. (2012). DOMA and presidential discretion: Interpreting and enforcing federal law. *Fordham Law Review, 81*(2), 619–647.

Landolt, M. A., Bartholomew, K., Saffrey, C., Oram, D. & Perlman, D. (2004). Gender nonconformity, childhood rejection, and adult attachment: A study of gay men. *Archives of Sexual Behavior, 33*(2), 117–128.

Langbein, L., & Yost, M. A. Jr. (2015). Still no evidence of negative outcomes from same-sex marriage. *Scholarly Comments on Academic Economics, 12*(2), 161–163.

Lehavot, K., & Simoni, J. M. (2011). The impact of minority stress on mental health and substance use among sexual minority women. *Journal of Consulting and Clinical Psychology, 79*(2), 159–170.

Lewis, N. M., Bauer, G. R., Coleman, T. A., Blot, S., Pugh, D., Fraser, M., & Powell, L. (2015). Community cleavages: Gay and bisexual men's perceptions of gay and mainstream community acceptance in the post-AIDS, post-rights era. *Journal of Homosexuality, 62*(9), 1201–1227.

Liau, A., Millett, G., & Marks, G. (2006). Meta-analytic examination of online sex-seeking and sexual risk behavior among men who have sex with men. *Sexually Transmitted Diseases, 33*(9), 576–584.

Lindhorst, T. (1998). Lesbians and gay men in the country. *Journal of Gay & Lesbian Social Services, 7*(3), 1–11.

Lune, H. (2007). *Urban action networks: HIV/AIDS and community organizing in New York City.* Lanham, MD: Rowman & Littlefield.

Madigan, S. (2010). *Who has the story-telling rights to the story being gold: Narrative therapy theory and practice.* Washington, DC: American Psychological Association.

Manalansan, M. (2006). Intersextions: Sexuality and gender in migration studies. *International Migration Review, 40*(1), 224–249.

Mancoske, R., & Lindhorst, T. (1994). Group work practice in an HIV/AIDS outpatient clinic. *Tulane Studies in Social Welfare, 19,* 71–81.

Martin, J., & Dean, L. (1993). Bereavement following death from AIDS: Unique problems, reactions and special needs. In M. S. Stroebe, W. Stroebe, & R. O. Hansson (Eds.), *Handbook of bereavement: Theory, research and intervention* (pp. 317–330). New York: Cambridge University Press.

Masuda, A. (2014). *Mindfulness & acceptance in multicultural competency: A contextual approach to sociocultural diversity in theory & practice.* Oakland, CA: New Harbinger.

McLean, R., & Marini, I. (2008). Working with gay men from a narrative counseling perspective: A case study. *Journal of LGBT Issues in Counseling, 2*(3), 243–257.

Meneses, C., & Grimm, N. (2012). Heeding the cry for help: Addressing LGBT bullying as a public health issue through law and policy. *University of Maryland Law Journal of Race, Religion, Gender, and Class, 12*(1), 140–168.

Meyer, I. H. (2003). Prejudice, social stress, and mental health in lesbian, gay, and bisexual populations: Conceptual issues and research evidence. *Psychological Bulletin, 129*(5), 674–697.

Meyer, I. H., & Dean L. (1995). Patterns of sexual behavior and risk taking among young New York City gay men. *AIDS Education and Prevention, 7*(5 Suppl.), 13–23.

Miller, R. (2013). Gay men: Practice interventions. In *Encyclopedia of social work.* Retrieved from http://socialwork.oxfordre.com/view/10.1093/acrefore/9780199975839.001.0001/acrefore-9780199975839-e-548.

Mills, D. (2015, June 26). Supreme court ruling makes same sex marriage a right nationwide. *The New York Times,* pp. A-1.

Mitchell, J. W., Harvey, S. M., Champeau, D., & Seal, D. W. (2012). Relationship factors associated with HIV risk among a sample of gay male couples. *AIDS Behavior, 16,* 404–411.

Morin, S. F., & Rothblum, E. D. (1991). Removing the stigma: Fifteen years of progress. *American Psychologist, 46*(9), 947–949.

Morrow, D. (2001). Older gays and lesbians: Surviving a generation of hate and violence. *Journal of Gay & Lesbian Social Services, 13*(1–2), 151–169.

Murphy, T. F. (1992). Redirecting sexual orientation: Techniques and justifications. *Journal of Sex Research, 29*(4), 501–523.

National Association of Social Workers. (2008). *Code of ethics.* Washington, DC: Author.

National Association of Social Workers. (2015). *Sexual orientation change efforts (SOCE) and conversion therapy with lesbians, gay men, bisexuals, and transgender persons.* Washington, DC: Author.

Ostrow, D. G., & Stall, R. (2008). Alcohol, tobacco, and drug use among gay and bisexual men. In R. J. Wolitski, R. Stall, & R. O. Valdiserri (Eds.). *Unequal opportunity: Health disparities affecting gay and bisexual men in the United States* (pp. 121–158). New York: Oxford University Press.

Pachankis, J. E. (2014). Uncovering clinical principles and techniques to address minority stress, mental health, and related health risks among gay and bisexual men. *Clinical Psychology: Science & Practice, 21*(4), 313–330.

Pachankis, J. E., & Goldfried, M. R. (2004). Clinical issues in working with lesbian, gay, and bisexual clients. *Psychotherapy: Theory, Research, Practice, Training, 41*(3), 227–246.

Paulson, R. (1991). Addressing the public mental health personnel crisis through systematic reform and public-academic linkages. *Community Mental Health Journal, 27,* 393–409.

Perry-Argüello, T. (2008). *Contagious communication: The mediatization, spatialization, and commercialization of "HIV."* (Unpublished doctoral dissertation). University of Washington, Seattle.

Phillips, M. J., & Ancis, J. R. (2008). The process of identity development as the parent of a lesbian or gay male. *Journal of LGBT Issues in Counseling, 2*(2), 126–158.

Pierceson, J. (2014). *Same-sex marriage in the United States: The road to the Supreme Court and Beyond.* Lanham, MD: Rowman & Littlefield.

Plant, R. (2011). *The pink triangle: The Nazi war against homosexuals.* New York: Macmillan.

Potârcă, G., Mills, M., & Neberich, W. (2015). Relationship preferences among gay and lesbian online daters: Individual and contextual influences. *Journal of Marriage and Family, 77*(2), 523–541.

Rahman, Q., & Wilson, G. (2003). Born gay? The psychobiology or human sexual orientation. *Personality and Individual Differences, 34,* 1337–1382.

Reilly, A., & Rudd, N. A. (2006). Is internalized homonegativity related to body image? *Family and Consumer Sciences, 35*(1), 58–73.

Rönn, M., White, P. J., Huges, G., & Ward, H. (2014). Developing a conceptual framework of seroadaptive behaviors in HIV-diagnosed men who have sex with men. *JID* (Suppl. 2), S586–S593.

Russel, G. M., & Bohan, J. S. (2006). The case of internalized homophobia: Theory and/as practice. *Theory & Psychology, 16,* 343–366.

Saari, C. (2001). Counteracting the effects of invisibility in work with lesbian patients. *Journal of Clinical Psychology, 57,* 645–654.

Samji, H., Cescon, A., Hogg, R. S., Modur, S. P., Althoff, K. N., . . . Klein, M. (2013) Closing the gap: Increases in life expectancy among treated HIV-positive individuals in the United States and Canada. *PLoS ONE, 8*(12), e81355.

Sanchez, F. J., Bocklandt, S., & Vilain, E. (2009). Gender role conflict, interest in casual sex, and relationship satisfaction among gay men. *Psychology of Men and Masculinity, 10*(3), 237–243.

Schuck, K., & Liddle, B. (2000). Religious conflicts experienced by lesbian, gay, and bisexual Individuals. *Journal of Gay & Lesbian Psychotherapy, 5*(2), 63–82.

Sears, J. T., & Williams, W. L. (1997). *Overcoming heterosexism and homophobia: Strategies that work.* New York: Columbia University Press.

Sepkowitz, K. A. (2001). AIDS—the first 20 years. *The New England Journal of Medicine, 344*(23), 1764–1772.

Shelp, S. G. (2002). Gaydar: Visual detection of sexual orientation among gay and straight men. *Journal of Homosexuality, 44*(1), 1–14.

Shernoff, M. (2006). Negotiated non-monogamy and male couples. *Family Process, 45*(4), 407–418.

Shilts, R. (1982). *The mayor of Castro Street: The life and times of Harvey Milk,* Vol. 12. New York: Macmillan.

Schumer, T. (2014). Abusing our LGBT youth: The criminalization of sexual orientation change reports. *Southern California Review of Law & Social Justice, 24,* 53–80.

Siconolfi, D., Halkitis, P. N., Allomong, T. W., & Burton, C. L. (2009). Body dissatisfaction and eating disorders in a sample of gay and bisexual men. *International Journal of Men's Health, 8*(3), 254–264.

Smith, R. A., & Siplon, P. D. (2006). *Drugs into bodies: Global AIDS treatment activism.* Westport, CT: Praeger.

Spector, A. Y., & Pinto, R. M. (2011). Let's talk about sex: Helping substance abuse counselors address HIV prevention with men who have sex with men. *Culture, Health, & Sexuality, 13*(4), 399–413.

Stampley, C. D. (2008). Social workers' culture-based countertransferences. *Journal of Ethnic and Cultural Diversity in Social Work, 17*(1), 37–59.

Substance Abuse and Mental Health Services Administration. (2012). *Top health issues for LGBT populations information & resource kit.* HHS Publication No. 12-4684. Rockville, MD: Author.

Tan, P. P. (2005). The importance of spirituality among gay and lesbian individuals. *Journal of Homosexuality, 49*(2), 135–144.

Thompson, B. L., Luoma, J. B., & LeJeune, J. T. (2013). Using ACT to guide exposure-based interventions for posttraumatic stress disorder. *Journal of Contemporary Psychotherapy, 43*(3), 133–140.

Tilsen, J., & Nylund, D. (2010). Resisting normativity: Queer musings on politics, identity, and the performance of therapy. *The International Journal of Narrative Therapy and Community Work, 3,* 64–70.

US Department of Health and Human Services. (2013). *2020 topics & objectives.* Retrieved from www.healthypeople.gov/2020/topicsobjectives2020/default.aspx

Van Den Bergh, N., & Crisp, C. (2004). Competent practice with sexual minorities: Implications for social work education and practice. *Journal of Social Work Education, 40*(2), 221–238.

Vetri, D. (1998). Almost everything you always wanted to know about lesbians and gay men, their families, and the law. *Southern University Law Review, 26,* 1–91.

Warner, M. (2002). *Publics and counterpublics.* New York: Zone Books.

Weeks, J. (1989). AIDS: The intellectual agenda. In P. Aggleton, G. Hart, & P. Davies (Eds.), *AIDS: Social representation, social practices* (pp. 5–31). Lewes, UK: Falmer Press.

Weeks, J., (1998). The sexual citizen. *Theory, Culture & Society, 15*(3–4), 35–52.

Weststrate, N. M., & McLean, K. C. (2010). The rise and fall of gay: A cultural-historical approach to gay identity development. *Memory, 18*(2), 225–240.

Williams, M. E., & Freeman, P. A. (2007). Transgender health. *Journal of Gay & Lesbian Social Services, 18*(3–4), 93–108.

Williamson, I. R. (2000). Internalized homophobia and health issues affecting lesbians and gay men. *Health Education Research, 15*(1), 97–107.

Wiseman, M. C., & Moradi B. (2010) Body image and eating disorder symptoms in sexual minority men: A test and extension of objectification theory. *Journal of Counseling Psychology, 57*(2), 154–166.

Wolpe, R. (2002). Treatment, enhancement, and the ethics of neurotherapeutics. *Brain and Cognition, 50*(3), 387–395.

Wolpe, R. (2004). Ethics and social policy in research on the neuroscience of human sexuality. *Nature Neuroscience, 7*(10), 1031–1033.

Woods, W. J., & Binson, D. (2003). Public health policy and gay bathhouses. *Journal of Homosexuality, 44*(3–4), 1–21.

World Heart Federation. (2012). *Cardiovascular disease risk factors.* Retrieved from http://www.world-heartfederation.org/cardiovascular-health/cardiovascular-disease-risk-factors/

CHAPTER 15

PRACTICE WITH THE BISEXUAL COMMUNITY

Kristin S. Scherrer and Lacey D. Clark

INTRODUCTION

Amongst the lesbian, gay, and bisexual (LGB) community in the United States, bisexual individuals are the largest demographic group (Egan, Edelman, & Sherrill, 2007; Hebenick et al., 2010; Mosher, Chandra, & Jones, 2005). Therefore it is particularly important for social workers to be knowledgeable about the unique needs of bisexual people, even within broader lesbian, gay, bisexual, transgender, and queer (LGBTQ) communities. Research suggests that bisexual individuals face unique challenges relative to their lesbian and gay counterparts. For instance, bisexual individuals are at higher risk for mental health issues than heterosexual, lesbian, and gay individuals (Dodge & Sandfort, 2007; Jorm, Korten, Rodgers, Jacomb, & Christensen, 2002; Kertzner, Meyer, Frost, & Stirratt, 2009). Other research suggests that culturally constructed notions of bisexuality shape myriad dimensions of social life, including coming out to families (Scherrer, Kazyak, & Schmitz, 2015), experiences with therapists (Dworkin, 2001; Page, 2007; Scherrer, 2013), and connections to community (Bradford, 2011; McLean, 2008). Despite the unique challenges faced by bisexual people and the ongoing need to serve this community, bisexuality remains an underexamined concept, relative to gay and lesbian identities (Scherrer & Woodford, 2013), underscoring the need for empirical and theoretical scholarship that focuses more specifically on bisexuality.

There is no universally agreed-on definition of bisexuality; the concept remains mercurial in academic scholarship as well as in everyday life (Esterberg, 2006; Halperin, 2009). Some research has focused on bisexual behaviors or on same- and different-sex attractions, while other scholarship examines those who adopt bisexuality as a self-identity. Self-identification represents a particularly salient classification for social workers as a person's bisexual identification conveys meaning about the self, internally as well as within a social and cultural context. While conceptualizations of bisexuality remain contested, this discussion illustrates the limitations of these concepts in contemporary society where "we cannot make our sexual concepts do all the descriptive and analytic work we need them to do, but in which we can neither manage to do without them . . . nor simply jettison them" (Halperin, 2009, p. 454). In other words, this scholarship encourages critical, contextual understandings of bisexuality, as the meanings and salience of this identity are likely to vary for individual bisexual people. Despite the variation among definitions of bisexuality, many would conceptualize their bisexual identity as indicating attraction to people of one's own gender and people of other genders.

A discussion of social work practice with bisexual populations would be neglectful without an examination of *biphobia*, a concept that describes the stereotypes and negative attitudes that people hold about bisexuality (Israel & Mohr, 2004; Ochs, 1996; Rodríguez-Rust, 2002). One common stereotype about bisexuality is the idea that bisexual people are simply in transition toward their "authentic" heterosexual or gay/lesbian identity. Bisexual people may be viewed as duplicitous, in seeking to avoid the stigma of identifying as gay/lesbian, or as at an early stage in their identity development and naïve to their true sexual orientation (Ochs, 1996; Rodríguez-Rust, 2002). These beliefs stem from the expectation that individuals should only be romantically attracted to people of one gender, a concept that has been described as *monosexism* (Bradford, 2004; Rodríguez-Rust, 2002). A corollary concept, *monosexual* can be understood as an individual who experiences attraction to members of only one gender category. Monosexist views convey the disbelief that bisexuality is a "real" sexual orientation and that individuals adopting this identity are motivated to do so because of fear, confusion, or naiveté. Another biphobic stereotype centers on their strong, deviant sexual drives, which are understood as even more hedonistic than lesbian or gay individuals (Israel & Mohr, 2004). People who hold this stereotype often express disbelief that a bisexual person could ever be satisfied in a monogamous relationship. Bisexual people are seen as sexually indiscriminate, and libel to have sex with "anything that moves" (Ochs, 1996). Related to this stereotype is the assumption that bisexual people are carriers of sexually transmitted infections (Eliason, 2001; Mohr, Weiner, Chopp, & Wong, 2009). As a result of this stereotype, bisexual people are often confronted by others' assumptions about their issues with commitment, fidelity, and trustworthiness (Eliason, 2001; Spalding & Peplau, 1997).

This chapter reviews existing literature on bisexuality with a focus on how such scholarship informs social work practice. The review of extant literature on social work practice focuses on bisexual populations, drawing on analytic and empirical insights from related fields (e.g., public health, counseling, sociology) as is fruitful to this analysis. This review is organized to focus on multiple practice domains, including practice with individuals, intimate relationships, families, groups, communities, and policy. For analytic clarity, the discussion of these practice domains remained separate, although it is recognized that there is often a great deal of overlap across these practice domains. In our review, a social constructivist lens was adopted to examine how (bi) sexual identities are constructed and reproduced in everyday interactions between individuals and social structures (Scherrer et al., 2015). In particular, a constructivist lens is employed to explicate how social, cultural, and historical contexts shape social work practice interventions with bisexual populations.

BISEXUAL INDIVIDUALS

The majority of existing literature on working with bisexual people focuses on practice with individuals. Previous scholarship has addressed several important domains relative to practice with bisexual individuals, including practitioners' own attitudes and beliefs about bisexuality, the unique needs of bisexual clients, and interventions with bisexual individuals. While practice with bisexual individuals could address a range of practice domains including clinical practice, advocacy, or case management, the vast majority of this previous literature focuses on clinical practice. This section focuses on clinical practice with bisexual individuals and highlights implications for advocacy or case management, as relevant.

PRACTITIONER ATTITUDES

A common theme in this scholarship is the role that biphobia plays in the clinical needs of bisexual clients. Research indicates that biphobic beliefs are pervasive (Herek, 2002; Spalding & Peplau, 1997) and can be internalized by bisexual people as well as shape their interactions with heterosexual and lesbian/gay people. Understanding how these biphobic beliefs shape interpersonal interactions represents a first step toward culturally competent practice with bisexual individuals.

One salient way that these biphobic stereotypes shape practice with bisexual individuals is in practitioners' attitudes about bisexual clients. Bisexual specific attitudes are rarely addressed in research that examines practitioners' attitudes toward sexual minorities (Bieschke, Paul, & Blasko, 2007; Mohr et al., 2009). Research that does focus on practitioners' attitudes about bisexuality finds that clinicians' beliefs generally mirror biphobic stereotypes (Eliason & Hughes, 2004; Mohr, Israel, & Sedlacek, 2001; Mohr et al., 2009; Page, 2007) and are generally more negative than attitudes about lesbian/gay identities (Eliason & Hughes, 2004). Furthermore, biphobic beliefs negatively shape practitioners' work with clients, as stereotypes about bisexuality negatively shape counselors' perceptions about their clients' overall functioning, feelings about treating the client, and assessment of the seriousness of their problems (Bowers & Bieschke, 2005; Mohr et al., 2009; Mohr et al., 2001; Murphy, Rawlings, & Howe, 2002).

Not only does research indicate that clinical practitioners are likely to have biphobic beliefs that negatively affect their work with clients, but bisexual people report that their sexual orientation presents unique challenges in experiences with psychotherapists (Page, 2007). Page conducted a mixed-method survey with 217 self-identified bisexual people who had experiences working with a mental health practitioner. This research indicates that one of the most commonly reported issues bisexual people face in psychotherapy is having their sexual orientation invalidated by their clinician (42% described this as the greatest problem in their work with a mental health professional; Page, 2007). Participants also reported experiencing challenges with practitioners' lack of knowledge about bisexuality or bisexual issues (26%) or the practitioner's belief that bisexuality is unhealthy (19%; Page, 2007). These views create a barrier for bisexual clients, not only in regard to developing trust and rapport with a mental health practitioner but also in that the practitioner's focus on the client's bisexuality may detract from the client's presenting issue (Scherrer, 2013).

Specialized training and education is likely key to overcoming these stereotypes. Research indicates that most mental health practitioners lack knowledge about issues regarding bisexuality (Murphy et al., 2002). Among clinicians that reported receiving training in regard to LGB issues, only 30% reported receiving training on bisexuality (Mohr et al., 2001). The need for bisexual specific training represents a challenge for social work practitioners since there is a relative lack of attention to bisexuality (as compared with lesbian or gay identities) in social work research (Scherrer & Woodford, 2013). Most research indicates a critical need to continue developing scholarly knowledge about bisexuality, so that we may educate one another about the strengths and needs of this identity group. A first step in providing culturally competent practice with bisexual individuals involves critical self-reflection about one's own, often unconscious, beliefs about bisexuality. Above and beyond individual practitioners, organizations can also make strides to promote bi-affirming practices among their practitioners. For instance, it is suggested that service-based organizations revise their materials (e.g., intake forms, nondiscrimination policy statements, website content) to reflect their inclusion and affirmation of bisexual identities. Organizations should seek out expert consultation when working with challenging cases involving bisexual clients or provide staff trainings on the health and mental health needs of bisexual individuals.

UNIQUE NEEDS OF BISEXUAL CLIENTS

Bisexual individuals enter into helping relationships with social workers for myriad reasons. Practitioners should be cautioned not to assume that a bisexual client's needs are necessarily related to their bisexuality, per se (Dworkin, 2001; Scherrer, 2013). That said, practitioners should also be knowledgeable about the range of issues that are likely to be relevant to bisexual clients (Page, 2007). Some of these issues are briefly discussed next, while suggesting that in individual work with bisexual clients "Bisexuality must not be either overemphasized or diminished, but definitely explored" (Dworkin, 2001, p. 674).

One unique challenge bisexual clients potentially face is related to mental health. Recent comparative studies of mental health indicators find that bisexual people experience higher levels of anxiety, depression, and suicidality than gay, lesbian, or heterosexual people (Dodge & Sandfort, 2007; Jorm et al., 2002; Kertzner et al., 2009). As a result, social workers should be attentive to possible mental health issues. Scholars theorize that these issues may stem from biphobic stereotypes and beliefs (Page, 2007). Aside from diagnosable mental health issues, bisexual people also report higher levels of stress related to their sexual orientation than their gay/lesbian counterparts; this finding is heightened for bisexual men (Page, 2007).

Stereotypes about bisexuality not only impact mental health practitioners but may also affect bisexual individuals, as these beliefs may be internalized and negatively shape their self-esteem or self-concept (Page, 2007; Scherrer, 2013). Internalized biphobia may lead bisexual individuals to believe that they are incapable of forming healthy, long-term relationships or that they are less psychologically developed and must eventually choose a monosexual identity. In working with bisexual clients, "Therapists need to remain alert to ways that bisexual clients may have internalized cultural bias deeply into their sense of self and sense of well-being" (Page, 2007, p. 67). Knowledge about biphobic stereotypes is key to this endeavor.

Although bisexual people have many similarities, the needs of this population are not monolithic and should be examined through the lens of intersectionality. In taking an intersectional approach to this identity group, we examine how other social identities shape individuals' experiences (Collins, 2004; Rust, 1996). Particularly relevant to bisexual clients is the role that gender plays in biphobic stereotypes. For example, women are often assumed to be "experimenting" with female partners and thus ultimately heterosexual. In contrast, men's bisexuality is more likely to be interpreted as stemming from a reluctance to claim a gay identity. While both men and women's bisexuality are delegitimized, the ways that these invalidations manifest are gendered (Eliason, 2001; Esterberg, 2006; Scherrer, 2013). Race is also likely salient to bisexual people's experiences of their sexual orientation (Collins, 2004; Israel, 2004). Israel describes the complex identity development processes that many bisexual people of color engage in as race and sexual orientation (as well as other social identities) all shape how one's identity is interpreted in a social and cultural context. In addition to gender and race, practitioners should be aware of how other social identities (e.g., urban/rural geographic location, religious/spiritual identity, ability status, age) may contribute to disparate experiences of biphobia.

PRACTICE IMPLICATIONS

Strengths-based practice approaches are a fundamental component of social work practice approaches (Saleebey, 1996) and should guide practitioners' work with bisexual clients. Although bisexual people face many unique challenges, there are also unique strengths associated with adopting a bisexual identity. Firestein (2007) suggests that some of these psychological strengths may include "the sense of freedom to define oneself, the satisfaction of having the ability to function as a bridge between straight and gay worlds, and the richness of being able to develop relationships with either sex" (p. 129). Adopting a strengths-based approach may also illuminate bisexual clients' proactive and ongoing engagement in self-discovery or their resilience in light of biphobic cultural stereotypes (Scherrer, 2013).

Addressing biphobic beliefs explicitly is likely critical to working with clients who identify as bisexual or may be considering adopting a bisexual identity (Dworkin, 2001; Firestein, 2007; Scherrer, 2013). Discussing biphobic stereotypes, and contextualizing them as socially constructed, will provide a safe space for bisexual people to examine possible internalized biphobia. Dworkin (2001) provides several examples of how these stereotypes may manifest for bisexual clients:

> Bisexuals may internalize that: bisexuals cannot make relationship commitments; bisexuals must have simultaneous relationships with both genders in order to be content; bisexuality is really a way to avoid coming to terms with a lesbian or gay identity; and bisexuals will leave a partner for the other gender if in a same gender relationship and for the same-gender if in a relationship with the other gender (p. 673).

While biphobic beliefs may represent a challenge for those who adopt a bisexual identity, understanding these beliefs as socially and culturally constructed may empower bisexual people to discard elements of these constructions that do not fit with their sense of self. Biphobia may also provide motivation for further advocacy and education efforts as clients are empowered to rewrite some of the problematic representations of bisexuality. When conducting advocacy efforts with, or on behalf of, bisexual clients, social workers may need to educate others about bisexuality or bisexual issues. However, it may be incumbent upon practitioners to dispel biphobic stereotypes among other helping professionals.

In consideration of the cultural roadblocks one may face in adopting a bisexual identity, a focus on identity development may be a fruitful tool for individual work with bisexual clients. Scherrer (2013) suggested that conceptual models that provide context for understanding one's bisexuality can be useful for extending client's understandings of their sexual identities. The Klein Sexual Orientation Grid (Klein, 1993) is one such tool. The Klein Sexual Orientation Grid enables clients to discuss their desires and experiences in nuanced ways, as they incorporate their past, present, and imagined future across domains such as sexual attraction, sexual behavior, sexual fantasies, emotional preferences, social preferences, and self-identification. A second identity development tool is Rust's (2007) conceptualization of identities as relative to a shifting social, political, and historical "landscape." This model invites a constructivist view of identity as socially and culturally situated and may provide clients a mechanism to examine how identities may shift over time and geographies (without necessarily representing a change in one's underlying sense of self).

These tools are congruent with an affirmative practice approach, a social work practice approach that was designed to alleviate the stressors associated with a stigmatized identity. Gay affirming practice prompts practitioners to

> Celebrate and advocate the validity of lesbian, gay, and bisexual persons and their relationships. Such a therapist goes beyond a neutral or null environment to counteract the lifelong messages of homophobia and heterosexism that lesbian, gay, and bisexual individuals have experienced. (Tozer & McClanahan, 1999, p. 736)

In adopting affirming practices with bisexual individuals, practitioners can assure clients that one need not be attracted to members of only one gender (Rodríguez-Rust, 2007). Practitioners can support clients in continuing their sexual identity discovery across their life course (Rodríguez-Rust, 2007). Knowing about the socially constructed nature of sexual identities, practitioners can assist clients in disentangling the meanings attached to sexual or emotional attractions or sexual behaviors. Suspending assumptions about how these experiences attach to particular identity labels, or what they may mean for a client's life, may offer a client the opportunity to examine thoughts or experiences without the social "baggage" that often accompanies them (Rodríguez-Rust, 2007). Social workers should provide additional resources to bisexual clients, such as bisexual community support groups or Internet-based information about bisexuality. Affirming practice with bisexual people should also attend to multiple dimensions of their social identities (e.g., race, gender, religion/spirituality, age, geographic locale). For example, bisexual clients with religious or spiritual beliefs may wish to be connected to a leader of their faith background for additional support. Furthermore, older bisexual people may feel particularly isolated and may benefit from additional social support (Scherrer, in press).

INTIMATE RELATIONSHIPS

This section discusses social work practice with bisexual people with regard to intimate relationships. Although much of this section discusses dyadic intimate relationships, the authors recognize that not all bisexual people seek out "coupled" relationships. Our intention is to be as inclusive as possible in attending to the myriad types of intimate relationships that bisexual people may form, including dyadic, nonmonogamous, and/or polyamorous relationships. We employ the term "nonmonogamous" to indicate an umbrella concept for all relationship statuses that are not intentionally monogamous, including those in open or swinging relationships. Polyamory is a related but somewhat more specific term that indicates "having multiple emotionally intimate relationships simultaneously. Often, though not always, these relationships are sexual in nature; the emphasis in polyamory is generally on the presence of multiple romantic partners" (Fierman & Poulsen, 2011, p. 17). The following section outlines scholarship on bisexual relationships alongside a description of social work practice implications.

Research indicates that misconceptions about bisexuality affect individual's interests in forming intimate relationships with bisexual people (Armstrong & Reissing, 2014; Eliason, 1997; McLean, 2007; Rodríguez-Rust, 2002; Spalding & Peplau, 1997). Spalding and Peplau found that heterosexual people believe bisexual individuals to be nonmonogamous, unfaithful, sexually risky, and more likely to spread sexually transmitted infections. Similarly, Eliason (1997) found that heterosexual undergraduate students were reluctant to engage in a relationship with a fictitious bisexual person to whom they were attracted. Other research has found that participants who were asked to pair up profiles of single people were more likely to match a bisexual profile to bisexual profile and less likely to match a bisexual profile to either a lesbian or gay profile or a heterosexual profile (Breno & Galupo, 2008), indicating the belief that bisexual people are less desirable potential partners for monosexual individuals. Taken together, this research indicates that bisexual people are often stereotyped as undesirable romantic partners.

Once in a relationship, stereotypes about bisexuality also shape bisexual people's experiences in intimate relationships (McLean, 2007; Rodríguez-Rust, 2002). One way that these stereotypes manifest is that bisexual people may not feel comfortable disclosing their identity to a partner, fearing stigma or rejection (McLean, 2007). The stereotype that bisexual people are sexually promiscuous, sexually insatiable, or nonmonogamous may also manifest in concerns that a bisexual person may not honor agreements about monogamy or exclusivity. Stereotypes that bisexual people are confused or unsettled about their sexual orientation also shapes one's experiences in intimate relationships. This may manifest as the monosexual partner may fear that the bisexual person may decide that he or she is no longer attracted to the monosexual partner's gender identity category.

Not all bisexual people are desirous of monogamous dyadic relationships (Kleese, 2005; Rodríguez-Rust, 2002; Rust, 2003). Bisexual people may be more likely than heterosexual or gay/lesbian individuals to seek out nonmonogamous relationships and less likely to regard monogamy as an idealized relationship form (Rodríguez-Rust, 2002; Rust, 2003). Forming and maintaining polyamorous and nonmonogamous relationships in a cultural context that privileges monogamy represents a potential source of stress for bisexual people who prefer nonmonogamous relationships.

PRACTICE IMPLICATIONS

Social workers practicing with couples where one partner is bisexual might expect that stereotypes about bisexuality may negatively shape the relationship quality. For instance, in some relationships a bisexual person may not even feel comfortable in disclosing his or her identity. Practitioners may be helpful in talking with the bisexual partner about possible coming out strategies, as well as potentially working with the (presumably) monosexual partner on his or her stereotypical beliefs about bisexuality. "Because trust and intimacy are usually needed to sustain intimate relationships, these relationships may be particularly difficult for bisexual people partnering with individuals who do not believe in a 'real' bisexual identity" (Scherrer, 2013, p. 244). Practitioners should encourage clients to openly discuss biphobic attitudes and examine how these stereotypes may shape partners' expectations of one another. Individuals who have indicated a nonmonogamous or polyamorous identity may wish to discuss the challenges associated with these identities, particularly in a cultural context that devalues these relationships (Rust, 2003). Social work practitioners should take advantage of clinical supervision, particularly as a way to practice critical self-reflection vis-à-vis one's own attitudes about bisexuality (and related areas of bias).

FAMILIES

There is a relative paucity of literature about the family relationships of bisexual people (Goldberg, 2010; Ross & Dobinson, 2013; Scherrer et al., 2015); however, existing literature generally falls into one of two categories: bisexual people's relationships with families of origin or bisexual people's parenting experiences. By families of origin, we are referring to the family members to whom we were assigned at birth. Families of origin may also be considered biological kin. The following section reviews existing literature on bisexual people's families of origin and experiences with family creation and parenting alongside a discussion of practice implications. As this chapter previously discussed bisexual people's experiences with significant others, the next section focuses on a discussion of families of choice on bisexual people's experiences with parenting and other creative family formations.

BISEXUALITY AND FAMILIES OF ORIGIN

Coming out to families of origin can be an emotionally fraught process for sexual minority individuals. LGB people may anticipate encountering negative responses from family members, strained family relationships, being forced out of the family, or violence (D'Augelli, 2005; Morrow, 2000; Savin-Williams & Ream, 2003). While these experience are shared by many LGB people, bisexual people also navigate unique stereotypes about bisexuality making coming out, or disclosing one's identity to one's family, particularly challenging. Research indicates that bisexual people may be less likely than their gay or lesbian counterparts to disclose their identity to family members (McLean, 2007). Furthermore, bisexual people's disclosure decisions are likely to be strongly mediated by their relationships status (e.g., those with partners are more likely to disclose their identity) and, in particular, the gender of their significant other (e.g., male bisexuals are more likely to disclose their identity if partnered with a female bisexual; Costello, 1997; Scherrer et al., 2015).

Stereotypes about bisexuality shape bisexual people's disclosure experiences with their families of origin, as it influences how bisexual people may choose to come out to their families (Scherrer et al., 2015; Watson, 2014). One of the only studies to empirically examine bisexual people's experiences coming out in families, Scherrer et al. detail the deliberation that went into their 45 bisexual-identified participants' disclosure processes, as bisexual people sought to adopt a disclosure strategy that would maximize desirable outcomes in their family relationships. The researchers found that "circulating discourses about bisexuality impact the strategies that individuals employ" (p. 692), as many bisexual people "simplified" their identity when coming out by describing themselves as gay or lesbian, often seeking to avoid negative conceptions about bisexuality. For example, some bisexual people reported coming out as lesbian/gay to avoid family members' "hopes" that they would eventually end up in a heterosexual relationship, mirroring findings in related studies (Lannutti, 2008). When bisexual people do come out *as bisexual* to members of their family of origin, they anticipated negative responses based on biphobic stereotypes (Scherrer et al., 2015; Watson, 2014).

Not only do stereotypes about bisexuality shape bisexual people's coming out strategies, but they also shape how family members respond to learning about a bisexual family member's sexual identity (Scherrer et al., 2015). Scherrer et al.'s research indicates that families were (surprisingly) knowledgeable about stereotypes about bisexuality, most often as they described bisexuality as a temporary identity on the way to a stable gay/lesbian/heterosexual identity (e.g., "I thought it was a phase"). When their participants came out as bisexual, family members engaged with these stereotypes, both explicitly and implicitly, to try to understand their bisexual family member (Scherrer et al., 2015). Taken together these data indicate that social constructions of bisexuality are important factors for understanding bisexual people's experiences in families of origin.

BISEXUALITY AND CREATING FAMILY

The decision to parent (or not to parent) is often central as sexual minorities create their own families. As in other domains, knowledge about bisexual people's parenting experiences is a relatively unexplored scholarly topic (Goldberg, 2010); when it is acknowledged it is usually subsumed under a broader discussion of LGBT parenting, which may obfuscate differences between these identity groups and render the experiences of bisexual parents in heterosexual relationships invisible (Ross & Dobinson, 2013). Thus much of what is known about bisexual parents is based on the experiences of bisexual people who are embedded in lesbian/gay communities.

Despite the substantial body of literature that examines the outcomes for children raised by gay/lesbian parents, little attention has been paid to child-level outcomes for bisexual-identified parents (Ross & Dobinson, 2013). Research that does exist on bisexual people and parenting suggests that bisexual people may be more likely to parent than their lesbian or gay counterparts, although there may be little difference in the desire to parent across LGB populations (Ross & Dobinson, 2013). A recent review of this topic suggests that "additional research with the children of bisexual parents, drawing upon a lens that explores and celebrates potential differences associated with being raised by a bisexual parent, would be of interest" (Ross & Dobinson, 2013, p. 96).

Finding ways to talk to children about one's sexual minority identity is a challenge for many sexual minority people in a social and cultural context that normalizes different-sex families (heteronormativity). However, unlike lesbian or gay identified parents who have readily available age-appropriate materials that describe same-sex families (e.g., children's stories such as *And Tango Makes Three* [Richardson & Parnell, 2005]), similar resources that explain bisexual identities do not currently exist (Ross & Dobinson, 2013). Finding ways to explain one's bisexual identity to children is one challenge that likely differs from lesbian or gay parents.

As with other facets of one's life, a bisexual person's family relationships are also shaped by other identities. For instance, for those bisexual people who also identify as polyamorous, the creation of families of choice may involve additional challenges (as well as strengths) relating to having multiple partners of different genders (Rust, 1996; Weitzman, 2006). Similarly, race is also salient to bisexual people's family relationships. As Israel (2004) finds in her examination of the overlaps between bisexual and biracial identities, both identities have implications for family relationships, including feelings of belonging, visibility, or misrepresentation.

PRACTICE IMPLICATIONS

Bisexual clients struggling with family relationships may benefit from being able to explore how stereotypes about bisexuality may shape their familial relationships. This may provide an opportunity for bisexual clients to describe experiences of familial support as well as marginalization and ultimately provide a better understanding of the client's familial context. Practitioners may helpfully affirm that there is no "wrong" or "right" way to come out to one's family members (nor is there an imperative to disclose one's identity to one's family). Rather, social workers can more fruitfully assist clients in examining some of the positive and negative potential outcomes of different types of disclosure strategies.

Practitioners working with the families of bisexual people may benefit from examining stereotypes about bisexuality with their clients. Conceptualizations of bisexual people as promiscuous, nonmonogamous, or untrustworthy may contradict family members' expectations of what constitutes "good" family members, interfering with bisexual people's abilities to maintain positive family relationships. At the same time, stereotypes about bisexual people as early in their sexual identity development or that they are "really" heterosexual, may lead to more affirming responses from family members. Addressing these stereotypes directly will enable family members to better understand how cultural constructions of bisexuality may shape their expectations of their bisexual family member. These expectations are likely to shape familial experiences above and beyond the disclosure moment, including interactions with a new partner, decisions around parenting, entering into a marriage relationship, or other similar familial events.

A prominent theme in research on the family relationships of bisexual people concerns the conflict that many bisexual people feel in regard to how to be authentically themselves with their family members (Firestein, 2007; Scherrer et al., 2015). For those bisexual clients who are interested, social work practitioners who are working with the families of bisexual individuals may seek to foster a dialogue where bisexual people can fully explain their identity to their families. Creating opportunities where bisexual people may be authentically themselves and safely explain their identities to children, parents, or other family members would potentially alleviate some of these challenges for bisexual individuals.

Family systems approaches have been identified as a potentially fruitful approach for working with families with a bisexual family member (Scherrer et al., 2015), as well as more generally with LGB families (Baptist & Allen, 2008; Heatherington & Lavner, 2008; Scherrer, 2013). Research indicates that coming out in families may be best understood as a process, whereby family members do disclosure, educate one another, or otherwise influence one another's thoughts and beliefs about having an LGB family member (Baptist & Allen, 2008; Heatherington & Lavner, 2008; Scherrer, 2013; Scherrer et al., 2015). Using a family systems practice approach provides an opportunity to understand coming out experiences as a complex, interdependent process with implications that unfold over time. Utilizing a family systems perspective enables practitioners to view the family outside of the moment of disclosure and instead view a person's bisexuality as an identity that will shape myriad family experiences, such as parenting, introducing new partners, separating with a significant other, or sexual health issues.

GROUP WORK

Feeling invisible and alone as a bisexual person is a critical issue for many bisexual people (Bradford, 2011). Groups are likely an important source of support for bisexual people, given monosexist beliefs within both heterosexual and gay/lesbian communities. Indeed, research indicates that lesbian/gay groups may not always feel safe for bisexual people to discuss sexual orientation issues (McLean, 2008). Existing research on group work with sexual minority populations primarily focuses on lesbian and gay individuals (Ball & Lipton, 2011; Engelhardt, 2011); to the best of our knowledge, there has been no empirical or theoretical scholarship that focuses on group work with bisexual people.

Despite the lack of research on group work with bisexual people, social support groups for bisexual individuals are provided at many LGBTQ organizations. These groups often include individuals who identify as bisexual, with those who may identify as "bi-curious" or "questioning." Although some bisexual people may benefit from group support in identity exploration, this grouping problematically implies that bisexual people are curious about or exploring their sexual identity. Other organizations provide social support groups for bisexuality, alongside other identity categories such as fluid, pansexual, or queer. These identities share many similar experiences, as they challenge monosexist assumptions about sexuality. It is suggested that organizations seeking to provide support groups for bisexual people create distinct groups for those seeking to explore their identities and for those that are seeking community or support for an identity that is already solidified.

While face-to-face groups may be a preferred mechanism for building community and finding social support, Internet-based groups may also be useful for bisexual people. Recent research finds that bisexual people are likely to use social media to create supportive groups or communities to seek out social support in regard to biphobia (Crowley, 2010). These findings indicate the group need not be limited to bisexual people but also include those who identify as lesbian or gay and share supportive ideas about bisexuality—as they may likely be supportive and affirming group participants (Crowley, 2010). Internet-based groups are likely to be particularly salient for bisexual people in more geographically rural spaces who may face additional barriers to finding lesbian/gay or bisexual groups. Readers are encouraged to explore bisexual specific online resources, such as the Bisexual Resource Center or the American Institute of Bisexuality, which are included in Appendix D of this text.

PRACTICE IMPLICATIONS

Groups are a potential source of support for bisexual people, although future research is needed as to how practitioners may most effectively leverage group work with this identity group. Practitioners may need to employ creative strategies in these groups, potentially using technology to enable greater reach to their services or adopting flexibility in terms of group inclusion.

COMMUNITIES

Identity-based communities are often a source of support for sexual-minority individuals who face marginalization among heterosexual individuals and communities. The issue of community support is more fraught for bisexual people, who are often marginalized in heterosexual communities as well as gay/lesbian communities (Bradford, 2004, 2011; Green, Payne, & Green, 2011; McLean, 2001; McLean, 2008; Miller, 2008; Ochs, 1996; Rodríguez-Rust, 2002). Research indicates that bisexual people have fewer community connections and experience more social isolation than their gay/lesbian counterparts (Balsam & Mohr, 2007). For those bisexual people who are involved in gay/lesbian communities, the fear of biphobia may mean that bisexual people do not feel comfortable to be their authentic (bisexual) selves (Scherrer, 2013). Rather, depending on the gender of their current partner, bisexual people may be misidentified as heterosexual or lesbian/gay, so "their bisexuality was never seen unless they made a point of talking about it" (Bradford, 2004, p. 14).

The invisibility of bisexuality is not only an individual-level issue but is constituted and reproduced within the broader US culture. This invisibility of bisexuality in the media and lack of bisexual representation in other cultural milieu contributes to the difficulties that bisexual people face in finding and creating community (McLean, 2001; Miller, 2008). In a recent review of bisexuality research, Bradford (2011) finds that bisexual visibility remains a central issue for bisexual people, particularly as their identities are often rendered invisible within their relationships with significant others or based on their community involvement.

PRACTICE IMPLICATIONS

The creation and maintenance of bisexual affirming community spaces is a significant practice issue for social workers. On a community level, social workers may seek to provide visibility and inclusion for bisexual identities in advertising events and seek to promote values of inclusion and diversity within sexual minority communities. Although creating bisexual specific spaces and events may be useful for some bisexual individuals who are seeking community support, research indicates that, for many bisexual people, having a community that is affirming of bisexual identities meets many of the needs that bisexual people have in seeking community support (Crowley, 2010). Technological innovations may facilitate the creation and maintenance of bisexual affirming communities, which may be of particular value for those in geographically rural or otherwise isolated areas.

POLICY

Though not abundant, existing literature addressing policy related to bisexual people has focused primarily on the domains of employment (Chamberlain, 2009; Green et al., 2011; Köllen, 2013; Tweedy & Yescavage, 2013), education (Jones, 2014; Kennedy & Fisher, 2010; Marshall, 2014), and relationship recognition (Battalora, 2008; Gammon & Isgro, 2006; Messinger, 2012). Common themes in the literature that examines how social policy can best support bisexual individuals primary focus on issues of visibility, identity recognition, and training.

EMPLOYMENT

A handful of studies have specifically focused on the need for employment policy to adopt more affirming policies for bisexual employees (Chamberlain, 2009; Green et al., 2011); Köllen, 2013; Tweedy & Yescavage, 2015). Bisexual people experience biphobia (and homophobia) at their workplaces (Chamberlain, 2009). As a result, "bisexual employees have a vital need to be appreciated as bisexuals and not as a part of the so-called LGBT group" (Köllen, 2013, p. 132). Workplace policies are important mediators for bisexual employees' workplace experiences (Green et al., 2011). Specifically, employers that adopt more inclusive language vis-à-vis gender as well as sexual orientation fosters greater feelings of safety amongst bisexual employees (Green et al., 2011). Furthermore, the inclusion of bisexual people in policy statements was related to a greater satisfaction with work life, as well as greater likelihood that bisexual people would be "out" to one's colleagues (Green et al., 2011).

EDUCATION

Educational settings are an important context to attend to issues of safety and inclusion for sexual minority students (Fisher et al., 2008; Henning-Stout, James, & Macintosh, 2000; Nichols, 1999). Although there are many similarities of the experience of LGBT students, bisexual students face unique challenges (Oswalt, 2009; Sheets & Mohr, 2009). Some of these challenges can be ameliorated through policy-level interventions (Jones, 2014; Kennedy & Fisher, 2010; Marshal, 2014). Antidiscrimination policies are one such policy intervention that can foster feelings of inclusion and safety for sexual-minority students. Yet these policies do not always explicitly include bisexual identities alongside other sexual or gender identities. This may present a challenge for bisexual students, as research indicates that they may be confused as to if they are included in their school's antidiscrimination policies if these policies do not explicitly mention bisexuality (Jones, 2014). Staff training is another important policy domain in educational settings (Kennedy & Fisher, 2010). Trainings that address homophobia in school settings should also provide information about bisexual identities, as well as some of the unique challenges that bisexual students may face. Similarly, educational institutions should also provide education to students about bisexuality alongside other sexual health materials or in trainings about bullying prevention (Kennedy & Fisher, 2010). Bisexual affirming policies may also emerge in the form of introducing changes to the curriculum or by using bisexual-inclusive language in mission statements, online materials, and other school materials (Kennedy & Fisher, 2010).

RELATIONSHIP RECOGNITION

The vast majority of policy literature on relationship recognition concerns same-sex marriage policy implications for bisexual people (Battalora, 2008; Gammon & Isgro, 2006; Messinger, 2012). In consideration of recent policy changes that recognize same-sex marriages by the US federal government, many of the policy recommendations of this research are obsolete. However, several implications for bisexual people remain. For instance, some scholars suggest that the binary language of same- and different-sex marriages is itself a problematic binary that reinforces binaristic constructions of sexuality and contributes to the invisibility of bisexuality (Battalora, 2008; Gammon & Isgro, 2006; Messinger, 2012). Rather, policies that involve intimate relationships should avoid assumptions about the similarities between lesbian/gay and bisexual constituents (Battalora, 2008; Gammon & Isgro, 2006; Messinger, 2012).

PRACTICE IMPLICATIONS

Across each of these domains several key policy recommendations emerge. Social workers who are responsible for policy development ought to acknowledge the unique challenges faced by bisexual people instead of assuming similarities to lesbian, gay, or transgender populations (Jones, 2014). Organizations should seek to identify the unique needs of bisexual constituents and adopt policies and practices that affirm and support these identities. In developing policy statements, social workers should seek to avoid binaristic language (e.g., heterosexual and homosexual) and instead incorporate more inclusive conceptualizations of sexual orientation and gender (Jones, 2014; Kennedy & Fisher, 2010; Marshall 2014). Specifically including the term "bisexual" or the phrase "gender identity and expression" in antidiscrimination statements has been identified as particularly useful, affirming, and effective language (Green et al., 2011). When needed, community leaders or experts may be brought in to assist in developing inclusive policy statements for bisexual constituents (Kennedy & Fisher, 2010).

CONCLUSION

Bisexuality remains a critical, yet underexplored, dimension of sexual diversity in the field of social work (Scherrer & Woodford, 2013). There remains significant need for social research focusing on bisexual individuals' health and mental health needs, the romantic and familial relationships of bisexual people, bisexual people's group and community experiences, and policy issues affecting bisexual individuals. In addition to empirical and theoretical social research on bisexuality, there is also a need for practice-oriented research on bisexuality to inform multiple domains of social work practice, including clinical practice as well as more macro-oriented practice domains. In order to appropriately represent the diversity of experiences within sexual-minority identities, greater attention to bisexual (as well as queer, pansexual, omnisexual, and other nonmonosexual identities) ought to be integrated into the field of social work and related health and social sciences.

REFERENCES

Armstrong, H. L., & Reissing, E. D. (2014). Attitudes toward casual sex, dating, and committed relationships with bisexual partners. *Journal of Bisexuality, 14*(4), 236–264.

Ball, S., & Lipton, B. (2011). Group work with gay men. In G. L. Greif & P. H. Ephross (Eds.), *Group work with populations at risk* (pp. 339–361). New York: Oxford University Press.

Balsam, K. F., & Mohr, J. J. (2007). Adaptation to sexual orientation stigma: A comparison of bisexual and lesbian/gay adults. *Journal of Counseling Psychology, 54*(3), 306–319.

Baptist, J. A., & Allen, K. R. (2008). A family's coming out process: Systemic change and multiple realities. *Contemporary Family Therapy, 30*(2), 92–110.

Battalora, J. (2008). Supremacy by law: The one man one woman marriage requirement and antimiscegenation law. *Journal of Bisexuality, 7*(3–4), 145–169.

Bieschke, K. J., Paul, P. L., & Blasko, K. A. (2007). Review of empirical research focused on the experience of lesbian, gay, and bisexual clients in counseling and psychotherapy. In K. J. Bieschke, R. M. Perez, & K. A. DeBord (Eds.), *Handbook Of Counseling And Psychotherapy With Lesbian, Gay, Bisexual, And Transgender Clients* (2nd Ed., pp. 293–315). Washington, DC, US: American Psychological Association, xviii, 442 pp. http://dx.doi.org/10.1037/11482-012

Bowers, A., & Bieschke, K. J. (2005). Psychologists' clinical evaluations and attitudes: An examination of the influence of gender and sexual orientation. *Professional Psychology: Research and Practice, 36*(1), 97–103.

Bradford, M. (2004). The bisexual experience: Living in a dichotomous culture. *Journal of Bisexuality, 4*(1–2), 7–23.

Bradford, M. (2011). Reflections on the bisexual experience. *Journal of Bisexuality, 11*(4), 509–512.

Breno, A. L., & Galupo, M. P. (2008). Bias toward bisexual women and men in a marriage-matching task. *Journal of Bisexuality, 7*(3–4), 217–235.

Chamberlain, B. (2009). *Bisexual people in the workplace: Practical advice for employers.* Retrieved from http://www.biresource.net/Bisexuals_in_Workplace.pdf

Collins, J. F. (2004). The intersection of race and bisexuality: A critical overview of the literature and past, present, and future directions of the "borderlands." *Journal of Bisexuality, 4*(1–2), 99–116.

Crowley, M. S. (2010). Experiences of young bisexual women in lesbian/bisexual groups on MySpace. *Journal of Bisexuality, 10*(4), 388–403.

Costello, C. Y. (1997). Conceiving identity: Bisexual, lesbian and gay parents consider their children's sexual orientations. *Journal of Sociology and Social Welfare, 24*(3), 63–89.

D'Augelli, A., Grossman, A., & Starks, M. (2005). Parents' awareness of lesbian, gay, and bisexual youths' sexual orientation. *Journal of Marriage and Family, 67*(2), 474–482.

Dodge, B., & Sandfort, T. (2007). A review of mental health research on bisexual individuals when compared to homosexual and heterosexual individuals. In B. Firestein (Ed.), *Becoming visible: Counseling bisexuals across the lifespan* (pp. 28–51). New York: Columbia University Press.

Dworkin, S. H. (2001). Treating the bisexual client. *Journal of Clinical Psychology, 57*(5), 671–680.

Egan, P. J., Edelman, M. S., & Sherrill, K. (2007). Findings from the Hunter College Poll of Lesbians, Gays, and Bisexuals: New discoveries about identity, political attitudes, and civic engagement. Hunter College, CUNY. Retrieved from http://as.nyu.edu/docs/IO/4819/hunter_college_poll.pdf

Eliason, M. (1997). The prevalence and nature of biphobia in heterosexual undergraduate students. *Archives of Sexual Behavior, 26*(3), 317–326.

Eliason, M. (2001). Bi-negativity: The stigma facing bisexual men. *Journal of Bisexuality, 19*(2–3), 137–154.

Eliason, M., & Hughes, T. (2004). Treatment counselor's attitudes about lesbian, gay, bisexual, and transgendered clients: Urban vs. rural settings. *Substance Use & Misuse, 39*(4), 625–644.

Engelhardt, B. J. (2011). Group work with lesbians. G. L. Greif & P. H. Ephross (Eds.), *Group work with populations at risk* (pp. 362–384). New York: Oxford University Press.

Esterberg, K. (2006). The bisexual menace revisited; or shaking up social categories is hard to do. In S. Seidman, N. Fisher, & C. Meeks (Eds.), *Handbook of the new sexuality studies: Original essays and interviews* (pp. 169–176). New York: Routledge Press.

Fierman, D. M., & Poulsen, S. S. (2011). Open relationships: A culturally and clinically sensitive approach. *American Family Therapy Academy Monograph Series, 7*, 16–24.

Firestein, B. A. (Ed.). (2007). *Becoming visible: Counseling bisexuals across the lifespan.* New York: Columbia University Press.

Fisher, E. S., Komosa-Hawkins, K., Saldana, E., Hsiao, C., Miller, D., Rauld, M., & Miller, D. (2008). Promoting school success for lesbian, gay, bisexual, transgendered, and questioning students: Primary, secondary, and tertiary prevention and intervention strategies. *The California School Psychologist, 13*(1), 79–91.

Gammon, M. A., & Isgro, K. L. (2006). Troubling the canon: Bisexuality and queer theory. *Journal of Homosexuality, 52*(1–2), 159–184.

Goldberg, A. E. (2010). *Lesbian and gay parents and their children: Research on the family life cycle.* Washington, DC: American Psychological Association.

Green, H. B., Payne, N. R., & Green, J. (2011). Working bi: Preliminary findings from a survey on workplace experiences of bisexual people. *Journal of Bisexuality, 11*(2–3), 300–316.

Halperin, D. (2009). Thirteen ways of looking at a bisexual. *Journal of Bisexuality, 9*(3–4), 451–455.

Heatherington, L., & Lavner, J. A. (2008). Coming to terms with coming out: Review and recommendations for family systems-focused research. *Journal of Family Psychology, 22*(3), 329–343.

Hebernick, D., Reece, M., Schick, V., Sanders, S.A., Dodge, B., & Fortenberry, J.D. (2010). Sexual behavior in the United States: Results from a national probability sample of men and women ages 14–94. *Journal of Sexual Medicine, 7*, 255–265. http://dx.doi.org/10.1111/j.17436109.2010.02012.x Medline:21029383

Henning-Stout, M., James, S., & Macintosh, S. (2000). Reducing harassment of lesbian, gay, bisexual, transgendered, and questioning youth in schools. *School Psychology Review, 29*(2), 180–191.

Herek, G. M. (2002). Heterosexuals' attitudes toward bisexual men and women in the United States. *Journal of Sex Research, 39*(4), 264-274.

Israel, T. (2004). Conversations not categories: The intersection of biracial and bisexual identities. *Women & Therapy, 27*(1–2), 173–184.

Israel, T., & Mohr, J. J. (2004). Attitudes toward bisexual women and men: Current research, future directions. *Journal of Bisexuality, 4*(1–2), 117–134.

Jones, T., & Hillier, L. (2014). The erasure of bisexual students in Australian education policy and practice. *Journal of Bisexuality, 14*(1), 53–74.

Jorm, A. F., Korten, A. E., Rodgers, B., Jacomb, P. A., & Christensen, H. (2002). Sexual orientation and mental health: Results from a community survey of young and middle-aged adults. *British Journal of Psychiatry, 180*(5), 423–427.

Kennedy, K. G., & Fisher, E. S. (2010). Bisexual students in secondary schools: Understanding unique experiences and developing responsive practices. *Journal of Bisexuality, 10*(4), 472–485.

Kertzner, R., Meyer, I. H., Frost, D. M., & Stirratt, M. J. (2009). Social and psychological well-being in lesbians, gay men, and bisexuals: The effects of race, gender, age and sexual identity. *American Journal of Orthopsychiatry, 79*(4), 500–510.

Klein, F. (1993). *The bisexual option* (2nd ed.). Binghamton, NY: Harrington Park Press.

Kleese, C. (2005). Bisexual women, non-monogamy and differentialist anti-promiscuity discourses. *Sexualities, 8*(4), 445–464.

Köllen, T. (2013). Bisexuality and diversity management—addressing the B in LGBT as a relevant "sexual orientation" in the workplace. *Journal of Bisexuality, 13*(1), 122–137.

Lannutti, P. J. (2008) "This is not a lesbian wedding": Examining same-sex marriage and bisexual-lesbian couples, *Journal of Bisexuality, 7*, 237–260.

Marshall, D. (2014). Queer contingencies: Bifurcation and the sexuality of schooling. *Journal of Bisexuality, 14*(1), 126–145.

McLean, K. (2001). Living life in the double closet: Bisexual youth speak out. *Hecate, 27*(1), 109–118.

McLean, K. (2007). Hiding in the closet? Bisexuals, coming out and the disclosure imperative. *Journal of Sociology, 43*(2), 151–166.

McLean, K. (2008). Inside, outside, nowhere: Bisexual men and women in the gay and lesbian community. *Journal of Bisexuality, 8*(1-2), 63–80.

Messinger, J. L. (2012). Antibisexual violence and practitioners' roles in prevention and intervention: An ecological and empowerment-based approach in public health social work. *Journal of Bisexuality, 12*(3), 360–375.

Miller, M. (2008). "Ethically questionable?": Popular media reports on bisexual men and AIDS. *Journal of Bisexuality, 2*(1), 93–112. doi:10.1300/J159v02n01_08

Mohr, J. J., Israel, T., & Sedlacek, W. E. (2001). Counselors' attitudes regarding bisexuality as predictors of counselors' clinical responses: An anlogue study of a female bisexual client. *Journal of Counseling Psychology, 48*(2), 212.

Mohr, J., Weiner, J. L., Chopp, R. M., & Wong, S. J. (2009). Effects of client bisexuality on clinical judgment: When is bias most likely to occur? *Journal of Counseling Psychology, 56*(1), 164–175.

Morrow, D. (2000) Coming out to families: Guidelines for intervention with gay and lesbian clients. *Journal of Family Social Work, 5*(2), 53–66.

Mosher, W. D., Chandra, A., & Jones, J. (2005). *Sexual behavior and selected health measures: Men and women 15–44 years of age, United States, 2002.* Atlanta, GA: US Department of Health and Human Services, Centers for Disease Control and Prevention, National Center for Health Statistics.

Murphy, J. A., Rawlings, E. I., & Howe, S. R. (2002). A survey of clinical psychologists on treating lesbian, gay, and bisexual clients. *Professional Psychology: Research and Practice, 33*(2), 183–189.

Nichols, S. L. (1999). Gay, lesbian, and bisexual youth: Understanding diversity and promoting tolerance in schools. *Elementary School Journal, 99*, 505–519.

Ochs, R. (1996). Biphobia: It goes more than two ways. In B. A. Firestein (Ed.), *Bisexuality: The psychology and politics of an invisible minority* (pp. 217–239). Thousand Oaks, CA: SAGE.

Oswalt, S. (2009). Don't forget the "B": Considering bisexual students and their specific health needs. *Journal of American College Health, 57*(5), 557–560. Retrieved from: http://www.acha.org/Publications/JACH.cfm

Page, E. (2007). Bisexual women's and men's experiences of psychotherapy. In B. Firestein (Ed.), *Becoming visible: Counseling bisexuals across the lifespan* (pp. 52–71). New York: Columbia University Press.

Richardson, J., & Parnell, P. (2005). *And tango makes three.* New York. Little Simon.

Rodríguez-Rust, P. (2002). Bisexuality: The state of the union. *Annual Review of Sex Research, 13,*180–240. doi:10.1080/10532528.2002.10559805

Rodríguez-Rust, P. (2007). The constructing and reconstructing of bisexuality: Inventing and reinventing the self. In B. Firestein (Ed.), *Becoming visible: Counseling bisexuals across the lifespan* (pp. 3–27). New York: Columbia University Press.

Ross, L. E., & Dobinson, C. (2013). Where is the "B" in LGBT parenting? A call for research on bisexual parenting. In A. E. Goldberg & K. R. Allen (Eds.), *LGBT-parent families* (pp. 87–103). New York, NY: Springer.

Rust, P. C. R. (1996). Monogamy and polyamory: Relationship issues for bisexuals. In B. A. Firestein (Ed.), *Bisexuality: The psychology and politics of an invisible minority* (pp. 127–148). Thousand Oaks, CA: SAGE.

Rust, P. C. R. (2003). Monogamy and polyamory: Relationship issues for bisexuals. In L. Garnets & M. Kimmel (Eds.), *Psychological perspectives on lesbian, gay and bisexual experiences* (pp. 127–148). New York: Columbia University Press.

Saleebey, D. (1996). The strengths perspective in social work practice: Extensions and cautions. *Social Work, 41*(3), 296–305.

Savin-Williams, R., & Ream, G. (2003). Sex variations in the disclosure to parents of same-sex attractions. *Journal of Family Psychology, 17*(3), 429–438.

Scherrer, K. S. (2013). Clinical practice with bisexual identified individuals. *Clinical Social Work Journal. 41*(3), 238–248.

Scherrer, K. S. (in press). Bisexual elders. In K. Hash & A. Rogers (Eds.), *Annual Review of Gerontology and Geriatrics (ARGG): LGBT elders.* New York: Springer.

Scherrer, K. S., Kazyak, E. A. & Schmitz, R. (2015). Getting "bi" in the family: Bisexual people's disclosure strategies within the family. *Journal of Marriage and Family. 77*(3), 680–696.

Scherrer, K. S., & Woodford, M. (2013). Incorporating content on gay, lesbian, bisexual, transgender, and queer issues in leading social work journals. *Social Work Research. 37*(4), 423–431.

Sheets, R. L., & Mohr, J. J. (2009). Perceived social support from friends and family and psychosocial functioning in bisexual young adult college students. *Journal of Counseling Psychology, 56*(1), 152–163.

Spalding, L. R., & Peplau, L. (1997). The unfaithful lover: Heterosexuals' stereotypes of bisexuals and their relationships. *Psychology of Women Quarterly, 21*(4), 611–625.

Tozer, E. E., & McClanahan, M. K. (1999). Treating the purple menace: Ethical considerations of conversion therapy and affirmative alternatives. *Counseling Psychologist, 27*(5), 722–742.

Tweedy, A. E., & Yescavage, K. M. (2013). Employment discrimination against bisexuals: An empirical study. *William & Mary Journal of Women and the Law, 21*(3), 1–45.

Watson, J. B. (2014). Bisexuality and family: Narratives of silence, solace, and strength. *Journal of GLBT Family Studies, 10,* 101–123.

Weitzman, G. (2006). Therapy with clients who are bisexual and polyamorous. *Journal of Bisexuality, 6*(1–2), 137–164.

CHAPTER 16

PRACTICE WITH TRANSGENDER AND GENDER-NONCONFORMING CLIENTS

Ashley Austin

INTRODUCTION

Effective social work practice with transgender and gender nonconforming (TGNC) communities necessitates a comprehensive understanding of the environmental and contextual issues impacting their overall health and well-being. A clear understanding of gender identity development and the range of gender experiences is a prerequisite for all discussions of gender identity specific to practice needs and potential interventions with this widely diverse community. Gender typically refers to the attitudes, feelings, and behaviors that are associated with an individual's biological sex. Behavior that is compatible with societal and cultural expectations is referred to as gender-normative, while behavior viewed as incompatible with these expectations is perceived as gender nonconforming. Gender identity is one's internal sense of identity (e.g., male, female, or something else). Contemporary gender identities beyond the binary include but are certainly not limited to terms such as bigender, genderqueer, gender creative, gender fluid, gender expansive, gender neutral, and transgender. "Transgender" is the commonly used umbrella term referring to any individual whose gender identity is incongruent with sex assigned at birth. As gender is increasingly recognized as a multidimensional spectrum, rather than a male–female binary, the terms "transgender," "trans," and "TGNC" are used in this discussion to encompass the wide array of binary and nonbinary gender identities. The term "cisgender" is used to refer to individuals whose assigned birth sex and gender identity are aligned (e.g., nontransgender individuals). This chapter begins by examining disparities in health and well-being among TGNC individuals through the lens of minority stress, attending to the impact of stigma, discrimination, and victimization. This is followed by an exploration of resilience and sources of support that may mitigate the adverse effects of minority stress. Discussion then focuses on the ways in which social workers can support TGNC individuals, their families, and significant others, as they move through their journey to live authentically. The chapter concludes with an overview of TGNC affirmative practice.

DISPARITIES IN HEALTH AND WELLNESS

There is a host of evidence indicating disparate health outcomes within TGNC communities. In particular, TGNC individuals experience disproportionate rates of psychological distress including suicidality, as well as risk for HIV/AIDS (Grant et al., 2011; Grossman & D'Augelli, 2007; Nuttbrock et al., 2010). Rates of depression and anxiety are significantly higher among TGNC individuals when compared with their cisgender counterparts (Budge, Adelson, & Howard, 2013; Nemoto, Bodeker, & Iwamoto, 2011; Nuttbrock et al., 2010). TGNC young people, in particular, have an exceptionally high risk of suicidality and other negative health outcomes (Grant et al., 2011; Grossman & D'Augelli, 2007; Nuttbrock et al., 2010). Findings from a study ($N = 55$) conducted by Grossman and D'Augelli indicate that nearly 50% of TGNC youth had strongly contemplated suicide. Similarly, among National Transgender Discrimination Survey (NTDS) respondents ages 18 to 24 ($n = 1,099$) approximately 45% reported having attempted suicide (Haas, Rodgers, & Herman, 2014) and nearly 50% of participants under the age of 25 ($n = 66$) in a study conducted by Clements-Nolle, Marx, and Katz (2006) had attempted suicide.

In addition to mental health risks, TGNC individuals, particularly transwomen of color, experience a disproportionate burden of HIV risk. Specifically, findings from a systematic review of 29 studies indicate that HIV prevalence rates are nearly 28% among transgender women in general, with HIV infection rates among African American transgender women three times as high (56%) as rates among Latino (16%) and White transgender women (17%; Herbst et al., 2008). Transfeminine youth are at similarly high risk for HIV infection, with study findings from a sample of transfeminine youth ages 15 to 24 indicated that 19% self-reported being HIV-positive and 67% reported engaging in sex work (Wilson et al., 2009); moreover, because of developmental factors associated with adolescence, HIV risk behaviors may be considerably exacerbated among this group (Wilson, Iverson, Garofalo, & Belzer, 2012). However, as a cautionary note, it should not be assumed that only transfeminine youth engage in sex work; practitioners should understand that many of the co-factors that increase the likelihood for sex work can include experiences of discrimination, harassment in schools and/or jobs, a lack of family and/or peer support, homelessness, among other factors.

RURAL POPULATIONS

While there is little data examining health and well-being among rural TGNC individuals, research suggests that rural communities may not be able to meet the health-care needs of underserved lesbian, gay, bisexual, transgender, and queer (LGBTQ) populations (Drumheller & McQuay, 2010). The social and economic realities of living in rural communities may make it particularly challenging for TGNC individuals to leave hostile working environments, come out safely, and find accessible TGNC specific support, creating additional risks for TGNC individuals. The only published study to date (Horvath, Iantaffi, Swinburne-Romine, & Bockting, 2014) that explores mental health, substance use, and sexual risk behaviors among rural and nonrural TGNC adults ($N = 1,229$) suggests that rural and nonrural TGNC adults have similar rates of substance use, with particularly high rates of marijuana use. Transwomen in both rural and nonrural communities reported concerning rates of unprotected sex in the past three months (42% rural, 45% nonrural). Moreover, data from this study indicates that rural transmen face exacerbated risk across some dimensions of well-being; specifically, Horvath and colleagues found that rural transmen had significantly higher rates of depression and anxiety. Given the barriers to accessible information, support, and services for rural TGNC individuals, elevated behavioral and mental health risks are of serious concern.

DISCRIMINATION AND VICTIMIZATION

Transgender individuals report pervasive discrimination and victimization across the life span (Grant et al., 2011; Grossman & D'Augelli, 2007; Mizock, & Lewis, 2008; Nuttbrock et al., 2010). Discrimination rooted in transphobia and cisgender privilege begins early. For instance, results from the NTDS ($N = 6,456$) indicate that alarming rates of harassment (78%), physical assault (35%), and sexual violence (12%) during K-12 education were reported by TGNC adults (Grant et al., 2011). Similarly, in a sample of TGNC young adults ($n = 290$), 44.5% reported experiencing in-school gender-based violence during their teen years (Goldblum et al., 2012). The 2013 GLSEN National School Climate Survey explored feelings of safety and experiences of school-based victimization among 7,898 LGBTQ students. Findings indicate that a troublesome majority experienced verbal harassment as a result of their gender expression (56%), including from teachers/staff (55%), and a third (33.1%) heard negative remarks specifically about transgender people frequently or often (Kosciw, Greytak, Palmer, & Boesen, 2013).

While schools are the scenes for a staggering amount of identity-based bullying and mistreatment, the victimization of TGNC youth is not limited to "any particular social context as it pervades their school, family, religious, and community environments" (Dragowski, Halkitis Grossman, & D'Augelli, 2011, p. 228). Dragowski et al. found that nearly three-quarters of gender nonconforming youth ($N = 350$) were verbally victimized (72%), had objects thrown at them (13%), and/or were physically attacked (11%) because of their TGNC identities. Notably, research indicates that gender nonconforming youth are at particular risk, encountering higher rates of all forms of victimization (physical, sexual, verbal, and psychological) by family members (D'Augelli et al., 2006; Roberts et al., 2012) than youth whose presentation and behavior are more gender typical. Furthermore, statistics documenting lifetime experiences of sexual violence among transgender people indicate shockingly high levels of sexual abuse and assault, with data suggesting that one in two transgender individuals has experienced sexual abuse and/or assault (Kenagy, 2005).

Data related to transphobic victimization and hate crimes provide a perspective on the scope and severity of hate-based crimes in the lives of TGNC people. While transgender individuals constitute only an estimated 0.3% of the population (Gates, 2011), findings from the National

Coalition of Anti-Violence Programs (NCAVP) exploring hate violence perpetrated against LGBTQ individuals found that transgender people, and particularly transwomen of color, are disproportionately impacted by the most violent hate crimes. Of the 20 reported hate homicides perpetrated against sexual and gender minority individuals in 2014, more than half (55%) were transgender women, and 50% were transgender women of color (NCAVP, 2015). Similarly, TGNC individuals are disproportionately represented among victims of police-involved hate crimes with transgender women being 5.8 times as likely to experience police violence compared to cisgender survivors/victims (NCAVP, 2015).

MINORITY STRESS MODEL

The minority stress model (Meyer, 2003) has increasingly been used to explain the heightened risk for negative health outcomes and maladaptive behaviors among LGBTQ people. According to minority stress theory, members of sexual and gender minority groups experience chronic stressors associated with identity-based stigma and prejudicial encounters, which in turn contribute to a higher prevalence of mental health and behavioral issues (Meyer, 2003). While this model was not specifically developed to explain stressors among TGNC individuals, several studies support the notion that TGNC individuals experience disproportionate rates of minority stressors, including physical and sexual violence, discrimination, stigma, and microaggressions (Bockting, Miner, Swinburne-Romine, Hamilton, & Coleman, 2013; Grant et al., 2011; Marcellin, Scheim, Bauer, & Redman, 2013; Hendricks & Testa, 2012). Recent cross-sectional data from a large, diverse sample of transgender individuals ($N = 1,093$) found that psychological distress was associated with experiences of rejection and discrimination and perceived transphobic stigma (Bockting et al., 2013). Thus, for TGNC individuals, the often daily onslaught of transphobic stigma and discriminatory treatment leads to pervasive experiences of minority stress that impacts emotional and behavioral health. For more information on the minority stress model, see chapter 12 in this text.

A TRAUMA-INFORMED PERSPECTIVE

It is well recognized that trauma results from adverse life experiences that overwhelm an individual's capacity to cope (Van der Kolk, 1996). Stress becomes trauma when it threatens one's physical or psychological integrity and when an individual's response includes intense fear, helplessness, and thoughts that one's survival may possibly be in danger (Herman, 1992; Van Horn & Lieberman, 2008; Van der Kolk, 2014). Consistent with conceptualizations of the trauma associated with experiences of interpersonal and systemic racism (Bryant-Davis & O'Campo, 2005), there is mounting recognition that transphobic stigma, discrimination, and victimization may be have a traumatic impact on TGNC individuals (Burnes, Dexter, Richmond, Singh, & Cherrington, 2016; Richmond, Burnes, & Carroll, 2012). Advances in knowledge and understanding regarding the detrimental cognitive, emotional, physical, and neurobiological effects of traumatic experiences (Centers for Disease Control and Prevention, 2013; Felitti et al., 1998; Herman, 1992; Van der Kolk, 2014) underscore the importance of utilizing a trauma-informed perspective when working with TGNC clients. An affirming and trauma-informed perspective recognizes that traumatic events and experiences may have threatened TGNC clients' sense of safety, power, and control over their lives, often undermining self-determination and dignity. Trauma-informed practice aims to provide services within a strengths-based therapeutic context that promotes safety, trust, collaboration, empowerment, and client choice (Hopper, Bassuk, & Olivet, 2010), factors that are critical for engaging and supporting TGNC clients.

SOURCES OF RESILIENCE

Many TGNC individuals demonstrate notable strength in the face of adversity, achieving success and embracing a positive sense of self and community in the face of high levels of minority stress (Austin, 2016; Beemyn & Rankin, 2011; McFadden, Frankowski, Flick, & Witten, 2013; Singh, 2013; Singh, Hays, & Watson, 2011; Singh & McKleroy, 2011). In particular, mounting qualitative research highlights unique aspects of resiliency among diverse samples of transgender individuals. In a recent grounded theory study of TGNC young people ($N = 13$), participants recounted stories of notable patience, perseverance, strength, and emerging confidence despite long and often protracted journeys toward authenticity frequently steeped in experiences of oppression (Austin, 2016). Other research findings highlight sources of resilience among TGNC populations, which include a sense of hope for the future, social activism, and being a positive role model for others (Singh et al., 2011; Singh & McKleroy, 2011).

THE IMPACT OF SOCIAL SUPPORT AND CONNECTEDNESS

Burgeoning research points to the importance of social support and acceptance for well-being and resilience among TGNC people even in the face of pervasive mistreatment and discrimination outside of the home (Budge et al., 2013; Ryan, Huebner, Diaz, & Sanchez, 2009; Ryan, Russell, Huebner, Diaz, & Sanchez, 2010; Simons, Schrager, Clark, & Olson, 2013). Research suggests that social support may foster the use of healthy coping mechanisms, reduce depression and psychological distress, and promote positive mental health (Budge et al., 2013; Sánchez & Vilain, 2009) among TGNC people. In one study of TGNC sex workers ($N = 573$), higher social support was associated with less depression (Nemoto, Bodeker, & Iwamoto, 2011). Similarly, in a recent study of TGNC adults ($N = 865$), higher levels of general social support protected against both depression and anxiety (Pflum, Testa, Balsam, Goldblum, & Bongar, 2015). Moreover, a study by Budge and colleagues (2013) found that social support was directly negatively correlated with anxiety and depression among TGNC adults ($N = 351$) but also found that lower levels of social support negatively impacted psychological distress through its indirect effects on coping style (e.g., greater use of avoidant coping strategies). Finally, research with a sample ($N = 66$) of transgender-identified adolescents (ages 12–24) receiving care associated with medically transitioning found that greater parental support was significantly and positively correlated with life satisfaction and less depression (Simons et al., 2013).

Accruing evidence suggests that positive connection to a supportive community and a sense of social connectedness may be particularly important sources of well-being for members of the TGNC community (Bariola et al., 2015; Frost & Meyer, 2012, Sánchez & Vilain, 2009; Testa, Jimenez, & Rankin, 2014). Findings from both Frost and Meyer and Sánchez & Vilain suggest that positive mental health among TGNC individuals is correlated with a connectedness to a community of similar others (e.g., TGNC support groups and TGNC social networks, social media groups). Additionally, survey research conducted by Bariola and colleagues with a sample of Australian transgender adults ($N = 169$) found that connecting frequently with LGBT peers was a significant correlate of resilience.

Testa et al. (2014) found that connection with other TGNC-identified individuals was notably important for both transfeminine and transmasculine participants. Specifically, the authors found that having prior engagement or connection with other TGNC people during early stages of identity development significantly predicted decreased psychological distress (anxiety and suicidality) and increased comfort with one's TGNC identity. Interestingly, a recent study conducted by Pflum et al. (2015) found that transgender community connectedness was negatively associated with anxiety and depression among transfeminine identified participants ($N = 865$), but the relation was not significant for transmasculine participants. Taken together, findings are consistent with the minority stress framework, which suggests that minority group connection and involvement may defend against the negative impact of identity-based discrimination (Meyer, 2003; Szymanski & Owens, 2009).

INFORMATION AND COMMUNICATION TECHNOLOGIES

The use of information and communication technologies (ICTs) in the TGNC community, which developed as a result of the scarcity of local TGNC specific resources, discriminatory practices in health-care settings, and the absence of TGNC community support and/or social groups, is regularly utilized to obtain transgender specific knowledge (e.g., understand TGNC identities) and resources (e.g., locate trans-affirming doctors, therapists, and clinics), as well as to connect and socialize with other TGNC individuals (Austin, 2016; Horvath, Iantaffi, Grey, & Bockting, 2012; Mizock & Lewis 2008). Examples of ICTs used by TGNC individuals include transgender-specific YouTube channels and blogs, TGNC-specific Facebook groups and organizations, online resource lists and guides to TGNC services, family support groups, TGNC-specific dating sites, as well as videos describing and sharing detailed information related to medical, legal, and social aspects of transitioning. ICTs facilitate resilience among TGNC populations by providing opportunities to form community, build individualized support networks, develop coping skills, engage in identity development activities, and seek information in an environment that is often notably safer and more accessible than one's physical environment (Craig & McInroy, 2013). While ICTs are particularly salient sources of support for young people navigating a TGNC identity (Austin, 2016; Craig & McInroy, 2013), data suggests the importance of these resources for TGNC individuals across the lifespan (Austin, Craig, & Goodman, 2016), as well as for parents and family members of TGNC individuals (Riley, Sitharthan, Clemson, & Diamond, 2013). TGNC-affirming social work practitioners should be well versed in web and technology-based sources of support. Taken together, the literature demonstrates strong evidence for the role of social support and acceptance, social connectedness, and technology and social media in fostering resilience among TGNC individuals. Such findings should guide social work practice and programming targeting TGNC communities, particularly those with the least access to in-person support (e.g., youth, individuals living within rural communities).

LIVING AUTHENTICALLY

There are many TGNC specific needs that may emerge as individuals navigate identity development and strive to live an authentic life. Historically, the journey toward living authentically has been perceived as synonymous with "transitioning," which is the process of aligning one's external gender presentation and role in society with one's internal gender identity. Transitioning may, but does not necessarily, include changing one's hair, clothing, and accessories; modifying one's physical appearance through the use of hormones/hormone blockers; gender-confirming surgeries; and hair removal procedures, as well as changing one's name and/or gender marker on legal documents. Increased recognition and validation of nonbinary gender identities has broadened understanding of what it means for a TGNC person to live authentically. A growing number of TGNC individuals achieve authenticity without any medical interventions, conveying a more flexible and expansive range of gender expressions. Despite the increased diversity of TGNC experiences, the need to transition physically, legally, and socially remains an important need for many TGNC youth and adults.

PHYSICAL TRANSITION & AFFIRMATION NEEDS

Transgender clients face significant barriers to receiving appropriate medical services related to their transition. They are often reluctant to seek medical care due to past rejection, trauma, and fear of disclosure of their transgender status (Spicer, 2010). In the absence of consistent and trans-affirmative care, medical settings can become sites of traumatization for transgender clients. In fact, the NTDS found that among transgender individuals accessing health care, 28% were harassed and experienced violence in medical settings, 19% were denied care, and 2% were victims of violence in doctor's offices (Grant et al., 2011). These findings underscore the pivotal need for advocacy around issues of health and medical care. There are several fundamental aspects of transgender affirmative social work practice related to medical aspects of transitioning. One of the first steps may be to facilitate client understanding of the guidelines for medical treatment according to Version 7 of the Standards of Care (World Professional Association for Transgender Health [WPATH], 2011). Often social workers are called upon to provide a referral to initiate medical treatment once a client determines whether or not he or she is interested in pursuing medical interventions aimed at bringing about congruity between physical body and gender identity. According to existing standards of care, a practitioner working with a client interested in pursuing medical intervention may need to (a) identify dysphoria and make the appropriate diagnosis,

(b) assess and provide treatment for any comorbid mental health issues, (c) provide (or refer clients to reliable sources for) information and education about the medical treatments under consideration, and (d) provide a formal referral letter regarding the client's need and readiness for medical intervention (WPATH, 2011).

LEGAL TRANSITION & AFFIRMATION NEEDS

For many transgender individuals, their legal name corresponds with their assigned sex at birth but not with their gender identity or expression, which can cause significant distress, threats to safety, and barriers to employment. In fact, the NTDS found that that 40% of TGNC individuals who presented IDs that did not match their gender identity/expression were harassed, 15% were asked to leave the setting in which they had presented incongruent identification, and 3% were attacked or assaulted (Grant et al. 2011). Unfortunately, legally changing one's name can be a complicated and cost-prohibitive process for many TGNC people. Procedures for changing names on various documents vary greatly from state to state, and navigating these processes can often be quite daunting, requiring that individuals explain their situation (e.g., out themselves) to individuals across a variety of settings (e.g., social security office, department of motor vehicles, and court personnel) who may or may not be transgender affirming. National data suggests that among TGNC individuals who have transitioned, only 21% were able to update all identification and records, while 33% had updated none of their documents (Grant et al. 2011). Only 59% reported updating the gender on their driver's license/state ID, suggesting that 41% live without a primary form of identification that matches their gender identity (Grant et al. 2011). It is critical that social work practitioners understand these unique challenges faced by TGNC clients and take the initiative to learn about the policies and procedures for name/gender marker changes in their counties and states, as well as local organizations that offer transgender-specific legal services. For instance, in some cities legal aid organizations will work with TGNC clients at no cost to facilitate the legal name change process in the courts.

SOCIAL TRANSITION & AFFIRMATION NEEDS

For most TGNC individuals, an early step toward living authentically includes changes in the ways that they may present themselves and engage in the social world. This process is often referred to as socially transitioning and generally includes several components (Collazo, Austin, & Craig, 2013). Changing one's hairstyle and manner of dress to be more consistent with one's gender identity is often a key aspect of socially transitioning. In addition, many TGNC individuals will often select a new name and/or personal pronouns that are more congruent with their gender identity and expression. These changes may happen gradually, whereby an individual begins dressing in a gender-confirming way and using chosen name and gender-confirming personal pronouns at home with family and close friends and then ease into socially transitioning at work, at school, and within the larger community.

Social workers can play an instrumental role in ensuring that social transitions for TGNC individuals within the community are smooth and safe. For instance, prior to socially transitioning at home or in the community, the social worker may facilitate disclosure planning. Social work practitioners should help clients determine their level of readiness to come out, as well as assess the relative safety of coming out to others about one's TGNC identity and/or the decision to begin socially and/or medically transitioning. Discussions should explore disclosure across social and cultural communities (e.g., family of origin and/or choice, friends, colleagues, ethno/cultural community, and faith community; White-Holman & Goldberg, 2006). Affirmative social workers should reinforce client empowerment and self-determination by ensuring that clients remain in control of all aspects of the disclosure process. For example, a clinician can assist clients in developing a timeline by which they would like to begin disclosing gender identity and/or plans to begin the transition process to loved ones. The clinician can also assist by helping clients decide how they wish to disclose this information to others (e.g., in person, via letter, email, text, or over the phone) and engaging in role plays that allow clients the opportunity to practice various scenarios associated with disclosure.

In addition to supporting clients in coming out in their social environments as TGNC, affirmative social workers may need to engage in education and advocacy work with organizations/institutions. For example, it may be important to help a client's health-care provider understand the importance of using clients' chosen names rather than their legal names on various documents. Likewise, helping others recognize the importance of using gender-neutral pronouns (e.g., ze/zir or they/them/their) for a genderqueer client can be an instrumental form of advocacy. Such advocacy may be particularly important for TGNC youth and families when youth are socially transitioning within school settings. Teachers, staff, and administrators may need to be educated on the guidelines and strategies for creating inclusive environments for TGNC students (see Orr, Baum, Brown, Gill, & Kahn, 2015). Overall, as many individuals find it problematic or bothersome to use pronouns that challenge binary-gender norms in any form or fashion, practitioners and educators alike should model affirming pronoun use across all settings as well as advocate for respect in using one's pronouns whether or not they identify as TGNC.

DEVELOPMENTAL CONSIDERATIONS OF TGNC CHILDREN AND ADOLESCENTS

The medical needs of gender-diverse children and adolescents may vary considerably based on many factors. Awareness of gender identity occurs relatively young as children can identify themselves as a boy or girl by age three, and gender identity is generally stable by age four (American Pediatric Association Committee on Adolescence [APACA], 2013; Menvielle, 2009). Of children who present at clinics with gender nonconforming behaviors, self-expression, or identities, research suggests that a transgender, gender-nonconforming, or gender-diverse identity does not persist for a majority of them by adolescence (APACA, 2013; Zucker, 2010). However, there is increasing speculation that these numbers may be an underestimate of the true percentage as a result of skewed research processes, as well as the possibility that children as a result of the implicit and explicit pressure to conform to behavioral expectations associated with assigned sex at birth were reluctant to share persisting experiences of gender dysphoria

(Substance Abuse and Mental Health Services Administration [SAMHSA], 2015). To date, the correlates of persisting or desisting gender nonconformity remain unknown (APACA, 2013) but emerging research suggests that it is likely the result of a complex interplay between biological, environmental, and psychological factors (Steensma, Kreukels, deVries, & Cohen-Kettnis, 2013). It appears that dysphoria during childhood, which intensifies during adolescence, is unlikely to abate, and gender TGNC identities, which present during puberty (10–12 for natal females and 12–14 for natal males), appear to remain stable throughout the lifespan (Spack et al., 2011; Steensma, McGuire, Kreukels, & Cohen-Kettenis, 2013; Zucker, 2010). Because the emergence and stability of TGNC identities varies across the developmental lifespan of children and adolescents, the health-care needs of these youth also vary. For example, reversible pubertal suppression (e.g., hormone blockers) for TGNC youth is identified as an important and often critical medical intervention for children during puberty but typically not prior to that life stage (WPATH, 2011; Spack et al., 2011). Similarly, for adolescents interested in transitioning, hormone therapy to initiate pubertal development of the desired other sex is recommended for adolescents around the age 16 but never prior to puberty (Edwards-Leeper & Spack, 2012; Hembree et al., 2009). Individuals in the United States are generally unable to undergo gender confirming surgeries until the age of consent (e.g., 18); however, increasingly, some doctors in the United States will perform gender-confirming surgeries with youth assent and parental consent. It is anticipated that the standards of care will continue to evolve in response to increasingly affirmative stances from the medical and mental health communities around transgender identities, as well as to accruing knowledge about the particular benefits associated with early medical intervention for TGNC children.

SUPPORT FOR PARENTS OF TGNC CHILDREN

As social and cultural attitudes toward TGNC individuals become more accepting, and knowledge about TGNC identities becomes more widespread, it will likely become easier for parents of TGNC children and adolescents to understand, affirm, and support gender nonconformity with their children. However, recent qualitative research suggests that parents may experience uncertainty, loss, and ambivalence before they move toward acceptance of a child's TGNC identity (Gregor, Hingley-Jones, & Davidson, 2015). These findings are consistent with Lev's (2004) model of transgender emergence in families. In this model, the first stage known as *discovery and disclosure* occurs when the family first identifies and names the child's identity issues. During the second stage, *turmoil*, families are often highly emotional as they struggle to make sense of their child's gender identity. *Negotiation* is the phase in which families explore strategies for managing a child's gender identity in a manner that feels safe and appropriate for the child and family. Lev describes the final stage as *finding balance* for a family with a TGNC child. However, not all parents are able to achieve acceptance or find balance with a TGNC child. As such, some express the hope and/or request that a social work practitioner "fix" their child through the use of conversion or reparative therapies. Competent and TGNC-affirming practitioners should be able to validate parental feelings of concern, fear, and desperation while clearly explaining that ethical practice guidelines for working with TGNC children and teens renounce the use of reparative and conversion therapies (Council on Social Work Education, 2015; SAMHSA, 2015).

Instead, parental support rooted in a TGNC-affirmative practice framework should be provided. The type of support should be associated with a parent's level of understanding and acceptance of the child's gender identity, as well as specific needs. Research suggests that parents may have several specific needs including (a) current and accurate information about the needs, experiences, and care guidelines for TGNC children; (b) contact with and support from other parents of TGNC children; (c) skills to counteract bullying and stigma toward their children and/or their families; (d) access to competent and affirming medical and mental health professionals; (e) the coping skills necessary to deal with uncertainty; and (f) school, community, family, and religious communities that are supportive and affirming of TGNC identities (Riley et al., 2013). For instance, a family who is struggling to accept their child's identity and feels very isolated with their experience of parenting a TGNC child may find a local or online support group of parents of TGNC youth to be particularly helpful. Other parents may need less help accepting their child's TGNC identity but instead are struggling to locate competent medical information and/or providers to facilitate their child's transition. Finally, in some instances parents may need the social worker to provide support in the form of advocacy for their children in schools or with extracurricular activities. As such, it is critical that trans-affirming social workers are aware of existing community and online resources, as well as policies and guidelines that can support parents and families of TGNC children.

AFFIRMATIVE PRACTICE APPROACHES

Affirmative approaches to care for TGNC individuals are markedly different than damaging and unethical practices, which try to change sexual orientation and gender identity. The potential harm associated with reparative or conversion therapy is well documented (Newman & Fantus, 2015) and recent SAMHSA (2015) guidelines eschew the use of these practices with TGNC children and adolescents. Additionally, such therapies must not be part of social work practice or referral mechanisms. In contrast, affirmative interventions, which support and validate the identities, strengths, and experiences of TGNC populations, are increasingly important in the provider landscape. Such interventions can counter minority stressors and promote the health and well-being of this population (Horn, 2010).

A social worker may be the first point of contact for individuals as they attempt to identify and navigate a TGNC identity. As such, the adoption of an affirming clinical position, which acknowledges all experiences of gender as equally healthy and valuable, is critical (Austin & Craig, 2015). This affirmative approach is consistent with SAMHSA (2015) guidelines that condemn as unethical and harmful any practices that coerce or support the coercion of gender conformity among TGNC children and adolescents. Unconditional positive regard for the diversity of TGNC identities and expressions is fundamental to creating an affirmative practice context for TGNC clients. Affirmative social work practice must acknowledge and counter the oppressive contexts in which patients may have previously experienced services by creating an affirmative culture at the onset of the clinical relationship (Craig, Austin, & Alessi, 2012).

A first step is to help individuals overcome reticence or distrust by creating a visibly affirmative and inclusive context during the first session. For instance, a practitioner may consider introducing oneself in the following manner: "Hello, my name is Ashley and I use she, her, and hers pronouns." Similarly, social workers can create a TGNC-affirming space by having posters or handouts that embrace diverse gender identities, utilizing inclusive intake forms that allow for the use of preferred names and pronouns, as well as a diverse and inclusive range of gender and sexual identities (American Academy of Pediatrics, Committee on Adolescence, 2013). In the same fashion, practitioners should attend to structural inclusivity for TGNC clients by ensuring that TGNC individuals can take part in programming based on gender identity rather than assigned sex at birth (e.g., live-in residential programs and/or participate in support groups consistent with gender identity), as well as replacing sex-segregated spaces with gender-inclusive spaces whenever possible (e.g., gender-neutral restrooms). Finally, interventions attending to the specific needs of TGNC individuals should be implemented and practiced with competency.

TRANSGENDER-AFFIRMATIVE CBT

Increasingly, research points to the effectiveness of emerging affirming cognitive behavioral interventions (Austin & Craig, 2015; Craig & Austin, 2016). Transgender affirmative cognitive behavior therapy (TA-CBT) represents a particularly promising intervention for TGNC youth and adults. TA-CBT is a version of CBT that has been adapted to ensure an affirming stance toward gender diversity, as well as to competently target the unique sources of stress experienced by TGNC individuals (e.g., transphobia, gender dysphoria, systematic identity-based oppression). CBT encourages individuals to formulate alternative ways of thinking about situations and problems, which in turn prompts emotional and behavioral changes (Beck, 2011). As result of pervasive exposure to transphobic attitudes, beliefs, and behaviors, transgender individuals may develop negative patterns of thinking about themselves and their futures, which in turn affect emotional and behavioral responses. Fostering a transgender-affirming view of TGNC identities and experiences may help clients overcome negative self-perceptions and/or outlooks for the future. This more positive way of thinking about oneself can influence maladaptive behavioral responses associated with negative emotions. Given the ubiquitous experience of minority stress among TGNC individuals, TA-CBT is rooted in understanding the pervasiveness and consequences of transgender stigma and prejudice. The intervention is aimed at promoting positive change and healthy coping in the face of notable individual, social, and structural oppression. Nevertheless, TA-CBT is intended to be implemented flexibly to meet the distinct needs of each client, differentially engaging dimensions of risk and resilience within the social work practice setting based on each client's unique needs and circumstances (Austin & Craig, 2015; Craig & Austin, 2016; Craig et al., 2012).

Certain components of TA-CBT make it particularly helpful for TGNC clients. Psychoeducation in TA-CBT is key to helping clients recognize and understand the relationship between minority stress and feelings associated with anxiety, depression, hopelessness, or suicidality. This component of TA-CBT offers the opportunity for the client to identify and explore traumatic experiences with discrimination, harassment, microaggressions, and violence within a context of safety and validation. Social work practitioners help clients to process these experiences through a trauma-informed, minority stress lens, allowing clients to better understand the development and maintenance of existing mental health concerns. In this way, clients begin to move away from a view of themselves as "weak" or "disordered" toward an affirming view of themselves as "resilient and resourceful" individuals navigating complex and often perilous situations (Austin & Craig, 2015).

TA-CBT is particularly well suited to help modify cognitive cycles that promote hopelessness. For many TGNC clients there are periods of time in which they feel hopeless or discouraged about the possibility of being able to live authentically and/or transition; these feelings of despair may be particularly pronounced among TGNC young people (Grossman & D'Augelli, 2007). Hopelessness is one of the primary predictors of suicidality (McMillan, Gilbody, Beresford, & Neilly, 2007; Ribeiro, Bodell, Hames, Hagan, & Joiner, 2013) and as TGNC individuals have disproportionately high rates of suicide ideation, attempts, and completions, this is a critical target for intervention. TA-CBT helps client recognize the flaws in their thinking. For instance, if clients are thinking: "If I socially transition, I will lose all my friends," they can learn to modify their thinking style: "Although I may lose some people, I will always have my trans friends from YouTube that are going through the same thing and will totally be there for me." Likewise, if a genderqueer client who does not ascribe to the gender binary is thinking: "I am not trans enough; I don't really belong anywhere," they can learn to modify their black-and-white thinking: "While some people may not get me, I know there is not one right way to be trans and my experience of gender is just as valid as others."

One consequence of transphobia and marginalization from mainstream society may be feelings of discomfort and social anxiety around others. As such, some transgender individuals struggle for a sense of belonging and social connectedness (Grant et al., 2011; Ryan et al., 2010). As social support and social connectedness are crucial to resilience and well-being among TGNC individuals, TA-CBT focuses on developing such resources. Social work practitioners using TA-CBT can help clients explore and recognize the ways in which previous experiences of transphobic discrimination may be impacting current feelings of isolation and disconnectedness. Once internal and external barriers to connection and support are identified, the practitioner can reinforce the development of affirming people, places, and activities. Because disconnectedness is related to hopelessness and even suicide (Ribeiro et al., 2013), such strategies are of great clinical importance. For individuals with few social resources, helping clients identify sources of support locally (e.g., attending local TGNC events, joining a GSA or TGNC support group) or virtually (e.g., joining online support groups, blogs, or social networking sites) can be effective in fostering identity-affirming friendships and social networks. If TGNC clients have a great deal of social anxiety, social work practitioners can engage in troubleshooting and role-play activities to facilitate the process.

USE OF A GROUP FORMAT

Utilizing group formats to deliver affirmative interventions may be particularly effective for TGNC clients (Dickey and Lowey, 2010). Group work can promote mutual aid and help clients recognize they are not alone with their challenges—as well as foster group members' ability to give and receive support—which can be very important for TGNC clients who may be isolated or disconnected from others. As TGNC individuals are often incredibly knowledgeable about transgender issues and available local, national, and international resources, groups can serve as portals for important information and knowledge sharing. Dickey and Loewy (2010) discuss the importance of attending to TGNC specific issues when deciding on group type, membership, format, and location. For instance, some groups may be open to all TGNC individuals across identities and age groups, while in other instances it may be appropriate to have separate groups (e.g., a psychoeducational group specific to transmasculine participants that focuses on the physical/medical transition; or a therapeutic play group for gender diverse children under the age of 12).

While there few studies exploring group-based interventions for TGNC individuals, emerging studies are promising. Craig and Austin (2016) found that a group-based version of affirmative CBT for sexual and gender minority youth was effective in promoting positive change (decreased depression) among TGNC participants. Moreover, TGNC youth in the study reported high levels of satisfaction and acceptability. Similarly, preliminary findings from a psychotherapy group with transgender adults in Montana indicated that the group had a high level of cohesion and participants were highly engaged in the therapeutic process—many demonstrated efforts at positive self-change (Heck, Croot, & Robohm, 2015).

CONCLUSION

TGNC-affirming approaches for social work practice are consistent with the core values of the social work profession and paramount to socially just practice with TGNC populations. A commitment to TGNC-affirmative practice requires that social work practitioners embrace an inclusive and affirming perspective of gender, gender identity, and expression, along with approaching clinical practice with an understanding of the potentially traumatic impact of TGNC-specific minority stressors on well-being. Affirming social workers must also be able to identify, acknowledge, and honor the unique sources of strength and resilience exhibited among TGNC clients. Finally, TGNC-affirming social workers must possess ample knowledge regarding the health, mental health, social, and legal issues associated with living authentically in a society that continues to marginalize TGNC experiences, as well as the specific assessment and intervention skills necessary to address challenges frequently experienced by TGNC individuals (e.g. depression, anxiety, social isolation). With growing awareness of TGNC experiences among the general public, TGNC individuals and their family members will likely seek supportive services in the community at greater rates and earlier than in previous decades. Ultimately, it remains imperative that social work practitioners be prepared to competently meet the needs of all TGNC clients.

REFERENCES

American Academy of Pediatrics, Committee on Adolescence. (2013). Position paper: Office-based care for lesbian, gay, bisexual, transgender, and questioning youth. *Pediatrics, 132,* 198–203.

Austin, A. (2016). "There I am": A grounded theory study of young adults navigating a transgender or gender nonconforming identity within a context of oppression and invisibility. *Sex Roles, 75*(5), 215–230. doi: 10.1007/s11199-016-0600-7

Austin, A., & Craig, S. L. (2015). Transgender affirmative cognitive behavioral therapy: Clinical considerations and applications. *Professional Psychology: Research and Practice, 46*(1), 21–29.

Austin, A., Craig, S. L., & Goodman, R. (2016, January). *Bridging efforts to enhance support for the transgender community: A grand challenge for social work.* Paper presented at the Society for Social Work Research 20th Annual Conference. Washington DC.

Bariola, E., Lyons, A., Leonard, W., Pitts, M., Badcock, P., & Couch, M. (2015). Demographic and psychosocial factors associated with psychological distress and resilience among transgender individuals. *American Journal of Public Health, 105*(10), 2108–2116.

Beck, J. S. (2011). *Cognitive behavior therapy: Basics and beyond.* New York: Guilford Press.

Beemyn, G., & Rankin, S. (2011). *The lives of transgender people.* New York: Columbia University Press.

Bockting, W. O., Miner, M. H., Swinburne-Romine, R. E., Hamilton, A., & Coleman, E. (2013). Stigma, mental health, and resilience in an online sample of the U.S. transgender population. *American Journal of Public Health, 103*(5), 943–951. doi:10.2105/AJPH.2013.301241

Bryant-Davis, T., & Ocampo, C. (2005). The trauma of racism: Implications for counseling, research, and education. *Counseling Psychologist, 33*(4), 574.

Budge, S. L., Adelson, J. L., & Howard, K. A. (2013). Anxiety and depression in transgender individuals: The role of transition status, loss, social support, and coping. *Journal of Consulting and Clinical Psychology, 81*(3), 545–557.

Burnes, T. R., Dexter, M. M., Richmond, K., Singh, A. A., & Cherrington, A. (2016). The experiences of transgender survivors of trauma who undergo social and medical transition. *Traumatology, 22*(1), 75–84.

Centers for Disease Control and Prevention. (2013). *Adverse Childhood Experience Study: Major findings.* Retrieved from http://www.cdc.gov/ace/findings.htm

Clements-Nolle, K., Marx, R., & Katz, M. (2006). Attempted suicide among persons: The influence of gender-based discrimination and victimization. *Journal of Homosexuality, 51*(3), 53–69.

Collazo, A., Austin, A., & Craig, S. L. (2013). Facilitating transition among transgender clients: Components of effective clinical practice. *Clinical Social Work Journal, 41*(3), 228–237. doi:10.1007/s10615-013-0436-3

Council on Social Work Education. (2015). *Position statement on conversion/reparative therapy.* Retrieved from http://www.cswe.org/File.aspx?id=85010

Craig, S. L., & Austin, A. (2016). The AFFIRM open pilot feasibility study: A brief affirmative cognitive behavioral coping skills group intervention for sexual and gender minority youth. *Child and Youth Services Review, 64,* 136–144. doi:10.1016/j.childyouth.2016.02.022

Craig, S. L., Austin, A., & Alessi, E. (2012). Gay affirmative cognitive behavioral therapy for sexual minority youth: A clinical adaptation and approach. *Clinical Social Work Journal, 41*(3), 258–266. doi:10.1007/s10615-012-0427-9

Craig, S. L., & McInroy, L. (2013). The relationship of cumulative stressors, chronic illness, and abuse to the self-reported suicide risk of black and Hispanic sexual minority youth. *Journal of Community Psychology, 41*(7), 783–798. doi:10.1002/jcop.21570

D'Augelli A. R., Grossman, A. H., & Starks, M. T. (2006). Childhood gender atypicality, victimization, and PTSD among lesbian, gay, and bisexual youth. *Journal of Interpersonal Violence, 21*(11), 1462–1482.

Dickey, L. M., & Loewy, M. I. (2010). Group work with transgender clients. *The Journal for Specialists in Group Work, 35*(3), 236–245.

Dragowski, E. A., Halkitis, P. N., Grossman, A. H., & D'Augelli, A. R. (2011). Sexual orientation victimization and posttraumatic stress symptoms among lesbian, gay, and bisexual youth. *Journal of Gay & Lesbian Social Services, 23*(2), 226–249.

Drumheller, K., & McQuay, B. (2010). Living in the buckle: Promoting LGBT outreach services in conservative urban/rural centers. *Communication Studies, 61*(1), 70–86.

Edwards-Leeper, L., & Spack, N. P. (2012) Psychological evaluation and medical treatment of transgender youth in an interdisciplinary "gender management service" (GeMS) in a major pediatric center. *Journal of Homosexuality, 59*(3), 321–336. doi:10.1080/00918369.2012.653302

Felitti, V. J., Anda, R. F., Nordenberg, D., Williamson, D. F., Spitz, A. M., Edwards, V., . . . Marks, J. S. (1998). Relationship of childhood abuse and household dysfunction to many of the leading causes of death in adults. *American Journal of Preventive Medicine, 14*, 245–258. doi:10.1016/S0749-3797(98)00017-8

Frost, D. M., & Meyer, I. H. (2012). Measuring community connectedness among diverse sexual minority populations. *Journal of Sex Research, 48*, 36–49.

Gates, G. (2011). *How many people are gay, lesbian, bisexual and transgender?* Williams Institute. Retrieved from http://williamsinstitute.law.ucla.edu/research/census-lgbt-demographics-studies/how-many-people-are-lesbian-gay-bisexual-and-transgender/

Goldblum, P., Testa, R., Pflum, S., Hendricks, M., Bradford, J., & Bongar, B. (2012). Gender-based victimization and suicide attempts among transgender people. *Professional Psychology: Research and Practice, 43*(5), 465–475.

Grant, J. M., Mottet, L. A., Tanis, J., Harrison, J., Herman, J. L., & Keisling, M. (2011). *Injustice at every turn: A report of the National Transgender Discrimination Survey.* Washington, DC: National Center for Transgender Equality and National Gay and Lesbian Task Force. Retrieved from http://endtransdiscrimination.org/report.html

Gregor, C., Hingley-Jones, H., & Davidson, S. (2015). Understanding the experience of parents of pre-pubescent children with gender identity issues. *Child and Adolescent Social Work Journal, 32*(3), 237–246.

Grossman, A. H., & D'Augelli, A. R. (2007). Transgender youth and life-threatening behaviors. *Suicide and Life-Threatening Behavior, 37*(5), 527–537.

Haas, A. P., Rodgers, P. L., & Herman, J. (2014). Suicide attempts among transgender and gender non-conforming adults: Findings of the national transgender discrimination survey. *Work, 50*, 59.

Heck, N. C., Croot, L. C., & Robohm, J. S. (2015). Piloting a psychotherapy group for transgender clients: Description and clinical considerations for practitioners. *Professional Psychology: Research and Practice, 46*(1), 30–36.

Hembree, W. C., Cohen-Kettenis, P., Delemarre-van de Waal, H. A., Gooren, L. J., Meyer III, W. J., Spack, N. P., . . . Montori, V. M. (2009). Endocrine treatment of transsexual persons: An Endocrine Society clinical practice guideline. *The Journal of Clinical Endocrinology & Metabolism, 94*(9), 3132–3154.

Hendricks, M. L., & Testa, R. J. (2012). A conceptual framework for clinical work with transgender and gender nonconforming clients: An adaptation of the minority stress model. *Professional Psychology: Research and Practice, 43*(5), 460–467. doi: 10.1037/a0029597

Herbst, J. H., Jacobs, E. D., Finlayson, T. J., McKleroy, V. S., Neumann, M. S., Crepaz, N., & HIV/AIDS Prevention Research Synthesis Team. (2008). Estimating HIV prevalence and risk behaviors of transgender persons in the United States: A systematic review. *AIDS and Behavior, 12*(1), 1–17.

Herman, J. (1992). *Trauma and recovery: From domestic violence to political terrorism.* New York: Basic Books.

Hopper, E. K., Bassuk, E. L., & Olivet, J. (2010). Shelter from the storm: Trauma-informed care in homelessness services settings. *The Open Health Services and Policy Journal, 3*(2), 80–100.

Horn, S. S. (2010). Attitudes about sexual orientation. In: C. Patterson & A. D'Augelli (Eds.), *The handbook for the psychology of sexual orientation* (pp. 239–251). Oxford: Oxford University Press.

Horvath, K. J., Iantaffi, A., Grey, J. A., & Bockting, W. (2012). A review of the content and format of transgender-related webpages. *Health Communication, 27*(5), 457–466.

Horvath, K. J., Iantaffi, A., Swinburne-Romine, R., & Bockting, W. (2014). A comparison of mental health, substance use, and sexual risk behaviors between rural and non-rural transgender persons. *Journal of Homosexuality, 61*(8), 1117–1130.

Kenagy, G. P. (2005). Transgender health: Findings from two needs assessment studies in Philadelphia. *Health & Social Work, 30*(1), 19–26.

Kosciw, J., Greytak, E., Palmer, N., & Boesen, M. (2013). *GLSEN National School Climate Survey.* Retrieved from https://www.glsen.org/sites/default/files/2013%20National%20School%20Climate%20Survey%20Full%20Report_0.pdf

Lev, A. I. (2004). *Transgender emergence: Therapeutic guidelines for working with gender-variant people and their families*. New York: Haworth Clinical Practice Press.

Marcellin, R., Scheim, A., Bauer, G., & Redman, N. (2013). Experiences of transphobia among trans Ontarians. *Trans PULSE e-Bulletin, 3*(2). http://www.transpulseproject.ca

McFadden, S. H., Frankowski, S., Flick, H., & Witten, T. M. (2013). Resilience and multiple stigmatized identities: Lessons from transgender persons reflections on aging. In J. D. Sinnott (Ed.), *Positive psychology: Advances in understanding adult motivation* (pp. 247–267). New York: Springer Science & Business Media.

McMillan, D., Gilbody, S., Beresford, E., & Neilly, L. I. Z. (2007). Can we predict suicide and non-fatal self-harm with the Beck Hopelessness Scale? A meta-analysis. *Psychological Medicine, 37*(6), 769–778.

Menvielle, E. (2009) Transgender children: Clinical and ethical issues in prepubertal presentations. *Journal of Gay & Lesbian Mental Health, 13*(4), 292–297. doi:10.1080/19359700903165357

Meyer, I. H. (2003). Prejudice, social stress, and mental health in lesbian, gay, and bisexual populations: Conceptual issues and research evidence. *Psychological Bulletin, 129*, 674–697. doi.org/10.1037/00332909.129.5.674

Mizock, L., & Lewis, T. K. (2008). Trauma in transgender populations: Risk, resilience, and clinical care. *Journal of Emotional Abuse, 8*(3), 335–354.

National Coalition of Anti-Violence Programs. (2015). *Lesbian, gay, bisexual, transgender, queer and HIV-affected hate violence in 2014*. Retrieved from http://www.avp.org/storage/documents/Reports/2014_HV_Report-Final.pdf

Nemoto, T., Bodeker, B., & Iwamoto, M. (2011). Social support, exposure to violence, and transphobia: Correlates of depression among male-to female transgender women with a history of sex work. *American Journal of Public Health, 101*, 1980–1988.

Newman, P. A., & Fantus, S. (2015). A social ecology of bias-based bullying of sexual and gender minority youth: Toward a conceptualization of conversion bullying. *Journal of Gay & Lesbian Social Services, 27*(1), 46–63.

Nuttbrock, L., Hwahng, S., Bockting, W., Rosenblum, A., Mason, M., Macri, M., & Becker, J. (2010). Psychiatric impact of gender-related abuse across the life course of male-to-female transgender persons. *Journal of Sex Research, 47*, 12–23.

Orr, A., Baum, J., Brown, J., Gill, E., & Kahn, E. (2015). *Schools in transition: A guide for supporting transgender students in K-12 schools*. Retrieved from https://www.genderspectrum.org/staging/wp-content/uploads/2015/08/Schools-in-Transition-2015.pdf

Pflum, S., Testa, R., Balsam, K., Goldblum, P., & Bongar, B. (2015). Social support, trans community connectedness, and mental health symptoms among transgender and gender nonconforming adults. *Psychology of Sexual Orientation and Gender Diversity, 2*(3), 281–286.

Ribeiro, J. D., Bodell, L. P., Hames, J. L., Hagan, C. R., & Joiner, T. E. (2013). An empirically based approach to the assessment and management of suicidal behavior. *Journal of Psychotherapy Integration, 23*(3), 207–221.

Richmond, K. A., Burnes, T., & Carroll, K. (2012). Lost in trans-lation: Interpreting systems of trauma for transgender clients. *Traumatology, 18*(1), 45–57.

Riley, E. A., Clemson, L., Sitharthan, G., & Diamond, M. (2013). Surviving a gender-variant childhood: The views of transgender adults on the needs of gender-variant children and their parents. *Journal of Sex & Marital Therapy, 39*(3), 241–263.

Roberts, A. L., Rosario, M., Corliss, H. L., Koenen, K. C., & Austin, S. B. (2012). Elevated risk of posttraumatic stress in sexual minority youths: mediation by childhood abuse and gender nonconformity. *American Journal of Public Health, 102*(8), 1587–1593.

Ryan, C., Huebner, D., Diaz, R. M., & Sanchez, J. (2009). Family rejection as a predictor of negative health outcomes in white and Latino lesbian, gay, and bisexual young adults. *Pediatrics, 123*(1), 346–352.

Ryan, C., Russell, S. T., Huebner, D., Diaz, R., & Sanchez, J. (2010). Family acceptance in adolescence and the health of LGBT young adults. *Journal of Child and Adolescent Psychiatric Nursing, 23*(4), 205–213.

Sánchez, F., & Vilain, E. (2009). Collective self-esteem as a coping resource for male-to-female transsexuals. *Journal of Counseling Psychology, 56*(1), 202–209.

Simons, L. Schrager, S. M., Clark, L. F., Belzer, M., & Olson, J. (2013). Parental support and mental health among transgender adolescents. *Journal of Adolescent Health, 53*, 791–793.

Singh, A. A. (2013). Transgender youth of color and resilience: Negotiating oppression and finding support. *Sex Roles, 68*(11–12), 690–702. doi:10.1007/s11199-012-0149-z

Singh, A. A., Hays, D. G., & Watson, L. S. (2011). Strength in the face of adversity: Resilience strategies of transgender individuals. *Journal of Counseling & Development, 89*, 20–27. dx.doi.org/10.1002/ j.1556-6678.2011.tb00057.x

Singh, A. A., & McKleroy, V. S. (2011). Just getting out of bed in the morning is a revolutionary act: The resilience of trans people of color who have survived traumatic life events. *Traumatology, 17*(2), 34–44.

Spack, N. P., Edwards-Leeper, L., Feldman, H. A., Leibowitz, S., Mandel, F., Diamond, D. A., & Vance, S. R. (2011). Children and adolescents with gender identity disorder referred to a pediatric clinic. *Pediatrics, 129*(3), 418–425.

Spicer, S. S. (2010). Healthcare needs of the transgender homeless population. *Journal of Gay & Lesbian Mental Health, 14*, 320–339. doi.org/10.1080/19359705.2010.505844

Steensma, T. D., Kreukels, B. P., de Vries, A. L., & Cohen-Kettenis, P. T. (2013). Gender identity development in adolescence. *Hormonal Behavior, 64*(2), 288–297.

Steensma, T. D., McGuire, J. K., Kreukels, B. P., Beekman, A. J., & Cohen-Kettenis, P. T. (2013). Factors associated with desistence and persistence of childhood gender dysphoria: A quantitative follow-up study. *Journal of the American Academy of Child & Adolescent Psychiatry, 52*(6), 582–590.

Substance Abuse and Mental Health Services Administration. (2015). *Ending conversion therapy and affirming LGBTQ youth.* HHS Publication No. 15-4928. Rockville, MD: Author.

Szymanski, D., & Owens, G. (2009). Group level coping as a moderator between heterosexism and sexism and psychological distress in sexual minority women. *Psychology of Women Quarterly, 33*(2), 197–205. doi:10.1111/j.1471-6402.2009.01489.x

Testa, R., Jimenez, C., & Rankin, S. (2014). Risk and resilience during transgender identity development: The effects of awareness and engagement with other transgender people on affect. *Journal of Gay & Lesbian Mental Health, 18*, 31–46. doi:10.1080/19359705.2013.805177.

Van der Kolk, B. (1996). *Traumatic stress: The effects of overwhelming experience on mind, body, and society.* New York: Guilford Press.

Van der Kolk, B. (2014). *The body keeps the score: Brain, mind, and body in the healing of trauma.* New York: Penguin.

Van Horn, P., & Lieberman, A. (2008). Using dyadic therapies to treat traumatized young children. In D. Brom, R. Pat-Horenczyk, & J. D. Ford (Eds.), *Treating traumatized children: Risk, resilience, and recovery* (pp. 210–224). London: Routledge.

White-Holman, C., & Goldberg, J. M. (2006). Social and medical transgender case advocacy. *International Journal of Transgenderism, 9*(3–4), 197–217.

Wilson, E. C., Garofalo, R., Harris, R. D., Herrick, A., Martinez, M., Martinez, J., . . . Adolescent Medicine Trials Network for HIV/AIDS Interventions. (2009). Transgender female youth and sex work: HIV risk and a comparison of life factors related to engagement in sex work. *AIDS and Behavior, 13*(5), 902–913.

Wilson, E. C., Iverson, E., Garofalo, R., & Belzer, M. (2012). Parental support and condom use among transgender female youth. *Journal of the Association of Nurses in AIDS Care, 23*(4), 306–317.

World Professional Association for Transgender Health. (2011). *Standards of care for the health of transsexual, transgender, and gender nonconforming people, 7th version.* Retrieved from www.wpath.org

Zucker, K. J. (2010) The DSM diagnostic criteria for gender identity disorder in children. *Archives of Sexual Behavior, 39*(2), 477–498.

CHAPTER 17

PRACTICE WITH THE QUEER COMMUNITY

M. Alex Wagaman

INTRODUCTION

Understanding queer identities and people who claim them is an important part of practicing within lesbian, gay, bisexual, transgender, and queer (LGBTQ) communities and populations. However, queerness is often intended to be elusive, in motion, and unable to be understood in the traditional sense of understanding identity formation, sexual orientation, gender, gender identity, and expression (Jagose, 1996; Sullivan, 2003). In fact, queer is an identity that can be used to refer to sexual orientation, gender identity, or both. Queer identities are often both personal and political and are the embodiment of resistance to social structures that are limiting or oppressive (Jagose, 1997). Queerness itself, and the use of the term "queer," is highly contextual. Responses to the term or identity label vary dramatically based on generation, geography, and other factors. While many LGBTQ people have embraced the reclamation of the term, for many it is still viewed as derogatory. As such, it is important to understand the history and theoretical framework underlying the use and meaning of "queer" in order to best understand how to practice effectively in queer communities and queer spaces.

This chapter differs from the previous chapters focused on practicing with various subpopulations of the broader LGBTQ population. This is due in part to the fact that very little research or empirical evidence exists about people who identify as queer that is distinct from the other subpopulations that are reflected in the LGBTQ acronym. In fact, "queer" has often been used to refer to all people falling under the LGBTQ umbrella of identities. The limited research is a reflection of the fluid and ever-changing nature of queerness and queer identities, which is discussed in this chapter. It also reflects an ongoing dialogue among social scientists who conduct research on LGBTQ issues and populations about how we identify our research population, how we categorize or identify people, and how we can truly come to know and understand such a dynamic community of people.

For many, the use of "queer" as an identity stands in opposition to categorization and to make visible the ever-present heteronormative and cisnormative structures and practices in society. This chapter explores the resistance that underlies queerness and queer identities and offers practice approaches that are built on an understanding of the oppressive context within which queer people come to know and authentically live their identities. Because of the nature of queerness, in its intentional complexity and fluidity, this chapter does not offer simple answers about how to "categorize" people who identify as queer or strategies for serving all queer people effectively. As with the previous chapters, it is important to understand that in a national and global context, there is as much diversity within the population of queer-identifying people as in any other population of people.

Queer identities encompass a broad array of identities and are at the heart of the complexity of gender identity and sexual orientation. As such, queer people and communities are often invisible. Because of the broad diversity within queer communities and the limited research, this chapter focuses on primary considerations for approaching and serving queer people and communities, with a recognition that these considerations serve as a framework and context for assessing how best to serve each individual most effectively, rather than specific prescriptions for practice.

HISTORY OF THE TERM "QUEER"

Historically, the term "queer" was used to refer to something that seemed odd, out of place, or outside of the norm (Dentato, 2014). It then was assigned as a term that was used to refer directly to homosexuals, or people who were viewed as deviating from the norm sexually through an expression of sexual attraction to the same sex. This usage of the term "queer" sanctioned, through language, the identification and marginalization of LGBTQ people as being intentionally deviant or different (Bronski, 2011). Use of "queer" as an offensive or derogatory term (circa 1920s–1980s) created a social discourse that allowed for the perpetration of violence and social isolation of LGBTQ people (Jagose, 1997). Such violence occurred (e.g., the lavender scare of the 1940s and 1950s), and continues to occur (e.g., employment discrimination, hate crimes), in systemic ways. In turn, some individuals within the larger society did not, and do not, want to be associated with anything viewed as queer for fear that they, in turn, would be labeled as such. This kind of societally sanctioned discrimination has resulted in practices that further marginalize LGBTQ people from their support networks, including, for example, families shunning their own children or relatives who are perceived to be LGBTQ (Ryan, Huebner, Diaz, & Sanchez, 2009). It also resulted in the policing of public spaces that were often used as meeting places for LGBTQ people, such as bars, parks, and restrooms, in order prevent and disrupt any type of queer activities. Halberstam (1998) writes about the gender policing that happens in public restrooms and its detrimental impact on individuals. For queer people whose gender expression is outside of the binary norm, going into a public bathroom often results in having to cope with being stared at, harassed, or suffering verbal or physical assault. Such behaviors send a clear message that queerness is not welcome within such spaces and promotes a sense of unfounded fear and illogical threat to the "well-being" of those not identified as queer. This message has been a large part of the present day rhetoric associated with political efforts in a number of US states (e.g., North Carolina) and localities to prevent transgender people from using public restrooms that align with their gender identity. In these political campaigns, fear is a driving factor that emphasizes the importance of (a) knowing someone's gender, biological sex, or sexuality and (b) being able to dictate a person's behavior based on this knowledge.

People who are identifiably queer are subject to daily microaggressions and threats of violence (Nadal, Rivera, & Corpus, 2010; Sue, 2010). In such a context, queer visibility has become a bodily form of resistance to the social norms that attempt to dictate who we can be and who we can love. As is discussed in greater depth later in the chapter, these norms were instrumental in fracturing many support networks among and between LGBTQ people.

As with other terms intended to denigrate a certain group of people, there came a time when some people in the LGBT community decided to reclaim the term "queer" in an effort to take away its power and challenge the oppressive standards of mainstream normativity (Jagose, 1997; Peters, 1997). In 1987, activists involved in the HIV/AIDS movement in New York City formed an organization called AIDS Coalition To Unleash Power (ACT UP). This organization engaged in direct actions to raise awareness of the US government's limited response to the HIV/AIDS crisis, which was disproportionately impacting the LGBT community. From the membership of those within ACT UP came another organization known as Queer Nation. Queer Nation's primary purpose was to increase visibility of queer people and identities in all of their diversity (Fox, 2007).

At that time, activists used the well-known chant "We're here. We're queer. Get used to it!" to reflect their decision to use "queer" on their own terms and create a collective visibility. Part of this reclamation and political activism included the message that queers are everywhere—that queer people are in every community, family, and demographic subgroup. During this time, the emphasis was on queer visibility. As a political identity, queerness was seen as an embrace of being outside of and resistance to the conventions of normative sexuality and gender (Tilsen & Nylund, 2011). It is also used, however, as a way of identifying a much broader community of LGBTQ people under one umbrella term (e.g., the queer community). In using queer to include many different nonnormative sexual and gender identities, the LGBTQ community created an inclusive space for building political momentum and power.

Similarly, the term queer was then taken up by mainstream media in shows such as *Queer Eye for the Straight Guy* and *Queer as Folk*. While some believe that greater representation in mainstream media is a step in the right direction toward the destigmatization of queer people, others raise concerns about the possible detrimental impact of unsavory or stereotypical portrayals (Gray, 2009). Without an analysis of the messages being sent to society about who queer people are (and are not) and how they behave, it is easy to overlook the ways that media representation can thwart efforts toward queer visibility and acceptance.

LABELING IDENTITY

Research suggests that identity labels limit our ability to fully understand the experiences of LGBTQ people and may limit people's abilities to fully live in their authentic identities (Abes, Jones, & McEwen, 2007). For example, Diamond's (2006) research on sexual-minority women suggests that there is a great deal of fluidity in identity, attraction, and sexual behaviors during a woman's lifetime. Based on this research, it is important for practitioners to understand that identity labels chosen by a client may only temporarily reflect one's sense of self. Research conducted by Savin-Williams (2009) suggests that sexual-minority youth may no longer resonate with traditional identity labels or categories such as gay or lesbian, particularly as society changes and gay culture becomes more visible and incorporated into the broader culture of the United States. This research raises questions about the function of identity labels and their importance over time. Does an identity label only serve a purpose for marginalized communities of people to help build a shared identity? What happens if the identity is no longer marginalized? Queer theorists have questioned the role of utilizing sexual and gender identity categories that were socially constructed and serve to uphold power structures in society (Butler, 2004).

Other research has challenged the notion that existing identity categories are no longer relevant to the lives and experiences of sexual and gender minorities, particularly for people who live at the intersections of multiple oppressed identities, including people of color and people from working-class backgrounds (McInroy & Craig, 2012; Wagaman, 2014). The importance and role of identity labels differ across time, space, and other aspects of identity. As practitioners, we cannot assume the primacy of one identity over another for a client or community, and we cannot know the meaning of a client's sexual or gender identity without getting to know the person and creating a space for dialogue.

REJECTING BINARY STRUCTURES

In the United States and many Western countries, the dominant understanding of gender and sexual orientation have been limited to binary thinking (Halberstam, 1998; Rand, 2005). For example, people are believed to fall into sex categories of male or female and the corresponding gender categories of masculine or feminine. Within dominant cultural narratives, transgender people are still assumed to revolve around the gender binary: transgender individuals assigned male at birth are expected to transition to a female identity and vice versa. Within this binary way of thinking, understandings of gender and sex are often conflated (Calhoun, 1995). It is assumed that if one's sex is assigned male at birth then one will identify as a man and will take on the norms and practices associated with maleness. As normative, binary understandings of gender identity and sexual orientation have been contested in society, many theorists have shifted to a continuum model of gender and sexual identity (Hawkesworth, 1997). For example, more recent categories of sexual orientation have replaced the mutually exclusive and oppositional division of heterosexual/homosexual with more fluid and expansive categories that include bisexuality and pansexuality. These identities, however, are often still based on a binary understanding of gender identity. For example, if a person's identity is male and he is attracted to males, then he is typically labeled gay. Examining such diverse identities along a rigid and binary continuum creates challenges to a fully inclusive understanding of gender and sexual orientation.

INTERSECTING IDENTITIES

More complex ways of thinking about identities and the ways that they intersect are important to understanding where queerness lies (Wiegman, 2001). For example, if gender identity and gender expression are thought of as separate yet interconnected aspects of gender then we can better understand the role that gender plays in how people identify and interact with the world. These identities also must be considered as separate from sex that is assigned at birth. Similarly, sexual attraction should be considered as separate from yet interconnected with emotional or romantic attraction. When we begin to intersect all of these aspects of identity, we can understand the complexity that exists well beyond the L, G, B, T, and Q. It may be interesting to imagine the full spectrum of such unique identities that have existed over time yet remained invisible to many people within society (Halberstam, 1998). As an example, imagine the person who presents with a male-centric gender expression but identifies as a woman. This person is romantically and emotionally attracted to people of all genders (including male, female, transgender, genderqueer, etc.) but is primarily sexually attracted to transgender women. This person's identity exists in the margins of many other identity labels and pushes the boundaries of our traditional understanding of the intersections of these aspects of identity—they are both distinct and interrelated and must be understood as such in order to adequately and appropriately serve individuals from both within and outside of the LGBTQ community.

What becomes challenging for those serving or working with people with queer identities is that most of us function in a society that still is structured in fairly binary terms. We have also been taught to think about these aspects of identity as fixed or unchangeable. This is reflected in our language, thinking, and behavior, and it is a hard pattern to change because it is reinforced in many overt and covert ways within society. Many people who do not have the language or label that reflects their sense of self or their experience respond by taking on a queer identity label. Some people prefer the flexibility and vagueness of the term "queer," while others continue to create their own identity labels, and still others remain silent about their experiences and identities.

CASE EXAMPLE

In a qualitative study (Wagaman, 2013) conducted with a sample ($N = 15$) of LGBTQ youth, a young woman was interviewed who described how her identity labels changed over time until she found herself at a place in her life for which there was no identity label. She described how, as a teenager, it had been difficult to take on a lesbian identity because of the social stigma and family isolation she encountered. Once she did take on a lesbian identity, it had meaning for her that was connected to her personal history and ability to overcome its related challenges. Then she began a relationship with someone who, after being together for a couple of years, decided to begin transitioning from living as a woman to living authentically as a man. The young woman shared that she wanted an identity that she could use to describe herself when talking with others. So, for her, a label or category was important. But she was not sure what identity would fit. She had spent a considerable amount of time connecting with the LGBTQ community in her city and felt like that was something she wanted to maintain. Yet she also wanted to reflect her partner's identity in her own because her relationship was a defining aspect of her own identity. Together they decided that she would identify as "trans-straight," an identity label that they created together. This example reflects the many layers that are involved in identity—personal sense of self, connection to others, sense of belonging to a community, intimate relationships, and having a term that fully reflects one's experience. It is in these kinds of spaces where queerness often lies. For many people, queer is an identity label that captures the lives and identities of those who exist in the margins of the larger LGBT community.

It is also important to note that a queer identity label may also be embraced by people who make a decision to use the term or label as a political statement. It is noted here because many people who identify as queer are doing so as a form of personal resistance to the existing structures and categories in society that limit them or others. It can be easier to understand this stance when one has a working knowledge of the history of LGBTQ people in the United States and understands the role of identity within such a sociohistorical context.

QUEERNESS IN THE LGBT COMMUNITY

The original political reclamation of the term "queer" described previously was an effort to call into question normative ideas about sexuality and gender. People took up the term to call into question existing social categories such as "lesbian, gay, or bisexual" and to highlight the existence of people for whom these categories are limiting or oppressive. However, the term "queer" was used by LGBT activists and advocates as an umbrella term causing political and philosophical conflicts to emerge. Queer activists, generally speaking, are not interested in strategies that will make LGBT people more accepted and acceptable within the existing structures of society such as prioritizing efforts like gay marriage (Shah, 2006). However, many queer activists are quite involved with fighting against oppressive societal structures such as heteronormativity, racism, sexism, and so on.

As Judith Butler (2004) points out in *Undoing Gender*, when we work to gain entry into institutions where some people are deemed worthy of being "in" and others are kept "out," then we further entrench those systems and perpetuate the invisibility of lives and experiences of those who are not recognized as fully human. For example, genderqueer people of color cannot walk down the street without fearing for their personal safety. Yet their experiences are not at the forefront of our mainstream LGBTQ movements and activism. In the past few decades, the political agenda for LGBT people became less about embracing queerness in all of its forms and more about fitting into and being accepted by heteronormative institutions. In essence, queerness is about disrupting collective politics founded on identities such as "gay" or "lesbian" (Sullivan, 2003). If an LGBTQ movement relies on a collective identity, something that LGBTQ people can come together around, then queer theory's deconstruction of existing identity categories puts this in flux. It is these differences in how identity is viewed, the meaning it is given, and the political priorities that emerge from it that cause some LGBTQ people to be hesitant to use the term "community" when referring to the population of people with sexual and gender minority identities.

This dynamic within the broader LGBTQ population is further complicated by other aspects of identity and the forms of discrimination that exist among and between LGBTQ people. Racism, classism, ableism, and other forms of oppression and discrimination exist within LGBTQ communities in the same way that they do in the broader society (Caluya, 2006; Han, 2007). Similarly, people whose identities are already seen to exist outside of the norm in mainstream culture are often marginalized by the LGBTQ community, including bisexual and transgender people. This is often a result of internalized oppression, a process by which people begin to internalize the dominant messages that exist about their identity groups, including their inferiority or dysfunction (Mizock & Mueser, 2014; Morrow, 2004). When this happens, people can respond by trying to conform to patterns of normative behavior or presentation and seeking to distance themselves from those who are outside of such norms. These responses to what is perceived as "guilty by association" can play out in dating preferences, exclusion from community events, and other forms of marginalization.

For queer people aiming to live authentically in an oppressive society, the dynamic of internalized oppression complicates the relationship with LGBT people. For example, many transgender people work hard to meet social expectations for presenting as male or female. This is about aligning with one's gender identity, but it is also sometimes related to a need to minimize very real threats of violence and harassment. When interacting with queer people who may be intentionally and visibly pushing boundaries of social norms and expectations about gender presentation or other aspects of identity, other LGBT people might feel a sense of fear or even anger if their safety is perceived as being put in jeopardy.

Practitioners need to educate themselves about oppression and the variety of ways that it can impact people—intrapersonally and interpersonally. It is also important to understand that people who experience oppression may not be aware or educated about it. This requires patience and empathy.

QUEER THEORY AS A FRAMEWORK FOR UNDERSTANDING QUEER IDENTITIES

Throughout this chapter thus far, aspects of queer theory have been introduced and explored. This section aims to summarize queer theory as a framework that can be applied in practice with people identifying as queer. Queer theory, in its simplest form, challenges us to question constructs and concepts that have previously been taken for granted (Sullivan, 2003). It is a lens through which we can call into question social structures that may bind us unnecessarily and that are the fabric underlying systems of oppression (Butler, 2004). A theoretical framework such as queer theory offers us an understanding of how theory can play out in action and oftentimes assist in the decision to take on a queer identity (Abes et al., 2007).

For a person who does not or will not ascribe to the expectations associated with the gender binary, a queer identity creates spaces and opportunities that did not previously exist. By taking on a queer or genderqueer identity in the face of a society that functions under the assumption of the gender binary is to call into question, with one's personhood, an ingrained social construct. This is what Duong (2012) refers to as "queer world-making," which happens when people live into the identities and communities that they wish existed rather than waiting for them to become a reality. In this sense, a queer identity is a political identity. Queerness begins by acknowledging that what exists in society, in terms of identity categories and the ability to fully express oneself free from fear, is limited. Queerness then pushes those limits by inserting something that can disrupt the status quo. In our example of the gender binary, a person who takes on a genderqueer identity is in essence making a statement—"I don't see myself reflected in the gender options presented to me. So I will create my own space and identity, rather than being forced to fit something that limits my sense of self." Some people queer multiple identities simultaneously and without limitations. Because of this, it would be fruitless to attempt to develop a list of identities that could be considered queer identities. Particularly among LGBTQ youth, identities are being created and "played" with daily (Saltzburg & Davis, 2010), and the language is ever-changing.

Queer theory also functions in action through the personal and social interactions of people who take on queer identities. When a person lives out or expresses a queer identity, the identity can serve as a beacon for others for whom their expression of identity is not aligned with who they know themselves to be. For example, if a person lives in an openly, visibly queer way, others will see this and their options for living and expression may be expanded. This is true not only for other queer people. From an anti-oppression framework, oppressive social structures and categories like the gender binary are harmful and limiting for all people (Burdge, 2007). Even if people live comfortably within acceptable norms of their gender, they are often aware that they must self-monitor in order to stay within those norms. This could be as simple as making sure that they are wearing colors that are acceptable for their gender. For these people, interactions with visibly queer people opens up new opportunities for expression. It also causes people to pause and question the importance of what they have come to expect in gendered interactions. For example, is it important to know someone's gender as soon as one sees or meets them? Why? This is queer theory in action (Abes, 2007). The act of living out one's queerness helps others begin to question the validity and importance of social norms like the gender binary.

Another important aspect of queer theory is the emphasis on the importance of language as a source of power. Those who control language control knowledge, and knowledge is power. When social categories exist that do not include all people, then the existing language is literally erasing the existence of some people. This has a number of implications in a society. Language is also used to tell stories and shape narratives about groups of people, such as those that exist about LGBTQ people (Goltz, 2013; Hillier & Harrison, 2004). Queer theory calls us to deconstruct these uses of language and examine the attitudes, beliefs, and values that underlie them (Jagose, 1997; Owens, 2010). This is called discourse analysis and is discussed further as an approach to working with queer people.

EFFECTIVE AND BEST PRACTICE APPROACHES

Despite the limited empirical knowledge that exists about people who identify as queer, there are a number of important considerations for practice that can be taken from a deeper understanding of queerness as distinct from LGBT identities. How these considerations can be incorporated into practice approaches using a queer theory framework are discussed next.

PRACTICING PRONOUN USE

The practice of asking clients what their pronouns are reflects a basic understanding on the part of the practitioner that assumptions about identity cannot be taken for granted. As previously discussed, people who identify as queer may experience an invisibility that asking pronouns can begin to address in a clinical relationship or other service setting. Practitioners should understand that pronouns, like identities, do not exist on a binary. While many people use he/him or she/her pronouns, others use pronouns that reflect identities outside of the binary, including they/them or zi/hir, among many others. Some individuals prefer that pronouns not be used at all when they are referred to. It may be helpful to ask individuals how they would prefer to be addressed in oral or written form (e.g., by first name only, or using "they"). Pronoun use is an important shift in one on one interactions, as well as at programmatic or organizational levels. Practitioners can identify forms (such as intake or assessment forms) and other ways in which clients interact with the service provider that may need to be changed to reflect queer identities. At a program or agency level, the practice of moving away from assuming what a person's pronouns are based on gender presentation is also a way to begin to "queer" the environment. By challenging assumptions about identity, and opening oneself to the idea that we are not the experts, queer-identified clients will be more likely to feel affirmed in their identities.

UNDERSTANDING THE ROLE OF FLUIDITY

As previously described, research suggests that our identities are not fixed and are rather fluid in nature. Queer theory calls into question the idea that, once we claim a sexual or gender identity, it defines us as a person throughout the lifespan. Practitioners and programs often function based on assumptions that a client's identity is an unchangeable characteristic. Demographic information may be gathered from a client at intake but not be revisited throughout the course of service over weeks, months, or even longer. Without spaces and opportunities to reflect upon changes in identity, clients may not volunteer such information, which may in turn impact the established therapeutic relationship or rapport.

As practitioners and program managers begin to consider how they can alter current processes to honor queer identities, it is important to acknowledge that queer people grow up in the same society as those who are not queer. That means that they receive the same messages about identity, sexual orientation, gender, and gender roles and may have some internalized shame or stigma associated with identity fluidity. In fact, even within the LGBT community there has been stigma placed upon individuals with identities, sexual partners, or sexual activities that are seen to be out of alignment with others' perceived or proclaimed identities. As such, it is important to consider ways to take the burden of initiating conversations about identity or placing descriptions of identity upon a client. Rather, such conversations should be incorporated as standard practice with all clients—that stems from initiation by the practitioner. Honoring identity fluidity requires such practices to be incorporated at multiple points in the client–practitioner relationship. As an example from one LGBTQ youth-serving organization, staff began the practice of having youth sign in and include their preferred gender pronouns each time they came in to participate in programs. What they found was that youth often would change their pronouns and their names from week to week. By having this documented, they were able to train volunteers on sensitivity related to identity fluidity with evidence to back up the need. They also were able to honor the young person's identity as it was in that moment without much fanfare.

HONORING THE IMPORTANCE OF QUEER VISIBILITY

If providers of programs and services are to engage in anti-oppressive practice, then creating spaces for queerness and queer identities to emerge is an important part of that process. The practices described previously illustrate ways to support queer visibility in a therapeutic relationship or client–practitioner interaction. But queer visibility extends beyond these interactions. Agencies within which practitioners work and deliver services need to examine ways that they might perpetuate queer invisibility. This can, in fact, come as a result of efforts to become more LGBT affirming and inclusive. For example, if images in offices or on agency materials only reflect people who present their genders in very binary ways, this can reinforce queer invisibility. Similarly, use of language can reinforce queer invisibility. This can be as simple as calling people "sir" or "ma'am" based on gender presentation, using traditional salutations to greet someone, or addressing them in writing using "Mr." or "Ms." This is where discourse analysis, or analyzing our use of language in a way that helps us to examine the underlying messages, can provide a useful tool to assess the extent to which individuals and agencies either support or interrupt queer invisibility. This type of analysis can be done at an agency level with support and direct input from queer clients, community leaders, and agencies that work with the queer community. This is important as we often do not include the "voice" of our clients in decision-making with regard to agency policy and procedures.

RESISTING BINARIES

We have explored ways that practitioners can engage in resisting binary thinking with regard to their clients, such as asking and honoring pronoun use and acknowledging that people are not confined to being either gay or straight with nothing in between. The practice of resisting binaries also encourages us to consider ways that we create or reinforce other kinds of boundaries. For example, when we talk about family or relationship dynamics, it may be easy to label situations as either functional or dysfunctional without considering that these options are limiting and create little room for exploring behaviors in different contexts or from other perspectives. Queer theory's call to resist binaries challenges us to question where and why binary categories might have been constructed and for whose benefit. Foucault's (1988) work encourages us to consider the ways that socially constructed identity categories set up systems that coerce people into distinguishing themselves from whatever identity, characteristic, or experience is deemed as negative, such as mental illness. It is only in this kind of a social structure that we can imagine parents of queer youth turning out their children into the streets, or people responding with such intense fear and hatred of another human being's existence that they would violently attack them. While we may not be directly confronting these kinds of behaviors in our own practice, we can engage in self-reflection that allows us and those around us to question the existing categories and their role in the well-being of our society.

RETHINKING RELATIONSHIPS AND FAMILY

Now that we have considered basic practices that we can use to engage queer clients and create queer affirming spaces, we must reconsider the ways that we think about families and relationships (Oswald, Blume, & Marks, 2005). As previously described, queer people express their sexual and romantic affections and attractions in multiple ways. Part of a queer identity often includes the queering of these private spaces—family, intimacy, relationships—in ways that have been and continue to be socially stigmatized in the United States. Queer people push the boundaries of monogamy and family structure in ways that can create discomfort in practitioners not prepared to examine their beliefs and values about what defines a "family" or a "healthy" relationship. Queer families may look like what we consider a traditional family, and they might have multiple (more than two) parents raising children. They might also be chosen families—groups of people who have created their own family structure outside of birth or marriage. Queer relationships can be as complex as queer identities. Just as with queer identities, people need spaces to safely talk about their families and relationships free from judgement.

QUEER THEORY AS A PRACTICE FRAMEWORK

While queer theory informs the practice strategies described previously, it can also be a useful framework for engaging and practicing with queer clients (Tilsen & Nylund, 2011). Practitioners who understand the principles of queer theory can educate and engage clients in dialogue about the ways in which the principles reflect or resonate with their own experiences. For many queer people, the existing social categories of identity for sexual orientation and gender identity may feel limiting and restrictive. By simply acknowledging this possibility, clients may feel a freedom to fully explore their own sense of identity and to imagine it beyond the existing categories (Abes, 2007). This process is similar to Freire's (1973) concept of consciousness raising. By increasing their consciousness about social structures and dominant narratives around identity, people come to understand that their experiences of oppression are not related to whether or not they are good or worthy people but rather that they are common experiences that are externally imposed upon them. Supporting clients through such a process is a form of liberatory practice and can be empowering in many ways.

Another application of queer theory as a framework for practice is through the use of discourse analysis and narrative therapy. Discourse analysis is a process of identifying and deconstructing the messages and stories that are told in society about an issue or population (Gee, 2014). Deconstruction is a process of unpacking underlying beliefs and values of dominant stories or narratives and evaluating how those beliefs and values position groups of people in certain ways in society (White, 1993). For LGBTQ people, the underlying belief that queerness is associated with deviance establishes a clear role of queer people as "less than" others and outside of the norm of society.

An example of a dominant narrative about LGBTQ youth is that they all face rejection by their families and experience suicide ideation. While these situations may be true for some LGBTQ youth, they are not true for all. However, LGBTQ youth who learn the narrative may perceive that their experiences are not "queer enough" or that they "aren't doing queerness right." This internalization can be damaging to a person's well-being. Another way that this narrative can impact LGBTQ people is by seeing the journey into queerness as being full of sadness and pain. Another dominant narrative that exists about LGBTQ people is that life is hard when one is young but "it gets better." Again, this may be true for some LGBTQ people but may not be true for others. In fact, this narrative has been criticized as centering the experiences of LGBTQ people who have race and class privilege and hence access to the resources to make life better despite certain forms of social exclusion (Majkowski, 2011). By naming and analyzing these dominant discourses, people can deconstruct them and explore their impact.

Narrative therapy can play a role in the analysis of dominant discourses with queer people (Willis, 2007). Queer people can be encouraged by practitioners to write or tell their own narratives, which may or may not align with the dominant narratives that exist in society. The process of telling one's own story, and in some cases using it to create queer visibility in contrast to dominant narratives, can be empowering and therapeutic (Llera & Katsirebas, 2010). Queer people have used their stories to interrupt dominant discourses through film, poetry, music, and other forms of expression (Wernick, Woodford, & Kulick, 2014).

ONGOING TRAINING AND EDUCATION

Perhaps what is evident at this point is that practitioners working with queer clients and communities must engage in their own process of learning and unlearning. Training and supervision are needed to support awareness raising about one's own beliefs and values related to gender identity and sexual orientation and their role and function in society. Practitioners who can raise their consciousness to a level at which they are able to monitor their own unconscious thoughts and behaviors are best equipped to engage sensitively with queer communities and clients. For example, most people look at a person whose gender presentation is not clearly masculine or feminine and wonder what gender they are. What is important in these instances is for a practitioner to notice, examine, and critically question these thoughts before acting on them. Similarly, unpacking one's biases about people whose identities exist outside of societal norms is a crucial part of this process. Understanding how we have been socialized to think in certain ways about queer people, or even about the term "queer," can be useful. Considering queer behavior has historically been defined as abnormal and suspicious is an important piece of the puzzle.

While practitioners are ethically bound to engage in self-assessment, it is vital that agencies provide the appropriate training and supervision necessary to support increased competency, along with self-assessment skills and techniques, among practitioners employed within their setting(s). Often within social service agencies, there are one or two practitioners who are seen as the "go to" people for serving LGBT and/or queer clients. While this may be appropriate at one level to ensure competent care, agencies and organizations should explore ways that all clinicians and practitioners are adequately trained to reflect affirmation and respect for queer clients. This can be reinforced by shifts in agency policies and processes, forms, and materials as previously discussed. Affirming organizations are also available to help agencies assess their ability to be LGBTQ inclusive. Such a process can assist with making visible the often unconscious ways that queer people can be marginalized or silenced.

CONCLUSION

Practice with queer people and communities, as distinct from those within the larger LGBT community, requires an understanding of queerness from historical, contextual, and theoretical perspectives. Queerness often resists reduction to a list of identities or practice behaviors. Rather, it requires the application of queer theory principles to open up spaces and dialogues that increase opportunities for queer people to emerge and examine their existence and experiences within the broader social context. Such a process requires practitioners who are willing and able to examine and challenge their own assumptions, values, and beliefs on an ongoing basis to increase their competency and ability to be affirming to members of the queer community.

REFERENCES

Abes, E. S., Jones, S. R., & McEwen, M. K. (2007). Reconceptualizing the model of multiple dimensions of identity: The role of meaning-making capacity in the construction of multiple identities. *Journal of college student development*, 48(1), 1–22.

Bronski, M. (2011). *A queer history of the United States.* Boston: Beacon Press.

Burdge, B. J. (2007). Bending gender, ending gender: Theoretical foundations for social work practice with the transgender community. *Social Work, 52*(3), 243–250.

Butler, J. (2004). *Undoing gender.* New York: Routledge.

Calhoun, C. (1995). The politics of identity and recognition. In C. Calhoun (Ed.), *Critical Social Theory: Culture, History, and the Challenge of Difference* (pp. 193–230). Cambridge, MA.

Caluya, G. (2006). The (gay) scene of racism: Face, shame and gay Asian males. *Australian Critical Race and Whiteness Studies Association e-Journal, 2*(2), 1–14.

Dentato, M. P. (2014). Queer communities (competency and positionality). In *Encyclopedia of social work.* Oxford: Oxford University Press. doi:10.1093/acrefore/9780199975839.013.881

Diamond, L. M. (2006). What we got wrong about sexual identity development: Unexpected findings from a longitudinal study of young women. In A. M. Omoto & H. S. Kurtzman (Eds.), *Sexual orientation and mental health: Examining identity and development in lesbian, gay, and bisexual people,* (pp. 73–94). Washington, DC: American Psychological Association.

Duong, K. (2012). What does queer theory teach us about intersectionality? *Politics & Gender, 8*(3), 370–386.

Foucault, M. (1988). *Madness and civilization: A history of insanity in the age of reason.* New York: Vintage.

Fox, R. C. (2007). Gay grows up: An interpretive study on aging metaphors and queer identity. *Journal of Homosexuality, 52*(3–4), 33–61.

Freire, P. (1973). *Education for critical consciousness*. New York: Continuum.

Gee, J. P. (2014). *An introduction to discourse analysis: Theory and method*. New York: Routledge.

Goltz, D. B. (2013). It gets better: Queer futures, critical frustrations, and radical potentials. *Critical Studies in Media Communication, 30*(2), 135–151.

Gray, M. L. (2009). *Out in the country: Youth, media, and queer visibility in rural America*. New York: New York University Press.

Halberstam, J. (1998). *Female masculinity*. Durham, NC: Duke University Press.

Han, C. S. (2007). They don't want to cruise your type: Gay men of color and the racial politics of exclusion. *Social Identities, 13*(1), 51–67.

Hawkesworth, M. (1997). Confounding gender. *Signs, 22*, 649–713.

Hillier, L., & Harrison, L. (2004). Homophobia and the production of shame: Young people and same sex attraction. *Culture, Health & Sexuality, 6*(1), 79–94.

Jagose, A. (1996). *Queer theory: An introduction*. New York: New York University Press.

Llera, D., & Katsirebas, E. (2010). Remapping the journey of lesbian youth through strength and "truth telling". *Journal of Lesbian Studies, 14*(1), 26–35.

Majkowski, T. (2011). The "It Gets Better campaign": An unfortunate use of queer futurity. *Women & Performance: A Journal of Feminist Theory, 21*(1), 163–165.

McInroy, L., & Craig, S. L. (2012). Articulating identities: Language and practice with multiethnic sexual minority youth. *Counselling Psychology Quarterly, 25*(2), 137–149.

Mizock, L., & Mueser, K. T. (2014). Employment, mental health, internalized stigma, and coping with transphobia among transgender individuals. *Psychology of Sexual Orientation and Gender Diversity, 1*(2), 146–158.

Morrow, D. (2004). Social work practice with gay, lesbian, bisexual, and transgender adolescents. *Families in Society: The Journal of Contemporary Social Services, 85*(1), 91–99.

Nadal, K. L., Rivera, D. P., & Corpus, J. H. (2010). Sexual orientation and transgender microaggressions. In D. W. Sue (Ed.), *Microaggressions and marginality: Manifestation, dynamics, and impact* (pp. 217–240). Hoboken, NJ: John Wiley.

Oswald, R. F., Blume, L. B., & Marks, S. R. (2005). *Decentering heteronormativity: A model for family studies*. In V. L. Bengtson, A. C. Acock, K. R. Allen, P. Dilworth-Anerson, & D M. Klein (Eds.), *Sourcebook of Family Theory & Research* (pp. 143–165). Thousand Oaks, CA: Sage Publications, Inc.

Owen, G. (2010). Queer theory wrestles the "real" child: Impossibility, identity, and language in Jacqueline Rose's the case of peter pan. *Children's Literature Association Quarterly, 35*(3), 255–273.

Peters, A. J. (1997). Themes in group work with lesbian and gay adolescents. *Social Work with Groups, 20*(2), 51–69.

Rand, E. (2005). Getting dressed up: The displays of Frank Woodhull and the policing of gender. In *The Ellis Island Snow Globe* (pp. 67–106). Durham, NC: Duke University Press.

Ryan, C., Huebner, D., Diaz, R. M., & Sanchez, J. (2009). Family rejection as a predictor of negative health outcomes in white and Latino lesbian, gay, and bisexual young adults. *Pediatrics, 123*(1), 346–352.

Saltzburg, S., & Davis, T. S. (2010). Co-authoring gender-queer youth identities: Discursive tellings and retellings. *Journal of Ethnic & Cultural Diversity in Social Work, 19*(2), 87–108.

Savin-Williams, R. C. (2009). *The new gay teenager*, Vol. 3. Cambridge, MA: Harvard University Press.

Shah, N. (2006). Adjudicating intimacies on U.S. frontiers. In A. L. Stoler (Ed.), *Haunted by empire: Geographies of intimacy in North American history* (pp. 116–139). Durham, NC: Duke University Press.

Sue, D. W. (2010). *Microaggressions in everyday life: Race, gender, and sexual orientation*. Hoboken, NJ: John Wiley.

Sullivan, N. (2003). *A critical introduction to queer theory*. New York: New York University Press.

Tilsen, J. & Nylund, T. (2011). *Queer theory in action: Theoretical resources for therapeutic conversations. Part One.* Retrieved from http://search.alexanderstreet.com/preview/work/bibliographic_entity|video_work|1779215

Wagaman, M. A. (2013). *Exploring intersections of identity and service provision among LGBTQ young adults: A participatory action research approach* (Doctoral dissertation). Arizona State University.

Wagaman, M. A. (2014). Understanding service experiences of LGBTQ young people through an intersectional lens. *Journal of Gay and Lesbian Social Services, 26,* 111–145. doi:10.1080/10538720.2013.866867

Wernick, L. J., Woodford, M. R., & Kulick, A. (2014). LGBTQQ youth using participatory action research and theater to effect change: Moving adult decision-makers to create youth-centered change. *Journal of Community Practice, 22*(1–2), 47–66.

White, M. (1993). *Deconstruction and therapy.* In S. Gilligan, & R. Price (Eds.), *Therapeutic Conversation* (pp. 22–61). New York: W.W. Norton.

Wiegman, R. (2001). Object lessons: Men, masculinity, and the sign women. *Signs: Journal of Women in Culture and Society, 26*(2), 355–388.

Willis, P. (2007). "Queer eye" for social work: Rethinking pedagogy and practice with same-sex attracted young people. *Australian Social Work, 60*(2), 181–196.

CHAPTER 18

BUILDING STRENGTHS-BASED AND EMPOWERING CONTINUUMS OF CARE FOR LGBTQ YOUTH

Shelley L. Craig and Lauren B. McInroy

INTRODUCTION

Lesbian, gay, bisexual, transgender, and queer (LGBTQ) youth experience a range of stressors, including increased risk of social exclusion and isolation, familial and peer rejection, and poor academic outcomes. LGBTQ youth are also at increased risk of discrimination, harassment, and violence (Burton, Marshal, & Chisolm, 2014; Starks, Newcomb, & Mustanski, 2015; Ylioja & Craig, 2014). Despite these complex challenges, few programs created specifically for LGBTQ youth are adequately described throughout the literature. Such gaps may result in an unequitable service delivery system that could exacerbate the negative health outcomes of LGBTQ youth. To address these concerns, this chapter describes a comprehensive model of service provision. It illustrates the model's applicability for LGBTQ youth through a real-world case example and provides a number of specific illustrations of successes and challenges experienced by the providers and administrators from the time of the model's conception throughout its implementation.

A continuum of care (CoC)—also referred to as a network of care or system of care—is generally considered a collection of integrated and collaborative services designed to meet the complex needs of a specific population (Matarese, 2012; McBryde-Foster & Allen, 2005). Throughout this chapter the term "CoC" is used for consistency whether referring to one specific CoC or a larger genre or category of CoC. A CoC approach has also been defined as a conceptual ideology beneficial to community-level planning for the prevention of poor health outcomes among vulnerable populations (Stroul, Blau, & Friedman, 2010). A CoC designed for young people should be "community-based, family-driven . . . youth-guided, and culturally and linguistically competent" (Stroul et al., 2010, p. 3) for the specific youth population(s) being served. Furthermore, a CoC should also constantly evolve to adapt to the current needs of these specific population(s), and respond to the broader socio-political climate (Miller, Blau, Christopher, & Jordan, 2012).

Although Stroul and Friedman (1986) initially proposed the concept of a CoC to support children and youth with severe emotional concerns, communities have utilized this model to serve many different populations (Stroul et al., 2010). Existent literature describes CoC for older adults (Palley, 2003), children and youth (Grimes, Kapunan, & Mullin, 2006; Stroul et al., 2010), mothers and infants (Kikuchi et al., 2015), HIV positive youth and adults (Christopoulous et al., 2013; Woods et al., 1998; Woods et al., 2002), and specific to HIV prevention and education for LGBTQ youth (Cranston, 1992). More recently, HIV CoC have been adapted and specifically designed to address pre-exposure prophylaxis (PrEP) treatments in the hope of increasing its overall effectiveness in the prevention of HIV transmission (Dvora, Bustamante, Wang, Young, & Klausner, 2016; Kelley et al., 2015). For more information about HIV/AIDS, PrEP, and related topics see chapter 24 in this text.

COC MODELS AND SPECIFIC YOUTH EXAMPLES

While over two dozen articles pertaining to CoC were identified and reviewed for this chapter, only one article and one edited book included LGBTQ youth specifically. Woods et al. (1998, 2002) described a CoC that focused on HIV prevention. Fisher, Poirier, and Blau's (2012) edited volume is an insightful approach to the development and evaluation of CoC, particularly for specific populations of LGBTQ youth (e.g., transgender, Native American, homeless). None of these resources, however, clearly described a "working" CoC model for LGBTQ youth, and few provided detailed examples of services. However, from the extant literature reviewed, two models emerged as beneficial illustrations of CoC.

Grimes et al. (2006) described a CoC for children and youth, the Mental Health Services Program for Youth (MHSPY), which offered services to youth with severe mental health issues. The MHSPY served children and youth (ages 3–17.5), residing in certain counties within Massachusetts, meeting the following criteria: (a) severe emotional disturbances for a minimum of six months, (b) a minimum IQ of 70, and (c) conclusive results from the Child and Adolescent Functional Assessment Scale, which identified a "need for intensive services" (Grimes et al., 2006, p. 314). The CoC included services for primary health care, mental health, substance use, criminal justice involvement, educational support, and community resources. After acceptance into the MHSPY, a care manager was appointed to each family to offer support and help the family build an interdisciplinary care team, which was comprised of professional and personal supports. The MHSPY emphasizes the role of youth and their families as the primary decision-makers of their own care (Grimes et al., 2006), which aligns with the current definition of CoC suggested by Stroul and colleagues (2010).

Similarly, Woods and colleagues (2002) discuss a CoC for youth who are HIV positive or at high risk of acquiring sexually transmitted infections. Key organizational partners included hospitals, public and community health centers, and outreach agencies. Each setting offered unique services, with a few offering key programs (e.g., HIV testing) at multiple venues. The features of this CoC included targeted HIV-related services that integrated mental and sexual health counseling, optional HIV testing, educational outreach by trained peer educators, primary health and dental care, case management by a multidisciplinary team, referrals and resourcing, and follow-up care (Woods et al., 2002). This CoC explicitly included youth in the processes of developing, implementing, and delivering services (Woods et al., 1998). For example, youth focus groups were created to identify needs and evaluate services, a youth advisory board was formed, and young people were hired as peer educators. Further, this CoC intentionally incorporated prevention, a harm-reduction approach, and education into the various interactions with youth. The importance of utilizing such a participatory approach is further discussed throughout this chapter.

RESPONDING TO SOCIAL PROBLEMS: BUILDING SUPPORTIVE NETWORKS

A CoC can serve as a community response to social problems and broad population needs (Palley, 2003). As a planned and synchronized effort by various agencies and stakeholders (Dentato, Craig, & Smith, 2010), a CoC can actively create and build a network of supports for marginalized or vulnerable groups (Stroul & Friedman, 1986). These efforts are made with the hope of creating efficacious services that consider the strengths and unique needs (e.g., social, cultural, linguistic) of the population requiring services (Stroul et al., 2010). A CoC could be considered an alternative service delivery model, one that has the potential to improve access for populations that have significant health and mental health disparities yet infrequently utilize traditional services—such as the widely diverse and expansive LGBTQ youth community (Miller et al., 2012; Stroul et al., 2010).

Moving from an ideology where the organization fundamentally functions as an individual entity, collaboration within an effective CoC requires that administrators and providers think expansively and encourage cooperation within and between organizations to more fully meet the needs of various populations. CoC are complex networks, which require providers to consider the critical services in their service context as well as the process of navigating these services (McBryde-Foster & Allen, 2005) experienced by their specific client population(s). It is essential to understand the limits of a single organization and the necessity of collaboration across the CoC (Dentato et al., 2010). Woods and colleagues (1998) stress the importance of collaboration between various types of youth services, spanning health and social services. Miller and colleagues (2012) further describe current models of CoC that integrate child welfare, youth criminal justice, substance abuse, mental health, and educational systems. Thus CoCs are unique to each community and require a wide range of stakeholder involvement. Depending on the needs of each unique community, a CoC may need to include political and community leaders, funders, and/or criminal justice services in addition to health and mental health services. A CoC could also have a positive and systemic impact on the overall service delivery environment and may even encourage other providers and agencies to deliver a variety of LGBTQ youth-friendly and LGBTQ-positive services. This could serve to create awareness within mainstream services that lead to the creation of welcoming and inviting spaces for LGBTQ youth (Crisp & McCave, 2007) or specialized services (Lazear, Pires, Forssell, & Mallery, 2012).

USE OF INTERNET AND TECHNOLOGY

Beyond creating awareness within traditional and mainstream services, it is also important to consider the potential for utilizing innovative methods to promote services. Raising the visibility and awareness of CoC may be enhanced through the use of traditional media sources (e.g., newspapers, television, radio) as well as through social media platforms (e.g., Facebook, Twitter, Tumblr). Kelley et al. (2015) propose the usefulness of awareness raising campaigns (at both the local and national level) to increase the knowledge and effectiveness of PrEP among men who have sex with men. Providers within a CoC should assess how to best promote their individual and collective services by understanding where each unique population is most likely to receive information. For example, LGBTQ youth have been found to be particularly active users of the Internet (Gay, Lesbian & Straight Education Network, 2013), indicating the potential of social media to promote youth-specific CoC. Internet promotion efforts can be both targeted advertisement of services (e.g., to a specific population and/or geographic region) and/or widespread awareness raising initiatives.

Additionally, the potential of emerging technology to promote practitioner education and training, reduce practitioner burden, facilitate more effective assessment of clients' risks and needs, and encourage treatment adherence also requires consideration (Kelley et al., 2015). A scoping review by Boydell et al. (2014) found that a diverse range of information and communication technologies (ICTs; e.g., mobile devices, Internet-based applications, video-conferencing) are used to provide mental health services and supports to young people. ICTs are being used to provide delivery of "prevention, assessment, diagnosis, counseling and treatment programs" (p. 87) to children, youth, and young adults on an increasingly global scale. Findings from the scoping review indicate encouraging conclusions; including the preference of young people for ICT-based services, the increased capacity of practitioners, positive mental health outcomes (e.g., decreased symptoms, increased access to services), positive outcomes for clients and their families, and cost savings (Boydell et al., 2014).

RELEVANCE OF COC FOR LGBTQ YOUTH POPULATIONS

There are several key characteristics of a CoC that make this framework appropriate for LGBTQ youth. Services typically originate from population needs, require family and community collaboration, and empower users (Stroul, et al., 2010). Ideally, a CoC for LGBTQ youth would strive to bridge existing gaps in service utilization in a particular context (Center for Mental Health Services, 2004; Dentato et al., 2010; Stroul et al., 2010). Barriers to traditional (i.e., non-LGBTQ) service use for LGBTQ youth include feeling unwelcome, perceiving the provider to be incompetent, and confusion regarding appropriate and accessible programs (Craig, 2011). When they do obtain traditional services, the sexual orientation, gender identity, and/or gender expression of LGBTQ youth frequently remain unacknowledged (Lazear et al., 2012). This lack of acknowledgement often renders them invisible within health, mental health, wellness, and social programs, and their unique concerns and assets are overlooked. For example, LGBTQ youth do not always have their concerns met when pursuing counseling services, which often results in their dissatisfaction (Lazear et al., 2012), disempowerment, and lack of consistent utilization.

ROLE OF FAMILIES AND CAREGIVERS

CoC are expected to be family driven—as caregivers and families typically make the most important decisions about their child's care (Stroul et al., 2010). Miller and colleagues (2012) advocate for practitioners to understand the particular context of each diverse family as a whole during assessment and treatment planning, which allows for the unique strengths and resources of the family unit to be incorporated into care. Wilber, Ryan, and Marksamer (2006) similarly advocate for specifically including families and caregivers into CoC for LGBTQ youth. A supportive caregiver or family member can be particularly critical for an LGBTQ youth who is coping with the regular hardships of being an adolescent while also contending with stigma and discrimination related to their sexual orientation, gender identity, and/or gender expression. Ryan, Russell, Huebner, Diaz, and Sanchez (2010) describe the benefits that family support has upon the lives of LGBTQ youth, including promoting higher self-esteem, overall health, and a stronger support system. A supportive family environment can also shield LGBTQ young adults from substance abuse, depression, and suicide ideation and/or attempts, which unfortunately are often present among LGTBQ young people with unsupportive families (Ryan et al., 2010).

ASSESSING FOR SAFETY AND OUTNESS

While it can be beneficial for both LGBTQ youth as well as their caregivers/families to be included in a CoC, it is imperative that a youth's emotional and/or physical safety is not placed at risk. Whether an LGBTQ youth's family is able to be involved or not, it is valuable for care to be provided in such a manner that the youth's caregiver/family context is fully considered and understood (Ryan et al., 2010). If a family system is unsupportive and the LGBTQ youth gives permission to work with them, it may be helpful for the provider to meet with family members and provide education and resources to help them fully understand the impact of their behavior on their child. If an LGBTQ youth's family member(s) or caregiver(s) are not able to be involved because of abusive or unhealthy treatment of the youth, the service provider and youth can identify supportive individuals and/or alternative affirming supports and environments (Wilber et al., 2006). Similarly, if youth have not disclosed their LGBTQ status to their family, a provider may assist with helping them find appropriate services that will not necessarily "out" them to unsupportive parents or caregivers. In fact, providers and practitioners alike should always be sensitive to a youth's level of outness with regard to their sexual orientation and/or gender identity. Assessing for such factors can impact referrals as well as access to and utilization of care and protect the youth's privacy and safety for both the short term and long term.

A final characteristic of CoCs is that they empower service participants. For LGBTQ youth, this may mean there are multiple opportunities for them to become involved in programming efforts (Pires, 2002; Pires & Silber, 1991). This can be accomplished through a participatory process, by asking service users (e.g., LGBTQ youth and their families/caregivers) their vision and expectations of effective services, as well as involving them in planning and (as available) in the delivery of services (Lazear et al., 2012; Matarese, 2012; Stroul et al., 2010; Woods et al., 1998). Such involvement ultimately creates a pivotal space for youth to exercise self-determination in their lives (Pires, 2002; Pires & Silber, 1991). As there has been a lack of attention paid to the strengths of LGBTQ youth in service models (Craig, 2012; Lazear & Gamache, 2012), and few opportunities for LGBTQ youth involvement in planning their own services (Craig, 2011), a CoC could provide a clear framework for youth engagement and empowerment.

COMMON ELEMENTS: FROM PEOPLE TO ENVIRONMENT, EVENTS, AND TIME

Although a CoC framework necessitates that it be unique to the population and community that it is created in partnership with, some common elements have been identified within the literature. A key commonality is the underlying value of community responsibility that shapes how continuums of care are created and adapted to best meet stakeholders' needs (Stroul, 2002). Miller and colleagues (2012) boldly suggest that as almost all communities have embraced and implemented some degree of CoC, it may be useful to regularly examine which components are being addressed (Minnick, 1997; Stroul, 2002) consistently and competently, as well as where gaps may exist in current services.

McBryde-Foster and Allen (2005) describe a CoC as having four common elements that include: "people, environment, events and time" (p. 629). It should be noted that the following examples provided in this chapter are specific to LGBTQ youth populations. *People* refers to the youth, their family members and peers, as well as the providers and stakeholders involved in the CoC. *Environment* refers to the variety of settings in which an LGBTQ youth might be cared for within the CoC, which can include community organizations, schools, hospitals, as well as other agencies. Practitioners must always understand the unique connections between an individual and their environment (e.g., family, school, and community), known as the ecological model or framework. *Events* refer to the "care events" that take place as the LGBTQ youth and their provider navigate the CoC, both as a unit and as separate entities (McBryde-Foster & Allen, 2005, p. 629). These care events range from individual counseling, to supportive interventions in schools, to treatment within health-care settings. A CoC considers the interactions of the various stakeholders as a sequence of "initiating, continuing and concluding care events" (McBryde-Foster & Allen, 2005, p. 630) between organizations that may occur as a youth receives services from multiple care settings. Finally, *time* refers to the amount of time a youth spends within the CoC, which could range from one visit of a short duration, such as one group counseling session, to participation in concurrent services (e.g., multiple services utilized by the youth and/or by their family/caregiver[s]) such as individual counseling, family counseling, case management, and/or prevention education over a period of several years. Ultimately, there are endless possibilities for the configuration of a CoC, as a result of the variety of youth and community needs and the types of people, environments, events, and time frames that might be involved (McBryde-Foster & Allen, 2005).

THE STRENGTHS-BASED PERSPECTIVE: AN EMPOWERING AND PARTICIPATORY APPROACH

Utilizing a strengths-based perspective is a critical component for any proposed CoC model, as it fully aligns with the key elements of CoC previously described. As CoCs are unique to their communities, it makes sense to utilize all the strengths and resources of such communities to develop, implement, and maintain the continuum (Dentato et al., 2010; Pires & Silber, 1991; Stroul et al., 2010). Empowerment can be attained through the logical involvement of service users (Pires & Silber, 1991), in a participatory manner that allows them to assert their strengths, such as asking them about their past or current experiences in programs and adapting programs to better meet their needs (Austin & Craig, 2015). A strengths-based perspective is appropriate for the LGBTQ youth population as it provides an opportunity for their voices to be heard and to underscore youth as experts (Craig, 2013; Lazear & Gamache, 2012). Incorporating the feedback of LGBTQ youth can ultimately help maintain a CoC (Woods et al., 1998) by ensuring that the services provided are affirming, appropriate, and helpful (Dentato et al., 2010; Miller et al., 2012).

CASE EXAMPLE OF A STRENGTHS-BASED CoC

To provide a specific model of a CoC for LGBTQ youth, an example of one strengths-based, resiliency-focused CoC established within a large, multicultural, urban city is provided. The CoC incorporates resilience "as an important element to maintaining and promoting child and youth mental health, and as a life-long buffer to potential threats to wellbeing over time and transition" (Khanlou & Wray, 2014, p. 65). While resilience emphasizes individual strengths, it is best understood as a process of positively responding (i.e., overcoming or adapting) to challenges or adversity, rather than an individual trait or capacity. Following an extensive mixed methods community needs assessment (Craig, 2011), a CoC for LGBTQ youth was developed based on the conceptualization of the core components of a CoC found in the literature (McBryde-Foster & Allen, 2005). Table 18.1 illustrates how this case example fits into the model (McBryde-Foster & Allen, 2005) previously described.

The eight integrated programs in the CoC (see Figure 18.1) include the following:

1. *Prevention Education Workshops.* These workshops were designed to increase service provider awareness of LGBTQ youth issues and were delivered in a variety of community-based environments. The flexible curriculum included an overview of LGBTQ youth risks, resiliencies, and identity development; direct strategies for inclusive programming and affirming service provision; and an opportunity to discuss inclusivity challenges in the context of organizational or personal barriers. Workshops were tailored to both the type of organization within the CoC (e.g., school, hospital, community mental health organization) and the specific audience (e.g., clinicians, administrators, physicians, students).

TABLE 18.1 Elements of a CoC for LGBTQ Youth

Elements of a CoC

Elements	The CoC
People	**Service Users:** LGBTQ youth, families, and caregivers **Service Providers:** Social workers, administrators, guidance counselors, lawyers, health professionals, students, teachers
Environment	Included a Jewish family and children's services organization, a telephone counseling, crisis and referral agency, an LGBTQ policy and advocacy organization, a safe schools organization, a training organization focusing on LGBTQ issues, an LGBTQ hub organization that provided direct services to youth and their families, a school of social work within a university, a nonprofit consulting agency, and a youth drop-in center for LGBTQ youth
Events	Eight integrated programs for prevention and early intervention at the individual, family, and community level (see Figure 18.1). They ranged from tertiary service provider training to high intensity direct services for homeless LGBTQ youth.
Time	Varying times for each youth client depending on the number of care events and services

Note: CoC = continuum of care.

2. *Youth Speaker Trainings.* These trainings consisted of public-speaking preparation to empower LGBTQ youth to share their stories in a narrative intervention. Youth were trained on enhancing their public speaking and presentation skills related to organizing their personal narratives, engaging audiences, responding to questions and answers, managing anxiety and stress when presenting, and co-facilitating a presentation, among other skills. Trained youth presented as part of the prevention education workshops to LGBTQ and non-LGBTQ youth, adults, parents, allies, and other community members.

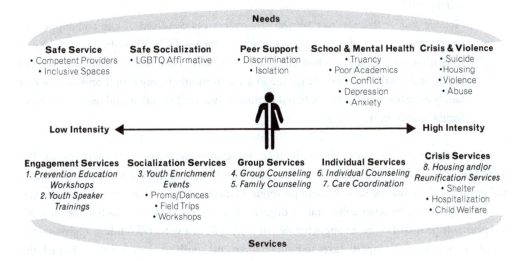

FIGURE 18.1: Eight integrated programs for prevention and early intervention at the individual, family, and community level

3. *Youth Enrichment Events.* These events included safe socialization and skill-building programs that encouraged youth leadership development and self-expression. Activities such as LGBTQ youth proms and dances, community field trips, artistic workshops, advocacy trainings, and educational sessions were delivered through various provider agencies at unique locations across the city and county.

4. *Community-Based Group Counseling.* Group counseling consisted of six to eight sessions of socioemotional and prevention-focused discussions in open-ended school and community-based groups with specifics described elsewhere (Craig, Austin, & McInroy, 2013). To access an intervention manual for this program, Affirmative Supportive Safe and Empowering Talk (ASSET), see www.projectyouthaffirm.org/asset (Craig, Thompson, & McInroy, 2016). These weekly youth groups were offered in various locations throughout the county. Topics such as healthy relationships, substance abuse prevention, healthy decision-making, and coping skills were discussed within these confidential group settings, led by graduate level social workers, mental health counselors, and interns.

5. *Family Counseling.* Within the context of the CoC, one clinician was specifically trained to work with families in the role of a "family specialist" who provided services to parents and caregivers that were struggling with issues related to their LGBTQ child and wished to obtain assistance and support.

6. *Individual Counseling.* Individual counseling was provided by a mental health professional and offered for youth at CoC provider agencies. Counseling was individually tailored to address the needs of LGBTQ youth clients, as collaboratively determined during an initial comprehensive psychosocial assessment.

7. *Care Coordination.* Care coordination consisted of individualized guidance, support, and critical linkage to services in the community. Highly trained case managers assisted LGBTQ youth to navigate a range of challenges on the path toward a healthy adulthood and independence while underscoring resilience and using a strengths-based approach (Craig, 2012).

8. *Housing and/or Reunification Services.* These services consisted of safe and supportive short-term shelter and housing programs for homeless LGBTQ youth in a unique collaboration between a youth homeless shelter and care coordinators. In extreme cases of family and youth separation (e.g., due to a youth running away from home or due to a family member throwing a youth out of their home, etc.) clients would receive intensive family reunification services.

All of these services were provided without any initial or ongoing costs to the participants. The hub organization provided direct services (i.e., care coordination, a limited amount of individual and group level counseling sessions, and prevention education) while the remainder of the services were provided by other collaborating organizations within the CoC. Funding for the CoC was primarily provided via grant opportunities stemming from a voter referendum approving the use of a certain level of property taxes to fund children and youth services as well as through the local United Way and supplemented with existing agency partner funding sources.

This CoC for LGBTQ youth has achieved positive outcomes in core programs.

1. *Care Coordination*: The multiethnic LGBTQ youth participants ($N = 162$) in the "Strengths First" program experienced statistically significant increases in self-esteem and self-efficacy (Craig, McInroy, Austin, Smith, & Engle, 2012).
2. *Community-Based Group Counseling.* The multiethnic LGBTQ youth ($N = 263$) that participated in ASSET, the first affirmative group counseling intervention created specifically to promote resilience in LGBTQ youth, reported significant increases in proactive coping and self-esteem (Craig et al., 2014).
3. *Prevention Education Workshops.* A diverse sample of White non-Hispanic (29%), Black/African American (20%), Hispanic (49%), and Haitian (3%) adult multidisciplinary professionals ($N = 2,850$) participated in the CoC community-based educational intervention designed to improve service provision for LGBTQ youth. As a result of the training, nearly 80% of participants reported that they intended to take at least one action to improve the lives of LGBTQ youth. Participants also agreed that their knowledge and skills increased after the intervention (Craig, Dorion, & Dillon, 2015).

While these findings cannot be considered reflective of the effectiveness of the CoC as a comprehensive system, some of the program components that comprise the whole have been found to be effective. Further, at least 46% of the youth receiving services within the CoC identified that they had used at least one other CoC program. A large majority of youth stated that they had learned about the variety of programs offered through the CoC and would be willing to attend available programs if they identified a need.

IMPLICATIONS FOR PRACTICE

This case example provides several key considerations in the development of a CoC for LGBTQ youth, including a focus on collaboration among service providers; training and skill enhancement of practitioners, staff members, and administrators; and the importance of incorporating service user feedback. The following sections examine each of these three key areas along with examples from the CoC for LGBTQ youth.

A FOCUS ON SERVICE PROVIDER COLLABORATION

As mentioned earlier in this chapter, an essential component of working with service providers is facilitating their understanding of the importance of modifying their existing organizational ideology associated with functioning as an individual entity to thinking and acting more expansively and cooperatively to meet the needs of diverse population(s). Thus there is no doubt that an effective CoC requires productive collaboration, effective communication, and trust in order to share knowledge, resources, and infrastructure. From the initial meeting of service providers to create a shared vision for a CoC to service coordination for an individual LGBTQ youth, effective communication was essential (Dentato et al., 2010). These considerations also emphasize the values of inclusivity and transparency necessary for continuum building. For instance, the use of consensus building can help ensure each member of the partnership has a voice in all matters, and keeping extensive records can promote transparency and equal access to decisions by all involved. Those working within CoC cite the benefits of collaborative planning and shared responsibility for vulnerable populations as strengths within this framework (Stroul, 2002).

CoCs often include a variety of providers from different disciplines. In a strengths-based approach, providers recognize the distinct expertise that each brings to the continuum and highlight that diversity within a collaborative framework. Further, within a CoC there may be conflicting perspectives on both participant needs and service delivery (McBryde-Foster & Allen, 2005). Without self-reflection and communication with colleagues, as suggested by Minnick (1997), contradictory perspectives between service providers could influence the quality of services received by clients (McBryde-Foster & Allen, 2005). Such concerns should be considered during the inception of a CoC and should be carefully integrated into planning.

A KEY CONSIDERATION: NEGOTIATING PARTNERSHIPS

From the very beginning of the process of conceiving and planning for the CoC, the key stakeholders discussed how to manage the various partners and build relationships among all staff members across agencies. It became clear that a series of individual and joint meetings had to be scheduled as an essential component to listening to provider's needs, thoughts, wishes, and challenges in order to gain perspective about where tensions may lie and/or collaboration could be fostered. To encourage a sense of community, meals were often provided at these meetings. Where tensions did exist or arise, the challenge of always remaining focused on the end goal of establishing the CoC for LGBTQ youth was instilled among all partners. At the forefront of the planning and implementation process, the vital skills necessary for negotiating these essential partnerships included active listening, networking, brokering, and building consensus along with understanding each unique personality and their histories of working within the community.

ENHANCING SKILLS: ORGANIZATIONAL AND PRACTITIONER TRAINING

To achieve optimal effectiveness, providers within the CoC should consider training in population-specific care as well as working within the collaborative framework. It is important for service providers to be culturally competent in working with LGBTQ youth. Matarese (2012) suggests ongoing training and professional development for those working with LGBTQ youth in conjunction with the development of LGBTQ antidiscrimination policies (Craig, Dentato, Messinger & McInroy, 2014; Council on Social Work Education, 2015). Within the context of a CoC, trainings to ensure culturally competent service delivery should be offered to all organizations serving LGBTQ youth, including service providers, fiscal agents, and funders, among others.

Interprofessional groups working in CoC can utilize affirmative practice. Such a framework can "celebrate, advocate and validate the identities" of LGBTQ clients (Crisp & McCave, 2007, p. 405). This could mean supporting and empowering LGBTQ individuals in exploring their identities and/or examining issues within the context of homophobia and transphobia (Craig, Austin, & Alessi, 2013). Affirmative practice requires three components: specialized knowledge, affirming skills, and supportive attitudes. Acquiring specialized knowledge related to LGBTQ youth may include learning and using preferred identity language (e.g., sexuality terms, gender pronouns); understanding experiences of diversity, oppression, and resilience; and having a strong sense of the supportive resources available. Important and affirming skills include the ability to create affirming LGBTQ-positive spaces, the avoidance of assumptions and imposition of labels, and the consideration of a client's issues within the context of their intersecting identities (Crisp & McCave, 2007). Last, with regard to demonstrating supportive attitudes, service providers must acknowledge and address their biases to better serve LGBTQ youth (Alessi, 2014). Affirmative practice can be tailored to develop community competence to deliver services to LGBTQ youth within the framework of a CoC. In addition, collaborating agencies should consider an evaluation of their own services, practices, and policies prior to participating in a CoC to determine if they are anti-oppressive and affirmative (Crisp & McCave, 2007; Matarese, 2012; Pawley Helfgott & Gonsoulin, 2012).

Specific programmatic skills are also important. Many programs, such as case management, are consistent with services offered by other CoCs (Grimes et al., 2006; Palley, 2003; Woods et al., 1998) and may require a focus on continuing education in effective case management. The inclusion of training programs to facilitate the development of staff, student, and volunteer competencies in counseling and supporting youth as peer educators is also warranted. Educational initiatives for LGBTQ youth to become peer educators may offer opportunities for them to develop leadership, public speaking, and other transferable skills, which will ultimately be useful for pursuing education and/or employment.

In the context of allied health, Minnick (1997) suggests several important skills that are critical to working within a CoC. These include the ability to motivate, communicate, and analyze. Motivational skills can be used to inspire and encourage individuals and groups to act (Minnick, 1997), which can be applied to organizations and governmental agencies of various levels— encouraging them to deliver services to LGBTQ youth while supporting youth in their efforts to secure services and opportunities internal and external to the network. For social workers, motivation could include the empowerment perspective, which entails providing opportunities for individuals and groups to have more control over their daily lives (Boehm & Staples, 2004). Minnick (1997) describes communication as including "system building and application of information system skills" (p. 45), which means that providers should consider the full CoC when delivering services. In addition to communication among service providers within the CoC, communication skills include explaining the various stages of the CoC to the client (Craig, 2012). Analysis skills can include management of client and administrative concerns, evaluating program effects, and the need for adaptation (Matarese, 2012). In addition, strong evaluation measures to capture the impact of individual LGBTQ services and the need for CoC development are necessary, as such efforts may result in increased utilization by youth (Goode & Fisher, 2012).

A KEY CONSIDERATION: TRAINING AGENCIES AND FUNDERS ALIKE

Upon initiation of the implementation stages of the CoC, it was essential that a plan for training be established. This plan included not only existing partners within the CoC but a variety of other external partners, organizations, consultants, schools, churches, as well as funders. It became apparent quite early in the process that understanding the unique identities of LGBTQ youth had to start with discussions surrounding issues of oppression, discrimination, heteronormativity, cisnormativity, homophobia, transphobia, and microaggressions in order to build a knowledge base for understanding how to create affirming agencies, programs, and funding opportunities. When a local funder held a public meeting to discuss a notice of funding availability, members of the team seeking to develop a CoC had to advocate by publicly speaking up and addressing the fact that while other minority groups were included in the call for funding, there was absolutely no mention of the LGBTQ community. When the funder responded that all groups would *naturally* be considered, regardless of being listed in the actual funding call, the CoC development team stated it was essential that the lack of inclusion and visibility of LGBTQ populations be addressed. Ultimately, the funding opportunity was modified to include the LGBTQ community, and the CoC development team succeeded in receiving some of those funds to support the CoC for LGBTQ youth. Therefore, while education and trainings can be planned effectively with members of the CoC or external agencies, they can also occur extemporaneously (e.g., such as in the midst of a public meeting) in order to best meet the needs of the CoC and diverse populations being served.

A PARTICIPATORY AND EMPOWERING APPROACH: INCORPORATING FEEDBACK FROM SERVICE USERS

It is asserted that a CoC can improve the quality of life of the population served (Stroul et al., 2010). However, there is a notable gap in the CoC literature that articulates clients' perspectives (McBryde-Foster & Allen, 2005). This gap is likely to be even more pronounced for LGBTQ youth who often experience invisibility within services (Lazear et al., 2012). A current CoC should be "youth-guided" with the engaged involvement of youth in all stages of the CoC (Miller et al., 2012; Stroul et al., 2010). This includes creating opportunities for youth to provide feedback, such as involving them in needs assessments and program evaluations (Miller et al., 2012). For LGBTQ youth, providers may consider the various ways to engage with youth who are "out," those who are not, and those who are questioning their sexual orientation and/or gender identity (Lazear et al., 2012). A study conducted by Bundock et al. (2011) examining youth and young adults ($n = 60$)

found that young people valued being included in the treatment choices that affected them, feeling heard by their provider(s), and accessing services in a safe space free of discrimination. Thus, in order to ensure the utility of CoC for LGBTQ youth, it is critical to solicit their perspective throughout the development process.

A KEY CONSIDERATION: CREATING A NEEDS ASSESSMENT

While the CoC was established in 2006, a more recent needs assessment discovered that LGBTQ youth had drastically different ideas from the service providers about the types of programs they would access or need (Craig, 2011). Such divergent perceptions might create obstacles between clients and providers during the administration of services. Thus ongoing needs assessments in a CoC should be developed in collaboration between providers and those being served. In an ideal situation, service users, such as LGBTQ youth, ought to take a leadership role in the development of needs assessments to encourage ownership of the process and to ensure findings are congruent with their perspective (Dobell & Newcomer, 2008; Stroul et al., 2010).

CONCLUSION

The collaborative framework, contextual approach, and potential for empowerment of a CoC makes it a good option for service delivery for LGBTQ youth. This chapter has examined the current literature surrounding CoC and proposed a strengths-based CoC model for LGBTQ youth, illustrated by a case example that ultimately became a successful nonprofit organization within a large city. It is clear that providing services through a CoC can contribute to meeting the immediate needs of the population served, while also serving as a form of capacity-building to better support organizations to provide competent services to LGBTQ youth. Community and youth involvement and leadership is crucial in all steps of the design, delivery, and implementation of the CoC services offered, in order to ensure its appropriateness and helpfulness (Dentato et al., 2010; Lazear et al., 2012; Matarese, 2012; Pires, 2002; Woods et al., 1998). Ultimately, social workers and other professionals working with LGBTQ youth must recognize their vital roles as allies and create opportunities for service provision to leverage the strengths of a community.

ACKNOWLEDGMENTS

This chapter was adapted from a previously published article: Craig, S. L., Dentato, M. P. & Iacovino, G. E. (2015). Patching holes and integrating community: A strengths-based continuum of care for lesbian, gay, bisexual, transgender and questioning youth. *Journal of Gay & Lesbian Social Services* 27(1), 100–115.

REFERENCES

Alessi, E. J. (2014). A framework for incorporating minority stress theory into treatment with sexual minority clients. *Journal of Gay & Lesbian Mental Health, 18*(1), 47–66.

Austin, A., & Craig, S. L. (2015). Adapting empirically supported interventions for sexual and gender minority youth: A stakeholder driven model. *Journal of Evidence-Based Social Work, 12*(6), 567–578.

Boehm, A., & Staples, L. H. (2004). Empowerment: The point of view of consumers. *Families in Society: The Journal of Contemporary Social Services, 85*(2), 270–280.

Boydell, K. M., Hodgins, M., Pignatiello, A., Teshima J., Edwards, H., & Willis, D. (2014). Using technology to deliver mental health services to children and youth: A scoping review. *Journal Canadian Academy of Child Adolescent Psychiatry, 23*(2), 87–99.

Bundock, H., Fidler, S., Clarke, S., Holmes-Walker, D. J., Farrell, K., McDonald, S., . . . Foster, C. (2011). Crossing the divide: Transition care services for young people with HIV—their views. *AIDS Patient Care and STDs, 25*(8), 465–473.

Burton, C., Marshal, M., & Chisolm, D. (2014). School absenteeism and mental health among sexual minority youth and heterosexual youth. *Journal of School Psychology, 52*(1), 37–47.

Center for Mental Health Services. (2004). *The Comprehensive Community Mental Health Services for Children and Their Families Program Evaluation Findings. Annual Report to Congress* (pp. 1–125). Atlanta, GA: Macro International. Retrieved from https://store.samhsa.gov/shin/content/SMA-CB-E2004CD/SMA-CB-E2004CD.pdf

Christopoulous, K. A., Massey, A. D., Lopez, A. M., Geng, E. H., Johnson, M. O., Pilcher, C. D., . . . Dawson-Rose, C. (2013). "Taking a half day at a time": Patient perspectives and the HIV engagement in care continuum. *AIDS Patient and STDs, 27*(4), 223–230. doi:10.1089/apc.2012.0418

Council on Social Work Education. (2015). *Position statement on conversion/reparative therapy*. Retrieved from http://www.cswe.org/File.aspx?id=85010

Craig, S. L. (2011). Precarious partnerships: Designing a community needs assessment to develop a system of care for gay, lesbian, bisexual, transgender and questioning (GLBTQ) youth. *Journal of Community Practice, 19*, 1–18.

Craig, S. L. (2012). Strengths-first: An empowering case management model for multiethnic sexual minority youth. *Journal of Gay and Lesbian Social Services, 39*(3), 274–288.

Craig, S. L. (2013). Affirmative Supportive Safe and Empowering Talk [ASSET]: Leveraging the strengths and resiliencies of sexual minority youth in school-based groups. *Journal of LGBT Issues in Counseling, 7*, 1–15.

Craig, S. L., Austin, A., & Alessi, E. (2013). Gay affirmative cognitive behavioral therapy for sexual minority youth: A clinical adaptation. *Clinical Social Work, 41*(3), 25–35.

Craig, S. L., Austin, A., & McInroy, L. (2014). School-based groups to support multiethnic sexual minority youth resiliency: Preliminary effectiveness. *Child and Adolescent Social Work, 30*(4), 87–106.

Craig, S. L., Dentato, M. P., & Iacovino, G. E. (2015). Patching holes and integrating community: A strengths-based continuum of care for lesbian, gay, bisexual, transgender and questioning youth. *Journal of Gay & Lesbian Social Services, 27*(1), 100–115.

Craig, S. L, Dentato, M. P., Messinger, L., & McInroy, L. B. (2014). Educational determinants of readiness to practice with LGBTQ clients: Social work students speak out. *British Journal of Social Work*, 1–20. doi:10.1093/bjsw/bcu107

Craig, S. L., Doiron, C., & Dillon, F. (2015) Cultivating multiethnic professional allies for sexual minority youth: A community-based educational intervention. *Journal of Homosexuality, 62*(12), 1703–1721.

Craig, S. L., McInroy, L., Austin, A., Smith, M., & Engle, B. (2012). Promoting self-efficacy and self-esteem for multiethnic sexual minority youth: An evidence-informed intervention. *Journal of Social Service Research, 38*(5), 688–698.

Craig, S. L., Thompson, M., & McInroy, L. B. (2016). Affirmative Supportive Safe and Empowering Talk (ASSET) group manual. Toronto, ON: Authors. Retrieved from www.projectyouthaffirm.org/asset

Cranston, K. (1992). HIV education for gay, lesbian, and bisexual youth: Personal risk, personal power, and the community of conscience. *Journal of Homosexuality, 22*(3–4), 247–259.

Crisp, C., & McCave, E. L. (2007). Gay affirmative practice: A model for social work practice with gay, lesbian, and bisexual youth. *Child and Adolescent Social Work Journal, 24*, 403–421.

Dentato, M. P., Craig, S. L., & Smith, M. (2010). The vital role of social workers in community partnerships: The alliance for gay, lesbian, bisexual, transgender youth. *Child and Adolescent Work Journal, 22*(5), 323–334.

Dobell, L. G., & Newcomer, R. J. (2008). Integrated care: Incentives, approaches, and future considerations. *Social Work in Public Health, 23*(4), 25–47.

Dvora, J. D., Bustamante, M. J., Wang, D., Young, S., & Klausner, J. D. (2016). PrEP continuum of care for MSM in Atlanta and Los Angeles County. *Clinical Infectious Diseases, 62*, 402–403.

Fisher, S. K., Poirier, J. M., & Blau, G. M. (Eds.). (2012). *Improving emotional and behavioral outcomes for LGBT youth: A guide for professionals*. Baltimore, MD: Brookes.

Gay, Lesbian & Straight Education Network, Center for Innovative Public Health Research, & Crimes Against Children Research Center. (2013). *Out online: The experiences of lesbian, gay, bisexual and transgender youth on the Internet*. Gay, Lesbian & Straight Education Network. Retrieved from http://www.glsen.org/sites/default/files/Out%20Online%20FINAL.pdf

Goode, T. D., & Fisher, S. K. (2012). Conducting cultural and linguistic competence self-assessment. In S. K. Fisher, J. M. Poirier, & G. M. Blau (Eds.), *Improving emotional and behavioural outcomes for LGBT youth: A guide for professionals* (pp. 127–140). Baltimore, MD: Paul H. Brookes.

Grimes, K. E., Kapunan, P. E., & Mullin, B. (2006). Children's health services in a "system of care": Patterns of mental health, primary and specialty use. *Public Health Reports, 121*, 311–323.

Khanlou, N., & Wray, R. (2014). A whole community approach toward child and youth resilience promotion: A review of resilience literature. *International Journal of Mental Health Addiction, 12*, 64–79.

Kelley, C. F., Kahle, E., Siegler, A., Sanchez, T., del Rio, C., Sullivan, P. S., & Rosenberg, E. S. (2015). Applying a PrEP continuum of care for men who have sex with men in Atlanta, Georgia. *Clinical Infectious Diseases, 61*(10), 1590–1597.

Kikuchi, K., Ansah, E. K., Okawa, S., Enuameh, Y, Yasuoka, J., Nanishi, K., ... Ghana EMBRACE Implementation Research Project Team. (2015). Effective linkages of continuum of care for improving neonatal, perinatal, and maternal mortality: A systematic review and meta-analysis. *PLoS ONE, 10*(9), e0139288. doi:10.1371/journal.pone.0139288

Lazear, K. J., & Gamache, P. (2012). The resilience U-turn: Understanding the risks and strengths to effectively support LGBT youth and families in systems of care. In S. K. Fisher, J. M. Poirier, & G. M. Blau (Eds.), *Improving emotional and behavioural outcomes for LGBT youth: A guide for professionals* (pp. 111–126). Baltimore, MD: Paul H. Brookes.

Lazear, K. J., Pires, S. A., Forssell, S. L., & Mallery, C. J. (2012). Building systems of care to support effective therapeutic and behavioural interventions and resources for LGBT youth and their families. In S. K. Fisher, J. M. Poirier, & G. M. Blau (Eds.), *Improving emotional and behavioural outcomes for LGBT youth: A guide for professionals* (pp. 127–140). Baltimore, MD: Paul H. Brookes.

Matarese, M. (2012). Improving outcomes for LGBT youth in out-of-home care settings: Implications and recommendations for systems of care. In S. K. Fisher, J. M. Poirier, & G. M. Blau (Eds.), *Improving emotional and behavioural outcomes for LGBT youth: A guide for professionals* (pp. 173–187). Baltimore, MD: Paul H. Brookes.

McBryde-Foster, M., & Allen, T. (2005). The continuum of care: A concept development study. *Journal of Advanced Nursing, 50*(6), 624–632.

Miller, B. D., Blau, G. M., Christopher, O. T., & Jordan, P. E. (2012). Sustaining and expanding systems of care to provide mental health services for children, youth and families across America. *American Journal of Community Psychology, 49*, 566–579.

Minnick, A. (1997). Key issues in building a continuum of care. *Nursing Administration Quarterly, 21*(4), 41–46.

Palley, H. A. (2003). Long-term care policy for older Americans: Building a continuum of care. *Journal of Health & Social Policy, 16*(3), 7–18.

Pawley Helfgott, K., & Gonsoulin, S. G. (2012). Standards of care for LGBT youth. In S. K. Fisher, J. M. Poirier, & G. M. Blau (Eds.), *Improving emotional and behavioural outcomes for LGBT youth: A guide for professionals* (pp. 141–158). Baltimore, MD: Paul H. Brookes.

Pires, S. A. (2002). *Building systems of care: A primer.* Retrieved from http://gucchd.georgetown.edu/products/PRIMER_CompleteBook.pdf

Pires, S. A., & Silber, J. (1991). *On their own: Runaway and homeless youth and programs that serve them.* Washington, DC: Georgetown University Child Development Center.

Ryan, C., Russell, S. T., Huebner, D., Diaz, R., & Sanchez, J. (2010). Family acceptance in adolescence and the health of LGBT young adults. *Journal of Child and Adolescent Psychiatric Nursing, 23*(4), 205–213.

Starks, T. J., Newcomb, M. E., & Mustanski, B. (2015). A longitudinal study of interpersonal relationships among lesbian, gay, and bisexual adolescents and young adults: Mediational pathways from attachment to romantic relationship quality. *Archives of Sexual Behavior, 44*, 1821–1831

Stroul, B. A. (2002). *Issue brief—Systems of care: A framework for system reform in children's mental health.* Washington, DC: Georgetown University Child Development Center, National Technical Center for Children's Mental Health.

Stroul, B. A., Blau, G., & Friedman, R. (2010). *Updating the system of care concept and philosophy.* Washington, DC: Georgetown University Center for Child and Human Development, National Technical Assistance Center for Children's Mental Health.

Stroul, B. A., & Friedman, R. (1986). *A system of care for children and youth with severe emotional disturbances* (rev. ed.). Washington, DC: Georgetown University Child Development Centre, National Technical Assistance Centre for Children's Mental Health.

Wilber, S., Ryan, C., & Marksamer, J. (2006). A family-centered approach to serving LGBT youth. In *Best practice guidelines: Serving LGBT youth in out-of-home care* (pp. 15–25). Atlanta: Child Welfare League. Retrieved from https://familyproject.sfsu.edu/sites/default/files/bestpracticeslgbtyouth.pdf

Woods, E. R., Samples, C. L., Melchiono, M. W., Keenan, P. M., Fox, D. J., Chase, L. H., . . . Goodman, E. (1998). Boston HAPPENS program: A model of health care for HIV-positive, homeless, and at-risk youth. *Journal of Adolescent Health, 23*(2 Suppl.), 37–48.

Woods, E. R., Samples, C. L., Melchiono, M. W., Keenan, P. M., Fox, D. J., Harris, S. K., & Boston HAPPENS Program Collaborators. (2002). Initiation of services in the Boston HAPPENS program: Human immunodeficiency virus-positive, homeless, and at-risk youth can access services. *AIDS Patient Care and STDs, 16*(10), 497–510.

Ylioja, T., & Craig, S. L. (2014). Exclusionary health policy: Responding to the risk of poor health among sexual minority youth in Canada. *Social Work in Public Health, 29*, 1–6.

CHAPTER 19

THE INTERSECTION OF POLICY AND PRACTICE

Advancing Civil Rights Equality and Equity

Anthony P. Natale, Kirsten Havig, Megan Gandy-Guedes, and David A. McLeod

INTRODUCTION

While the civil rights of lesbian, gay, bisexual, transgender, and queer (LGBTQ) individuals have grown at an unprecedented rate for any minority group in American history over the past four decades, several key protections remain elusive. Without doubt, the LGBTQ civil rights movement has heeded the lessons learned from the African American civil rights movement from the generation before. The US Supreme Court's 2015 decision to clear the way for gays and lesbians to obtain a federally recognized marriage is the pinnacle in the movement, but LGBTQ civil rights across the United States remain unequal and inequitable. The Court's decision leaves out other essential protections in education, employment, housing, health care, and public accommodations (Badgett, 2009; Fidas & Cooper, 2015). Until LGBTQ populations are fully covered under federal nondiscrimination policies that are comprehensive in scope, as other protected groups already are, much work remains.

This chapter outlines practice at the macro or policy level, through advancement of LGBTQ civil rights. First, it provides a brief historical overview of key LGBTQ civil rights developments beginning in the United States during the 1950s while also including global trends through the present decade. Next is a review of data on LGBTQ hate crimes, education access, employment barriers, housing obstacles, health-care access, and barriers to public accommodations that highlight the enduring social, institutional, and interpersonal oppression directed at LGBTQ individuals. Human ecological systems theory and intersectionality theory provide a framework for policy assessment and a call to action is grounded in the National Association of Social Workers (NASW) Code of Ethics. The chapter closes with 10 goals for advancing LGBTQ civil rights, accompanied by practical practice strategies.

LGBTQ CIVIL RIGHTS HISTORY IN THE UNITED STATES AND ABROAD

The second half of the twentieth century and beginning of twenty-first century brought about considerable advances in civil rights for LGBTQ individuals, both in the United States as well as around the world. The protections and legal supports championed by LGBTQ activists and advocates during this time period paved the way for numerous laws and policies that have become critical fixtures in the modern era.

1950s–1960s

The 1950s were a period marked by mostly restrictive and quite limited LGBTQ civil protections. Despite this, Harry Hay founded the Mattachine Society in 1950, one of the first national gay rights organization (Richards, 2005). The American Psychiatric Association first classified homosexuality as a mental illness in the *Diagnostic and Statistical Manual of Mental Disorders*, a handbook used by mental health professionals to diagnose mental health and related disorders, listing it as a "sociopathic personality disturbance" in 1952. This allowed President Dwight Eisenhower through executive order to ban employment of homosexuals within the federal government or any of its contractors (Richards, 2005). A trend of restricting LGBTQ civil protections grew in scope abroad as well. In 1953, Thailand became the first country to ban LGBTQ people in the military. The African country of Eritrea became the first in a fast-growing trend to make homosexual behavior illegal and subject to imprisonment and punishment in 1957. The next year Eritrea started another global trend—outlawing same sex-marriage ("Timeline of LGBTQ Rights," 2015).

By 1958, one of the first LGBTQ civil rights cases came before the US Supreme Court, which upheld the first amendment rights of freedom of speech and press for *ONE: The Homosexual Magazine* (Eaklor, 2008). This decision was instrumental in promoting visibility of LGBTQ people and allowed other publications that catered to LGBTQ people and communities to flourish. Illinois became the first state to remove sodomy from its criminal code in 1962 (Richards, 2005).

Globally, the early 1960s brought a trend of unequal consent laws across Europe and Asia, making consent for heterosexual sex at age 16 while for homosexual sex at age 21—adopted by the United Kingdom as law in 1967. The same year, Italy became the first to outlaw same-sex adoption (Adam, Duyvendak, & Krouvel, 2009).

Police brutality was already festering in San Francisco in 1966 when patrons, many of whom were transgender, rioted after an officer manhandled a patron in a restaurant. The riots led to development of the National Transsexual Counseling Unit, a peer-run support and advocacy group serving transgender people. Despite the global trend of restricting LGBTQ civil rights, Poland became the first nation in 1964 to provide the right to legally change gender assigned at birth, although it required gender reassignment surgery for eligibility (Adam et al., 2009).

The Stonewall Riots of June 28, 1969, served as the birth of the modern LGBTQ civil rights liberation movement (Richards, 2005). Leading up to that night, police frequently raided the Stonewall and other bars in major cities while patrons decried police brutality. Patrons of the Stonewall Inn clashed with police during another routine raid, which was meant to cleanse the neighborhood of "sexual deviants" (Manalansan, 1995). The riots flared for a week in the Greenwich Village area of New York City (Carter, 2004). In the weeks following the riots, village residents organized to create LGBTQ safe spaces and later marked the anniversary of the riots with the first gay pride march the next year (Poindexter, 1997). The Stonewall Riots coincided with an emerging trend for nations to remove criminal restrictions on homosexual activity (Manalansan, 1995).

1970s–1980s

The civil protections of LGBTQ people remained uneven throughout the globe in the 1970s (Richards, 2005). For example, Egypt became the first country in 1971 to *remove* LGBTQ discrimination protections in housing and employment. Meanwhile, the decade in the United States was marked by the advancement of some state-level civil rights protections (e.g., California, Maine, Colorado, and Alaska) including removing bans on homosexual activity (Adam et al., 2009). Though not a gain in civil rights but in human dignity, the American Psychiatric Association removed "homosexuality" as a mental illness from the third edition of the *Diagnostic and Statistical Manual of Mental Disorders* in 1973 (Stein, 2004). Minneapolis became the first city to offer discrimination protections for transgender people two years later (Stein, 2004). Harvey Milk won an election in 1977 to the San Francisco board of supervisors and championed employment protections for gays and lesbians while working against bans on homosexual teachers (Shilts, 1982). He served in that role for 11 months before he was assassinated along with the San Francisco mayor.

In 1981, reports emerged of a deadly pneumonia and skin cancer found among gay men, which was initially identified as gay related immune deficiency (GRID) and later changed to acquired immune deficiency syndrome (AIDS) only after it was found in populations beyond gay men (Forbes, Blanshard, & Gazzard, 1993). The majority of the 1980s focused on the growing AIDS epidemic and the public health panic that resulted. By 1982, nearly every state in the nation had banned gay men from donating blood (Shilts, 2007).

Wisconsin became the first state to ban discrimination on the basis of sexual orientation in 1982, at the same time that Louisiana ended its ban on same-sex adoption ("Timeline of LGBTQ Rights," 2015). In 1986, in *Bowers v. Hardwick* the Supreme Court upheld a Georgia law banning homosexual sex. The next year, in a national march on Washington, D.C., hundreds of thousands demanded that President Ronald Reagan publicly speak of AIDS and address the growing public health crisis (Shilts, 2007). The following year, each American home was canvased with the brochure *Understanding AIDS*. As the decade closed, LGBTQ protections began to grow globally as seen in housing protections in Ireland and same-sex civil unions in Denmark ("Timeline of LGBTQ Rights," 2015).

In 1990, the Ryan White CARE ACT was enacted, which provided federal funds for Americans living with HIV and AIDS (Parham & Conviser, 2002). In 1993, Minnesota passed the first law prohibiting discrimination of transgender people (Eaklor, 2008). The military directive and Clinton era policy known as "Don't Ask, Don't Tell" (DADT) was issued in 1993, which forbade inquiring of, or disclosing of, sexual orientation while still maintaining the military standard forbidding homosexual activity (Britton & Williams, 1995).

Three years later, in 1996, the Supreme Court decided in *Romer v. Evans* that forbidding gays and lesbians from receiving discrimination protections is a violation of the Fourteenth Amendment's Equal Protection Clause (Stein, 2004). That same year President Bill Clinton signed the Defense of Marriage Act (DOMA) into law, thereby prohibiting federal same-sex marriage (Rimmerman, Wald, & Wilcox, 2000). Also in 1996, homosexual activity was made legal in China, a nation home to one-third of the global population ("Timeline of LGBTQ Rights," 2015). Meanwhile, South Africa became the first to include constitutional civil protections for LGBTQ people.

Brazil became the first nation to ban conversion/reparative therapy in 1998 (Haldeman, 2002). The next year, California became the first state to legalize same-gender domestic partnerships (Natale & Miller-Cribbs, 2012). As the decade closed, Switzerland passed a broad scope of civil protections for LGBTQ people including employment and housing, forecasting a trend in the next decade ("Timeline of LGBTQ Rights," 2015).

The first decade of the twenty-first century saw rapid civil rights development for LGBTQ populations. Around the globe, bans once making homosexuals ineligible for military service were struck down (Natale & Miller-Cribbs, 2012). Stateside, growth of civil unions was evident at the same time as restrictions on same-sex marriage. In 2000, Vermont became the first state to legalize same-gender civil unions (Natale & Miller-Cribbs, 2012). Two years later, Belgium became the first nation to allow same-sex marriage ("Timeline of LGBTQ Rights," 2015).

Also in 2002, New Mexico began a trend for states to expand employment and housing protections to include gender identity. In *Lawrence v. Texas*, the Supreme Court declared antisodomy laws unconstitutional in 2003, thereby decriminalizing homosexual behavior between two men (Tribe, 2004). The next year, Massachusetts became the first state in the union to legalize same-sex marriage (Natale & Miller-Cribbs, 2012). By the end of the decade, a growing trend for nations to legalize same-sex marriage was evident—the United Kingdom and Canada did so in 2005 in addition to Mexico in 2009 ("Timeline of LGBTQ Rights," 2015).

The second decade of the twenty-first century has been marked by increases in employment, marriage, and housing protections for LGBTQ people across the globe. In 2010, President Obama signed the law ending Don't Ask, Don't Tell, thereby allowing lesbian, gay, and bisexual-identified individuals to openly serve in the military. Two years later, New Jersey banned conversion therapy while also allowing same-sex marriage ("Timeline of LGBTQ Rights," 2015). At least six other states have passed similar anticonversion therapy laws since that time.

In *United States v. Windsor* (2013), the Supreme Court ruling held that restricting an interpretation of marriage and spouse to only a heterosexual union is unconstitutional, thereby invalidating the Defense of Marriage Act (Peralta, 2013). In 2015, the Supreme Court decided in *Obergefell v. Hodges* that marriage is a fundamental right guaranteed to same-sex couples under the Constitution, thereby making same-sex marriage possible in all 50 states. Also in 2015, Ireland became the first to provide the right to legally change one's gender assigned at birth without requiring surgery, and France lifted its ban on gay men from donating blood ("Timeline of LGBTQ Rights," 2015). In 2016, the US Department of Defense issued policy statements allowing transgender service members the right to enlist and serve openly in the military.

This overview of the LGBTQ civil rights movement from the 1950s forward reveals remarkable progress despite several persistent challenges in the United States and abroad. Most notably, attempts to include LGBTQ populations in nondiscrimination laws have fallen short for 40 years. However, progress continues in the form of the Equality Act, proposed legislation that is comprehensive in scope and would provide for LGBTQ people the civil rights in the form of nondiscrimination in employment, housing, health care, education, and public services (Human Rights Campaign, 2016).

LGBTQ DISCRIMINATION

The need for civil rights legislation inclusive of sexual orientation and gender identity and expression is evident when reviewing the data on hate crimes and discrimination based on employment, housing, health care, adoption, public accommodations, and education. Disparities in each of these areas and their impact upon LGBTQ populations are examined in more detail next.

HATE CRIMES

A prejudice-motivated crime is a *hate crime* that includes different types of offenses (e.g., physical assault, damage to property, bullying, harassment, verbal abuse or insults, or offensive graffiti or letters) against a person from a protected status category (e.g., race, religion, ethnicity, nationality, gender, sexual orientation, gender identity, and disability). Hate crimes tend to carry longer sentences of a year on average (Herek, 2009). The federal government can prosecute hate crime cases using federal law or assist states that have state-level hate crimes laws with resources and support. By far, most criminal cases are prosecuted at the state level using existing state law; the same is true of criminal hate crimes. Most states (45 as of the time of this writing) have already criminalized hate crimes motivated by race, religion, ethnicity, and national origin (Federal Bureau of Investigations [FBI], 2014). Presently, only 31 states identify a crime motivated by sexual orientation as a hate crime, thereby leaving prosecution of these hate crime cases to the federal government, which it rarely does. The situation is worse for other vulnerable groups as only 28 states include gender protections, and 17 include gender identity protections (FBI, 2014).

The FBI produces the Uniform Crime Report, which is comprised of aggregate data information from law enforcement agencies from the all over the nation (FBI, 2014). This report reveals that 20% of hate crimes are motivated by sexual orientation and 0.5% by gender identity, and these are likely to be underreported. While hate crimes overall have decreased, not all categories have experienced the same results. Along with marriage equality in 2015 came increases in assaults on gay men and lesbians, and the growing trend of assaults and murders of transgender women remains deeply troubling (FBI, 2014; "Hate Violence," 2015). The disproportionate impacts of physical violence on transgender women of color highlights the intersections of minority statuses of race and gender identity; both face oppression resulting from different forms of discrimination. A closer examination of hate crime data reveals that violence severity including homicide has increased, disproportionately affecting HIV-affected individuals, transgender women, communities of color, young LGBTQ adults, and low-income people ("Hate Violence," 2015).

EMPLOYMENT

Up to 40% of LGBTQ workers have reported being harassed, fired, or denied promotion in the workplace (Sears & Mallory, 2011). Over half of LGBTQ people live in states without employment protections, and presently only 19 states include nondiscrimination employment policies for sexual orientation and gender identity. Gay and bisexual men earn between 10% to 32% less than their similarly qualified heterosexual counterparts. This is true even when controlling for education, race, and occupation in years worked ("Hate Violence," 2015). Transgender women face barriers in the workplace including significant wage disparities, termination during transition, lack of health-care access, and high unemployment rates. Up to 15% of transgender people make less than $10,000 a year, a rate of poverty four times that of the general population (Davis & Wertz, 2010). This is noteworthy considering transgender people face double the rate of unemployment (Grant et al., 2011).

HOUSING

Discrimination in housing can take various forms such as verbal harassment from a landlord because of sexual orientation or gender identity, a realtor refusing to show or sell a home or rental to same-sex couples, or application of discriminatory financial tests such as refusing recognizing dual incomes of unmarried same-sex couples. One in five sexual minorities report being refused an apartment, while 11% indicated this occurred because of their gender identity ("Hate Violence," 2015). Presently only 19 states prohibit discrimination in housing based on sexual orientation and gender identity, which is particularly troubling because 40% of homeless youth identify as LGBTQ. Older LGBTQ adults are more susceptible to poverty and homelessness due to lack of social support systems (Gay & Network, 2004). Older gays and lesbians also report experiencing discrimination in the retirement care facilities in which they live (Johnson, Jackson, Arnette, & Koffman, 2005).

HEALTH CARE

More than half of LGBTQ people report experiencing discrimination from their health-care provider, including refusal of needed care, refusal to touch a patient, using excessive precautions, using harsh or excessive language, blaming the patient for their health status, or excessive physical roughness (Grant et al., 2011). Up to 70% of transgender individuals report the same discrimination. In every discrimination category, a higher proportion of LGBTQ respondents were also people of color or low income (Brooks, Etzel, Hinojos, Henry, & Perez, 2005; Diamant, Wold, Spitzer, & Gelberg, 2000). These institutional health-care barriers are palpable for LGBTQ individuals (Sanchez, Sanchez, & Danoff, 2009) particularly those living with challenging illnesses such as HIV (Kinsler, Wong, Sayles, Davis, & Cunningham, 2007). LGBTQ people are at a higher risk for a variety of poor health outcomes including mental illness, cancer, smoking, and other drug and alcohol use (Krehely, 2009). LGBTQ people of color experience greater risks. This is troubling given that LGBTQ ethnic minorities are the least likely to have health insurance while being the most likely to delay or not seek health care (Krehely, 2009).

ADOPTION

A legal parent has a series of rights including living with their child and making education, health, and well-being decisions, as well as the financial responsibility to support the child. In the event of divorce, legal parents' rights are typically maintained. Historically, many same-sex parents had no way to become a legal parent because same-sex marriage was not legal until 2015. Many same-sex relationships that ended in separation or legal divorce did not result in both parents maintaining their rights. This left the child (or children) with the loss of a parental figure and no legal recourse for maintaining involvement in their life. In the United States, same-sex couples who have adopted children head 20,000 households, representing 4% of all adoption households (Gates, 2013). Approximately 25% of transgender individuals report having biological or adopted children (Stotzer, Herman, & Hasenbush, 2014). These numbers would likely be greater than those reported if same-sex households were not historically banned from adopting or fostering children. In fact, in past years, some states banned single-parent adoptions as a way of indirectly barring same-sex couples that were not legally married to adopt a child by having only one member of the couple identify as the adopting parent. Fortunately, this trend has reversed with the passage of marriage equality, giving legal recourse for couples to adopt and legally divorced same-sex parents to both retain legal parental rights. In addition, it is estimated that there are 14 million biological children of gays and lesbians (Gates, 2013), some of which were conceived in a previous heterosexual relationship or were conceived in same-sex relationships through various artificial insemination or surrogate methods. Often, these biological children are raised in same-sex households or share custody with their heterosexual parent. From a global perspective, joint adoption is legal in 21 countries, with second-parent adoption allowed in 7 countries (Gates, 2013).

PUBLIC ACCOMMODATIONS

Public accommodations are places, either public or private, that are used by members of the community, including retail stores; rental establishments; service establishments such as restaurants, hotels, and museums; educational institutions; recreational facilities; and parks and libraries (Keck, 2009). About 38% of lesbians and gays report being verbally harassed in public accommodations, while the rate for transgender people rises to 53% (Grant et al., 2011). Almost half of transgender individuals reported being refused services in public accommodations, a rate of 6% for lesbians and gay men. The most severe form of harassment—physical assault—occurred for 5% of gays and lesbians and 8% of transgender persons (Grant et al., 2011). Federal law already prohibits discrimination in public accommodations for race, color, disability, religion, or national origin. At the time of this writing there are 28 states that allow discrimination against LBGT people in public accommodations. Conversely, only 19 states plus Washington, D.C., provide nondiscrimination laws protecting all citizens (Keck, 2009).

EDUCATION

Heterosexist discrimination occurs in schools every day, with over half of LGBTQ students reporting feeling unsafe (Thapa, Cohen, Guffey, & Higgins-D'Alessandro, 2013). Almost 70% of LGBTQ students report hearing slurs such as "gay" or "tranny." Over half of LGBTQ youth report hearing homophobic and transphobic remarks from teachers or staff. Over a third of sexual minorities report being physically assaulted at school, with 23% of transgender students reporting the same. Students impacted by such discrimination have greater absences, lower grade point averages, lower self-esteem, and lower self-confidence in higher education (Thapa et al., 2013). At the time of this writing, only 14 states currently ban discrimination based on sexual orientation and gender identity in education institutions (Thapa et al., 2013).

APPLYING THEORY

Theoretical application can provide a tangible way to formulate policy when working with LGBTQ populations. Intersectionality, Ecological Systems, as well as Microsystem, Mesosystem, Exosystem, and Macrosystem theoretical orientations all provide frameworks to guide avenues for social, political, and economic change.

INTERSECTIONALITY THEORY

Intersectionality theory is a conceptual tool that highlights the multiple identities and interconnectedness of various systems of oppression and privilege that contextualize an individual's world experience. First put forth as an analytical framework within feminist theory, it allows for a more complex understanding of the many facets of intersecting identities (Collins, 2000; Crenshaw, 1991), and it has great applicability to the promotion of LGBTQ civil rights. Identity politics bear the risk of universalizing the experiences of those who identify as part of a group, when accounting for in-group differences is a critical step for the promotion of policies that are inclusive and relevant to all members (Collins, 2000). Characteristics including race and ethnicity, socioeconomic status, geographical location, religious affiliation, ability, and age intersect with gender identity and sexual orientation to create complex experiences of both privilege and disadvantage (Crenshaw, 1991). Some elements of identity may serve as mediators to risk rooted in other

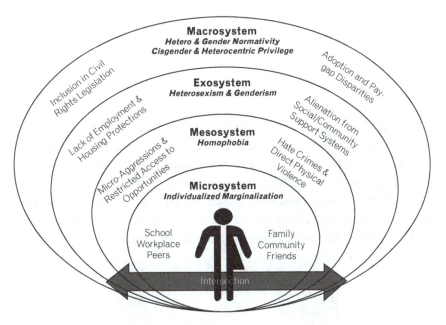

Macrosystem
Hetero & Gender Normativity
Cisgender & Heterocentric Privilege

Inclusion in Civil Rights Legislation

Adoption and Pay-gap Disparities

Exosystem
Heterosexism & Genderism

Lack of Employment & Housing Protections

Alienation from Social/Community Support Systems

Mesosystem
Homophobia

Micro-Aggressions & Restricted Access to Opportunities

Hate Crimes & Direct Physical Violence

Microsystem
Individualized Marginalization

School
Workplace
Peers

Family
Community
Friends

Intersection

FIGURE 19.1: Policy, marginalization, and ecological systems for LGBTQ people

identity categories, while others are likely to increase the risk of harm when coupled with LGBTQ identity. It is critical to inclusive policy practice that these differences be considered when analyzing or advocating for policy that impacts civil rights.

ECOLOGICAL SYSTEMS THEORY

Ecological systems theory or human ecological theory posits that human development is influenced by interlocking environmental systems that span from micro to macro (Bronfenbrenner, 1979). Intersectionality theory along with ecological systems theory presents a complex framework for understanding the impacts of policy upon LGBTQ people. Ecological systems theory is particularity adept at examining factors that exert direct or indirect influence on the individual's life, and as shown in Figure 19.1, these theories can be used to try and communicate the complexity of experiences among LGBTQ people.

MICROSYSTEM

The microsystem can include the workplace, school, family, peers, community agencies, and any additional supports. At the individual level it is important to note that most human life exists in multiple microsystem intersections (Germain & Bloom, 1999). That is to say that rather than treat age, race, disability, gender, gender identity, gender expression, socioeconomic status, sexual orientation, and documentation status as distinct identities, it is more correct to recognize the unique combination of these intersecting identities of the individual (Bronfenbrenner, 1979). At this level, certainly workplace protections are critical for LGBTQ communities. In addition, it is evident that protections for public accommodations by LGBTQ individuals are especially critical in education, social service, and health-care institutions. (Germain & Bloom, 1999).

MESOSYSTEMS

The mesosystem is focused on interactive relationships between the elements of the microsystem; these interactions have a direct and indirect influence on the individual (Bronfenbrenner, 1979). Using the case of a family headed by an LGBTQ individual, we can highlight the relationship between the family and the workplace at the mesosystem level. Without employment protections for LGBTQ individuals, families headed by these individuals face greater workplace uncertainty. For transgender women, mesosystem interactions are underscored by high unemployment that correspond to greater dependence on community agencies for financial support, health care, and housing.

EXOSYSTEM

The exosystem binds the micro- and mesosystem together by public policies including health care, education, and employment policies (Germain & Bloom, 1999). The exosystem does not include active participation by the individual, yet this system level still has a direct impact on the individual (Bronfenbrenner, 1979). While the US Supreme Court decision allowing marriage equality enhanced the functioning of that portion of the exosystem of lesbians and gay men, other civil protections in health care, public accommodations education, and employment remain absent.

MACROSYSTEM

The macrosystem includes economic, historical, and cultural contacts (Bronfenbrenner, 1979). The cultural environment for LGBTQ individuals is uneven, as evidenced by the abundance of cisgender and heterocentric privilege (Germain & Bloom, 1999). Examples include documentation using birth gender markers, restroom use for gender nonconforming individuals, workplace protections, pay-gap disparities, and health-care access. In the case of LGBTQ people, homophobia and heterosexism diminish social, political, and economic justice. Additionally, transphobia threatens the civil rights of transgender and gender nonconforming individuals.

Ecological systems theory is helpful given its focus on the macro level that dovetails with the advancement of civil rights for LGBTQ people (Germain & Bloom, 1999). Lack of discrimination protections for LGBTQ people in the workplace, housing, education, and in health care remain macro-practice problems and will require policy practice strategies. Without a macro-level intervention approach, equity for LGBTQ people will remain forever elusive. Advancement of civil rights for LGBTQ groups at the macro level has the ability to improve the functioning of the individual at all other levels. The absence of these protections has the alternate effect by stressing each system independently and collectively (Bronfenbrenner, 1979).

SOCIAL WORK ETHICS AND
A CALL TO ACTION

The NASW Code of Ethics squarely places social and political action at the center of social work practice (NASW, 1999). Beyond the key values outlined as guideposts of the profession, the Code delineates a number of ethical standards. Key among these in terms of policy practice includes Section 6: Social Workers' Ethical Responsibilities to the Broader Society, which addresses social welfare (6.01), public participation (6.02), and social and political action (6.04). Social workers must work to promote the general welfare from local to global society for social justice by supporting informed public participation and through taking a role in shaping social policies and institutions. The code also highlights equal access, individual and community development, choice, the challenging of oppressive conditions, the empowerment of vulnerable and marginalized groups, and the elimination of all forms of discrimination, including discrimination on the basis of sexual orientation and gender identity.

TARGETED GOALS AND STRATEGIES
FOR LGBTQ CIVIL RIGHTS

Policy advocacy on behalf of a group or issue requires a contextualized understanding of the strengths and needs of that group, the history and impact of social policy for that group, and up-to-date information about proposed legislation. Interest groups are a key source of such information and include those specifically focused on LGBTQ issues, such as GLAAD, the National LGBTQ Task Force, the Equality Federation, and the Gay and Lesbian Victory fund, a political action committee devoted to increasing political leadership representation. Additionally, broadly engaged groups that work toward equity and representation across groups like Human Rights Campaign and the American Civil Liberties Union provide resources for action. The NASW falls into the second category, providing educational materials for policy practice and advocacy to assist social workers in meeting ethical obligations to clients, the profession, and the broader society. NASW-PACE (Political Action for Candidate Election), a 501(c)(4) organization, engages in targeted lobbying and action on behalf of candidates who endorse views and policies that are in line with social work values and ethics.

NASW also publishes *Social Work Speaks* (NASW, 2015) now in its 10th edition, which articulates policy statements rooted in the NASW Code of Ethics. Through these statements, NASW provides guidance for social workers in interpreting ethics and values for application through policy at the agency, local, state, and federal levels. The current edition includes sections that address specifically policy issues pertaining to gay, lesbian, and bisexual people as well as regarding transgender and gender identity issues. Additionally, sections covering topics such as social work education, family policy, social services, bullying, the criminal justice system, the child welfare system, prostituted and exploited people, and parenting specifically include recommendations for greater inclusivity and recognition of the needs and essential rights of LGBTQ individuals, families, and groups. Critical impacts for LGBTQ individuals of discrimination, both at the individual and institutional levels, include comparatively higher rates of violence across the lifespan, depression and suicide, homelessness, high school dropout, employment barriers, poverty, health disparity, and limits to reproductive freedom. NASW (2015) provides five key areas of recommended focus for policy practice around issues relevant to the LGBTQ population that include:

- *Nondiscrimination and equality:* Endorses agency-level policy and position statements that mandate nondiscrimination; international, federal, state, and local-level policies that ban all forms of discrimination for LGBTQ individuals and their children; proactive efforts at preventing harassment of LGBTQ youth in schools; and representation of LGBTQ individuals in leadership and across all levels of employment.

- *Professional and continuing education:* Encourages proactive efforts to include nondiscrimination content and instructional materials pertaining to the LGBTQ population in examination and continuing education required for professional licensure; also identifies the importance of self-awareness for the elimination of bias for social workers. Efforts under this category are critical for informing social workers of issues relevant to the LBGTQ community in order to analyze and advocate around key social policies.

- *Education and public awareness:* Promotes the development and delivery of training and informational materials on critical topics for the LGBTQ population such as antibullying, injustice awareness, LGBTQ-positive messages, and the unique needs and strengths of LGBTQ individuals and families. Public opinion is an important contextual factor for policy advocacy and for generating collective action and political power.

- *Health and mental health services:* This section addresses issues relevant for both LGBTQ individuals in the social work workforce, such as the right to choose whether or not to disclose one's sexual orientation to colleagues, as well as service users and clients. Of note, the NASW specifically denounces the use of policies in support of, or public funding for "reparative" or conversion-based therapies, as a response to the mental health needs of lesbian, gay, and bisexual people. Additionally, policy recommendations are provided that underscore the importance of culturally competent training and practice, including the importance of multiple intersecting identities to this work, support for the continued development of services targeting LGBTQ individuals across the lifespan, better recognition of the participation of LGBTQ individuals in reproductive technologies, and protection for LGBTQ individuals in the United States and globally from criminalization.

- *Political action and advocacy:* This section provides key strategies for policy work in support of LGBTQ individuals, families, and groups and outlines areas of focus and strategies for social workers to engage in policy practice that supports the rights and well-being of LGBTQ people. Included are recommendations that social workers create and become actively involved in coalitions aimed at lobbying and carrying out social action that opposes efforts to limit the rights of LGBTQ people; to work toward funding for antihate groups and legislation; to seek parity for LGBTQ people in the areas of health and mental health; to support policies that recognize the full parental rights of LGBTQ people, including adoption rights; to enhance research efforts focused on better understanding issues the needs and strengths of LGBTQ people across fields of practice; and to support the expansion of

TABLE 19.1 10 Key Strategies to Advance LGBT Civil Rights

Strategy	Desired Outcome
1. Foster Legislative Action	• Expansion of federal and state protections for LGBT people
2. Engage in Policy Analysis	• Increased policy refinement with social justice implications
3. Expand Existing Legislation	• Include LGBT people in existing protected class legislation
4. Use Democratic Process	• Improved political involvement and advising on LGBT issues
5. Lobby	• Increased involvement in explicit lobby advocacy for LGBT protections
6. Provide Issue Advocacy and Education	• Increased understanding of the criticality of LGBT protections and impact of issues for the population
7. Encourage Voter Participation	• Increased voter participation among LGBT people and allies
8. Increase Electoral Representation	• Increased numbers of LGBT candidates in office
9. Develop Client and Citizen Empowerment	• Improved self-efficacy in regard to involvement in the political process
10. Agency-Level Policy Advocacy	• Increased LGBT inclusiveness at agency and institutional levels

the Employment Non-Discrimination Act (ENDA) to include full recognition and protection for LGBTQ people in education, employment, housing, and other services.

The historical review, theoretical analysis, and grounding in the profession of social work has led to the final portion of this chapter, a detailed overview of 10 key strategies to advance LGBTQ civil rights. Table 19.1 displays these 10 key strategies along with desired outcomes for each.

STRATEGY 1—FOSTER LEGISLATIVE ACTION

Social workers have both a duty to take political and social action on behalf of vulnerable and oppressed populations and the knowledge and insight needed to translate the impact of such oppression for individuals, families, and communities (Abramovitz, 1998). Legislative action is critical at all levels of government including federal, state, and local-level policy, and social workers should understand where to direct advocacy efforts based on the levels and branches of American government. The 10th Amendment to the US Constitution defines the concept of federalism and outlines the purview of states in terms of policymaking. It delegates specific areas in which the federal government may enact policies that impact all states in the union and reserves the power for lawmaking outside of that purview to each separate state. The federal government retains the power to make treaties, regulate foreign and domestic commerce, impose and regulate taxation, declare war and maintain a military, and enact other laws necessary to meet the responsibilities set forth in the Constitution (Abramovitz, 1998).

Concurrent powers exist that are shared by the states and the federal government including taxation, bank regulation, establishment of a judiciary, and making and enforcing laws. The powers of the state government protected by the 10th Amendment include many of those that impact the daily lives of citizens, such as the establishment of local governments; public education; elections; the protection of health, safety, and public morals; the regulation of marriage; professional licensure; and all other powers not delegated to the federal government. It is important that social workers understand the capabilities and limitations of advocacy work at each level of government so that advocacy may be directed appropriately and effectively (Abramovitz, 1998).

While there is great value to contextualizing policy and considering the uniqueness of different states, the 10th Amendment also sets the stage for unequal protection and rights for individuals based on geography. As a result, federal-level policies such as ENDA take on great importance and value as pathways to ensuring protection for all across the nation (Figueira-McDonough, 1993). Additionally, the judicial branch of government plays a key role in interpreting the US Constitution and ruling on contested cases. The US Supreme Court has played an instrumental role in the evolution of rights and policies impacting the LGBTQ community, as evidenced by the marriage equality decision that, in effect, equalized protection under the law for all citizens, in every state. Social workers must understand the complex interaction of the judicial and legislative branches of government to best target their advocacy efforts. With these structures in mind, there are many strategies that social workers can employ to harness our collective power to impact policies for all people, and specifically for LGBTQ populations.

STRATEGY 2—ENGAGE IN POLICY ANALYSIS

Policy analysis is a powerful tool for influencing both legislative action and public opinion. Social workers bring a particular values-based orientation to the task of policy analysis (Chambers, 1993). Social workers also possess knowledge of the experiences of diverse and vulnerable populations relevant to the impact of actual and proposed legislation that other interest groups and policymakers themselves do not possess or do not consider (Figueira-McDonough, 1993). Policy analysis performed through a social justice framework has the ability to highlight the factors that create and sustain key social problems as well as the often-disparate impact experienced by vulnerable and oppressed populations of unjust policy.

Bardach and Patashnik (2016) outline the "Eightfold Path" to policy analysis with these key activities: defining the problem, assembling evidence, constructing alternatives, selecting evaluative criteria, projecting possible outcomes, confronting the trade-offs, focusing and deciding on recommendations, and telling the story. While this model is broadly applicable, understanding local contextual factors and feasibility are also important elements for an effective contribution to the policymaking process via policy analysis. Other nuances in policy analysis include strategizing relevant to real-world constraints and capacities; application of social work values and ethics as a specific framework, decision-making around level of analysis pertaining to root causes of social problems, weighing of often competing forces such as safety versus liberty, and timing and coordination of policy analysis and recommendations (Bardach & Patashnik, 2016; Kraft & Furlong, 2015; Meenaghan, Kilty, & McNutt, 2009). Social workers may apply policy analysis skills to proposed legislation such as a bill in the state legislature or to an existing statute in order to assess the efficacy and equity of a law. For example, a number of state-level bills have been introduced around the United States in response to the Supreme Court ruling in favor of marriage equality that seek to provide protection to businesses and even public employees who wish to deny service to and access for same-sex couples (e.g., religious freedom laws). Through a systematic process of policy analysis, social workers can craft responses rooted in a careful examination of the contexts (social, economic/fiscal, technological, political) and impact (for individuals, families, and communities) of a policy, that consider its projected efficacy and possible unintended consequences as well as its constitutionality and equity based on the social justice frame. Such a process allows for this key information-gathering process as the foundation for generating alternatives (including no policy action by the government) and for making policy recommendations rooted both in evidence and in the social work value frame.

STRATEGY 3—SEEK TO EXPAND EXISTING LEGISLATION

The passage of the Violence Against Women Act (VAWA) 2013 reauthorization represented only the second LGBTQ-inclusive federal law, following suit after the 2011 enactment of the Matthew Shepard and James Byrd Jr. Hate Crimes Prevention Act. The VAWA reauthorization was successful despite Republican opposition to new inclusions for tribal citizens, immigrants, and LGBTQ individuals and will provide $650 million to states over five years for transitional housing, legal assistance, and other services for people who have experienced intimate partner violence (Modi, Palmer, & Armstrong, 2014). The law expressly prohibits any denial of services on the basis of race, religion, national origin, sexual orientation, or disability, critical protections for LGBTQ individuals who previously may have been turned away from shelters or denied protection orders. Specifying inclusion of groups that have experienced exclusion from key protections and benefits is an important strategy for improving the lives of sexual and gender minorities through legislation.

The 2013 VAWA reauthorization also highlighted political opposition to such efforts, and while the outcome was positive, the process exposed some legislators' willingness to turn lifesaving policy into a wedge issue (Modi et al., 2014). Social workers should continue to advocate for inclusion of LGBTQ individuals and families in federal-level legislation that aims to protect people from harm, to fund services, and to assure equal access under the law. Social workers can support inclusion of LGBTQ persons or advocate for their addition to any federal, state, or local legislation where protected status on the basis of other social categories (age, religion, race, etc.) is explicitly mentioned as a policy goal.

STRATEGY 4—USE THE DEMOCRATIC PROCESS

As citizens and as social workers, the ability to communicate directly with policymakers is a critical pathway to improving legislation impacting the LGBTQ community. It is not necessary to follow the lead of lawmakers from a reactive stance, as we may also lead by offering information that can inform the crafting of new laws and by providing legislators with model language that can be adapted across the states (Chambers, 1993). Interest groups such as the Human Rights Campaign work at the national level tracking successful and supportive legislation and provide examples and language that can be utilized in other locales. Websites like that of the National Conference of State Legislatures also provide specific information about laws passed at the state level so that social workers can both stay up to date with key issue responses across the nation as well as to access examples of legislation that can be used as a model for action in other areas that may directly impact the lives of LGBTQ individuals. Legislators rely on experts to assist in their understanding of the broad and complex range of issues on which they must act, and this provides the opportunity to be proactive in establishing new laws that are in line with the positions outlined previously (Abramovitz, 1998).

STRATEGY 5—LOBBY FOR A BILL

Lobbying is an important element of the legislative process (Abramovitz, 1998). Many social workers report their hesitance to engage in lobbying due to a lack of understanding of laws governing nonprofits and public employees. There are many misconceptions about what 501(c)(3) organizations can and cannot do under the policies put forth by the Internal Revenue Service. Unfortunately, this lack of clarity results in avoidance of lobbying legislators and mobilizing supporters. Two types of lobbying exist: direct, which involves communication with legislators around a specific bill or law, and grassroots, which centers on educating and influencing the public to engage with lawmakers around a certain issue. The latter can be understood as a call to action.

A major barrier for social worker involvement in policy practice is widespread misunderstanding about the limits for nonprofit organizations in the area of lobbying; social workers tend to think there are more limitations than actually exist (Rocha, Poe, & Thomas, 2010). 501(c)(3) organizations measure their lobbying to help ensure they are acting within the bounds of the law: The "insubstantial part" test is the default method and requires that lobbying be an insubstantial part of an organization's overall activity (US Internal Revenue Service, 2015). While no clear guidelines exist to concretize the meaning of this, it can be understood as being a minimal element of the overall mission and activities of an organization. A second method of examining a nonprofit organization's lobbying activity is the 501(h) expenditure test is the second method of measuring lobbying activity. With more clarity to these guidelines, it provides an exact dollar-based limit based upon an organization's expenditures as follows: 20% of the first $500,000 of an organization's budget is allowable for lobbying, with 15% of the next $500,000, 10% of the next $500,000, and 5% of the remaining. Additionally, only 25% of spending on lobbying can target grassroots lobbying. Other options for nonprofits is to seek a 501(h) election, which provides additional guidelines around allowable lobbying, or to establish a 501(c)(4) tax status (US Internal Revenue Service, 2015).

To simplify, nonprofits can limit their efforts to those that do not advocate for or against a specific legislation. Nonprofits may also avoid electoral advocacy or campaigning on behalf of a particular candidate. There are no limits to providing educational materials to the public and to lawmakers around a specific issue and its impact for people (US Internal Revenue Service, 2015). For instance, a nonprofit organization concerned about operating within the confines of the law might choose to work on providing information about the harmful impact of conversion or reparative approaches with LGBTQ youth as a general issue versus taking action around a specific bill intended to protect the right of families or providers to engage in this unethical and harmful practice. Lobbying within the bounds of the law can also include the provision of alternative pathways to achieving a policy goal, rooted in sound policy analysis.

STRATEGY 6—PROVIDE ISSUE ADVOCACY AND EDUCATION

With these factors in mind, there are many strategies that social workers can utilize to advocate around an issue (Schneider & Lester, 2001). These include communication with legislators to provide statistics and insight pertaining to the impact of an issue or proposed legislation; giving testimony to a legislative committee during the session or for interim studies held by the state legislature that are intended to educate lawmakers between sessions on key LGBTQ issues; working with the press via op-ed pieces and coverage of LGBTQ community events and agency services; identifying and tracking bills in order to draw attention to key areas of focus; performing policy analysis, which can be communicated in the form of issue briefs; and educating clients and other stakeholders about how to find and track proposed legislation as well as about strategies that citizens can engage in to impact the process (Schneider & Lester, 2001).

The empowerment of clients and, more broadly, vulnerable populations is a key social work avenue with multiple benefits that reach beyond a single legislative issue (Schneider & Lester, 2001). Voter registration drives and workshops on topics such as parliamentary process, the legislative process, communication with legislators, how to write an opinion piece, and how to interact with the media are activities that are well within the bounds of those allowable for nonprofits and that will help people feel more prepared and more confident when engaging in the legislative process at the local, state, and federal levels in the area of concerns relevant to the LGBTQ population and beyond. It is imperative that both social workers and LGBTQ stakeholders feel empowered to act in the political arena.

STRATEGY 7—ENCOURAGE VOTER PARTICIPATION

A simple strategy in which social workers can engage is the promotion of voter participation. Little research exists to date on voter turnout within the LGBTQ population and its impact on electoral politics (Perez, 2014). Existing studies have revealed that LGBTQ people range from as likely to more likely to register and to vote compared to the general population, are more politically engaged, and tend toward Democratic and liberal partisan preferences (Egan, Edelman, & Sherrill 2008). Based on measures of citizen political participation, LGB individuals display higher levels in a number of key areas, including direct communication with a policymaker; attendance at a political rally, speech, or organized protest; writing a letter to the editor of a newspaper or magazine; working for a political party or candidate; active membership in any group that tries to influence public policy; regularly reading local and national publications and other news outlets; and authoring blogs or communicating on social media about political issues (Egan et al., 2008). Voter registration drives and voter education are key strategies that LGBTQ communities and allies can utilize to enhance the political voice and influence of historically marginalized populations and are made even more critical when issues pertaining to LGBTQ civil rights and inclusion are routinely being taken up in the political arena.

STRATEGY 8—INCREASE ELECTORAL REPRESENTATION

LGBTQ candidates pursuing elected office are an effort social workers can proactively support as citizens and professionals (Schneider & Lester, 2001). Organizations like the Victory Fund offer support including initial assessments of candidate viability; campaign organization and intensive candidate and campaign training; financial support at the level of an organized individual donor base as well as from an established political action committee; and focused strategic and technical support for planning, fundraising, message development, voter contact, and advertising. Enhancing elected representation for the LGBTQ community is a key pathway for bringing the perspectives of the community to the legislative process. Elected officials are empowered to introduce new legislation, pass or oppose bills that would impact the LGBTQ community, inspire voters, and simply be a presence in our governmental institutions.

STRATEGY 9—DEVELOP CLIENT AND CITIZEN EMPOWERMENT

Empowerment is a primary goal and method of the social work profession (Abramovitz, 1998). Empowerment theory is especially salient for application with the most vulnerable groups in our society, those most in need of a social work profession committed to social justice. The main concepts of empowerment in social work practice concern partnership with and active participation of the client in consciousness-raising, overcoming barriers and oppressive forces, and the endowment of self-efficacy, a sense of belonging, and access to personal power (Payne, 2005). Empowerment is highlighted as a process, not necessarily an outcome, with the goal for clients of gaining influence in their own lives and the ability to improve their circumstances (Barker, 1995). Consciousness-raising involves education toward the ability to analyze the intersection between individual disempowerment with systems and structures of oppression (Gutierrez et al., 1995). Boehm (2004) differentiates two types of empowerment: personal and collective.

First, *personal empowerment*, related to individual capacities such as the ability to look critically at the world, self-esteem, self-determination, a sense of responsibility, the ability to engage productively with others, assertiveness, and hope for the future. Second, *collective empowerment* relates to the ability to act collectively for the shared benefit and to support one another in struggle (Boehm, 2004). These concepts point to the applicability of the theory not only to social work practice for client empowerment but to its utility as a lens through which to view social workers' own ability to wield influence and to act as collective change agents in the sociopolitical context.

Knowledge and self-efficacy are key to empowerment. Social workers, when politically empowered, can act to facilitate others to be empowered to impact social policy. Education and awareness-raising is one method through which social workers can assist others in becoming empowered for political action (Abramovitz, 1998). More targeted strategies exist to enhance LGBTQ client empowerment including inclusion of client groups in decision-making bodies, as well as provision of training in parliamentary procedure, lobbying activities such as direct communication with lawmakers, working with the press, and community organizing for impacted groups. Such strategies are aimed at empowering people in the community to enhance their own political voice and power. A more specific example might be a workshop to help community members write letters to elected officials explaining support for (inclusion in antidiscrimination protections) or opposition to (protecting the practice of reparative or conversion approaches with LGBTQ youth) a proposed policy action. It is critical to grow political participation as there truly is power in numbers, and social workers can promote not only targeted policy action but broad political capital of a community through such capacity-building.

STRATEGY 10—KNOW AGENCY-LEVEL POLICY AND PROCEDURES

Social workers can affect policies that exist at the agency level to directly impact the experience of LGBTQ people with services. By making LGBTQ welcoming and inclusiveness a priority at the agency level, through institutional policies, we can make an immediate impact for service users (Abramovitz, 1998). Such efforts can include intake forms that include gender identification options beyond the male–female binary, that are inclusive for all kinds of families, and that allow for preferred names and variant gender identity; the provision of a client bill of rights that reflects the agency's commitment to equal treatment, addresses confidentiality, and outlines a procedure for grievance for unfair treatment; evaluation of outcomes and client satisfaction that includes areas specific to the treatment of LGBTQ people; the establishment of a welcoming environment expressed through agency literature, environment, and approach; clear nondiscrimination statements in regard to hiring practices; service provision criteria that do not exclude or disadvantage LGBTQ people; the maintenance of referral lists that include LGBTQ-relevant services and that exclude organizations that do not support the needs and dignity of the population; staff training that includes topics specific to the LGBTQ community; active recruitment of LGBTQ board members and staff; use of nongendered language; and sustainable coalition with LGBTQ organizations in the community.

CONCLUSION

Recent years have brought many advances with regard to policy development and implementation that benefits the LGBTQ community. With the passage of marriage equality for same-sex couples, workplace insurance access, expansion of local hate crimes protections, and other similar policies, some progress is being made to secure civil rights through extensive integrated efforts in policy practice. However, far more is needed in order to secure those rights for the LGBTQ community and maintain them in perpetuity across the United States and internationally. Just as many other marginalized groups of people in the United States, the LGBTQ community will continue to face significant challenges across multiple bands of society and will have to deal with backlash with regard to such newly found protections. Continued policy advocacy by all social workers, from those in direct practice as well as those with a macro focus, will be needed not only to advance LGBTQ rights but also to protect those rights already granted. Critical policy analysis and inclusive policy development and implementation will be key in maintaining and advancing opportunities and protections for the LGBTQ community, and social workers should play vital roles, at multiple levels, in the pursuit of these goals.

REFERENCES

Abramovitz, M. (1998). Social work and social reform: An arena of struggle. *Social Work, 43*(6), 512–526.

Adam, B. D., Duyvendak, J. W., & Krouwel, A. (2009). *The global emergence of gay and lesbian politics: National imprints of a worldwide movement.* Philadelphia, PA: Temple University Press.

Badgett, M. V. (2009). Bias in the workplace: Consistent evidence of sexual orientation and gender identity discrimination 1998–2008. *Chicago-Kent Law Review, 84,* 559–595.

Bardach, E., & Patashnik, E. M. (2016). *A practical guide for policy analysis: The eightfold path to more effective problem solving* (5th ed.). Los Angeles, CA: SAGE.

Barker, R. L. (1995). *The social work dictionary* (3rd ed.). Washington, DC: National Association of Social Workers.

Boehm, A. (2004). Empowerment: The point of view of consumers. *Families in Society, 85*(2), 270–280.

Britton, D. M., & Williams, C. L. (1995). "Don't ask, don't tell, don't pursue": Military policy and the construction of heterosexual masculinity. *Journal of Homosexuality, 30*(1), 1–21.

Brooks, R. A., Etzel, M. A., Hinojos, E., Henry, C. L., & Perez, M. (2005). Preventing HIV among Latino and African American gay and bisexual men in a context of HIV-related stigma, discrimination, and homophobia: Perspectives of providers. *AIDS Patient Care and STDs, 19*(11), 737–744.

Bronfenbrenner, U. (1979). *The ecology of human development: Experiments by nature and design.* Cambridge, MA: Harvard University Press.

Carter, D. (2004). *Stonewall: The riots that sparked the gay revolution,* New York: St. Martin's Press.

Chambers, D. E. (1993). *Social policy and social programs: A method for the practical public policy analyst.* Boston: Macmillan.

Collins, P. H. (2000). *Black feminist thought: Knowledge, consciousness, and the politics of empowerment* (2nd ed.). New York: Routledge.

Crenshaw, K. (1991). Mapping the margins: Intersectionality, identity politics, and violence against women of color. *Stanford Law Review, 43*(6), 1241–1299. doi:10.2307/1229039

Davis, M., & Wertz, K. (2010). When laws are not enough: A study of the economic health of transgender people and the need for a multidisciplinary approach to economic justice. *Seattle Journal for Social Justice, 8*(2), 467–495.

Diamant, A. L., Wold, C., Spritzer, K., & Gelberg, L. (2000). Health behaviors, health status, and access to and use of health care: A population-based study of lesbian, bisexual, and heterosexual women. *Archives of Family Medicine, 9*(10), 1043–1051.

Eaklor, V. L. (2008). *Queer America: A GLBT history of the 20th century.* Westport, CT: Greenwood Press.

Egan, P. J., Edelman, M. S., & Sherrill, K. (2008). *Findings from the Hunter College Poll of Lesbians, Gays and Bisexuals: New discoveries about identity, political attitudes, and civic engagement.* New York: Hunter College.

Federal Bureau of Investigations. (2014). *Uniform Crime Reports: Hate crime statistics.* Retrieved from https://www.fbi.gov/about-us/cjis/ucr/hate-crime/2014.

Fidas, D., & Copper, L. (2015). *The cost of the closet and the rewards of inclusion: Why the workplace environment for LGBTQ people matters to employees.* Washington, DC: Human Rights Campaign.

Figueira-McDonough, J. (1993). Policy practice: The neglected side of social work intervention. *Social Work, 38*(2), 179–188.

Forbes, A., Blanshard, C., & Gazzard, B. (1993). Natural history of AIDS related sclerosing cholangitis: A study of 20 cases. *Gut, 34*(1), 116–121. doi:10.1136/gut.34.1.116

Gates, G. J. (2013). *LGBTQ parenting in the United States.* Retrieved from http://williamsinstitute.law.ucla.edu/wp-content/uploads/LGBTQ-Parenting.pdf

Gay, L., & Network, S. E. (2004). *State of the states 2004: A policy analysis of lesbian, gay, bisexual and transgender (LGBTQ) safer schools issues.* New York: Author.

Germain, C. B., & Bloom, M. (1999). *Human behavior in the social environment: An ecological view.* New York: Columbia University Press.

Grant, J. M., Motter, L. A., Tannis, J., Harrison, J., Herman, J., & Keisling, M, (2011). *Injustice at every turn: A report of the National Transgender Discrimination Report 51.* National Center for Transgender Equality & the Gay and Lesbian Task Force. Retrieved from http://www.thetaskforce.org/downloads/reports/reports/ntds_full.pdf

Gutierrez, L. M., DeLois, K. A., & GlenMaye, L. (1995). Understanding empowerment practice: Building on practitioner knowledge. *Families in Society: The Journal of Contemporary Human Services, 76*(8), 543–542.

Haldeman, D. C. (2002). Gay rights, patient rights: The implications of sexual orientation conversion therapy. *Professional Psychology: Research and Practice, 33*(3), 260–264.

Hate violence in 2014. (2015) National Coalition of Anti-Violence Programs. Retrieved from http://www.avp.org/storage/documents/Reports/2014_HV_Report-Final.pdf

Herek, G. M. (2009). Hate crimes and stigma-related experiences among sexual minority adults in the United States: Prevalence estimates from a national probability sample. *Journal of Interpersonal Violence, 24*(1), 54–74.

Human Rights Campaign. (2016). *Support the Equality Act.* Retrieved from http://www.hrc.org/campaign/support-the-equality-act

Johnson, M. J., Jackson, N. C., Arnette, J. K., & Koffman, S. D. (2005). Gay and lesbian perceptions of discrimination in retirement care facilities. *Journal of Homosexuality, 49*(2), 83–102.

Keck, T. M. (2009). Beyond backlash: Assessing the impact of judicial decisions on LGBTQ rights. *Law & Society Review, 43*(1), 151–186.

Kinsler, J. J., Wong, M. D., Sayles, J. N., Davis, C., & Cunningham, W. E. (2007). The effect of perceived stigma from a health care provider on access to care among a low-income HIV-positive population. *AIDS Patient Care and STDs, 21*(8), 584–592.

Kraft, M. E., & Furlong, S. R. (2015). *Public policy: Politics, analysis, and alternatives* (5th ed.). Los Angeles, CA: SAGE.

Krehely, J. (2009). *How to close the LGBT health disparities gap: Disparities by race and ethnicity.* Center for American Progress. Retrieved from https://cdn.americanprogress.org/wp-content/uploads/issues/2009/12/pdf/lgbt_health_disparities_race.pdf

Manalansan, M. F. (1995). In the shadows of Stonewall: Examining gay transnational politics and the diaspora dilemma. *GLQ: A Journal of Lesbian and Gay Studies, 2*(4), 425–438.

Meenaghan, T. M., Kilty, K. M., & McNutt, J. G. (2009). *Social policy analysis and practice.* Chicago: Lyceum Books.

Modi, M. N., Palmer, S., & Armstrong, A. (2014). The role of Violence Against Women Act in addressing intimate partner violence: A public health issue. *Journal of Women's Health, 23*(3), 253–259.

Natale, A. P., & Miller-Cribbs, J. E. (2012). Same-sex marriage policy: Advancing social, political, and economic justice. *Journal of GLBT Family Studies, 8*(2), 155–172.

National Association of Social Workers. (1999). *Code of ethics of the National Association of Social Workers.* Washington, DC: Author.

National Association of Social Workers. (2015). *Social work speaks* (10th ed.). NASW Policy Statements. Washington, DC: Author.

Parham, D., & Conviser, R. (2002). A brief history of the Ryan White CARE Act in the USA and its implications for other countries. *AIDS Care, 14*(Suppl. 1), 3–6.

Payne, M. (2005). *Modern social work theory* (3rd ed.). Chicago: Lyceum Books.

Peralta, E. (2013, June 26). Court overturns DOMA, sidesteps broad gay marriage ruling. National Public Radio.

Perez, V. M. (2014, June). Political Participation and LGBT Americans. Retrieved from http://www.projectvote.org/wp-content/uploads/2014/06/RESEARCH-MEMOLGBT-PARTICIPATION-June-20-2014.pdf

Poindexter, C. C. (1997). Sociopolitical antecedents to Stonewall: Analysis of the origins of the gay rights movement in the United States. *Social Work, 42*(6), 607–615.

Richards, D. A. (2005). *The case for gay rights: From Bowers to Lawrence and beyond.* Lawrence: University Press of Kansas.

Rimmerman, C. A., Wald, K. D., & Wilcox, C. (2000). *The politics of gay rights.* Chicago: University of Chicago Press.

Rocha, C., Poe, C., & Thomas, V. (2010). Political activities of social workers: Addressing perceived barriers to political participation. *Social Work, 55*(4), 317–325.

Sanchez, N. F., Sanchez, J. P., & Danoff, A. (2009). Health care utilization, barriers to care, and hormone usage among male-to-female transgender persons in New York City. *American Journal of Public Health, 99*(4), 713–719.

Schneider, R. L., & Lester, L. (2001). *Social work advocacy: A new framework for action.* Belmont, CA: Brooks/Cole.

Sears, B., & Mallory, C. (2011). *Documented evidence of employment discrimination & its effects on LGBT people.* Williams Institute. Retrieved from https://escholarship.org/uc/item/03m1g5sg

Shilts, R. (1982). *The mayor of Castro Street: The life and times of Harvey Milk.* New York: St. Martin's Griffin.

Shilts, R. (2007). *And the band played on: Politics, people, and the AIDS epidemic, 20th-anniversary edition.* New York: St. Martin's Press.

Stein, M. (2004). *Encyclopedia of lesbian, gay, bisexual, and transgender history in America.* New York: Charles Scribner's.

Stotzer, R. L., Herman, J. L., & Hasenbush, A. (2014). *Transgender parenting: A review of existing research.* Williams Institute. Retrieved from https://williamsinstitute.law.ucla.edu/research/parenting/transgender-parenting-oct-2014/

Thapa, A., Cohen, J., Guffey, S., & Higgins-D'Alessandro, A. (2013). A review of school climate research. *Review of Educational Research, 83*(3), 357–385.

Timeline of LGBTQ rights. (2015, November 4). Retrieved from http://equaldex.com/timeline

Tribe, L. H. (2004). *Lawrence v. Texas*: The" fundamental right" that dare not speak its name. *Harvard Law Review, 117*(6), 1893–1955.

US Internal Revenue Service. (2015). *Lobbying*. Retrieved from https://www.irs.gov/Charities-&-Non-Profits/Lobbying

PART IV

HEALTH AND MENTAL HEALTH FACTORS

AN EXAMINATION OF HEALTH AND MENTAL HEALTH FACTORS IMPACTING THE LGBTQ COMMUNITY

Sarah R. Young and Marcie Fisher-Borne

INTRODUCTION

Lesbian, gay, bisexual, transgender, and queer (LGBTQ) people have long been on the margins of health care, faced with both overt as well as subtle forms of discrimination and stigma, resulting in significant disparities along a variety of health outcomes (Herek, Capitanio, & Widaman, 2002; Institute of Medicine [IOM], 2011; Lambda Legal, 2010). LGBTQ people represent a broad range of experiences and identities that cross race, class, and cultural lines. As such, it is impossible to characterize a singular experience (or set of experiences) for LGBTQ people and health. Even so, discrimination, stigma, and challenges with access to care are often common denominators for members of the LGBTQ community (IOM, 2011). This chapter offers a broad exploration of health and mental health issues for LGBTQ people. Exploring the multitude of facets that shape the health and mental health of LGBTQ individuals is beyond the scope of the chapter; however, we offer context and a conceptual framework for approaches to addressing health disparities within LGBTQ communities

FRAMING HEALTH: UNDERSTANDING UNIQUENESS AND INTERSECTIONALITY

Defining the LGBTQ community as a singular unified group can be problematic, as it often leads to a static and oversimplified view of complex and evolving health-care issues. In fact, practitioners should clearly understand that LGBTQ populations are not homogenous. Within the LGBTQ community one will find the needs and experiences of health care are defined and evolve based on one's age, socioeconomic status, race, geographic location, ability, and nationality, among other demographic concerns. For example, the health-care needs of a low-income, middle-aged white lesbian in the rural South may be quite distinct from the needs of a young, African American, middle-class lesbian living in an urban area. Therefore, when talking about LGBTQ health, it is critical to acknowledge significant subgroup variation based on age, race, income, geographic location, and a host of other cultural and social influences (IOM, 2011). As a practitioner, this vantage means continually assessing how multiple intersecting identities may impact an individual's health and access to adequate health care.

MOVING AWAY FROM A PATHOLOGY PERSPECTIVE

The World Health Organization (2003, 2006) defines health as a "state of complete physical, mental, and social well-being and not merely the absence of disease or infirmity." Historically, LGBTQ health issues and research on health disparities have largely been defined by the presence of disease and disease outcomes and have not fully addressed social well-being and resiliency. While the experience of an unequal disease burden should be recognized and understood, solely addressing LGBTQ health issues as a long laundry list of illnesses and deficiencies is problematic for a number of reasons.

Social work, along with other health and mental health professions, has a history of viewing the LGBTQ community through a lens of deviance and a desire to diagnose and reform "risk" behaviors (Herrick, Stall, Goldhammer, Egan, & Mayer, 2014; Vaughan & Rodriguez, 2014). This has led, in many ways, to ignoring how the larger social and political environment impact and stigmatize an LGBTQ identity that contributes to a variety of undesirable health and mental health outcomes (McClain, Hawkins, & Yehia, 2016). Focusing merely on "risk behavior" and specific disease types with an absence of focus on the systems, policies, or social determinants of health that negatively impact health and wellness paints an incomplete picture of LGBT individuals and communities (Herrick et al., 2014; Mulé et al., 2009). When practitioners adopt a micro-level diagnosis orientation and exclude an awareness of macro-level changes that impact people's well-being, they contribute to the extension of stigma and discrimination that LGBTQ people face under the guise of trying to be helpful and provide support. While professionally our focus on individual "client" outcomes devoid of a systems perspective may have been harmful, the overall "illness-based" perspective of LGBTQ communities runs counter to the strengths-based perspective inherent to the profession of social work (Rapp, Saleebey, & Sullivan, 2005). This focus disregards the body of evidence that shows the LGB community as adaptive, resilient and resourceful (Butler, 2004; Connolly, 2005; Gonzalez et al., 2004; Meyer, 2003). Building on the lens of a strengths perspective and underscoring an LGBTQ client's resilience should be considered among other best practices. Such best practices are reviewed later on in this chapter.

UNDERSTANDING ACCESS AND BARRIERS TO CARE AND UTILIZATION: THE IMPACT OF POLICIES AND PROVIDERS

The IOM report along with the Department of Health and Human Services (DHHS) Healthy People 2020 initiative have highlighted disparities in LGBT care and called for steps to address these challenges (DHHS, 2011; IOM, 2011). Understanding the social and structural forces that impact all aspects of health is critical to approaching LGBTQ health and mental health. While the policy landscape for LGBT individuals is changing rapidly, growing research is demonstrating how social policies impact health (Fredriksen-Goldsen & Espinoza, 2014; Hatzenbuehler, McLaughlin, Keyes, & Hasin, 2010; Hatzenbuehler et al., 2012; Williams, Costa, Odunlami, & Mohammed, 2008).

For example, a study of US adults ($N = 34,653$) found that LGB residents in states that had anti-same-sex marriage amendments in 2004 demonstrated significant increases in anxiety and substance disorders in contrast to LGB individuals in states without these amendments (Hatzenbueler, 2010). Similar research has found lower levels of psychological distress among LGB individuals in states with supportive LGBT legislation (Russ et al., 2012) and reduced medical visits and mental health care visits following the enactment of same-same sex marriage laws (Hatzenbueler et al., 2012). Interestingly, Hatzenbueler and colleagues found that when Massachusetts legalized same-sex marriage in 2004, the reduction in medical visits and expenditures were seen even for single gay male clients 12 months following the policy change, thus suggesting that legal protections have a protective effective on health.

IDENTITY, MENTAL HEALTH, AND THE DSM

While homosexuality was removed from the *Diagnostic and Statistical Manual of Mental Disorders* (DSM) in 1973, the legacy of sexual minorities being labeled as ill and deviant, along with discriminatory laws and policies, have influenced LGBTQ peoples' interaction with providers and the broader health-care system. It is important to note that transgender individuals, whose sex assigned at birth does not align with their current identity, are typically diagnosed with gender dysphoria in the fifth edition of the DSM.

REPARATIVE THERAPY

Born from the desire to change or "fix" LGBTQ people, instead of a desire to affirm and support them, sexual orientation change therapy has had a particularly negative impact on LGBTQ people's mental health. Public condemnation of reparative therapy from professional organizations is still relatively recent. However, a number of leading professional organizations, including the American Academy of Pediatrics (1993), the American Counseling Association (2013), the

American Psychiatric Association (2000), the American Psychological Association (2009), and the National Association for Social Workers (2005) have released policy and position statements condemning the harmful effects this therapy can have on individuals. A public outcry over its use, along with a number of lawsuits brought against social workers and other professionals who are using this discredited therapy, highlights how this once accepted form of "therapy" has no role in helping LGBTQ people.

THE ROLE OF HEALTH-CARE PROVIDERS

Health-care providers play a pivotal role in connecting individuals to treatment and prevention resources (DHHS, 2011; IOM, 2011). Strengthening the quality of relationship between provider and client is essential to the work of culturally competent care. In a landmark study of LGBT people and experiences with health-care providers (N = 4,916), almost 56% of LGB adults and 70% of transgender individuals reported discrimination in health-care settings (Lambda Legal, 2010). Disturbingly, 36% of respondents living with HIV reported that health-care providers refused to touch them, and 7.8% of transgender and gender-nonconforming respondents described experiences of physical abuse by providers. A study involving 4,385 clinicians in California found that doctors reported being "sometimes" or "often" uncomfortable in dealing with LGBT patients (Smith & Mathews, 2007). Part of this discomfort may be connected to a lack of formal medical training related to working with LGBTQ people.

LGBTQ health and mental health needs are often not fully addressed in medical and nursing education. A recent study in the *Journal of the American Medical Association* surveyed 150 academic medical schools in the United States and found a paucity of teaching and clinical training on LGBT issues (Obedin-Maliver et al., 2011). Almost one-third reported no LGBT-related content during clinical years, and schools taught a median of only five hours throughout medical school (Obedin-Maliver et al., 2011). Given the evidence that stigma and discrimination related to sexual orientation and gender identity impact health (IOM, 2011), provider and clinician training are critical to changing the landscape of LGBTQ health.

FACTORS THAT IMPACT HEALTH AND MENTAL HEALTH

Social work, as a distinguishing professional characteristic, examines people within the context of their environments. While we can examine health and mental health outcomes on a micro level exclusively, and this is sometimes appropriate for tasks within our profession, the National Association of Social Workers Code of Ethics implores us to challenge systems that oppress and undermine the well-being of minority groups, including sexual and gender minorities. While there are a multitude of such structural challenges for members of the LGBTQ community that impact health and mental health, here we explore the key issues of socioeconomic status, rural/urban location, stigma, and LGBT-specific health concerns.

SOCIOECONOMIC STATUS

Poverty and income inequality are associated with poorer health and mental health outcomes in the general population. Specifically, higher rates of infant mortality, shorter life expectancy, obesity, diabetes, and heart disease are connected to poverty (Braveman et al., 2010). In order to understand the health and mental health of LGBTQ communities, the experiences of poverty and income inequality need to be examined. LGBT people experience poverty at higher rates compared to heterosexual and cisgender peers. Gallup surveyed 121,290 people and found that LGBT people experienced poverty at a higher rate of 21.5% for women and 20.1% for men compared to cisgender and/or heterosexual women and men who had poverty rates of 19.1% and 13.4%, respectively (Gates & Newport, 2012). Given that poverty is experienced at higher rates, it deserves a closer examination in terms of how it impacts the health and mental health of LGBTQ people.

The stereotype that the LGBTQ community is affluent and has "high disposable income" has been disproved generally and among specific subsections of the community (Badgett, Durso, & Sheneebaum, 2013). For example, lesbians and bisexual women are more likely to live in poverty than gay and bisexual men or heterosexuals according to recent Census data compiled by the Williams Institute (Badgett et al., 2013; Short, 2012). With regard to the impact of socioeconomic status on the transgender community, research suggests that transgender people have lower incomes compared to their cisgender peers (Grant et al., 2011). This disparity is likely impacted by the high rates of unemployment and underemployment among transgender people, particularly for transgender people of color (Grant et al., 2011).

Same-sex couples and the children of same-sex couples appear to be at particular risk of poverty when compared to opposite-sex couples and their children (Badgett et al., 2013). Children of same-sex couples are twice as likely to be living in poverty when compared to the children of married, different-sex couples (Badgett et al., 2013). African American children of gay male parents experience the highest rates of poverty at 52.3% (Badgett et al., 2013). Social workers should be aware of how child poverty impacts health and mental health and should know that children of same-sex couples may be at particular risk. For a deeper discussion of the importance of LGBTQ identity and intersections with racial and ethnic identity, see chapter 21 of this text.

Experiences of discrimination (e.g., housing, police violence, sexual violence, and being kicked out of a family home for being LGBTQ) and poverty are also connected. Given that discrimination can impact socioeconomic status, which in turn can impact health and mental health outcomes, combatting discrimination through policy and regulation can be one way to improve health-related outcomes for the LGBTQ community. This can include ensuring policies of non-discrimination exist and are followed in public housing, in how police interact with the public, and in response to calls investigating sexual and intimate partner violence. The full impact of national marriage equality as a poverty intervention with potential health and mental health outcomes has yet to be fully understood or analyzed.

RURAL AND URBAN HEALTH-RELATED CONCERNS

US census data confirms what most social work practitioners know—that LGBTQ people live in all types of communities and across all 50 US states (US Census Bureau, 2013). Despite this evidence, research tends to predominantly emphasize the existence and needs of urban LGBTQ people. In the process, this research seems to reinforce the invisibility of LGBT people living in rural areas (Fisher, Irwin, & Coleman, 2014). This invisibility reinforces what many researchers have noted as the "myth" of the rural LGBT person (Fisher et al., 2014; Wrathall, 2000). While there are a number of practical and methodological reasons why there is a paucity of research on rural LGBT people (including but not limited to a lack of community resources, small sample sizes, and a lack of organizations from which researchers can recruit participants), we do know some of what may make the health and mental health needs of rural LGBTQ people different from (and in some ways the same as) their urban counterparts.

In general, individuals living in rural areas have unique health concerns when compared to their urban counterparts, such as lower access to primary care providers, poorer health behaviors such as smoking and drinking to excess, and higher rates of mortality and morbidity for a variety of illnesses such as diabetes and asthma (Hartley, 2004). Although more research is needed, it does appear that rural LGBT people mirror these concerns when compared to their urban LGBT counterparts (Fisher et al., 2014). In their convenience sample of 770 LGBT Nebraskans, Fisher and colleagues (2014) found that respondents in rural areas had higher rates of smoking, lower rates of health insurance, and higher rates of binge drinking when compared to their urban counterparts. Only rates of being uninsured were statistically significant in their model. It is worth noting that, in this particular sample, most rural participants in this study identified as white men.

Horvath, Iantaffi, Swinburne-Romine, and Bockting (2014) examined national survey responses of 1,229 transgender people and found several significant differences between rural and urban transgender respondents. First, although there was a small difference between lifetime suicide attempts between rural and urban transgender women, rural transgender men fared poorly on several indicators compared to their urban counterparts. This included higher scores on depression, somatic, and anxiety scales and significantly lower self-esteem compared to urban transgender men in the sample. This study did not note any significant differences between urban and rural participants with regard to substance use and risky sexual behaviors.

People living in urban areas also have unique health and mental health needs. In the same study of 1,229 transgender people, Horvath and colleagues (2014) found that transgender people in urban areas had higher rates of health-care utilization, which corresponded to lower health risk-taking behaviors (such as unprotected sex and intravenous drug use). In an examination of the Urban Men's Health Study, Stall and colleagues (2008) found that while HIV and other sexually transmitted infections impacted gay and bisexual men, that there was also a certain level of resilience found among those residing within urban settings. This research implies that there is health-related resilience that is possible in cities that may not be possible rural areas (Stall et al., 2008). Having an awareness of the unique needs and experiences of rural versus urban LGBTQ individuals lives and lifestyles is of critical importance for future social work professionals.

STRESS AND STIGMA

Social workers should also pay special attention to stress and stigma among people who have multiple oppressed identities. Stress has contributed to negative health outcomes for LGBTQ people in a demonstrable way. This includes increased depression and anxiety, decreased self-esteem, and a sense of isolation (Berger, Ferrans, & Lashley, 2001). Minority stress theory (Meyer, 2003) can help us explain why those who live at multiple margins often fare poorer when it comes to health and well-being. For more information about minority stress theory, see chapter 12 in this text.

For LGBTQ people, stress can come from the mezzo, or family, level and can have an impact on health and well-being. Research from the Family Acceptance Project and social worker Dr. Caitlyn Ryan has demonstrated that the degree to which family members support or affirm a person's LGBTQ identity can have a demonstrable impact on the individual's health and mental health (Ryan, 2010). For example, in a study of 245 youth, those who came from "highly rejecting" families had an 8.5 times higher likelihood of attempting suicide over the course of their lives when compared to youth who came from "highly accepting" families. From the same study, youth from highly accepting families were 3.5 times less likely to be at risk for HIV infection when compared to youth from highly rejecting families (Ryan, 2010). Examples of rejecting behaviors, according to the Family Acceptance Project, include physically punishing youth for their identity, isolating LGBTQ youth from their LGBTQ friends, and "blaming LGBTQ youth for the discrimination" they face (Ryan, 2010, p. 12). Examples of accepting family behaviors include communicating with their child about their LGBTQ identity, standing up for their child if they faced discrimination, and working through any discomfort the parents may feel about their child's LGBTQ identity (Ryan, 2010). This research, which shows a direct connection between stigma, rejection, and negative health outcomes (and a connection between acceptance and healthier outcomes) suggests that assessing and fostering family acceptance for LGBTQ youth may be an important health intervention that social workers should be providing to families.

HIV-RELATED STIGMA

Given the impact that HIV has had on gay and bisexual men, transgender women, and men who have sex with men (MSM), it is unsurprising that in addition to the challenges that accompany being HIV-positive (HIV+), stigma adds an extra layer of challenge. In particular, the level of stigma that HIV+ individuals perceive appears to influence health and mental health outcomes in significant ways. For example, in their survey of 637 HIV+ individuals who were homeless or housing vulnerable (of whom 41% identified as MSM), higher levels of stigma were associated with poorer health and mental health, as well as lower adherence to HIV treatment. Similar links between higher rates of stigma and poorer health and mental health have been found throughout the literature (see Aidala, Abramson, Messeri, & Siegler, 2007; Murphy et al., 2006; Valdiserri, 2002). To capture HIV-related stigma, Berger and colleagues (2011) developed a psychometric assessment of HIV stigma and its impact on health and found four concepts to be significant: personalized stigma, disclosure concerns, negative self-image, and concern with public attitudes toward HIV. Social workers should assess for both the source and level of stigma their HIV+ clients experience, as this may be an important health-related piece of information that can influence any treatment planning with their LGBTQ clients.

POPULATION-SPECIFIC HEALTH
AND MENTAL HEALTH CONCERNS

As has been mentioned at several points in this chapter, the LGBTQ community is diverse and the needs of LGBTQ subpopulations both overlap with and diverge from other subpopulations and from heterosexual and/or cisgender people. The Gay and Lesbian Medical Association has excellent resources directed both at LGBTQ health providers and LGBTQ patients that highlight common health and mental health concerns that should be discussed as a part of the continuum of care. The following sections highlight some of the population-based health and mental health concerns for each subgroup across the LGBT community.

LESBIANS

While lesbians have health and mental health challenges that overlap with bisexual and heterosexual women, they also have health and mental health challenges that are unique. Lesbians are less likely to seek life-saving cancer screenings such as mammograms, pap smears and colonoscopies (Substance Abuse and Mental Health Services Administration [SAMHSA], 2012). Lesbians have higher rates of tobacco use, estimated at twice the rate as heterosexual women (Nyitray, Corran, Altman, Chikani, & Negrón, 2006). Lesbians also experience higher rates of obesity and lower rates of exercise compared to heterosexual women, although some women report that structural barriers (such as a lack of lesbian-inclusive fitness opportunities or lack of same-sex partner/spouse gym memberships) may play into this (Brittain, Baillargeon, McElroy, Aaron, & Gyurcsik, 2006).

Lesbians have disparate mental health challenges when compared to heterosexual women. For example, lesbians report higher rates of anxiety and depression related to chronic stress and experiences of discrimination (Poteat, 2012). Alarmingly, related to stress and discrimination, lesbians have higher rates of heavy drinking and binge drinking compared to bisexual women and heterosexual women (Poteat, 2012). For more information on the specific health and mental health needs of lesbians, see chapter 13 in this text.

GAY MEN

HIV/AIDS has disproportionately impacted gay and bisexual men. The lack of concern for the lives of those immediately impacted by HIV in the early stages of the disease is often blamed for allowing the disease to continue to spread so quickly among gay and bisexual men (Herek et al., 2002). Gay men and other MSM remain at elevated risk for contracting HIV, accounting for 78% of new infections in men compared to 22% in heterosexual men in 2010 (Centers for Disease Control and Prevention, 2015). Young gay men and MSM of color (particularly Black and Latino men) are at highest risk of infection—with an estimated 36% of new HIV infections in 2010 among Black MSM and 22% of new HIV infections among Latino MSM (Centers for Disease Control and Prevention, 2015). While some of this disparity of HIV infection for men of color can be explained by targeted HIV testing campaigns, it also suggests a need for racially and culturally sensitive prevention and treatment options (Centers for Disease Control and Prevention, 2016; Wolitski & Fenton, 2011). These options may have been slow to develop due to elements of racism and an overall lack of inclusion in developing HIV prevention and treatment efforts for this racial/ethnic minority group of gay men and MSM.

Gay men are at risk of contracting various strains of Hepatitis (such as B, C, and D), which is commonly spread through sexual contact. Hepatitis impacts liver functioning and is often co-morbid with HIV (World Health Organization, 2010). Certain types of cancer, such as prostate, testicular, and colon cancer, are also more common in gay men compared to heterosexual men (SAMHSA, 2012). The ability to be out and open about one's sexual orientation and sexual behavior can provide an opportunity for the patient to share and receive key information about their health status and risk factors. As discussed earlier in the chapter, health-care providers (which may include medical social workers) are crucial in creating an environment where patients can be open about who they are and what behaviors they engage in.

Gay men experience disparate mental health outcomes as well. In one sample of 230 men of varying sexual orientations, being gay was significantly associated with eating disorder criteria (Boisvert & Harrell, 2010). This finding has been consistent across other empirical studies (Mosher et al., 2005, Wichstrom, 2006). Low self-esteem and body image issues are related to the development of eating disorders (Carper, Negy, & Tantleff-Dunn, 2010). These issues can be perpetuated in certain elements of gay culture that prize fit and lean bodies that are often unrealistic for most men to safely achieve (Carper et al., 2010). In addition to eating disorders, gay men are also more likely than straight men to experience depression and anxiety (Mosher et al., 2005; Wichstrom, 2006). In one sample of 198 gay and bisexual men, 10% of those with an eating disorder also experienced an anxiety disorder, and 37% of those diagnosed with an eating disorder experienced a diagnosis of panic disorder specifically (Feldman & Meyer, 2010). It would behoove social workers to pay attention to comorbid mental health diagnoses. For more information on the specific health and mental health needs of gay men, see chapter 14 in this text.

BISEXUAL MEN AND WOMEN

Lack of access to health care is a theme for the LGBTQ community generally, and it particularly impacts bisexual people (SAMHSA, 2012). According to Diamant, Wold, Spritzer, and Gelberg (2000), bisexual women are more likely to be uninsured when compared to both heterosexuals and gays and lesbians. Of course, this lack of health-care access can contribute to later health challenges for this population.

High rates of cancer impact members of the bisexual community. In one sample of 90,823 women (317 of whom identified as bisexual), bisexual women in particular reported higher rates of having cancer of any type and had higher rates of breast cancer specifically when compared to heterosexual women (Case et al., 2004). Similar to lesbians, one associated factor includes low cancer screening rates (SAMHSA, 2012). Bisexual men who have male sexual partners report higher rates of anal cancer, likely related to HPV infection, when compared to heterosexual men (SAMHSA, 2012). Bisexual MSM also have HIV infection rates that are higher compared to heterosexual men (Winn, 2012). Interestingly, bisexual women report getting tested for HIV at higher rates than heterosexual women (58.9% compared to 38.6% in a total sample size of 16,970), which is important for social workers to share with their clients, while always encouraging HIV testing as well (VanKim & Padilla, 2010). While this information is encouraging, bisexual women report lower rates of having ever had a pap screening, an important prevention measure against developing cervical cancer (SAMHSA, 2012). Bisexuals have similarly high rates as lesbians and gay men of heart disease, tobacco use, high blood pressure, alcohol use, and high cholesterol when compared to heterosexuals.

The mental health of bisexual individuals should also be of concern to social workers. Bisexual people report higher rates of intimate partner violence compared to heterosexuals. In a sample of 16,970 people in New Mexico, researchers found that 47.4% of bisexual men and women reported experiencing some form of intimate partner violence in their lifetime, compared to 17.5% of heterosexuals in the same sample (VanKim & Padilla, 2010). For more information on the specific health and mental health needs of bisexuals, see chapter 15 in this text.

TRANSGENDER INDIVIDUALS

Transgender and gender-nonconforming people experience a unique set of health and mental health needs and challenges that social workers and other professionals should be sensitive to. This includes access to—and utilization of—health care as well as services provided by transgender affirming and knowledgeable health-care staff, specific health concerns related to the experience of being transgender (particularly when living in a society that may not affirm their needs and existence) and disparate health and mental health outcomes, including trauma, victimization, and violence (Grant et al., 2011).

For many transgender people, the term "transition" exists along a spectrum. Some transgender individuals have little interest in obtaining medical care (such as hormones and surgeries) related to their transition. Others may wish to medically transition but lack the resources (such as finances and health insurance coverage) or lack access to care that they require. For those who wish to medically transition, they may be met with medical providers who are not knowledgeable about transgender health needs. Alarmingly, according to the National Center on Transgender Equality (2011), in a sample of 6,400 transgender adults, 19% had been denied health care based on their transgender status.

Lack of access to health care, coupled with health-care providers who may not offer the most competent care, appears to contribute to a number of health and mental health concerns that impact transgender people. Increasingly, states are passing oppressive antitransgender bathroom bills that would deny transgender people the right to use the public restroom that matches their gender identity. Already, according to one survey of 93 people, 18% of the overall sample of transgender respondents had been denied access to public bathrooms, and 25% of Black respondents reported being denied use of a public bathroom (Herman, 2013). It is unclear whether these bills, if passed, would pass legal muster and if so how they would contribute to transgender health and mental health challenges. The inability to use a restroom of one's choosing has led to higher rates of kidney infections and urinary tract infections related to holding one's bladder, so it is assumed that further barriers and increased stigma could have an impact on transgender health and mental health (Herman, 2013).

Unsurprisingly, given high rates of oppression and discrimination, transgender people face disproportionate rates of both suicide attempts and suicidal ideation (Grossman & D'Augelli, 2007). Relatedly, transgender people face a disproportionate rate of violence and hate crimes (Stolzer, 2009). The experiences of living in fear, facing stigma, and societal rejection mean that as social workers we need to expand protections for transgender and gender-nonconforming people while working to dismantle the societal and structural experience of oppression that they face. For more information on the specific health and mental health needs of the transgender community, see chapter 16 in this text.

In conclusion, the health and mental health concerns for LGBTQ people are both similar to and distinctive from the concerns of heterosexual and cisgender individuals. The ability to be out as LGBTQ with one's health-care provider can lead to better care for the client (IOM, 2011). If social workers understand that many negative health and mental health outcomes are the result of systemic oppression and discrimination, it makes intervening at the micro, mezzo, and macro levels a necessary part of social work practice. The amelioration of structural and cultural oppression would likely lead to better health outcomes for many of our LGBTQ clients.

KEY POLICY CONSIDERATIONS: THE AFFORDABLE CARE ACT

While 82% of heterosexual adults have health insurance, less than 77% of lesbian, gay, and bisexual adults and only 52% of transgender adults have health coverage (Krehely, 2009). Additional research suggests that same-sex couples with children may have additional disparities in health insurance coverage and access as they are less likely to have insurance when compared to heterosexual couples (Buchmueller & Carpenter, 2010). Lack of insurance is a major impediment to health-care access. The implementation of the Affordable Care Act (ACA) in 2014 brought an expansion of rights and protections for LGBT people that have reduced a number of barriers to health care (Durso, Baker, & Cray, 2013).

For example, insurance plans through the health marketplace can no longer deny health coverage due to existing conditions (e.g., HIV status). Additionally, the ACA includes nondiscrimination protections based on gender identity for insurance purchased through the health marketplace or insurers receiving federal funds (i.e. Medicaid and Medicare). Hospitals and long-term care facilities can no longer deny visitation rights to same-sex couples regardless of marital status nor can they deny individuals the right to choose who can make medical decisions on their behalf, regardless of sexual orientation or gender identity.

Section 1557 of the ACA bars discrimination by any entity receiving federal funds. This includes hospitals, primary care clinics, and all entities that receive Medicaid or Medicaid funding (DHHS, n.d.). While no federal protections currently exist related to sexual orientation, ACA Section 1557 has been interpreted to included discrimination based on gender identity

(DHHS, n.d.). This is a significant milestone in health access for transgender and gender-nonconforming individuals.

DO ASK, DO TELL: WHY DEMOGRAPHIC DATA MATTERS

The 2011 IOM report on the health of LGBT people highlighted major challenges with collecting demographic data of LGBT people and recommended the standardization of data collection to strengthen information gathering specifically related to gender identity and sexual orientation (IOM, 2011). Additionally, Healthy People 2020, which provides a roadmap for improving public health for all people over the next decade, calls on providers to gather information on sexual orientation and gender identity (SO/GI) (DHHS, 2011). The justification for collecting these data is similar to the need to gather demographic data that captures race and ethnicity. According to the Joint Commission (2010), a US nonprofit that accredits more than 21,000 health care organizations:

> Hospitals must collect patient-level demographic data on race and ethnicity to identify the needs of individual patients and to eliminate disparities in the patient population. These critical data provide hospitals with information on the potential cultural needs of each patient, as well as an opportunity to monitor and analyze health disparities at the population level. (p. 11)

Collecting broad-based demographic data on LGBTQ people will create a more accurate picture of the community and highlight their unique health needs (Cahill & Makadon, 2014). Deliberate and systematic data collection within health-care systems that is inclusive of sexual orientation, gender identity, and gender expression will provide justification for research funding, service expansion, and how specific interventions and treatment plans should be tailored to meet the unique needs of LGBTQ people.

In 2015, new rules from the Centers for Medicare and Medicaid Services will require all electronic health record systems certified under Stage 3 of "Meaningful Use" to allow users to record, change, and access structured data on SO/GI (Cahill, Baker, Deutsch, Keatley, & Makadon, 2016). These requirements will go into place in 2018 and mark a critical step forward in being able to understand LGBT health disparities. As part of this change in LGBTQ data collection, the Fenway Institute in Boston and Center for American Progress in Washington, D.C., developed the "Do Ask, Do Tell" project, which provides tools and resources to support providers and health systems in integrating LGBT data collection into practice (Do Ask, Do Tell, 2015). One challenge for health systems involves figuring out how to ask specific questions related to sexual orientation, gender identity, and gender expression.

Based on a multiclinic study at Fenway Institute, as well as research conducted by the Center of Excellence for Transgender Health at the University of California at San Francisco

TABLE 20.1 Questions to Utilize when Asking about Sexual Orientation and Gender Identity

	Questions to include in patient information forms and in clinical appointments
Sexual Orientation	**Do you think of yourself as** • Lesbian, gay, or homosexual • Straight or heterosexual • Bisexual • Something else (please specify): _____ • Don't know
Gender Identity	**What is your current gender identity?** • Male • Female • Female-to-male (FTM)/Transgender Male/Trans Man • Male-to-Female (MTF)/Transgender Female/Trans Woman • Genderqueer, neither exclusively male nor female • Additional gender category/(or Other), please specify:_____ • Decline to answer **What sex were you assigned at birth on your original birth certificate? (Check one)** • Male • Female • Decline to answer **What is your preferred gender pronoun?** • He/Him • She/Her • Something else (Specify:_____)

Source: Cahill, S., Singal, R., Grasso, C., King, D., Mayer, K., Baker, K., & Makadon, H. (2014). Do ask, do tell: high levels of acceptability by patients of routine collection of sexual orientation and gender identity data in four diverse American community health centers. *PloS one, 9*(9), e107104.

on collecting information on gender identity in clinical settings (Cahill et al., 2014; Deutsch et al., 2013), Table 20.1 outlines tested questions to use when asking about SO/GI. Questions related to gender identity include capturing information related to sex assigned at birth as well as current gender identity. This information provides clinically relevant information that can help providers identify a patient's clinical needs. For example, a transgender female may need to be offered a prostate screening and a transgender male client may need to be offered a cervical cancer screening exam. Asking a question about gender identity alone would not provide clinicians important information.

RECONCEPTUALIZING MENTAL HEALTH

It is clear from a review of relevant literature that an overwhelming focus on LGBTQ mental health, like that of physical health, is on experiencing risk, harm, and challenge (Russell, 2005). Likewise, public discourse and media attention often focus on the most challenging and violent aspects of LGBTQ mental health such as suicide, victimization, and hate crimes. Very little discussion reframes LGBTQ mental health from the perspective of strength and resilience, which LGBTQ people and their families often possess. In addition to ignoring strengths, these narratives may fail to spotlight the larger contextual factors, such as stigma, family rejection, and discrimination that may contribute to overall mental health and wellness. Linking pathology and disease to sexual and gender minority status may happen automatically in the minds of the general public and even in the minds of social work professionals (Tan, 2014). This link, of course, can be harmful to LGBTQ people's mental health and well-being and may skew the treatment they receive from social work professionals.

Social work practitioners and researchers may be in a unique position to change the narrative from risk to resilience. Several promising theories and practices attempt to do just that. Structures and systems that were once seen solely as sources of pain and distress, such as faith communities and families, may be viewed as having the potential to serve as a source of support for LGBTQ people. Whereas faith and family were once seen as an inevitable "lost cause"—such systems are now being engaged in strength-based and effective ways. Although rejection from faith and family may still be an experience that many LGBTQ people share, narratives of hope and acceptance are also making their way into research. Social work practice should focus on fostering acceptance and building resilience whenever possible. The following sections review building resilience, fostering family acceptance, and connecting LGBTQ clients to faith-based communities as promising practices for social work with LGBTQ people.

IDENTIFYING AND BUILDING RESILIENCE

While the vast number of risks and risk factors for LGBTQ mental health are well documented, Russell (2005) reminds us that "[w]e know much less about resilience, the characteristics and factors that explain or predict the health of adolescent and adult lives of most sexual minorities," (p. 6). So much has changed in the macro, sociopolitical context that impacts LGBTQ people, their families, and their employment possibilities in recent decades. Social workers need to remember that older LGBTQ people have often demonstrated great resilience in the face of blatant homophobia, transphobia, and other forms of oppression and ignorance. Coming of age during a time when discrimination and prejudice was much more pronounced may mean that older LGBTQ people have had to adapt to more challenging conditions than their contemporaries and that their resilience in the face of such challenges goes unrecognized (Dentato, Orwat, Spira, & Walker, 2014).

Given that LGBTQ people have multiple intersecting identities, the needs and experiences of one subgroup of individuals within the community may vary according to factors such as race, class, religious beliefs, and geography. Social workers should assess several elements of information at once, such as age of the LGBTQ client and era in which they came of age, specific racial, class, religious beliefs, and so on. All of these factors, and how they intersect to form specific lived experiences for clients, is crucial to understanding and building resilience. As Russell (2005) reminds us, we need to have a working theory of "why the *majority* of sexual minority young people grow up to be healthy and contributing members of society despite widespread heterosexism and homophobia," (p. 8) to which we would add widespread incidence of cissexism and transphobia as well. A deeper understanding of successful development and the factors that foster it would help social workers build upon the strengths of the client, something our profession is widely recognized for.

PROMOTING FAMILY ACCEPTANCE FOR MENTAL WELLNESS

The Family Acceptance Project, discussed earlier in this chapter, examines the concept of "family acceptance" of LGBTQ people as important in improving the health and mental health of this diverse community. Developed by social worker Dr. Caitlyn Ryan, the Family Acceptance Project has empirically demonstrated the health and mental health impacts that rejection can have on LGBTQ youth. For example, youth who come from highly rejecting families have a 3.5 times greater incidence of suicide attempts across their lifespan (Ryan, 2010). Viewed from a strengths perspective, that same data can showcase that youth from highly accepting homes are 3.5 times less likely to attempt suicide over the course of their lives. More than semantics, a focus on acceptance and resilience can offer a goal for social workers who want to build wellness. It is also important to remember that acceptance from family members should be thought of as a spectrum ranging from full rejection to full acceptance. Since the level of family acceptance can impact mental health across the lifespan, a focus on how to increase such support should be a main target for social work practitioners who work with the families of LGBTQ people. Ultimately, the Family Acceptance Project and other similar programs view the possibilities for change within a family instead of viewing families solely as a source of pain and rejection for LGBTQ people.

Community-based programs, such as Parents, Families and Friends of Lesbians and Gays (PFLAG), offer peer-based support groups that assist the families and friends of all LGBTQ people in accepting and supporting their loved ones. PFLAG chapters are widespread nationally and may be an important referral to make for families and friends who are struggling to accept their LGBTQ loved one (see http://community.pflag.org/). While the direct benefit may be for the individual friends and family members, there may be an overall mental health impact for the LGBTQ person who then benefits from the increased support and understanding that they receive.

FINDING FAITH IN RELIGIOUS AND SPIRITUAL COMMUNITIES

Estimates are that as many as 80% of all Americans identify as religious (Kosmin, Keysar, Cragun, & Navarro-Rivera, 2009). In the general population, religious identity and spiritual practice has been associated with a variety of positive mental health impacts (Hamblin & Gross, 2014). For example, religious beliefs and coping mechanisms have been associated with reduced symptoms of panic disorder, anxiety, and depression. The positive impact of religion on mental health seems to strengthen when individuals are in the midst of a major life event, such as a terminal illness, death of a loved one, or the loss of a job (Smith et al., 2003). It should serve as no surprise that participation in a faith community can help people connect, reduce stress, and increase positive coping behaviors (Smith et al., 2003). These benefits have been reported across race, age, and gender (Hamblin & Gross, 2014). The specific impact of faith on mental health for LGBTQ people remains underexplored (Hamblin & Gross, 2014).

LGBTQ people have not always had a warm reception within various communities of faith. In fact, certain denominations remain indifferent to their LGBTQ members while others may be hostile. Still, most LGBT people identify as religious, and yet 79% of the over 35,000 people sampled by the Pew Research Center also felt that most major religious communities have negative views of LGBT people (Murphy, 2015). In addition to having the perception that major faith groups are unwelcoming to LGBT people, 30% of the sample reported that they had personally experienced an instance of discrimination from a faith organization (Murphy, 2015). Despite LGBT people identifying as people of faith at similar rates as the general population, they face particular barriers to full inclusion and acceptance in their faith community and the mental health benefits that this inclusion can provide (Murphy, 2015). In recent times, religious denominations have clarified their stance on LGBTQ inclusion. The Human Rights Campaign website, in a section called "Faith Positions," has cataloged major faith traditions and their specific LGBTQ position statements as a reference. Social workers may want to consider what a profaith or prospiritual LGBTQ approach can look like for clients who seek such an intervention while becoming more knowledgeable about the intersection between LGBTQ people and faith.

There are several suggestions for how to join LGBTQ people with their faith communities for the purpose of improved mental health. First, social work practitioners should assess the role that faith or religion has played in the lives of their LGBTQ clients. This can mean assessing for ways that faith has helped, harmed, or been absent in their client's life. It should also include assessing the desired relationship that a client wishes to have with a faith community. This may be an opportunity to explore with LGBTQ clients which faith tradition might fit their beliefs and their identity. For clients who wish to take an activist stance on challenging bigotry within religious communities toward LGBTQ people, organizations like Soulforce train people of faith to work from the inside of their communities to educate their peers and clergy on the importance of LGBT inclusion (www.soulforce.org).

CONCLUSION

While research has not always led the way in reframing the narrative of health and mental health of LGBTQ people from one of pathology to one of power and resilience, social work practitioners can take the lead. Social work and other health and mental health practitioners are well-positioned to refocus the conversation and subsequent interventions for LGBTQ people on health, wellness, and resilience. By engaging people and systems that were formerly thought of as obstacles to support—such as faith and family systems—social workers can open up new possibilities for the physical and mental well-being of their LGBTQ clients. Finally, a holistic view of LGBTQ people means recognizing that various identities and communities often bring strength and support. When social workers can assume strengths and resilience rather than deficits in communities who have experienced systemic oppression, better health and mental health outcomes will certainly follow.

REFERENCES

Aidala, A. A., Lee, G., Abramson, D. M., Messeri, P., & Siegler, A. (2007). Housing need, housing assistance, and connection to HIV medical care. *AIDS and Behavior, 11*(Suppl. 2), S101–S115. doi:10.1007/s10461-007-9276-x.

American Academy of Pediatrics. (1993). Homosexuality and adolescence. *Pediatrics, 92,* 631–634. Retrieved from http://pediatrics.aappublications.org/content/92/4/631.full.pdf

American Counseling Association. (2013). *ethical issues related to conversion or reparative therapy.* Retrieved from http://www.counseling.org/news/updates/2013/01/16/ethical-issues-related-to-conversion-or-reparative-therapy

American Psychiatric Association. (2000). *Position statement on therapies focused on attempts to change sexual orientation (reparative or conversion therapies).* Retrieved from http://www.psychiatry.org/File%20Library/Advocacy%20and%20Newsroom/Position%20Statements/ps2000_ReparativeTherapy.pdf

American Psychological Association. (2009). *Resolution on appropriate affirmative responses to sexual orientation distress and change efforts.* Retrieved from http://www.apa.org/about/policy/sexual-orientation.pdf

Badgett, M. V., Durso, L. E., & Sheneebaum, A. (2013). *New patterns of poverty in the lesbian, gay, and bisexual community.* Los Angeles, CA: Williams Institute.

Berger, B. E., Ferrans, C. E., & Lashley, F. R. (2001). Measuring stigma in people with HIV: Psychometric assessment of the HIV stigma scale. *Research in Nursing & Health, 24*(6), 518–529.

Boisvert, J. A., & Harrell, W. A. (2010). Homosexuality as a risk factor for eating disorder symptomatology in men. *The Journal of Men's Studies, 17*(3), 210–225.

Brittain, D. R., Baillargeon, T., McElroy, M., Aaron, D. J., & Gyurcsik, N. C. (2006). Barriers to moderate physical activity in adult lesbians. *Women Health, 43*(1), 75–92.

Buchmueller T., & Carpenter C. S. (2010). Disparities in health insurance coverage, access, and outcomes for individuals in same-sex versus different-sex relationships, 2000-2007. *American Journal of Public Health, 100*(3), 489–495.

Butler, S. S. (2004). Gay, lesbian, bisexual and transgender (GLBT) elders: The challenge and resilience of this marginalized group. *Journal of Human Behavior in the Social Environment, 9,* 25–44. doi:10.1300/J137v09n04_02

Cahill, S., & Makadon, H. (2014). Sexual orientation and gender identity data collection in clinical settings and in electronic health records: A key to ending LGBT health disparities. *LGBT Health, 1*(1), 34–41.

Cahill, S., Singal, R., Grasso, C., King, D., Mayer, K., Baker, K., & Makadon, H. (2014). Do ask, do tell: High levels of acceptability by patients of routine collection of sexual orientation and gender identity data in four diverse American community health centers. *PLoS ONE, 9*(9), e107104.

Cahill, S. R., Baker, K., Deutsch, M. B., Keatley, J., & Makadon, H. J. (2016). Inclusion of sexual orientation and gender identity in stage 3 meaningful use guidelines: A huge step forward for LGBT health. *LGBT Health, 3*(2), 100–102. doi:10.1089/lgbt.2015.0136

Carper, T. L. M., Negy, C., & Tantleff-Dunn, S. (2010). Relations among media influence, body image, eating concerns, and sexual orientation in men: A preliminary investigation. *Body Image, 7*(4), 301–309.

Case, P., Austin, S. B., Hunter, D. J., Manson, J. E., Malspeis, S., Willett, W. C. & Spiegelman, D. (2004). Sexual orientation, health risk factors, and physical functioning in the Nurses' Health Study II. *Journal of Women's Health, 13,* 1033–1047.

Centers for Disease Control and Prevention. (2015). HIV among gay and bisexual men. Retrieved from http://www.cdc.gov/hiv/group/msm/

Centers for Disease Control and Prevention. (2016). HIV among African American gay and bisexual men. Retrieved from http://www.cdc.gov/hiv/group/msm/bmsm.html

Connolly, C. M. (2005). A qualitative exploration of resilience in long term lesbian couples. *The Family Journal, 13*, 266–280. doi:10.1177/ 1066480704273681

Department of Health and Human Services. (2011). *Lesbian, gay, bisexual, and transgender health.* Retrieved from https://www.healthypeople.gov/2020/topics-objectives/topic/lesbian-gay-bisexual-and-transgender-health

Department of Health and Human Services. (n.d.). *Frequently asked questions: Section 1557 of the affordable care act.* Retrieved from http://www.hhs.gov/civil-rights/for-individuals/section-1557/section-1557-proposed-rule-faqs/index.html[

Dentato, M. P., Orwat, J., Spira, M., & Walker, B. (2014). Examining cohort differences and resilience among the aging LGBT community: Implications for education and practice among an expansively diverse population. *Journal of Human Behavior in the Social Environment, 24*, 316–238.

Deutsch, M. B., Green, J., Keatley, J., Mayer, G., Hastings, J., Hall, A. M., . . . Fennie, K. (2013). Electronic medical records and the transgender patient: Recommendations from the World Professional Association for Transgender Health EMR Working Group. *Journal of the American Medical Informatics Association, 20*(4), 700–703.

Diamant, A. L., Wold, C., Spritzer, K., & Gelberg, L. (2000). Health behaviors, health status, and access to and use of health care: A population-based study of lesbian, bisexual, and heterosexual women. *Archives of Family Medicine, 9*(10), 1043–1051.

Do Ask, Do Tell. (2015). *A toolkit for collecting data on sexual orientation and gender identity in clinical settings.* Retrieved from www.doasktell.org

Durso, L. Baker, K., & Cray, A. (2013). *LGBT communities and the Affordable Care Act.* Retrieved from https://www.americanprogress.org/wp-content/uploads/2013/10/LGBT-ACAsurvey-brief1.pdf

Feldman, M. B., & Meyer, I. H. (2010). Comorbidity and age of onset of eating disorders in gay men, lesbians, and bisexuals. *Psychiatry Research, 180*(2), 126–131.

Fisher, C. M., Irwin, J. A. & Coleman, J. D. (2014). LGBT health in the Midlands: A rural/urban comparison of basic health indicators. *Journal of Homosexuality, 61*, 1062–1090.

Fredriksen-Goldsen, K. I., & Espinoza, R. (2014). Time for transformation: Public policy must change to achieve health equity for LGBT older adults. *Generations, 38*(4), 97–106.

Gates, G. J., & Newport, F. (2012). *Special report: 3.4% of U.S. adults identify as LGBT.* Gallup Polling. Retrieved from www.gallup.com/poll/158066/special-report-adults-identify-lgbt-aspx.

Gonzalez, J. S., Penedo, F. J., Antoni, M. H., Duran, R. E., McPherson-Baker, S., Ironson, G., . . . Schneiderman, N. (2004). Social support, positive states of mind, and HIV treatment adherence in men and women living with HIV/AIDS. *Health Psychology, 23*(4), 413–418.

Grant, J. M., Mottet. L. A., Tanis, J. Harrison, J., Herman, J. L., & Keisling, M. (2011). *Injustice at every turn: A report of the National Transgender Discrimination Survey.* Washington, DC: National Center for Transgender Equality and National Gay and Lesbian Task Force.

Grossman, A. H., & D'Augelli, A. R. (2007). Transgender youth and life-threatening behaviors. *Suicide and Life-Threatening Behavior, 37*(5), 527–537.

Hamblin, R. J., & Gross, A. M. (2014). Religious faith, homosexuality, and psychological well-being: A theoretical and empirical review. *Journal of Gay & Lesbian Mental Health, 18*, 67–82.

Hartley, D. (2004). Rural health disparities, population health, and rural culture. *American Journal of Public Health, 94*(10), 1675–1678.

Hatzenbuehler, M. L., McLaughlin, K. A., Keyes, K. M., & Hasin, D. S. (2010). The impact of institutional discrimination on psychiatric disorders in lesbian, gay, and bisexual populations: A prospective study. *American Journal of Public Health 100*(3), 452–459.

Hatzenbuehler, M. L., O'Cleirigh, C., Grasso, C., Mayer, K., Safren, S., & Bradford, J. (2012). Effect of same-sex marriage laws on health care use and expenditures in sexual minority men: A quasi-natural experiment. *American Journal of Public Health, 102*(2), 285–291.

Herek, G. M., Capitanio, J. P., & Widaman, K. F. (2002). HIV-related stigma and knowledge in the United States: Prevalence and trends, 1991–1999. *American Journal of Public Health, 92*(3), 371–377.

Herman, J. L. (2013). Gendered restrooms and minority stress: The public regulation of gender and its impact on transgender people's lives. *Journal of Public Management & Social Policy, 19*(1), 65–80.

Herrick, A. L., Stall, R., Goldhammer, H., Egan, J. E., & Mayer, K. H. (2014). Resilience as a research framework and as a cornerstone of prevention research for gay and bisexual men: Theory and evidence. *AIDS and Behavior, 18*(1), 1–9.

Horvath, K. J., Iantaffi, A., Swinburne-Romine, R., & Bockting, W. (2014). A comparison of mental health, substance use, and sexual risk behaviors between rural and non-rural transgender persons. *Journal of Homosexuality, 61*, 1117–1130.

Human Rights Campaign. (n.d.). *Faith positions*. Retrieved from http://www.hrc.org/resources/faith-positions

Institute of Medicine. (2011). *The health of lesbian, gay, bisexual, and transgender people: Building a foundation for better understanding*. Washington, DC: National Academies Press.

Joint Commission. (2010). *The Joint Commission: Advancing effective communication, cultural competence, and patient-and family-centered care: A roadmap for hospitals*. Oakbrook Terrace, IL: Author.

Kosmin, B. A., Keysar, A., Cragun, R., & Navarro-Rivera, J. (2009). *American nones: The profile of the no religion population, a report based on the American religious identification survey 2008*. Hartford, CT: Trinity College.

Krehely, J. (2009, December 21). *How to close the LGBT health disparities gap*. The Center for American Progress. Retrieved from https://www.americanprogress.org/issues/lgbt/report/2009/12/21/7048/how-to-close-the-lgbt-health-disparities-gap/

Lambda Legal. (2010). *When health care isn't caring: Lambda Legal's survey of discrimination Against LGBT people and people with HIV*. Retrieved from www.lambdalegal.org/health-care-report

Meyer, I. H. (2003). Prejudice, social stress, and mental health in lesbian, gay, and bisexual populations: Conceptual issues and research evidence. *Psychological Bulletin, 129*, 674–697.

McClain, Z., Hawkins, L. A., & Yehia, B. R. (2016). Creating welcoming spaces for lesbian, gay, bisexual, and transgender (LGBT) patients: An evaluation of the healthcare environment. *Journal of Homosexuality, 63*(3), 387–393.

Mosher, W. D., Chandra, A., & Jones, J., (2005). *Sexual behavior and selected health measures: Men and women 15–44 years of age, United States, 2002*. Advance Data from Vital and Health Statistics 362. Hyattsville, MD: National Center for Health Statistics.

Mulé, N. J., Ross, L. E., Deeprose, B., Jackson, B. E., Daley, A., Travers, A., & Moore, D. (2009). Promoting LGBT health and wellbeing through inclusive policy development. *International Journal for Equity in Health, 8*(1), 1–11.

Murphy, C. (2015). *Lesbian, gay and bisexual Americans differ from general public in their religious affiliations*. Pew Research Center. Retrieved from http://www.pewresearch.org/fact-tank/2015/05/26/lesbian-gay-and-bisexual-americans-differ-from-general-public-in-their-religious-affiliations/

Murphy, D. A., Austin, E. L., & Greenwell, L. (2006). Correlates of HIV-related stigma among HIV-positive mothers and their uninfected adolescent children. *Women and Health, 44*, 19–42. doi:10.1300/J013v44n03_02.

National Association of Social Workers. (2005). *Policy statement: Lesbian, gay, and bisexual issues.* Retrieved from http://www.socialworkers.org/da/da2005/policies0505/documents/lgbissues

Nyitray, A., Corran, R., Altman, K., Chikani, V., & Negrón, E. V. (2006). *Tobacco use and interventions among Arizona lesbian, gay, bisexual and transgender people.* Phoenix, AZ: Arizona Department of Health Services. Retrieved from http://www.lgbttobacco.org/files/Arizona_smoking_lgbt_report.pdf

Obedin-Maliver, J., Goldsmith, E. S., Stewart, L., White, W., Tran, E., Brenman, S., . . . Lunn, M. R. (2011). Lesbian, gay, bisexual, and transgender–related content in undergraduate medical education. *JAMA, 306*(9), 971–977.

Poteat, T. (2012). *Top 10 things lesbians should discuss with their healthcare provider.* Gay and Lesbian Medical Association. Retrieved from http://www.glma.org/_data/n_0001/resources/live/Top%2010%20forlesbians.pdf

Rapp, C. A., Saleebey, D., & Sullivan, W. P. (2005). The future of strengths-based social work. *Advances in Social Work, 6*(1), 79–90.

Russ, T. C., Stamatakis, E., Hamer, M., Starr, J. M., Kivimäki, M., & Batty, G. D. (2012). Association between psychological distress and mortality: Individual participant pooled analysis of 10 prospective cohort studies. *BMJ, 345*, e4933.

Russell, S.T. (2005). Beyond risk: Resilience in the lives of sexual minority youth. *Journal of Gay and Lesbian Issues in Education, 2*(3), 5–18.

Ryan, C., Russell, S. T., Huebner, D., Diaz, R., & Sanchez, J. (2010). Family acceptance in adolescence and the health of LGBT young adults. *Journal of Child and Adolescent Psychiatric Nursing, 23*(4), 205–213. doi:10.1111/j.1744-6171.2010.00246x

Short, K. (2012). *The research supplemental poverty measure: 2011.* Current Population Reports. Washington, DC: US Census Bureau.

Smith, D. M., & Mathews, W. C. (2007). Physicians' attitudes toward homosexuality and HIV: Survey of a California medical society-revisited (PATHH-II). *Journal of Homosexuality, 52*(3–4), 1–9.

Smith, T. B., McCullough, M. E., & Poll, J. (2003). Religiousness and depression: Evidence for a main effect and the moderating influence of stressful life events. *Psychological Bulletin, 129*(4), 614–636.

Soulforce. (n.d.). *What we do.* Retrieved from http://www.soulforce.org/#!what-we-do/clm2

Stall, R., Friedman, M., & Catania, J. A. (2008). Interacting epidemics and gay men's health: A theory of syndemic production among urban gay men. In R. J. Wolitski, R. Stall, & R. O. Valdiserri (Eds.), *Unequal opportunity: Health disparities affecting gay and bisexual men in the United States,* (pp. 251–274). New York: Oxford University Press.

Stolzer, R. L. (2009). Violence against transgender people: A review of United States data. *Aggression and Violent Behavior, 14*(3), 170–179.

Substance Abuse and Mental Health Services Administration. (2012), *Top health issues for LGBT populations information & resource kit.* HHS Publication No. 12-4684. Rockville, MD: Author.

Tan, A. M. (2014). Understanding the tension: Christian practitioner perspectives on working with LGBT clients. In A. B. Dessell & R. M. Bolen (Eds.), *Conservative Christian beliefs and sexual orientation in social work: Privilege, oppression, and the pursuit of human rights* (pp. 273–287). Alexandria, VA: CSWE Press.

US Census Bureau. (2013). *Frequently asked questions about same-sex couple households.* Retrieved from http://www.census.gov/hhes/samesex/files/SScplfactsheet_final.pdf

Valdiserri, R. O. (2002). HIV/AIDS stigma: An impediment to public health. *American Journal of Public Health, 92*, 341–342.

VanKim, N. A. & Padilla, J. L. (2010). *New Mexico's progress in collecting lesbian, gay, bisexual, and transgender health data and its implications for addressing health disparities.* Albuquerque: New Mexico Department of Health, Chronic Disease Prevention and Control Bureau.

Vaughan, M. D., & Rodriguez, E. M. (2014). LGBT strengths: Incorporating positive psychology into theory, research, training, and practice. *Psychology of Sexual Orientation and Gender Diversity, 1*(4), 325–334.

Wichstrom, L. (2006). Sexual orientation as a risk factor for bulimic symptoms. *International Journal of Eating Disorders 39*, 448–453.

Williams, D. R., Costa, M. V., Odunlami, A. O., & Mohammed, S.A. (2008). Moving upstream: How interventions that address the social determinants of health can improve health and reduce disparities. *Journal of Public Health Management Practice, 14,* S8–S17.

Winn, R. J. (2012). *Ten things bisexuals should discuss with their healthcare provider.* Gay and Lesbian Medical Association.

Wolitski, R. J., & Fenton, K. A. (2011). Sexual health, HIV, and sexually transmitted infections among gay, bisexual, and other men who have sex with men in the United States. *AIDS and Behavior, 15*(1), 9–17.

World Health Organization. (2003). *WHO definition of health.* Retrieved from http://www.who.int/about/definition/en/print.html

World Health Organization. (2006). *Constitution of the World Health Organization.* Retrieved from www.who.int/govemance/eb/who_constitution_en.pdf

World Health Organization. (2010). *Hepatitis: Frequently asked questions.* Retrieved from http://www.who.int/csr/disease/hepatitis/world_hepatitis_day/question_answer/en/

Wrathall, J. D. (2000). Reading the silences around sexuality. In K. Peiss (Ed.), *Major problems in the history of American sexuality* (pp. 16–24). New York: Houghton Mifflin.

CHAPTER 21

LGBTQ PEOPLE OF COLOR WITH MENTAL HEALTH CONDITIONS

Considering Intersectionalities

Lynn C. Holley and De'Shay Thomas

INTRODUCTION

Reporting that one has experienced racism and/or heterosexism has been found to be associated with negative psychological and physical health outcomes (Assari, Watkins, & Caldwell, 2015; Balsam, Molina, Beadnell, Simoni, & Walters, 2011; Boyle & Omoto, 2014; Denton, Rostosky, & Danner, 2014; Pascoe & Richman, 2009; Schmitt, Branscombe, Postmes, & Garcia, 2014; Szymanski & Henrichs-Beck, 2014; Velez, Moradi, & DeBlaere, 2015; Williams, Neighbors, & Jackson, 2008). Therefore, it is important to consider the experiences of lesbian, gay, bisexual, transgender, and queer/questioning (LGBTQ) people of color with mental health conditions. Informed by an intersectionality perspective, the focus of this chapter is to understand the experiences that LGBTQ people of color may have with heterosexism, racism, and mental illness discrimination and to consider the implications of these experiences for social work practice.

We first describe an *intersectionality* perspective and the concept of *microaggressions*. Unfortunately, the knowledge base about mental illness discrimination is largely separate from research about heterosexism and racism. We therefore present literature about heterosexism and racism experienced by LGBTQ people of color, followed by examining mental illness discrimination, and include the few studies that have considered people who are LGBTQ or people of color. We then present an overview of research about mental illness, heterosexist, and racist discrimination within mental health treatment settings. We conclude with implications for working with LGBTQ people of color who are living with mental health conditions.

Several issues related to terminology need to be clarified. Throughout this chapter, we use terms such as LGT, LGB, Asian Americans, and people of color depending on the populations that were in included in the respective studies. This does not suggest that there are no differences within these categories (e.g., that lesbian, gay, and transgender individuals or Japanese Americans and Chinese Americans have identical experiences). Moreover, we use the term *mental health conditions* rather than *mental illnesses* for two primary reasons. First, we recognize that people experience depression, anxiety, and other negative mental health outcomes that do not meet the socially constructed criteria for mental illnesses. Second, some people with conditions that professionals label as mental illnesses do not consider themselves to have an illness (e.g., http://www.intervoiceonline.org). Finally, some authors use the term *microaggressions* to describe the types of discrimination that are likely to occur today; we use these terms when present in the literature. Sue (2010) defined microaggressions as "brief, everyday exchanges that send denigrating messages to certain individuals because of their group membership" (p. 24). He described three categories of microaggressions. One type is a *microassault*, which is an often conscious, overt, blatantly derogatory comment or other behavior. The second type is a *microinsult*, when a person makes comments or engages in other behaviors that are demeaning to people based on their identity group membership. *Microinvalidations* occur when people's behaviors indicate that they do not consider the perspectives or experiences of members of the targeted identity group to be valuable. Persons engaging in microinsults and microinvalidations may not be aware that they are being discriminatory.

AN INTERSECTIONALITY PERSPECTIVE

In the United States—as well as in other nations—people who are members of certain identity groups have less access to power. These less powerful groups include LGBTQ people, people of color, persons with mental health conditions or physical disabilities, women, and others. Members of these groups experience micro-level prejudice and discrimination in addition to being subject to unfair social structures that may limit their opportunities. In contrast, members of other identity groups such as cisgender heterosexuals, Whites, people without mental health conditions or physical disabilities, and men experience privilege in relation to these marginalized groups.

An intersectionality perspective[1] recognizes that everyone has multiple identities simultaneously, some of which lead to disadvantage and discrimination and some of which offer relative advantages and privileges (Bowleg, 2008; Cole, 2009). Looking at identities separately (e.g., considering only LGBTQ identities) gives an incomplete picture of people's lives because individuals' experiences are contingent on their multiple identities (Bowleg, 2008; Cole, 2009; Mehrotra, 2010; Warner, 2008). These identities may be fluid and change over time and in different contexts (Hulko, 2009; Mehrotra, 2010; Warner, 2008). There are both similarities and differences

1. What is now called an intersectionality perspective arose from the experiences of African American women (e.g., Beale, 1970; Combahee River Collective, 1983; Crenshaw, 1989, 1991; Hill Collins, 1990), including lesbians, who asserted that critical race theory focused on men and feminist theories focused on Whites; their experiences were not addressed.

in how people at different intersections experience oppression and privilege (Cole, 2009), and recognizing similarities can help bridge differences (Warner, 2008), whether in developing change coalitions or in one-on-one situations. In addition, although individuals experience identity-based discrimination at the micro level, these experiences can be understood only by considering the social and historical contexts, including identity groups' access to economic, social, and political resources and power (Bowleg, 2008; Cho, Crenshaw, & McCall, 2013; Cole, 2009; Hulko, 2009; Mehrotra, 2010). Systems of oppression cannot be ranked (Bowleg, 2008); for example, we cannot say that heterosexism is worse than racism or vice versa. Instead, we focus on the interconnectedness of multiple forms of oppression. Finally, rather than seeking only to understand people's experiences or helping people deal with discrimination, the purpose of an intersectionality analysis is to achieve social justice for members of oppressed identity groups (Cho et al., 2013; Mehrotra, 2010).

In considering discrimination, an intersectionality perspective helps to understand that, for example, African American cisgender lesbians with mental health conditions do not simply experience racism, sexism, heterosexism, and mental illness discrimination. Rather, their experiences with these forms of discrimination are contingent (or interdependent) on their intersection of identities. Their experiences with heterosexism, for example, may be different from those of White cisgender lesbians without mental health conditions. In this same example, if these women are wealthy, Christian, US-born citizens without physical or intellectual disabilities then these identities will provide access to privileges and influence their experiences with and responses to heterosexism.

LGBTQ COMMUNITIES OF COLOR: EXPERIENCES WITH RACISM AND HETEROSEXISM

Experiencing heterosexist discrimination has been associated with negative mental health outcomes (Mays & Cochran, 2001; Szymanski & Henrichs-Beck, 2014), as has experiencing racist discrimination (US Department of Health and Human Services, 2001; Williams & Mohammed, 2009). Considering intersecting identities, mental health concerns such as anxiety, depression, suicidal ideation, and severe psychological distress are common among LGBTQ people of color (Balsam et al., 2011; Bazargan & Galvan, 2012; Bostwick, Boyd, Hughes, West, & McCabe, 2014; Diaz, Ayala, Bein, Henne, & Marin, 2001; Schmitt et al., 2014; Whitbeck, McMorris, Hoyt, Stubbern, & Lafromboise, 2002). Bostwick et al. (2014) examined the relationship between discrimination and the intersections of sexual orientation, race/ethnicity, and gender among a sample of 577 lesbian, gay, and bisexual adults. They found that participants who experienced two forms of discrimination, such as both heterosexism and racism, were more likely to report negative mental health outcomes compared to participants who reported only one form of discrimination.

INTRAGROUP DISCRIMINATION

Similar to their experiences in the larger society, LGBTQ people of color may experience heterosexism within their racial and ethnic communities and racism in the larger LGBTQ community (Balsam et al., 2011). Intragroup discrimination, or "the downgrading and discrimination that more privileged group members have toward other, less privileged group members" often leaves LGBTQ people of color feeling excluded and marginalized (Harris, 2009, p. 431).

HETEROSEXISM WITHIN COMMUNITIES OF COLOR

Scholars argue that racial/ethnic intragroup heterosexist discrimination of LGBTQ people is related to conservative value systems (Akerlund & Cheung, 2000; Constantine-Simms, 2001; Harris, 2009). In particular, African American, Latina/o, and Asian American communities are traditionally noted to hold conservative beliefs about family and sexual practices (e.g., heterosexual relationships) that are rooted in religious ideologies and biblical interpretations (Akerlund & Cheung, 2000; Barnes & Meyer, 2012; Constantine-Simms, 2001; Douglas, 1999; Harris, 2009). Catholic and many Protestant Christian religious traditions—common in African American, Latina/o, and some Asian American communities—believe same-sex attraction and sexual practices to be "sinful" and to go against appropriate heterosexual relationships (Akerlund & Cheung, 2000; Douglas, 1999). This antigay religious rhetoric has contributed to the internalization of homophobia and heterosexism (Barnes & Meyer, 2012; Ward, 2005) and results in feelings of guilt and shame due to perceptions that same-sex attraction is deviant (Akerlund & Cheung, 2000; Diaz et al., 2001; Ward, 2005).

LGBTQ people of color who deviate from conservative or heteronormative gender and sexual roles may experience a number of challenges. For instance, African American LGBTQ people often experience rejection from their social support networks such as their nuclear family and religious communities (Graham et al., 2014; Greene, 2000, Ward, 2005), which are known to protect against the negative effects of racist oppression (Graham, 2014; Greene, 2002). Many African Americans believe that homosexuality is a "White problem" and African Americans who identify as LGBTQ are "traitors to their race" (Douglas, 1999; Harris, 2009, p. 235). As a result, LGBTQ people of African descent are more likely to conceal their sexual and gender identities from members of their racial community and depend on institutions (e.g., affirming churches, African American LGBTQ communities, and ballroom culture [Bailey, 2013]) that affirm their intersecting identities as sources of support (Graham, 2014; Greene, 2002).

Likewise, Latina/o sexual minorities may believe their sexual identities are an embarrassment to their families and often leave their families in order to live out their LGBTQ identities (Diaz et al., 2001, Marsiglia, 1998). Latina/o families may uphold strong gender roles where men are expected to be hypermasculine (e.g., *machismo*) and considered superior to women (Estrada, Rigali-Oiler, Arciniega, & Tracey, 2011; Marsiglia, 1998). The cultural expectations of Latina women include being sexually pure and spiritual as well as to marry a "man who is serious" (Marsiglia, 1998, p. 119; also see Bonilla & Porter, 1990; Estrada et al., 2011). Lesbian and gay Latinas/os who do not follow these cultural norms ascribed to women and men (e.g., Latinas who are "masculine," Latinos who are "feminine") may be excluded from their communities (Estrada et al., 2011).

Within Asian American cultures, lesbian and bisexual women report pressure to conform to traditional gender and family norms, experiences of parental conflict, and nonacceptance from their families due to their sexual orientation and gender expression (Chung & Szymanzki, 2006; Sung, Szymanski, & Henrichs-Beck, 2015; Szymanski & Sung, 2010). Similar to African American and Latina/o family expectations, Asian Americans are expected to participate in reproductive roles such as marrying and rearing children out of obligation to further the family lineage (Chung & Szymanzki, 2006). Asian Americans concerned with not following family expectations, coupled with potential familial conflict, may respond by "camouflaging" (i.e., concealing) or avoiding discussions about their sexuality (Sung et al., 2015).

RACISM WITHIN LGBTQ COMMUNITIES

Within the larger society, African American, Asian American, Latina/o, and indigenous people experience microaggressions that portray them as second-class citizens, devalue their racial/ethnic cultures, and assign racial ascriptions about their intellectual ability (Hill, Kim, & Williams, 2010; Sue et al., 2008, 2009). They also experience invisibility in dialogues about race (Sue, Bucceri, Lin, Nadal, & Torino, 2009) and LGBTQ identities (Harper, Jernewall, & Zea, 2004; Sung et al., 2015). African Americans are assumed to possess a criminal status, be intellectually inferior, and have a universal experience (Sue et al., 2008). Asian Americans, on the other hand, are assumed to be intelligent and are assigned a pan-Asian identity (i.e., interethnic differences among Asians Americans are not acknowledged; Sue et al., 2009). Furthermore, Latina/o people are assumed to be immigrants and are seen as not "Real Americans" (Rivera, Forquer, & Rangel, 2010) while indigenous people experience a "collective lack of concern" and misrepresentation in the media (see Hill et al., 2010; Walters, Evans-Campbell, Simoni, Ronquillo, & Bhuyan, 2006). People of color often experience feelings of anger, shame, frustration, and belittlement while also being faced with discrimination such as subtle microaggressions (Hill et al., 2010; Rivera et al., 2010; Sue et al., 2008, 2009).

These racist microaggressions also occur within LGBTQ communities. People of color report experiences of overt racism and of exclusion and invisibility within the broader LGBTQ community (Balsam et al., 2011; Han, 2007; Lehavot, Balsam, & Ibrahim-Wells, 2009). Racist discrimination can take a blatant or more subtle form (Han, 2007; Lehavot et al., 2009). Signs of racism include lack of leadership and inclusion of people of color in predominately White LGBTQ spaces (Han, 2007) and negative stereotypes about certain racial or ethnic groups (Hill et al., 2010; Rivera et al., 2010; Sue et al., 2009; Sue, Nadal, Capodilupo, Lin, Torino, & Rivera, 2008; Sung et al., 2015) that are present in the larger LGBTQ community (Balsam et al., 2011).

MENTAL ILLNESS DISCRIMINATION

As described already, due to experiences with heterosexist and racist discrimination LGBTQ people of color are at risk of having negative mental health outcomes. It is critical that people working with these communities understand mental illness discrimination, another type of discrimination that may negatively affect their lives. An intersectionality perspective helps us to understand that to the extent that LGBTQ people of color have higher rates of negative psychological outcomes, they likely will be disproportionately affected by mental illness discrimination.

Although not commonly viewed as an oppressed identity group, people who are perceived to have mental health conditions meet Sue's (2010) definition of a marginalized group as one that is "confined to existing on the margins of our social, cultural, political, and economic systems" (p. 5) (Gonzales, Davidoff, Nadal, & Yanos, 2015; also see Holley, Stromwall, & Tavassoli [2015] and Young [1998] regarding the definition of an oppressed group).[2] Multiple studies have found that mental illness discrimination is common (Corker et al., 2013; Hansson, Stjernswärd, & Svensson, 2014; Lasalvia et al., 2013). People with mental health conditions report that family and friends who know about their condition avoid them or treat them negatively (Corker et al., 2013; Hamilton et al., 2014; Hansson et al., 2014; Lasalvia et al., 2013; Świtaj et al., 2012), that their experiences are invalidated and they are assumed to be inferior and dangerous (Gonzales et al., 2015), that others convey that having a mental health condition is something to be ashamed of (Gonzales et al., 2015), and that they have trouble finding or maintaining employment because of mental illness discrimination (Corker et al., 2013; Hamilton et al., 2014; Świtaj et al., 2012). Outcomes of mental illness microaggressions may include frustration, alienation, lowered self-esteem, and discontinuing mental health treatment (Gonzales et al., 2015).

In addition to experiencing one-on-one discrimination, people with mental health conditions must deal with pervasive media portrayals that create and perpetuate negative stereotypes (e.g., that they are dangerous) and with laws that limit their civil rights (Corrigan, Markowitz, & Watson, 2004). Use of language provides insight into another source of mental illness discrimination (Holley, Stromwall, & Bashor, 2012). For example, common derogatory use of words such as "crazy," "psycho," and "whacko"; referring to people by their diagnoses (e.g., referring to "schizophrenics" rather than "people with schizophrenia," saying a person "is bipolar" rather than "has bipolar disorder"); and advertisers' use of phrases such as "insane deals" reinforce negative images of people with mental health conditions as unstable, dangerous, and "Other" than normal. These forms of blatant institutional discrimination, combined with the prevalence of overt one-on-one discrimination, are evidence that mental illness discrimination "still is considered to be socially acceptable" (Gonzales et al., 2015, p. 239).

2. We consider people with mental health conditions as a marginalized social group and thus use an anti-oppression framework to understand their experiences. Other theorists in this field use stigma models. For example, see Link and Phelan (2001), Corrigan (2005), and Pescosolido, Martin, Lang, and Olafsdottir (2008).

Family members of LGBTQ people with mental health conditions also may experience mental illness discrimination, sometimes called "stigma by association" (Quinn & Chaudoir, 2009; Schulze & Angermeyer, 2003; van der Sanden, Stutterheim, Pryor, Kok, & Bos, 2014). For example, family members have reported that they were not taken seriously and were avoided, blamed, and accused of being overprotective toward their family member who had a mental health condition (van der Sanden et al., 2014).

MENTAL HEALTH CONDITIONS AND DISCLOSURE/NONDISCLOSURE

The prevalence of mental illness discrimination leads to decisions related to identity management—whether to "come out" as a person with a mental health condition. Practitioners working with LGBTQ people of color with mental health conditions thus need to understand the possible ramifications of disclosure and nondisclosure of having a mental health condition in addition to those related to disclosing sexual orientation and/or gender identities.

In research considering a range of concealable devalued identities (e.g., being lesbian or gay, having a mental health condition), Quinn and Chaudoir (2009) found that anticipating discrimination (when one reveals an identity that is not valued by others) was associated with increased levels of anxiety and depression. In addition, family members of people with a concealable devalued identity also experienced increased anxiety and depression due to anticipating discrimination but not as much as people with the concealable identity. As noted by Quinn and Chaudoir, if one conceals such an identity then access to identity group support is not available; one thus may experience more negative psychological outcomes if this identity is a central aspect of one's self-definition.

Research has found that people with mental health conditions may conceal this identity and hide their symptoms; combined with anticipating discrimination, these behaviors prevented them from seeking help for their mental health conditions (Clement et al., 2015). As with LGBTQ individuals, people with mental health conditions may selectively disclose this identity. One study of 500 people with mental health conditions in the Netherlands found that most participants were out to their parents and partners and were least likely to be out to their acquaintances and colleagues (Bos, Kanner, Muris, Janssen, & Mayer, 2009). Participants who disclosed to parents and partners reported increased support and less discrimination, while those who disclosed to acquaintances and colleagues reported less support and more discrimination (Bos et al., 2009). In addition, the more open participants were about having mental health conditions, the more likely they were to report that experiencing discrimination negatively affected their self-esteem (Bos et al., 2009). We could find no research that examined issues related to disclosure of mental health conditions by LGBTQ people of color. Practitioners also should keep in mind that depending on their symptoms, people with mental health conditions do not always have the choice of whether to conceal this identity (Gonzales et al., 2015; Holley, Tavassoli, & Stromwall, 2016).

MENTAL ILLNESS DISCRIMINATION AND INTERSECTING IDENTITIES

People with mental health conditions who are of color and/or LGB commonly report experiencing mental illness discrimination in addition to racial, heterosexist, and/or other forms of discrimination (Gabbidon et al., 2014; Sanders Thompson, Noel, & Campbell, 2004; Zerger et al., 2014). Those who report experiencing multiple types of discrimination (e.g., both mental illness and heterosexist discrimination) report more anxiety and depression symptoms than those who report only one type of discrimination (Sanders Thompson et al., 2004).

LGBTQ PEOPLE WITH MENTAL HEALTH CONDITIONS

In a study of LGT people with mental health conditions, Kidd, Veltman, Gately, Chan, and Cohen (2011) found that participants experienced both heterosexist/gender identity discrimination and mental illness discrimination, with some study participants reporting more mental illness discrimination than LGT discrimination. Participants in this study said that they were not accepted by LGBT communities due to their mental health condition or by others with mental health conditions due to their LGT status, though fewer lesbians than gay and transgender individuals experienced mental illness discrimination in the LGBT community. Further, each of these identities had led to rejection by some of their families. Participants said they concealed these identities in some contexts to avoid discrimination and that doing so worsened their mental health.

PEOPLE OF COLOR WITH MENTAL HEALTH CONDITIONS

African Americans, Asian Americans, and people of Arabic descent are among the groups that are more likely to report that mental illness prejudice or discrimination is a barrier to seeking mental health treatment (Clement et al., 2015). People of color with mental health conditions who have close connections to their ethnic or national origin groups may isolate themselves from their families due to mental illness prejudice and discrimination within these communities or because their communities do not believe in the Western, medicalized view of mental illness (Zerger et al., 2014). This self-isolation may protect their families from disappointment or worry and help people with mental health conditions to maintain a positive self-image but also may lead to loss of sources of support (Zerger et al., 2014).

African Americans may avoid mental health treatment because having a mental health condition is considered a weakness, it causes associative stigma for their families, and it is important to keep problems within the family (Clement et al., 2015). But a study of older adults found that although African Americans associated more shame with having a mental health condition than did Whites, they nevertheless indicated they had more comfort than Whites about speaking with mental health professionals about these conditions (Jimenez, Bartels, Cardenas, & Alegría, 2013).

Other communities of color also may consider having a mental health condition as causing associative stigma for their families (Clement et al., 2015). Family members of Mexican-origin, Spanish-speaking Latinas/os with mental health conditions may experience shame or embarrassment due to anticipated reactions of family members (Hernandez & Barrio, 2015; also see Jimenez et al., 2013), along with conflicts related to beliefs about whether mental health conditions have spiritual/religious, neurobiological, or both spiritual/religious and neurobiological origins (Marquez & Ramírez García, 2013). But despite the possibility of associative stigma, Jimenez and colleagues found that older Latinas/os were more comfortable than older Whites speaking with mental health professionals.

Asian Americans may hold stronger negative attitudes toward people with mental health conditions than do Whites (Cheng, 2015). Asian Americans in one study reported a desire for greater social distance from and more anger toward people with depression; they also blamed them for their condition and were less willing to rent to or hire a person with depression (Cheng, 2015). Compared to White older adults, Asian American older adults report more embarrassment and shame associated with having a mental health condition (Jimenez et al., 2013). In addition, Asian Americans and Pacific Islanders who hold traditional Asian values may perceive that their families' reputations will be harmed if other community members learn they have a mental health condition; they thus may avoid participating in mental health treatment (Choi & Miller, 2014).

We are not aware of studies focusing on mental illness discrimination within indigenous communities. According to Thompson, Walker, and Silk-Walker (1993, as cited in Abdulla & Brown, 2011) some indigenous communities do not discriminate against people with mental health conditions; others discriminate against people with some, but not all, conditions; and others discriminate against people with any mental health condition.

DISCRIMINATION IN MENTAL HEALTH TREATMENT SETTINGS

Mental health providers and organizations are not immune from internalizing society's prejudices and thus exhibiting heterosexist, racist, and mental illness microaggressions and other forms of discrimination. With few exceptions, studies about discrimination in mental health treatment settings have examined mental illness, heterosexist, or racist discrimination rather than the presence of multiple forms of discrimination. In this section we describe findings from the literature in these primarily separate areas of research, specifying when a study considered the intersection of two or more identities.

MENTAL ILLNESS DISCRIMINATION

People with mental health conditions commonly report experiencing discrimination from service providers (e.g., Hansson et al., 2014); one study found that the most common source of mental illness microaggressions was in mental health treatment settings (Gonzales et al., 2015). Mental health service participants have reported that providers treat them like children (Angell, Cooke, & Kovac, 2005; Holley et al., 2016), assume they are not intelligent (Gonzales et al., 2015; Holley et al., 2016), have low expectations for their recovery (Angell et al., 2005; Charles, 2013; Schulze & Angermeyer, 2003), minimize their experiences (Gonzales et al., 2015), exhibit irritation or annoyance toward them (Charles, 2013), view them as diagnoses rather than as complex individuals (Holley et al., 2016), and do not listen to their perspectives—including their treatment preferences (Holley et al., 2016).

Experiencing these behaviors from providers is likely to negatively affect treatment. Service participants have reported having a "detached relationship" with providers when the provider was viewed as "indifferent, hostile, or unwilling to understand the person and her or his experiences" (Eriksen, Arman, Davidson, Sundfør, & Karlsson, 2014, p. 113). This description of the provider is consistent with literature about microaggressions. In their study of mental illness microaggressions, Gonzales et al. (2015) found that when service participants were treated as if their experiences and perspectives were not important they felt "a lack of control over their own treatment and recovery" (p. 238).

HETEROSEXIST AND RACIST DISCRIMINATION

LGBT people of color with mental health conditions are more likely than heterosexual Whites to report dissatisfaction with services of mental health treatment programs (Avery, Hellman, & Sudderth, 2001). Delphin-Rittmon et al.'s (2013) study utilizing 22 focus groups that included 210 mental health service participants, including people of color and LGBTQI (I is the abbreviation for intersex) individuals, found that shared provider/client identities aided in building trust, though providers who were not members of the same identity group also could be effective if they conveyed an understanding of clients' identity-related experiences; participants did not disclose important aspects of their lives—including issues related to their LGBTQI identities—to their providers, often because of a lack of trust or because they did not think the provider would understand; and they felt that providers stereotyped them and treated them dismissively or with disrespect.

All participants in Kidd et al.'s (2011) study of LGT mental health service participants reported experiencing discrimination by mental health providers due to their LGT status. For example, they said that providers ignored their sexual orientation (also see Holley et al., 2016), assumed their mental health conditions were related to these identities, and did not allow displays of affection.

People of color report experiencing various forms of racial discrimination when seeking or receiving mental health treatment and services. Some service participants and their families may view the lack of providers of color or of services grounded in their cultures as evidence of subtle racist discrimination (Holley et al., 2016). African American service participants have described the system as a "White system" with primarily middle- and upper-class White providers who do not understand their problems (Newhill & Harris, 2007). The focus on medications as a primary intervention may be viewed by African Americans as evidence of White bias, in that they may prefer counseling instead of medications because "wellness" means dealing with issues in counseling rather than masking problems with medication (Jones, Hopson, Warner, Hardiman, & James, 2015). African American service participants have reported not having a voice in their treatment (Newhill & Harris, 2007), that providers lack empathy and treat them in a "rushed and impersonal manner" (Newhill & Harris, 2007, p. 119), and that providers stereotype them by assuming that all Black people are the same (Jones et al., 2015). African American women have reported that providers avoided discussing race or gender issues and did not understand that race was an important context of their mental health and substance use issues, and they thought their mental health problems were not taken seriously leading some to falsely claim they were considering suicide in order to get treatment they knew they needed (Jones et al., 2015).

RECOMMENDATIONS FOR PRACTICE

We do not know of any outcome-based research that addresses practice with LGBTQ people of color with mental health conditions. However, an intersectionality perspective informed by research about microaggressions and other forms of discrimination that LGBTQ people of color with mental health conditions may experience suggests that five major areas should be considered for effective social work practice with people living at these intersections of identities: (a) knowledge about experiences related to intersecting identities, (b) disclosure decisions, (c) reducing internalized oppression, (d) social workers' awareness of their own intersecting identities, and (e) addressing microaggressions within mental health services organizations. Woven throughout these five areas is attention to working toward macro-level change.

Before discussing these areas, it is important to note several limitations in the content of this chapter. First, we have focused on possible negative experiences and outcomes of structural oppression. Research is needed to learn about factors that promote resiliency and healthy development in the face of oppression and on ways to reduce oppression. Second, much less research is available about the experiences of transgender individuals, so the following implications may not be as applicable in practice with members of this identity group. Third, we have limited our focus to LGBTQ people of color with mental health conditions, with some attention to religious group membership. Practitioners also need to consider the importance of additional intersecting identities, perhaps especially those related to social class; physical (dis)ability; immigrant, citizenship, and national origin identities; and age/cohort identities in working with LGBTQ people of color with mental health conditions. Finally, we think that some of the content of this chapter may be useful in understanding the experiences of those living at other intersections. For example, White LGBTQ individuals with mental health conditions who are members of families or communities that espouse antigay and gender-restrictive religious rhetoric or in which mental illness discrimination is prevalent may experience heterosexism and mental illness discrimination in similar ways to LGBTQ people of color with mental health conditions. But these experiences will not be identical for those who are White. For example, access to White privilege means that they do not require family and community support to offer protection from the harmful effects of racism, they are more likely to find antiheterosexism support in primarily White LGBTQ spaces, and mental health treatment programs may be more likely to offer interventions grounded in White culture. The following narrative examines the five key areas to consider for effective practice with LGBTQ people of color with mental health conditions: knowledge about experiences related to intersecting identities, disclosure decisions, reducing internalized oppression, social workers' awareness of their own intersecting identities, and addressing microaggressions within mental health services organizations.

EXPERIENCES RELATED TO INTERSECTING IDENTITIES

Social workers should recognize that LGBTQ people of color with mental health conditions have unique identity-related life experiences, including those related to systemic oppression and possible sources of support. For example, experiences of Chinese American transgender heterosexual women living with anxiety will be very different from those of Vietnamese American cisgender gay men living with depression. Though not discussing mental health conditions, Bowleg's (2008) explanation of the importance of considering intersections is useful for practitioners:

> Black lesbian poet Audre Lorde's (1984) description of "... constantly being encouraged to pluck out some aspect of myself and present this as the meaningful whole, eclipsing and denying the other parts of the self" (p. 120) highlights eloquently the complexity of intersectionality. For Lorde and other Black lesbians, one's identity as a Black lesbian is the meaningful whole; it is not a mere addition of ethnicity, sexual orientation, and sex/gender. (p. 312)

Informed by an intersectionality perspective with attention to microaggressions, culturally grounded practice with members of these communities requires knowledge about cultures and experiences related to identity intersections of these identities and attention to social change efforts involving these identities.

Thus social workers need to seek out knowledge about the lives of the groups with whom they practice. In addition to staying up to date on research reported in peer-reviewed journal articles and other scholarly sources, developing connections with clients' identity communities can help in this area (Delphin-Rittmon et al., 2013). Through extensive research about and interactions within identity communities, providers can learn about shared experiences and variations that are present within communities—critical to correct misinformation, prevent stereotyping, and develop skills in avoiding unconscious microaggressions. As noted by Gonzales et al. (2015) in discussing mental illness microaggressions, providers who engage in microaggressions likely will seriously harm their relationships with clients, thus decreasing the effectiveness of interventions and presenting a "barrier to recovery" (p. 239).

Social workers need to understand the personal perspectives and the meaning of intersecting identities because identity-specific experiences might be related to clients' stress (Jones et al., 2015). To do this, social workers need to be trained in ways to ask identity-related questions respectfully (see Kidd et al., 2011) as a way to allow clients to talk about experiences related to their mental health conditions within their racial, ethnic, and LGBTQ communities; experiences related to their sexual orientation within their racial, ethnic, and mental health communities; and experiences related to their sexual orientation within their racial, ethnic, and mental health communities in addition to experiences with intersecting identities in these communities and the larger society.

Such dialogue will serve many purposes. It will allow social workers to learn and use clients' language in discussing their mental health conditions, which has been found to be a nonstigmatizing approach (Clements et al., 2015). In addition, Kidd et al. (2011) reported:

> when providers were accepting, validating, and understanding [of LGT identities], participants described this as being a core aspect of effective clinical intervention. It resulted in their feeling more engaged in treatment, experiencing direct benefits in terms of their emotional state, and feeling like a "real person" (p. 33).

We assume that similar outcomes will occur when providers are affirming toward racial, ethnic, and mental health condition identities and conscious of microaggressions people may have experienced related to these identities. This dialogue also may reveal strengths such as effective strategies they have used to cope with negative experiences and sources of support for their intersecting identities, in addition to identifying areas that require family, community, institutional, and societal-level interventions. Further, it will allow program participants to tell practitioners about their achievements in multiple areas, preventing practitioners from assuming that people living at these intersections continually "suffer" and lack the ability to stand strong in the face of oppression.

Note that while an intersectionality framework focuses on experiences with oppression and privilege, attention to *culture* related to sexual orientation, gender identity/expression, race, ethnicity, gender, social class, religion, and other identities should not be considered irrelevant, either in assessment or in identifying individual, family, community, organizational, and social/cultural level interventions. An effective practitioner will work with people to identify relevant aspects of their intersecting identity groups' cultures that might provide tools and support for resisting oppression and working to change oppressive structures and practices.

DISCLOSURE DECISIONS

Based on knowledge about discrimination that may be experienced by LGBTQ people of color with mental health conditions and on an individual's unique experiences, providers can play critical roles in helping people decide whether to disclose their mental health conditions (Clement et al., 2015; Gonzales et al., 2015) as well as other identities. To support informed decision-making, providers need to be familiar with possible advantages and disadvantages of disclosure and concealment. For example, advantages of disclosing that one has a mental health condition might include access to support from others with mental health conditions (Quinn & Chaudoir, 2009) or from some parents and partners (Bos et al., 2009). On the other hand, concealing this identity might result in decreased discrimination for people with mental health conditions (Bos et al., 2009) and their families (Choi & Miller, 2014; Clement et al., 2015; Hernandez & Barrio, 2015; Jimenez et al., 2013). With an understanding of individuals' unique social positions and skills, providers can assist in identifying possible sources of support if they choose to disclose their mental health condition within their racial, ethnic, and/or LGBTQ communities, to close family and friends, in their employment or educational setting, and/or in other important venues.

Beyond considering possible effects on individuals who disclose or conceal their identities, social workers may want to discuss possible macro-level effects of disclosure. At least two issues need to be considered in this area. First, if people stay "in the closet" about their oppressed identities, identity group members and the larger society are prevented from seeing members of these groups as "normal" and opportunities to decrease oppression are reduced. Second, others who are members of oppressed identity groups are prevented from having "out" role models who could potentially reduce internalized oppression.

REDUCING INTERNALIZED OPPRESSION

Whether or not people voluntarily disclose their mental health conditions, providers may need to focus on reducing internalized mental illness oppression, including by "normalizing" this identity (Clement et al., 2015). Practitioners can assist individuals in developing responses to mental illness and other forms of discrimination, including identifying opportunities for involvement in education, policy advocacy, and other social change efforts. These efforts might be of particular importance when working with African Americans whose racial community may consider a mental health condition to be a sign of weakness (Clement et al., 2015); Asian Americans whose ethnic communities might believe mental health conditions to be the fault of individuals (Cheng, 2015); African Americans, Asian Americans, or Mexican-origin Spanish-speaking Latinas/os whose mental health condition might bring shame to their families (Choi & Miller, 2014; Clement et al., 2015; Hernandez & Barrio, 2015; Jimenez et al., 2013); those who are not accepted by LGBTQ communities because of their mental health conditions (Kidd et al., 2011; or with those who have experienced mental illness discrimination by other treatment providers or organizations (Gonzalez et al., 2015; Holley et al., 2016).

Practitioners also should be prepared to help reduce internalized heterosexism, particularly among African Americans, Asian Americans, and Latinas/os whose communities accept conservative beliefs about family and sexual practices (Akerlund & Cheung, 2000; Barnes & Meyer, 2012; Constantine-Simms, 2001; Douglas, 1999; Harris, 2009) or among those who have experienced heterosexism perpetrated by mental health professionals or others with mental health conditions (Kidd et al., 2011). Practitioners should not assume, though, that LGBTQ people have color have internalized their racial or ethnic community's heterosexism, as LGBT people of color in Balsam et al.'s (2011) study did not do so.

Practitioners also should be prepared to support people of color if they have internalized racism due to the prevalence of racism with LGBTQ communities (Balsam et al., 2011; Han, 2007; Lehavot et al., 2009), the larger society (Hill et al., 2010; Sue et al., 2008, 2009), and in mental health treatment programs (Delphin-Rittmon et al., 2013; Holley et al., 2016; Jones et al., 2015; Newhill & Harris, 2007). If they have been rejected by their families of origin and religious communities because of heterosexism (Graham et al., 2014; Greene, 2000, Ward, 2005), they may have lost an important source of support for dealing with racist discrimination (Graham, 2014; Greene, 2002).

To support people in reducing internalized oppression related to intersecting identities, it is critical that providers affirm their identities and assist in identifying other sources of support—from other LGBTQ people with mental health conditions who are members of their specific racial or ethnic communities if possible, and identify avenues for educating families and communities about LGBTQ issues and mental health conditions. Developing partnerships among groups focusing on issues related to LGBTQ people, people of color, and people with mental health conditions might be useful. (See Kidd et al. [2011] regarding the need for LGBT-focused groups to include people with mental health conditions and vice versa.)

SOCIAL WORKERS' AWARENESS OF THEIR OWN INTERSECTING IDENTITIES

In addition to considering the experiences of their clients, social workers need to be conscious of ways in which their own intersecting identities may contribute to covert and overt bias against LGBTQ people of color with mental health conditions. Even if a practitioner lives at the intersection of multiple oppressed identities, completing a baccalaureate, master's, or doctoral education brings social class privileges that may affect one's ability to build relationships with some clients. In addition, regardless of their personal identities, educational content may better prepare graduates to practice with White heterosexuals (see Newhill & Harris, 2007); graduates might accept White, male, heterosexual values and perspectives about the people with whom they practice and about appropriate interventions. For example, education might lead social workers to place more focus on the person rather than the environment in assessing the sources of clients' problems, to ignore the roles of systems of oppression and privilege that affect people's lives, to place higher value on the expertise of professionals than on the perspectives of clients, to implement "evidence-based" interventions that have not been evaluated for use with communities of color and/or LGBTQ communities, and to select only individual-level interventions. Effective, anti-oppressive practice requires awareness of one's own privileged identities and constant reflection on ways in which one's intersecting identities effect personal biases, relationships, and practice in both positive and negative ways.

MICROAGGRESSIONS WITHIN MENTAL HEALTH SERVICES ORGANIZATIONS

In addition to focusing on individual-level bias and behaviors of service providers, social workers need to evaluate their workplaces for the presence of organizational-level microaggressions toward LGBTQ people of color with mental health conditions. An assessment would include attention to many areas. For example, does leadership include people who are out as LGBTQ people of color with mental health conditions? Do training and supervision promote staff self-awareness and help them avoid racist, heterosexist, and mental illness microaggressions? Does the organization include peer-led programs (i.e., programs led by people who identify as having mental health conditions) staffed by LGBTQ people of color? If so, are leaders of these groups treated as experts?

Organizations serving LGBTQ people of color with mental health conditions also need to assess whether their programs are grounded in the values and experiences of the specific communities they serve, as not doing so may be evidence of microinvalidation. It is beyond the scope of this chapter to describe the characteristics of providers, interventions, or organizations that may be preferred by members of various racial, ethnic, sexual orientation, gender identity or expression, or mental health condition identity groups. With conscious efforts to learn about these communities (see "Experiences Related to Intersecting Identities" section) and collaboration with peer-run, LGBTQ, and racial- and ethnic-focused community groups, organizations can develop programs and initiatives that have the potential to lead to change at multiple levels.

One element of culturally grounded programming is to work with families (origin and/or choice) of LGBTQ people of color with mental health conditions—not only to help them support their family members—but also to provide support when families experience discrimination due to their loved one's identity or mental health status. Psychoeducational family interventions using an anti-mental illness discrimination approach (see Hansson et al., 2014) are recommended for helping families understand mental health conditions, as are interventions focusing on emotional support and coping strategies (van der Sanden et al., 2014), though further research is needed to learn the most effective interventions for families of LGBTQ individuals from specific communities of color. For example, it is possible that a psychoeducational family intervention that focuses solely on educating family members about the Western (i.e., White professional) understanding of the causes of and treatment for mental health conditions without an equal focus on understanding families' perspectives may be experienced as a microinvalidation.

Finally, recognizing that macro changes are required to reduce experiences with discrimination that occurs at the micro level (Bowleg, 2008; Cho et al., 2013; Cole, 2009; Hulko, 2009; Mehrotra, 2010), organizations that serve LGBTQ people of color with mental health conditions need to work with service participants, community organizations, policymakers, media, and others to effect change that will benefit LGBTQ people of color with mental health conditions and their families. That is, rather than helping people only to resist the negative effects of discrimination, we need to work to reduce oppression from multiple interacting sources—from individuals and families, LGBTQ and racial/ethnic communities, and institutions such as media, law enforcement and legal systems, religious institutions, and education and employment. Based on the similarities across oppression related to race, ethnicity, sexual orientation, gender identity/expression, and mental health condition status, intergroup coalitions may be effective in working toward social change that creates equality for LGBTQ people of color with mental health conditions.

CONCLUSION

In summary, effective practice with LGBTQ people of color with mental health conditions requires recognition that people living at different intersections have unique identity-related life experiences, including those related to systemic oppression and privilege. Thus social workers and other mental health service providers must constantly strive to learn more about the lives of those with whom they practice, increase awareness of their own privileges and unconscious participation in creating and recreating oppression, work to build anti-oppressive organizations, and partner with individuals, families, and communities to identify sources of discrimination and support and develop interventions to effect change at multiple levels.

REFERENCES

Akerlund, M., & Cheung, M. (2000). Teaching beyond the deficit model: Gay and lesbian issues among African Americans, Latinos, and Asian Americans. *Journal of Social Work Education, 36*(2), 279–292.

Angell, B., Cooke, A., & Kovac, K. (2005). First person accounts of stigma. In P. W. Corrigan (Ed.), *On the stigma of mental illness: Practical strategies for research and social change* (pp. 69–98). Washington, DC: American Psychological Association.

Assari, S., Watkins, D. C., & Caldwell, C. H. (2015). Race attribution modifies the association between daily discrimination and major depressive disorder among Blacks: The role of gender and ethnicity. *Journal of Racial and Ethnic Health Disparities, 2*, 200–210. doi:10.1007/s40615-014-0064-9

Avery, A. M., Hellman, R. E., & Sudderth, L. K. (2001). Satisfaction with mental health services among sexual minorities with major mental illness. *American Journal of Public Health, 91*(6), 990–991.

Bailey, M. M. (2013). *Butch queens up in pumps: Gender, performance, and ballroom culture in Detroit.* Ann Arbor: University of Michigan Press.

Balsam, K. F., Molina, Y., Beadnell, B., Simoni, J., & Walters, K. (2011). Measuring multiple minority stress: The LGBT People of Color Microaggressions Scale. *Cultural Diversity and Ethnic Minority Psychology, 17*(2), 163–174.

Barnes, D. M., & Meyer, I. H. (2012). Religious affiliation, internalized homophobia, and mental health in lesbians, gay men, and bisexuals. *American Journal of Orthopsychiatry, 82*(4), 505–515.

Bazargan, M., & Galvan, F. (2012). Perceived discrimination and depression among low-income Latina male-to-female transgender women. *BMC Public Health, 12*(663), 1–8.

Beale, F. (1970). Double jeopardy: To be Black and female. In T. C. Bambara (Ed.), *The Black woman: An anthology* (pp. 90–100). New York: Signet.

Bonilla, L., & Porter, J. (1990). A comparison of Latino, Black, and non-Hispanic White attitudes toward homosexuality. *Hispanic Journal of Behavioral Sciences, 12*(4), 437–452.

Bos, A. E. R., Kanner, D., Muris, P., Janssen, B., & Mayer, B. (2009). Mental illness stigma and disclosure: Consequences of coming out of the closet. *Issus in Mental Health Nursing, 30*, 509–513. doi:10.1080/01612840802601382

Bostwick, W. B., Boyd, C. J., Hughes, T. L., West, B. T., & McCabe, S. E. (2014). Discrimination and mental health among lesbian, gay, and bisexual adults in the United States. *American Journal of Orthopsychiatry, 84*(1), 35–45.

Bowleg, L. (2008). When Black + lesbian + woman ≠ Black lesbian woman: The methodological challenges of qualitative and quantitative intersectionality research. *Sex Roles, 59*, 312–325. doi:10.1007/s11199-008-9400-z

Boyle, S. C., & Omoto, A. M. (2014). Lesbian community oughts and ideals: Normative fit, depression, and anxiety among young sexual minority women. *Psychology of Women Quarterly, 38*, 33–45. doi:10.1177/0361684313484900

Charles, J. L. K. (2013). Mental health provider-based stigma: Understanding the experience of clients and families. *Social Work in Mental Health, 11*, 360–375. doi:10.1080/15332985.2013.775998

Cheng, Z. (2015). Asian Americans and European Americans' stigma levels in response to biological and social explanations of depression. *Social Psychiatry & Psychiatric Epidemiology, 50*, 767–776. doi:10.1007/s00127-014-0999-5

Cho, S., Crenshaw, K. W., & McCall, L. (2013). Toward a field of intersectionality studies: Theory, applications, and praxis. *Signs, 38*, 785–810. Retrieved from http://www.jstor.org/stable/10.1086/669608

Choi, N.-Y., & Miller, M. J. (2014). AAPI college students' willingness to seek counseling: The role of culture, stigma, and attitudes. *Journal of Counseling Psychology, 61*, 340–351. doi:10.1037/cou0000027

Chung, Y. B., & Szymanski, D. M. (2006). Racial and sexual identities of Asian American gay men. *Journal of LGBT Issues in Counseling, 1*, 67–93.

Clement, S., Schauman, O., Graham, T., Maggioni, F., Evans-Lacko, S., Bezborodovs, N., . . . Thornicroft, G. (2015). What is the impact of mental health-related stigma on help-seeking? A systematic review of quantitative and qualitative studies. *Psychological Medicine, 45*, 11–27. doi:10.1017/S0033291714000129

Cole, E. R. (2009). Intersectionality and research in psychology. *American Psychologist, 64*, 170–180. doi:10.1037/a0014564

Combahee River Collective. (1983). The Combahee River Collective statement. In B. Smith (Ed.), *Homegirls: A Black feminist anthology* (pp. 272–282). New York: Kitchen Table Press.

Constantine-Simms, D. (2001). *The greatest taboo: Homosexuality in Black communities* (1st ed.). Los Angeles: Alyson Books.

Corker, E., Hamilton, S., Henderson, C., Weeks, C., Pinfold, V., Rose, D., . . . Thornicroft, G. (2013). Experiences of discrimination among people using mental health services in England 2008–2011. *The British Journal of Psychiatry, 202*, s58–s63. doi:10.1192/bjp.bp.112.112912

Corrigan, P. W. (Ed.). (2005). *On the stigma of mental illness*. Washington, DC: American Psychological Association.

Corrigan, P. W., Markowitz, F. E., & Watson, A. C. (2004). Structural levels of mental illness stigma and discrimination. *Schizophrenia Bulletin, 30*, 481–491.

Crenshaw, K. (1989). Demarginalizing the intersection of race and sex: A Black feminist critique of antidis-crimination doctrine, feminist theory and antiracist politics. *University of Chicago Legal Forum, 1989*(1), 139–167.

Crenshaw, K. (1991). Mapping the margins: Intersectionality, identity politics, and violence against women of color. *Stanford Law Review, 43*, 1241–1299. http://www.jstor.org.ezproxy1.lib.asu.edu/stable/1229039

Delphin-Rittmon, M., Bellamy, C. D., Ridgway, P., Guy, K., Ortiz, J., Flanagan, E., & Davidson, L. (2013). "I never really discuss that with my clinician": U.S. consumer perspectives on the place of culture in behavioural healthcare. *Diversity and Equality in Health and Care, 10*, 143–154.

Denton, F. N., Rostosky, S. S., & Danner, F. (2014). Stigma-related stressors, coping self-efficacy, and physical health in lesbian, gay, and bisexual individuals. *Journal of Counseling Psychology, 61*, 383–391. doi:10.1037/a0036707

Diaz, R. M., Ayala, G., Bein, E., Henne, J., & Marin, B. V. (2001). The impact of homophobia, poverty, and racism on the mental health of gay and bisexual Latino men: Findings from 3 US cities. *American Journal of Public Health, 91*(6), 927–932.

Douglas, K. B. (1999). *Sexuality and the Black church: A womanist perspective*. Maryknoll, NY: Orbis Books.

Eriksen, K. Å., Arman, M., Davidson, L, Sundfør, & Karlsson, B. (2014). Challenges in relating to mental health professionals: Perspectives of persons with severe mental illness. *International Journal of Mental Health Nursing, 23*, 110–117. doi:10.1111/inm.12024

Estrada, F., Rigali-Oiler, M., Arciniega, G. M., & Tracey, T. J. (2011). Machismo and Mexican American men: An empirical understanding using a gay sample. *Journal of Counseling Psychology, 58*(3), 358–365.

Gabbidon, J., Farrelly, S., Hatch, S. L., Henderson, C., Williams, P. Bhugra, D., . . . Clement, S. (2014). Discrimination attributed to mental illness or race-ethnicity by users of community psychiatric services. *Psychiatric Services, 65*, 1360–1366.

Gonzales, L., Davidoff, K. C., Nadal, K. L., & Yanos, P. T. (2015). Microaggressions experienced by persons with mental illnesses: An exploratory study. *Journal of Psychiatric Rehabilitation, 38*, 234–241. doi:10.1037/prj0000096

Graham, L. F. (2014). Navigating community institutions: Black transgender women's experiences in schools, the criminal justice system, and churches. *Sexuality Research and Social Policy, 11*(4), 274–287.

Graham, L. F., Crissman, H. P., Tocco, J., Hughes, L. A., Snow, R. C., & Padilla, M. B. (2014). Interpersonal relationships and social support in transitioning narratives of Black transgender women in Detroit. *International Journal of Transgenderism, 15*(2), 100–113.

Greene, B. (2000). African American lesbian and bisexual women. *Journal of Social Issues, 56*(2), 239–249.

Greene, B. A. (2002). Heterosexism and internalized racism among African Americans: The connections and considerations for African American lesbians and bisexual women: A clinical psychological perspective. *Rutgers Law Review, 54*(4), 931–957.

Hamilton, S., Lewis-Holmes, E., Pinfold, V., Henderson, C., Rose, D., & Thornicroft, G. (2014). Discrimination against people with a mental health diagnosis: Qualitative analysis of reported experiences. *Journal of Mental Health, 23*, 88–93. doi:10.3109/09638237.2014.880408

Han, C. S. (2007). They don't want to cruise your type: Gay men of color and the racial politics of exclusion. *Social Identities, 13*(1), 51–67.

Hansson, L., Stjernswärd, S., & Svensson, B. (2014). Perceived and anticipated discrimination in people with mental illness—An interview study. *Nordic Journal of Psychiatry, 68*, 100–106. doi:10.3109/08039488.2013.775339

Harper, G. W., Jernewall, N., & Zea, M. C. (2004). Giving voice to emerging science and theory for lesbian, gay, and bisexual people of color. *Cultural Diversity and Ethnic Minority Psychology, 10*(3), 187–199.

Harris, A. C. (2009). Marginalization by the marginalized: Race, homophobia, heterosexism, and "the problem of the 21st century." *Journal of Gay & Lesbian Social Services, 21*(4), 430–448.

Hernandez, M., & Barrio, C. (2015). Perceptions of subjective burden among Latino families caring for a loved one with schizophrenia. *Community Mental Health Journal, 51*, 939–948. doi:10.1007/s10597-015-9881-5

Hill, J. S., Kim, S., & Williams, C. D. (2010). The context of racial microaggressions against indigenous peoples. In D. W. Sue (Ed.), *Microaggressions and marginality: Manifestation, dynamics, and impact* (pp. 105–122). Hoboken, NJ: John Wiley.

Hill Collins, P. (1990). *Black feminist thought: Knowledge, consciousness, and the politics of empowerment.* New York: Routledge.

Holley, L. C., Stromwall, L. K., & Bashor, K. E. (2012). Reconceptualizing stigma: Toward a critical anti-oppression paradigm. *Stigma Research and Action, 2*, 51–61. doi:10.5463/SRA.v1i1.9

Holley, L. C., Stromwall, L. K., & Tavassoli, K. (2015). Teaching note—Oppression of people with mental illnesses: Incorporating content into multiple-issue diversity courses. *Journal of Social Work Education, 51*, 398–406. doi:10.1080/10437797.2015.1012940

Holley, L. C., Tavassoli, K. Y., & Stromwall, L. K. (2016). Mental illness discrimination in mental health treatment programs: Intersections of race, ethnicity, and sexual orientation. *Community Mental Health Journal, 52*(3), 311–322.

Hulko, W. (2009). The time- and context-contingent nature of intersectionality and interlocking oppressions. *Affilia: Journal of Women and Social Work, 24*, 44–55. doi:10.1177/0886109908326814

Jimenez, D. E., Bartels, S. J., Cardenas, V., & Alegría, M. (2013). Stigmatizing attitudes toward mental illness among racial/ethnic older adults in primary care. *International Journal of Geriatric Psychiatry, 28*, 1061–1068. doi:10.1002/gps.3928

Jones, L. V., Hopson, L., Warner, L., Hardiman, E. R., & James, T. (2015). A qualitative study of Black women's experiences in drug abuse and mental health services. *Affilia: Journal of Women and Social Work, 30*, 68–82. doi:10.1177/0886109914531957

Kidd, S. A., Veltman, A., Gately, C., Chan, K. J., & Cohen, J. N. (2011). Lesbian, gay, and transgender persons with severe mental illness: Negotiating wellness in the context of multiple sources of stigma. *American Journal of Psychiatric Rehabilitation, 14*, 13–39. doi:10.1080/15487768.2011.546277

Lasalvia, A., Zopei, S., Van Bortel, T., Bonetto, C., Cristofalo, D. Wahlbeck, K., . . . ASPEN/INDIGO Study Group. (2013). Global pattern of experienced and anticipated discrimination reported by people with major depressive disorder: A cross-sectional survey. *The Lancet, 381*, 55–62. doi:10.1016/S0140-6736(12)61379-8

Lehavot, K., Balsam, K. F., & Ibrahim-Wells, G. D. (2009). Redefining the American quilt: Definitions and experiences of community among ethnically diverse lesbian and bisexual women. *Journal of Community Psychology, 37*(4), 439–458.

Link, B. G., & Phelan, J. C. (2001). Conceptualizing stigma. *Annual Review of Sociology, 27*, 363–385. Retrieved from http://www.jstor.org/stable/2678626

Marquez, J. A., & Ramírez García, J. I. (2013). Family caregivers' narratives of mental health treatment usage processes by their Latino adult relatives with serious and persistent mental illness. *Journal of Family Psychology, 27*, 398–408. doi:10.1037/a0032868

Marsiglia, F. F. (1998). Homosexuality and Latinos/as: Towards an integration of identities. *Journal of Gay & Lesbian Social Services, 8*(3), 113–125.

Mays, V., & Cochran, S. (2001). Mental health correlates of perceived discrimination among lesbian, gay, and bisexual adults in the United States. *American Journal of Public Health, 91*, 1869–1876.

Mehrotra, G. (2010). Toward a continuum of intersectionality theorizing for feminist social work scholarship. *Affilia: Journal of Women and Social Work, 25*, 417–430. doi:10.1177/0886109910384190

Newhill, C. E., & Harris, D. (2007). African American consumers' perceptions of racial disparities in mental health services. *Social Work in Public Health, 23*, 107–124. doi:10.1080/19371910802151861

Pascoe, E. A., & Richman, L. S. (2009). Perceived discrimination and health: A meta-analytic review. *Psychological Bulletin, 135*, 531–554. doi:10.1037/a0016059

Pescosolido, B. A., Martin, J. K., Lang, A., & Olafsdottir, S. (2008). Rethinking theoretical approaches to stigma: A Framework Integrating Normative Influences on Stigma (FINIS). *Social Science & Medicine, 67*, 431–440. Retrieved from http://dx.doi.org/10.1016/j.socscimed.2008.03.018

Quinn, D. M., & Chaudoir, S. R. (2009). Living with a concealable stigmatized identity: The impact of anticipated stigma, centrality, salience, and cultural stigma on psychological distress and health. *Journal of Personality and Social Psychology, 97*, 634–651. doi:10.1037/a0015815

Rivera, D. P., Forquer, E. E., & Rangel, R. (2010). Microaggressions and the life experience of Latina/o Americans. In D. W. Sue (Ed.), *Microaggressions and marginality: Manifestation, dynamics, and impact* (pp. 59–84). Hoboken, NJ: John Wiley.

Sanders Thompson, V. L., Noel, J. G., & Campbell, J. (2004). Stigmatization, discrimination, and mental health: The impact of multiple identity status. *American Journal of Orthopsychiatry, 74*, 529–544. doi:10.1037/0002-9432.74.4.529

Schmitt, M. T., Branscombe, N. R., Postmes, T., & Garcia, A. (2014). The consequences of perceived discrimination for psychological well-being: A meta-analytic review. *Psychological Bulletin, 140*(4), 921–948.

Schulze, B., & Angermeyer, M. C. (2003). Subjective experiences of stigma: A focus group study of schizophrenic patients, their relatives and mental health professionals. *Social Science & Medicine, 56*, 299–312.

Sue, D. W. (2010). *Microaggressions in everyday life: Race, gender, and sexual orientation.* Hoboken, NJ: John Wiley.

Sue, D. W., Bucceri, J., Lin, A. I., Nadal, K. L., & Torino, G. C. (2009). Racial microaggressions and the Asian American experience. *Asian American Journal of Psychology,* S(1), 88–101.

Sue, D. W., Nadal, K. L., Capodilupo, C. M., Lin, A. I., Torino, G. C., & Rivera, D. P. (2008). Racial microaggressions against Black Americans: Implications for counseling. *Journal of Counseling and Development: JCD, 86*(3), 330–338.

Sung, M. R., Szymanski, D. M., & Henrichs-Beck, C. (2015). Challenges, coping, and benefits of being an Asian American lesbian or bisexual woman. *Psychology of Sexual Orientation and Gender Diversity, 2*(1), 52–64.

Świtaj, P., Wciórka, J., Grygield, P., Anczewska, M., Schaeffer, E., Tyczyński, K., & Wiśniewski, A. (2012). Experiences of stigma and discrimination among users of mental health services in Poland. *Transcultural Psychiatry, 49*, 51–68. doi:10.1177/1363461511433143

Szymanski, D. M., & Henrichs-Beck, C. (2014). Exploring sexual minority women's experiences of external and internalized heterosexism and sexism and their links to coping and distress. *Sex Roles, 70*, 28–42. doi:10.1007/s11199-013-0329-5

Szymanski, D. M., & Sung, M. R. (2010). Minority stress and psychological distress among Asian American sexual minority persons. *The Counseling Psychologist, 38*(6), 848–872.

US Department of Health and Human Services. (2001). *Mental health: Culture, race and ethnicity—A supplement to mental health: A report of the Surgeon General.* Rockville, MD: Author.

van der Sanden, R. L. M., Stutterheim, S. E., Pryor, J. B., Kok, G., & Bos, A. E. R. (2014). Coping with stigma by association and family burden among family members of people with mental illness. *The Journal of Nervous and Mental Disease, 202*, 710–717. doi:10.1097/NMD.0000000000000189

Velez, B. L., Moradi, B., & DeBlaere, C. (2015). Multiple oppressions and the mental health of sexual minority Latino/a individuals. *The Counseling Psychologist, 43*, 7–38. doi:10.1177/0011000014542836

Walters, K. L., Evans-Campbell, T., Simoni, J. M., Ronquillo, T., & Bhuyan, R. (2006). "My spirit in my heart": Identity experiences and challenges among American Indian two-spirit women. *Journal of Lesbian Studies, 10*(1–2), 125–149.

Ward, E. G. (2005). Homophobia, hypermasculinity and the US black church. *Culture, Health & Sexuality, 7*(5), 493–504.

Warner, L. R. (2008). A best practices guide to intersectional approaches in psychological research. *Sex Roles, 59*, 454–463. doi:10.1007/s11199-008-9504-5

Whitbeck, L. B., McMorris, B. J., Hoyt, D. R., Stubben, J. D., & LaFromboise, T. (2002). Perceived discrimination, traditional practices, and depressive symptoms among American Indians in the upper Midwest. *Journal of Health and Social Behavior, 43*(4), 400–418.

Williams, D. R., & Mohammed, S. A., (2009). Discrimination and racial disparities in health: Evidence and needed research. *Journal of Behavioral Medicine, 32,* 20–47. doi:10.1007/s10865-008-9185-0

Williams, D. R., Neighbors, H. W., & Jackson, J. S. (2008). Racial/ethnic discrimination and health: Findings from community studies. *American Journal of Public Health, 98,* S29–S37. doi:10.2105/AJPH.93.2.200

Zerger, S., Bacon, S., Corneau, S., Skosireva A., McKenzie, K., Gapka, S., … Stergiopoulos, V. (2014). Differential experiences of discrimination among ethnoracially diverse persons experiencing mental illness and homelessness. *BMC Psychiatry, 14,* 1–22. doi:10.1186/s12888-014-0353-1

CHAPTER 22

SUBSTANCE USE AND ADDICTION

Natasha S. Mendoza

INTRODUCTION

Viewing the world from a person-in-environment lens, social work practitioners are uniquely positioned to deliver behavioral health interventions to lesbian, gay, bisexual, transgender, and queer (LGBTQ) individuals. Working with members of the LGBTQ community who struggle with behavioral health issues like substance use disorders (SUD) requires additional knowledge and information about population-specific risk, assessment, intervention, and prevention. To that end, this chapter begins with a discussion of the sociohistorical context of substance use among individuals in the LGBTQ community including a focus on the development of strong social bonds within settings that serve alcohol or promote the use of illicit drugs. It appears that factors contributing to current-day epidemiology of substance abuse patterns include a substantial emphasis on community. According to the Substance Abuse and Mental Health Services Administration ([SAMHSA], 2012), clear empirical evidence suggests that members of the LGBTQ community are at risk of developing SUDs. Care is taken to report factors specific to lesbians and bisexual women, gay and bisexual men, and transgender individuals. Moreover, physiological development is considered with a focus on substance use in adolescence and late adulthood. While public health information is becoming more available, significant gaps remain in the empirical literature regarding specific subpopulation risk factors. Drawing from available information, the chapter offers a section on evidence-based approaches to the treatment of SUDs including specific diagnostic criteria, recommendations for screening and brief interventions, assessment, and, broadly, individual and group interventions. Last, we offer a note about substance abuse prevention, the first step in addressing the complex needs of the LGBTQ community.

SOCIOHISTORICAL CONTEXT

Bars and clubs have played an important part of the sociohistorical context of the modern LGBTQ movement. Early in the twentieth century, LGBTQ people were forced to invent ways to meet and socialize as a result of puritanical "new patterns of living" (Wolf, 2009, p. 59). Following the Second World War, LGBTQ people were drawn to places like San Francisco where they could be open in communities of people with whom they shared commonalities. The first bars serving LGBTQ people began opening just after World War II and were eventually found in nearly every major American and European city by midcentury (Wolf, 2009). Historically, bars and clubs have served as a veritable respite for the LGBTQ community, where logical families could be built and friendships fostered. Settings served as safe spaces to socialize and escape public ridicule (Wolf, 2009) and arguably continue to be an important setting for social network building and connection. Not only have such socialized settings offered community and camaraderie, but they have allowed patrons to find themselves and one other. Often segregated by gender (e.g., lesbian versus gay men), alcohol-serving establishments were—and still are—a primary setting for socializing among LGBTQ people.

While bars have served as important community centers, establishments serving LGBTQ communities have experienced a tumultuous past. During the 1960s, bars also served as an easily identified collective where patrons were harassed by law enforcement (Wolf, 2009). In the late 1960s police raids on gay bars were a common occurrence because it was illegal for bars to serve gay people or for gay people to dance with one another (Bronski, 2011). In one such instance in 1969, law enforcement in New York City raided the Stonewall Inn, which resulted in a bold rebellion by patrons fighting back against the oppression. Essentially, the Stonewall Inn served as a symbol of hard-won civil rights (Duberman, 1993).

Apart from the sociohistorical importance and connection of the LGBTQ civil rights movement with bars, drinking establishments have served as important spaces for empowerment and social interaction (Valentine & Skelton, 2003). Such paradoxical spaces can be both liberating and supportive with building community, while also provide a "range of social risks" . . . including . . . "abusive relationships and social exclusion" (Valentine & Skelton, 2003, p. 863) among other dangers. Since the 1970s certain "club drugs" such as amyl nitrite "poppers" and cocaine have been used to reduce sexual inhibition (Race, 2009). Over time, through the 1980s and 1990s the use of other club drugs (e.g., ecstasy, ketamine) and methamphetamine have become a common occurrence within club settings (Race, 2009). As a result of evolving use and social connection, LGBTQ communities experience prevalence and tolerance of use, coupled with sexual risk behaviors—unparalleled to substance use and behavior within the general population.

Ensconced in sociocultural importance, entering environments such as bars and clubs, in which alcohol and drugs are typically consumed, can elevate the potential for use among LGBTQ patrons. Coupled with the psychosocial components found therein, such as strong social and felt-family bonds, LGBTQ people can often be subject to an increased risk of problematic substance use. This decades-long trend may have led to networks of heavy substance users and could add to increased challenges in avoiding problematic use among members of the LGBTQ community (Green, 2012).

As the LGBTQ community evolves, the means through which community members interact continues to change. While a sociohistorical context lays a foundation from which to view problematic substance use, it is important to recognize the ever-changing means through which adults (and especially young adults) socialize. Ingram (2012) posits that relationships in queer communities have moved from "[sic] half-hidden networks relying on strategic sites to visible defended queer space to more ubiquitous, queer systems of overlapping ecologies" (p. 54). Virtual systems have taken on an entirely new and different role, serving as social catalysts though which social interaction will continue to change with applications (e.g., Scruff, Grindr), which help individuals (gay men in particular) find one another using GPS coordinates (Blackwell, Birnholtz, & Abbott, 2014). Thus a designated space, such as a bar, is not necessarily needed. As this evolution takes place, it is wholly unclear how substance use behavior will be impacted.

EPIDEMIOLOGY

Data from the National Survey on Drug Use and Health ([NSDUH], Center for Behavioral Health Statistics and Quality, 2015) indicates that more than half (52.7%) of Americans over age 12 report being current drinkers of alcohol, while approximately 17 million of these individuals meet the diagnostic criteria for having an alcohol use disorder as defined by the *Diagnostic and Statistical Manual of Mental Disorders* (5th ed. [DSM-5], American Psychiatric Association, 2013). The NSDUH also reports that 4.2 million people meet the criteria for SUD based on marijuana use. Furthermore, 476,000 people meet the criteria for a stimulant use disorder as a result of cocaine and 569,000 as a result of methamphetamine. Last, 1.9 million people meet the criteria for an opioid use disorder related to prescription drugs (Center for Behavioral Health Statistics and Quality, 2015).

However, the NSDUH does not include sexual orientation and gender identity in their demographic surveys (Healthy People, 2010). According to the Centers for Disease Control and Prevention when compared to heterosexual people—gay and bisexual men, lesbians, and transgender people are more likely to use alcohol and drugs, demonstrate higher use rates, and continue heavy drinking into later life (SAMHSA, 2012). Research related to the epidemiology of substance use among LGBTQ people is increasing in momentum, albeit slowly. While public health empiricists value this line of inquiry, there are relatively few sources of information related to the substance use patterns of LGBTQ people. The assessment of sexual orientation is not often part of population-based studies (McCabe, Hughes, Bostwick, West, & Boyd, 2009), and the assessment of gender identities other than male or female is even more rare. The next section of this chapter highlights specific epidemiological rates of substance use patterns among gender and sexual minorities in the United States.

LESBIANS AND BISEXUAL WOMEN

Research conducted by Flentje, Hech, and Sorensen (2015) indicated that there were no marked differences between the substance use patterns of lesbian, bisexual, and heterosexual women in a study of adults entering substance abuse treatment in San Francisco ($N = 1,441$). However, other research suggests that women who identify as lesbian or bisexual appear to be at increased risk of alcohol and other drug abuse. In a 2013 study utilizing data from over 34,000 adults, McCabe and colleagues (2009) found that female sexual minorities (approximately 2% of the total population of women in the study) had a greater likelihood of lifetime SUDs and earlier age of drinking onset. Moreover, the odds of SUD outcomes were significantly greater for nonheterosexual women than for heterosexual women. Specifically, lesbians had more than three times greater odds for a lifetime SUD than did heterosexual women.

Cochran and Mays (2009) examined the associations between sexual orientation, mental health, and substance use morbidity using data from 2,272 individuals in California. Results from this study indicated that sexual minorities demonstrated increased risk of psychiatric morbidity. The researchers found that women with sexual-minority status were more likely to meet the criteria for all mental health disorders except for drug dependency when compared to heterosexual counterparts—but this differed by identity (Cochran & Mays, 2009). They remarked that bisexual women were more likely to meet the criteria for several disorders including alcohol dependency. Women identifying primarily as heterosexual but with previous homosexual experiences demonstrated higher rates of alcohol dependency when compared to heterosexual women overall. Additionally, Cochran and Mays demonstrated that sexual-minority women were more likely than heterosexual women to have received treatment in the past year for SUDs. Similarly, a study conducted by Drabble, Midanik, and Tocki (2005) utilizing the National Alcohol Survey ($N = 7,612$) found that lesbian and bisexual women were more likely than heterosexual women to seek treatment.

GAY AND BISEXUAL MEN

In Flentje, Heck, and Sorenson's (2015) study evaluating the sexual orientation-specific differences in substance use behaviors among adults entering treatment in San Francisco ($N = 1,441$), bisexual males demonstrated a higher prevalence of methamphetamine use. The study also found that gay and bisexual men demonstrated higher rates of primary methamphetamine use when compared to heterosexual men (44.5% and 21.8%, respectively, compared to 7.7%). Research conducted by McCabe, Hughes, Bostwick, West, and Boyd (2013) found that gay and bisexual men (approximately 2% of more than 14,000 men) had significantly higher odds of lifetime drug use disorders (but not alcohol) compared with heterosexual men. The authors highlighted that men with histories with male sexual partners had significantly lower rates of alcohol use across their lifetimes when compared to men with only female partners.

Cochran and Mays (2009) found that heterosexual identified men who have sex with men (MSM) demonstrated higher risk for alcohol and drug dependency when compared to exclusively heterosexual men. While gay and bisexual men in the study demonstrated higher rates of psychological disorders than heterosexual men, they did not show significantly higher rates of alcohol or drug dependency. Last, research has demonstrated little evidence indicating that sexual minority men access or seek treatment for SUDs at rates different from those of heterosexual men (Cochran, Keenan, Schober, & Mays, 2000; Drabble et al., 2005).

TRANSGENDER INDIVIDUALS

It may be that the use of alcohol and other illicit drugs among transgender individuals is similar to that of members of the larger LGB community; however, empirical data related to drug behaviors and use among transgender individuals is scant. Moreover, data on drug use related to transgender men is nearly nonexistent. Herbst and colleagues (2008) conducted a comprehensive systematic review of the available literature that included 29 research studies. Across all of the studies included in the meta-analysis, transgender female participants demonstrated rates of injecting street drugs such as heroin or crack at 12% with 2% reporting rates of sharing needles. Nearly 44% of participants reported consuming alcohol, 30% reported using crack or other illicit drugs, and 20% reported smoking marijuana. Two studies reported no injection drug use while three studies reported rates from 4 to 21% (Herbst et al., 2008). Herbst and colleagues also reported high rates of mental health issues including suicide attempts in the transgender female studies reviewed (54%). Sample sizes ranged between 19 and 515, with nearly half (48%) having fewer than 100 participants.

Research conducted by Reback and Fletcher (2014) using outreach encounters with transgender women ($N = 2,136$) indicated relatively high rates of recent alcohol use (57%), followed by marijuana (26%), and methamphetamine (22%). Moreover, lifetime injection drug or illegal hormone use was reported among 66% of participants. A major finding from the study related to substance use was the significant association with odds of reporting an HIV-positive status. Among the transgender women in the study, alcohol was the most frequently reported substance but differed significantly by HIV status with negative status being more so associated with recent alcohol use. HIV positive women were more likely to report methamphetamine use in the past 30 days when compared to women with HIV-negative status. Lifetime injection drug use was reported by two-thirds of the sample and was significantly more likely to be reported by HIV-positive women.

DEVELOPMENTAL CONSIDERATIONS

Substance abuse may manifest differently among various LGBTQ subpopulations (e.g., gay men compared to lesbians), as evidenced in earlier sections. In the same fashion, substance abuse clearly may arise in different ways as a function of developmental stage across the lifespan. Given the unique standpoint of LGBTQ youth and older adults, the following sections highlight patterns of use and epidemiology among these two groups. In addition, discussion surrounding the neurological effects of substance use is included as a cautionary note to practitioners who must consider the biological and deleterious effect upon an individual's brain and stage of development.

ADOLESCENTS

Adolescence is typically defined as the developmental stage between ages 12 and 18 (Erikson, 1950, 1968), though some developmental theory suggests that adolescence reaches well into the early 20s (Arnett, 2000, 2014). It is a time period typically wrought with new life challenges, and this is especially true for LGBTQ youth and young adults. Adolescence is a period of transition to adulthood when individuals attempt to define themselves; however, if young adults are not yet fully self-aware with respect to sexual orientation or gender identity or they experience some measure of internalized phobia, the transition may involve risk. Specifically, youth may be at risk for a host of psychosocial problems including depression, anxiety, social stress, and substance abuse. With a focus on substance abuse, this section delineates risk of adolescent substance use and abuse.

LGBTQ youth are subject to regular psychosocial stressors and trauma that could exacerbate a need to escape or self-medicate with substances. For example, youth are routinely harassed because of sexual orientation (Kosciw, Greytak, Palmer, & Boesen, 2014). The Gay, Lesbian, and Straight Education Network reported that 74.1% of LGBTQ students experienced verbal harassment, 55% felt unsafe, and 30.3% skipped school because of safety concerns ($N = 7,898$ students between the ages of 13 and 21; Kosciw et al., 2014). Youth must contend with family rejection, physical, sexual, and emotional abuse associated with emerging sexual orientation and gender identity (Killen-Harvey, 2006). National research suggests that youth may engage in health and sexual health risk behaviors as a way to cope with solidifying their self-identities (Killen-Harvey, 2006); substance use and abuse may exacerbate the problem.

Meta-analysis indicated that young sexual minorities reported greater substance use than their heterosexual counterparts ($N = 20$ studies; Marshal et al., 2008) including drinking alcohol and using marijuana/cocaine and other street drugs, especially among those who experienced high levels of victimization. Furthermore, in comparison to girls, sexual-minority boys may be at greater risk for drinking, marijuana, and cocaine use, as well as legal problems related to substance use. However, some research reports that girls ($n = 47$) experiencing increased substance use compared to boys ($n = 64$) and their heterosexual counterparts ($n = 1,279$; Hatzenbuehler, Corbin, & Fromme, 2008).

A study with 105 youth ages 14 to 21 demonstrated that, compared to youth with same-sex sexual partners, bisexual adolescents are at increased risk of ever having used alcohol, marijuana, crack, or heroin (Moon, Fornili, & O'Briant, 2007). Overall, bisexual youth may express more risk-taking behaviors than others including higher levels of substance use experimentation that could result in higher risk profiles (Moon et al., 2007). Meta-analysis ($N = 20$ studies) related to sexual orientation and substance use found that the odds of substance use for LGB youth were, on average, 190% higher than for heterosexual youth. For bisexual youth, odds were 340% higher and, for females, 400% higher (Marshal et al., 2008).

Data related to transgender youth substance use patterns is rare yet these youth may represent the most vulnerable individuals. In a recent study, Coulter and colleagues (2015) compared the drinking patterns and prevalence of alcohol-related problems of 175 transgender-identified young adults with non-transgender-identified males and females. Results indicated that non-transgender individuals reported less drinking and had lower odds of past-year alcohol-related sexual assault and suicidal ideation. Transgender-identified youth who were sexually or verbally assaulted demonstrated significantly higher use than individuals who did not experience victimization. Research focused on young transgender women has demonstrated that more than 90% have used substances during their lifetime (Wilson et al., 2009) and that sexual intercourse under the influence of substances may be occurring 50% of the time (Garofalo, Osmer, Sullivan, Doll, & Harper, 2007).

In a comprehensive review of the substance abuse and gerontological literature, Rosen and colleagues (2013) examined the presence of research (i.e., 634 articles) associated with gerontology and substance abuse. Less than 1% of all of the articles published addressed substance use among older adults. It stands to reason that the literature about LGBTQ older adults and their substance abuse patterns is even more so limited. Over a decade ago, the Institute of Medicine called for an increasing focus on the health needs of LGB older adults (2001). Historically, research in this area is severely lacking and overwhelmingly limited to small non-population-based samples.

Recently, Fredriksen-Goldsen, Kim, Barkan, Muraco, and Hoy-Ellis (2013) investigated health disparities among LGB adults ages 50 and older ($N = 2,560$) in the state of Washington. Results indicated higher risk of disability, poor mental health, smoking, and excessive drinking when compared to heterosexuals. With respect to substance use risk, lesbians reported a higher rate of excessive drinking than did bisexual women. Other research on older lesbian and bisexual women has found excessive drinking among multiple physical and mental health concerns (Conron, Mimiaga, & Landers, 2010; Dilley, Simmons, Boysun, Pizacani, & Stark, 2010). Although Fredriksen-Goldsen, Kim, et al. found comparable substance use rates between older and younger gay and bisexual men (in comparison to other research), they reported that there were in fact higher rates among older gay and bisexual men compared to heterosexual men. The researchers pointed out that excessive drinking and smoking are major concerns for this population, and this is particularly problematic because most prevention targets younger adults.

With a different focus, Fredriksen-Goldsen, Cook-Daniels, et al. (2013) examined the physical and mental health of transgender older adults utilizing data from a cross-sectional survey of over 2,500 LGBT individuals aged 50 and older. Though the researchers did not find salient results related to alcohol or other drug use, the study indicated higher risk of poor physical health, disability, depressive symptomatology, and perceived stress compared to nontransgender participants, outcomes that could have a comorbid association with SUD. The researchers also pointed out that transgender people demonstrate higher rates of smoking, but research related to other areas of substance use continues to be lacking.

CONSIDERING NEUROLOGICAL IMPACT

Alcohol and drugs impact brain development across the lifespan, and over time the negative effect on the brain may further become compounded by long-term use. While substance misuse may cause a state of euphoria in the user at first, continued use may have significant and deleterious effects such as seizures, stroke, and brain damage affecting every aspect of an individual's life (National Institute on Drug Abuse [NIDA], 2014). The NIDA's and other empirical evidence highlight the following drugs that can cause significant neurological problems:

- Alcohol: May cause changes in emotion, personality, perception, learning, and memory. May cause atrophy of nerve cells and brain shrinkage (Oscar-Berman, Shagrin, Evert, & Epstein, 1997).

- Cocaine: Blocks the removal of dopamine from synapse causing an accumulation of dopamine. Long-term cocaine use may lead to severe cognitive dysfunction which may persist despite abstinence (Enevoldson, 2004).
- Gamma hydroxybutyrate and rohypnol: Causes excess sedation, disorientation, and vomiting. Seizures may occur especially if used with alcohol (Enevoldson, 2004).
- Inhalants (e.g., amyl nitrate): May cause convulsions or seizures as a result of abnormal electrical discharges in the brain. Toxic inhalants may damage parts of the brain that control cognition, movement, vision, and hearing. May also cause asphyxiation, suffocation, coma, or fatal injury (NIDA, 2014).
- Marijuana: May effect attention, memory, or learning, which could reduce intellectual levels (NIDA, 2014).
- Methylenedioxymethamphetamine (e.g., MDMA, ecstasy, molly): May cause reduction in mental capacity including memory. Information processing is significantly impacted. May cause shifts in mood including feelings of anxiety, irritability, and sadness (NIDA, 2014).
- Methamphetamine: Causes the release of very high levels of dopamine. Long-term effects include changes in brain structure and function, deficits in motor skills, memory loss, increased distractibility, and mood disturbance (NIDA, 2014).
- Nicotine: Causes a decrease in important enzymes that are responsible for the breakdown of dopamine in addition to multiple other physiological effects including heart disease, stroke, heart attack, aneurysm, and cancer (NIDA, 2014).
- Prescription stimulants: Can cause seizures, hostility, paranoia, or psychosis (NIDA, 2014).

EVIDENCE-BASED APPROACHES: ASSESSMENT, DIAGNOSIS, AND TREATMENT OF ADDICTION

The evidence base for interventions specifically tailored to the unique needs of LGBTQ people continues to be limited in comparison to the evidence base of knowledge related to treating heterosexual people. While research is gaining momentum, much of it is focused on the experience of MSM. Very little research exists examining treatment for members of gender-minority communities or sexual-minority women. Thus the following sections highlight the evidence base as it stands offering exemplars of research with members of gender and sexual minority groups. A review of the diagnostic criteria is offered as a reference followed by a section on the relevance of affirmative practice in the addictions. Screening and assessment recommendations are made in the context of working with members of the LGBTQ community. While several interventions exist to treat SUDs, the section on individual interventions focuses on cognitive behavioral and motivational enhancement techniques.

In the United States, social work practitioners primarily use the DSM-5 (American Psychiatric Association, 2013) to diagnose a host of behavioral health and mental health disorders. The most recent version of the DSM-5 is used to guide practitioners in clinical decision-making. In the DSM-5, a pattern of substance use leading to significant impairment or distress is manifested by two or more of 11 criteria within a 12-month period (see Box 22.1).

If two to three criteria are endorsed, a mild SUD may be present. If four to five criteria are endorsed, a moderate SUD may be present. Six or more criteria may indicate a severe SUD.

BOX 22.1 DSM-5 CRITERIA FOR SUBSTANCE USE DISORDER

1. The substance is often taken in larger amounts or over a longer period than was intended.
2. There is a persistent desire or unsuccessful efforts to cut down or control substance use.
3. A great deal of time is spent in activities necessary to obtain the substance, use the substance, or recover from its effects.
4. Recurrent substance use resulting in a failure to fulfill major role obligations at work, school, or home (e.g., repeated absences or poor work performance related to substance use; substance-related absences, suspensions, or expulsions from school; neglect of children or household).
5. Continued substance use despite having persistent or recurrent social or interpersonal problems caused or exacerbated by the effects of the substance (e.g., arguments with spouse about consequences of intoxication, physical fights).
6. Reduction or abandonment of social, occupational, or recreational activities because of substance use.
7. Recurrent substance use in situations in which it is physically hazardous.
8. The substance use is continued despite knowledge of having a persistent or recurrent physical or psychological problem that is likely to have been caused or exacerbated by the substance.
9. Tolerance, as defined by a need for markedly increased amounts of the substance to achieve intoxication or desired effect or markedly diminished effect with continued use of the same amount of the substance.
10. Withdrawal symptoms or use to avoid withdrawal.
11. Craving or a strong desire or urge to use a specific substance.

LGBTQ-AFFIRMATIVE PRACTICE
FOR TREATING SUDS

When assessing, diagnosing, or treating individuals, psychotherapist attitudes in any behavioral health setting may have adverse effects upon the client (American Psychological Association, 2012). Research over the past two decades related to attitudes among treatment providers indicated that negative attitudes or endorsement of heterosexist belief systems may be translated as homophobia or, at least, lack of empathy (see Ben-Ari, 2001; Hayes & Erkis, 2000, McHenry & Johnson, 1993). In the 1990s Davies (1996), Tozer and McClanahan (1999), and Appleby and Anastas (1998) began to form what is currently known as affirmative practice. "[Affirmative practitioners] celebrate and advocate the validity of lesbian, gay, and bisexual persons and their relationships" (Tozer & McClanahan, 1999, p. 736), The practice "affirms a lesbian, gay, or bisexual identity as an equally positive human experience and expression to heterosexual identity" (Davies, 1996, p. 25).

In application to the treatment of SUDs, affirmative practice is essential. Crisp and McCave (2007) encourage the use of affirmative strategies across behavioral health settings for several reasons. In a substance abuse treatment setting, it may involve affirming sexual-minority status (e.g., voicing an appreciation of the role of logical or felt families who play a part in substance use patterns), utilizing a strengths perspective when helping clients build strategies for recovery, supporting self-determination while recognizing and identifying homophobic forces that play a role in problematic use, and considering substance abuse within the context of homophobia and discrimination (see Crisp & McCave, 2007). Interventions considered herein must be applied from an affirmative standpoint. In other words, behavioral interventions utilized with LGBTQ individuals must start with an affirmative foundation.

SCREENING AND BRIEF INTERVENTION

Screening for a SUD is critical in any health-care setting. For members of the LGBTQ community, risks associated with problematic substance use (as evidenced in the current chapter) are pervasive. Evidence-based methods for screening can and should be incorporated into health-care settings serving members of the LGBTQ community. According to a recent publication by the Fenway Institute regarding LGBT health (Makadon, Mayer, Potter, & Goldhammer, 2015), the most important step in assessing problematic substance use is simply asking about it.

Inquiring about substance use behaviors across all health-care settings should be the norm. With this in mind, the Fenway Institute guides practitioners to make use of a model known as SBIRT: Screening, Brief Intervention, and Referral to Treatment. SBIRT is described as an early intervention for individuals with SUD or those at risk of developing SUDs by the SAMHSA (2016). Over two decades of research has demonstrated that substance use may be effectively identified in primary care settings; research related to SBIRT has demonstrated its effectiveness with alcohol screening in particular and may increase the percentage of people who access care (Babor, McRee, Kassebaum, et al., 2007). It involves a standardized means of quickly assessing severity of use to identify appropriate treatment options; brief interventions that focus on insight, awareness, and motivation; and then referral to treatment for those in need of more extensive services. For more SBIRT information, training, and resources, see www.integration.samhsa. gov/clinical-practice/SBIRT. Moreover, the Fenway Institute has developed an LGBT-specific training webinar regarding the use of SBIRT (www.lgbthealtheducation.org). While SBIRT was developed as a multimodal screening process, there are many other evidence-based screening tools available for use. The NIDA developed a list of instruments that may be found at www. drugabuse.gov.

ASSESSMENT

The purpose of screening for SUDs is to determine the presence or potential for a SUD. After a screen determines potential for use, the LGBTQ individual must be assessed. "Assessment is the act of determining the nature and causes of a client's problem . . . to understand our clients' substance abuse problems, we must try to understand our clients" (Lewis, Dana, & Blevins, 2015, p. 82). Assessment usually involves interviewing the client about their biopsychosocial history including their substance use history. A multidimensional assessment should focus on physiology of the user, behavioral patterns, psychological and social factors (National Institute on Alcohol Abuse and Alcoholism [NIAAA], 2005).

Multiple standardized, evidence-based tools are available for practitioners. A useful resource for practitioners seeking tailored assessment instruments is the Alcohol and Drug Abuse Institute at the University of Washington (lib.adai.washington.edu/instruments/). The advantage of using developed measures is that they tend to be manualized with measured reliability and validity (NIAAA, 2005). One of the most commonly used assessments in addiction treatment is the Addiction Severity Index ([ASI], McLellan, Luborsky, O'Brien, & Woody; 1980). The ASI is a semistructured interview guide that assesses medical status, employment and support, drug use, alcohol use, legal status, family/social status, and psychiatric status. Client history is gathered for both past 30-day and lifetime use.

While the ASI is a good example of a comprehensive assessment instrument, clinicians may wish to build a more comprehensive assessment including components related to *brief screening for referral* (see The Alcohol Use Disorders Identification Test (AUDIT) developed by Saunders, Aasland, Babor, de la Fuente, & Grant [1993] and the Drug Abuse Screening Test (DAST) developed by Skinner [1982]), *treatment history* (see The Treatment Services Review developed by McLellan, Alterman, Cacciola, Metzger, & O'Brien [1992]), *psychological functioning* (see The Brief Symptom Inventory developed by Derogatis [1975]), *trauma* (see The Modified PTSD Symptom Scale Self-Report developed by Resick, Falsetti, Resnick, & Kilpatrick [1991]), and *stages of change* (see The University of Rhode Island Change Assessment developed by Dozois, Westra, Collins, Fung, & Garry [2004] and McConnaughy, Prochaska, & Velicer [1983]) to name a few. Ultimately, the NIAAA (2005) notes that LGBT-specific or culturally sensitive assessments are lacking, creating a potential barrier to community members. Most important, practitioners and clinicians are cautioned to avoid marginalization, making assumptions, and scapegoating

1. What are the differences between a client's life as it is now and what he or she [they] would like it to be?
2. What strategies are most likely to help clients achieve their goals?
3. What barriers might stand in the way of clients' progress?
4. How can these barriers be lessened?
5. What internal and external resources can help clients reach their goals?
6. How can these resources be used effectively?

during the assessment process while finding ways to effectively provide LGBTQ-affirming assessment processes and best practice standards.

Substantial information may be gleaned utilizing assessment instruments. However, Lewis, Dana, and Blevins (2015, p. 78) assert that the following questions must be included (see Box 22.2).

In consideration of LGBTQ risk factors discussed herein, the questions in Box 22.2 are particularly powerful. Assessing substance abuse patterns among sexual and gender minorities must include an appreciation of the individual's status. Specifically, practitioners are encouraged to consider substance use and abuse in the context of each individual's development and ecology as a gender and/or sexual minority. For example, assessment should involve an appreciation of how the individual managed or is managing the coming out process. It should involve an appreciation of the strong social networks that might be built within substance use environments. For transgender people, assessment may involve conversations about substance interactions with hormone replacement therapies.

INDIVIDUAL INTERVENTIONS

Individual interventions for the treatment of SUD vary as a function of the individual's assessed severity of use. As with any social work intervention, the best individual intervention is one that is tailored to the individual person understanding the key role of environment and in consideration of the complex ecological systems in which the client operates. For LGBTQ individuals this means holistic interventions in the form of treatment that celebrates identity. Said another way, behavioral therapies and recovery maintenance are highly effective interventions that should be delivered to members of the LGBTQ community honoring sexual orientation and gender identity development within and across service systems.

BEHAVIORAL INTERVENTIONS

Clinicians engaged in behavioral therapies with LGBTQ clients must approach their work from a biopsychosocial perspective, ensuring that interventions are in consideration of individual factors including (but not limited to) gender identity and expression, sexual orientation, and the associated developmental processes. Moreover, working with clients who possess comorbid diagnoses (e.g., mental health issues such as posttraumatic stress disorders or physical health issues such as HIV-positive status) may require additional consideration. With respect to behavioral approaches, the NIDA (2012) offers the following statement:

> Behavioral approaches help engage people in drug abuse treatment, provide incentives for them to remain abstinent, modify their attitudes and behaviors related to drug abuse, and increase their life skills to handle stressful circumstances and environmental cues that may trigger intense craving for drugs and prompt another cycle of compulsive abuse. (n.p.)

In consideration of this purpose of behavioral approaches in concert with LGBTQ population-specific needs, this section focuses on motivational enhancement therapy and cognitive-behavioral therapy (CBT). It should be noted that few behavioral interventions for SUDs have been adapted and empirically tested for use with LGBT populations. Moreover, many behavioral approaches exist to treat SUDs, not only those presented herein.

MOTIVATIONAL ENHANCEMENT INTERVENTIONS

At the core of motivational enhancement therapy with LGBTQ individuals is the resolution of ambivalence about substance abuse. The client is guided toward motivation to change problematic substance use behaviors through a variety of techniques including elicitation of motivational statements (NIDA, 2012). The person-centered techniques, based on motivational interviewing, were developed originally by Miller in 1983 and involve an appreciation of the stage of change in which the client exists (i.e., precontemplation, contemplation, preparation, action, maintenance, and relapse; Prochaska, DiClemente, & Norcross, 1992). Moyers and Rollnick (2002) adapted the techniques to include four key principles: (a) express empathy, (b) develop discrepancy, (c) roll with resistance, and (d) support self-efficacy. Essentially, the responsibility for change is elicited from the client. For more in-depth study, see Miller and Rollnick (2013).

While motivational techniques have been empirically reviewed for effectiveness (see Smedslund et al., 2011), there are few empirical sources that test the intervention with members of the LGBTQ community; those that do exist are focused on the behavior and outcomes of gay and bisexual men. In a recent randomized controlled trial, Parsons, Lelutiu-Weinberger, Botsko, and Golub (2014) tested motivational techniques among a sample of non-treatment-seeking young gay and bisexual men ($N = 143$). Participants were followed for one year while researchers examined behavior change across conditions. Ultimately, findings indicated that participants in the motivational condition were 18% less likely to use drugs and 24% less likely to engage in unprotected intercourse. Another randomized study assessing motivational techniques with the behaviors of MSM (N = 150) found that on average club drug use declined (Morgenstern et al., 2009). In sum, motivational techniques used alone or in addition to cognitive behavioral techniques may be highly effective for members of the LGBTQ community (Anderson, 2009), but there is a substantial lack of available evidence tailored to subpopulations.

COGNITIVE-BEHAVIORAL THERAPY

Fundamentally, CBT is a technique that allows LGBTQ clients to address substance abuse through the identification of maladaptive thinking patterns and correction of behaviors using learned coping skills to address problems associated with use (e.g., identifying triggers; NIDA, 2012). Cognitive-behavioral techniques—developed from foundations provided by Beck (1970) and Ellis (1962)—are used with clients to change behavior and address emotional distress. The overall goals of any variant forms of cognitive-behavioral techniques are to decrease symptoms, improve functioning, and lead to remission (Hofmann, Asnaani, Vonk, Sawyer, & Fang, 2012).

In 2006 researchers conducted an influential review of 16 meta-analyses, finding support for the efficacy of CBT with many different disorders (Butler, 2006); however, substance abuse was not included. In 2012 Hofmann and colleagues conducted a review including SUDs. Ultimately, their study examining 269 meta-analyses found support for the efficacious use of CBT across multiple disorders including SUDs. Specifically, researchers noted efficacy related to cannabis dependence and multiple sessions (versus single sessions) and a lower dropout rate compared to control conditions. They noted however, that the effect size was smaller than with some other interventions (e.g., motivational approaches).

Similar to empirical evidence related to motivational enhancement therapy, evidence related to CBT is often a product of data collected among sexual-minority men. In a systematic review of cognitive-behavioral interventions (i.e., 70 articles) for HIV risk reduction in substance-using MSM, Melendez-Torres and Bonell (2013) found mixed results indicating that CBT may reduce MSM risk-taking behaviors—but findings were speculative. Other research with LGB clients suggests that the best standpoint from which to conduct CBT is an affirmative one. Balsam, Martell, and Safren (2006) highlight several major advantages for using CBT with sexual-minority clients. First, there is a strong empirical foundation for its use with issues often faced by sexual minorities such as depression and anxiety; second, CBT is grounded in the social context of the individual's life; third, it's a collaborative approach; fourth, it offers concrete coping mechanisms; fifth, CBT does not qualify behavior as good or bad, rather, it is functional or nonfunctional; and sixth, CBT allows the client to challenge internalized homophobia. The authors also noted a few limitations related to historical use of CBT to challenge sexual orientation or promote a heterosexist agenda.

Recent work in the area of CBT with transgender people includes the development of transgender-affirming CBT (TA-CBT; Austin & Craig, 2015). Austin and Craig noted that TA-CBT "recognizes the interpersonal, social, cultural, and political barriers to safety and well-being experienced by individuals whose experiences lie outside of the gender binary and actively works to intervene upon these barriers" (p. 21). Austin and Craig focused on TA-CBT in the treatment of depression, anxiety, and/or suicidality. However, given the overall CBT evidence base related to SUDs, suggested techniques remain apropos. Specifically, tenets related to psychoeducation (e.g., understanding the role between transphobic experiences), cognitive disconnects between thoughts and feelings (e.g., understanding the effect of minority stress), and developing safe, supportive, and affirmative networks can and should be woven in the treatment of SUDs.

PHARMACOTHERAPY

The best therapeutic strategies for SUDs are those that employ behavioral and pharmacological interventions (NIDA, 2012). When behavioral therapies and pharmacology are combined, clients benefit from medication-assisted treatment. Primarily, pharmacotherapies are used to address treatment of opioid addiction but are also effective for treating alcohol use disorder (SAMHSA, 2015). SAMHSA reports that medication-assisted treatment is greatly underused and that

> slow adoption of these evidence-based treatment options for alcohol and opioid dependence is partly due to misconceptions about substituting one drug for another ... instead, these medications relieve the withdrawal symptoms and psychological cravings that cause chemical imbalances in the body. (n.p.)

There are three types of pharmacotherapies: symptom amelioration, agonist substitution, and agonistic therapies (Lewis, Dana, & Blevins, 2015). Amelioration is related to addressing withdrawal symptoms (e.g., antidepressants); substitution is related to replacing the effect of the source drug (e.g., methadone); and agonistic therapies block the effect of the source drug (e.g., naltrexone, disulfiram; Lewis, Dana, & Blevins, 2015). Several medications are available for the treatment of opioid and alcohol addiction including Methadone (opioid), Buprenorphine (opioid), Naltrexone (opioid and alcohol), Disulfiram (alcohol), and Acamprosate (alcohol; SAMHSA, 2015). There are no available pharmacotherapies for stimulants, cannabis, or hallucinogens (Makadon et al., 2015).

CONSIDERING RELAPSE AND ASSOCIATED TRAUMA HISTORY

For clients exiting treatment for SUDs, relapse occurs more than half the time; thus continuing care (i.e., less intensive treatment) is extended to reinforce recovery (Blodgett, Maisel, Fuh, Wilbourne, & Finney, 2014). Meta-analysis of the empirical evidence about the efficacy of continuing care indicates significant positive effects, suggesting that there is a benefit for continuing care after initial treatment, though the effect was modest (Blodgett et al., 2014). Specific techniques such as relapse prevention incorporates strategies for the client and therapist to address the relapse process—interventions include identifying high-risk situations, enhancing coping skills, increasing self-efficacy, eliminating myths, managing lapses, and restructuring client perceptions (Larimer & Palmer, 1999). Various relapse prevention or continuing care methods have been shown effective over the past decade; however, methods may only be as effective as their adaptability. Arguably, in consideration of an LGBTQ client base, both treatment and continuing care must include attention to trauma history.

Empirical evidence related to the effectiveness of relapse prevention or continuing care with LGBTQ clients is limited; however, there are important factors that must be taken into consideration when addressing potential for relapse among such minority-community members. For instance, trauma history appears to be a salient indicator for relapse among treatment seekers across the board. In a study examining relapse probability and trauma history among treatment seekers, Farley, Golding, Young, Mulligan, and Minkoff (2004) examined demographic differences including sexual orientation. Data were collected from 959 treatment seekers, with 13% identifying as gay or lesbian and 4% bisexual. Lesbian, gay, and bisexual seekers reported significantly more violence-related trauma compared to their counterparts. For bisexual treatment seekers in particular, trauma history had a strong connection to relapse.

Trauma history is of critical concern when working with transgender clients (Mizock & Lewis, 2008); thus it is an important consideration for relapse. Implications for practitioners working with transgender clients to avoid relapse may include the recommendations offered by Richmond, Burnes, and Carroll (2012; see Box 22.3).

MUTUAL-HELP OR 12-STEP GROUP INTERVENTIONS

For many LGBTQ individuals working toward recovery from alcohol and/or drug addictions, mutual-help and 12-step groups (e.g., Alcoholics Anonymous, Narcotics Anonymous, Crystal Meth Anonymous) may serve as important foundations to lasting change. Often, mutual-help groups are part of a comprehensive treatment plan for individuals accessing treatment; individuals who participate in ongoing group involvement demonstrate better outcomes than individuals who do not (see Moos & Timko, 2008). Outcomes may hinge on individual-level engagement or buy-in. Several factors are related to engagement including steps completed, acceptance of 12-step ideology, self-identification as a group member, belief in a need for lifelong attendance, and need to surrender to a higher power (Moos & Timko, 2008). In each predictive area, there are concerns for the outcomes that may be experienced by members of the LGBTQ community. Practitioners are urged to help clients identify welcoming and LGBTQ-friendly or specific mutual-help groups especially if individuals experience trepidation about attendance.

According to SAMHSA (2012), LGBTQ people may feel a sense of moral condemnation if they connect 12-step models to religious dogma. However, many 12-step groups are open to everyone, and in many communities there exist LGBTQ-specific affirming mutual-help groups such as Alcoholics Together or there are Lambda Centers dedicated to serving LGBTQ communities. Often many 12-step groups support participants in defining their "higher power" quite broadly to encompass all religions, spiritualities, and even atheists and agnostics. As noted in one of Alcoholics Anonymous's program brochures (1989):

> Faith is a personal thing and it is not necessary to believe in God or in any form of religion to be a member of AA. All you need to be a member of AA. is a desire to stop drinking. Atheists, agnostics, and believers of all religions have a place in AA—provided they wish to stay away from the first drink.

Ultimately, practitioners should always assist their LGBTQ clients with finding an affirming 12-step group, other support group, or Al-ANON meeting for family members, if possible within their local area.

TREATMENT CHALLENGES IN RURAL ENVIRONMENTS

For members of the LGBT community, living in a rural environment may introduce additional biopsychosocial hurdles to substance abuse treatment. The Human Rights Campaign reports that in rural environments: "Discrimination in health care, housing and employment often leads to increased risk for poverty and social isolation for LGBT families, and also creates an additional barrier to accessing critical state and federal social services" (Maril, 2014, n.p.). Arguably social stressors highlighted by Human Rights Campaign may play a role in the substance-abusing behaviors of LGBTQ people living in rural areas. In these communities, potential for lack of social networks, increased isolation, and lack of health related-information may increase challenges faced by LGBTQ people seeking treatment services. Additional issues may arise when clinicians in rural environments are not equipped with work with gender and sexual minorities. Willging and colleagues (2006) examined mental health care for sexual and gender minorities living in a rural state. Using ethnographic techniques with 20 service providers in rural areas, the researchers found that LGBT clients had been denied services, discouraged from broaching sexual and gender issues, and secluded in residential settings. They noted that challenges to care in the community "magnified by provider neutrality" or claims that the provider sees and experiences no difference between the sexual- and gender-minority clients they serve. Practitioners treating substance abuse in rural environments must ultimately be disavowed of provider neutrality.

SUBSTANCE ABUSE PREVENTION

According to the SAMHSA (2015), a comprehensive approach to addressing public health involves prevention or efforts "delivered prior to the onset of a disorder . . . intended to prevent or reduce the risk of developing a behavioral health problem" (www.samhsa.gov/prevention). In 2010, the federal government (Healthy People, 2010) released a monograph related to reducing substance abuse and protecting the health, safety, and quality of life for all. Included in the monograph were several recommendations for the prevention of substance abuse among LGBTQ communities based on the following objectives:

- *Increase the age and proportion of adolescents who remain alcohol and drug free.* A first step in this effort is to build the data collection infrastructure to better understand the substance use patterns of LGBTQ youth. Specifically including items in national surveys that assess gender- and sexual-minority status.
- *Reducing use of illicit substances and average alcohol consumption.* In order to measure decreases in population use, there must be comprehensive community-level assessments in place. Assessments must include standardized LGBTQ-specific data from across the country as well as qualitative methods to elicit information about effective prevention efforts.
- *Increase the proportion of adolescents who perceive great risk associated with substance abuse.* Prevention efforts in this domain include community education efforts aimed at clarifying associated risk within youth populations. Youth may be best informed by adults who are in regular contact and may communicate information related to risk.
- *Increase the number of communities using partnerships and coalition models to conduct comprehensive substance prevention efforts.* Community-based efforts have a shared vision, core partners, mechanisms for conflict resolution, locally tailored programming, clearly defined and implemented agreements, and extensive prevention policies.

In sum, substance abuse and addiction within the LGBTQ community may be best addressed through community prevention efforts that include comprehensive data collection strategies and holistic research designs that allow prevention practitioners a place to start. In the meantime, prevention of problematic use among LGBTQ adolescents may be best addressed by trusted adults within their own family system and through the community via social service agencies. Last, prevention efforts must be organized within and by members of the LGBTQ community, so that it is tailored to meet the unique needs of individuals within specific locales.

CONCLUSION

The treatment of substance use and addiction is a complex undertaking, therefore social workers and practitioners engaged with LGBTQ clients who are challenged with substances must approach assessment, treatment, and interventions carefully. To this end, this chapter began with the sociohistorical context of substance use and settings in which substances are used, setting the stage for modern-day manifestations of addiction. Currently, epidemiological reports confirm a bleak picture of substance abuse and addiction among LGBTQ populations and highlight an overwhelming need for more data and information to fully understand and appreciate the scope of the problem. Irrespective of problem scope, however, the fact remains; evidence-based assessment, diagnosis, and treatment tailored to the unique needs of the LGBTQ population are paramount. Resources remain limited with regard to local, state, and federal funding for such services as well as amply LGBTQ-affirming service providers. While this chapter delineates often used strategies for treatment, much work remains in order to determine the most efficacious treatment approaches for LGBT individuals. In that regard, major gaps continue to exist in epidemiology and evidence-based treatment domains, yet one truth remains steadfast: the treatment of substance use and addiction among LGBTQ populations must occur from a person-in-environment perspective while consistently utilizing affirmative practice tenets.

REFERENCES

Alcoholics Anonymous. (1989). *AA and the gay/lesbian alcoholic.* New York: Author. Retrieved from http://www.aa.org/assets/en_US/P-32_AAandtheGayLesbianAlcoholic.pdf

American Psychiatric Association. (2013). *Diagnostic and statistical manual of mental disorders* (5th ed.). Washington, DC: American Psychiatric Association.

American Psychological Association. (2003). Guidelines for psychological practice with lesbian, gay, and bisexual clients. *American Psychologist, 67,* 10–42.

American Psychological Association. (2012). *Recognition of psychotherapy effectiveness.* Retrieved from http://www.apa.org.ezproxy1.lib.asu.edu/about/policy/resolution-psychotherapy.aspx

Anderson, S. C. (2009). *Substance use disorders in lesbian, gay, bisexual, and transgender clients: assessment and treatment.* New York: Columbia University Press.

Appleby, G. A., & Anastas, J. W. (1998). *Not just a passing phase: Social work with gay, lesbian, and bisexual people.* New York: Columbia University Press.

Arnett, J. J. (2000). Emerging adulthood: A theory of development from the late teens through the twenties. *American Psychologist, 55*(5), 469–480.

Arnett, J. J. (2014). *Emerging adulthood: The winding road from the late teens through the twenties* (2nd ed.). Oxford: Oxford University Press.

Austin, A., & Craig, S. L. (2015). Transgender affirmative cognitive behavioral therapy: Clinical considerations and applications. *Professional Psychology: Research and Practice, 46*(1), 21–29.

Babor, T. F., McRee, B. G., Kassebaum, P. A., Grimaldi, P. L., Ahmed, K., & Bray, J. (2007). Screening, Brief Intervention, and Referral to Treatment (SBIRT) toward a public health approach to the management of substance abuse. *Substance Abuse, 28*(3), 7–30.

Balsam, K. F., Martell, C. R., & Safren, S. A. (2006). Affirmative cognitive-behavioral therapy with lesbian, gay, and bisexual people. In P. A. Hays & G. Y. Iwamasa (Eds.), *Culturally responsive cognitive-behavioral therapy: Assessment, practice, and supervision* (pp. 223–243). Washington, DC: American Psychological Association.

Beck, A. T. (1970). Cognitive therapy: Nature and relation to behavior therapy. *Behavior Therapy, 1,* 184–200.

Ben-Ari, A. (2001). Homosexuality and heterosexism: Views from academics in the helping professions. *British Journal of Social Work, 31,* 119–131.

Blackwell, C., Birnholtz, J., & Abbott, C. (2014). Seeing and being seen: Co-situation and impression formation using Grindr, a location-aware gay dating app, *New Media & Society*, 7(7), 1117–1136.

Blodgett, J. C., Maisel, N. C., Fuh, I. L., Wilbourne, P. L., & Finney, J. W. (2014). How effective is continuing care for substance use disorders? A meta-analytic review. *Journal of Substance Abuse Treatment*, 46(2), 87–97.

Bronski, M. (2011). *A queer history of the United States*. Boston: Beacon Press.

Butler, A. C., Chapman, J. E., Forman, E. M., & Beck, A. T. (2006). The empirical status of cognitive-behavioral therapy: A review of meta-analysis. *Clinical Psychology Review*, 26(1), 17–31.

Center for Behavioral Health Statistics and Quality. (2015). *Behavioral health trends in the United States: Results from the 2014 National Survey on Drug Use and Health* (HHS Publication No. SMA 15-4927, NSDUH Series H-50). Rockville, MD: Substance Abuse and Mental Health Services Administration, Department of Health & Human Services.

Cochran, S. D., Keenan, C., Schober, C., & Mays, V. M. (2000). Estimates of alcohol use and clinical treatment needs among homosexually active men and women in the U. S. population. *Journal of Consulting and Clinical Psychology*, 68(6), 1062–1071.

Cochran, S. D., & Mays, V. M. (2009). Burden of psychiatric morbidity among lesbian, gay and bisexual individuals in the California Quality of Life Survey. *Journal of Abnormal Psychology*, 118, 647–658.

Conron, K. J., Mimiaga, M. J., & Landers, S. J. (2010). A population based study of sexual orientation identity and gender differences in adult health. *American Journal of Public Health*, 100 (10), 1953–1960.

Coulter, R. W. S., Blosnich, J. R., Bukowski, L. A., Herrick, A. L., Siconolfi, D. E., & Stall, R. D. (2015). Differences in alcohol use and alcohol-related problems between transgender- and non-transgender-identified young adults. *Drug and Alcohol Dependence*, 154, 251–259.

Crisp, C., & McCave, E. (2007). Gay affirmative practice: A model for social work practice with gay lesbian, and bisexual youth. *Child and Adolescent Social Work Journal*, 24, 403–421.

Davies, D. (1996). Towards a model of gay affirmative therapy. In D. Davies & C. Neal (Eds.), *Pink therapy: A guide for counselors and therapists working with lesbian, gay, and bisexual clients* (pp. 24–40). Philadelphia, PA: Open University Press.

Derogatis, L. R. (1975). *Brief Symptom Inventory*. Baltimore, MD: Clinical Psychometric Research.

Dilley, J. A., Simmons, K. W., Boysun, M. J., Pizacani, B. A., & Stark, M. J. (2010). Demonstrating the importance and feasibility of including sexual orientation in public health surveys: Health disparities in the Pacific Northwest. *American Journal of Public Health*, 100(3), 460–467.

Dozois, D. J. A., Westra, H. A., Collins, K. A., Fung, T. S., & Garry, J. K. F. (2004) Stages of change in anxiety: Psychometric properties of the University of Rhode Island Change Assessment (URICA) scale. *Behavior Research & Therapy*, 42(6), 711–729.

Drabble L., Midanik, L. T., & Tocki, K. (2005). Reports of alcohol consumption and alcohol-related problems among homosexual, bisexual, and heterosexual respondents: Results from the 2000 National Alcohol Survey. *Journal of Studies on Alcohol*, 66(1), 111–120.

Duberman, M. B. (1993). *Stonewall*. New York: Dutton.

Enevoldson, T. P. (2004). Recreational drugs and their neurological consequences. *Journal of Neurology, Neurosurgery & Psychiatry*, 75(Suppl. 3), iii9–iii15.

Ellis, A. (1962). *Reason and emotion in psychotherapy*. New York: Lyle Stuart.

Erikson, E. H. (1950). *Childhood and society*. New York: Norton.

Erikson, E. H. (1968). *Identity: Youth and crisis*. New York: Norton.

Farley, M., Golding, J. M., Young, G., Mulligan, M., & Minkoff, J. R. (2004). Trauma history and relapse probability among patients seeking substance abuse treatment. *Journal of Substance Abuse Treatment*, 27(2), 161–167.

Flentje, A., Hech, N. C., & Sorensen, J. L. (2015). Substance use among lesbian, gay, and bisexual clients entering substance abuse treatment: Comparisons to heterosexual clients. *Journal of Consulting and Clinical Psychology*, 83(2), 325–334.

Fredriksen-Goldsen, K. I., Cook-Daniels, L., Kim, H., Erosheva, E. A., Emlet, C. A., Hoy-Ellis, C. P., ... Muraco, A. (2013). Physical and mental health of transgender older adults: An at-risk and underserved population. *The Gerontologist, 54*(3), 488–500.

Fredriksen-Goldsen, K. I., Kim, H., Barkan, S. E., Muraco, A., & Hoy-Ellis, C. P. (2013). Health disparities among lesbian, gay, and bisexual older adults: Results from a population-based study. *American Journal of Public Health, 103*(10), 1802–1809.

Garofalo, R., Osmer, E., Sullivan, C., Doll, M., & Harper, G. (2007). Environmental, psychosocial and individual correlates of HIV risk in ethnic minority male-to- female transgender youth. *Journal of HIV AIDS Prevention in Children and Youth, 7*(2), 89–104.

Green, K. E., & Feinstein, B. A. (2012). Substance use in lesbian, gay, and bisexual populations: An update on empirical research and implications for treatment. *Psychology of Addictive Behaviors, 26*(2), 265–278.

Hayes, J. A., & Erkis, A. J. (2000). Therapist homophobia, client sexual orientation, and HIV infection as predictors of therapist reaction to clients with HIV. *Journal of Counseling Psychology, 47*, 71–78.

Hatzenbuehler, M. L., Corbin, W. R., & Fromme, K. (2008). Trajectories and determinants of LGB young adults and their heterosexual peers: Results from a prospective study. *Developmental Psychology, 44*(1), 81–90.

Healthy People 2010. *Lesbian, gay, bisexual, and transgender health*. Washington, DC: US Department of Health and Human Services, Office of Disease Prevention and Health Promotion. Retrieved from https://www.nalgap.org/PDF/Resources/Substance_Abuse.pdf.

Herbst, J. H., Jacobs, E. E., Finlayson, T. J., McKleroy, V. S., Newmann, M. S., & Crepaz, N. (2008). Estimating HIV prevalence and risk behaviors of transgender persons in the United States: A systematic review. *AIDS Behavior, 12*, 1–17.

Hofmann, S. G., Asnaani, A., Vonk, I. J., Sawyer, A. T., & Fang, A. (2012). The efficacy of cognitive behavioral therapy: A review of meta-analyses. *Cognitive Therapy Research, 36*(5), 427–440.

Ingram, G. B. (2012). From queer spaces to queerer ecologies: Recasting Gregory Bateson's steps to an ecology of mind to further mobilise & anticipate historically marginal stakeholders in environmental planning for community development. *European Journal of Ecopsychology, 3*, 53–80.

Institute of Medicine. (2001). *The health of lesbian, gay, bisexual and transgender people: Building a foundation for better understanding*. Washington, DC: National Academics Press.

Killen-Harvey, A. (2006, June). *Trauma among lesbian, gay, bisexual, transgender, or questioning youth*. NCTSN Culture and Trauma Briefs. Retrieved from http://www.nctsnet.org/nctsn_assets/pdfs/culture_and_trauma_brief_LGBTQ_youth.pdf.

Kosciw, J. G., Greytak, E. A., Palmer, N. A., & Boesen, M. J. (2014). *The 2013 National School Climate Survey: The experiences of lesbian, gay, bisexual and transgender youth in our nation's schools*. New York: GLSEN.

Larimer, M. E., & Palmer, R. S. (1999). Relapse prevention: An overview of Marlatt's cognitive-behavioral model. *Alcohol Research and Health, 23*(2), 151–160.

Lewis, J. A., Dana, R. Q., & Blevins, G. A. (2015). *Substance Abuse Counseling* (5th ed.). Stamford, CT: Cengage.

Makadon, H. J., Mayer, K. H., Potter, J., & Goldhammer, H. (2015). *Fenway guide to lesbian, gay, bisexual, and transgender health* (2nd ed.). Philadelphia, PA: American College of Physicians.

Maril, R. (2014). *Bringing equality home: LGBT people in rural America*. Human Rights Campaign. Retrieved from http://www.hrc.org/blog/bringing-equality-home-lgbt-people-in-rural-america.

Marshal, M. P., Friedman, M. S., Stall, R. King, K. M., Miles, J., Gold, M. A., ... Morse, J. Q. (2008). Sexual orientation and adolescent substance use: A meta-analysis and methodological review. *Addiction, 103*(4), 546–556.

McCabe, S. E., Hughes, T. L., Bostwick, W., West, B. T., & Boyd C. J. (2009). Sexual orientation, substance use behaviors and substance dependence in the United States. *Addiction, 104*, 1333–1345.

McCabe, S. E., West, B. T., Hughes, T. L., & Boyd, C. J. (2013). Sexual orientation and substance abuse treatment utilization in the United states: Results from a national survey. *Journal of Substance Abuse Treatment, 44*, 4–12.

McConnaughy, E. A., Prochaska, J. O., & Velicer, W. F. (1983). Stages of change in psychotherapy: Measurement and sample profiles. *Psychotherapy: Theory, Research, and Practice, 20,* 368–375.

McHenry, S. S., & Johnson, J. W. (1993). Homophobia in the therapist and gay or lesbian client: Conscious and unconscious collusions in self-hate. *Psychotherapy, 30,* 141–151.

McLellan, A. T., Alterman, A. I., Cacciola, J., Metzger, D., & O'Brien, C. P. (1992). A new measure of substance abuse treatment: Initial studies of the Treatment Services Review. *Journal of Nervous and Mental Disease, 180,* 101–110.

McLellan, A. T., Luborsky, L., O'Brien, C. P., & Woody, G. E. (1980). An improved diagnostic instrument for substance abuse patients: The addiction severity index. *Journal of Nervous & Mental Diseases, 168,* 26–33.

Melendez-Torres, G., & Bonell, C. (2013). Systematic review of cognitive behavioural interventions for HIV risk reduction in substance-using men who have sex with men. *International Journal of the Study of AIDS, 25*(9), 627–635.

Miller, W. R. (1983). Motivational interviewing with problem drinkers. *Behavioural Psychotherapy, 11,* 147–172.

Miller, W. R., & Rollnick, S. (2013). *Motivational interviewing: helping people change* (3rd ed.). New York: Guilford Press.

Mizock, L., & Lewis, T. K. (2008). Trauma in transgender populations: Risk, resilience, and clinical care. *Journal of Emotional Abuse, 8*(3), 335–354.

Moon, M. W., Fornili, K., & O'Briant, A. L. (2007). Risk comparison among youth who report sex with same-sex versus both-sex partners. *Youth and Society, 38*(3), 267–284.

Moos, R. H., & Timko, C. (2008). Outcome research on 12-step and other self-help programs. In M. Galanter & H. D. Kleber (Eds.), *The American Psychiatric Publishing textbook of substance abuse treatment* (4th ed., pp. 511–521). Arlington, VA: American Psychiatric Publishing.

Morgenstern, J., Bux, D. A., Parsons, J., Hagman, B. T., Wainberg, M., & Irwin, T. (2009). Randomized trial to reduce club drug use and HIV risk behaviors among men-who-have-sex-with-men (MSM). *Journal of Consulting and Clinical Psychology, 77*(4), 645–656.

Moyers, T. B., & Rollnick, S. (2002). A motivational interviewing perspective on resistance in psychotherapy. *Journal of Clinical Psychology, 58*(2), 185–193.

National Institute on Alcohol Abuse and Alcoholism. (2005). *Social work education for the prevention and treatment of alcohol use disorders. Module 10G: Sexual orientation and alcohol use disorders.* Retrieved from http:// pubs.niaaa.nih.gov/publications/Social/Module10GSexualOrientation/Modu le10G.html.

National Institute on Drug Abuse. (2012). *Principles of drug addiction treatment: A research-based guide* (3rd ed.). Washington, DC: National Institutes of Health.

National Institute on Drug Abuse. (2014). *Drugs, brains, and behavior: The science of addiction.* Washington, DC: National Institutes of Health.

Oscar-Berman, M., Shagrin, B., Evert, D. L., & Epstein, C. (1997). Impairments of the brain and behavior: The neurological effects of alcohol. *Alcohol Health & Research World, 21*(1), 65–75.

Parsons, J. T., Lelutiu-Weinberger, C., Botsko, M., & Golub, S. A. (2014). A randomized controlled trial utilizing motivational interviewing to reduce HIV risk and drug use in young gay and bisexual men. *Journal of Consulting and Clinical Psychology, 82*(1), 9–18.

Prochaska, J. O., DiClemente, C. C., & Norcross, J. C. (1992). In search of how people change. Applications to addictive behaviors. *American Psychology, 47*(9), 1102–1114.

Race, K. (2009). *Pleasure consuming medicine: The queer politics of drugs.* Durham, NC: Duke University Press.

Reback, C. J., & Fletcher, J. B. (2014). HIV prevalence, substance use, and sexual risk behaviors among transgender women recruited through outreach. *AIDS Behavior, 18,* 1359–1367.

Resick, P. A., Falsetti, S. A., Resnick, H. S., & Kilpatrick, D. G. (1991). *The Modified PTSD Symptom Scale–Self Report.* Charleston: Crime Victims Treatment and Research Center, Medical University of South Carolina.

Richmond, K. A., Burnes, T., & Carroll, K. (2012). Lost in trans-lation: Interpreting systems of trauma for transgender clients. *Traumatology: An International Journal, 18*(1), 45–57.

Rosen, D., Engel, R. J., Hunsaker, A. E., Engel, Y., Detlefsen, E. G., & Reynolds, C. F. (2013). Just say know: An examination of substance use disorders among older adults in gerontological and substance abuse journals. *Social Work in Public Health, 28*(3–4), 377–387.

Saunders, J. B., Aasland, O. G., Babor, T. F., de la Fuente, J. R., & Grant, M. (1993). Development of the Alcohol Use Disorders Screening Test (AUDIT). WHO collaborative project on early detection of persons with harmful alcohol consumption. II. *Addiction, 88,* 791–804.

Skinner, H.A. (1982). *The Drug Abuse Screening Test (DAST): Guidelines for administration and scoring.* Toronto: Addiction Research Foundation.

Smedslund, G., Berg, R. C., Hammerstrom, K. T., Steiro, A., Leiknes, K. A., Dahl, H. M., & Karlsen, K. (2011). Motivational interviewing for substance abuse (Review). *Cochran Database of Systematic Reviews, 5,* CD008063.

Substance Abuse and Mental Health Services Administration. (2012). *A provider's introduction to substance abuse treatment for lesbian, gay, bisexual, and transgender individuals.* Rockville, MD: US Department of Health and Human Services.

Substance Abuse and Mental Health Services Administration. (2015). *Medication and counseling treatment.* Retrieved from http://www.samhsa.gov/medication-assisted-treatment/treatment.

Substance Abuse and Mental Health Services Administration. (2016). *Screening, brief intervention, and referral to treatment (SBIRT).* Retrieved from http://www.samhsa.gov/sbirt.

Tozer, E., & McClanahan, M. (1999). Treating the purple menace: Ethical considerations of conversion therapy and affirmative alternatives. *The Counseling Psychologist, 27,* 722–742.

Valentine, G., & Skelton, T. (2003). Finding oneself, losing oneself: The lesbian and gay 'scene' as a paradoxical space. *International Journal of Urban and Regional Research, 27*(4), 849–866.

Wilson, E. C., Garofalo, R., Harris, Herrick, A., Martinez, M., Martinez, J., . . . Transgender Advisory Committee and the Adolescent Medicine Trials Network for HIV/AIDS Interventions. (2009). Transgender female youth and sex work: HIV risk and a comparison of life factors related to engagement in sex work. *AIDS Behavior, 13*(5), 902–913.

Willging, C. E., Salvador, M., & Kano, M. (2006). Brief reports: Unequal treatment: Mental health care for sexual and gender minority groups in a rural state. *Psychiatric Services, 57*(6), 867–870.

Wolf, S. (2009). *Sexuality and socialism: History, politics, and theory of LGTB liberation.* Chicago: Haymarket Books.

CHAPTER 23

UNDERSTANDING THE IMPACT OF INTIMATE PARTNER VIOLENCE

Trends, Frameworks, and Treatments

David A. McLeod, Kirsten Havig, Megan Gandy-Guedes,
and Anthony P. Natale

INTRODUCTION

The epidemic of intimate partner violence (IPV) is not a new phenomenon, with recognition from the US Centers for Disease Control and Prevention (CDC) declaring it a public health priority area over three and a half decades ago (Dahlberg & Mercy, 2009). Although the majority of service delivery systems established to address IPV in the United States have been constructed to provide assistance to women in heterosexual relationships, the phenomenon is not isolated to that population alone. When exploring the occurrence of IPV in American society it would be ill-advised to suggest heterosexual women are not a high-risk group, as data has indicated around one-third will experience IPV within their lifetime (Black et al., 2011). However, it is the intent of this chapter to pull back the curtain and provide additional context for understanding the experiences of IPV among people within the lesbian, gay, bisexual, transgender, and queer (LGBTQ) community, where this *openly* accepted public health epidemic has largely remained a closeted issue (Talicska, 2012).

Research findings from the National Violence Against Women Survey ($N = 16,000$) suggested that among those respondents who identified as living in same-sex partnership households, roughly 22% of men ($n = 65$) and 35% of women ($n = 79$) experienced IPV within their lifetimes (Tjaden & Thoennes, 2000). These numbers are slightly higher for women, and more than double for men, when compared to heterosexual partnerships (Tjaden & Thoennes, 2000). To add even more complexity to the issue, the CDC's 2010 National Intimate Partner and Sexual Violence Survey ($N = 16,507$) produced compelling findings with 43.8% of lesbians, 61.1% of bisexual women, and 26% of gay men reporting experiences related to some combination of stalking, physical, and/or sexual violence by an intimate partner at some point during the participant's lifetime, as compared to 35% of heterosexual women and 29% of heterosexual men who experienced the same (National Coalition of Anti-Violence Programs [NCAVP], 2013). Additionally, Brown and Herman (2015) found in their meta-analysis of the literature that 25% to 40% of transgender people reported experiencing dating violence or IPV across the course of their lifetimes.

This chapter begins by exploring the theoretical origins of domestic violence and defining and conceptualizing violence within relationships. Extended frameworks to assist in making meaning in violent relationships are provided. From there the chapter moves into an exploration of the prevalence of IPV within LGBTQ relationships and outlines multiple types of violence and the specific implications that may be critical for LGBTQ populations. Barriers to seeking care are discussed and recommendations for intervention work specific to LGBTQ individuals, families, and communities are provided.

DEFINING IPV AND RELATIONAL VIOLENCE

Clearly defining IPV is an endeavor still in process, and achieving consensus around the most appropriate terminology can be difficult. This may also complicate various factors when working to identify strategies to combat such significant social and behavioral problems. These challenges leave many advocates struggling to understand how to develop interventions that address IPV, find common language, and identify exactly what IPV means for this population. Conceptually, this is an area that in its origins was defined as "wife battering" or "spousal abuse" and has continually evolved as the context has shifted across the past several decades. To make matters more complicated, the criminal justice system has functioned as the primary mechanism for intervention with regard to domestic, family, interpersonal, relational, dating, and intimate partner violence. This type of approach reduces consistency due to the nature of our legal system in the United States. Each individual state has had the opportunity to define IPV in its own way, which has often been through heteronormative and cisnormative frameworks. The lack of both consistency and inclusivity in legal definitions confounds not only effective interventions but research using common variables to build the knowledge base. In an attempt to foster inclusivity and bring together the vast array of conceptualizations around the meaning of IPV, the CDC presented an official definition for IPV, which included many emerging elements associated with all types of intimate relationships including those with dynamics unique to relationships between transgender and same-sex individuals (Breiding, Basile, Smith, et al., 2015).

In this definition the CDC posits "intimate partner violence includes physical violence, sexual violence, stalking, and psychological aggression (including coercive tactics) by a current or former intimate partner (i.e. spouse, boyfriend/girlfriend, dating partner, or ongoing sexual partner)" (Breiding et al., 2015, p. 11). It is through this definition that we can begin to reconceptualize IPV from the ground up. Of the highest importance, close attention should be paid to the expanded recognition of who an intimate partner can be and the included emphasis on psychological aggression and coercive tactics. Even though the definitional origins of IPV have been strongly rooted in discrete acts of physical violence, over the past decade researchers have begun to recognize the importance of acknowledging the psychological, emotional, coercive, and controlling components of IPV. In the context of IPV, the phenomenon of coercive control can be defined as a pattern of behavior that is developed over time and focused on the intentional disempowerment and marginalization of a victim through the application of psychological force in an attempt to achieve a reduction of an intimate partner's liberty, freedom, independence of thought or action, or self-efficacy (Stark, 2007). This framework for coercive control can be framed as a response to an earlier call from the CDC for a refinement in the way IPV is conceptualized, to include enacted, threatened, or implied or physical, sexual, or psychological abuse (Saltzman, Fanslow, McMahon, et al., 1999).

RECONCEPTUALIZING IPV

If we are to begin to examine IPV in an inclusive, contextual, and holistic way, it could prove valuable to add to previous frameworks that have explained IPV based on recognition of specific physical acts of violence. Starting in 1979 with the seminal work of Lenore Walker, the cycle of violence theory began its permeation of the IPV lexicon. This theory suggests that a cycle of domestic and IPV includes tension building in a relationship, which then leads to a violent eruption or outburst, followed by a honeymoon period during which an absence of violence would be present in the relationship. The theory further suggests, though each relationship is unique, that after some period of time that tension would begin to build again, and eventually the cycle would repeat. Much attention has been given to this cyclical interpretation of IPV as it has been widely adopted in interventional and prevention circles. While these conceptualizations have been remarkably helpful in furthering discussions of the complexity surrounding IPV, they could be interpreted to suggest a perception of a lack of violence during periods between explicit physical acts. More recent research related to the importance of understanding coercive control in violent relationships, and its components of psychological and emotional violence, could be used to reconceptualize experiences of IPV as systemic rather than cyclical.

Figure 23.1 illustrates the model of systemic relational violence, which was developed by Dr. David McLeod (2016). This model is focused on conceptualizing IPV as a system of continued dominance over another, rather than a repeating cycle of violence in a relationship. In this conceptualization there is no expectation of relief from violence after specific physical or sexual acts of aggression have occurred. Rather, it is suggested that violence, through the psychologically and emotionally abusive components of coercive control, is always present within abusive relationships and escalates or deescalates over time. It is only when tension rises, due to a longing for or attempt to gain autonomy on the part of the disempowered partner, that the controlling or

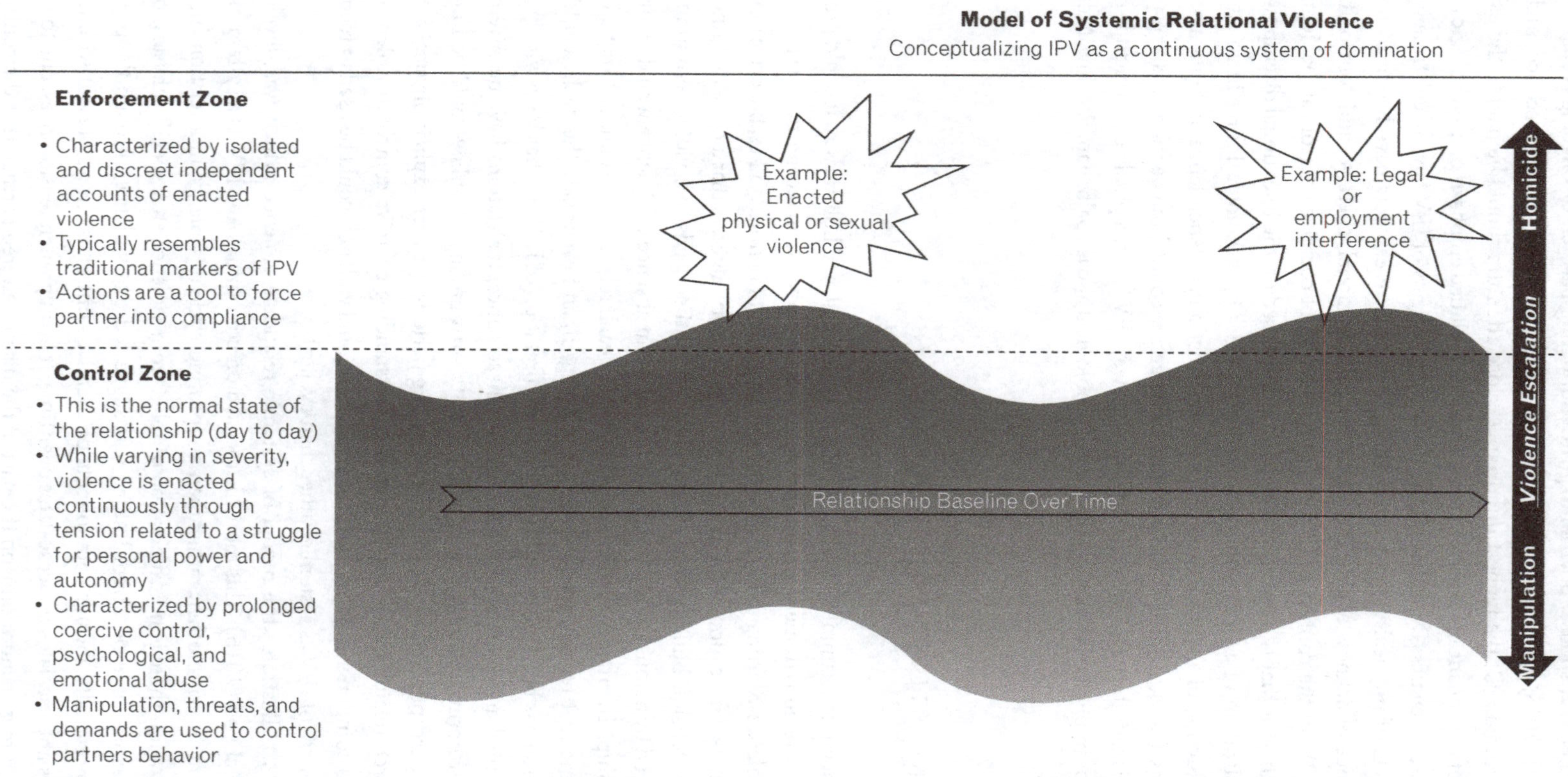

Model of Systemic Relational Violence
Conceptualizing IPV as a continuous system of domination

Manipulation ◄——— *Violence Escalation* ———► **Homicide**

Example: Legal or employment interference

Example: Enacted physical or sexual violence

Relationship Baseline Over Time

Enforcement Zone

- Characterized by isolated and discreet independent accounts of enacted violence
- Typically resembles traditional markers of IPV
- Actions are a tool to force partner into compliance

Control Zone

- This is the normal state of the relationship (day to day)
- While varying in severity, violence is enacted continuously through tension related to a struggle for personal power and autonomy
- Characterized by prolonged coercive control, psychological, and emotional abuse
- Manipulation, threats, and demands are used to control partners behavior

FIGURE 23.1: The model of systemic relational violence

dominant partner enforces power through explicit accounts of discreet and direct enacted violence, such as a physical assault or other external behavior that will cause direct harm. From the perspective of this model, these traditional markers of IPV are merely enforcement actions in a larger system of violence, which are used to force a disempowered partner into a state of compliance. This represents a continuum of control where the demands, needs, or desires of the abusive partner continually influence and guide the behavior(s) of the abused or marginalized partner.

This model holds the potential for conceptualizing relationships along a spectrum and over time while also allowing for the conceptualization of how relationships may or may not involve intimacy, cohabitation, or traditional concepts of domestication across their full course. Respecting that relationships change and evolve over time, this model allows for flexibility by reducing the reliance on specific details of the relationship or on actions the model defines as external mechanisms of enforcement. Rather, the focus of the model is on capturing the evolution of relationships and the constant, but fluctuating, tension associated with enforced control across the spectrum of violence.

Conceptualizing IPV in this way could be helpful in understanding the unique dynamics of violence in the relationships of LGBTQ people. Just as in heterosexual and cisgender relationships, violence in LGBTQ relationships is highly connected to a pattern of conscious manipulation and control and in the use of threats and other mechanisms of enforcement to perpetuate a system of domination over one's partner (Hart, 1986; Letellier, 1996). Such a model of systemic relational violence emphasizes the reality of violence as it exists beneath the surface of external control enforcement. Throughout this chapter we present multiple examples of how traditional conceptualizations of domestic violence, which quantify the phenomenon solely through the existence of physical or sexual aggression in relationships, fall short of understanding and describing the experiences of IPV in their totality. This is particularly important when trying to understand the phenomenon of IPV in the context of populations or groups of people who are experiencing, or have experienced, multidimensional marginalization throughout their lives.

PREVALENCE OF IPV WITHIN LGBTQ POPULATIONS

A report by the Williams Institute (Brown & Herman, 2015) gave an overview of current research on the prevalence of IPV in LGBT populations. The report examined both representative samples and purposive samples to estimate lifetime IPV experienced by these groups and compared those estimates to lifetime IPV estimates in heterosexual and cisgender populations. Brown and Herman found that across all reviewed research studies ($n = 42$), the range of prevalence of IPV among sexual-minority women (lesbian and bisexual) spans from 8.5% to 55%, and for sexual-minority men (gay and bisexual) from 13.9% to 44%. Only three studies existed at the time of this report that examine IPV in the transgender population, noting a range of 31.1% to 50% of lifetime IPV (Brown & Herman, 2015). The authors of this report went on to create an estimated average of lifetime IPV for each of the LGBT subgroups and compared them to the general population

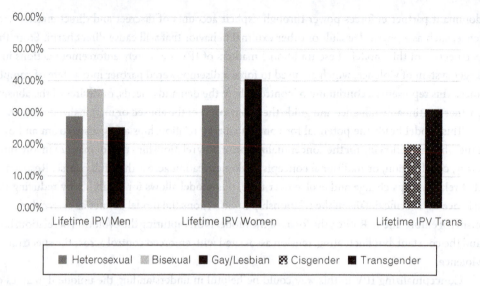

FIGURE 23.2: Prevalence of lifetime IPV and IPSV by sexual orientation and gender (National Intimate Partner and Sexual Violence Survey, 2010)

(see Figure 23.2). The estimates suggest that there is no statistically significant difference between heterosexual, bisexual, and gay men. However, bisexual women are 1.8 times more likely to experience IPV than heterosexual women, a finding that is statistically significant. Both men and women contribute to the IPV experienced by sexual-minority women: almost 90% of bisexual women and approximately 33% of lesbian women reported a male perpetrator. The only study to date that compared lifetime IPV between transgender and cisgender people found that 20.4% of cisgender people versus 31.1% of transgender people reported ever experiencing IPV in their lifetimes ($N = 1,139$; Langenderfer-Magruder, Whitfield, Walls, Kattari, & Ramos, 2016). These results suggest that bisexual populations and transgender populations are at disproportionate risk of lifetime IPV compared to lesbian women, gay men, heterosexual men and women, and cisgender populations. These estimates are based on available data only and are likely lower than the actual experiences of LGBTQ individuals due to a number of factors such as a historic mistrust of law enforcement (leading to lower reporting levels), the lack of same-sex relationship definitions in IPV laws, and the general difficulty researchers have noted on accessing LGBTQ individuals for research due to the hidden nature of their identities and the stigmatizing and potentially legal consequences of coming out.

The NCAVP has published a report each year since 2012 on national person-level data related to IPV survivors in LGBTQ populations. It analyzes the experiences of LGBTQ and HIV-affected IPV survivors who sought services from 16 NCAVP member organizations and thus cannot be considered representative of the general population of LGBTQ individuals. However, the goal of the report is to highlight disparities within the LGBTQ population of individuals who experience higher rates of certain kinds of violence. Over the four years of reporting, subpopulations that are more severely affected by IPV include people of color, HIV-infected persons, youth and young adults, bisexual individuals, transgender individuals, and gay men (NCAVP, 2015). The report defines more severely affected such as homicide victims of IPV and also as the highest percentage of survivors in certain demographic areas (i.e., racial, age, sexual orientation, gender identity, etc.).

There are several types of violence to be considered when examining incidence of IPV in LGBTQ populations. Not only does physical violence account for IPV but also sexual, emotional/verbal, financial, and identity abuse come into play for LGBTQ persons (National Coalition Against Domestic Violence, n.d.). The identity form of abuse is unique to hidden populations such as LGBTQ individuals because it uses the threat of "outing" someone as a coercive form of abuse (i.e., threatening to "out" a partner to their workplace or to other family members), usually intended to control the victim. Also unique to some members of the transgender population is coercive control exerted by threats of, or actually withholding, hormone therapy or access to other resources necessary to express gender according to one's identity.

There is a dearth of representative research on the prevalence of each type of abuse in the LGBTQ community. However, data collected by the NCAVP for the year 2014 suggest that physical violence is the most common form of abuse (20%), followed by verbal abuse such as threats and intimidation (16%), verbal harassment (15%), and sexual violence (4%; NCAVP, 2015). Although there is no direct data on identity abuse, the NCAVP collected data on survivors experiencing anti-LGBTQ bias in their relationship and found that 38% reported experiencing such bias (NCAVP, 2015). Along similar lines, 8% of those surveyed reported experiencing anti-immigrant bias, 15% reported experiencing antitransgender bias, and 11% reported experiencing HIV/AIDS-related bias. As these numbers indicate, there are many types and manifestations of abuse. LGBTQ communities likely face more complex types of abuse due to their multiple intersecting identities, resulting in a compounded impact.

UNIQUE EXPERIENCES OF RELATIONAL VIOLENCE AMONG THE LGBTQ COMMUNITY

Homophobia, biphobia, and transphobia are each palpable barriers for LGBTQ individuals in addressing partner violence within their own relationships. Taken with that is the omnipresence of cissexisim and heterosexism in limiting IPV to a concern for heterosexuals and cisgender individuals and thereby minimizing solutions for the LGBTQ communities. Until individual and structural barriers to reducing IPV among LGBTQ people are addressed, the problem will continue, with devastating effects. Whether an LGBTQ individual can access a protection order for domestic violence remains unclear. Three states have instituted a ban on same-sex survivors' protection orders, while 18 states have gender-neutral laws but they apply to only those living in the home. Another 30 states and the District of Columbia have gender-neutral domestic violence protection orders available regardless of cohabitation (National Gay and Lesbian Task Force, 2005). The following sections examine unique experiences of relational violence among members of the LGBTQ community, including psychological, economic, physical, and sexual violence.

PSYCHOLOGICAL VIOLENCE

Forms of psychological violence that can impact members of the LGBTQ community may include verbal and emotional abuse (including both expressive aggression and coercive control). This will be followed by a discussion surrounding other forms of violence related to economic abuse, physical and sexual abuse, and societal forces that impact IPV among members of the LGBTQ community.

VERBAL AND EMOTIONAL ABUSE

IPV within LGBTQ relationships most often takes the form of psychological violence, which includes verbal and emotional abuse (Greenwood et al., 2002). Verbal abuse is understood as the use of words, voice volume, action, or lack of action that is intended to hurt, control, or demean another person (Ard & Makadon, 2011). The intent of the verbal abuse is often to intimidate and control the actions of the victim. Verbal and emotional attacks are often a prelude to physical aggression (Stephenson, Rentsch, Salazar, & Sullivan, 2011) and serve to reinforce control in the absence of physical acts. For LGBTQ victims, when verbal abuse occurs in public, it holds the potential to reveal the sexual orientation or gender identity of the victim, thereby increasing their vulnerability to societal oppression (Aulivola, 2004; Elliott, 1996).

Verbal abuse can be especially hostile when it reflects experiences the victim might have received from the family of origin. Chen, Jacobs, and Rovi (2013) remind us that sexual orientation stigma remains a barrier to seeking professional assistance. They underscore that, for transgender victims, leaving an IPV situation can often entail leaving the support system behind. In addition, it is important to consider that outing of one's positive HIV status as another means of verbal abuse can have profound effects for that individual.

EXPRESSIVE AGGRESSION

Emotional abuse typically takes two primary forms—*expressive aggression* and *coercive control* (Hamel, Desmarais, & Nicholls, 2007). Expressive aggression occurs when a partner uses hateful and derogatory names (e.g., faggot, tranny, queer, crazy, homo, ugly, fat, whore) to insult or humiliate. In the case of a transgender individual, the offending behavior may be the intentional misgendering of the victim or claims that they are not "woman or man enough" to claim the gender they identify with. The effects of verbal abuse can be lifelong including hopelessness, lack of confidence, and poor self-esteem and self-worth (Otis & Skinner, 1996). While the scars of physical abuse are often more noticeable with a specified healing timetable, scars acquired from verbal abuse can be sustained over the life course with little if any healing (Garnets, Herek, & Levy, 1990), making the damage caused by their reopening all the more devastating.

COERCIVE CONTROL

The second form of emotional abuse is called coercive control, which is when abusers keep their partner from seeing family or friends or engaging in decision-making for themselves by threatening an undesirable course of action (Hamel, Desmarais, & Nicholls, 2007). Examples include threats of harm to themselves or to others that the victim cares for. This can include threats to harm or remove children or pets from the home. For transgender women, coercive control threats are supported by the notion that most shelters for IPV are designed for females only, thereby denying access to transgender people (McClennen, 2005). Consequently, IPV perpetrators could verbally abuse their transgender partner by stating "Where would you go? No one will take you." In this case, the perpetrator is correct in the limited options for the victim, a chilling truth.

ECONOMIC VIOLENCE

While the scars of physical abuse are often visible and the scars of emotional and verbal abuse are omnipresent but invisible, perhaps the least understood while the most insidious of all are the scars left from economic violence (Postmus, Plummer, McMahon, et al., 2012). Economic abuse is most often found within a larger pattern of IPV where control is a predominant feature (Baker, Buick, Kim, et al., 2013). Economic abuse is when one partner has control over the economic resources of the other. This control functions to minimize the problem-solving options of the victim while maximizing the power of the perpetrator over the victim (Baker et al., 2013).

Common behaviors of economic abuse include making victims ask for money, even if they earned it themselves; using a victim's credit cards without permission; or forcing the victim to work while the perpetrator does not (Anderson, 2010). It also includes denying access to education for victims, which has the potential to impact their self-sufficiency and capacity for independence. Destroying property such as cell phones or transportation are other examples. An often-used economic abuse strategy is to threaten the victim with eviction and homelessness. This threat has even more power in the case where children are in the home under the care of the victim (Anderson, 2010). Economic abuse includes not only controlling one's current resources but also impacting the victim's ability to seek employment or increase potential for future financial independence (Heintz & Melendez, 2006). By denying the victim access to resources or the potential to accumulate resources, essentially, the perpetrator makes the victim financially dependent on the perpetrator for food, shelter, and clothing into the foreseeable future. The inability to financially plan for the future leaves the victim in a perpetual state of vulnerability (Heintz & Melendez, 2006).

For many LGBTQ individuals, financial vulnerability is already pronounced due to higher rates of unemployment in the face of a lack of employment protections (Pizer, Sears, Mallory

& Hunter, 2011). This is especially true for lesbian, gay, and bisexual people of color. It is even more pronounced for transgender women of color, whose intersecting identities compound the oppression they experience compared with the individual components of race, gender identity, and perhaps sexual orientation alone (Parry & O'Neal, 2015). LGBTQ financial stability may already be at risk in terms of loss of families of origin at the time of disclosure of sexual orientation or gender identity (McClennen, 2005). This can mark the loss of an important support network, which often provides economic assistance or a safety net in times of need. As a result, the social and economic resources available to them are diminished, increasing the vulnerability of LGBTQ individuals who do not have robust social and economic support networks.

PHYSICAL AND SEXUAL VIOLENCE

Although this chapter has focused so far on conceptualizations of IPV in a more holistic fashion, when it comes to traditional markers of violence within relationships, research has continually suggested LGBTQ people suffer at rates comparable to and exceeding that of the general population in the United States (Brown & Herman, 2015). Numerous factors contribute to the differences seen in these numbers, including differential interpretations of what constitutes enacted violence as well as the many barriers that could impede IPV reporting for LGBTQ people.

PHYSICAL VIOLENCE

Physical violence is likely the single most identified characteristic of IPV. Many individuals often erroneously characterize physical violence as the only expression of what is, in reality, a much more complex web of behaviors. While we know relational violence is a far more contextual and nuanced phenomenon, incidents involving physical violence as a contributing factor to this overall experience are profound among LGBTQ people. As introduced earlier in the chapter, recent research has suggested that just over 26% of men identifying as gay have experienced IPV in their lifetimes, with over 12% of the sample disclosing experiences within the past year (Goldberg & Meyer, 2013). These findings mirror those associated with the CDC National Intimate Partner and Sexual Violence Survey, which goes on to add that approximately 40% of women identifying as lesbian and almost 57% of women identifying as bisexual have also reported experiences of physical violence at the hand of their partner during their lifetime (CDC, 2010). While findings associated with transgender people tend to be far more limited, they are just as disturbing in the numbers they report. One study ($N = 1,139$) identified approximately 31% of the transgender participants reporting experiences of physical violence in their intimate relationships, compared to approximately 20% of the cisgender participants in the study (Langenderfer-Magruder et al., 2016). Across the spectrum of the available research, findings consistently support that between 25% to 47% of transgender people report having experienced physical violence in their relationships (Brown & Herman, 2015).

SEXUAL VIOLENCE

Not unlike physical violence, sexual violence is a tremendous assault on bodily integrity that also holds specific psychological implications within the context of intimate relationships. The frequency of intimate partner sexual assault in LGBTQ relationships is substantial and well-quantified in the 2015 meta-analysis report by Brown and Herman (2015), where it is suggested up to 30% of women identifying as lesbian, 22% of women identifying as bisexual, 14% of men identifying as gay, 14.3% of people identifying as bisexual, and 47% of individuals identifying as transgender report having been sexually assaulted by an intimate partner. To add additional context to these numbers it should be understood that research has often identified sexual minorities to have extensive histories of relationship-based victimization at the hands of both men and women throughout the course of their lives (Messinger, 2011; Walters, Chen, & Breiding, 2013).

SOCIETAL FORCES THAT INFLUENCE IPV IN LGBTQ POPULATIONS

Heterosexism and cissexism have an influence on the occurrence of and response to IPV in LGBTQ intimate relationships (Guadalupe-Diaz, 2013; Herek, 1990; Kubicek, McNeeley, & Collins, 2015). As Guadalupe-Diaz states:

> Specifically, homophobia, heterosexism, and transphobia structurally disadvantage LGBT victims and also foster opportunities for abuse that rely on this power structure. The marginalization of LGBT individuals may fuel intimate abuse through the isolation and shaming of victims as well as present barriers to help-seeking. (p. 12)

Heterosexism and cissexism impact IPV in LGBTQ people in two ways: by making them more susceptible and by providing a perpetrator with a significant pathway of power. Some LGBTQ people become more susceptible to being victims of IPV due to lower self-esteem and greater feelings of powerlessness as a result of internalized negative messages shared by society (i.e., internalized homophobia, internalized transphobia). Perpetration of IPV by LGBTQ intimate partners can be more likely by providing a pathway for the abuser with unique sources of power and control. The perpetrator can play on the power dynamics that exist within the broader society, including perceptions of LGBTQ people as less-than (and therefore using that dynamic to verbally put down the victim), and also using threats to the victim such as outing, which could result in fall-out with family members or friends, in educational and employment settings, and in other relationships (Guadalupe-Diaz, 2013).

Minority stress theory (see chapter 12) could also explain the experiences of LGBTQ people in relation to IPV. This theory relates the stressors of minority status resulting in oppression and marginalization to the higher rates of health and mental health problems in minority populations (Meyer, 1995). Thus LGBTQ people as a minority experience higher rates of stress and as a result also experience higher rates of problems such as IPV (Pimentel, 2015). The minority stress model helps provide a framework for understanding the impact of stigma for gender and sexual minorities and reluctance to talk about violence in their private lives and the resulting internalized oppression that may occur (Hendricks & Testa, 2012). A member of a gender- or sexual-minority group may also hesitate to come out to service providers, fearing possible discrimination, leaving them in a position where it may be assumed they are heterosexual or cisgender and, in turn, at risk for receiving services that are not relevant or appropriate to actual needs (FORGE, 2013; Gentlewarrior & Fountain, 2009).

Experiences of IPV by people who identify as transgender, genderqueer, or gender nonconforming are differentially impacted with an additional layer of influence associated with gender norms, stereotypes, and power. Genderism has long purported the idea that IPV occurs only between a "powerful" male and a "powerless" female, thus entrenching gender norms into its explanation of IPV (Walker, 2015). However, once the field acknowledged IPV among same-sex couples, this gendered explanation, while still applicable in some cases, became less useful, particularly when applied to intimate partner relationships where one or both members are transgender. Walker (2015) suggests that rather than seeing IPV as an issue of masculinity and patriarchal motivation for control over a weaker, feminine partner, this vision may be reimagined to see the problem in a hierarchical fashion. In this context, perpetrators already feel weakened by society (for any reason) and then turn to someone who has even less power than themselves to exert their own power and control. So it is not so much an issue of gender norms and masculinity but rather of the struggle for power in the midst of real or perceived powerlessness.

Walker (2015) goes on to describe three specific stages at which transgender people have unique vulnerabilities to IPV: (a) during the initial phases of transitioning, whether that be by the use of medication or surgeries to alter physical appearance; (b) while living full-time as their new gender identity in public, including changes in dress, name, pronoun, and so on; and (c) when dealing with coming out to family and friends. During these times of transition, transgender people face transphobia in social settings and in relationships, thus leaving them more vulnerable than ever. Therefore, the penchant for their partner to turn to power and control is heightened.

BARRIERS TO SEEKING SUPPORT AND CARE

LGBTQ individuals encounter unique obstacles to their efforts at seeking help. The gendered norms entrenched in policies, such as using pronouns to identify the perpetrator (he) versus the victim (she), automatically excludes many LGBTQ people's realities (Walker, 2015). Also entrenched in survivor-supportive services is the assumption of a female gender identity (i.e., women's resource center, women's aid, women and children shelter, etc.). While such services have great value in the landscape of IPV responses, the reality is that those who do not identify or express a female gender are left with few resources geared toward their needs.

Another barrier to seeking help is the decision to come out or stay closeted. If a lesbian woman is experiencing partner abuse but is not out to any family or friends, she may not be willing to disclose her sexual orientation, or she may not even mention the abuse for fear of risking accidental disclosure. Indeed, a perpetrator may even use this closeted status as a form of coercion and control, threatening to out the victim, as described elsewhere in this chapter.

Social isolation is a problem faced by transgender people in particular. They are shunned from common spaces where cisgender and gender-normative people do not think twice about occupying—a grocery store, drugstore, park, church, work, bathroom, bar, and so on. Thus transgender people can easily lose the social connections that were once afforded to them before they came out or transitioned. Some transgender people express, in weighing the risks and rewards of disclosure, that it is more worthwhile in their view to stay with an abusive partner than to face total social isolation (Walker, 2015).

The mistrust of police officers and others in authority is another reason that LGBTQ people are hesitant to seek support in response to IPV. For a transgender person, if there is an investigation that involves a bodily examination (to document bruises or collect evidence for a sexual assault or rape kit), they might be very uncomfortable revealing their bodies to cisgender law officers or medical professionals, especially given the frequency of transphobic responses by those service providers (Oregon State Attorney Generals Sexual Assault Task Force, 2010). Indeed, this reason alone might prevent transgender people from seeking to report abuse and assault—if they are not willing to give physical documentation of the incident, they may not be taken seriously by the authorities. LGBTQ individuals have experienced a historic mistrust of police due to incidents of brutality in response to their stigmatized identities. Thus, as has been reported by women of color regarding utilization of established systems for IPV, LGBTQ people may never see police and other authorities as a safe or effective option.

The lack of spaces that can accommodate LGBTQ victims is yet another problem. Women's shelters tend to be exclusive to female-bodied individuals; in the case of transgender women who have not had gender reassignment surgery, they are likely to be turned away. This outlook is changing as policies and regulations shift to require safe spaces that accommodate LGBTQ people; yet there are anecdotal reports that some service organizations advertise a safe space for a LGBTQ person but when it comes time to access such services, the reality is that there are none available.

RECOMMENDATIONS

As new information and awareness of IPV in the LGBTQ community emerges, so do many challenges for service providers, policymakers, and victims of IPV. LGBTQ individuals impacted by IPV may not recognize the signs or symptoms themselves or even name it as such. LGBTQ victims may have a difficult time recognizing abuse because of the lack of information, education, and community discussion around transgender and same-sex IPV. Without education to contextualize violence, or even an understanding of the LGBTQ community itself rooted in stereotypes, misinformation, and internalized negative self-image, people may believe such behaviors are normal. Coupled with the impact of childhood exposure to violence, such misinformation only furthers the likelihood of continuing sustained engagement in violent relationships in one's own adult life. Prevention programs may not recognize or include LGBTQ individuals and families, in effect excluding many from education relevant to their own lives and leaving support systems and service providers equally unprepared to respond (National Sexual Violence Resource Center and Pennsylvania Coalition Against Rape, 2012). Isolation experienced by many victims of IPV may be further heightened due to marginalization connected to being LGBTQ, as discussed earlier in the chapter.

Perpetrators of abuse may use these contexts as weapons against partners as tools of control; for instance, telling victims that there are no services available to help them, or that judgment and discrimination await them within domestic violence agencies. In some situations, this may still be the case, leaving many victims without refuge. LGBTQ victims may choose not to report crimes against them committed by an intimate partner in fear of further stigmatizing the community or "airing the dirty laundry." Additionally, the historical context of discrimination and violence from law enforcement further discourages reporting and help-seeking (Native American Program of Legal Aid Services of Oregon, 2013). Whether real or perceived, these psychological barriers afford abusers greater power over their partners.

One of the first and most difficult challenges domestic violence service providers may face in working with LGBTQ individuals and couples is the ability to simply recognize the unique dynamics that may be present. While many similarities exist with heterosexual cisgender-based IPV, there are distinctions that challenge the assumptions and established protocols service providers are accustomed to. Research indicates that IPV among same-sex couples occurs at similar or higher rates compared to straight couples; unfortunately, domestic violence victims in same-sex relationships do not consistently receive the help they need. Key dynamics include gender norms and stereotypes that make it harder to see women as aggressors and men as victims; perceptions of power equity in same-sex couples (i.e., men fighting with one another is viewed differently than the more obvious power differential perceived between a woman and a man); and a lack of legal protection and value for transgender individuals (Goodmark, 2013). Emerging research helps to shed light on these dynamics as they manifest in system responses to IPV. For instance, in some cases the victim of IPV has been detained instead of the aggressor because the latter was physically smaller. In a 2013 report, NCAVP indicated that only 16.5% of IPV victims reported interacting with the police, but in one-third of those cases, the survivor was arrested instead of the abuser. A mere 3.7% of survivors reported seeking access to shelters. Authorities often lack the knowledge of how to handle domestic violence cases involving people of the same gender. Victims may not file a report of domestic violence since the two parties involved may be unwilling to divulge their relationship status. Same-sex victims have been found in some research to be more likely to abuse alcohol and drugs as a coping mechanism, further muddying the waters for law enforcement responses.

Domestic violence programs that include residential shelter face unique challenges in responding to the LGBTQ community's needs. Many domestic violence shelters are increasingly responsive to the needs of lesbian victims; however, services for gay men are practically nonexistent in environments built as female-specific. Shelter services targeting LGBTQ victims are lacking in number and accessibility, with such lack of access to safety only exacerbating the risk and impact of violence to the community (GLBT Domestic Violence Coalition and Jane Doe Inc., n.d.) Another element of service provision for lesbian and transgender individuals now occurring in traditional female-serving IPV programs is the perpetrator posing as a victim in order to gain access to the victim in shelter or in service settings. For reasons of both safety and sound service provision, these dynamics are important to recognize and plan for in shelter settings. Training and referral resources available to shelter staff are important elements of broadening the response to IPV. While female-only programs remain critical to the landscape of IPV service, agencies can also work toward building community support and resources for the establishment of safe housing that is gender-neutral, transinclusive, and male-specific (Ford, Slavin, Hilton, & Holt, 2012; Munson, 2014).

Despite gains made in terms of marriage equality for same-sex couples, survivors of same-sex domestic violence may still lack the same legal recognition and protection as heterosexual survivors. Currently, a patchwork of state laws exist that offer some protections to gay and lesbian victims of IPV. Some laws cover gay and lesbian victims explicitly in their anti-domestic violence legislation, while others do so though gender-neutral language. This may be further compounded in areas with a high Native American population due to tribal laws and jurisdictional challenges, which can create gaps in enforcement and prosecution. The 2013 reauthorization of the Violence Against Women Act represented a big step toward closing these gaps, both for LGBTQ individuals as well as tribal citizens.

First responders, court personnel, and social service providers are critical to improving services and protection for LGBTQ people in terms of IPV prevention and response. Three elements of culturally competent practice—self-awareness, knowledge, and skills—are as critical to service with LGBTQ victims of IPV as with any other group (Gentlewarrior & Fountain, 2009) and should guide efforts to not only incorporate new knowledge but to examine our own biases and limitations as social workers. While specific training within and across multidisciplinary professionals is key, there are a number of recommendations that are relevant across systems as seen in Table 23.1.

CONCLUSION

Moving forward, it is important to recognize the complexity that exists when addressing the phenomenon of relational violence, particularly in the context of the lives of LGBTQ people. Not only are there multiple constructs that can be used to describe the specific details of these violent exchanges in relationships, but there are also are a great many social and organizational constructs that can complicate and restrict intervention for those in crisis. In the origins of the language used to describe relational violence in our society, recognition was seldom if ever given to LGBTQ people, and the uniqueness of the relationships of sexual minorities was rarely given consideration. However, the knowledge revealed throughout this chapter gives recognition to a substantial, even epidemic, problem that many people across our country are facing, including LGBTQ people. As diverse people of all types struggle to find ways to deal with these complicated problems, we must work together to ensure the service delivery mechanisms that we implement to address IPV and relational violence are inclusive and supportive of all who are impacted.

TABLE 23.1 Key Recommendations for Working with LGBTQ Populations Dealing with Relational Violence

Become familiar with the history, language, struggles, and resilience of the LGBTQ community

Advocate for ongoing training in social work settings relevant to the history of and current experiences of LGBTQ people

Work toward inclusivity of LGBTQ staff and perspectives in agencies and decision-making processes

Measure and monitor LGBTQ-affirming practice among staff (the Gay Affirmative Practice Scale [Crisp, 2006] is one example of a tool)

Become familiar with the unique dynamics of intimate partner violence in the LGBTQ community, keeping in mind, however, that there are more similarities than differences

Gain an understanding of identity formation and the coming out process to inform sensitive interactions and contextualized decision-making

Do not assume that every victim you come into contact with is heterosexual or cisgender

Do not pressure the survivor to file a police report or follow up on legal action

Respect each survivor's individuality and recognize the diversity *within* populations of LGBTQ people

Do not minimize fears and concerns

Make connections with local LGBTQ organizations to share resources and to collaborate on outreach efforts and community education

Create a safe environment for LGBTQ survivors that includes, for example, inclusive literature and signage/art, gender-neutral restrooms, and intake forms that offer options beyond male/female (FORGE, n.d.)

Consider instituting a bill of rights and/or nondiscrimination pledge in agency consent forms (FORGE, n.d.)

Have appropriate and inclusive information and referrals on hand to provide to clients and colleagues

Consider your agency policies and protocols—are there unintentional barriers that may disproportionately impact LGBTQ people or prevent service provision? (i.e., no services offered to men or transgender people; housing/residential services for transgender individuals in a traditional women's space; how to approach treatment and intervention when the batterer is a woman)

When safety planning, take into consideration the unique threats and barriers that LGBTQ individuals may face, including identification documents, resources related to gender identity, and a potential lack of social support

Increase survivor-led programming to empower survivors as well as enhance inclusivity of agencies (National Coalition of Anti-Violence Programs, 2013)

Examine state-level policies that may limit response to LGBTQ victims; educate policymakers and advocate for equitable laws

Examine how your community views LGBTQ people—is there stigma associated with agencies who serve them? Does that stigma impact staff or funding source? Again, education and advocacy within and outside of the organization may be needed to build understanding and support

Include LGBTQ individuals in prevention materials and efforts across settings to better equip potential victims as well as the community to recognize and respond to intimate partner violence

Ask if you are not sure how a person identifies, preferred terms or pronouns, and experience with exposure to violence

Remember compassion and the right to live free from violence should be available to all people regardless of sexual orientation, gender identity, or gender expression

REFERENCES

Ard, K. L., & Makadon, H. J. (2011). Addressing intimate partner violence in lesbian, gay, bisexual, and transgender patients. *Journal of General Internal Medicine, 26*(8), 930–933.

Anderson, K. L. (2010). Conflict, power, and violence in families. *Journal of Marriage and Family, 72*(3), 726–742.

Aulivola, M. (2004). Outing domestic violence. *Family Court Review, 42*(1), 162–177.

Oregon State Attorney Generals Sexual Assault Task Force. (2010). *Advocacy manual 2010: LGBTQ survivors of sexual assault.* Oregon Department of Justice. Retrieved from http://www.doj.state.or.us/victims/pdf/lgbtiq_survivors_of_sexual_assault.pdf

Baker, N. L., Buick, J. D., Kim, S. R., Moniz, S., & Nava, K. L. (2013). Lessons from examining same-sex intimate partner violence. *Sex Roles, 69*(3–4), 182–192.

Black, M. C., Basile, K. C., Breiding, M. J., Smith, S. G., Walters, M. L., Merrick, M. T., & Stevens, M. R. (2011). *National intimate partner and sexual violence survey.* Atlanta, GA: CDC. Centers for Disease Control and Prevention. Retrieved from http://www.cdc.gov/violenceprevention/pdf/nisvs_report2010-a.pdf

Breiding M. J., Basile K. C., Smith S. G., Black M. C., Mahendra R. R. Intimate Partner Violence Surveillance: Uniform Definitions and Recommended Data Elements, Version 2.0. Atlanta (GA): National Center for Injury Prevention and Control, Centers for Disease Control and Prevention; 2015.

Brown, T. N. T., & Herman, J. L. (2015). *Intimate partner violence and sexual abuse among LGBT people: A review of existing research.* Los Angeles, CA: Williams Institute. Retrieved from http://williamsinstitute.law.ucla.edu/wp-content/uploads/Intimate-Partner-Violence-and-Sexual-Abuse-among-LGBT-People.pdf

Chen, P. H., Jacobs, A., & Rovi, S. L. (2013). Intimate partner violence: IPV in the LGBT community. *FP Essentials, 412,* 28–35.

Crisp, C. (2006). The Gay Affirmative Practice Scale (GAP): A new measure for assessing cultural competence with gay and lesbian clients. *Social Work, 2*(51), 115–126.

Dahlberg, L. L., & Mercy J.A. (2009). *History of violence as a public health issue.* US Centers for Disease Control. Retrieved from http://www.cdc.gov/violenceprevention/pdf/history_violence-a.pdf

Ford, C. L., Slavin, T. Hilton, K. L. & Holt, S. L. (2013). Intimate partner violence prevention services and resources in Los Angeles: Issues, needs, and challenges for assisting lesbian, gay, bisexual, and transgender clients. *Health Promotion Practice, 14*(6), 841–849.

FORGE (n.d.). *Creating a trans-welcoming environment: A tips sheet for sexual assault service providers.* Milwaukee, WI: Author.

FORGE (n.d.). *Is your agency ready to serve transgender survivors?* Milwaukee, WI: Author.

FORGE (2013). *Safety planning with transgender clients FAQ* (Victim Service Providers' Fact Sheet 9). Milwaukee, WI: Author.

Elliot, P. (1996). Shattering illusions: Same-sex domestic violence. *Journal of Gay & Lesbian Social Services, 4*(1), 1–8.

Garnets, L., Herek, G. M., & Levy, B. (1990). Violence and victimization of lesbians and gay men mental health consequences. *Journal of Interpersonal Violence, 5*(3), 366–383.

Gentlewarrior, S., & Fountain, K. (2009). *Culturally competent service provision to lesbian, gay, bisexual and transgender survivors of sexual violence.* National Online Resource Center on Violence Against Women. Retrieved from http://www.vawnet.org/print-document.php?doc_id=2099&find_type=web_sum_AR

Goldberg, N. G., & Meyer, I. H. (2013). Sexual orientation disparities in history of intimate partner violence: Results from the California Health Interview Survey. *Journal of Interpersonal Violence, 28*(5), 1109–1118.

Goodmark, L. (2013) Transgender people, intimate partner abuse, and the legal system. *Harvard Civil Rights-Civil Liberties Law Review, 48,* 51–104. Retrieved from http://harvardcrcl.org/wp-content/uploads/2013/04/Goodmark_51-104.pdf

GLBT Domestic Violence Coalition and Jane Doe Inc. (n.d.). *Shelter/housing needs for gay, lesbian, bisexual and transgender (GLBT) victims of domestic violence.* Boston, MA: Author.

Greenwood, G. L., Relf, M. V., Huang, B., Pollack, L. M., Canchola, J. A., & Catania, J. A. (2002). Battering victimization among a probability-based sample of men who have sex with men. *American Journal of Public Health, 92*(12), 1964–1969.

Guadalupe-Diaz, X. L. (2013). *Victims outside the binary: Transgender survivors of intimate partner violence* (PhD dissertation). University of Central Florida, Orlando.

Hamel, J., Desmarais, S. L., & Nicholls, T. L. (2007). Perceptions of motives in intimate partner violence: Expressive versus coercive violence. *Violence and Victims, 22*(5), 563–576.

Hart, B. (1986). Lesbian battering: An examination. In K. Lobel (Ed.), *Naming the violence* (pp. 173–189). Seattle, WA: Seal Press.

Heintz, A. J., & Melendez, R. M. (2006). Intimate partner violence and HIV/STD risk among lesbian, gay, bisexual, and transgender individuals. *Journal of Interpersonal Violence, 21*(2), 193–208.

Hendricks, M. L., & Testa, R. J. (2012). A conceptual framework for clinical work with transgender and gender nonconforming clients: An adaptation of the minority stress model. *Professional Psychology: Research and Practice 43*(5), 460–467.

Herek, G. M. (1990). The context of anti-gay violence: Notes on cultural and psychological heterosexism. *Journal of Interpersonal Violence, 5*(3), 316–333. http://doi.org/10.1177/088626090005003006

Kubicek, K., McNeeley, M., & Collins, S. (2015). "Same-sex relationship in a straight world": Individual and societal influences on power and control in young men's relationships. *Journal of Interpersonal Violence, 30*(1), 83–109. http://doi.org/10.1177/0886260514532527

Langenderfer-Magruder, L., Whitfield, D. L., Walls, N. E., Kattari, S. K., & Ramos, D. (2016). Experiences of intimate partner violence and subsequent police reporting among lesbian, gay, bisexual, transgender, and queer adults in Colorado: Comparing rates of cisgender and transgender victimization. *Journal of Interpersonal Violence, 31*(5), 855–871.

Letellier, P. (1996). Twin epidemics: Domestic violence and HIV infection among gay and bisexual men. In C. Renzetti & C. Miley (Eds.), *Violence in lesbian and gay domestic partnerships* (pp. 53–59). New York: Haworth Press.

McClennen, J. C. (2005). Domestic violence between same-gender partners: Recent findings and future research. *Journal of Interpersonal Violence, 20*(2), 149–154.

Messinger, A. (2011). Invisible victims: Same-sex IPV in the National Violence against Women Survey. *Journal of Interpersonal Violence, 26*(11), 2228–2243.

Meyer, I. H. (1995). Minority stress and mental health in gay men. *Journal of Health and Social Behavior, 36*(1), 38–56.

Munson, M. (2014). *Sheltering transgender women: Providing welcoming services.* National Resource Center on Domestic Violence and FORGE. Retrieved from http://www.vawnet.org/Assoc_Files_VAWnet/NRCDV_TAG-TransWomenShelter-Sept2014.pdf

National Coalition of Anti-Violence Programs. (2013). *Lesbian, gay, bisexual, transgender, queer, and HIV-affected intimate partner violence in 2012.* Retrieved from http://www.avp.org/storage/documents/ncavp_2012_ipvreport.final.pdf

National Coalition of Anti-Violence Programs. (2015). *Lesbian, gay, bisexual, transgender, queer, and HIV-affected intimate partner violence in 2014.* New York: Author. Retrieved from http://www.avp.org/storage/documents/2014_IPV_Report_Final_w-Bookmarks_10_28.pdf

National Coalition Against Domestic Violence. (n.d.) *Fact sheet: Domestic violence and lesbian, gay, bisexual, and transgender relationships*. Washington, DC: Author. Retrieved from http://www.uncfsp.org/projects/userfiles/file/dce-stop_now/ncadv_lgbt_fact_sheet.pdf

National Resource Center on Domestic Violence. (2007). *Lesbian, gay, bisexual and trans (LGBT) communities and domestic violence: Information and resources*. Retrieved from http://www.vawnet.org/summary.php?doc_id=1210&find_type=web_desc_NRCDV.

National Sexual Violence Resource Center and Pennsylvania Coalition Against Rape. (2012). *Guide for transformative prevention programming: Sexual violence and individuals who identify as LGBTQ*. Enola, PN: Author. Retrieved from http://www.nsvrc.org/sites/default/files/Publications_NSVRC_Guides_Transformative-Prevention-Programming.pdf

Native American Program of Legal Aid Services of Oregon, Indigenous Ways of Knowing Center at Lewis and Clark College, Western States Center, Pride Foundation, & Basic Rights Oregon. (2013). *Tribal equity kit: Tribal resolutions and codes to support two spirit and LGBT justice in Indian country*. Seattle, WA: Pride Foundation and Western States Center. Retrieved from https://graduate.lclark.edu/live/files/15810-tribal-equity-toolkit-20

Otis, M. D., & Skinner, W. F. (1996). The prevalence of victimization and its effect on mental well-being among lesbian and gay people. *Journal of Homosexuality, 30*(3), 93–121.

Parry, M. M., & O'Neal, E. N. (2015). Help-seeking behavior among same-sex intimate partner violence victims: An intersectional argument. *Criminology, Criminal Justice, Law, and Society, 16*, 51–67.

Pimentel, M. L. (2015). A review of the syndemic components of male same-sex intimate partner violence. *Journal of Nursing Education and Practice, 5*(1), 19–25.

Pizer, J. C., Sears, B., Mallory, C., & Hunter, N. D. (2011). Evidence of persistent and pervasive workplace discrimination against LGBT people: The need for federal legislation prohibiting discrimination and providing for equal employment benefits. *Loyola of Los Angeles Law Review, 45*, 715–779.

Postmus, J. L., Plummer, S. B., McMahon, S., Murshid, N. S., & Kim, M. S. (2012). Understanding economic abuse in the lives of survivors. *Journal of Interpersonal Violence, 27*(3), 411–430.

Saltzman L. E., Fanslow J. L., McMahon P. M., Shelley G. A. Intimate Partner Violence Surveillance: Uniform definitions and recommended data elements, Version 1.0. Atlanta (GA): National Center for Injury Prevention and Control, Centers for Disease Control and Prevention; 1999.

Stark, E. (2007). *Coercive control: How men entrap women in personal life*. New York: Oxford University Press.

Stephenson, R., Rentsch, C., Salazar, L. F., & Sullivan, P. S. (2011). Dyadic characteristics and intimate partner violence among men who have sex with men. *Western Journal of Emergency Medicine, 12*(3), 324–332.

Talicska, J. D. (2012). Out of one closet and into another: Why abused homosexual males refrain from reporting their abuse and what to do about it. *The Modern American, 8*, 21–34.

Tjaden, P., & Thoennes, N. (2000). Extent, nature, and consequences of rape victimization: Findings from the National Violence Against Women Survey. NIJ Research Report. NIJ Office of Justice Programs and Center for Disease Control. Retrieved from https://www.ncjrs.gov/pdffiles1/nij/181867.pdf

Walker, J. K. (2015). Investigating trans people's vulnerabilities to intimate partner violence/abuse. *Partner Abuse, 6*(1), 107–125.

Walker, L. E. (1979). *The battered woman*. New York: Harper & Row.

Walters, M. L., Chen J., & Breiding, M. J. (2013). The National Intimate Partner and Sexual Violence Survey (NISVS): 2010 findings on victimization by sexual orientation. Atlanta, GA: National Center for Injury Prevention and Control, Centers for Disease Control and Prevention. Retrieved from http://www.cdc.gov/violenceprevention/pdf/nisvs_sofindings.pdf

CHAPTER 24

HEALTH DISPARITIES, HIV/AIDS, AND FRAMING A PUBLIC HEALTH AGENDA

Ian W. Holloway and Sid P. Jordan

INTRODUCTION

Health and wellness are critical concerns for social work practitioners and policymakers. In evaluating the health and wellness of individuals, social workers might think about a range of physical, psychological, and behavioral factors. Yet these considerations are situated within a complex set of social, political, economic, and environmental conditions that underpin an individual's health and create distinctive patterns across groups, neighborhoods, and communities. The causes and consequences of health disparities have become a focus of much interdisciplinary research, from public health and medicine to sociology and urban planning. Efforts to identify and understand health inequities and their root causes can direct social work practices and policies toward promoting equity and disease prevention and improving access to culturally relevant, affordable, proximate, and high-quality health care.

Health disparities among lesbian, gay, bisexual, transgender, and queer (LGBTQ) people in the United States are increasingly well documented. There are various conditions that appear to impact LGBTQ people more frequently or with differing consequences when compared to non-LGBTQ people, including some forms of traumatic injury, cancers, and sexually transmitted infections (STIs), as well as heart disease, substance addiction, anxiety, and depression. The complex causes of LGBTQ health disparities are tied to social, cultural, political, and economic conditions that overlap and interplay with the health inequities experienced among women, communities of color, rural communities, poor people, and other marginalized groups. Therefore, understanding LGBTQ health disparities is most useful insofar as these efforts adopt a complex and intersectional analysis of the social and structural determinants of individual and community health. By taking such an approach, social workers can play an important role in improving health outcomes for LGBTQ people, from advocating for individual patients in medical settings to helping frame environmental justices campaigns, and from supporting the independence of people with chronic health conditions to strengthening community and social support networks.

In social work education, learning about LGBTQ health disparities is a relatively new framework foregrounded by earlier efforts to train social workers in HIV prevention and patient advocacy from the early 1980s to today. This chapter first introduces and contextualizes LGBTQ health disparities–related research for social workers by situating LGBTQ health in a sociopolitical history, with a focus on the impact of HIV/AIDS. Next, the chapter briefly introduces recent evidence related to some of the known health burdens that disproportionately impact LGBTQ people and connects them to existing theories in public health. Last, opportunities for social work practitioners to address barriers and promote health equity are discussed, from micro-oriented practice to community-level social change. Because LGBTQ health disparities are complex and research in this area is relatively recent and unfolding, this chapter is an introduction that hopes to inspire the reader to further inquiry, investigation, and continuing education.

As examined in more depth in other chapters of this volume, gender and sexuality norms are ever evolving and the language and identities used by gender and sexual minorities is deeply embedded in their cultural, generational, and regional contexts. There are numerous questions of whom, how, and when to count LGBTQ people and communities in health-related research, and this remains a relatively unsettled area of debate. This chapter uses the acronym LGBTQ, as is consistent with this volume; however, it is important in a chapter on health disparities to remember that there is no singular LGBTQ community or experience. The phrase "gender and sexual minorities" is also used, relatively interchangeably, as this has alternatively been embraced within public health and social work and intends here to refer more broadly to those who may experience similar health burdens but who may not identify as LGBTQ. When possible, this chapter utilizes the language of the sources it references, and, in this way, the relatively dynamic and unstable nature of queer terminology is embraced.

SOCIOPOLITICAL HISTORY AND CONTEXT

Societal recognition and acceptance of the LGBTQ community has clearly evolved over time. The health and mental health communities alike have moved from the often unethical, harmful treatment and pathologizing of LGBTQ relationships, sexual attitudes and behaviors to understanding the need for empowerment and affirming practice skills when framing the diverse health needs of this diverse community.

Same-sex sexuality, nonbinary gender expressions, and myriad forms of coupling and kinship have been elements of human experience since antiquity. The language and social meanings ascribed to gender variance, gendered expressions, sexual desire, and sexual behavior change over time and between cultures. In fact, the concept of "homosexuality" as a social category is traced in part to Western medical literature of the late nineteenth century that linked same-sex sexuality and gender variance to mental weakness and disease (Weeks, 1977). Along with new consumer economies of the same period, the medical model of homosexuality facilitated concepts of sexual orientation and consolidated social and moral values around a superior heterosexual norm (Katz, 1990).

The incipient belief that homosexuality was a fixed congenital medical condition generated research and medical experimentation from the late nineteenth through the twentieth century often aimed at the identification, prevention, and possible "cures" for those believed to be "afflicted." Among various etiological theories, concepts of "inversion" linked same-sex sexuality to cross-gender phenotypical traits. For example, in studies on same-sex desire among women, researchers assumed that lesbian women had inherent masculine characteristics and were thereby puzzled to account for feminine women who pursued same-sex sexual partners (Terry, 1990). Physical examinations of human subjects were a primary mode of research in efforts to categorize "homosexual" bodies as anatomically distinguishable from a "normal" body, an approach that built on nineteenth-century scientific racism (Somerville, 1994). The assertion of racial and sexual inferiority under the guise of biomedical expertise provided an authoritative justification for a range of inhumane policies and treatments with little supporting and flawed evidence, including immigration and social welfare exclusions, experimental and coercive psychiatric treatments, and so-called corrective surgeries for infants born as intersex (Canaday, 2009; Reis, 2009; Terry, 1999). In these strands of research, particularly in studies of the brain, the search for biological clues to explain sexual orientation and transgender identities are increasingly overshadowed by theories that interrogate the social, cultural, and political constructions of heterosexual norms and binary/fixed gender and sex categories.

Psychiatric abuse and related health-care issues were among the concerns of gay and lesbian activists in the late 1960s and 1970s, predating and prefiguring responses to the HIV/AIDS crisis. By 1970, for example, gay and lesbian liberationists began protesting the American Psychological Association (APA) to remove homosexuality from the *Diagnostic and Statistical Manual of Mental Disorders*, which was ultimately approved by a 1973 vote of the APA board (Drescher, 2015). However, political compromises of the time resulted in new APA diagnostic criteria describing a mental disorder involving an individual who sought to change their sexual orientation (Spitzer, 1981). These criteria were also eventually abandoned and homosexuality was removed altogether in the revised third edition of the *Diagnostic and Statistical Manual of Mental Disorders* (DSM) in 1987. However, a new set of gender identity disorders appeared in the 1980 manual, signaling an expanding medicalized framework for gender variance (Drescher, 2010). In 2013, gender identity disorders was altered and replaced with the term "gender dysphoria" in the fifth edition of the DMS, and many debates continue over its inclusion (Drescher, 2015). The documentary film *Diagnosing Difference* (Ophelian, 2009) features perspectives of some transgender activists' perspectives about the meaning and consequences of the DSM classification.

THE IMPACT OF HIV/AIDS ON LGBTQ HEALTH FRAMEWORKS

Around 1980, physicians and hospitals in southern California were responding to a number of sick and dying patients who would later be understood as early cases of the AIDS epidemic in the United States, soon to be linked to HIV (Grmek, Maulitz, & Duffin, 1993). By June 1981, the Centers for Disease Control and Prevention (CDC) reported five independent cases of gay men with pneumocystis pneumonia in Los Angeles (Weekly, 1981), a rare infection linked to compromised immune systems. Because the symptoms were first identified among gay men, the unknown cause of rapid immune deficiency became informally referred to as a "gay cancer" and in the early medical literature, "gay related immune deficiency" ([GRID]; Self, Filardo, & Lancaster, 1989). Popular narratives and biomedical discourses about the growing epidemic as linked exclusively to gay male sexuality were fueled by and perpetuated homophobic moral condemnation more broadly (Treichler, 1987). Despite early reports of AIDS cases among people with hemophilia, intravenous drug users, infants, and women, among others (US Department of Health and Human Services, 2011), the myths and stigma related to the nature of transmission of the disease had flourished and produced dynamics that have continued to vex prevention and treatment efforts for decades.

Despite a rapidly mounting count of AIDS-related deaths, grassroots demands for a federal response in the first years of the crisis were met with a resounding silence and inaction. The lack of effective federal responses for years into the epidemic can only be explained within the context of the pervasive homophobia in American culture. It was not until 1985 that US President Ronald Reagan first mentioned AIDS in a public address, and it was not until two years later that he would make his first public speech about the epidemic, the same year the CDC launched the first public awareness campaign "America Responds to AIDS" (US Department of Health and Human Services, 2011). By 1995, the CDC reported more than half a million known AIDS patients in the United States. For more information about the early timeline of the AIDS crisis in the United States, the Department of Health and Human Services has published an interaction timeline and other information on the aids.gov website.

In response to the failed mainstream health systems and often in the absence of resources, community-based organization led primarily by gay and lesbian volunteers created some of the first AIDS-related health clinics and services organizations, such as the Shanti Project in San Francisco, Gay Men's Health Crisis in New York, the Health Education Resource Organization in Baltimore, and AIDS Project Los Angeles. These groups developed safer-sex education campaigns and needle exchanges, established health clinics and care facilities, and pursued legal cases fighting rampant discrimination against people living with AIDS. Among the many grassroots efforts, AIDS Coalition to Unleash Power (ACT UP), which began in New York and proliferated chapters in many major cities, is one of the most documented and notable for inventive civil disobedience strategies and for building connections about the disparate impact of HIV among and between gay men, Black and Latino communities, and poor people. The group's history and activism is featured in a number of films about the early years of the epidemic, such as *United in Anger: A History of ACT UP* (Hubbard, 2012) and *How to Survive a Plague* (France, 2012).

Demands for a federal response to the HIV/AIDS crisis eventually forged new relationships between biomedical researchers, policymakers, and gay and lesbian communities. Their efforts, combined with a number of other forces in the late twentieth century, would ultimately lead to the incorporation of LGBT communities as a federally recognized underserved health population (Epstein, 2003). The institutionalization of LGBT health as part of a national health agenda has focused most centrally on HIV/AIDS and has included the designation of significant federal, local, and private foundation funding for HIV/AIDS-related research and services, such as testing sites, targeted health campaigns, case management services, social centers, and funding mechanisms. Today, this large network of research institutes and organizations includes gay and bisexual men's health centers, AIDS service organizations, and other service providers dedicated to providing health care and other social services to people living with HIV/AIDS (Panel on Opportunistic Infections in HIV-Infected Adults and Adolescents, 2015) and those at high risk for acquiring and transmitting HIV, as well as related chronic health issues.

ESTABLISHING A FEDERAL PUBLIC HEALTH AGENDA

The National Institutes of Health (NIH) has described health disparities as "differences in the incidence, prevalence, mortality, and burden of diseases and other adverse health conditions that exist among specific population groups in the United States" (US Department of Health and Human Services, 2000, p. 4). The NIH has identified racial and ethnic minorities, people with low social economic status, and rural persons as "health disparity populations" (US Department of Health and Human Services, 2008). Federal recognition of LGBT health disparities is a relatively recent arrival within the public health landscape. A federally funded comprehensive white paper on LGBT health was published in 2000 and drew on existing research to define several key health issues, including cancer, HIV/AIDS, mental health, suicide among youths, substance abuse, and access to quality care (Dean et al., 2000).

Prior to 2000, the bulk of LGBT-related public health research focused on HIV/AIDS and other STIs among gay and bisexual men (Boehmer, 2002). However, lesbian health services and research has been continuously active since the 1970s despite systematic barriers such as limited funding and research infrastructures for lesbian health researchers (Bradford, 1999). The American Association of Physicians for Human Rights, a subsection of the American Medical Association that would eventually be renamed the Gay and Lesbian Medical Association (GLMA), established a Lesbian Health Fund in 1992, which continues to fund research on health disparities among sexual-minority women. In 1997, a commissioned study by the Institute of Medicine (IOM) brought together lesbian health researchers and practitioners to assess the state of the field and identify future priorities (Bradford, 1999). The final report identified a range of specific health risks, including "cancer, sexual transmitted disease, HIV/AIDS, mental health and substance abuse problems" (IOM Committee on Lesbian Health Research Priorities, 1999, p. 6), and concluded that additional research and improved methodologies were needed to better understand disparities, risks and protective factors, and barriers to care for sexual-minority women.

The US Department of Health and Human Services produces a 10-year plan for national health promotion and disease prevention, *Healthy People*, which focuses on eliminating health disparities. In 2001, GLMA produced a companion document to *Healthy People 2010*, which identified recommendations for LGBT health within the key objectives of the plan (GLMA, 2001). Perhaps most significant to social workers is the focus on improving access to health-care services, as well as public health infrastructure that can address health disparities. This was followed by a seminal report published by the IOM (2011), which set an agenda for future research that can specifically address health-care inequities and social influences that affect health. In assessing gaps in the current research, the IOM recommended studies that can increase participation of sexual and gender minorities in research, advance knowledge about transgender-related health needs, and improve methodologies for understanding how LGBT health is shaped by race, socioeconomic status, age, geography, and other factors.

Healthy People 2020 incorporates key objectives related to LGBT health disparities, specifically to develop and implement standardized questions to identify LGBT people in population-based data collected to evaluate the full range of Healthy People objectives (Office of Disease Prevention and Health Promotion, 2012). As part of this goal, the CDC has added questions related to sexual orientation and to some extent gender identity into population-based surveys used to monitor health-related issues, which are optional for states to collect (Office of Disease Prevention and Health Promotion, 2012). In August 2015, the NIH announced a new supplementary funding stream for research partners to add sexual- and gender-minority health questions to existing research programs. In particular, the NIH (2015) sought studies with a focus on "increased disease risk, behavioral and social health; approaches to personalized medicine; access to care; reproductive and sexual development; and resilience." Many health researchers and practitioners believe that these efforts, along with ongoing efforts of community-based researchers, may rapidly advance evidence and understanding of LGBTQ health disparities in the next decade.

FRAMING LGBTQ HEALTH

While LGBTQ people are increasingly recognized and culturally embraced in the United States, legal battles over protections from discrimination are contested in many jurisdictions and barriers and inequities remain in terms of access to resources and services. Health knowledge and medical practices are profoundly influenced by the legacies of pathology and exclusion of those who fail to conform to dominant normative expectations of binary gender or heterosexuality. The persistent belief in fixed and meaningfully dichotomous sex categories (male and female) and compulsory heterosexuality continue to structure much scientific inquiry, biomedical research, medical education, public health campaigns, and health-care information. Ongoing bias, stigma, and invisibility of LGBTQ people and relationships, along with the interrelated and compounding effects of medical racism, are significant to understanding contemporary LGBTQ health disparities (e.g., Bauer et al., 2009; Lambda Legal, 2010).

Therefore, we can view "LGBTQ health" as an important yet also imprecise taxonomy for framing questions about health needs and health disparities. In health and social equity–related research, significant challenges about who should be counted as LGBTQ and how, when, and why to collect, analyze, and report data are dynamically debated among researchers and scholars (e.g., Currah & Stryker, 2015; Young & Meyer, 2005). Among the many challenges is the vast number of intergroup differences between LGBT people. Lesbian women, for example, have both similar and different health risks and protective factors than bisexual men or those with nonbinary gender identities. Moreover, a poor, White, middle-aged lesbian in a rural area may experience vastly different health determinants than a middle-class, young, Latina lesbian in a major metropolitan area.

Because much of the health research has focused on HIV/AIDS and gay and bisexual men (and/or men who have sex with men [MSM]), there is less information about LGBTQ health disparities among LGBQ women and transgender people overall. There is also a paucity of research on the health differences among people who may consider themselves queer or questioning, and, when included, these identities are increasingly collapsed into a composite category (e.g., "LGBTQ-identified"). The focus on categorizing and amalgamating LGBTQ identities can ignore, erase, and subsume non-Western and indigenous concepts (e.g. two-spirit, Māhū, fa'afafine), intersex embodiments, and a range of other gender- and sexual-minority identities and experiences (nonbinary genders, asexuality, polyamory, etc.).

The discordance between behavior, experiences, and identities pose further unsettled debates in conceptualizing LGBTQ health. The inclusion of people who do not self-identify as LGBTQ as gender and sexual minorities has been a common practice in HIV and other STI-related research, promulgated in part through the use of behavior-related nomenclature, such as MSM (and to some extent, women who have sex with women [WSW]). While behavior-related categories function to focus on how sexuality, sexual practices, and relationships may impact health risks and disparities, such categorization may obscure or undermine the salience of LGBTQ identity and overshadow a more complex view of LGBTQ health that can account for geographic factors, affiliation networks, and community relationships. Incorporating an understanding of social identity may not only help explain health disparities but may also support the development of health promotion prevention and intervention strategies (Young & Meyer, 2005). Conversely, the orientation toward LGBT identity as opposed to sexual behavior has been shaped in part by efforts to desexualize LGBTQ health research for purposes of political viability (Epstein, 2003).

HEALTH DISPARITIES

LGBTQ health and wellness are considered throughout this volume and particularly in chapter 20. This section provides a broad and brief overview of a few of the commonly researched dimensions LGBTQ health, followed by some of the dominant theories related to LGBTQ health disparities. While this section focuses on some of the known disproportionate health burdens of LGBTQ people, it is crucial to note that an increasing number of scholars are examining resiliency and related protective factors that shape positive LGBTQ health outcomes (Herrick, Stall, Goldhammer, Egan, & Mayer, 2013; Meyer, 2003; Wexler, DiFluvio, & Burke, 2009).

VICTIMIZATION

Experiences of violence and abuse can lead to acute traumatic injury, as well as contribute to negative health outcomes across the life course. While injuries are frequently framed and treated at the individual level, patterns of violence among groups are influenced by gender, race, access to resources, and numerous other factors. While portrayals of violence experienced by LGBTQ people often focus on hate crimes by strangers, most people experience victimization by someone they know. Studies of sexual-minority youth indicate a greater likelihood of childhood physical and sexual abuse, as well as parental rejection, when compared to heterosexual peers (Alvy, Hughes, Kristjanson, & Wilsnack, 2013; Friedman et al., 2011). The vast majority of LGBT youth report experiences of targeted harassment and violence in schools (Kosciw, Greytak, Bartkiewicz, Boesen, & Palmer, 2012). Family rejection and school victimization among sexual-minority youth has been linked to higher rates of depression, suicidal ideation, substance abuse, HIV, and other serious health issues (Burton, Marshal, Chisolm, Sucato, & Friedman, 2013; Ryan, Huebner, Diaz, & Sanchez, 2009).

Intimate partner and domestic violence are discussed more thoroughly in chapter 23 of this text, and these forms of violence can have significant health consequences that are often overlooked and misunderstood in health-care settings. In the first national probability study on interpersonal violence to include sexual orientation, gay and lesbian adults reported histories of intimate partner and sexual violence at similar or greater rates than non-LGB adults of the same gender. Prevalence was higher among all women and bisexual women, who reported significantly greater lifetime prevalence than lesbian and heterosexual women (Walters, Chen, & Breiding, 2013). While there are no similar national probability surveys on victimization that include indicators for gender identity beyond male/female, researchers indicate that transgender people face profound risks for physical and sexual assault both by known people (e.g., intimate partners and family members) and strangers (Stotzer, 2009). In a study investigating cyber-bullying, sexual coercion, and sexual abuse among adolescents, LGBT youth reported higher prevalence rates of victimization when compared to non-LGBT peers (Dank, Lachman, Zweig, & Yahner, 2014).

Victimization and trauma can increase risks for numerous other health-related symptoms. In addition to mental health disparities discussed already, studies have linked experiences of child neglect, victimization, and discrimination to higher rates of substance abuse and tobacco use among sexual minorities (McCabe, Bostwick, Hughes, West, & Boyd, 2010). For these and other reasons, sexual-minority youth and adults report higher levels of substance and tobacco use when compared to the general population, and substance use trends appear to be most pronounced among bisexual people and women (Blosnich, Lee, & Horn, 2013; Conron, Mimiaga, & Landers, 2010; Marshal et al., 2008; Marshal et al., 2011; McCabe, Hughes, Bostwick, West, & Boyd, 2009).

MENTAL HEALTH

Rates of depression, mood or anxiety disorders, suicidal ideation, and other mental health symptoms are higher among LGBT people when compared to the general population (Bockting et al., 2013; Bostwick, Boyd, Hughes, & McCabe, 2010; Budge, Adelson, & Howard, 2013; Clements-Nolle, Marx, & Katz, 2006). A 2011 review of 24 existing studies found that suicidality was nearly three times more prevalent among sexual-minority youth when compared to their peers, with bisexual youth at particular risk (Marshal et al., 2011). Studies of bisexual adults also indicate a greater prevalence of suicidal ideation and mood disorders when compared to both heterosexual and gay and lesbian adults (Cohen, Blasey, Taylor, Weiss, & Newman, 2016; Conron et al., 2010).

At least one recent study of suicide mortalities among 17,886 participants found significant disparities between sexual-minority and heterosexual women but did not find a similarly significant pattern between sexual-minority and heterosexual men (Cochran & Mays, 2015). In contrast, a study based on the National Latino and Asian American Survey, a national probability sample of 4,488 participants on psychiatric health, found that gay and bisexual men were more likely than heterosexual men to report a recent suicide attempt (Cochran, Mays, Alegria, Ortega, & Takeuchi, 2007), suggesting the salience of race and gender in understanding suicide risk of sexual minorities.

Transgender youth and adults, and particularly those of color, are at significant risk for psychiatric diagnosis and multiple mental health symptoms (Clements-Nolle et al., 2006; Reisner et al., 2016). Among respondents of the 2008 National Transgender Discrimination Survey, including US territories, approximately 41% of 6,456 survey respondents reported a history of attempting suicide, with an even higher prevalence among those who identified as American Indian (56%) or multiracial (54%; Grant et al., 2011).

SEXUAL HEALTH

Among new HIV infections in the United States today, more than 60% occur among gay and bisexual men and other MSM, an incidence rate 44 times that of their heterosexual counterparts (CDC, 2013; Purcell et al., 2012). Young gay and bisexual men between the ages of 13 and 24 account for nearly one-fifth of new infections (CDC, 2013). The 2015 National HIV/AIDS Strategy for the United States addresses the ongoing high burden of HIV particularly among Black gay and bisexual men and transgender women, reflecting the need for approaches to HIV prevention and care that better serve people based on their race/ethnicity, gender identity, sexual orientation, and socioeconomic backgrounds (Office of National HIV/AIDS Policy, 2015).

Although transgender women make up a smaller number of the overall population, the odds of HIV-positive status is estimated as 50 times higher among transgender women than other adults of a similar age (CDC, 2015). Rates of unidentified HIV infection are also sharply elevated (CDC, 2008b; Herbst et al., 2008; Operario, Nemoto, Iwamoto, & Moore, 2011; Sevelius, Keatley, & Gutierrez-Mock, 2011), which means that many transgender women are often delayed in receiving HIV primary care. While substantial research has shown the disproportionate burden of HIV among transgender women, and especially women of color, few culturally relevant interventions have been developed to address these disparities. The prevalence of HIV among sexual-minority women and transgender men has been thought to be low. However, this is based on generalizations about sexual health, and there are unique risks for subgroups including intravenous drug users and those who have sex with men (Lemp, et al., 1995; Sevelius, 2009).

While preliminary research suggests higher rates of various cancers among sexual minorities, awareness and action of this issue has been limited (Boehmer & Elk, 2016). Higher rates of cancer may be due to barriers to care but also overlap with social and structural factors including lower income and higher rates of poverty among LGBT adults (IOM, 2011) and less health-care seeking behavior (Buchmueller & Carpenter, 2010). LGBT survivors of cancer may experience higher levels of distress, which may compromise long-term and overall health (Kamen, Mustian, Dozier, Bowen, & Li, 2015). While there are a variety of cancers that LGBTQ people appear to be at greater risk of developing, this section focuses on breast and anal cancer.

Lesbian and bisexual women face higher rates of breast cancer than their heterosexual peers (IOM, 2011). Although research is still inconclusive about the origins of these disparities (Quinn et al., 2015) contributing factors may include higher rates of nulliparity, alcohol use and tobacco use, and body weight (Zaritsky & Dibble, 2010). Barriers to accessing screening services may also be a critical determinant, as lesbian and bisexual women may be less likely to utilize screening services due in part to poor relationships with health-care providers (Hart & Bowen, 2009). Racial and economic disparities in breast cancer survival rates have also been linked to early detection. While there is a paucity of research on cancer risks and disparities among transgender people, a study of 3,102 transgender women and men showed that cross-sex hormones did not elevate risks for breast cancer (Gooren, van Trotsenburg, Giltay, & van Diest, 2013). Nevertheless, transgender people may face unique barriers to breast cancer screenings, including provider bias and insurance exclusions for those whose are designated male on health-care identity documents, which can contribute to disparities in early detection.

MSM are more at risk for anal cancer, a relatively rare form of cancer, which has been linked to higher number of lifetime sexual partners and higher rates of HIV, other STIs, and cigarette smoking. A significant factor for the development of anal cancer is the contraction of human papillomavirus (HPV), although there is limited awareness about this connection (Fenkl, Jones, Schochet, & Johnson, 2016). HPV vaccination among gay and bisexual men is a suggested health promotion strategy (Hawkes & Lewis, 2014), but there have been barriers in uptake because the vaccine is most effective when administered in adolescence. The Advisory Committee on Immunization Practices (2011) of the CDC has recommended that HPV vaccinations for males at ages 11 to 12, a time when many young people are unaware of, or unable to disclose, sexual orientation or gender identity to parents and health-care providers. The Advisory Committee on Immunization Practices recommends that MSM, particularly those with HIV infection, through the age of 26 receive the HPV vaccine.

THEORIZING LGBT HEALTH DISPARITIES

Examining social determinants of health can be helpful for practitioners to consider the many factors that disproportionately impact LGBTQ people with a range of health and mental health conditions when compared to the general population, heterosexuals, etc. In the same regard, minority stress theory and syndemic theory can provide useful insight related to understanding access and barriers to education, prevention, treatment and care for members of the LGBTQ community.

SOCIAL DETERMINANTS OF HEALTH

Efforts to address and overcome LGBTQ and other health disparities requires policymakers and practitioners to examine why and how health is structured by the unequal distribution of resources and other social inequities. The World Health Organization ([WHO], 2011) defines "social determinants of health" as arising "from the conditions in which people are born, grow, live, work, and age" and as a "shorthand to encompass the social, economic, political, cultural, and environmental determinants of health" (p. 2). According to the WHO, structural determinants are stratification factors "such as the distribution of income; discrimination on the basis of factors such as gender, ethnicity, or disability; and political and governance structures that reinforce rather than reduce inequalities in economic power" (p. 7). These definitions can be helpful in thinking about the ways in which LGBTQ people are disproportionately impacted by a range of health conditions compared to their heterosexual and cisgender counterparts.

In developing a framework for explaining health disparities among racial minorities, the NIH points to the role of biological, cultural, political, and socioeconomic factors, including racism, in effecting health-related practices, psychological and environmental stress, psychological resources, and medical care (US Department of Health and Human Services, 2000). Understanding LGBTQ health disparities can build on this framework to account for how heterosexism and cissexism influence not only medical knowledge and practice but the social and structural determinants of health in everyday life. To understand how social factors (e.g., stigma, discrimination) "get under the skin" to create negative health outcomes among LGBTQ people and contributing to disparities in disease prevalence among LGBTQ populations, a number of other theoretical frameworks have been proposed.

MINORITY STRESS THEORY

Minority stress theory is covered extensively in chapter 12 and offers one explanatory framework that has been used in LGBTQ health disparities research. Applied first to psychological distress experienced by lesbian women (Brooks, 1981), it has since been applied to theorize a number of negative mental health outcomes for LGBT people. Minority stress theory generally posits that prejudice and social stress experienced by gender and sexual minorities within dominant culture are key to understanding disparities and resiliency factors among LGB people (Meyer, 2003). Minority stress theory has also been adapted to theorize stress and resiliency factors among transgender people (Testa, Habarth, Peta, Balsam, & Bockting, 2015).

Stress theory, in general, states that as major life events and chronic circumstances accumulate, an individual becomes less equipped to adapt, adjust, and tolerate continued life stress experiences (Brown & Harris, 1978). In general population studies, minority individuals repeatedly show increased stress and psychological vulnerability when compared to their majority-group peers

(Thoits, 1991). Minority stress theory suggests that societal oppression and chronic victimization lead to significant distress for LGBT people and result in poorer health and mental health outcomes. Related stressors, including negative events, negative attitudes, and discomfort (Rosario, Schrimshaw, Hunter, & Gwadz, 2002), have been extensively linked with negative behavioral health outcomes (e.g., Goldbach, Tanner-Smith, Bagwell, & Dunlap, 2014; Marshal et al., 2008; Rosario et al., 2002).

A number of studies have linked the stress of coming out (i.e., fear of family disapproval, loss of close friendships) to negative mental health (D'Augelli, Hershberger, & Pilkington, 1998; Russell & Joyner, 2001). In fact, nearly 67% of LGBT individuals report coming out to their family to be somewhat or extremely troubling (Pilkington & D'Augelli, 1995). Further, sexual minorities may fear disclosure because of real and perceived impact on their ability to maintain a supportive social network, creating opportunities for further social isolation. While Meyer's original work focused on understanding negative mental health outcomes among LGB people, minority stress theory serves as a basis for emerging research on physical health outcomes, as well as transgender individuals and communities.

SYNDEMIC THEORY

Syndemics refer to the presence of two or more diseases that overlap and intersect to create a synergistic effect that exacerbates the negative health outcomes of disease and lowers the overall health profile of the individual. The term "syndemic" was originally used by Singer (1994) to explain the co-occurrence of substance use, HIV risk, and violence within poor urban communities. A syndemic has been defined as "two or more afflictions, interacting synergistically, contributing to excess burden of disease in a population" (Milstein, 2008, p. 7) or, in the words of Singer, "[disease] entwinement with each other and with the social conditions and biopsychological consequences of disparity, discrimination, and structural violence" (p. 423). When applied to LGBTQ communities, syndemic theory refers to both the interaction of the range of diseases that are disproportionately concentrated within sexual and gender minority communities (described in detail previously) and also the societal factors, such as systemic discrimination and exclusion, that exacerbate those diseases. Syndemic theory has been applied most often in the extant literature related to LGBTQ populations in order to describe a constellation of diseases and other negative experiences that put gay and bisexual men at higher risk for contracting HIV disease.

Stall, Friedman, and Catania (2008) applied the theory of syndemics to explain the pronounced and varied health disparities among American gay men through a developmental lens. Evidence of a syndemic of psychosocial health problems leading to HIV risk has been demonstrated in both MSM in general (Stall et al., 2008) and young MSM (YMSM) specifically (Mustanski, Garofalo, Herrick, & Donenberg, 2007). The theory of syndemic production described by Stall and colleagues (2008) postulates that as some YMSM are introduced to gay communities, they are exposed to opportunities for both risk and resilience. Engagement in gay communities may offer social supports that are unavailable in families of origin or other communities in which YMSM are connected; however, due to the high prevalence of substance use, mental health issues, HIV, and other STIs, in addition to permissive norms related to risk taking, YMSM may also be exposed to a range of health risks.

ACCESS TO CARE

LGBTQ health disparities are both reflective of and intensified by numerous barriers to accessing affordable, culturally appropriate, and proximate health care. Individual experiences with health-related services vary tremendously and are influenced by race, ethnicity, language, socioeconomic status, geography, education, and other factors. Increasingly prohibitive costs of care and the curtailment of social welfare benefits are some of the major political and economic trends that have had a disproportionate impact on LGBTQ health. In particular, transgender people, lesbian and bisexual women, and people of color are more likely be unemployed, underemployed, and/or live in poverty (Albelda, Badgett, Schneebaum, & Gates, 2009; Conron et al., 2010; Grant et al., 2011) and therefore may have less access to employer-sponsored health insurance plans. The Patient Protection and Affordable Care Act (ACA) of 2010 critically expanded Medicaid benefits to the uninsured and within its first years of implementation increased access to care and improvements in self-reported health (Sommers, Baicker, & Epstein, 2012). While the ACA has mitigated some factors impacting entry to care, many challenges to accessing and utilizing affordable, high-quality, culturally appropriate health care remain. Ongoing barriers for the most economically vulnerable continue to impact access to health-care services, including limited availability of nearby services in rural areas, the costs of transportation and childcare, and inability to take time off from work.

Health-care providers are increasingly cognizant that they may encounter LGBTQ patients. However, medical education and training is often premised on heterosexual norms and biologically determined gender with relatively little, if any, acknowledgement of gender and sexual diversity, LGBTQ families, and relevant health concerns. When LGBTQ health is included in medical education, it is often introduced as supplementary, rather than integrated throughout the broader curricula. Institutionalized bias and invisibility of LGBTQ people and families can facilitate misinformation, contributing to health risks and reducing quality of care.

Medical racism and the ongoing unequal treatment of communities of color in health-care settings (Nelson, Smedley, & Stith, 2002) creates profound barriers for LGBTQ people of color when accessing care. In a 2009 survey conducted by Lambda Legal with nearly 5,000 respondents, LGB and transgender nonconforming (TGNC) people of color were more likely than LGB and TGNC White respondents to report discrimination and mistreatment by medical providers, as well as substandard care (Lambda Legal, 2010). More than a quarter of TGNC people of color in the study reported that health-care providers used harsh or abuse language or that they were refused care. These overt forms of discrimination in health-care settings indicate a critical need for increased cultural competency training of providers and front-line staff in addition to policies that prevent prejudice and harassment of all patients. In addition, more research on and trainings to prevent covert forms of bias toward LGBTQ people in health-care settings is crucial to ensuring equal access to health care for all.

From emergency rooms to general public health clinics to specialty care, LGBTQ people and their families often navigate questions including "if, when, and how" to disclose information about transgender identity, sexuality, and relationships. Such calculations can lead to stress and anxiety among patients, create intrapersonal barriers between provider and patient, and ultimately depreciate quality of care. Some health clinics use visual cues or messaging to encourage disclosure and allay patient concerns of bias. However, disclosure alone does not lead to effective care unless providers are also equipped with accurate medical information and prepared to deliver culturally appropriate care. Many transgender patients report having to educate their providers about their health-care needs (Bauer et al., 2009), pursuing self-education through medical journals, community health organizations, patient advocacy groups, word of mouth, and other networks. While medical providers are often aware of their own limitations in understanding transgender health care (Snelgrove, Jasudavisius, Rowe, Head, & Bauer, 2012), the professionalized context of health-care settings can create power dynamics that tend to endorse medical authority over patient knowledge (Poteat, German, & Kerrigan, 2013). Some of the testimonies of barriers faced by transgender people in medical settings have been popularized and archived using social media under the hashtag #transhealthfail. Social media campaigns are one way in which transgender people are raising awareness about the ways in which medical professionals can better recognize and address their needs.

Community-based organizations, grassroots groups, and informal health information networks have led to significant policy change efforts and advanced access to LGBTQ-specific health information and quality care. LGBTQ health centers, such as the Los Angeles LGBT Center, Fenway Health in Boston, Mazzoni Center in Philadelphia, Center for Transyouth Health and Development at the Children's Hospital Los Angeles, Center on Halsted in Chicago, and Callen-Lorde Health Center in New York City, to name a few, have filled an important role by providing free or low-cost culturally tailored services. Not only do these centers provide affirming environments for LGBTQ patients to receive services, but they have also situated practitioners to develop health-related best practices and standards for the field. Because these services tend to only be available in large metropolitan areas, can have heavy caseloads, and often offer a limited scope of services, advocates have sought to expand governmental funding for LGBTQ-specific health and wellness services. The expansion of these services is critical in smaller cities and rural communities throughout the United States, where many LGBTQ people have no access to culturally appropriate care. Narratives of LGBTQ people in rural communities have been documented in films such as *Forbidden: Undocumented and Queer in Rural America* (Rhynard, 2016), *Passing Ellenville* (Centore & Fischer, 2016), and *Southern Comfort* (Davis, 2001) and highlight the absence of supportive services for LGBTQ people in these settings.

INFORMED CONSENT FOR TRANSGENDER HEALTH CARE

Many medical professionals and health insurance companies require transgender people to receive a mental health diagnosis for gender dysphoria as a prerequisite for accessing gender confirmation medical services (e.g., hormones, surgical treatments). Documentation from a medical professional is also required under many state laws in order to change a sex designation (M or F) on various identification documents. This medical gatekeeping system creates steep barriers to care by adding layers of scrutiny and exclusion for transgender people from medical treatments that are otherwise widely available to non-transgender people without a mental health diagnosis (e.g., hormone replacement therapies, plastic surgeries, etc.). Many of these standards were developed or endorsed by World Professional Association for Transgender Health (W-PATH), a professional group on transgender health. However, W-PATH and other professional groups have increasingly embraced informed consent as a standard of care for transgender health. Informed consent centers the knowledge and needs of transgender people in decision-making about their treatment, which is more consistent with social work ethics and values.

HIV PREVENTION AND TREATMENT

A chapter on LGBTQ health disparities would be incomplete without a discussion of the significant advances that have been made in improving HIV prevention and treatment among gay and bisexual men and, by extension, for many other people living with HIV or at high risk for acquiring the disease. Indeed, in recent years HIV prevention and treatment has become one of the most significant issues on the national and global health agenda. In the United States, the CDC estimates that 1.2 million people are living with HIV, with about 50,000 new cases identified each year (CDC, 2015b). HIV is an enduring health problem, especially for marginalized people. Biomedical advances in HIV care, including antiretroviral therapies have significantly increased the life expectancy for all those living with HIV and AIDS. In fact, most people who are infected can remain healthy if they have access to early and ongoing care. The initiation of these pharmaceutical interventions are recommended for all HIV-positive people immediately upon diagnosis in order to achieve viral suppression (Panel on Opportunistic Infections in HIV-Infected Adults and Adolescents, 2015). Viral suppression is considered the ideal endpoint in the HIV treatment cascade—a model whereby all people at risk for HIV are routinely tested and those who test positive are referred to treatment in order to receive antiretroviral therapy and are retained in care to ensure adherence and ultimate viral suppression.

For HIV-negative MSM, a number of harm reduction–based behavioral strategies have been discussed to prevent HIV transmission. Serosorting, defined as "a person choosing a sexual partner known to be of the same HIV serostatus, often to engage in unprotected sex, in order to reduce the risk of acquiring or transmitting HIV" (CDC, 2009) and strategic positioning (or seropositioning) where an HIV-positive partner takes the receptive role during unprotected anal intercourse with an HIV-negative partner (Parsons et al., 2005) potentially reducing HIV transmission risk (Jin et al., 2010; Vittinghoff et al., 1999) are two such strategies. These practices are preferred by many gay and bisexual men in serodiscordant (where one partner is positive and the other is negative) relationships and for whom consistent condom use is not possible; however, some public health practitioners discourage their use as studies have demonstrated the relative risk of HIV transmission when practicing serosorting compared to consistent condom use (Fengyi et al., 2009; Golden, Stekler, Hughes, & Wood, 2008; Marks et al., 2010; WHO, 2011b).

Additionally, biomedical HIV prevention strategies have been added to the arsenal of HIV prevention approaches for those at risk of acquiring HIV. Perhaps most promising is an intervention called pre-exposure prophylaxis (PrEP). PrEP is an HIV medication taken on a daily basis that has been shown to be extremely effective even when an occasional dose is missed. Several randomized, placebo-controlled clinical trials have reported that with high medication adherence, PrEP reduced new HIV infections by over 90% among gay and bisexual men (Grant et al., 2010) and heterosexual men and women (Baeten et al., 2012), and over 70% among people who inject drugs (Choopanya et al., 2013). Most recently, researchers at Kaiser Permanente San Francisco Medical Center found no new HIV infections among over 600 PrEP patients during more than two and a half years of observation (Volk et al., 2015). Clinical guidelines for PrEP recommend its use by MSM who are at high risk for acquiring HIV (e.g., those who describe inconsistent condom use with partners of unknown serostatus). However, major challenges to widespread PrEP use by MSM, especially racial/ethnic minority MSM, have been documented. These include concerns about accessibility, affordability, health insurance coverage, and a range of attitudes about PrEP that may decrease its use and acceptability among MSM (Hoff et al., 2015; Mimiaga, Case, Johnson, Safren, & Mayer, 2009). That said, PrEP and other biomedical prevention strategies are important tools to reduce the disproportionate burden of HIV among gay and bisexual men.

THE ROLE OF SOCIAL WORKERS

Social workers have the capacity to address LGBTQ health disparities in a variety of practice settings, such as clinical work with individuals, social services program development, community mobilization, and policy development, to change cultural conditions and social structures that perpetuate disparities. The National Association of Social Workers Code of Ethics (2008) reminds us that social justice is at the core of our professional identity stating, "social workers pursue social change, particularly with and on behalf of vulnerable and oppressed individuals and groups of people. Social workers' social change efforts are focused primarily on issues of poverty, unemployment, discrimination, and other forms of social injustice." It is the mandate of every social worker to understand how structural and intersecting oppression impacts LGBTQ people and to work toward a society where all people are afforded the equitable access to high-quality health care and accompanying social services.

According to the US Bureau of Labor Statistics (2015), there are nearly 160,000 social workers employed in health-care settings across the country who work in diverse practice contexts including hospitals, outpatient care centers, community clinics, home healthcare, and skilled nursing facilities. Social workers employed outside health-care settings will often interface with health-care systems or support clients or community members in accessing care. The Standards and Indicators of Culturally Competent Practice (National Association of Social Workers, 2015) includes possessing and continuing to develop knowledge and practice skills regarding sexual orientation and gender identity or expression, among others. This mandate is one critical step in addressing health disparities across LGBTQ populations, as social workers with a nuanced understanding of LGBTQ health-care needs can better tailor their efforts to explicitly address the health of LGBTQ people, families, and communities.

CONTINUING EDUCATION

It is critical that social workers familiarize themselves with a diversity of positive personal and community narratives about LGBTQ experiences, as well as relevant LGBTQ community resources, through ongoing and proactive continuing education. Given the dynamic evolution of LGBTQ communities and the regional and cultural contexts to which they are tied, continuing education must be viewed as an ongoing process that can include exploring literature, art, films, and media, as well attending community events, talks, and political events. Many professional groups provide trainings for social workers on special topics related to working with LGBTQ communities, and some states require modules on sexuality that include content related to LGBTQ experiences prior to licensing (e.g., Cal. Code Regs., tit. 16, § 1807).

AFFIRMING PRACTICE

In micro-level practice, social workers are called upon to help individuals, families, and groups through bolstering human relationships and focusing on the inherent dignity and worth of the person. When working with LGBTQ people, social workers should adhere to the principles outlined in this volume and other sources regarding LGBTQ-affirmative practice (Appleby & Anastas, 1998; Crisp & McCave, 2007; Morrow, 2004). Social workers should also learn about and follow principles of informed consent when supporting transgender people in accessing health-related care.

TALKING ABOUT GENDER AND SEXUALITY

LGBTQ people often face discrimination and stigma regarding their sexual and gender minority identities. As a result, clients may fear disclosing critical health information to health-care professionals. Social workers across a variety of practice settings should learn how to talk openly about gender and sexuality and, when appropriate, conduct culturally sensitive assessment that includes questions about gender and sexual identity. In health-care settings in particular, social workers should strive to create openings and opportunities for clients to provide relevant information about whether sexual orientation and gender identity may be relevant to their health-care needs and overall functioning. Consistent with minority stress theory, disclosure or "coming out" may provide some people with a feeling of relief, as well as help facilitate connections to competent health resources and social support networks. Self-disclosure may be one of a number of protective factors to negative health outcomes such as depression and substance abuse (D'Augelli et al., 1998). However, disclosure to social workers can entail weighing perceived and actual risks, which vary greatly. Some LGBTQ youth, for example, may face additional forms of violence or exclusion within their families or in foster care, while other LGBTQ individuals within institutional settings such as prisons, mental health or rehabilitations centers, or elder care facilities may be at risk for LGBTQ people are often subjected to targeted mistreatment or abuse.

Many social workers perform psychosocial assessments as part of their role in a range of agency settings. Building rapport and creating openings for disclosure of sexual orientation and gender identity should be ongoing; however, direct questions related to sexual orientation and gender identity, (such as asking preferred names and pronouns) of all clients may be one way of enabling LGBTQ people to discuss these issues openly with social workers.

UNETHICAL AND HARMFUL TREATMENT

Recently the Council on Social Work Education released a formal position statement opposing the use of conversation/reparative therapy in social work practice, specifying that this approach, which attempts to "change" or "repair" the sexual orientation and/or gender identity of LGBTQ people is "not only associated with psychological harm, but also violate[s] the Code of Ethics of the National Association of Social Workers" (2015). With this statement, the Council on Social Work Education joined a number of other professional associations, including the American Psychological Association and the American Psychiatric Association, in opposing this approach to the treatment of LGBTQ people. Despite this significant policy milestone, questions remain regarding the accreditation of social work programs that continue to teach conversion/reparative therapy and licensing sanctions for social workers who continue to use these practices despite their harm to LGBTQ people.

RESILIENCE

While this chapter focused largely on how LGBTQ people are disproportionately impacted by disease, social workers might also elicit information about resilience from their LGBTQ clients, who may develop positive self-image and coping strategies related to overcoming significant adversity. Adaptive coping strategies may reduce the negative effects of stigma. In order to make effective referrals to an affirming health-care provider, social workers should be knowledgeable of affirming local health-care providers or clinics that specialize in LGBTQ health and mental health as well as LGBTQ-affirming recovery groups, family support groups for parents, youth support and social groups, elder care providers, and other LGBTQ networks. Social workers should be especially aware of culturally specific resources for LGBTQ people of color and services for people with disabilities that are LGBTQ affirming. Gaining consent prior to making a referral is vital, as clients may not want to be referred to local LGBTQ organizations or have concerns related to anonymity or privacy, particularly in smaller communities.

AFFIRMING PRACTICE SETTINGS

At the mezzo level, organizations that provide social and health services must make an explicit commitment to access to services for LGBTQ people. Nondiscrimination policies and ongoing provider trainings are often an important step in making this commitment—but alone are wholly insufficient—to address the profound historical barriers to services that exist within social service agencies for LGBTQ people. Social workers employed within health-care settings can develop programming aimed at equipping health colleagues with knowledge and skills to identify and address the needs of LGBTQ people (Utamsingh, Richman, Martin, Lattanner, & Chaikind, 2016). Building meaningful collaborations with multiple LGBTQ organizations can help guide organizations in efforts to improve service delivery and outreach while also strengthening community-based referrals and co-advocacy relationships. Another critical step for organizations is to encourage LGBTQ people to respond to job announcements and to ensure that workplace culture is affirming for LGBTQ employees, particularly for transgender people. Ensuring that organizational facilities and programs can appropriately serve people of all genders, including bathrooms and overnight shelter space, is another critical step toward access. When appropriate, organizations that collect information on sexuality and gender identity through electronic health records may utilize this information to consider their organizational performance in serving LGBTQ organizations, as well as providing a valuable infrastructure for further health research on LGBTQ populations (Makadon & Cahill, 2013).

POLICY

At the macro level, social workers can work to address health disparities among LGBTQ people by working to change policies and shift cultural values that create barriers to adequate health care and distribute health and environmental risk based on race, gender, and other social hierarchies. Unfair and discriminatory policies targeting LGBTQ people have pernicious "downstream" consequences. For example, research examining the relationship between those residing in states that banned same-sex marriage and the prevalence of psychiatric disorders among LGBT people demonstrated increases in mood disorders, generalized anxiety disorder, alcohol use disorders, and psychiatric comorbidity between 2001 and 2005 (Hatzenbuehler, McLaughlin, Keyes, & Hasin, 2009). Similar research has shown declines in health-care expenditures, including mental health expenditures, among sexual-minority men in the years following enactment of same-sex marriage laws (Hatzenbuehler et al., 2011). This research provides compelling evidence for the importance of challenging discriminatory policies, which have very real consequences for the health and well-being of sexual- and gender-minority people. In 2013 the repeal of the Defense of Marriage Act enabled married gay couples to receive the same federal health, tax, social security, and other benefits that heterosexual couples receive. In 2016, with all 50 states recognizing same-sex marriage, these federal benefits are likely to impact the health of some LGBTQ people across the country in years to come. However, the distribution of health care and other federal benefits through marriage may tend to further disadvantage people who, for myriad reasons, do not get married or divorce (Beyond Marriage, 2006; Zissimopoulos, 2009), as well as survivors of intimate partner abuse.

There is much work to be done, and social workers can play a key role in advocating for policies that directly and indirectly impact the health of LGBTQ people. Perhaps one of the most pressing is access to health-care services for transgender people. Denial of care, provider bias, problems with "discrepancies" in personal identification documents, and the lack of training among medical providers and insurance staffers still remain significant barriers for transgender people navigating the health-care industry (Grant et al., 2010; Sanchez, Sanchez, & Danoff, 2009). The Transgender Law Center found pervasive discrimination in the private insurance market, including the denial of insurance coverage for transgender and gender-nonconforming people for a range of health-care services, including reproductive health, cancer screenings, mental health services, hormone therapy, and surgical treatments (Transgender Law Center, 2004). The ACA prevents insurance companies from discriminating on the basis of sex, which has been interpreted to include discrimination against transgender people and those who do not conform to gender stereotypes. However, transgender patients continue to encounter significant procedural barriers. For example, it is standard practice for most insurance companies and health-care providers to require transgender patients to "prove" their identity through documentation from a mental health provider. Many transgender people and health advocates view these extra requirements as an undue and discriminatory barrier. Not only can this process be demeaning and costly for transgender people, but it can prohibit some people from accessing care altogether and is particularly burdensome for transgender people who have another mental health diagnosis or for whom psychotherapy is not desired or culturally appropriate. Social workers can join in efforts to change these requirements by advocating for informed consent as an appropriate standard of care, ensuring their organizations are prepared to support transgender people in navigating systems of care while improving individual skills and knowledge.

CONCLUSION

This chapter provided a broad overview on the state of LGBTQ health disparities in the United States, the factors that contribute to these disparities, and the role of social workers in addressing health disparities among LGBTQ people. We paid particular attention to the HIV/AIDS epidemic, perhaps the most significant public health challenge for LGBTQ people to date based on its scope and intractability in the face of current prevention and treatment efforts. Where possible, we tried to highlight the experiences of LGBTQ people of color and those living in poverty, who face compounded health disparities due to racism and structural violence levied at the poor. Much work remains to realize health equity between LGBTQ people and their heterosexual counterparts. Social workers are uniquely positioned to address health and well-being among LGBTQ people across a range of practice settings.

REFERENCES

Advisory Committee on Immunization Practices. (2011). Recommendations on the use of quadrivalent human papillomavirus vaccine in males. *Morbidity and Mortality Weekly Report, 60*(50), 1705–1708.

Albelda, R., Badgett, M. V. L., Schneebaum, A., & Gates, G. (2009). *Poverty in the lesbian, gay, and bisexual community*. Retrieved from http://www.escholarship.org/uc/item/2509p8r5

Alvy, L. M., Hughes, T. L., Kristjanson, A. F., & Wilsnack, S. C. (2013). Sexual identity group differences in child abuse and neglect. *Journal of Interpersonal Violence, 28*(10), 2088–2111. doi:10.1177/0886260512471081.

Appleby, G. A., & Anastas, J. W. (1998). *Not just a passing phase: Social work with gay, lesbian, and bisexual people*. New York: Columbia University Press.

Baeten, J. M., Donnell, D., Ndase, P., Mugo, N. R., Campbell, J. D., Wangisi, J., . . . Celum, C. (2012). Antiretroviral prophylaxis for HIV-1 prevention among heterosexual men and women. *The New England Journal of Medicine, 367*(5), 399–401. doi:10.1056/NEJMoa1108524

Bauer, G. R., Hammond, R., Travers, R., Kaay, M., Hohenadel, K. M., & Boyce, M. (2009). "I don't think this is theoretical; this is our lives": How erasure impacts health care for transgender people. *Journal of the Association of Nurses in AIDS Care, 20*(5), 348–361.

Beyond Marriage. (2006). *A new strategic vision for all our families & relationships.* Retrieved from http://www.beyondmarriage.org/BeyondMarriage.pdf

Blosnich, J., Lee, J. G., & Horn, K. (2013). A systematic review of the aetiology of tobacco disparities for sexual minorities. *Tobacco Control, 22*(2), 66–73.

Bockting, W. O., Miner, M. H., Swinburne Romine, R. E., Hamilton, A., & Coleman, E. (2013). Stigma, mental health, and resilience in an online sample of the US transgender population. *American Journal of Public Health, 103*(5), 943–951.

Boehmer, U. (2002). Twenty years of public health research: Inclusion of lesbian, gay, bisexual, and transgender populations. *American Journal of Public Health, 92*(7), 1125–1130.

Boehmer, U., & Elk, R. (2016). LGBT populations and cancer: Is it an ignored epidemic? *LGBT Health, 3*(1), 1–2. doi:10.1089/lgbt.2015.0137

Bostwick, W. B., Boyd, C. J., Hughes, T. L., & McCabe, S. E. (2010). Dimensions of sexual orientation and the prevalence of mood and anxiety disorders in the United States. *American Journal of Public Health, 100*(3), 468–475.

Bradford, J. (1999). Emergence of an infrastructure for lesbian health research. *Journal of the Gay and Lesbian Medical Association, 3*(4), 115–117.

Brooks, V. R. (1981). *Minority stress and lesbian women.* Lexington, MA: Lexington Books.

Brown, G. W., & Harris, T. (1978). *Social origins of depression: A study of psychiatric disorder in women.* London: Tavistock.

Buchmueller, T., & Carpenter, C. S. (2010). Disparities in health insurance coverage, access, and outcomes for individuals in same-sex versus different-sex relationships, 2000–2007. *American Journal of Public Health, 100*(3), 489–495.

Budge, S. L., Adelson, J. L., & Howard, K. A. (2013). Anxiety and depression in transgender individuals: The roles of transition status, loss, social support, and coping. *Journal of Consulting and Clinical Psychology, 81*(3), 545–557.

Burton, C. M., Marshal, M. P., Chisolm, D. J., Sucato, G. S., & Friedman, M. S. (2013). Sexual minority-related victimization as a mediator of mental health disparities in sexual minority youth: A longitudinal analysis. *Journal of Youth and Adolescence, 42*(3), 394–402.

Canaday, M. (2009). *The straight state: Sexuality and citizenship in twentieth-century America.* Princeton, NJ: Princeton University Press.

Centers for Disease Control and Prevention. (2008). *HIV incidence.* Atlanta, GA: Author.

Centers for Disease Control and Prevention. (2009). *Consultation on serosorting practices among men who have sex with men.* Retrieved from http://www.cdc.gov/hiv/topics/research/resources/other/serosorting.htm.

Centers for Disease Control and Prevention. (2013). *HIV among gay and bisexual men.* Atlanta, GA: Author.

Centers for Disease Control and Prevention. (2015a). *HIV among transgender people.* Retrieved from http://www.cdc.gov/hiv/pdf/group/gender/transgender/cdc-hiv-transgender.pdf

Centers for Disease Control and Prevention. (2015b). *HIV in the United States: At a glance.* Retrieved from http://www.cdc.gov/hiv/statistics/overview

Centore, S., & Fischer, G. (Dirs.). (2016). *Passing Ellenville.* USA.

Choopanya, K., Martin, M., Suntharasamai, P., Sangkum, U., Mock, P. A., Leethochawalit, M., . . . Vanichseni, S. (2013). Antiretroviral prophylaxis for HIV infection in injecting drug users in Bangkok, Thailand (the Bangkok Tenofovir Study): A randomised, double-blind, placebo-controlled phase 3 trial. *The Lancet, 381*(9883), 2083–2090. http://dx.doi.org/10.1016/S0140-6736(13)61127-7

Clements-Nolle, K., Marx, R., & Katz, M. (2006). Attempted suicide among transgender persons: The influence of gender-based discrimination and victimization. *Journal of Homosexuality, 51*(3), 53–69.

Cochran, S. D., & Mays, V. M. (2015). Mortality risks among persons reporting same-sex sexual partners: Evidence from the 2008 general social survey—national death index data set. *American Journal of Public Health, 105*(2), 358–364.

Cochran, S. D., Mays, V. M., Alegria, M., Ortega, A. N., & Takeuchi, D. (2007). Mental health and substance use disorders among Latino and Asian American lesbian, gay, and bisexual adults. *Journal of Consulting and Clinical Psychology, 75*(5), 785–794. doi:10.1037/0022-006X.75.5.785.

Cohen, J. M., Blasey, C., Taylor, C. B., Weiss, B. J., & Newman, M. G. (2016). Anxiety and related disorders and concealment in sexual minority young adults. *Behavior Therapy, 47*(1), 91–101.

Conron, K. J., Mimiaga, M. J., & Landers, S. J. (2010). A population-based study of sexual orientation identity and gender differences in adult health. *American Journal of Public Health, 100*(10), 1953–1960.

Council on Social Work Education. (2015). *Position statement on conversion/reparative therapy.* Alexandria, VA: Author.

Crisp, C., & McCave, E. L. (2007). Gay affirmative practice: A model for social work practice with gay, lesbian, and bisexual youth. *Child and Adolescent Social Work Journal, 24*(4), 403–421.

Currah, P., & Stryker, S. (2015). Making transgender count. *TSQ: Transgender Studies Quarterly, 2*(1), 148–159.

Dank, M., Lachman, P., Zweig, J. M., & Yahner, J. (2014). Dating violence experiences of lesbian, gay, bisexual, and transgender youth. *Journal of Youth and Adolescence, 43*(5), 846–857.

D'Augelli, A. R., Hershberger, S. L., & Pilkington, N. W. (1998). Lesbian, gay, and bisexual youth and their families: Disclosure of sexual orientation and its consequences. *American Journal of Orthopsychiatry, 68*(3), 361–371.

Davis, K. (Dir.). (2001). *Southern comfort.* Los Angeles: Shout! Factory.

Dean, L., Meyer, I. H., Robinson, K., Sell, R. L., Sember, R., Silenzio, V. M., . . . Xavier, J. (2000). Lesbian, gay, bisexual, and transgender health: Findings and concerns. *Journal of the Gay and Lesbian Medical Association, 4*(3), 101–151.

Drescher, J. (2010). Queer diagnoses: Parallels and contrasts in the history of homosexuality, gender variance, and the *Diagnostic and Statistical Manual. Archives of Sexual Behavior, 39*(2), 427–460.

Drescher, J. (2015). Queer diagnoses revisited: The past and future of homosexuality and gender diagnoses in DSM and ICD. *International Review of Psychiatry, 27*(5), 386–395.

Epstein, S. (2003). Sexualizing governance and medicalizing identities: The emergence of state-centered LGBT health politics in the United States. *Sexualities, 6*(2), 131–171.

Fengyi, J., Crawford, J., Prestage, G. P., Zablotska, I., Imrie, J., Kaldor, J. M., & Grulich, A. E. (2009). Unprotected anal intercourse, risk reduction behaviours, and subsequent HIV infection in a cohort of homosexual men. *AIDS, 23*(2), 243–252. doi:10.1097/QAD.0b013e32831fb51a

Fenkl, E. A., Jones, S. G., Schochet, E., & Johnson, P. (2016). HPV and anal cancer knowledge among HIV-infected and non-infected men who have sex with men. *LGBT Health, 3*(1), 42–48. doi:10.1089/lgbt.2015.0086

France, D., (Dir.). (2012). *How to survive a plague.* New York: Sundance Selects.

Friedman, M. S., Marshal, M. P., Guadamuz, T. E., Wei, C., Wong, C. F., Saewyc, E. M., & Stall, R. (2011). A meta-analysis of disparities in childhood sexual abuse, parental physical abuse, and peer victimization among sexual minority and sexual nonminority individuals. *American Journal of Public Health, 101*(8), 1481–1494.

Gay and Lesbian Medical Association. (2001). *Healthy people 2010: Companion document for lesbian, gay, bisexual, and transgender (LGBT) health.* San Francisco, CA: Author.

Gay and Lesbian Medical Association. (2015). Lesbian Health Fund. Retrieved from http://www.glma.org/index.cfm?fuseaction=Page.viewPage&pageId=594

Goldbach, J. T., Tanner-Smith, E. E., Bagwell, M., & Dunlap, S. (2014). Minority stress and substance use in sexual minority adolescents: A meta-analysis. *Prevention Science, 15*(3), 350–363.

Golden, M., Stekler, J., Hughes, J., & Wood, R. W. (2008). HIV serosorting in men who have sex with men: Is it safe? *Journal of Acquired Immune Deficiency Syndromes, 49*(2), 212–218. doi:10.1097/QAI.0b013e31818455e8

Gooren, L. J., van Trotsenburg, M. A. A., Giltay, E. J., & van Diest, P. J. (2013). Breast cancer development in transsexual subjects receiving cross-sex hormone treatment. *The Journal of Sexual Medicine, 10*(12), 3129–3134. doi:10.1111/jsm.12319

Grant, J. M., Mottet, L. A., Tanis, J. E., Harrison, J., Herman, J., & Keisling, M. (2011). *Injustice at every turn: A report of the national transgender discrimination survey.* Washington, DC: National Center for Transgender Equality and National Gay and Lesbian Task Force.

Grant, R. M., Lama, J. R., Anderson, P. L., McMahan, V., Liu, A., Vargas, L., . . . Glidden, D. V. (2010). Preexposure chemoprophylaxis for HIV prevention in men who have sex with men. *The New England Journal of Medicine, 363*(27), 2587–2599. doi:10.1056/NEJMoa1011205.

Grmek, M. D., Maulitz, R. C., & Duffin, J. (1993). *History of AIDS: Emergence and origin of a modern pandemic.* Princeton, NJ: Princeton University Press.

Hart, S. L., & Bowen, D. J. (2009). Sexual orientation and intentions to obtain breast cancer screening. *Journal of Women's Health, 18*(2), 177–185.

Hatzenbuehler, M. L., McLaughlin, K. A., Keyes, K. M., & Hasin, D. S. (2009). The impact of institutional discrimination on psychiatric disorders in lesbian, gay, and bisexual populations: A prospective study. *American Journal of Public Health, 100*(3), 452–459. doi:10.2105/AJPH.2009.168815

Hatzenbuehler, M. L., O'Cleirigh, C., Grasso, C., Mayer, K., Safren, S., & Bradford, J. (2011). Effect of same-sex marriage laws on health care use and expenditures in sexual minority men: A quasi-natural experiment. *American Journal of Public Health, 102*(2), 285–291. doi:10.2105/AJPH.2011.300382

Hawkes, S., & Lewis, D. A. (2014). HPV vaccine strategies: Equitable and effective? *Sexually Transmitted Infections, 90*(7), 510–511. doi:10.1136/sextrans-2014-051637

Herbst, J. H., Jacobs, E. D., Finlayson, T. J., McKleroy, V. S., Neumann, M. S., & Crepaz, N. (2008). Estimating HIV prevalence and risk behaviors of transgender persons in the United States: A systematic review. *AIDS and Behavior, 12*(1), 1–17.

Herrick, A. L., Stall, R., Goldhammer, H., Egan, J. E., & Mayer, K. H. (2013). Resilience as a research framework and as a cornerstone of prevention research for gay and bisexual men: Theory and evidence. *AIDS and Behavior, 18*(1), 1–9.

Hoff, C. C., Chakravarty, D., Bircher, A. E., Campbell, C. K., Grisham, K., Neilands, T. B., . . . Dworkin, S. (2015). Attitudes towards PrEP and anticipated condom use among concordant HIV-negative and HIV-discordant male couples. *AIDS Patient Care and STDs, 29*(7), 408–417. doi:10.1089/apc.2014.0315

Hubbard, J. (Dir.). (2012). *United in anger: A history of ACT UP.* Film Collaborative.

Institute of Medicine. (2011). *The health of lesbian, gay, bisexual, and transgender people: Building a foundation for better understanding.* Washington, DC: National Academies Press.

Institute of Medicine Committee on Lesbian Health Research Priorities. (1999). *Lesbian health: Current assessment and directions for the future.* Washington, DC: National Academy Press.

Jin, F., Jansson, J., Law, M., Prestage, G. P., Zablotska, I., Imrie, J. C. G., . . . Wilson, D. P. (2010). Per-contact probability of HIV transmission in homosexual men in Sydney in the era of HAART. *AIDS, 24*(6), 907–913. doi:10.1097/QAD.0b013e3283372d90

Kamen, C., Mustian, K. M., Dozier, A., Bowen, D. J., & Li, Y. (2015). Disparities in psychological distress impacting lesbian, gay, bisexual and transgender cancer survivors. *Psycho-Oncology, 24*(11), 1384–1391.

Katz, J. N. (1990). The invention of heterosexuality. In M. L. Andersen (Ed.), *Race, class and gender: An anthology* (pp. 252–264). Chicago: University of Chicago Press.

Kosciw, J. G., Greytak, E. A., Bartkiewicz, M. J., Boesen, M. J., & Palmer, N. A. (2012). *The 2011 National School Climate Survey: The experiences of lesbian, gay, bisexual and transgender youth in our nation's schools.* New York: GLSEN.

Lambda Legal. (2010). *From when health care isn't caring: Lambda Legal's survey of discrimination against LGBT people and people with HIV.* Retrieved from www.lambdalegal.org/health-care-report

Lemp, G. F., Jones, M., Kellogg, T. A., Nieri, G. N., Anderson, L., Withum, D., & Katz, M. (1995). HIV seroprevalence and risk behaviors among lesbians and bisexual women in San Francisco and Berkeley, California. *American Journal of Public Health, 85*(11), 1549–1552.

Makadon, H., & Cahill, S. (2013). Sexual orientation and gender identity data collection in clinical settings and in electronic health records: A key to ending LGBT health disparities. *LGBT Health, 1*(1), 34–41. doi:10.1089/lgbt.2013.0001.

Marks, G., Millett, G., Trista, B., Lauby, J., Murrill, C. S., & Stueve, A. (2010). Prevalence and protective value of serosorting and strategic positioning among Black and Latino men who have sex with men. *Sexually Transmitted Diseases, 37*(5), 325–327. doi:10.1097/OLQ.0b013e3181c95dac

Marshal, M. P., Dietz, L. J., Friedman, M. S., Stall, R., Smith, H. A., McGinley, J., . . . Brent, D. A. (2011). Suicidality and depression disparities between sexual minority and heterosexual youth: A meta-analytic review. *Journal of Adolescent Health, 49*(2), 115–123. doi:10.1016/j.jadohealth.2011.02.005

Marshal, M. P., Friedman, M. S., Stall, R., King, K. M., Miles, J., Gold, M. A., . . . Morse, J. Q. (2008). Sexual orientation and adolescent substance use: A meta-analysis and methodological review. *Addiction, 103*(4), 546–556. doi:10.1111/j.1360-0443.2008.02149.x

McCabe, S. E., Bostwick, W. B., Hughes, T. L., West, B. T., & Boyd, C. J. (2010). The relationship between discrimination and substance use disorders among lesbian, gay, and bisexual adults in the United States. *American Journal of Public Health, 100*(10), 1946–1952.

McCabe, S. E., Hughes, T. L., Bostwick, W. B., West, B. T., & Boyd, C. J. (2009). Sexual orientation, substance use behaviors and substance dependence in the United States. *Addiction, 104*(8), 1333–1345.

Meyer, I. H. (2003). Prejudice, social stress, and mental health in lesbian, gay, and bisexual populations: Conceptual issues and research evidence. *Psychological Bulletin, 129*(5), 674–697.

Milstein, B. (2008). *Hygeia's constellation: Navigating health futures in a dynamic and democratic world.* Center for Disease Control, Syndemic Prevention Network. Retrieved from http://www.cdc.gov/syndemics/monograph/sections/systemdynamics.htm

Mimiaga, M. J., Case, P., Johnson, C. V., Safren, S. A., & Mayer, K. H. (2009). Pre-exposure antiretroviral prophylaxis (PrEP) attitudes in high risk Boston area MSM: Limited knowledge and experience, but potential for increased utilization after education. *Journal of Acquired Immune Deficiency Syndromes, 50*(1), 77–83. doi:10.1097/QAI.0b013e31818d5a27

Morrow, D. (2004) Social work practice with gay, lesbian, bisexual, and transgender adolescents. *Families in Society: The Journal of Contemporary Social Services, 85*(1), 91–99.

Mustanski, B., Garofalo, R., Herrick, A., & Donenberg, G. (2007). Psychosocial health problems increase risk for HIV among urban young men who have sex with men: Preliminary evidence of a syndemic in need of attention. *Annals of Behavioral Medicine, 34*(1), 37–45.

National Association of Social Workers. (2008). *Code of ethics.* Retrieved from http://www.socialworkers.org/pubs/code/code.asp

National Association of Social Workers. (2015). *Standards and indicators for cultural competence in social work practice.* Retrieved from https://www.socialworkers.org/practice/standards/Standards_and_Indicators_for_Cultural_Competence.asp

National Institutes of Health. (2015). *Administrative supplements for research on sexual and gender minority (SGM) populations.* Retrieved from http://grants.nih.gov/grants/guide/pa-files/PA-15-329.html

Nelson, A. R., Smedley, B. D., & Stith, A. Y. (2002). *Unequal treatment: Confronting racial and ethnic disparities in health care*. Washington, DC: National Academies Press.

Office of Disease Prevention and Health Promotion. (2012). 2020 topics and objectives: Lesbian, gay, bisexual, and transgender health. Retrieved from https://www.healthypeople.gov/2020/topics-objectives/topic/lesbian-gay-bisexual-and-transgender-health/objectives

Office of National HIV/AIDS Policy. (2015). *National HIV/AIDS strategy for the United States: Updated to 2020*. Washington, DC: Author.

Operario, D., Nemoto, T., Iwamoto, M., & Moore, T. (2011). Risk for HIV and unprotected sexual behavior in male primary partners of transgender women. *Archives of Sexual Behavior, 40*(6), 1255–1261.

Ophelian, A. (Dir.). (2009). *Diagnosing difference*. San Francisco, CA: Frameline.

Panel on Opportunistic Infections in HIV-Infected Adults and Adolescents. (2015). *Guidelines for the prevention and treatment of opportunistic infections in HIV-infected adults and adolescents: Recommendations from the Centers for Disease Control and Prevention, the National Institutes of Health, and the HIV Medicine Association of the Infectious Diseases Society of America*. Retrieved from http://aidsinfo.nih.gov/contentfiles/lvguidelines/adult_oi.pdf

Parsons, J., Schrimshaw, E., Wolitski, R., Halkitis, P., Purcell, D., Hoff, C., & Gomez, C. (2005). Sexual harm reduction practices of HIV-seropositive gay and bisexual men: Serosorting, strategic positioning, and withdrawal before ejaculation. *AIDS, 19*(1), 13–25.

Pilkington, N. W., & D'Augelli, A. R. (1995). Victimization of lesbian, gay, and bisexual youth in community settings. *Journal of Community Psychology, 23*(1), 34–56.

Poteat, T., German, D., & Kerrigan, D. (2013). Managing uncertainty: A grounded theory of stigma in transgender health care encounters. *Social Science & Medicine, 84*, 22–29.

California Code of Regulations. Professional and Vocational Regulations, § 1807, Human Sexuality Training, (2016). Retrieved at: https://govt.westlaw.com/calregs/Document/IEE7787F08D6111E095DEB89B5D26CB60?viewType=FullText&originationContext=documenttoc&transitionType=CategoryPageItem&contextData=(sc.Default)

Purcell, D. W., Johnson, C. H., Lansky, A., Prejean, J., Stein, R., Denning, P., . . . Crepaz, N. (2012). Estimating the population size of men who have sex with men in the United States to obtain HIV and syphilis rates. *The Open AIDS Journal, 6*(1), 98–107.

Quinn, G. P., Sanchez, J. A., Sutton, S. K., Vadaparampil, S. T., Nguyen, G. T., Green, B. L., . . . Schabath, M. B. (2015). Cancer and lesbian, gay, bisexual, transgender/transsexual, and queer/questioning (LGBTQ) populations. *CA: A Cancer Journal for Clinicians, 65*(5), 384–400.

Reis, E. (2009). *Bodies in doubt: An American history of intersex*. Baltimore, MD: Johns Hopkins University Press.

Reisner, S. L., Biello, K. B., Hughto, J. M. W., Kuhns, L., Mayer, K. H., Garofalo, R., & Mimiaga, M. J. (2016). Psychiatric diagnoses and comorbidities in a diverse, multicity cohort of young transgender women: Baseline findings from Project LifeSkills. *JAMA Pediatrics, 170*(5), 481–486.

Rhynard, T. (Dir.). (2016). *Forbidden: Undocumented and queer in rural America*. Boca Raton, FL: Sisters Unite Productions.

Rosario, M., Schrimshaw, E. W., Hunter, J., & Gwadz, M. (2002). Gay-related stress and emotional distress among gay, lesbian and bisexual youths: A longitudinal examination. *Journal of Consulting and Clinical Psychology, 70*(4), 967–975.

Russell, S. T., & Joyner, K. (2001). Adolescent sexual orientation and suicide risk: Evidence from a national study. *American Journal of Public Health, 91*(8), 1276–1281.

Ryan, C., Huebner, D., Diaz, R. M., & Sanchez, J. (2009). Family rejection as a predictor of negative health outcomes in White and Latino lesbian, gay, and bisexual young adults. *Pediatrics, 123*(1), 346–352.

Sanchez, N. F., Sanchez, J. P., & Danoff, A. (2009). Health care utilization, barriers to care, and hormone usage among male-to-female transgender persons in New York City. *American Journal of Public Health, 99*(4), 713–719.

Self, P., Filardo, T., & Lancaster, F. (1989). Acquired immunodeficiency syndrome (AIDS) and the epidemic growth of its literature. *Scientometics, 17*, 49–60.

Sevelius, J. M. (2009). There's no pamphlet for the kind of sex I have: HIV-related risk factors and protective behaviors among transgender men who have sex with non-transgender men. *Journal of the Association of Nurses in AIDS Care, 20*(5), 398–401. doi:10.1016/j.jana.2009.06.001.

Sevelius, J. M., Keatley, J., & Gutierrez-Mock, L. (2011). HIV/AIDS programming in the United States: Considerations affecting transgender women and girls. *Women's Health Issues, 21*(6), S278–S282.

Singer, M. (1994). AIDS and the health crisis of the U.S. urban poor: The perspective of critical medical anthropology. *Social Science and Medicine, 39*(7), 931–948.

Snelgrove, J. W., Jasudavisius, A. M., Rowe, B. W., Head, E. M., & Bauer, G. R. (2012). "Completely out-at-sea" with "two-gender medicine": A qualitative analysis of physician-side barriers to providing healthcare for transgender patients. *BMC Health Services Research, 12*, 110. doi:10.1186/1472-6963-12-110

Somerville, S. (1994). Scientific racism and the emergence of the homosexual body. *Journal of the History of Sexuality, 5*(2), 243–266.

Sommers, B. D., Baicker, K., & Epstein, A. M. (2012). Mortality and access to care among adults after state Medicaid expansions. *The New England Journal of Medicine, 367*(11), 1025–1034.

Spitzer, R. L. (1981). The diagnostic status of homosexuality in DSM-III: A reformulation of the issues. *American Journal of Psychiatry, 138*(2), 210–215.

Stall, R., Friedman, M., & Catania, J. A. (2008). Interacting epidemics and gay men's health: A theory of syndemic production among urban gay men. In R. J. Wolitski, R. Stall, & R. O. Valdiserri (Eds.), *Unequal opportunity: Health disparities affecting gay and bisexual men in the United States* (pp. 251–274). New York: Oxford University Press.

Stotzer, R. L. (2009). Violence against transgender people: A review of United States data. *Aggression and Violent Behavior, 14*(3), 170–179.

Terry, J. (1990). Lesbians under the medical gaze: Scientists search for remarkable differences. *Journal of Sex Research, 27*(3), 317–339.

Terry, J. (1999). *An American obsession: Science, medicine, and homosexuality in modern society.* Chicago: University of Chicago Press.

Testa, R. J., Habarth, J., Peta, J., Balsam, K., & Bockting, W. (2015). Development of the gender minority stress and resilience measure. *Psychology of Sexual Orientation and Gender Diversity, 2*(1), 65–77.

Thoits, P. A. (1991). On merging identity theory and stress research. *Social Psychology Quarterly, 54*(2), 101–112.

Transgender Law Center. (2004). *Transgender health and the law: Identifying and fighting health care discrimination.* Retrieved from http://transgenderlawcenter.org/issues/health/transgender-health-and-the-law-identifying-and-fighting-health-care-discrimination

Treichler, P. A. (1987). AIDS, homophobia and biomedical discourse: An epidemic of signification. *Cultural Studies, 1*(3), 263–305.

US Bureau of Labor Statistics. (2015). *Occupational outlook handbook, 2016–2017 edition.* Retrieved from http://www.bls.gov/ooh/community-and-social-service/social-workers.htm

US Department of Health and Human Services. (2000). *Strategic research plan to reduce and ultimately eliminate health disparities: Fiscal years 2002–2006.* Washington, DC: National Institutes of Health.

US Department of Health and Human Services. (2008). *Health disparities strategic plan and budget fiscal years 2009–2013.* Washington, DC: National Institutes of Health.

US Department of Health and Human Services. (2011). A timeline of HIV/AIDS. Retrieved from https://www.aids.gov/hiv-aids-basics/hiv-aids-101/aids-timeline/

Utamsingh, P. D., Richman, L. S., Martin, J. L., Lattanner, M. R., & Chaikind, J. R. (2016). Heteronormativity and practitioner-patient interaction. *Health Communications, 30*(5), 566–574.

Vittinghoff, E., Douglas, J., Judson, F. N., McKirnan, D., MacQueen, K., & Buchbinder, S. P. (1999). Per-contact risk of human immunodeficiency virus transmission between male sexual partners. *American Journal of Epidemiology, 150*(3), 306–311.

Volk, J. E., Marcus, J. L., Phengrasamy, T., Blechinger, D., Nguyen, D. P., Follansbee, S., & Hare, C. B. (2015). No new HIV infections with increasing use of HIV preexposure prophylaxis in a clinical practice setting. *Clinical Infectious Diseases; 61*(10), 1601–1603. doi:10.1093/cid/civ778

Walters, M. L., Chen, J., & Breiding, M. J. (2013). *The National Intimate Partner and Sexual Violence Survey (NISVS): 2010 findings on victimization by sexual orientation.* Atlanta, GA: National Center for Injury Prevention and Control, Centers for Disease Control and Prevention.

Weeks, J. (1977). *Coming out.* London: Quartet Books.

Weekly, M. M. W. R. (1981). Pneumocystis pneumonia—Los Angeles. *June, 5*(30), 21.

Wexler, L. M., DiFluvio, G., & Burke, T. K. (2009). Resilience and marginalized youth: Making a case for personal and collective meaning-making as part of resilience research in public health. *Social Science & Medicine, 69*(4), 565–570. doi:10.1016/j.socscimed.2009.06.022

World Health Organization. (2011a). *Closing the gap: policy into practice on social determinants of health: Discussion paper.* Geneva: Author.

World Health Organization. (2011b). *Prevention and treatment of HIV and other sexually transmission infections among men who have sex with men and transgender people: Recommendations for a public health approach.* Geneva: Author.

Young, R. M., & Meyer, I. H. (2005). The trouble with "MSM" and "WSW": Erasure of the sexual-minority person in public health discourse. *American Journal of Public Health, 95*(7), 1144–1149.

Zaritsky, E., & Dibble, S. L. (2010). Risk factors for reproductive and breast cancers among older lesbians. *Journal of Women's Health, 19*(1), 125–131.

Zissimopoulos, J. M. (2009). *Gain and loss: Marriage and wealth changes over time.* Ann Arbor: Michigan Retirement Research Center, University of Michigan.

PART V
APPENDICES

APPENDIX A

Signs, Symbols, and Subcultures

The following list briefly highlights some of the signs, symbols and subcultures of the LGBTQ community. Please note that this list is by no means exhaustive. For more information related to additional signs, symbols and subcultures of the LGBTQ community, See http://www.glaad.org/blog/mashable-publishes-date-compilation-lgbt-flags-and-symbols and http://www.algbtical.org/2A%20SYMBOLS.htm

PINK TRIANGLE

The history of the pink triangle stems from World War II during the Holocaust and the Nazi's use of this symbol on prisoner uniforms to identify homosexuals in concentration camps. The pink triangle has been reclaimed since the 1970s as a symbol of pride, solidarity, and remembrance. See https://www.geneseo.edu/safe_zone/triangle_history and http://www.legacyprojectchicago.org/The_Pink_Triangle.html

RAINBOW FLAG

The flag is comprised of six colors of the rainbow including red, orange, yellow, green, blue, and violet in a horizontal design with red on top and violet on the bottom. It was designed by Gilbert Baker (1951–2017), an artist from San Francisco, in 1978 to be used in social movements for

LGBTQ equality, during annual pride parades and marches, and also to represent LGBTQ pride. See http://www.sanfrancisco.travel/article/brief-history-rainbow-flag

TRANSGENDER PRIDE FLAG

The flag was designed to represent the transgender community consisting of five horizontal stripes of two light blue, two pink, and one white in the center. The transgender pride flag was designed by Monica Helms in 1999 and first shown at a pride parade in Phoenix, Arizona, in 2000. It is often flown during pride events or during the Transgender Day of Remembrance. There are several alternative designs used across the globe. See http://point5cc.com/the-history-of-the-transgender-flag/

TRANSGENDER UMBRELLA

"Transgender" may be used as an umbrella term for people whose gender identity and/or gender expression differs from what is typically associated with the sex they were assigned at birth. People under the transgender umbrella may describe themselves using one or more of a wide variety of terms—including *transgender*. In order to fully understand the diversity of the transgender community, it is important to learn about the umbrella. See http://www.transequality.org/issues/resources/transgender-terminology

LEATHER SUBCULTURE

Some members of the LGBTQ community may take part in the leather subculture. "Leather" is a blanket term for the community that includes a wide variety of sexual identities and preferences, relationships, and organizations that for some may or may not be associated with practices related to bondage, discipline, and sadomasochism. For other members of the leather community, participation may be related to the sociosexual sphere such as an Internet chat room, a leather bar or club, or within their own home and bedroom. See http://www.glbtqarchive.com/ssh/leather_culture_S.pdf

BEAR SUBCULTURE

Gay and bisexual men within the bear culture may be defined by their hairy bodies and facial hair, while being attracted to the same type of man. Many may have a stocky or muscular build and portray themselves as the epitome of masculinity through their rugged appearance and demeanor. These social and sexual networks of gay and bisexual men may also ascribe to a counterculture of gay men typically appearing neatly dressed and well manicured. See http://lgbt.wikia.com/wiki/Bear

LGBTQQIAA2S . . .

The ever-evolving acronym is often used in various forms within literature, research, and among community members to represent the widely diverse sexual and gender minority groups including but not limited to: lesbian (L), gay (G), bisexual (B), transgender (T), queer (Q), questioning (Q), intersex (I), asexual (A), allied (A), and Two-Spirit (2-S) communities. Combining and collapsing such diverse communities within one acronym can be quite difficult and is often met with resistance as it may confuse identities, relationships, and associations with sexual orientation, gender identity, gender, gender expression, sex, relationships, spirituality, and so on. See http://ok2bme.ca/resources/kids-teens/what-does-lgbtq-mean/

THE RED RIBBON

In 1991, a group of artists gathered to discuss a new project for Visual AIDS, a New York arts organization that raises awareness of HIV/AIDS. They came up with a simple idea that later became one of the most recognized symbols of the decade – the red ribbon, worn to signify awareness and support for people living with HIV and AIDS. The Red Ribbon continues to be a powerful and global force in the fight to increase public awareness of HIV/AIDS and in the lobbying efforts to increase funding for HIV/AIDS services and research. See https://www.worldaidsday.org/the-red-ribbon and https://www.visualaids.org/projects/detail/the-red-ribbon-project

APPENDIX B

Notable LGBTQ Individuals

Jane Addams (1860–1935). Addams won worldwide recognition in the first third of the twentieth century as a pioneer social worker in the United States and as a feminist, suffragette, and internationalist. In 1889, Addams and Ellen Star cofounded Hull House in Chicago, one of the first settlement houses in the United States. Mary Rozet Smith, a Chicago heiress, arrived at Hull House around the same time and became Addams' life partner for more than 40 years. In 1910, Addams received the first honorary degree ever awarded to a woman by Yale University and was awarded the Nobel Peace Prize in 1931. See http://www.legacyprojectchicago.org/Jane_Addams.html and http://www.nobelprize.org/nobel_prizes/peace/laureates/1931/addams-bio.html

Barbara Gittings (1932–2007). Gittings helped found the Daughters of Bilitis, later editing the organization's magazine, *The Ladder*. She marched in some of the earliest protests in Washington, D.C., at the White House and Pentagon, along with successfully lobbying the American Psychiatric Association to remove homosexuality as a mental disorder from its list of mental disorders. Gittings also helped start the organization that would become the National Gay and Lesbian Task Force. See http://www.legacyprojectchicago.org/Barbara_Gittings.html and http://www.nytimes.com/2007/03/15/obituaries/15gittings.html?_r=0

Harry Hay (1912–2002). Hay was born in London and later cofounded the Mattachine Society in 1950 as the first gay liberation group in the United States, which many call the beginning of the gay rights movement. He was an active member of the Communist Party and fought for workers' rights during the labor movement. In 1979 he cofounded the Radical Faeries. See http://www.harryhay.com/ and http://www.legacyprojectchicago.org/Harry_Hay.html

Marsha P. Johnson (1944–1992). Johnson was an African American transgender activist who survived living in New York by waitressing and panhandling. She was present during the Stonewall riots in 1969 and later cofounded Street Transgender Activist Revolutionaries (STAR) with Sylvia Rivera to assist homeless transgender women. See http://www.legacyprojectchicago.org/Marsha_ P_Johnson.html and http://www.outhistory.org/exhibits/show/tgi-bios/marsha-p-johnson

Frank Kameny (1925–2011). Kameny was dismissed from the Army Map Service and ultimately challenged his termination all the way to the US Supreme Court in 1961. He cofounded the Washington, D.C., chapter of the Mattachine Society, organizing some of the earliest protests at Independence Hall and the White House. He worked with Barbara Gittings to lobby the American Psychiatric Association to remove homosexuality from its list of mental disorders. Kameny was one of the first activists to challenge US military policy related to discrimination against gay service members. See http://www.legacyprojectchicago.org/Frank_Kameny.html and http://www. nytimes.com/2011/10/13/us/franklin-kameny-gay-rights-pioneer-dies-at-86.html

Audre Lorde (1934–1992). Lorde was a self-proclaimed Black, lesbian, mother, warrior, and poet. She was also a feminist, author, and civil rights activist. A featured speaker at the first March on Washington for lesbian and gay rights in 1979, Lorde later cofounded Kitchen Table: Women of Color Press in the late 1980s to promote the work of Black feminists. Lorde received the Walt Whitman citation of merit in 1991, which recognized her as poet laureate for the state of New York. See http://www.legacyprojectchicago.org/Audre_Lorde.html

Del Martin (1921–2008) and Phyllis Lyon (1924–). Del Martin and Phyllis Lyon founded the Daughters of Bilitis (DOB) with six other women and have fought for more than 50 years for the rights of lesbians and gays. DOB was the first social and political organization for lesbians in the United States, which soon established branches around the country. The name was taken from "Songs of Bilitis," a collection of lesbian love poems by Pierre Louys. On June 16, 2008, Martin and Lyon became the first gay couple to be legally married in California. See http://www.nytimes. com/2008/08/28/us/28martin.html?_r=0

Harvey Milk (1930–1978). Milk was a US Navy veteran from the Korean War and the first openly elected gay official to the San Francisco board of supervisors. Eleven months after taking office, Milk and San Francisco Mayor George Moscone were assassinated by disgruntled city supervisor Dan White. White was found guilty of voluntary manslaughter of the two murders, causing civil unrest and riots across the country. Milk was posthumously awarded the presidential medal of freedom in 2009. See http://www.legacyprojectchicago.org/Harvey_Milk.html and http://milkfoundation.org/about/harvey-milk-biography/

Sylvia Rivera (1951–2002). Rivera is a transgender Hispanic activist who was instrumental in leading the fight against police during the Stonewall riots in 1969. She would later join the Gay Liberation Front and start Street Transgender Activist Revolutionaries (STAR) with Marsha Johnson to assist homeless transgender women and fight for a New York City transgender rights bill and inclusion of transgender individuals in the New York state sexual orientation nondiscrimination act. See http://www.legacyprojectchicago.org/Sylvia_Rivera.html

Bayard Rusting (1912–1987). A leader of the civil rights, social justice, and gay rights movement, Rusting helped to initiate the Freedom Ride (1947) to challenge racial segregation related to busing. He promoted nonviolence and nonviolent resistance, becoming a leading strategist for the civil rights movement and chief organizer of the March on Washington (1963). Rusting was posthumously awarded the Presidential Medal of Freedom in 2013 by President Obama. See http://www.pbs.org/wnet/african-americans-many-rivers-to-cross/history/100-amazing-facts/who-designed-the-march-on-washington/

Alan Turing (1912–1954). A British computer scientist who created the Turing machine, which was the beginning of the development of the modern-day computer. During World War II he worked to intercept and decipher codes used by the Germans and was largely responsible for assisting the Allies in their defeat of Nazi forces. Turing was later prosecuted in 1952 for homosexual acts, chemically castrated, and committed suicide. He was later given a posthumous public apology and pardoned by Queen Elizabeth II. See http://www.biography.com/people/alan-turing-9512017#synopsis and http://www.legacyprojectchicago.org/Alan_Turing.html

Oscar Wilde (1854–1900). Wilde was a British dramatist, poet, and critic who authored *The Picture of Dorian Gray* and *The Importance of Being Earnest*, among other famous works. He was indicted on charges for "gross indecency between males" in a series of trials and found guilty and sentenced to two years of hard labor. See http://www.legacyprojectchicago.org/Oscar_Wilde.html and http://www.cmgww.com/historic/wilde/content/oscarwilde/biography.html

APPENDIX C

Important Modern LGBTQ Historical Events

Don't Ask, Don't Tell Policy. In 1993, President Clinton signed a defense directive and military policy known as "Don't Ask, Don't Tell" (DADT), which forbade service members from disclosing their LGBTQ identity lest they be discharged, as well as forbidding military command personnel from inquiring about any service member's sexual or gender minority status. The DADT policy was repealed by the US Senate and President Obama in 2010 and fully lifted in September 2011. See http://www.legacyprojectchicago.org/Gays_In_The_Military.html and http://www.washingtonpost.com/wp-srv/special/politics/dont-ask-dont-tell-timeline/

Employment Non-Discrimination Act (ENDA). In 2013, the US Senate passed ENDA, which would prohibit workplace and employment discrimination based on sexual orientation or gender identity. As of the writing of this text in 2017, the Republican-led House of Representatives has refused to bring ENDA to a vote on the house floor. In July 2015, President Obama signed two executive orders protecting transgender federal employees from workplace discrimination and prohibiting federal contractors from discriminating on the basis of sexual orientation or gender identity. The future of ENDA remains uncertain at this time. See https://www.washingtonpost.com/news/the-fix/wp/2013/11/04/what-is-the-employment-non-discrimination-act-enda/

Marriage Equality and Defense of Marriage Act (DOMA). DOMA was signed into legislation by President Clinton in 1996 stating that, under federal law, marriage would be defined and recognized as a union between "one man and one woman," as well as legislating that states would not have to recognize same-sex marriages or partnerships performed in other states. In 2013, the Supreme Court ruled that the federal government must recognize legal same-sex marriages regardless of what state they were performed in or in which the couples currently reside in the landmark case of *U.S v. Windsor*, striking down DOMA as unconstitutional. In 2015 during the case of *Obergefell v. Hodges*, the US Supreme Court ruled in favor legalizing same-sex marriages across the United States. See http://www.legacyprojectchicago.org/Marriage_Equality.html

Religious Freedom Legislation, "Bathroom" Bills, and Title IX Exemptions. As of the writing of this text in 2017, there has been a national movement in some states in the United States and across certain religious colleges and universities to openly oppress members of the LGBTQ community. Religious freedom bills have been moving through state legislatures (e.g., Indiana, Mississippi) for those with certain religious beliefs, giving them the right to refuse services to members of the LGBTQ community within their organizations (i.e., a florist, a local store, restaurant, etc.) due to their opposition to same-sex marriage or transgender individuals. See http://www.npr.org/sections/thetwo-way/2016/04/05/473107959/mississippi-governor-signs-religious-freedom-bill-into-law

So-called bathroom bills have been proposed and passed in the state of North Carolina (HB-2), for example, that legislate individuals use the bathroom of their birth gender and sex rather than their transgender sex or gender. See http://www.theatlantic.com/politics/archive/2016/05/hb2-is-a-constitutional-monstrosity/482106/

In addition, some 56 religiously affiliated colleges and universities across 26 states have requested exemption from Title IX of the Education Amendments of 1972 with regard to accepting, enrolling, and matriculating LGBTQ students within their schools. See http://www.hrc.org/blog/hrc-calls-on-department-of-education-to-take-action-following-anti-lgbt

Save Our Children Campaign. Anita Bryant (1940–) is a singer and former beauty contestant who was the spokesperson for the Florida Citrus Commission. She is an outspoken opponent of gay rights and started the "Save Our Children" campaign in the 1970s, which successfully repealed a sexual orientation discrimination law in Miami-Dade County, Florida. To counter the discrimination, the LGBT community ran a successful protest of orange juice. An antidiscrimination ordinance was successfully re-authorized in 1998 in Miami. Bryant also assisted in the effort to pass California Proposition 6 also known as the Briggs Initiative. The failed initiative would have banned gays and lesbians, and possibly anyone who supported gay rights, from working within California's public schools. See http://www.nndb.com/people/177/000024105/

Stonewall Inn Revolution. The legendary Stonewall Inn bar, located in the Greenwich Village neighborhood of New York City, is the birthplace of the modern LGBTQ rights movement for equality. On June 28, 1969, the patrons of the Stonewall Inn fought back against what had become regular, tolerated, city-sanctioned harassment by the police department. See http://www.history.com/this-day-in-history/the-stonewall-riot and http://www.thestonewallinnnyc.com/StonewallInnNYC/HISTORY.html and http://www.legacyprojectchicago.org/Stonewall_Riot.html

Transgender Day of Remembrance. The Transgender Day of Remembrance was set aside to memorialize those who were killed due to antitransgender hatred or prejudice. The event is held in November to honor Rita Hester, whose murder on November 28, 1998, kicked off the "Remembering Our Dead" web project and a San Francisco candlelight vigil in 1999. Rita Hester's murder—like most antitransgender murder cases—has yet to be solved. See https://tdor.info/

APPENDIX D

National and International Resources and Websites

AIDS Coalition To Unleash Power (ACT UP): http://www.actupny.org/
"Since its birth in March 1987 at the Lesbian and Gay Community Services Center in downtown Manhattan, the AIDS Coalition To Unleash Power has grown to have thousands of members in more than 70 chapters in the U.S. and worldwide. ACT UP's non-violent direct action, often using vocal demonstrations and dramatic acts of civil disobedience, focuses attention on the crucial issues of the AIDS crisis."

American Foundation for AIDS Research (amfAR): http://www.amfar.org/
"In the course of its 25-year history, amfAR has invested more than $366 million in its programs, spawning numerous significant advances in HIV prevention, treatment, and care. These accomplishments have helped extend, improve, and save the lives of countless people around the world living with HIV/AIDS or vulnerable to HIV infection."

Council on Social Work Education (CSWE): http://www.cswe.org/
"The Council on Social Work Education (CSWE) is a nonprofit national association representing more than 2,500 individual members, as well as graduate and undergraduate programs of professional social work education. Founded in 1952, this partnership of educational and professional institutions, social welfare agencies, and private citizens is recognized by the Council for Higher Education Accreditation as the sole accrediting agency for social work education in this country."

CSWE Council on Sexual Orientation and Gender Identity and Expression (CSOGIE): http://www.cswe.org/CentersInitiatives/Diversity/AboutDiversity/15550/15548/76545.aspx

"The Council on Sexual Orientation and Gender Identity & Expression, formerly the Commission on Gay Men and Lesbian Women, is a council of the Commission for Diversity and Social and Economic Justice. The council promotes the development of social work curriculum materials and faculty growth opportunities relevant to sexual orientation, gender identity and expression, and the experiences of individuals who are gay, lesbian, bisexual, transgender, or two-spirit. The council also works for the full participation of individuals who are gay, lesbian, bisexual, transgender, or two-spirit in social work education, facilitating mentorship of students and junior faculty who are gay, lesbian, bisexual, transgender, or two-spirit and offering assistance and consultation to educators and students concerning issues of sexual orientation and gender identity and expression."

Gay and Lesbian Alliance Against Defamation (GLAAD): http://www.glaad.org/
"GLAAD rewrites the script for LGBT acceptance. As a dynamic media force, GLAAD tackles tough issues to shape the narrative and provoke dialogue that leads to cultural change. GLAAD protects all that has been accomplished and creates a world where everyone can live the life they love."

Gay, Lesbian and Straight Education Network (GLSEN): http://www.glsen.org/
"At GLSEN, we want every student, in every school, to be valued and treated with respect, regardless of their sexual orientation, gender identity, or gender expression. We believe that all students deserve a safe and affirming school environment where they can learn and grow. We accomplish our goals by working in hallways across the country—from Congress and the Department of Education to schools and district offices in your community—to improve school climate and champion LGBT issues in K-12 education."

GLBT Historical Society: http://www.glbthistory.org/
"The GLBT Historical Society collects, preserves, and interprets the history of GLBT people and the communities that support them. Founded in 1985, we are recognized internationally as a leader in the field of GLBT public history. The GLBT Historical Society, located in San Francisco, CA is a registered 501(c)3 educational nonprofit organization."

Gay & Lesbian Medical Association: http://www.glma.org/
"Through the expertise of our members and in collaboration with other lesbian, gay, bisexual and transgender (LGBT) civil rights and health organizations as well as with health associations and policy-makers at all levels, GLMA is a major force in the effort to ensure the health and well-being of LGBT individuals and families."

Gay and Lesbian Victory Fund: https://victoryfund.org/
"Our mission is to change the face and voice of America's politics and achieve equality for LGBT Americans by increasing the number of openly LGBT officials at all levels of government. The Gay & Lesbian Victory Fund works to elect LGBT leaders to public office for one simple reason. They change America's politics."

Lesbian Herstory Archives: http://www.lesbianherstoryarchives.org/history.html
"The Lesbian Herstory Archives exists to gather and preserve records of lesbian lives and activities so that future generations will have ready access to materials relevant to their lives. The process of gathering this material will uncover and collect our herstory denied to us previously by patriarchal historians in the interests of the culture which they serve. We will be able to analyze

and reevaluate the Lesbian experience; we also hope the existence of the Archives will encourage Lesbians to record their experiences in order to formulate our living herstory."

Human Rights Campaign (HRC): http://www.hrc.org/
"The Human Rights Campaign is organized and will be operated for the promotion of the social welfare of the lesbian, gay, bisexual and transgender community. By inspiring and engaging individuals and communities, HRC strives to end discrimination against LGBT people and realize a world that achieves fundamental fairness and equality for all."

International Lesbian, Gay, Trans and Intersex Association (IGLA): http://ilga.org/
"ILGA is a worldwide federation of 1,200 member organizations from 125 countries campaigning for lesbian, gay, bisexual, trans and intersex rights since 1978. ILGA is an umbrella organization of more than 1,200 member organizations presented in six different regions including: Pan Africa ILGA, ILGA-Asia, ILGA-Europe, ILGA-LAC (Latin America and the Caribbean), ILGA North-America and ILGA-Oceania (Aotearoa/New Zealand, Australia and Pacific Islands). Established in 1978, ILGA enjoys consultative status at the UN ECOSOC, publishes an annual world report and a map on legislation criminalizing or protecting people on the basis of their sexual orientation or recognizing their relationships."

It Gets Better Project: http://www.itgetsbetter.org/
"The It Gets Better Project's mission is to communicate to LGBT youth around the world that it gets better and to create and inspire the changes needed to make it better for them."

Lambda Legal: http://www.lambdalegal.org/
"Lambda Legal, a 501(c)(3) nonprofit, is a national organization committed to achieving full recognition of the civil rights of lesbians, gay men, bisexuals, transgender people and those with HIV through impact litigation, education and public policy work. Lambda Legal was founded in 1973 as the nation's first legal organization dedicated to achieving full equality for lesbian and gay people. When founder Bill Thom filed an application in early 1972 to establish Lambda Legal Defense and Education Fund, he borrowed from the bylaws of another newly established organization—the Puerto Rican Legal Defense and Education Fund (now Latino Justice PRLDEF)."

Leather Archives and Museum: http://www.leatherarchives.org/
The mission of the leather archives and museum, located in Chicago, is: "The compilation, preservation and maintenance of leather lifestyle and related lifestyles [including but not limited to the Gay and Lesbian communities], history, archives and memorabilia for historical, educational and research purposes."

LGBTQ Parenting Network: http://lgbtqpn.ca/about-us/
"The LGBTQ Parenting Network is a program of Sherbourne Health Centre. We support lesbian, gay, bisexual, trans and queer parenting through training, research, resource development, and community organizing. We work with individuals, organizations, and communities from the local to the international."

Matthew Shepard Foundation: http://www.matthewshepard.org/
"The Matthew Shepard Foundation empowers individuals to embrace human dignity and diversity through outreach, advocacy and resource programs. We strive to replace hate with understanding, compassion, and acceptance."

Milk Foundation: http://milkfoundation.org/

"As a not-for-profit global organization, our program goals—to empower local, regional, national and global organizations so that they may fully realize the power of Harvey Milk's story, style, and collaborative relationship building—are as large and bold as Harvey taught us! The Foundation, through Harvey's dream for a just tomorrow, envisions governments that celebrate the rich and universally empowering diversity of humanity, where all individuals—gay, lesbian, bisexual, transgendered, racial and ethnic minorities, the elderly, the young, the disabled—all who had been excluded can fully participate in all societal rights without exception."

National Association of Social Workers (NASW): http://www.socialworkers.org/

"The National Association of Social Workers (NASW) is the largest membership organization of professional social workers in the world, with 132,000 members. NASW works to enhance the professional growth and development of its members, to create and maintain professional standards, and to advance sound social policies."

National LGBTQ Task Force: http://www.thetaskforce.org/

"The National LGBTQ Task Force advances full freedom, justice and equality for LGBTQ people. We're building a future where everyone is free to be themselves in every aspect of their lives. Today, despite all the progress we've made to end discrimination, millions of LGBTQ people face barriers in every aspect of their lives: in housing, employment, healthcare, retirement, and basic human rights. These barriers must go. That's why the Task Force is training and mobilizing millions of activists across our nation to deliver a world where you can be you."

National Center for Transgender Equality: http://www.transequality.org/

"NCTE has been at the forefront of changing laws, policies, and society to improve the lives of transgender Americans. From our early beginnings educating Hill staff about who we are, to the milestone inclusion of transgender people in the president's State of the Union speech a decade later, and to the dozens of policy wins that lined the pathway in between—NCTE has been a strategic force in our movement toward equality."

National Coalition of Anti-Violence Programs: http://www.avp.org/

"AVP empowers lesbian, gay, bisexual, transgender, queer, and HIV-affected communities and allies to end all forms of violence through organizing and education, and supports survivors through counseling and advocacy."

National Gay & Lesbian Chamber of Commerce: http://www.nglcc.org/

"The National Gay & Lesbian Chamber of Commerce (NGLCC) started in November 2002, when Justin Nelson and Chance Mitchell realized no one had really considered the economic equality of LGBT people or the impact economics could have on the equality movement. The two co-founders sought to showcase that LGBT people were business owners, employers, taxpayers, providers of healthcare—that they were a vibrant, essential part of the small business engine that makes the U.S. economy run and therefore, deserved a place at the equality table."

No H8 Campaign: http://www.noh8campaign.com/

"The NOH8 Campaign is a charitable organization whose mission is to promote marriage, gender, and human equality through education, advocacy, social media, and visual protest."

OK2BME: http://ok2bme.ca/

"The OK2BME project is operated by KW Counselling Services. OK2BME is a set of free, confidential services including counseling and a youth group for kids and teens wondering about their sexuality or gender identity. They may identify as lesbian, gay, bisexual, transgender, gender-variant, or they may just have questions."

Parents, Families, Friends and Allies United with LGBTQ People (PFLAG): https://community.pflag.org/

"PFLAG envisions a world where diversity is celebrated and all people are respected, valued, and affirmed inclusive of their sexual orientation, gender identity, and gender expression. By meeting people where they are and collaborating with others, PFLAG realizes its vision through support for families, allies, and people who are LGBTQ; education for ourselves and others about the unique issues and challenges facing people who are LGBTQ; and advocacy in our communities to change attitudes and create policies and laws that achieve full equality for people who are LGBTQ."

Queer Nation: http://queernationny.org/

"Queer Nation is a direct action group dedicated to ending discrimination, violence, and repression against the LGBT community."

Services and Advocacy for GLBT Seniors (SAGE): http://www.sageusa.org/

"Services & Advocacy for GLBT Elders (SAGE) is the country's largest and oldest organization dedicated to improving the lives of lesbian, gay, bisexual and transgender (LGBT) older adults. Our mission is to lead in addressing issues related to lesbian, gay, bisexual and transgender (LGBT) aging."

The 519: http://www.the519.org/

"The 519 is committed to the health, happiness, and full participation of the LGBTQ community. A City of Toronto agency with an innovative model of Service, Space and Leadership, we strive to make a real difference in people's lives, while working to promote inclusion, understanding and respect."

Southerners on New Ground: http://southernersonnewground.org/

"Southerners On New Ground (SONG) is a regional Queer Liberation organization made up of people of color, immigrants, undocumented people, people with disabilities, working class and rural and small town, LGBTQ people in the South."

Southern Poverty Law Center: https://www.splcenter.org/issues/lgbt-rights?gclid=CKXUxJf-l9MCFQYMaQodY1sBog

"Civil rights lawyers Morris Dees and Joseph Levin Jr. founded the SPLC in 1971 to ensure that the promise of the civil rights movement became a reality for all. Since then, we've won numerous landmark legal victories on behalf of the exploited, the powerless and the forgotten. Our lawsuits have toppled institutional racism and stamped out remnants of Jim Crow segregation; destroyed some of the nation's most violent white supremacist groups; and protected the civil rights of children, women, the disabled, immigrants and migrant workers, the LGBT community, prisoners, and many others who faced discrimination, abuse or exploitation.

The Trevor Project: http://www.thetrevorproject.org/

"Founded in 1998 by the creators of the Academy Award® winning short film TREVOR, The Trevor Project is the leading national organization providing crisis intervention and suicide prevention services to lesbian, gay, bisexual, transgender, and questioning (LGBTQ) young people ages 13–24."

Transgender Law Center: http://transgenderlawcenter.org/

"Transgender Law Center changes law, policy, and attitudes so that all people can live safely, authentically, and free from discrimination regardless of their gender identity or expression."

Williams Institute: http://williamsinstitute.law.ucla.edu/

"The Williams Institute is dedicated to conducting rigorous, independent research on sexual orientation and gender identity law and public policy. A think tank at UCLA Law, the Williams Institute produces high-quality research with real-world relevance and disseminates it to judges, legislators, policymakers, media, and the public. Experts at the Williams Institute have authored dozens of public policy studies and law review articles, filed amicus briefs in key court cases, provided expert testimony at legislative hearings, been widely cited in the national media, and trained thousands of lawyers, judges and members of the public."

INDEX

identity disorder
gender
   vs. gender dysphoria, 82
identity foreclosure, 76
identity formation
described, 98
as social narrative, 98–99
identity pride, 103–104
identity status
LGB (sic)
developing, 75
identity tolerance, 103
IGLA. *see* International Lesbian, Gay, Trans and
   Intersex Association (IGLA)
immigrant(s)
gay male, 296–297
undoumented
gay male, 296–297
immigration
by gay men, 296–297
inclusive language
learning and validating, 142–143
incongruence
in lesbian coming out and identity development,
   104, 105
indirect trauma, 123–125, 124*f*
individual counseling
in strengths-based CoCs for LGBTQ youth,
   373*f*, 374
information and communication
   technologies (ICTs)
in building strengths-based and
   empowering CoCs for LGBTQ
   youth, 369
in dating, socialization, and meeting others by
   LGBTQ persons, 167–168
in TGNC community, 338–339
information/reaching out
in lesbian coming out and identity
   development, 105
informed consent
for transgender health care, 507–508
insemination
among LGBTQ persons, 174–175
insidious trauma, 123–125, 124*f*
Institute of Medicine (IOM), 498
Committee on Lesbian, Gay, Bisexual, and
   Transgender Health Issues and Research
   Gaps and Opportunities of, 211
Institute of Sexual Science, 9
integration, acceptance, and posttransition
in lesbian coming out and identity development,
   105–106

intentional communities
social work practice with lesbian community in,
   273–274
intentionality
in coming out, 107
internalization/synthesis of love for women
in lesbian coming out and identity
   development, 104
internalized homophobia
defined, 255
minority stress among sexual-minority
   populations related to, 255–256
International Lesbian, Gay, Trans and Intersex
   Association (IGLA)
resources and websites for, 533
internet
in building strengths-based and empowering
   CoCs for LGBTQ youth, 369
interpersonal relationships
in assessment of stress in sexual-minority
   populations, 257
intersecting identities
LGBTQ persons of color with mental health
   conditions and, 437–438
experiences related to, 441–442
social workers' awareness of own, 444–445
intersectionality
of health and mental health factors impacting
   LGBTQ community, 409–410
of LGBTQ youth, 140
intersectionality perspective
on LGBTQ persons of color with mental health
   conditions, 431–432
intersectionality theory, 53*t*, 55
in advancing equality and equity of LGBTQ civil
   rights, 390–391, 391*f*
intersex
defined, 33–34
intimate partner violence (IPV), 122–123
CDC on, 475–476
defined, 122, 476–477
in LGBTQ community, 122–123, 475–493
awareness of, 487–489
barriers to seeking support and care for,
   486–487
coercive control, 483
economic violence, 483–484
expressive aggression, 482
lack of information, education, and community
   discussion related to, 487–489
physical violence, 484
prevalence of, 122, 479–481, 480*f*
psychological violence, 482–483

historical context of, 268–270
identity development among, 104–106
    in childhood and adolescence, 274–275
lifespan influences on, 274
marriage equality for, 271–272
mental health of, 278–279
partnership/marriage of, 277
prejudice against
    health and mental health effects of, 278–279
PSEs among, 170
raising children, 175–176
relationships of
    in adolescence, 276
repeal of DADT effect on, 271
sociopolitical context of, 270–271
substance use and addiction in, 454–455
tobacco use by, 279
victimization of
    bullying and, 275–276
workplace experiences of, 204
lesbian, gay, and bisexual (LGB) community. *see*
    LBG community; LGB persons
lesbian, gay, and bisexual (LGB) persons. *see* LGB
    persons
lesbian, gay, bisexual, and transgender (LGBT)
    persons. *see* LGBT community
lesbian, gay, bisexual, transgender, and queer/
    questioning (LGBTQ) persons. *see* LGBTQ
    community; LGBTQ persons
lesbian and gay (LG) community. *see* LG community
lesbian and gay (LG) development
    Cass homosexual identity formation model
        and, 76–77
lesbian and socially oriented models, 78–80
lesbian coming out model, 104–106
lesbian community. *see also* lesbian(s)
    social work practice with, 266–285
        in adulthood, 276–279
        aging, 279
        applied model of care in, 267–268, 268f
        building families, 277–278
        childhood and adolescence, 274–276
        community context, 272–274
        considerations related to, 279–281
        health and mental health, 278–279
        historical context of, 268–270
        intentional communities, 273–274
        introduction, 266
        lifespan influences, 274
        macro-practice considerations, 280–281
        marriage equality, 271–272
        mezzo-practice considerations, 280
        micro-practice considerations, 280

partnership/marriage, 277
repeal of DADT, 271
in rural and urban settings, 272–273
sociopolitical context of, 270–271
terminology related to, 267
theoretically informed conceptual
    framework, 267
lesbian feminism, 14–15
Lesbian Gay Aging Issues Network
    of American Society for Aging, 224
Lesbian Health Fund, 498
Lesbian Herstory Archives
    resources and websites for, 532–533
lesbian identity development, 78–80, 104–106,
    274–275
LGB–affirmative treatment
    examination of, 257–261
        addressing stigma in, 258
        building relationship in, 258–259
        focus on coping in, 260
        introduction, 257–258
        processing therapeutic relationship in, 260–261
        sexual orientation disclosure in, 259
        social skills improvement in, 260
LGB community, 75
LGB (sic) identity status
    developing, 75
LGB persons
    African-American
        stress in, 251–252
    becoming offspring, 75
    Caucasian
        stress in, 251–252
    entering LGB community, 75
    identity of
        developing, 75
    intimacy status of
        developing, 75
    Latino
        stress in, 251–252
    minority stress among, 251
    minority stress model in, 249–265
    processes experienced across lifespan, 75
LGB persons of color
    minority stress and, 251–252
LGBT community
    aging within, 211–231 *see also* aging, within LGBT
        community
    queerness in, 356–357
LGBTQ adolescents. *see also* LGBTQ youth
    acceptance and disclosure among, 101–102
    repression/denial among, 100–101
    suppression among, 101

neglect
    as factor in aging within LGBT community, 223
negotiating partnerships
    in strengths-based CoCs for LGBTQ youth, 376
neurologic system
    substance use and addiction effects on, 458–459
neuroscience
    in gay male community development, 291–292
    in sexual orientation development, 41–42, 86–87
New Leaf Outreach to Elders, 294
New Left, 239
NIAAA, 462–463
NIDA. *see* National Institute on Drug Abuse (NIDA)
No H8 Campaign
    resources and websites for, 534
nonconformity
    gender
        defined, 31
nondisclosure
    LGBTQ persons of color with mental health
        conditions and, 436
nondiscrimination
    for LGBTQ persons, 394
nonmonogamy
    among bisexual persons, 321–322
    among gay men, 170, 297–298
    among LGBTQ persons, 169
    consensual
        among LGBTQ persons, 170–171
normality
    from stigma to, 38–39
NSDUH. *see* National Survey on Drug Use and
    Health (NSDUH)
NTDS. *see* National Transgender Discrimination
    Survey (NTDS)

Obergefell v. Hodges, 3, 164, 295, 386–387
OK2BME
    resources and websites for, 535
older adults
    within LGBT community, 211–231 *see also* aging,
        within LGBT community
    abuse-related concerns, 223
    best practice considerations, 225–226
    coming out, 110–111, 220–221
    dating, relationships, and family issues effects
        on, 180–181
    families of origin impact on, 219–220
    grief, loss, death, and dying concerns, 225
    health and mental health of, 216–219
    health and provider concerns related to,
        221–222
    health-care workers' impact on, 221–222

HIV/AIDS impact on, 217
    legal concerns, 224
    neglect-related concerns, 223
    strengths and resilience of, 216
    substance use and addiction in, 458
ONE, Inc., 11
ONE: The Homosexual Magazine, 384
1, 112 and Counting, 239
online resources
    in coming out process, 108–109
"ontology of gender," 162
"open" relationships, 170
oppression
    conceptualizing structural components of
        in social and economic justice, 61
    gay male–related
        history of, 288
        racial and ethnic considerations in, 295
        religion and spirituality considerations in,
            295–296
    LGBTQ persons of color with mental health
        conditions–related
        reducing internalized, 443–444
    LGBTQ persons–related, 162–163
    to sexual health and practice, 26–48
    systems of, 28–29
    transgender persons–related, 50
    understanding, 26–30
outness
    defined, 204
    of LGBTQ workers at work, 204
    victimization experience related to degree
        of, 128
overall life satisfaction
    of LGBTQ workers, 203

pansexual
    defined, 34
Paragraph 175, 7
paraphilia, 171
parent(s)
    of TGNC children
        support for, 342–343
Parents, Families, Friends and Allies United with
    LGBTQ People (PFLAG)
    resources and websites for, 535
partnership(s)
    lesbian, 277
    in strengths-based CoCs for LGBTQ youth
        negotiation of, 376
Passing Ellenville, 507
Patient Protection and Affordable Care Act (ACA).
    see Affordable Care Act (ACA)